Edwidge Danticat

McFarland Companions to Young Adult Literature

Gary Paulsen: A Companion to the Young Adult Literature
by Mary Ellen Snodgrass (2018)

Marion Zimmer Bradley: A Companion to the Young Adult Literature
by Mary Ellen Snodgrass (2020)

Edwidge Danticat

A Companion to the Young Adult Literature

MARY ELLEN SNODGRASS

McFarland Companions to Young Adult Literature

McFarland & Company, Inc., Publishers
Jefferson, North Carolina

ALSO BY THE AUTHOR AND FROM MCFARLAND

Asian Women Artists: A Biographical Dictionary, 2700 BCE to Today (2022); *Octavia E. Butler: A Literary Companion* (2022); *Rachel Carson: A Literary Companion* (2021); *Television's* Outlander: *A Companion, Seasons 1–5* (2021); *Marion Zimmer Bradley: A Companion to the Young Adult Literature* (2020); *Rachel Carson: A Literary Companion* (2020); *Lee Smith: A Literary Companion* (2019); *Coins and Currency: An Historical Encyclopedia*, 2d ed. (2019); *Gary Paulsen: A Companion to the Young Adult Literature* (2018); *World Epidemics: A Cultural Chronology of Disease from Prehistory to the Era of Zika*, 2d ed. (2017); *Brian Friel: A Literary Companion* (2017); *Settlers of the American West: The Lives of 231 Notable Pioneers* (2015); *Who's Who in the Middle Ages* (2013; paperback 2001); *Isabel Allende: A Literary Companion* (2013); *World Epidemics: A Cultural Chronology of Disease from Prehistory to the Era of SARS* (2011; paperback 2003); *Encyclopedia of World Scriptures* (2011; paperback 2001); *Leslie Marmon Silko: A Literary Companion* (2011); *Peter Carey: A Literary Companion* (2010); *Jamaica Kincaid: A Literary Companion* (2008); *Kaye Gibbons: A Literary Companion* (2007); *Walter Dean Myers: A Literary Companion* (2006); *World Shores and Beaches: A Descriptive and Historical Guide to 50 Coastal Treasures* (2005); *Barbara Kingsolver: A Literary Companion* (2004); *August Wilson: A Literary Companion* (2004); *Amy Tan: A Literary Companion* (2004)

ISBN (print) 978-1-4766-8715-5
ISBN (ebook) 978-1-4766-4460-8

LIBRARY OF CONGRESS AND BRITISH LIBRARY
CATALOGUING DATA ARE AVAILABLE

© 2022 Mary Ellen Snodgrass. All rights reserved

No part of this book may be reproduced or transmitted in any form or by any means, electronic or mechanical, including photocopying or recording, or by any information storage and retrieval system, without permission in writing from the publisher.

Front cover: Housing stacked up a hillside
in Port-Au-Prince, Haiti (Shutterstock/ Sylvie Corriveau)

Printed in the United States of America

McFarland & Company, Inc., Publishers
Box 611, Jefferson, North Carolina 28640
www.mcfarlandpub.com

Try to tell your truth.
2019

Be bold. Be fearless. Be unafraid.
2016

Acknowledgments

Appalachian State University, Boone, North Carolina
Asheville-Buncombe Technical Community College, North Carolina
Cabarrus County Public Library, Concord, North Carolina
Central Piedmont Library, Charlotte, North Carolina
Davidson College Library, Davidson, North Carolina
Decker Library, Maryland Institute College of Art, Baltimore
Elon University Library, Elon, North Carolina
Greensboro Public Library, Greensboro, North Carolina
Heather Cole, archivist, John Hay Library, Brown University, Providence, Rhode Island
Hunter Library, Western Carolina University, Cullowhee, North Carolina
Joyner Library, East Carolina University, Greenville, North Carolina
Ken Carlson, reference archivist, Rhode Island Department of State, Providence
Lane Library, Georgia Southern University, Savannah
Lanham Bundy, reference librarian, Providence Public Library, Providence, Rhode Island
North Carolina State University, Raleigh
Patricia Brennan, reference, James P. Adams Library, Rhode Island College, Providence
Ridgeview Public Library, Hickory, North Carolina
Walter Clinton Jackson Library, University of North Carolina, Greensboro
Special thanks to reference librarian Martin Otts at Patrick Beaver Library, Hickory, North Carolina, and Mark Schumacher, retired reference librarian, UNC-Greensboro.

Table of Contents

Acknowledgments vi

Preface 1

Introduction 3

*A Biography of Edwidge Danticat
(January 19, 1969–)* 7

Edwidge Danticat Family Tree 41

THE COMPANION 43

Glossary 227

Appendix A: Aphorisms in Danticat's Writing 235

Appendix B: Historical References 236

Appendix C: A Guide to Places 241

*Appendix D: A Guide to Writing, Art
and Research Topics* 244

Bibliography 255

Index 269

Preface

A comet in the mounting firmament of third world, nonwhite, and female writers, Edwidge Danticat stands apart under professions as varied as trilingual children's and YA author, activist, op-ed and cinema writer, and keynote speaker. Much of her work introduces the world to the cultural uniqueness of Haiti, the first black republic, and the elements of African heritage, language, and Vodou that continue to color all aspects of island art and self-expression. Because of her great-heartedness toward the precarious refugee, she continues to examine areas of injustice that deny human rights to members of the Haitian diaspora.

The text of *Edwidge Danticat: A Companion to the Young Adult Literature* will prove essential to student reading and classroom lessons on a variety of genres. For the elementary school, *The Last Mapou* and *Eight Days* adapt themselves to lessons on self-sufficiency, storytelling, and survival. For stories of home hardships, the titles *My Mama Medicine, Mama's Nightingale,* and *Behind the Mountains* specify situations that children can appreciate and discuss from their own experience. The author extended genre and style with the historical novel *Anacaona,* the romanticized facts about a Taino queen, and *Célimène,* a French fairy tale suitable to a romance language class. For older teens, *Untwine* places the survivor of a car accident in the tough position of misidentified hospital patient and bereaved sister. The author's finest model of voicing and child psychology, the novel offers a fictional recovery for a troubled character. For a social studies introduction to Haiti, the abridged travelogue *A Walk Through Carnival* assesses a Lenten festival permeated with dance, singing, parade floats, and character parody. All entries incorporate citations of the author, literature experts, and journalists from news sources in New York, Chicago, Washington, Philadelphia, Brooklyn, Bronx, Miami, Fort Lauderdale, Boston, Los Angeles, Santa Fe, Salt Lake City, Minneapolis, St. Petersburg, Durham, Raleigh, Providence, Cleveland, Portland, London, Paris, Toronto, Montreal, Berlin, Canberra, and Nigeria.

The mature reader will find a variety of model short stories in *Krik? Krak!* and a mesmerizing escape motif in *The Farming of Bones,* which includes scenes of first aid, group psychology, and volunteer treatment for the traumatized. *Breath, Eyes, Memory* introduces the concept of matrilineage, virginity, and female heritage, an acclamation of noble womanhood through four generations. An experimental novel, *The Dew Breaker* allies character-rich events of the Duvalier regime and violence wrought by the Tonton Macoute, a diabolical paramilitary. For specifics on the author's loss of the two male authority figures in her life, *Brother, I'm Dying* explains the situation that deranges Edwidge in double deaths during expectation of a first child. Her most recent works alert the unwary to the difficulties of truth-telling in literature, the subject of *Create Dangerously*, and the interconnection of a seaside populace in coping with tragedy, the story of a motherless girl called by her mother *Claire of the Sea Light*. After an overview of candid reportage on mortality in *The Art of Death,* the writer collected stories, some old, some new, in an anthology, *Everything Inside.* She returned to professional philosophy with *Beginnings, Endings, and Salt,* an essay collection revealing the importance of mentors.

The text of *Edwidge Danticat: A Companion to the Young Adult Literature* opens on a preface and introduction guiding the reader to historical entries (colonialism, Tonton Macoute, Duvaliers, slavery), sources (music, children's literature, folklore, superstition, Creole), genealogies on *Krik? Krik!* and nine other fictional lineages, and background material on carnival, religion, Catholicism, cane, Vodou, and noirism. Gendered entries (women, adaptation, patriarchy) offer insight into essays on eighteen titles and their accompanying genealogies. Commentary on dreams, humor, health, couples, details, vulnerability, and coming of age add nuance to specific works and brief reviews of character names and

titles. A comprehensive biography of Edwidge Danticat isolates development that impacts her canon. A family tree identifies real characters from her autobiographical writings.

Following the A to Z entries, the companion lists 32 aphorisms from Danticat's fiction—nuggets of wisdom that contribute sage advice and comfort. The Historical Chronology names specific places and dates of events from the author's canon, beginning in ancient Egypt and continuing to a 2017 hurricane that devastated the West Indies. A glossary supplies a simple definition or translation of 388 terms in Creole, French, Japanese, Latin, Spanish, and Taino. A Guide to Place Names identifies locations and historical significance of towns and rural landmarks. As an aid to lesson planning, the text includes a Guide to Topics, which introduces literary terms and themes and character relationships for further research, discussion, comparative reading, or composition. The text concludes with primary and secondary sources and primary and secondary indexing by title (*Dreams Like Me,* "We Are Ugly, But We Are Here"), subject (grandparents, Arawak), and topic (shape-shifting, coming of age, abortion, literacy, language). Overall, the introduction enables the reader to add Edwidge Danticat to a bicultural list of classic authors.

Introduction

Obsessions breed writers. Edwidge Danticat's memories and concerns for her motherland block out most other issues, such as college in Providence, Rhode Island, life in New York City, and college teaching. From her first preteen juvenilia, she pictured herself and characters as immigrants journeying from cosmos to cosmos. Like time travelers, they faced the frustrations and fears of displacement—not just in locale, but in a social milieu that viewed them as non–English speakers and aliens with black skin and foul diseases. Accepting the crusader's challenge, she adopted the pose of stranger in a strange land and threaded twisting paths obstructed by xenophobia, persecution, and racism.

Naturally creative as Haitian women have to be, Edwidge treasured a mental cache of home tales recorded in Creole, her everyday speaking language. She skipped French as a communication medium and adopted English as the practical means of bridging the immigrant's two-stage route. Part of her way, she relied on the immersion of an extended family in prayer, hymns, and scripture. A livelier side of her upbringing incorporated neighborhood plays and masking, a preface to adult writings based on fantasy and imagination. Frustrating language conundrums required reading her impersonal correspondence from her father, André Mira Danticat, in New York and, in Haiti, assisting her disabled Uncle Joseph

Nozius Dantica in the daily struggle of the mute. (Note that the younger generation spells its surname with a final T.)

The year 1981 marked the dividing line between life in the Caribbean and a hyphenated Haitian-American existence with two parents and three brothers. From English language classes in Brooklyn, Edwidge progressed the way most writers grow—by internalizing the words of experts and by composing a journal and typing original stories. From Nancy Drew, she moved on to the purpose-driven works of Paule Marshall and Maya Angelou. In "Color Blocking," an interview in 2013 with *Arquitectonica,* Edwidge acknowledged, "I try to incorporate the visual in my writing because there's so much vibrancy; there's so much visual in daily life" (Danticat, 2013). The reflection reprised personal observations in "Westbury Court," a somber recounting of a Brooklyn fire that killed two boys. The ability to impart suffering in the young and vulnerable set a pattern that became her vocation—commiserating with victims without overloading text with unbearable hurt. By grooming compassion into a subtle flair, she eased readers into the worst of the worst—thuggery, rape, natural disaster, stillbirth, prison, torture, and loss at sea in both body and name.

A startling number of editors and publishers claim Edwidge as the voice for the pathfinder, the wanderer who accepts

4   **Introduction**

uneven odds of arriving safely on an unexplored shore. Behind fictional names, she relived scenarios in the life of cousin Marie Micheline Marole and in the street shootings that warned nonwhite Brooklynites of sudden death. From scattered newspaper writing for the *Providence Journal* and an office job, she edged surreptitiously past her parents' anticipation for a medical professional in the family into a feminist blockbuster. Her maiden novel, *Breath, Eyes, Memory,* scrutinized matriarchy soaked in more honesty than past Haitian authors had dared. Material came from one-on-one camaraderie with new arrivals at immigration offices and detention centers, the source of her op-ed letters that blazed with details the caliber of "starvation" and "bullets." Among the characters she pitied were an anonymous sex worker and single parent in "Night Women" and a would-be mother living a delusion in "Between the Pool and the Gardenias," both anthologized in *Krik? Krak!*

Rapid pacing toward character epiphanies dominated the 1990s, netting the writer fiction awards and hate mail. Collaboration with filmmaker Jonathan Demme and scenarist Patricia Benoit thrust Edwidge into a parallel universe of cinema art, a placement of theme and action in the words and movements of screen actors. Out of rage at Haitian archivists for shrouding the October 2–8, 1937, Parsley Massacre, she accepted the scut work—reading, research, and interview—that preceded *The Farming of Bones,* a split with the postcolonial world of sanitized history. By stacking doleful events on the shoulders of a domestic servant, she again elevated Haitian females for their willingness to tackle lethal threats that shred the subconscious, pocking it with land mines of regret and trauma. In the late 1990s, she acquired from interviews with Haitian artist Odilon Pierre the urgent need

for candor about island poverty and food insecurity. The decade ended with critical recognition—the American Book Award.

Back and forth visits to Haiti pumped nurturing insight into Edwidge's adult thoughts, aiding her continued ventures into long and short prose themes and classroom teaching at the University of Miami. By 2000, she had added young adult fiction to her résumé with *Behind the Mountains,* a "Swiss Family Robinson" account of Haitian repatriation in New York. A trip to Jacmel for Carnival 2001 provided details for *After the Dance* and the YA abridgement, *A Walk Through Carnival.* Returned to the vibrance of Little Haiti, her new home in Miami, she engaged the Caribbean soul that had anchored her pre-teen years. Thoughts on biracial communities broadened her audience through French translations, public readings, and lecturing in Tokyo, Japan. Colleges and universities lauded her resonant narrative and podium talks on the issues that drove her career.

The murder of radio activist Jean Léopold Dominique in Port-au-Prince and the reputation of Miami's Krome Detention Center for mistreating immigrants ate at Edwidge. From filming *The Agronomist,* she acquired notoriety as a one-women tocsin forcing Americans to hear dire truths about refugee persecution. The collection of related stories into *The Dew Breaker* and additional fiction citations and a fellowship preceded an unprecedented summer 2004. In the first weeks of pregnancy, she began accepting her father's decline from terminal lung fibrosis. In early fall, Uncle Joseph's scurry through the vicious underworld of Bel Air preceded his incarceration at Krome in November and resultant death from pancreatitis. Awaiting the birth of Mira Boyer, the author completed a second tween work, *Anacaona,* a fictionalized biography of a Taino queen murdered

Introduction   5

by Hispanic conquistadors under Christopher Columbus. At Mira Danticat's death in May 2005, she buried him alongside Uncle Joseph.

Edwidge's professional headway, sustained by joy in motherhood and unfathomable grief for the men in the family, ushered her into the planning of *Brother, I'm Dying* and testimony before a congressional hearing on the barbarous jailing of immigrants. Speeches filled her calendar. Newspapers embraced her themes and lacerating style for airing a pocket of rot in American democracy. She dug deeper into urban crime with the film *Poto Mitan* (Middle Pillar) and "Ghosts," her most memorable story about youth. She took hope from the U.S. election of black president Barack Obama. Exacting glimpses of *Create Dangerously* and terror in the child's picture book *Eight Days* grappled with the cataclysms that made Haiti the world's most blighted underdog.

From editing *Haiti Noir,* Edwidge pressed on with *Claire of the Sea Light* and op-ed essays for the *Miami Herald* and *New York Times* revealing the horror of collapsed buildings, hunger, tent cities, and contamination from unburied cadavers. She developed writing skills into new directions with poems for *Standing Tall* and return flights to write about tented communities and read to children whose schools lay pulverized. For a PBS documentary, outstanding work for young readers, speeches, border vigils, and TV orations on struggle and need in Haiti, the world could not deck her in honors fast enough. With the children's fable *The Last Mapou,* she moved beyond the earthquake and cholera epidemic to threats of ecological collapse from deforestation and climate change, subjects she broached in *After the Dance.*

A gentler side of Edwidge followed her mother's death from ovarian cancer in 2014, which she narrated in "Without Her" and *The Art of Death.* Back to island conflicts in 2015, the author joined Julia Alvarez, Vargas Llosa, and Junot Diaz in protests of arbitrary deportations. Publishing another children's book, *Mama's Nightingale,* and the op-ed pieces "Detention Is No Holiday" and "Mourning in Place," she posed the difficulties that families confront after parental jailing or a death from Covid. A cerebral classic, *Untwine* expressed survivor's guilt in an identical twin. Edwidge vaulted into a period of anxiety after the 2016 election of Donald Trump, a bigoted narcissist and anti-immigrationist. In 2018, she pushed back against a venal administration with the lecture "A Right to Be Here." The decade ended with accolades to the author's efforts for all human rights, not just Haiti's.

Critical attention tends toward superlatives. Because the tone and texture of Edwidge's canon prove unpredictable—from the essays in *Beginnings and Salt,* poem "On the Day of the Dead," film "Caroline's Wedding," vignette "Seven," cautionary tale "Water Child," and fairy tale *Célimène* to her satire "Tatiana, Mon Amour"—her flair for understatement often leaves readers nonplussed. Variances in media fiction critiques suggest that even experienced readers puzzle over open-endedness ("Sunrise, Sunset"), edgy humor ("The Port-au-Prince Marriage Special"), noirism ("Sawfish Soup"), and partially occluded narratives ("Dreams of the Butterflies"). She chooses individualized dilemmas and the input of secondary characters who may have a partial or distorted understanding of the situation ("Seven Stories"). Puns and word play add dimensions to titles as unique as *Untwine,* "Claire of the Sea Light," "Dosas," "Color Blocking," and "The Book of the Dead." Female characters battered by patriarchy (Sophie Caco, Louise George, Ka Bienaimé, Valencia Duarte, Flore Voltaire) manage to extricate themselves and progress toward self-rule. Enrichment of text with relevant names (Max, Jr., Marie Magdalène, Nadine, Faustin, Old Kongo) and fastidious details (adaptation, rituals, colors, memory, Catholicism) carry much of the weight of plot.

Reviewers and academic evaluators tend to lessen the weaknesses of Edwidge's canon, particularly the gullibility of the naive and the solitude of the loners. She repeats names, especially Rose, and revises and rewrites stories with new names and varied situations, the shifts that alter "Elsie"/"Dosas"; "Bastille Day"/"The Gift"; "The Wall of Fire"/"The Wall of Fire Rising"; "Quality Control"/"Seven Stories"; and the surge of "Claire of the Sea Light" (story) to *Claire of the Sea Light* (novel). Her travelogue *After the Dance* and writer's philosophy in *The Art of Death* lack the smooth integration of stories as fine as "Night Women" and "The Bridal Seamstress." Whatever her lapses, Edwidge excels at control, the reduction of diction and symbol to one fine polestar, and the patience to leave it to the reader to interpret.

Sources

Danticat, Edwidge. "Color Blocking," *Arquitectonica*, https://www.interiorsandsources.com/article-details/articleid/15929/title/color-blocking-edwidge-danticat (1 July 2013).

A Biography of Edwidge Danticat
(January 19, 1969–)

A national ambassador in the golden era of Haitian literati, Edwidge Danticat writes about conflict in black lives. From a trilingual thought process, her works, issued in some 25 publications, proclaim the worth of motherhood, human rights, and identity to descendants of the Afro-Caribbean diaspora. As a high-profile feminist writer, children's author, scenarist, essayist, editor, translator, dramatist, poet and young adult novelist, to broaden commentary on an island tainted by a desperate history, she varies genres, including oratory, translation, acting, and film scripting. She has edited anthologies, recovered the lost works of Haitian exiles, and submitted op-ed pieces to the *New York Times, Washington Post, Miami Herald, Gainesville Sun, Providence Journal, Toronto Star,* and *Los Angeles Times.* Collectors have translated her works into Creole, French, German, Italian, Japanese, Korean, Spanish, and Swedish. Like the classic authors of early imperial Rome after the fall of the Republic, she turns an era of despair and terror into a source of dynamism.

1915

July 28

Paternal grandfather Nozial Dantica, whose stories would instill a spirit of resistance, joined the *cacos* (guerrillas) opposing the 330 U.S. Marines occupying Port-au-Prince. Invasion forces withdrew nineteen years later, on August 15, 1934. During their tenure, Americans trained island military and forced work crews to build roads and bridges. For her first novel, *Breath, Eyes, Memory,* she chose Caco as a surname for characters as a gesture to her family's intransigence against American insurgents.

1933

During secret guerrilla missions preceding U.S. President Franklin D. Roosevelt's peace initiative, Granpè Nozial ordered ten-year-old son Joseph Nozius Dantica to avoid American Marines by staying in Beauséjour, southwest of Port-au-Prince. When Joseph walked to the market to get medicine for his sisters, he witnessed seven white soldiers kicking a decapitated head like a football, a motif that Edwidge incorporated in the story of Madam Roger in "Children of the Sea."

1946

May

Uncle Joseph Dantica met Denise and settled with her at Bel Air, a hilly slum

8   *A Biography*

in south central Port-au-Prince. Despite poverty, they reared son Maxo and numerous foster children.

1954

At age nineteen, André Miracin "Mira" Danticat quit school in Léogâne to run a home sweatshop manufacturing children's shirts at the rate of two dozen per day. With a profit of five cents per piece or $1.20 a day, over the next decade, he managed to buy a sewing machine and expand his business.

1957

As a result of the rigged election of François "Papa Doc" Duvalier on September 22 and the exile of opponent Louis Déjoie to Cuba, corruption in the Chamber of Deputies forced Uncle Joseph Dantica out of political activism and into the Baptist evangelical ministry.

1963

October 2

After Hurricane Matthew struck Haiti in 2016, Edwidge reflected on her parents' survival of Hurricane Flora in 1963, six years before she was born. The category four storm, with 145 mph winds, produced 57 inches of rain in three days and a 12-foot storm surge on the island's southern beaches. Some 5,000 residents and 400 more in the Dominican Republic died in floods and mudslides.

1964

November 12

"Treated like entertainment," the public execution of rebels Louis Drouin

and Marcel Numa under the command of François "Papa Doc" Duvalier shocked the Danticat family (Danticat, 2010, 12). A firing squad gathered outside the Grand Cemetery on Rue Alerte in front of school children assembled by principals for educational purpose. Edwidge's mother Rose Souvenance Napoléon, of Léogâne, in the Haitian mountains, thought the events tragic. Joseph Nozius Dantica believed that the brutal murders would influence a generation, a prophecy that affected his niece, author Edwidge, and convinced her parents to migrate to New York City, the American ideal that she later called "our city on the hill" (Danticat, 2004, CY1).

1965

Rose embroidered a trousseau for herself. She wed 29-year-old André, a handsome, mustachioed salesman of Italian shoes on the Port-au-Prince Grand Rue. At their Bel Air home, they began sewing flags and school uniforms for sale. André later became a tailor in a handbag factory, glass worker, and Brooklyn gypsy cab driver, whose job Edwidge's poem "Postscript" compared to "wanderers, nomads" (Danticat, 2010, 410). A devout Jehovah's Witness, Rose prayed for their daughter to be intelligent, an escape from her parents' daily grind.

1969

January 19

A working-class native of Port-au-Prince, Edwidge Rosa Danticat was born during the third year of the 29-year Duvalier regime of François "Papa Doc" and Jean-Claude "Baby Doc." Writers faced danger of persecution, murder and censored words, spoken or written.

Resistance, "forbidden and illegal," could precede arrest of a whole family and mass execution (Danticat, 2010, 65). Away from fears of the city, she spent summers at Beauséjour in the Léogâne mountains, where her maternal grandmother lived near a rushing stream.

Creativity marked the Danticats' free time. Rose made matching dresses for her and Edwidge. In oral tradition, the poor congregated *à la ou* (in courtyards) to tell "pumpkin stories" (Mirabal, 2007; Pierre-Pierre, 1995, C1). Amid histories of Taino queen Anacaona and the 1493 invasion of Christopher Columbus, Edwidge listened to her aunt Denise's mother, Granmè Melina, tell folk tales in Creole. Elders were cautious about too much talk in front of a nosy child. Edwidge admitted, "Adults were afraid to talk in front of me when I was a young girl because they knew I was relishing and loving every bit of information that came out of their mouths and they were suspicious of my curiosity" (Horn, 2001, 19). From oral instruction, she learned to value her paternal grandfather Nozial Dantica's rebel involvement against American insurgents.

1970

January 2

The Danticat family observed *Jour de Anciens* (Heroes and Ancestors Day) with a beefy squash soup. Children received coins, cake, and red, syrupy liqueur, a health tonic.

1971

Edwidge's brother Eliab André "Bob" was born the year André Danticat migrated on a one-month tourist visa to New York and settled in a Haitian-American enclave called the "tenth department." His motivation, the increasing intimidation by the Tonton Macoute, Duvalier's military police, made him seek a safer place for his family. Leaving Rose in Haiti until she could obtain travel papers, he accepted the new spelling of his name, "Danticat." He worked early hours driving drunks from clubs at 4:00 A.M. and dodging bullets from unknown assailants. According to the author's character study "Papi," the elder André suffered hair loss, psoriasis, and eczema from on-the-job stress.

In the story "Claire of the Sea Light," the author pictured a similar desperation in Gaspard, a character who must "chèche lavi," Creole for "search for life." The departure eased the burden of supporting two uncles and three aunts. Historically, cousin Maxo Dantica fled the island as a political exile because of his outspoken views on tyranny. Ironically, he died on January 12, 2010, when a four-story building fell on him during Haiti's devastating earthquake, which Edwidge described in "Our Guernica," a sardonic chapter in *Create Dangerously*. André clung to his faith, read from the Bible several times a day, attended Monday night prayer meetings, and served the congregation as deacon.

The siblings remained on the island in the Bel Air slum, where their parents sent monthly food, clothing, and school expense allowances. Members of the Tonton Macoute, Jean-Claude Duvalier's paramilitary, resided in neighboring houses. With Grandmé Melina, the siblings shared the pink house of Aunt Denise Dantica and paternal uncle Joseph Nosius Dantica, the 50-year-old Baptist pastor of L'Eglise Chrétienne de la Rédemption (Christian Church of the Redemption). A part of her connection with the church, attendance at funerals and burials became obligatory and taught her ancestral beliefs about death and mausoleum design. Joseph promoted Edwidge's language skills by giving her books; Denise supplied paper to stitch into notebooks to contain poems, stories, and stick figures. Edwidge and Bob fantasized that their handmade visas, passports, and immigration papers would end the family's separation by providing adequate documentation.

Edwidge's aunt and uncle also fostered cousins whose mothers and fathers had migrated to Canada, the Dominican Republic, France, and the U.S. Because of Joseph's pride, when the price of staples rose, they omitted meals rather than buy on credit. In the large household, Edwidge felt as though she had vanished into depression, sadness, and silence because she was too shy to speak. To the London *Independent* writer Christina Patterson, the author declared, "The years that you lose you never get back" (Patterson, 1999, 14). In addition to embroidering a traditional trousseau, she decided to write stories similar to her favorite book of girl adventures, Ludwig Bemelmans's *Madeleine*, a birthday gift from Uncle Joseph.

1972

Speaking Haitian Creole at home and enrolled with her parents' funding at the Collège Elliott Pierre, a private francophone school known for hard beatings, the author entered classes at age three. After school, she sat by cousin Marie Micheline, who taught her to read. Every Friday, the class attended mass at the national cathedral, Notre Dame de l'Assomption. In *The Art of Death*, she acknowledged, "The chimes of the church's bells had guided the routines of my childhood, even my most painful days" (Danticat, 2017, 66). The colonial school system offered the only exit

from struggle and poverty through rote memory work "in Haitian orality," but it ignored folk culture and focused on standard French titles—*Les Trois Mousquetaires* (The Three Musketeers) and *Fables de la Fontaine* (Fontaine's Fables) (Danticat, 2010, 62). She later regretted that "People who speak Creole are not validated and in some ways are being told their voice isn't heard" (Shea, 1996, 388).

In a free atmosphere, within the first year, the writer read educator Jacqueline Turian Cardozo's primer *Ti Malice au pays des lettres* (Little Malice in the Land of Letters). Her essay "Storybook Ending" for *Oprah* Magazine described the trickster Little Malis and his escapades. She advanced to French classics by male writers—Victor Hugo's classic *Les Miserables,* Alexandre Dumas's *Camille,* poet Charles Baudelaire, dramatist Jean Racine, satirist François Rabelais, novelist Emile Zola, and excerpts from essays by Voltaire and Blaise Pascal. As eldest child, she embraced the immigrant work ethic and applied herself to serious study.

In *The Art of Death,* Edwidge stated, "I grew up in a family that prayed all the time" (Danticat, 2017, 159). The family occupied themselves with daily devotions and religious activities, recitations of school lessons, kite wars, flag day parades, and an oral storytelling tradition that broadened to include songs and hymns. In a speech at Barnard College, she honored as best writing instructors the tellers of her childhood that fed her soul: "Some of them were not literate at all, but they carried stories inside" (Irwin, 2011, 25). Of her squalid home, she declared in an interview for the *Guardian*, "It's hard for me to recognise it as a slum, because I lived there. Most of us were poor; that was our world. But when you leave, you realise you were part of a population that's completely written off, as though they're not human" (Jaggi, 2004).

1973

Rose completed ten dresses for Edwidge with bows, collars, and ruffles, and made some large enough to last through growth spurts during Rose's absence. With two suitcases, she followed André to New York, where he invested in a car service. On Rose's departure, Edwidge clung to her at the airport. She repined the parting: "What does it feel like being left? Are you ever whole?" (Brown, 2007, M2). While her parents petitioned for their children's admission to the U.S., she observed "lines and lines of people stand in front of the U.S. consulate in Haiti, daily, in the sun, with a mustard-colored envelope full of their documents under their arms" (Berger, 2008, 34).

In an interview with writer Renee Shea of *Callaloo*, the author reflected on separation: "What happens if the mother is not there? Then we mother ourselves, or we look for that in somebody else…. Our mothers—Haitian mothers or mothers of immigrant daughters who are growing up in this culture—often suffer because, in their daughters' eyes, they become an anachronism" (Shea, 1996, 383).

The author loved masking and subversive plays read and staged in the neighborhood, bold anti-government texts that risked the lives of authors and translators into Creole. However daring their dramas, the island family avoided the militaristic extremes of Carnival season by attending mountain religious retreats. Workers communicated by call and response, the work rhythms of the tilling of spring gardens. Edwidge absorbed so many cautionary tales from her uncle that she hyperventilated in crowds and fainted from outsized fears. Seized by girlhood fears, she watched the *chaloska* (Charles Oscar) bands, military torturers who growled when they marched near her uncle's house. Edwidge read French literature and the children's classic *Madeline,* the adventurer who became her alter ego. She surveyed the religious and narrative culture recorded in French and Haitian creole and in Granmè Melina's stories—narratives "that didn't exist anywhere else" (Danticat, 2004). The student body incurred beatings from the staff and restrictions on participation at Lenten carnival, a pre–Easter spree of identity and belonging.

1975

Summer

Edwidge, Bob, and Cousin Nick visited Uncle Joseph in the hospital, where he trembled with malarial chills. News from New York reported Rose's pregnancy with a third child and jailing after immigration officials raided the factory where she worked. The author captured the terror of parental incarceration in the children's book *Mama's Nightingale*.

1976

As part of the Faustian bargain to separate from their son and daughter, Edwidge's parents communicated via phone calls, cassettes, and restrained letters in which the children "were constantly alive in each other's imagination" (Danticat, 2019, 58). The parents returned for their only visit to Haiti with her brothers, infant Karl and one-year-old Kelly, who was born missing a forearm. The author grieved for Rose and had no memory of her father, whom she feared.

1977

Summer

In the stories "Walk Straight" and "A Taste of Coffee," the author recalled

12 · A Biography

her first visit at age eight to Aunt Ilyana, a coffee grower in the mountains above Beauséjour and a night talker like Edwidge. A skilled reader, she read between the lines of her father's impersonal letters from New York. Her letters replied with news of high grades and requests for a typewriter, sewing machine, and gold earrings. Of the family's cyclical trips four or five times annually, she declared, "We are nomads constantly leaving and returning to these mountains either in actuality or in our dreams" (Danticat, 2001, 45).

November

Uncle Joseph began losing his voice, an ominous symptom of laryngeal cancer, which required a radical laryngectomy at Kings County Hospital in Brooklyn.

1978

In French and Creole on a Corsair typewriter from her father, at age nine, Edwidge began writing, a character trait she shared with the fictional Céliane Espérance in *Behind the Mountains*. She reproduced Belgian cartoonist Hergé's *Adventures of Tintin* comic books that her brother read, which Steven Spielberg filmed in 2011. In the mode of Céliane, she also typed letters for illiterate adults and read aloud their prescriptions, deeds, news clippings, and birth, marriage, and death documents, all sources of later stories. After her uncle's silencing, at age nine, she read his lips and spoke for him until he acquired an artificial voice box. To *New York Times* interviewer Garry Pierre-Pierre, she noted, "Without me he would have had no voice" (Pierre-Pierre, 1995, C1). He instructed her to speak French at the bank to ensure respectful treatment.

1979

After Uncle Joseph returned from the U.S., Edwidge shadowed him, serving as voice and interpreter. Meanwhile, Rose and Mira shared the destiny of New York immigrants: "If they were poor, they were likely to be working more hours than anyone else, for less money, and with few if any benefits" (Danticat, 2004). One brightener, the folktales of Granmè Melina, Denise's mother, relieved boredom and Edwidge's loneliness for her parents.

1980

Visa examinations disclosed inactive tuberculosis in Bob and Edwidge, who required a six-month treatment. The medication caused skin lesions, cold extremities, and suppressed appetites.

1981

March 21

At age twelve, the author flew to New York City. She later remarked, "There is a romance with this city for me that began with my imagining it as a little girl" (Danticat, 2011). She carried a gift—a pocketful of indigo balls that disintegrated and stained her new dress. She and Bob settled in a protective Haitian enclave in East Flatbush, Brooklyn, with her parents, five-year-old Karl, and seven-year-old Kelly. At the two-bedroom, sixth-floor apartment at Westbury Court overlooking Prospect Park, the city seemed fast and over-lighted. Residents practiced "it takes a village" in general babysitting and child discipline.

Mira walked his children to and from school and supported the family on cab fares he began collecting at 4:00 A.M. To ensure financial stability, he worked six ten-hour days per week, including holidays. Unwarranted police stops produced what Edwidge called "microaggressions" in the form of undeserved citations (Danticat, 2017, 209). Arriving with a wave of poor boat refugees, the author discovered "a strong and direct echo between migration patterns and the economic and political situation in Haiti" (Mirabal, 2007, 27). Far from island culture, she concluded, "Every meal is a reminder that we're not home" (*ibid.*).

In a personal essay, Edwidge recorded a first view of skyscrapers, a superhighway, elevator, fire escape, and escalator, which she described to her grandmother as a magic carpet. The period became memorable from discovery, imagination, ingenuity, and invention, especially Rose's manufacture of family clothing. While Rose struggled with the cold climate, treated Karl's frequent ear infections and Kelly's migraines, and sewed leg warmers to wear under dresses, the author learned from her the importance of imagination in solving problems, such as reducing her difficult first name to Edie. While supervising her family's home life, Rose ignored the doctor's directions to seek treatment for hypertension at Cumberland Hospital.

The reunion caused Edwidge to divide her life into "my actual age and my mama years" (Lyons, 2003, 196). To welcome her, André cooked island food. At the apartment among other Haitians, she recalled "an extraordinary amount of exchange of food" (Mirabal, 2007, 410). Hip New Yorkers ridiculed her hair style, clothes, and dialect, which earned taunts of arrival on a banana boat. Reunion of older siblings with their two youngest brothers shocked Kelly and Karl that they lost first place as eldest.

Regular prayers like those in Haiti joined congregants in homes for Monday night worship. At the Evangelical Crusade of Fishers of Men Church southeast of Brooklyn's Prospect Park on Flatbush Avenue, Edwidge had a crush on the choir director. Her parents dreamed of joining members on trips to Israel. Her mother's contribution to the Haitian community involved ritual: "She went to everybody's funeral because that's what you do to support the community whether you know them well or not" (Gleibermann, 2019, 73). Of commemoration, the author added, "The grace of life is having a proper funeral" (*ibid.*).

For solace in the new environment, Edwidge entered an English as a Second Language class at junior high. In transition, she fell "between languages ... [in] a creative collaboration with the new place I was in" (*BookBrowse,* 2004). Her family gravitated toward Pentecostalism and the scriptural injunction "Unto whom much is given, much is required" (Luke 12:48). For the first time, she read Gustave Flaubert and Emile Zola in translation. She familiarized herself with American domestic customs, absorbed the bold females in Edward Stratemeyer's Nancy Drew mysteries and Paule Marshall's *Brown Girl, Brownstones,* and kept a journal in blended Creole, French, and English. The works of Jacques Roumain, Marie Chauvet, and Jean Rhys influenced her to compose island imagery. In the August 2014 issue of *Essence,* the author's article "Our Maya" spoke of her admiration for Maya Angelou and her memoir, *I Know Why the Caged Bird Sings.*

1983

Living in the top floor across from Prospect Park above rattling subways, the author shared a blind alley for playing basketball. Daily, she hurried home down

14 *A Biography*

Flatbush Avenue to care for seven-year-old brother Karl and to watch *General Hospital.* To protect her from stabbings and shootings in rougher schools, her father enrolled her at Clara Barton High School in Crown Heights, over ten blocks from home. During rigorous honors courses, she spoke in whispers to conceal a West Indian dialect. She composed an essay on Thanksgiving in English. Classwork prepared her for a medical career and interning with a psychiatrist. She later acknowledged that "it might have been simpler, safer to have become the more helpful doctors, lawyers, engineers our parents wanted us to be" rather than artists (Danticat, 2010, 19).

Edwidge advanced to riding the city bus to classes and observing police violence against blacks. Racial demonstrations terrified her enough to cause hyperventilation and fainting. She regretted the lack of cell phones to record incidents and added, "Most of us were too terrified to demand a badge number" (Danticat, 2017, 208). After school, she volunteered at the Kings County Hospital geriatric ward to feed patients and read to them. In September, volunteering at a hospital sapped her strength: "Whenever any person died I cried and cried so much I came to realize I couldn't do it" (Spratling, 2002, C1). A fire in the six-story apartment house left little time for Edwidge and her three brothers to flee. She wrote of the blaze in a personal essay, "Westbury Court," which describes the deaths of two brothers.

For the first time, the writer faced discrimination as a francophone boat person arriving like bloated corpses on the beach at South Florida and an alleged spreader of HIV-AIDS, a charge by the Centers for Disease Control that kept Haitian-American children from a school trip to the Statue of Liberty. Rose encouraged her to look neat and be her best to present a positive image of Haitians to others. Still, whites hit and shoved her and accused her of having "dirty blood" (Danticat, 2019, 58). She reprised victimization of newcomers in the experience of Sophia Caco, protagonist of *Breath, Eyes, Memory.*

1984

Passing the Brooklyn Museum and Botanical Gardens on the way to the Brooklyn Public Library, Edwidge was surprised to find that she could check out ten titles at a time. She accessed French works by Haitian writers Jacques Roumain, Jan J. Dominique, and Marie Vieux Chauvet as well as English books by Paule Marshall and dramatist Arthur Miller, author of *Death of a Salesman* and *The Crucible.* In a special black history elective, she read classic Afro-American authors—novelists Zora Neale Hurston and Alice Walker and poet Nikki Giovanni.

The writer had never composed in Creole and lacked enough French to produce fiction, so she turned to English for creative efforts. She told interviewer Bonnie Lyons of *Contemporary Literature,* "My writing in English was as much an act of personal translation as it was an act of creative collaboration with the new place I was in" (Lyons, 187–188). As a journalist for the mimeographed newspaper *New Youth Connections,* the 18-year-old author poured her holiday rituals into prose—"A Haitian-American Christmas: Cremace and Creole Theatre" and "A New World Full of Strangers." While still at Clara Barton High School, she progressed from autobiography to fiction with the beginnings of *Breath, Eyes, Memory,* her debut novel.

Like Chicana writer Sandra Cisneros's use of Spanish in *The House on*

Mango Street, Edwidge's novel interspersed the language of the Dominican Republic. The story features Mother Haiti and Sophie Caco, a child of rape, a character similar in intensity to those of Alice Walker and Maya Angelou. She wrote of Sophie throughout her school years and later observed that fiction writing took a lot of effort. Christina Patterson, a book analyst for the London *Independent,* characterized the work as "poetic, pared-to-the-bone and moving narrative ... shot through with the folklore, stories and painful history of Haiti" (Patterson, 1999, 14).

1986

The Danticats moved into their own house in East Flatbush—a two-story, four-bedroom brick residence. The financial struggle seemed unending: "The mortgage was nearly double the amount they'd paid in rent, and some months my father drove his cab both at night and during the day to make the payment, which he then took to the bank, in person, during the final hours of the grace period" (Danticat, 2004, CY1). The constant juggling of funds raised her father to family hero, whom she described in the story "Papi," collected in *Family: American Writers Remember Their Own.*

The author recounted acceptance at the Wagner School of Public Service at New York University to study international affairs, but chose a Manhattan branch of Columbia University. Introduced to Barnard College with a full scholarship, she found an all-woman atmosphere relaxing: "The small class size and the all female atmosphere allowed me to find my voice" (Horn, 2001, 19). Against her father's wishes, she abandoned medicine to study French literature

and economics. She joined Alpha Kappa Alpha, the first black sorority, which began a charity for poor South African villages. The story "Tatiana, Mon Amour" for *Callaloo* satirized the sisterhood. She prepared for a literary career by reading the essays of Albert Camus, a philosopher from French Algeria, and the surreal experimentalists, Andre Breton of Bocage, France, and Parisian George Perec.

1987

November 2

Edwidge maintained a home office on Avenue D in Flatbush, where she relished island food and sounds of reggae, calypso, and konpa, an island dance similar to the calenda. She wrote in Creole for radio broadcasts, in which her father played a small part. Of her art, she told Jill Krementz, an interviewer for *The Writer,* that she sank into composition and let the world go by: "There are these blissful moments when you start writing and it's light outside; then you look out and it's dark, and you were just lost in this other place" (Krementz, 2004, 66). For a break, she read books like Toni Morrison's *Sula* or *Beloved* and viewed movies.

1989

April 17

Because of a shooting outside her home, cousin Marie Micheline Marole died from a seizure. A dream involved Edwidge in the death, which her parents concealed. Marie returned in the author's story "Children of the Sea" as a drowning victim.

August 23

The battery and shooting death of Yusuf K. Hawkins in Bensonhurst, Brooklyn, and the murder of Black Panther leader Huey P. Newton in Oakland, California, the previous day haunted Edwidge with memories of torture and executions during Haiti's Duvalier regime. She and her siblings joined the mile-long "Day of Outrage and Mourning" march at the Grand Army Plaza at 5 P.M. and chanted "No Justice, No Peace." The protest ended at 7:00 P.M. on the Brooklyn Bridge with police blocking approach of 7,500 blacks into Manhattan.

1990

After the author graduated Phi Beta Kappa with a degree in French literature and creative writing, she worked as administrative assistant in the Brown University financial aid office and wrote for the *Providence Journal.* The job gave her free tuition to Columbia's School of International Public Affairs, where she taught an undergraduate course. She read the works of nonwhite feminists—Maxine Hong Kingston, Julia Alvarez, and Amy Tan. After the office closed at 5:00 P.M., she wrote until 9:00, expressing themes of immigration, hyphenated citizenship, and family severance that she would have liked at age fifteen. She regretted that "My parents think that it's a hobby that ended up well" (Pierre-Pierre, 1995, C1).

1991

Entry to Brown University in Providence, Rhode Island, required no standardized Graduate Record Exam and awarded the author tuition and a small stipend. She encountered face-to-face heckling from football players, who called her a brown dog. She found a congenial congregation at a Haitian church. She elevated the city name for identifying "the creator, the Almighty" (Danticat, 1994, 70). Joseph Woods, the fictional musician in *Breath, Eyes, Memory,* equates the town with the serenity of the Seekonk River, a five-mile stretch bearing tides from Narragansett Bay. To fictional Sophie Caco, the town becomes a haven from her erratic mother Martine and a beginning of domestic life as Joseph Woods's wife and Brigitte's mother.

As a volunteer to illegal aliens, Edwidge aided a woman and her son after the father died before arriving through Miami. Their story reminded her, "There is a historical resonance with the Middle Passage, with how our ancestors got to this part of the world in the first place: on ships and on a terrible journey" (Misra, 2018). She collected stories on a congressional delegation to detention centers and from people while they talked to immigration attorneys.

Summer

The writer issued "A Wall of Fire" in *Cymbals,* the preface to "A Wall of Fire Rising," a seminal story of liberation and ideals collected in *Krik? Krak!*

November 10

In a first term of graduate study, the author composed an editorial, "Haiti: The Poetry behind the Bloodshed," for the *Providence Journal* on the deaths of 500 during the September 29 ouster of President Jean-Bertrand Aristide. With her homeland tyrannized by puppet president Joseph Nérette and General Raoul Cédras's military junta and a revival of the

Tonton Macoutes, she and other "mental refugees" viewed the islanders "slowly heading towards an Ethiopia-like stage of starvation while they wait for the storm of bullets to subside" (Danticat, 1991, D15).

1992–1993

The author produced the play *The Creation of Adam* at Rites and Reason Theater in Providence. Of her chosen career, she stated, "I'm totally compulsive. If something is on my mind, writing-wise, I have to do it and do it in the instant. I have to at least put down a first draft. Otherwise, I am so afraid I will lose it.... I live with the eternal fear that I am not supposed to be doing what I'm doing" (Danticat, 2007, 89).

Fall

Edwidge contributed one of her most famous stories, "The Missing Peace," to *Just a Moment,* a literary anthology. She reprised the story in *Caribbean Writer* (July 1994, and a collection, *Feminism 3: The Third Generation in Fiction.* Her popular stories in 1991 and 1992 appeared under engaging titles—"Dream of the Butterflies," "Graduation," and "Lost Shadows and Stick Figures."

1993

To earn an M.F.A. in creative writing from Brown University, Edwidge rejected an offer from NYU's business school and collected from Haitian Americans their memories. From the "communal endeavor," she began "Children of the Sea," the epistolary introit to a ten-story compendium, *Krik? Krak!,* composed on

her Mac computer over seven years (Shea, 1995, 15). She described in an interview with David Barsamian for *Progressive* how coarse, frowzy hair requires taming before braiding, a visualization of the author's work. Of the variety that results, she added, "Some of the braids are long, others are short. Some are thick, others are thin. Some are heavy. Others are light" (Barsamian, 2003). Her play *Dreams Like Me* opened at the Brown University New Plays Festival in Providence.

The author submitted fiction for a thesis: "My Turn in the Fire, an Abridged Novel," a metaphor based on women encircling a fire for storytelling by the one teller on the hot seat. She retitled the published work *Breath, Eyes, Memory.* Soho Press optioned the first 70 pages with a $5000 advance. She and Rose wrapped a copy as a Christmas gift for a factory seamstress so Rose could say "My daughter wrote this book" (Danticat, 2009, 36).

The *New York Times Book Review* complimented Edwidge's folk art for clear vision and resonance; a *Washington Post Book World* critic remarked on her creation of epiphanies. *Newsweek* compared her to North Carolina memoirist Thomas Wolfe, author of *Look Homeward, Angel* and *Of Time and the River.* She described her pacing as rapid: "I just wanted to write fast and finish quick" (Misra, 2018). In defense of later stories, she added that her narratives "have unity of themes: rites, rituals, notions and ideas that carry throughout most, if not all, the stories" (ibid.).

1994

At age 25, Edwidge published *Breath, Eyes, Memory,* a reflection on the 29-year Duvalier regime, the Haitian obsession with female virginity, and memories of a girl conceived by rape. Rose feared that her daughter faced execution for issuing personal comments on a dangerous subject. Duvalier rejected Creole speech, drove out intellectuals and professionals, and jailed as leftists anyone who advocated literacy. Of the era's "black holes," she remarked on the effects of dictatorship on fractured memories: "Maybe that's a bigger scar than even I realized when I was a child, or even now.... Maybe I was traumatized and that trauma is now surfacing" (Ibarrola-Armendáriz, 2011, 6).

The author's fresh take on Caribbean women's lives won the 1994 fiction prize from *The Caribbean Writer* along with hate mail for disclosing the shameful testing of young women for sexual impropriety. The *New York Times* listed her among thirty young, promising authors. Additional citations from *Essence* and *Seventeen* increased her notoriety. She redirected career plans to French literature, economics, and creative writing. Brown University's creative writing magazine *Clerestory* issued "Voices in a Dream," compiled in the anthology *Krik? Krak!* as "Children of the Sea."

January

A cinema research and production assistant, the author traveled to Haiti to collaborate with Jonathan Demme and Patricia Benoit's film company Clinica Estetico, which completed 56 films between 1993 and 2018. The collaborators produced *Courage and Pain,* a documentary on torture victims and the beginnings of Haitian movies. She attended the screening at the Walter Reade Theater in New York City on February 25.

October

On Edwidge's return visit to Haiti, stipends from the Barbara Deming Memorial Fund and the Barnard College alumnae Association underwrote travel while she researched the historiography and therapeutic benefit of rememory while writing *The Farming of Bones*. She toured the geographic site along the Massacre River, where up to 30,000 Haitians died under the machetes and rifle butts of Generalissimo Raphael Trujillo. To *Publishers Weekly* interviewer Mallay Charters, Edwidge reported the normality of swimmers, bathers, and launderers at a massacre site, which she perceived as "a huge mass grave" (Charters, 1998, 42). She encountered the myth of a Hawaiian hero, Sergeant Sam "The Cowboy" Makanani, one of the U.S. troops who arrived by helicopter to free Jacmel from oppressor Hugues Seraphin.

1995

The author's short fiction anthology *Krik? Krak!,* a twelve-story survey of female heritage, won a National Book Award shortlisting, a Barnard College Women of Achievement Award, and commendation from the *Washington Post Book World*. The story "Between the Pool and the Gardenias" earned a Pushcart Press prize. The French translation of *The Farming of Bones* received a nomination for the Prix littéraire des Caraïbes (Francophone Caribbean Literary Prize). On private time, she compiled stories from girlhood for daughters Mira and Leila in a notebook cobbled together from "fish wrappers, panty-hose cardboard" (Danticat, 1995, 192). Of her preservation of "oral tradition within an unwritten history," critic Xavier Navarro of the University of Puerto Rico at Rio Piedras acclaimed her Haitian characters "who wish to pass on a *new* history that breaks from the colonized mold, a history

A Biography

of their own, a reclamation of pride" (Navarro, 2015, 272).

March

Edwidge signed with independent agent Nicole Aragi to manage her next two titles. She visited Haiti four times a year and surveyed the Massacre River at Ouanaminthe to research *The Farming of Bones*. She quoted novelist Rene Philoctète's view of "a gory history" that had haunted Haitians for years: "Death seemed so tangible that it had set up shop everywhere" (Danticat, 2005, 8). Edwidge's book restored knowledge of the genocide and commemorated its victims.

1996

Granta 54 listed Edwidge among the twenty best young American novelists; the *New York Times* identified her as a culture changer. She also accepted acclaim from the American Literary Association Black Caucus and the Lila Acheson Wallace *Reader's Digest* grant. She began a three-year stint aiding the National Coalition for Haitian Rights, which honored martyr Jean Léopold Dominique and fought abuses against black Haitians in the Hispanic Dominican Republic. When she initiated a teaching career in creative writing at New York University, she thought of her job as midwifery—the birthing of a unique work.

Tributes accrued to Edwidge in her twenties, when she lived at her first apartment in New Rochelle. She presented the speech "Aha" at the Inter-American Development Banks Cultural Center in Washington, D.C. *Harper's Bazaar* listed her among twenty emergent people making a difference. *Jane* magazine named the author among the fifteen gutsiest women of the year.

1997

March 16

The writer produced the play *Children of the Sea* at Roxbury Community College in Boston, where she taught journalism and English literature.

Summer

On a flight home to teach a seaside course to American college students, the author shared the airways with 26-year-old Cousin Marius Dantica, Tante Zi's son. He returned in a casket after his death in Miami of *move malady ya* (the bad disease—AIDS).

1998

In the career overview *Odilon Pierre, Atis d'Ayiti* (Artist of Haiti), Edwidge and co-author Jonathan Demme presented forty-three of the naturalistic wood sculpting and oil portraits and landscapes by a dynamic Port-au-Prince surrealist and recluse in the city's *Marché de Fer* (Iron Market), constructed in Paris. Shortly before Odilon died in 1998 at age 53, he told the author of frustration with Haiti and an urgent intent to leave impressions of island history.

January

Edwidge played a small part in a crowd scene in the screen adaptation of Toni Morrison's *Beloved,* produced by Harpo Films. She left New Rochelle and rented a studio outside New York.

May

Oprah Winfrey chose *Breath, Eyes, Memory* for her book-of-the-month club.

Edwidge's objective tone reported severe housing shortages, causing people "to live in huts, shacks, or one-room houses that, sometimes, they had to build themselves" (Danticat, 1994, 11). The crude beginnings echoed the primitive efforts of Haiti's pre-Columbian Taino.

June 8

Edwidge published *The Farming of Bones,* historical fiction based on the 1937 massacre of some 30,000 black Haitians on the Dominican border. Funded by national authorities at the rate of 50¢ per head, the slaughter was the master stroke of the vainglorious dictator "Generalissimo Rafael Leonidas Trujillo Molina, Supreme Commander-in-Chief, President of the Republic" (Danticat, 1998, 17). He based his regime on ardent nationalism and rejection of immigrants, particularly people with dark skin. Nonetheless, the author chose not to pontificate: "I don't think the novel should have the burden of being a tool of activism" (Krug, 2015, 25).

The story characterizes the domestic Juana as a fanatic of hagiology, a personal trait that suits the author's intent to showcase "the person who is different from everybody else" (Charters 1998, 43). The title repeats a phrase referring to cutting jointed cane stalks, which resemble jointed human bones. Edwidge pursued the background as a tutorial to youth: "I wanted to popularize it with a larger audience as with younger people, like my brothers, who didn't know about it at all. It's a part of our history, as Haitians, but it's also a part of the history of the world. Writing about it is an act of remembrance" (Charters 1998, 43).

Novelist Julia Alvarez characterized the work as "clear as a bell, magical as a butterfly and resonant as drum talk" (Lyons, 2003, 183). Analyst Megan Feifer, a specialist in postcolonial feminism at Medaille College in Buffalo, New York, maintained that the author "[raised] questions about how society remembers historic events through archives" and "how survivors initiate acts of recovery by documenting pertinent details left out of the 'official' archive" (Feifer, 2020, 35).

June 18

The author appeared on Oprah Winfrey's show to receive acclaim for her debut novel, *Breath, Eyes, Memory.* The Oprah Book Club acknowledged the difficult themes of third-world political turmoil, sexual abuse, and rape and the grace with which the narrative hails suffering and courage.

1999

The Farming of Bones achieved an American Book Award and the Italian Super and International Flaiano Prize for Literature worth 5,000 Euros. The *New Yorker* selected her among twenty model American novelists of the future. Accolades poured in from *Newsweek, New York Times, People, Chicago Tribune, Time, Entertainment Weekly, Nation, Time Out New York, Wall Street Journal, Denver Post, Publishers Weekly, Cleveland Plain-Dealer,* and *Boston Globe.* Books on Tape issued an unabridged sound recording read by Rebecca Nicholas.

Summer

In the mountains above Beauséjour, Edwidge visited her 75-year-old Aunt Ilyana, who had called her the nickname Nounoune during a first meeting in summer 1977. During their stay, Uncle Joseph completed plans to add two rooms to a school he had started. Ilyana remained behind "to maintain our family's physical legacy, to guard the ancestral village," the subject of the story "Walk Straight" (Danticat, 2001, 47).

Edwidge and fiancé Fedo Boyer visited the Parc de la Visite in Seguin north of Jacmel and drove a pickup through craggy uphill pine trails, a side trip that she outlined in *After the Dance*. Along the way, she photographed graveyards. With Cousin Nick, she climbed hills to Beauséjour from Darbonne, in January 12, 2010, the epicenter of a devastating earthquake. With much effort, she reaches the burial place of her great grandparents, peasant farmer Osnac Dantica and his wife, who died in 1919. She reprised the visit in the story "A Taste of Coffee."

June 14

The *New Yorker* issued "The Book of the Dead," the first story anthologized in *Krik! Krak! The Farming of Bones,* translated as *La récolte douce des larmes* (The Sweet Harvest of Tears) in Paris by Jacques Chabert, earned the annual Prix Carbet de al Caraibe et Tout-Monde. While serving on the advisory board of *The Caribbean Writer* along with Derek Walcott, a Nobelist from Saint Lucia, and Jamaican poet Opal Palmer Adisa, Edwidge submitted a personal essay and recipe, "Plantains, Please."

2000

The author taught creative writing as a visiting professor at the University of Miami by assigning students to go outside, observe, and take notes. She acknowledged in an interview that classroom teaching cannot turn students into writers. They must discover composition within themselves.

September

Edwidge absorbed the volatility in Haiti during the election of Jean-Bertrand Aristide. Political crisis brought killings and pipe bombs, both part of her YA novel *Behind the Mountains*. She intended the novel to promote truth in families rather than shield against children's knowledge of political and social injustice.

September 4

The *New Yorker* published her story "Water Child," a portrait of loneliness and regret in a Haitian immigrant nurse.

November 1

The author left New Rochelle for Brooklyn.

2001

Mid–February

Edwidge visited Jacmel in southern Haiti to collect memories for her book *After the Dance: A Walk Through Carnival in Jacmel, Haiti,* composed with segments of memoir, history, and travelogue of Haiti's south coast. She incorporated facts about the island's French colonialism and war of independence in 1791, which prefaced the world's first black democracy. Of her own lineage, she compared the island's agricultural caste to her grandfather, Nozial Dantica, a Léogâne peasant who raised beans, coffee, corn, and plantains before moving his family to the Bel Air slums in Port-au-Prince.

Spring

The author moved to Miami's Little Haiti in Florida with fiancé Fedo Boyer and served the University of Miami as a visiting professor of creative writing. She felt at home in landscape similar to Haiti and observed people's movement, a familiar posture. Of her surroundings, she declared to Benjy Caplan, writer for the *Miami New Times,* "It feeds me" (Caplan, 2013, 28). The novelist Fièvre admired the results of observation: "Her words, they have in them the Haitian soul" (*ibid.*).

September 1–10

Edwidge and Rose Danticat flew from New Rochelle, New York, to Tokyo, Japan, for the author's speaking tour of American and Haitian embassies. She returned to news of 9/11 and the unknown whereabouts of brother Karl. She admired their father Mira, who navigated Manhattan to aid survivors of the World Trade Center collapse and take them safely home. Her personal reaction described in the *New Yorker* was "a certain urgency about life…. Not being alone seemed important and love was a bigger priority" (Danticat, 2011).

October 11

The author moved from Brooklyn to New York City. In editing *The Butterfly's Way: Voices from the Haitian Diaspora in the United States,* she provided an introduction that lists films on Haitian subjects: *Anita, Restavèk,* and *Masters of the Dew.* Of struggles within the diaspora, she asserted, "Our voices will not be silenced, our stories will be told" (Danticat, 2001, xvii).

2002

While living in Boston, Edwidge added to YA fiction *Behind the Mountains,* a semi-autobiographical diary

that received less acclaim than her adult works. The title acknowledged a life truth that one challenge precedes more challenges. With Carrol F. Coates, a French professor at Binghamton University, Edwidge co-translated the 1959 novel *L'espace d'un cillement* (In the Flicker of an Eyelid) by Jacques Stephen Alexis, a sensory story of Niña Estrellita, a refugee from Cuba's Fulgencio Batista regime. The plot summarized her love for El Caucho, a fellow Cuban exile. In the afterword, Edwidge preferred the author's spelling of Kreyòl and the use of footnotes to enhance glossing.

April 5

In Detroit, Marygrove College chose Edwidge for a dual honor—the featured 2002 author of its Contemporary American Authors series and the reader at the 75th anniversary celebration of the Sisters of the Immaculate Heart of Mary.

June

Accompanied by her father, the author flew to Haiti under UNESCO sponsorship during a Bel Air gang war and the World Cup to address a conference of young women on self-esteem. Her Uncle Joseph waited at the airport along with Tante Rézia, their youngest sister, Edwidge's confidante in *The Art of Death.* At Joseph's house, Aunt Estina Estème, protagonist of "Night Talkers," prompted tears from nephew Mira. He joined Edwidge for dinner at the lavish U.S. Embassy compound on the Route de Tabarre.

August

Marriage to Haitian teacher and commercial translator Faidherbe "Fedo" Boyer—with his dazzling Denzel Washington smile—and the mothering of Leila and Mira at their five-bedroom Miami home at 203 NE 44th Street on the edge of Little Haiti influenced the author's themes. By sharing the fruit of their avocado tree with neighbors, Fedo made her popular. She abandoned the Pentecostalism of her youth and embraced Unitarianism. Some Haitian readers protested when she expanded on Creole traditions in the travelogue *After the Dance: A Walk through Carnival in Jacmel, Haiti* (2002), her first nonfiction. Central to the feel of island life, she invoked the Haitian Revolution as well as the pre–Lenten Carnival, at which she became an outsider viewing some 40,000 natives. For *Progressive,* radio broadcaster David Barsamian characterized her reportage as rich and insightful. The Haitian culture ministry conferred on Edwidge the Prix Gouverneur de la Rosée du Livre et de la Littérature.

December 25

The author began spending holidays at her mother-in-law's house at Les Cayes, her husband's hometown on Haiti's southwestern shore. On Christmas Day, a shooter gunned down the bodyguard of Michèle Montas, the reporter and wife of martyr Jean Léopold Dominique, whom an assassin murdered at Radio Haiti-Inter in Port-au-Prince on April 3, 2000.

2003

Late February

The author, Jonathan Demme of ThinkFilm Inc., investigative radio reporters Jan "J.J." Dominique and stepmother Michele Montas, activist Marlene Bastien, and attorney Cheryl Little visited the Krome Detention Center. In the essay "No Greater Shame" for the *Haitian Boston Reporter,* Edwidge compared the infamous lockup to "a cross between Mount Olympus and hell" (Danticat, 2003). The group also toured a Dade County immigration complex holding Haitian women and children. In May, the newspaper dubbed Edwidge Haiti's most famous literary flag-bearer for divulging the underside of U.S. immigrant detainment prisons.

With Demme, Edwidge co-produced *The Agronomist,* a biography of radio reporter and activist Jean Léopold Dominique, owner of Radio Haiti-Inter. A defender of the poor agrarian class, he died of an assassin's bullets at Radio Hall. The 90-minute documentary debuted at the United Nations Headquarters on May 2004 and was featured at the Festival International du Film des Droits de l'Homme (Human Rights) de Paris. Accolades accompanied presentations in Brittany at the 2007 Festival International du Film des Droits de l'Homme de Bangui, the 2010 Festival de Cinéma du Duarnenez and the Festival International du Film Insulaire de l'île de Groix, and, in 2017, the Festival International du Film d'Amiens.

September 22

Edwidge continued a side career in acting with a bit part in *The Manchurian Candidate,* filmed in the Bronx by Paramount.

October 15

For a Caribbean Women Writers Series at Smith College in Northampton, Massachusetts, the author gave an afternoon reading and discussed personal and political consequences of writing and bilingualism in the postcolonial novel. In the roundtable discussion "Voices from Hispaniola," Edwidge appreciated the insider/outsider perspective on Haiti, which offered her "another kind of eye with which to examine things" (Danticat, 2004). The statement proved prophetic of a year of family and personal turmoil.

2004

Early March

Edwidge collected short fiction about a persecutor under the 29-year dictatorship of Papa Doc and Baby Doc Duvalier. She stated in *Create Dangerously,* "I have tried to maintain a silent conversation with Jacques Roumain" by arranging and interconnecting the stories into a unit in *The Dew Breaker,* which opens on "The Book of the Dead." Referring to political corruption, the layered text compounded her denunciations of tyranny by the men who stomp the dew, a Creole idiom for terrorists. In a cycle of revenge, dew becomes a symbol for unending gifts of nature and a token of mercy and forgiveness, a suggestion of playwright William Shakespeare's belief in *The Merchant of Venice* that "the quality of mercy is not strained" (IV, I, 173). The author won fiction citations from *Caribbean Writer, Essence,* and *Seventeen* and a Lannan Foundation Fellowship for Fiction of $150,000.

May 12–23

The author accepted a post as judge at the 57th annual Cannes Film Festival, which awards the coveted Palme d'Or (Gold Palm), presented to Michael Moore's *Fahrenheit 9/11.*

Early July

Edwidge confirmed her pregnancy the same day that she learned that pulmonary fibrosis doomed her father Mira, who had already made three diagnostic visits to Coney Island Hospital. In this same period, the French adaptation of *Children of the Sea* (Les Enfants de la Mer) opened in Avignon, France, at the Chapelle du Verbe Incarné.

July 15

Mira called his older brother, 81-year-old Joseph Dantica, in Haiti to urge him to leave Bel Air, a hillside Port-au-Prince slum turned into a battleground by police and U.N. raiders and gangs.

Late August

During Mira's first hospitalization, Uncle Joseph visited New York.

September

While armed gangs looted and burned Uncle Joseph's school and church in Port-au-Prince, for three days, he hid under a neighbor's bed. U.N. peacekeepers and island riot police stormed the church, calmed congregants, and fired on the criminals from the roof. While tanks parked on the street and blocked the Rue Saint Martin, gangs threw bottles and rocks at the pastor's house on the adjacent Rue Tirremasse. Believing Joseph had taken police bribes, thugs burned his office and demanded that he pay for burial of fifteen *chimères* (gang members).

Edwidge found disgraceful a dual assault on a sanctuary. She reported, "His church was desacralized not just by the gangs who pillaged it but by the police and peacekeepers who stormed it" (Miller, 2007). She summarized the result of turmoil: "If you've lived in a place like Haiti, which has experienced invasion, and whose destiny has always been grasped by

A Biography

others, you know people live with those scars for generations" (Jaggi, 2004).

October 24–29

For five days, a U.N. peacekeeping division of 300 soldiers attacked the gangs in Bel Air with tanks and bulldozed debris that blocked roads. Neighbors beat pots and pans to demand peace. The author's Uncle Joseph fled from the violence-ridden neighborhood and boarded a plane for Miami.

November

During her first pregnancy, the author joined Haitian American voting rallies in Miami's Little Haiti. She noted anger in residents over ballot confusion and asylum exclusions during a period of hurricanes, floods, and violence following the Haitian ouster of president Jean-Bertrand Aristide. She wrote of the cataclysm in "A Very Haitian Story," published in the *New York Times*. To harness local energies, she promoted Haitian Women for Haitian Refugees, Lambi Fund of Haiti, Haitian Neighborhood Center, Americans for Immigrant Justice, Equality Now, and Florida Immigrant Advocacy Center. Optimism filled her interview with E. Ethelbert Miller for *Foreign Policy in Focus,* to whom she exclaimed: "We are not complacent. We are fighting" (Miller, 2007).

November 3

For seeking asylum, Uncle Joseph Dantica entered jail among other immigrants. Of his collapse, his niece stressed, "Racism was probably a huge factor in my uncle's death" (Berger, 2008, 36). He had obtained a visa and adequate documentation for himself and 55-year-old son Maxo. Nonetheless, the Department of Homeland Security handcuffed the octogenarian for five days in the Krome immigrant detention center on NE Fourth Street adjacent to Miami Beach and the Miami International Airport.

Transported to nearby Jackson Memorial Hospital in shackles and prison overalls after suffering a seizure, severe vomiting, and coma, Joseph died from pancreatitis. Later in the story "Without Inspection," the author described the facility as "a prison for people like us," where her uncle arrived like a criminal under the designation Alien #27042999 (Danticat, 2018). Of the punitive treatment of black migrants, she concluded, "We all live with a certain level of risk in post-9/11 America" (Danticat, 2005, vi).

Immigration agents refused attorney Cheryl Little's intercession for Joseph and denied admittance to his hospital room by his son Maxo or niece Edwidge. In an interview with National Public Radio journalist Steve Inskeep, Edwidge added, "He died without his medications, which were taken away from him, five days later in a county hospital chained to a bed" (Inskeep, 2004). Because authorities accused Joseph of faking illness, the Danticat family pressed a lawsuit to gain details of the detainment. Nothing came of litigation, but the book *Brother, I'm Dying,* a documentation of the Danticat brothers' last days, enlightened readers on immigrant intimidation and racism.

2005

HBO optioned for screen *The Dew Breaker,* a cycle of nine stories and winner of the Anisfield-Wolf Book Awards. The collection earned a $5000 nomination for the PEN/Faulkner Award and a $20,000 Story Prize for defining the brutality of Haiti's paramilitary Tonton

Macoute under the Duvalier regimes. Edwidge wrote a second YA novel, *Anacaona: Golden Flower, Haiti, 1490,* a mythic Taino Indian ruler from Léogâne, 19 miles southwest of Port-au-Prince.

April

The author gave birth to Mira Boyer, a first child, whom she named for her father. The swirl of emotion in the baby's first month enabled Edwidge to "see that life takes place at the crossroad of joy and sorrow" (Santiago, 2005, PA26).

May 24

After a nine-month illness, pulmonary fibrosis from environmental impurities taken in during daily cab driving killed André Mira Danticat, Edwidge's father. The doctor told her the disease was terminal, but did not tell André. He lay buried beside his brother Joseph, interred five months earlier in Queens, New York. The author reprised the lung ailment for the story "Elsie" and revisited the disquieting intake of each breath in the cough, chills, and gasping of Uncle Matunherí in *Anacaona.*

Summer

Katharine Capshaw Smith, an English professor at the University of Connecticut, introduced an interview for *Children's Literature Association Quarterly* with compliments to Edwidge's grace and imagery and her use of fable and metaphor to disclose the trauma of deracination and political violence. Smith characterized the author's two-world view as "cultural liminality," a position at the juncture of two nations (Smith, 2005, 195). Edwidge asserted that her works for adults and young readers cover the African diaspora as well as Haiti and the Caribbean.

2006

May 30–June 3

The author attended the Association of Caribbean Women Writers & Scholars Conference in Miami. She spent time with novelist Toni Morrison, age 75, in Paris at the Denon wing of the Louvre, where her son Ford filmed the meeting.

2007

A cover story in *Poets and Writers Magazine* featured Edwidge. She provided the background voice for a 95-minute documentary *The Sugar Babies* (Les Enfants du Sucre). Filmed in the Dominican Republic by Amy Serrano for Siren Studios, the text protested the abuses and human trafficking perpetrated by cane magnates. After screenings in New Orleans and Delray Beach, Florida, it was a feature at the 3e édition du Festival International du Film Haïtien de Montréal.

January 8

Seattle Arts & Lectures invited Edwidge to speak at Benaroya Hall to challenge readers in the Puget Sound region with literature from current times.

May 30

The author praised *Callaloo,* a multicultural venue of Johns Hopkins University Press for issuing an outlet for diasporic cultures. She added that the publication offers "a home for what you write" (Collins, 2007, 674).

September 18

The author read from *Brother, I'm Dying* for a program at Brown University coordinated by Africana Studies and Literary Arts.

October 4

Before the House Subcommittee on Immigration, Citizenship, Refugees, Border Security, and International Law, Edwidge reported at the satirically named "Holiday on ICE" hearing, "Immigration detention is one of the fastest growing forms of incarceration in the United States" (Berger, 2008, 33). She predicted that more asylum seekers will die in custody of hostile, racist authorities and outside the knowledge of the media and families.

October 29

The author's memoir *Brother, I'm Dying* received nomination for a National Book Award and a National Book Critics Circle Award for summarizing her Uncle Joseph's flight from Haiti's Tonton Macoute and his death in custody of Miami immigration agents. Six newspapers declared the work a best book of the year: *Boston Globe, Chicago Tribune, Christian Science Monitor, Los Angeles Times, Miami Herald,* and *Washington Post.* The *New York Times* named it a notable work.

2008

Edwidge wrote *Create Dangerously* after presenting the Toni Morrison lecture on artistic ambivalence, sponsored by Princeton University Center for African American Studies.

March 1

In Miami, Florida, Edwidge established a quiet place filled with familiar possessions, where she worked at night one project at a time. The Dayton Literary Peace Prize honored *Brother, I'm Dying; Booklist* placed it among the top ten non-fiction works by black Americans.

March 10

Independent scenarist Zeinabu Irene Davis, a professor at the University of California, San Diego, proposed filming the author's story "The Secret Island."

November 24

To clarify the criminal underworld in Port-au-Prince, Edwidge published "Ghosts" in the *New Yorker.*

2009

January 1

The author reported to Opal Palmer Adisa, a writer for *African American Review,* "While I have left Haiti, it's never left me" (Adisa, 2009, 345). Edwidge scripted and narrated the feminist cinema *Poto Mitan: Haitian Women Pillars of the Global Economy,* a survey of globalization and its impact on five women from varied generations. The 50-minute documentary features activist factory worker Marie-Jeanne, rights activist and shanty town resident Solange, and Frisline, a divorced mother of three sons.

September 21

The author accepted "le prestigious Prix des génies de la foundation MacArthur, (the prestigious John D. and Catherine T. MacArthur Fellows Program Genius grant) of $500,000, the Best of Brooklyn Award, and the Nicolas Guillen

Philosophical Literature Prize from the Caribbean Philosophical Association.

November

Upon of the election of America's first black president, Edwidge gathered her daughter into her arms to commend the rise of Barack Obama. In the essay for *Progressive* "I Still Have a Dream," she attempted to echo Martin Luther King's famous sermons, but had to admit "this one man was not going to take all of us with him into the postracial promised land" (Danticat, 2015, 16).

2010

January 12

Critics and authors praised *Create Dangerously: The Immigrant Artist at Work,* a painfully explicit view of Gothic horror after a building collapses, leaving a stack of arms and legs "flesh-depleted" and dry (Danticat, 2010, 165). The story replicated the motif of her first picture book, *Eight Days: A Story of Haiti,* a child's version of terror under earthquake rubble after the cataclysm splayed Léogâne. He remembered spending his time playing, living in his imagination through fifty aftershocks. The disaster produced 200,000 deaths (including her cousin Maxo Dantica), 300,000 injured, and 1,500,000 displacements from home.

The author found her five-year-old daughter Mira confused by news of collapsed homes and fearful that her Haitian Grandmother Dantica lay under a house at Les Cayes. In an interview for *Granta* with Zimbabwean critic and publisher Ella Wakatama Allfrey, the author reported on working as a volunteer and witnessing increased peril among rural

females: "Rape has increased, especially in the displacement camps, as has prostitution and survival-sex" (Allfrey, 2011). She collected stories from seventeen fiction writers and edited the book *Haiti Noir* (Black Haiti), which contains her story "Claire of the Sea Light." The text defines the middle ground between morality and immorality. She added, "The trick is how to ... turn it into something truly worth sharing with others" (*ibid.*). Proceeds from the book went to the Lambi Fund, an educational outreach to rural people.

January 17

In the essay "Haiti: Bloodied, Shaken—and Beloved" for the *Miami Herald,* Edwidge poured out personal sorrows for islanders damaged or killed by the earthquake. She wrote about people sleeping outdoors, food shortages, and soil and air contamination from unburied corpses.

February 4

Edwidge flew to the island and occupied a sleeping bag on a relative's roof rather than risk dying under rubble dislodged by an aftershock.

August

The author returned to Port-au-Prince for the annual Fête Dieu Livres en Folie (the Feast of God Mad Books) book festival of 135 writers. At the summer camp Li Li Li (Read, read, read), Edwidge worked and visited family.

October 4

For First Readings, the author returned to Brown University in Providence, Rhode Island. To freshmen who were discussing *The Dew Breaker,* she lectured on themes of redemption, liberation, and the Haitian people's need for art. Students learned about the destruction of a Port-au-Prince hospital and the death of an entire class of graduate nurses.

October 20

A subsequent cholera epidemic killed 8,183 and sickened 665,000, largely because of Haiti's inadequate sanitation and waterworks. For an expert's opinion, the BBC, National Public Radio, and most international news gatherers turned to Edwidge for analysis. Authorities began calling her Haiti's voice.

November 18

Edwidge contributed poems to Bruce Weber's photo compendium *Standing Tall: Portraits of the Haitian Community in Miami, 2003–2010*, issued by the Miami Museum of Contemporary Art. The collection incorporates "Miras," a poem about *ras la fine* (the end of the race) originally published in the spring 2010 issue of *Callaloo*.

December

For reading to children in tent cities, *Foreign Policy,* a magazine sponsored by Wordpress, chose Edwidge as one of 100 global thinkers promoting art amid chaos. The *New York Times Book Review* awarded *Create Dangerously* the 2010 Editor's Choice. More book of the year citations arrived from *Mosaic Magazine, Miami Herald,* and a nomination from the 2010 Book the Year Award in Biography and Autobiography from ForeWord Reviews.

2011

January 11

For the Independent Lens series, the author narrated *Nou Bouke* (We're

Tired), a one-hour PBS documentary on the post-earthquake mood a year after the crisis. Sponsored by the *Miami Herald,* WPBT2, and *El Nuevo Herald*, the film debuted at the Little Haiti Cultural Center and received an Emmy. Profits aided Doctors Without Borders and Operation Helping Hands in answering unmet needs of survivors. In the aftermath, UNESCO named Jacmel a global heritage site.

April 12

In a speech in Lewisburg, Pennsylvania, at Bucknell University, the writer and speaker summarized the nonfiction work as an examination of "what it means to be an immigrant artist from a country in crisis" (Kopchik, 2011). For the forum "Creativity beyond the Box," she focused on the themes of two works: *Eight Days,* the story of a child's experience during the 2010 earthquake, and *Create Dangerously.*

May 20

At the 2011 commencement, Adelphi University in Uniondale, New York, conferred a degree in humane letters on Edwidge.

Summer

Skipping Stones Magazine, an outlet in Eugene, Oregon, for multicultural literature from writers eight to sixteen, chose *Eight Days* as one of thirty outstanding books and DVDs for students.

September 11

On the anniversary of 9/11, the author spoke over National Public Radio in Washington, D.C., to discuss her essay "Flight" in *New Yorker.* She noted the immigrants' disbelief that cataclysm could strike their haven in the U.S. To interviewer Audie Cornish, she described the terrorists' attack as a "rude awakening" to the fact that "every place is vulnerable" (Cornish, 2011). The result was accounts of "cultural trauma" from people who became storytellers of "collective grieving" (*ibid*.). Of the undocumented aliens who died in the towers, she regretted their invisibility: "it's like they were never here" (Danticat, 2011).

September 20

The author issued *Create Dangerously,* an overview of exiled writers and artists who continue to produce art revealing the miseries in their motherlands. For autobiography, she achieved the One Caribbean Media Bocas Prize for West Indian literature and received $10,000 for recalling vanishing cultures.

October 9–10

Edwidge edited the collection *Haiti Noir* and wrote an entry in *Tent Life: Haiti,* winner of the 2011 Best American Essays award. Of the lives of refugees from the earthquake, she observed, "Tent life is not to be idealized though. It is indeed about misery and pain," including crimes against the vulnerable (Danticat, 2011, 9). She listed fear of lightning, mudslide, decay and garbage, cholera, and possible rape. Water trucks relieved a crisis in Cité Soleil (Sunshine City), a trash-filled shantytown of 400,000 in Port-au-Prince. International agencies replaced scraps with stable tarps for building shelters.

November 18

City College of New York honored Edwidge with a Langston Hughes Medal, which she valued for the poet's promotion of Haitian culture in the 1920s during the Harlem Renaissance.

2012

Edwidge starred as Yannick in the cinema *Stones in the Sun,* shot in Brooklyn by Syncopated Films under director Patricia Benoit. The plot highlighted the post–Duvalier lives of Haitian immigrants in Brooklyn and the residuum of violence committed by the Tonton Macoute death squad. The title reflects the Haitian proverb "Stones in the water don't know the suffering of stones in the sun."

March 12

The author addressed students at the University of Michigan at Flint on *Brother, I'm Dying,* the book chosen for the campus read.

March 27–28

In "Detention Is No Holiday," an op-ed rebuttal for the *New York Times,* Edwidge challenged the U.S. Department of Homeland Security's standards of roundup and jailing for immigrants. She restated the directive as a dangerous message denying medical care to the vulnerable, aged, and sick. She rebuked the consortium for implying that "their very lives are luxuries, and that it is not our responsibility to protect them" ("Edwidge," 2016).

May 20

At commencement, Smith College in Northampton, Massachusetts, conferred an honorary doctorate on the author for her impact on female lives and education and for publicizing a nation's plight.

September 23

Edwidge appeared in *Hotel Haiti,* an 88-minute documentary shot in Germany by Alma Barkey, a Montreal company. A title at the Cinéma du Parc at the 8ème Festival International du Film Black de Montréal, it featured the Hotel Oloffson and glimpses of Vodou ritual in Jacmel and Pétionville.

October 1

In a National Public Radio interview with journalist Celeste Headlee, Edwidge joined Dominican-American novelist Julia Alvarez and U.S. poet laureate Rita Dove in recognizing the rescuers who saved Haitian-Dominicans from mass murder by machete, rifle butt, and drowning at the Massacre River on October 2–8, 1937. Edwidge noted the connection with German fascism: "The time of the massacre was a spread of Nazism throughout Europe and Trujillo was a great admirer, it turned out, of Hitler" (Headlee, 2012). In keeping with Hitler's drive for a light-skinned master race, Trujillo attempted to reduce the black population with a purge called "El Corte, the cutting" (*ibid.*). Edwidge blamed a "collaboration among the elites of both Haiti and the Dominican Republic" for victimizing peasants (*Ibid.*)

October 4–6

Edwidge and other islanders assembled at "The Border of Lights," an international vigil commemorating the "angelitos" who risked death to circumvent dictator Rafael Trujillo's "Parsley Massacre," the extermination of 30,000 black cane workers along the Massacre River on the Dominican-Haitian border.

December

"Giving and Receiving," Edwidge's autobiographical essay for *Progressive,* revered Joseph Nosius Dantica for a lifetime of charity that supported a church, two schools, and a trauma clinic in addition to his anonymous gifts to funeral costs, school fees, and medical care.

2013

January

The author published children's cultural fiction in *The Last Mapou,* a nature myth based on ecology and human mortality. A second honorary degree came from Yale for writing truthful stories the year that Edwidge scripted the film *Girl Rising,* starring Anne Hathaway, Liam Neeson, Cate Blanchett, Selena Gomez, Salma Hayek, and Meryl Streep. Nominated for an Emmy, the documentary shot by the Girl Rising project in New York City featured nine participants from Afghanistan, Cambodia, Egypt, Ethiopia, Haiti, India, Nepal, Peru, and Sierra Leone. The *Washington Post* commended the movie for promoting women's education worldwide.

April 25

Create Dangerously earned an Association of Caribbean Writers Grand Prize for Literature, presented in Deshaies, Guadeloupe.

Summer

Edwidge traveled to Tahiti, a francophone nation in the South Pacific.

August

Following a nine-year hiatus, Edwidge issued *Claire of the Sea Light,* a parable of a small life on the lush fictional beach of Ville Rose. The cover features the author's daughter Mira in Claire Limyè Lanmè Faustin's role. Based on *Haiti Noir* and Léogâne, her mother Rose's hometown, the tripartite hybrid of novel, fable, and story won a notable fiction selection from the *Washington Post,* a National Public Radio "Great Read," a *New York Times Book Review* notable work of 2013, and top picks from *Library Journal* and *Christian Science Monitor.* The controlling theme reflects on personal adaptations to grief and makes the community into a character. The story of Claire elicits from critics the adjectives wrenching, surprising, luminous, pulsing, hypnotic, precise, ethereal, and lyrical.

September 21–22

For the two-day Brooklyn Book Festival, the writer led the Haiti Cultural Exchange, which offered banners, drumming, storytelling, and a photo exhibit at Five Myles Gallery. She followed with a presentation entitled "Creating Dangerously in a Dangerous World," impetus to a subsequent nonfiction survey of candid art.

November 10

In a September ethnic purge of 400,000 Haitian-Dominicans, the Dominican Republic engaged in "institutionalized racism" or denationalization by deporting as aliens 250,000 birthright citizens born after 1929 to non–Hispanic parents (Danticat, 2013). Edwidge joined Julia Alvarez, Junot Diaz, and Mark Kurlansky in submitting "In the Dominican Republic, Suddenly Stateless," an op-ed piece for the *Los Angeles Times.* The text warned of a genocidal ploy from Nazi Germany in the 1930s—"[stripping] a people of their right to citizenship," a violation of international law (ibid.). The essay suggested that Western nations boycott travel and tourism among violators of human rights. It concluded with historic

comparisons to genocide in Germany, the Balkans, and South Africa.

November 16

In a subsequent response to Dominican racism, Edwidge joined Julia Alvarez and Junot Diaz in submitting an editorial to the *Providence Journal,* "Stateless in the Dominican Republic." The text characterized the Afro-Caribbean crisis as "near-slavery in Dominican agro-industry" and compared the purge to expulsion of Haitians from Miami (Danticat, 2013, 1).

2014

January

The writer edited the anthology *Haiti Noir 2: The Classics. Claire of the Sea Light* received short listing for the Andrew Carnegie Medal for Excellence in Fiction and the PEN Oakland Josephine Miles Literary citation.

May 10

At graduation at Miami's St. Thomas University, Edwidge received an honorary doctorate for her advocacy of Haitians at home and in the diaspora.

October 2

After Rose Danticat's death at Edwidge's home in Little Haiti, Miami, a neighbor sat with the family all night. The author composed for *Sojourners* a memoir, "The Possibility of Heaven."

November 14

Edwidge published "Quality Control" in the *Washington Post.* The story recurred in *Everything Inside* as "Seven

Stories," an account of two girls' friendship following the assassination of a Caribbean prime minister.

2015

May 7

The author wrote "A Prayer before Dying" for PEN World Voices and its chapbook, *A Book of Prayer and Meditation*. The lyrical ode in memory of her mother Rose reappeared in *The Art of Death* as "A New Sky."

June 17

After a court ruling stripped a half million black Haitian-Dominicans of their citizenship, Edwidge challenged the statelessness that left islanders fearful of mass roundups. Her speeches and essays decried denationalization, a form of ethnic and racial purging. Additional protest from nationally renowned authors Julia Alvarez, Vargas Llosa, and Junot Diaz compared the arbitrary deportation plan to the Nazi Holocaust. Edwidge charged the U.S. with provoking Dominican racism by subsidizing the sugar industry, the main employer of black day laborers.

September 18

Mama's Nightingale, a child's story of the separation of immigrant mother and daughter by border guards, appeared with illustrations by Leslie Staub. *Kirkus Reviews* named the work a best book of 2015. Edwidge narrated the work at the Young Readers Stage on Brooklyn Book Festival Children's Day.

October

The novel *Untwine* added to Edwidge's growing acclaim for YA fiction with positive reviews from the *New York Times, Kirkus, Audio File, School Library Journal, Philadelphia Inquirer, Publishers Weekly,* and *Bulletin of the Center for Children's Books.* The book won an National Association for the Advancement of Colored People Image Award for an outstanding literary work, a Voices of Young Advocates Perfect Ten, Bank Street College of Education Best Children's Books of 2016, New York Public Library best selection for teens, and a Cooperative Children's Book Center Choices selection. Key to acclaim lay thoughtful pacing of a serious emotional shift from twin to only child on the rim of womanhood.

2016

In Tucson, Arizona, Edwidge judged the Kore Press short fiction contest, a nonprofit publisher that annually promotes diversity, nonconformity, and literary activism in women.

March 20

The writer delivered the address "The Artist as Activist" at Case Western Reserve to the Cuyahoga County library Writers series in Cleveland, Ohio, about visiting displays of Southern migrant painter Jacob Lawrence's art featuring blacks relocating to the North. She found the series heartbreaking and beautiful for capturing "black bodies in motion, in transit, in danger, and in pain" (Long, 2016). Her salute to Lawrence dramatized the poor and hungry in the Great Migration of 1916–1970 for maintaining momentum as black Southerners pressed into urban areas toward prosperity, learning, and voting rights. Edwidge earned a 2016 Jane Addams Peace Prize honor for *Mama's Nightingale.*

March 30

At the closing of the Miami Book Fair Big Read, sponsored by Miami-Dade College, Edwidge shared a podium with her attorney, Cheryl Little. They discussed themes of *Brother, I'm Dying* and social concerns of immigrants.

April 7

Dickinson College in Carlisle, Pennsylvania presented Edwidge the Harold and Ethel L. Stellfox Visiting Scholars and Writers Program award, part of a $1.5 million estate.

May 25

Because of mounting anxiety at President Donald Trump's xenophobia, Edwidge addressed an audience at the University of California, Los Angeles, Fowler Museum at the Conference on Racialized State Violence in Global Perspective with a keynote speech: "Living with Uncertainty: Violence, Exile, and Black Life." The invitation established her prominence as vocal advocate for human rights.

2017

January 20

After Donald Trump's inaugural, Edwidge declared the president's speech hostile, xenophobic, and inhumane. She stated in a *New Yorker* article, "Poetry in a Time of Protest," a fear for refugees. She joined immigrants at a rally a week later at Miami airport. For self-care, she read novelists Maya Angelou, Judy Blume, and Paule Marshall and the verse of Gwendolyn Brooks, Langston Hughes, and Audre Lorde. All declared unity the soul of community.

March 30

Edwidge and Bahamian scenarist Easmanie Michel presented a table reading of "Caroline's Wedding," featuring Numa Perrier in the role of protagonist Gracina Azile. Easmanie hired writers France-Luce Benson and Darcy Miller to adapt the short story to the screen.

Summer

Out of 1,600 entries, the film version of "Caroline's Wedding" won the 2017 American Zoetrope Screenplay Contest and a $5,000 grand prize, presented by Judge Francis Coppola. The adapted short story was a finalist for the New York University Fusion Film Festival and a feature at the March 2016 Women at Sundance Financing and Strategy Intensive.

July

Edwidge compiled a biography, *The Art of Death: Writing the Final Story*, about her mother Rose's slow wasting from ovarian cancer in early 2014. A universal theme anchored the 2015 memoir "Without Her" for the April 25, 2015, issue of the *New York Times*, which she repeated as "Feetfirst." Of a family's acceptance of mortality, the writer stated, "Your parents can seem immortal, then they get terminally ill and they remove the possibility of either of you or them being immortal" (Danticat, 2017, 13). In the introduction to the book, Edwidge offered a personal testimony to the source of her career: "Writing has been the primary way I have tried to make sense of my losses, including death" (Danticat, 2017, 6).

October 8

To benefit the Haitian Women for Haitian Refugees, Edwidge hosted a reading of *Mama's Nightingale*, a discussion, and book signing at New York's Families for Freedom, a multi-ethnic human rights organization combatting deportation.

October 14

At the Open Campus of the University of the West Indies in Cave Hill, Barbados, Edwidge accepted a third honorary doctorate. The presentation occurred one month after the area incurred disaster following Maria, a category five hurricane that swept Barbuda, Dominica, Grenada, Puerto Rico, and U.S. Virgin Islands on September 18, killing students and destroying homes.

November 6

The author submitted to the *New York Times* "Dawn after the Tempests," a personal essay on a visit to Coyaba Beach, Grenada, where Hurricane Maria killed 39 residents and devastated nutmeg groves that produce one-fifth of the world's production of mace and nutmeg.

November 9

Edwidge's work won a Neustadt International Prize of $50,000 and a silver eagle feather from the University of Oklahoma and *World Literature Today* for outstanding literary merit.

2018

March

As the Robert L. Hess scholar in residence in black studies at Brooklyn College on Bedford Avenue, the author delivered the lecture "A Right to Be Here: Race, Immigration, and My Third Culture Kids."

April 10

Edwidge contributed to *The Foreigner's Home,* a feature film from Ice Lens Pictures in Cleveland, Ohio. It debuted at the Cleveland Museum of Art after a world premiere at the International Film Festival at Rotterdam.

June

To the interviewer Jivin Misra with the *Brooklyn Review*, the author stated her despair at the separation of parents and children at the Mexican border. Not only did U.S. President Donald Trump's policies create the nightmare, "This administration is using the Bible to justify it" (Misra, 2018). Of her career "in heartbreaking times," she saw herself doing the author's job—"bearing witness" to her journey (*ibid.*).

June 17

Edwidge delivered the "Message from the Brooklyn Public Library" lecture and urged listeners to guard their integrity during a period of mass shootings.

June 18

At Philipsburg, St. Martin, the author accepted the St. Martin Book Fair President's Award for activism toward Caribbean sovereignty and human rights. Presenters honored her for combining literary, cultural, and liberation components in the service of progress, of their people or nation, and of humanity.

September 6

The University of Kansas at Lawrence chose *Create Dangerously* as the common read for all first-year students to discuss. Edwidge presented a keynote address at the Lied Center on powerful storytelling.

October 2

In New York City, the Ford Foundation named Edwidge a fellow of the Art of Change along with writer Sandra Cisneros, dancer Mikhail Baryshnikov, filmmaker Ava Du Vernay, and poet Joy Harjo.

2019

February 18

In New York City, the eight-part collection *Everything Inside* received Edwidge's second National Book Critics Circle Award.

February 25

The American Academy of Arts and Letters in New York awarded Edwidge a second $20,000 Story Prize for *Everything Inside*. Judges named her "a harking angel. She comes to tell us that the world is new, again and again, and that stories will not lose their urgency, their necessity" ("Author," 2020). She is the only writer to achieve a second Story award (Author, 2020). She also completed a second mother-daughter picture book, *My Mommy Medicine,* which earned a 2019 Parent's Choice Recommended Award.

May 5

Edwidge narrated *My Mommy Medicine* at the Little Haiti Book Festival, a free segment of the ReadCaribbean program in cooperation with the Miami Book Fair. The gathering at the Little Haiti Cultural Center and Library Mapou incorporated immigrants and neighbors wanting to learn about island culture and seeking to make their children better narrators, readers, and writers. At 11:15 A.M. on the Target Stage, the author discussed with children's literature expert Andrea Davis Pinkney the worth of a giving relationship between mother and daughter.

May 8

Edwidge visited Chicago after Columbia College and the city library named *Brother, I'm Dying* the featured selection for the Big Read, sponsored by the National Endowment for the Arts. To Darcel Rockett, an interviewer from the *Chicago Tribune,* she spoke on the essence of the American Dream under anti-immigration president Donald Trump, who classed poor nations as "shithole countries" (Rockett, 2019). She accused the U.S. of being "a more closed place ... less friendly" and a promoter of anti-third world antagonisms (*ibid.*).

August

The public acclaimed the new short fiction anthology *Everything Inside.* The collection earned Best Books of the Year from Buzzfeed, *Esquire, Miami Herald, Milwaukee Journal Sentinel,* National Public Radio, Powell's City of Books, *St. Louis Post-Dispatch,* and *Time.*

August 29

National Public Radio listed *The Art of Death* among the year's best books. In an interview with journalist Steve Inskeep, she stated a truism about society: "Whether or not we belong is not defined by us" (Inskeep, 2019).

September

Everything Inside appeared in the compendium *New Daughters of Africa* and the first page of the September/October issue of *Poets & Writers.*

September 27–October 5

In Harrison, New York, Purchase College launched a program on international studies featuring Edwidge, the Roy and Shirley Durst Distinguished Chair in Literature. Directed by Alex Correia, Edwidge's play "Bastille Day," a revision of the story "The Gift" in *Everything Inside,* placed two expat Haitian couples discussing the island's destiny after the January 12, 2010, earthquake.

October 24

At the Sheldon Concert Hall, the St. Louis University Library named Edwidge its 2019 literary award winner. The university chose *Brother, I'm Dying* as the freshman read for small group discussion. Of the author's skill at short and long fiction, Abby Manzella, a book critic for the *St. Louis Dispatch,* emphasized the backstories of Haiti and the peril arising from "dictatorships, the devastating Haitian earthquake of 2010, the United States' restrictive immigration laws" and "the lasting effects of these events on all of our interactions" (Manzella, 2019, B8).

November 20

Edwidge joined TV star Oprah Winfrey and lecturer Angela Davis in New York's Cathedral of St. John for a tribute to Toni Morrison, who died on August 5, 2019.

2020
February

The American Academy of Arts and Letters inducted Edwidge into membership as a recognition of excellence. The New York State Council on the Arts bestowed an Individual Artist grant for the filming of "Caroline's Wedding."

February 5

In New York, the author earned a Vilcek Foundation Prize in Literature consisting of a trophy and $100,000, a reward for creative promise and excellence.

February 26

The American Academy of Arts and Letters named Edwidge a two-time winner of the Story Prize and granted her a purse of $20,000. The citation occurred fifteen years after she won the debut Story Prize for "The Dew Breaker," which the judges and media labelled "canonical."

March 12

For an art critique of Botswanan painter Pamela Phatsimo Sunstrum in *Paris Review,* the author imparted the influence of Nobelist Toni Morrison on her thorough understanding of Caribbean history. According to the journals of Christopher Columbus, black Africans had preceded the Genoan navigator in exploring Arawak and Taino strongholds. Proof lay in the alloyed copper, gold, and silver spear points that archeologists located in the West Indies.

May 10

Edwidge reported that the *Boston Globe, Miami Herald,* and *Washington Post* condemned the U.S. Immigration and Customs Enforcement for deporting children and families to Haiti, a nation unprepared for public health crises during the Covid-19 epidemic. In a letter to the *Miami Herald,* she charged: "With these ongoing deportations, the Trump Administration, the Department of Homeland Security, and ICE are not just endangering the lives of the men, women, and children on these flights, they are also potentially condemning entire communities to death" (Abbott, 2020). To interviewer Kamila Shamsie, a columnist for the *Guardian,* Edwidge declared it the work of artists to "make sense of our experiences" in the Trump and Covid eras (Shamsie, 2020).

June 8

The author joined protesters of White House charges that Haitian immigrants carried AIDS, a topic she covered the previous April 13 in the essay "Ripple Effects" for the *New Yorker.* Netflix removed an episode of *History 101* that stigmatized islanders.

June 19

For National Public Radio, Edwidge spoke for a half hour on loss and grief and on taking comfort and inspiration during the Covid-19 epidemic, the subject of her meditation "Mourning in Place" for the *New York Review of Books.* She reflected lockdowns that curtailed Haitian exuberance for storytelling, family festivities, funeral singing, and feasting.

August 19–22

Invited by the Royal Bank of Scotland, Edwidge spoke at the Edinburgh International Book Festival on climate change, the focus of the essay collection *Tales of Two Planets: Making Climate Change Personal.* On August 22, she presented the speech "Death Cannot Write Its Own Story." Buzzfeed, *Esquire,* National Public Radio*,* and *Time* also conferred annual best book honoraria on *Everything Inside* and *The Art of Death.*

September 10

In the two-week Albany Book Festival, sponsored by the New York State Writers Institute, Edwidge took part in the author discussion "The Joys of the Short Story Form."

September 19

At the Port of Spain in Trinidad-Tobago, Edwidge received a 2020 One Caribbean Media Bocas Literary Festival Award of $3,000 for the resonant short fiction in *Everything Inside.* Her acceptance speech of the second prize in nine years called for the kind of language that heals civilization. Three days later, the collection earned selection by the Reese Witherspoon Book Club.

October 8

The author joined 121 other readers in a Cornell University presentation of Nobelist Toni Morrison's poignant novel *The Bluest Eye.* The event initiated a twelve-month salute to Morrison.

October 27

The London *Times* listed Edwidge's story "Please Translate" among the best crime fiction.

November 18–19

At a national ceremony held online, Edwidge presented the National Book Foundation's Medal for Distinguished Contribution to American Letters to Walter Mosley. On the 19th, she presented the Decameron Project, a Books Are Magic anthology of 29 stories created by the *New York Times Magazine* in response to the Covid epidemic the previous March.

Sources

Abbott, Jeff. "The Other Americans: Trump Is Spreading the Virus," *Progressive* (14 May 2020).

Adisa, Opal Palmer. "Up Close and Personal," *African American Review* 43:2–3 (Summer/Fall 2009): 345–355.

Allfrey, Ella. "Interview," *Granta* (4 July 2011).

"Author Edwidge Danticat Wins $20,000 Story Prize," AP (26 February 2020).

Barsamian, David. "Interview," *Progressive* (1 October 2003).

Berger, Rose Marie. "Death by Asylum," *Sojourners Magazine* 37:4 (April 2008): 32–36.

Brown, DeNeen L. "Interview," *Washington Post* (14 October 2007): M2.

Caplan, Benjy. "Miami's Literary Genius," *Miami New Times* (29 August 2013): 28.

Charters, Mallay. "Edwidge Danticat: A Bitter Legacy Revisited," *Publishers Weekly* 245:33 (17 August 1998): 42, 43.

Collins, Michael S. "Interview," *Callaloo* 30:2 (Spring, 2007): 471–473, 674.

Cornish, Audie. "Marking the Events," *NPR Weekend Edition* (11 September 2011).

Danticat, Edwidge. "All Geography Is Within Me," *World Literature Today* 93:1 (Winter 2019): 58.

_____. *The Art of Death: Writing the Final Story.* Minneapolis, MN: Graywolf Press, 2017.

_____. *Breath, Eyes, Memory.* New York: Soho Press, 1994.

_____. *The Butterfly's Way: Voices from the Haitian Diaspora in the United States.* introduction. New York: Soho Press, 2001, ix–xvii.

_____. "Cane and Roses," *Small Odysseys.* Chapel Hill: Algonquin, 2022.

_____. *Create Dangerously: The Immigrant Artist at Work.* New York: Vintage, 2010.

_____. "Detention Is No Holiday," *New York Times* (28 May 2012): A27.

_____. *The Farming of Bones.* New York: Penguin, 1998.

_____. "Flight," *New Yorker* 87:27 (5 September 2011): 32.

_____. "Haiti: A Bi-Cultural Experience" (lecture). Washington, DC: IDB Cultural Center (7 December 1995): 1–9.

_____. "Haiti: Bloodied, Shaken—and Beloved," *Miami Herald* (17 January 2010).

_____. "Haiti: The Poetry Behind the Bloodshed," *Providence Journal* (10 November 1991): D15.

_____. "Hurricane Matthew's Devastating Toll in Haiti," *New Yorker* (6 October 2016).

_____. "In Flesh and Bone," *Tent Life: Haiti.* Brooklyn: Umbrage, 2011, 8–9.

_____. "In the Dominican Republic, Suddenly Stateless," (contributor) *Los Angeles Times* (10 November 2013).

_____. "I Still Have a Dream," *Progressive* 79:2 (February 2015): 15–17.

_____. "Junot Díaz," *BOMB* 101 (Fall 2007): 89–95.

_____. *Krik? Krak!* New York: Soho Press, 1995.

_____. *Massacre River.* preface. New York: New Directions, 2008, 7–10.

_____. "Message to My Daughters," *The Fire This Time: A New Generation Speaks about Race.* New York: Scribner, 2017, 205–216.

_____. "Mourning in Place," *New York Review of Books* (24 September 2020).

_____. "My Father Once Chased Rainbows," *Essence* 24:7 (November, 1993): 48.

_____. "New York Was Our City on the Hill," *New York Times* (21 November 2004): CY1.

_____. "No Greater Shame," *The Haitian Boston Reporter* (May 2003).

_____. "Our Maya," *Essence* 45:4 (August 2014).

_____. "Pamela Phatsimo Sunstrum: New and Recent Paintings," *Paris Review* 232 (Spring 2020): 105–121.

_____. "Papi," *Family: American Writers Remember Their Own.* Collingdale, PA: Diane, 2000.

_____. "Poetry in a Time of Protest," *New Yorker* (31 January 2017).

_____. "September 11th: Ten Years," *New Yorker* (5 September 2011).

_____. "Significant Others," *Sojourners* 38:10 (November 2009): 36–40.

_____. "Stateless in the Dominican Republic," (contributor) *Providence Journal* (16 November 2013): 1.

_____. "U.S. Deportations to Haiti during Coronavirus Pandemic Are 'Unconscionable,'" *Miami Herald* (10 May 2020).

_____. "Voices from Hispaniola," (contributor) *Meridians* 5:1 (2004): 68–91.

_____. "Without Inspection," *New Yorker* 94:13 (14 May 2018): 76–83.

Dyer, Erv. "Interview," *New Pittsburgh Courier* (20 September 2017): A9.

"Edwidge Danticat, Author and Activist, Speaks Out Against Racialized State Violence," *UCLA Center for the Study of Women,* https://csw.ucla.edu/

Feifer, Megan. "The Remembering of Bones," *Palimpsest* 9:1 (2020): 35–49.

Gleibermann, Erik. "The Story Will Be There When You Need It," *World Literature Today* 93:1 (Winter 2019): 68–73.

Handal, Nathalie. "We Are All Going to Die," *Guernica* (15 January 2011).

Headlee, Celeste. "Dominicans, Haitians Remember Parsley Massacre," NPR (1 October 2012): www.npr.org/2012/10/01/162088692/dominicans-haitians-remember-parsley-massacre.

Horn, Jessica. "Edwidge Danticat: An Intimate Reader," *Meridians* 1:2 (Spring 2001): 19–25.

Ibarrola-Armendáriz, Aitor. "Broken Memories of a Traumatic Past and the Redemptive Power of Narrative in the Fiction of Edwidge Danticat," *Cross/Cultures* 136 (2011): 3–27, 248.

Inskeep, Steve. "Whether or Not We Belong Is Not Defined by Us," NPR (30 August 2019).

"Interview," *BookBrowse* (2004), https://www.bookbrowse.com/author_interviews/full/

index.cfm/author_number/1022/edwidge-danticat.

Irwin, Demetria. "Barnard College Honors Edwidge Danticat," *Amsterdam News* (3 November 2011): 25.

Jaggi, Maya. "Island Memories," *Guardian* (19 November 2004).

Kopchik, Kathryn. "Bucknell Forum: Haitian-American Edwidge Danticat to Speak April 12," *Targeted News Service* (7 March 2011).

Krementz, Jill. "Interview," *The Writer* 117:12 (December 2004): 66.

Krug, Julie. "The Spectacular KICK," *The Writer* 128:11 (November 2015): 24–29.

Long, Karen R. "The Artist as Activist," Anisfield-Wolf Book Awards (23 March 2016): https://www.anisfield-wolf.org/2016/03/the-artist-as-activist-author-edwidge-danticat-in-cleveland/

Louisdhon-Louinis, Lucrèce. "Interview," *MediaSpace* (25 August 2013).

Lyons, Bonnie. "Interview," *Contemporary Literature* 44:2 (Summer 2003): 183–198.

Manzella, Abby. "Danticat's Love Stories Can't Escape Politics in 'Everything Inside,'" *St. Louis Post-Dispatch* (15 September 2019): B8.

Miller, E. Ethelbert. "Interview," *Foreign Policy in Focus* (16 October 2007).

Mirabal, Nancy Raquel. "Dyasporic Appetites and Longings," *Callaloo* 30:1 (Winter 2007): 26–39, 410.

Misra, Jivin. "Interview," *Brooklyn Review* (18 June 2018).

Munro, Martin. *Edwidge Danticat: A Reader's Guide*. Charlottesville: University of Virginia Press, 2010.

Murphy, Dwyer. "The Art of Not Belonging," *Guernica* (3 September 2013).

Navarro, Xavier. "Primal Scream? Rebel Yell! Correlations Between Death and Nostalgia and the Preservation of History in the Haitian Storytelling Tradition: *Krik? Krak!*," *Caribbean without Borders*. Cambridge: Cambridge Scholars, 2015.

Patterson, Christina. "Interview," (London) *Independent* (13 March 1999): 14.

Pierre-Pierre, Garry. "At Home with Edwidge Danticat: Haitian Tales, Flatbush Scenes," *New York Times* (26 January 1995): C1.

Rockett, Darcel. "Interview," *Chicago Tribune* (8 May 2019).

Shamsie, Kamila. "Memory, Ritual and Migration," *Edinburgh International Book Festival* (interview) (15 August 2020), https://www.edbookfest.co.uk/press-release/memory-ritual-and-migration-discussed-by-edwidge-danticat-and-kamila-shamsie.

Shea, Renee. "The Dangerous Job of Edwidge Danticat," *Callaloo* 19:2 (Spring, 1996): 382–389.

Smith, Katharine Capshaw. "Interview," *Children's Literature Association Quarterly* 30:2 (Summer, 2005): 194–205.

Spratling, Cassandra. "Haitian Heritage Author Edwidge Danticat Treats Poverty and Oppression in Plain Words," *Detroit Free Press* (1 April 2002): C1.

Edwidge Danticat Family Tree

Essential to Edwidge's autobiographical writing is a sense of clannishness and mutual support from generation to generation. The family tree on the following page indicates the members of her family over several generations.

Sources

Danticat, Edwidge. *Create Dangerously: The Immigrant Artist at Work*. New York: Vintage, 2010.
_____. "Edwidge Danticat," *Nation* 296:4 (28 January 2013): 18.
_____. "A Taste of Coffee," *Calabash* 1:2 (Spring-Summer 2001): 39–48.
Santiago, Soledad. "Danticat at the Crossroads," *Santa Fe New Mexican* (25 November 2005): PA26.

Osnac Dantica=wife

peasant farmer   d. 1919

Tonton Jean   Nozial Dantica=Lovana Saint Lot

Résina Beauchard=Elifa Napoléon   guerrilla | d. 1919 in Sejour

| Rezia   Zi   Tina   Luis | Ino | Granmé Melina   Franck |
| d. 2012 | | | b. ca. 1876 | husband=Ilyana
| | | | d. 1980 | b. 1924
| | | | | | | d. 2001
Marius Richard Marie			
b. 1971			
d. 1997			
Justin Therese Grace Rose=André Miracin "Mira" Joseph Nosius Dantica=Denise Léone	Linoir
1908- Souvenance	Danticat b. February 7, 1923	d. February		
2002 Napoléon	b. July 6, 1935 in Beauséjour	2003 George Liline
b. December 28, 1935	d. May 24, 2005 d. November 3, 2004	& Bosi _____
d. October 2, 2014				
_____   Renel   Marie Renel
		dentist Jeanne
Jean=/=Marie Micheline=Pressoir Maxo Dantica=Josiane
Pradel	Danticat Marol b. November 4, 1948 two
	b. 1952 d. January 12, 2010 sons
	d. April 17, 1989
	_____
_____				
				Monica Denise, Nozial Nick Maxime
Ruth Pouchon Marc Ronald   Gabrielle,   b. 2000
Nozial, &   d. January 12,
Joseph   2010

Grandma Issa		
_____		
Edwidge Rosa Danticat=Faidherbe "Fedo" G. Boyer   Estina   Eliab Andre "Bob"   Kelly E.   Karl
b. January 19, 1969   b. December 13, 1961   Estème   b. October 7, 1971 b. 1975   b. 1977
m. August 2002	in Les Cayes high school teacher musician broker
_____	_____
	Nadira Amaris	
    Mira   Leila   b. 2005   Ezekiel   Zora
    b. 5/2005   b. 2009   b. 2005

The Companion

Adaptation

Edwidge pictures characters accommodating change, the aim of Arnold, a refugee from Port-de-Paix, Haiti, in forming a new family with Miamians Darline and Paris in "Without Inspection" and the purpose of fisherman Nozias Faustin's urgent search for a mother to foster his seven-year-old, the title figure in *Claire of the Sea Light*. Without referring directly to advanced age and failing health, Grann's creation story to her granddaughter in *The Last Mapou* educates the girl on an alteration in her own future—the alarming disappearance of island habitats from deforestation. Contrasting gradual baring of topography, human versatility during a natural disaster in *Eight Days* enables Junior to survive the January 12, 2010, Haitian earthquake and forces short-term living arrangements in *Tent Life,* a photo essay in coping by rebuilding with materials at hand. Edwidge volunteered her expertise and read to children who had no classrooms. In each scenario, fictional and real islanders display inner strength and determination to endure, a contrast to the widow Morrissete in "Seven Stories," who retreats from public view and mourns selling her virtue to a border guard to escape assassins.

The author parallels a fifteenth-century Haitian girl's experience with coming of age, marriage to a Maguana dignitary, resettlement to his village, and young motherhood in *Anacaona* with the move of the title figure in *Célimène* from the town of Pik Rose (Rose Peak). The fairy tale bride migrates to the home of her husband Zaken, where newness introduces her to "une autre réalité, à une autre forme de vie" (another reality, another form of life) (Dumas and Chenald, 2011). Apart from brides in legend and fairy tales, the author turns to realism for the worries of Marie Micheline in "Dream of the Butterflies." With limited shelter, she rears two children in a violence-torn slum riddled each night with machine gun bursts. For each eyewitness, immediacy limits choice and forces characters to modify expectations and adjust to their environment.

In *A Walk Through Carnival,* a shortened version of *After the Dance*, the author divulged the fears instilled by her uncle Joseph Nosius Danticat before she was twelve. To discourage joining pre–Lenten festival excess, he cited examples of pummeling and groping women and a violation of Christian sacraments in "a *maryaj pou dis,* a ten-cent or ten-minute marriage," by which total strangers faked sex acts with young girls (Danticat, 2016, iii). The cautionary tales to a small-framed woman kept her out of the annual splurge until age thirty. As reviewed by Madison Smartt Bell for the *Washington Post,* adulthood freed the author to dance ecstatically, thus entering the spectacle as a tourist, not a writer.

Whole Body Pain

For maidservant Amabelle Desír, the protagonist of *The Farming of Bones,* survival of dictator Rafael Leónidas Trujillo Molina's slaughter of black Haitian field workers at the Massacre River over October 2–8, 1937, forces her to assess changes in self and outlook, particularly her love life. Safe in Cap Häitien among other refugees suffering exhaustion, horrific memories, and wounds from machete blows, she surveys the hurts—joint misalignment in jaw and knee, and the heartache of losing Sebastien Onius, her lover. In other situations, the author masters the range of diasporic emotions among people who refashion themselves from victim to survivor, a skill of teen painter Moy Espérance in *Behind the Mountains* and the "fat man," the teenage title figure in "The Dew Breaker." Of the two, Moy harmonizes a new home with art, while the fat man grabs the power of the Tonton Macoute and initiates a career in torture and slaughter. The contrast illustrates the grace of a positive, humanistic outlook.

Because the author reached New York City on the edge of womanhood, Edwidge felt less foreign amid multilingual communities of immigrants from numerous lands. She viewed the city as a microcosm of ethnicities who welcomed all newcomers. Thus freed from a dominant language and culture, she allowed a shared visual and sensory experience to set the tone and direction of her stories, which critics compare to the naif school of Haitian art. By revisiting Afro-Caribbean aphorism, such as the Guineans who carry the sky on their heads, she accounts for human idiosyncrasies, particularly the tendency of peasants to incur anguish.

Personalized Stories

Acclimation to motherhood in *Breath, Eyes, Memory* places serious stress on Martine Caco, an immigrant to New York. Recovering from rape by the Tonton Macoute in her teens and breast cancer in adulthood, she acquires a distorted outlook and struggles to forgive daughter Sophie for eloping, marrying, and producing daughter Brigitte Ifé Woods. After mother and daughter reunite in Haiti, Martine continues to batter personal demons, beginning with a late-in-life pregnancy and a compulsion to abort the fetus. While Sophie modifies her own domestic shortcomings, Martine refuses to think of the unborn baby as a person. Rejection of a second motherhood sparks the self-destructive fury that kills Martine along with the fetus in a grotesque rain of seventeen stab wounds.

Citing a psychological shift that Odile Ferly surveys in *A Poetics of Relation,* Janelle Martin, an English major at Wake Forest University, depicts Edwidge's concept of adaptation as a "redefinition of identity"—a reshaping of personhood that besets sixteen-year-old Gabrielle Boyer in *Untwine* after the death of her identical twin Isabelle (Martin, 2015). For Claude, a patricidal ex-con in "Night Talkers," progressing from selling drugs in New York to prison on a murder charge, homelessness in Port-au-Prince, and a return to the rural mountains constitutes a reverse immigration. He returns a stranger to mountainous Beau Jour. Amid a village welcome, he takes advantage of forgiveness "after everything I did, because my moms told them I was their blood," an unfailing link to his lineage (Danticat, 2004, 102). He summarizes the family reunion from a deportee's perspective: "I'm a puzzle and these people are putting me back together," the peasant method of reviving Claude's membership and giving him peace (*ibid.*).

The author introduces Claude with a swagger and big-city bluster, a means of concealing from fellow returnee Dany

Dorméus the long downward spiral of a criminal life. Because both youths admire Aunt Estina Estème, a beloved relative and village midwife, they find common ground at the seven-place mausoleum in Beau Jour to mourn her sudden passing and share cultural roots. Claude's ability to share friendship and diaspora memories helps him to conform to peasant standards of respect for others' sufferings and acts of kindness. In a rare positive conclusion, the author presents optimism in his readjustment as "one of them, a member of their tribe" (Danticat, 2004, 120). Unlike the hermetic widow in "Seven Stories," Claude's future holds promise.

See also Behind the Mountains, Carnival, Coming of Age, *Untwine.*

Sources

Bell, Madison Smartt. "Distant Drums," *Washington Post* (18 August 2002).
Danticat, Edwidge. *Breath, Eyes, Memory.* New York: Soho Press, 1994.
_____. *Célimène—Fairy Tale for the Daughter of Immigrants.* Montreal: Memoire d'Encrier, 2009.
_____. *The Dew Breaker.* New York: Abacus, 2004.
_____. *The Farming of Bones.* New York: Penguin, 1998.
_____. *A Walk Through Carnival.* New York: Vintage, 2016.
Dumas, Pierre-Raymond, and Augustin Chenald. "'Célimène' ou la problématique de l'exil au coeur du merveilleux," *Le Nouvelliste* (21 June 2011).
Martin, Janelle. "Wandering Bodies: The Disruption of Identities in Jamaica Kincaid's Lucy and Edwidge Danticat's *The Farming of Bones*" (dissertation) Wake Forest University, 2015.
Munro, Martin. *Exile and Post-1946 Haitian Literature.* Liverpool, UK: Liverpool University Press, 2007.

After the Dance: A Walk through Carnival in Jacmel, Haiti

After a pre–Karèm (Lenten) festival in southwestern Haiti, Edwidge turned a clutch of ambiguous anecdotes into a loose travelogue. She urged readers not to be easily offended. The introduction identified *After the Dance* as "a love story to Jacmel," a coastal resort and tourist attraction (Alexandre and Howard, 2007, 169). Among the narratives, she included "Carnivalia," issued in a 2002 edition of *Transition*, a journal issued by Indiana University Press. The author dedicated the work to husband Fedo Boyer, a business translator, and chose the memoir title from the West African aphorism, "Apre bal, tanbou lou" (After the dance the drum is heavy), a Creole reference to the island's crushing burdens that return to revelers after a holiday (Lyons, 2003, 195). The French translation appeared under the title *Après la Danse* (After the Dance).

In a pastiche of island history, the writer described how Arawak children syncretized cultural costume for the annual parade to depict African and Arawak beginnings of Haiti, a craft she repeats in fifteenth-century masking for the future Taino *cacica* (ruler) in *Anacaona* and Old Kongo's funereal mask for his son, sugar mill worker Joël Raymond Loner, in *The Farming of Bones*. The blending of themes and ethnicities exorcises outsiders' fears of the annual festival. Partakers flaunt Haiti's uniqueness and the willingness of float painters, historical costume and headdress designers, papier-mâché mask makers, makeup artists, and musicians to invest creative wealth all year in a one-time extravaganza. In an interview with journalist Michael S. Collins for *Callaloo,* Edwidge stressed the shaping and design of face disguises as a harmless means of maintaining the individual's role in culture.

Set in mid–February 2001 on the Rue de l'Eglise (Church Street) at the Hotel de la Place, an architectural relic of the French colonial era, the author's narrative concedes her ignorance of past carnivals. Analyst Daphne Lamothe, a cultural scholar at Smith College in Northampton, Massachusetts, stated that "Religious affiliation, age, gender, and class all conspired when [Edwidge] was young to prevent her from participating" (Lamothe, 2012). Because of a mass Lenten gala of global renown, her Aunt Denise and Uncle Joseph Nozius Dantica thought it too racy, too dangerous for so small and inexperienced a girl among drunks, shooters, and dirty old men. In adulthood, the yearning for "baptism by crowd among my own people" causes her to arrange the visit to the island's party city accompanied by an expert, historian Michelet Divers, the Minister of Culture of the Southeast who died in November 2017 (Danticat, 2002, 15). The concept of baptism merges her family's fanatic evangelicalism with elements of Vodou that emulate Catholic ritual.

A City Tour

In "Carnival of the Dead," the text incorporates landmarks and sights along a major thoroughfare, Barranquilla Avenue—assertive street evangelists, a mule in sneakers, iron gates, and vine-covered monuments in an historic graveyard. To illustrate the French era of tobacco and coffee planting, parade participants traditionally portray white owners and black slaves, the prime actors in Haiti's colonial agrarian beginnings. Aided by Ovid, a plantation laborer, the author sketches early history, especially for non-white islanders. Facts affirm that mulatto children educated in Europe were called *affranchis* (freed), but enjoyed limited privileges in public. Of the overall health and independence of the post-colonial nation in the twenty-first century, Edwidge found it "robust and stalwart at the core" (*ibid.*, 61).

Stars of the carnival parade include irrepressible magical realism—zombies cloaked in white sheets, a painted ghost, a sacrificial Yawe (god) in a cowhide, and masked versions of Sgt. Sam "The Cowboy" Makanani, an American soldier who arrived in Haiti by Humvee. Fabulous creatures wear the head coverings and body paint of alligators, lions, zebras, giraffes, frogs, parrots, and apes, a bestial disguise repeated in the story "Quality Control." Metaphysical revelers take operatic forms—wandering Jews, skeletons, devils, phantoms, dragons, Mathurin monks, archangels, and the abstract AIDS, a daunting presence in the early 2000s. Extending humor, cultural icons—Maypoles, cross-dressing May queens, and Lucifer posing as Ogun, the Vodou blacksmith—draw artists to craft shops to view costume making. Identifiable impersonations—politicians, South African president Nelson Mandela, India's hero Mohandas Gandhi, and Che Guevara, a rebel Argentine Marxist—bracket phantasms and legends with recent history. Artist Ronald Mevs, a local acrylic painter, defined the purpose of surreal festival art as a replacement for what is missing—ample food, home security, and trees from denuded hillsides. He revered drums, which Roman Catholicism banned in the 1940s as elements of superstition and Satanism.

Carnival Close Up

In the ancestral pine forest, Edwidge and fiancé Fedo Boyer divert their truck north into the high country to observe a watershed and a preserve of native birds and trees, which dictator Jean-Claude "Baby Doc" Duvalier shielded in 1983 from peasant clear-cutting for timber and charcoal. The couple returns to coastal Jacmel for a licentious Lenten weekend on Friday night, when fireworks open the pre–Easter festival. Giddy Haitians glorify the spree as a stimulus to art, music, and literature and to coronation of the newly elected carnival queen. The author compares the annual hoopla to a late medieval morality play, a theatrical presentation of abstractions such as Mr. Good Deeds and Mr. Envy as well as the specter of AIDS, punctuated with displays of condoms. A decade later, the phantasm of disease pictured cholera.

Following a silent protest of Coast Guard officers on a U.S. cutter forcing Haitian boat people to leap overboard, the procession lifted spirits with a giant butterfly representing optimism, a symbol that Edwidge reprises in "Dream of the Butterflies" and the YA novel *Untwine*. Viewers express joy in an improvisational street dance that continues until trucks run out of gas at 3:00 a.m. Of the gaiety, Edwidge summarized the seaside blow-out for the *Toronto Star* in the memoir "Haiti's Quiet Beauty Captivates in Jacmel." The article, a repeat of the essay "My Own Island" in the *New York Times,* declared the bash seductive, "like that flashy gentleman caller who demands a closer look, but is guaranteed to steal your heart" (Danticat, 2013, T3).

As depicted by an insider, the national fiesta becomes for the author a delayed and largely private coming of age in her homeland, where she grew up amid her Uncle Joseph Nozius Dantica's strict Baptist expectations. *Boston Herald* literary critic Judith Wynn regretted that Edwidge "is too grounded in Haiti's tragic politics, its poverty, and its health and environmental crises to resort to easy laughs" (Wynn, 2002, 61). Carole Goldberg, a reviewer for the *Chicago Tribune,* and Madison Smartt Bell, critiquing for the *Washington Post,* agreed that the travelogue fails to uplift.

See also Carnival, Vodou.

Sources

Alexandre, Sandy, and Ravi Y. Howard. "Interview," *Journal of Caribbean Literature* 4:3 (Spring 2007): 161–174.

Bell, Madison Smartt. "Distant Drums," *Washington Post* (18 August 2002).
Collins, Michael S. "Interview," *Callaloo* 30:2 (Spring, 2007): 471–473, 674.
Danticat, Edwidge. *After the Dance: A Walk Through Carnival in Jacmel, Haiti.* New York: Vintage, 2002.
_____. "Carnivalia," *Transition* 12:3 (2002): 40–49.
_____. "Haiti's Quiet Beauty Captivates in Jacmel," *Toronto Star* (28 December 2013): T3.
_____. "My Own Island" (contributor) *New York Times* (10 November 2013): TR8.
Lamothe, Daphne. "Carnival in the Creole City: Place, Race, and Identity in the Age of Globalization," *Biography* 35:2 (Spring 2012).
Wynn Judith. "Cruising Through Carnival; Prejudices Hinder Look at Famous Celebration," *Boston Herald* (1 September 2002): 61.

Anacaona

A Taino balladeer and choreographer, rock carver, jewelry maker, and ceramicist born in Haiti in 1474, the *cacica* (ruler) Anacaona, wife of *cacique* Caonabó, lived a short, dynamic life ending in 1503 at age 29. Edwidge intended the royal diary, written by a queen known as the tribal golden flower, to encapsulate an islander's agricultural lifestyle in the southwestern quadrant of Quisqueya (prehistoric Hispaniola). Most significant to the history of the West Indies is her personal experience with global cataclysm. She witnessed an age preceding literacy and Western calendars. Through ballad, rock carving, riddling, and storytelling, she recorded historic and cultural events, such as ball playing, sculpture, song and dance, choreographed combat, fishing, a royal wedding, and healing.

The blended history and fictional text gives the protagonist a charismatic background in a tight community of Taino, Caribbean aborigines from the Amazon Basin who infiltrated the Antilles, Bahamas, Cuba, Jamaica, and Puerto Rico. Much of the action derives from native creativity with materials from nature. For a coming-out rite, beneath a ritual outfit and masks, Anacaona wears a braid, ankle ribbons, and anatto paste that ornaments her skin with a crimson glow. Gifts of seafood, agricultural produce, and belts, headdresses, and jewelry made of indigenous shells and feathers tie her more closely to a matriarchal Caribbean heritage. Long into Haiti's future, women reprised the grace and beauty of the mythic queen in carnival parades and masquerades described in *After the Dance*.

New World and Old

As stated in the author's foreword to *Women: A Celebration of Strength*, Anacaona is best known for expiring while "fighting the genocide that followed Genoan navigator Christopher Columbus's arrival" on December 5, 1492 (Danticat, 2007). In the 2017 essay "We Are Ugly, But We Are Here," Edwidge identified the Taino ruler as one of the first victims of Spanish fortune hunters, who introduced sugarcane and tobacco planting on Hispaniola. Inklings of a crime to her person appear during her womanhood ritual. Through a specific death prophecy, she envisages "something painful ... done to my neck," a scenario that returns in a dream of a cannibalistic Kalina (Carib) invasion (Danticat, 2005, 27).

Details hint at the imminent carnage preceding permanent colonization of Hispaniola. Baba, Anacaona's father, proposes that dancers in choreographed combat protect the noble family from kidnappers, who value the traditional drama of bride capture, a violent form of concubinage practiced by Balinese and Japanese men, Amazon and African tribes, Greeks and Romans, Vikings, Gypsies, and Mormons. The omen of ritual lopping of the braid from Anacaona's head reminds her of cutting the umbilical cord, a female memento blessed with carved amulets, an effort to capture and transmit Native

American experience. Clairvoyance unites Anacaona with the wraith of her perceptive grandmother of Xaraguá, particularly the pregnancy that sister-in-law Yaruba conceals from her husband, Chief Behechio. In woman-to-woman tradition, Anacaona relies on a matrilineage based on trust and female intuition.

Sickness and death sharpen Anacaona's reportage with details of shamanic therapies for Uncle Matunherí via uplifted torches and transfers to a prayer house for breathing treatments with carved figurines. A merger of purgation and a mystic trance induced by inhaling tobacco dust restores Uncle Matunherí's health. His recovery strengthens the tribe to withstand a disastrous windstorm, a foreshadowing of devastation to come. Anacaona mourns three friends, Nahe, Piragua, and Yaybona. An unthinkable number of victims lie buried in caves or at sea or on altars with the laboring class to join the sky people in the form of smoke from funeral pyres. The concept of a pellucid vapor drifting upward replicates reverence in worldwide devotions over candle and torch flames, censers, and altar fires.

Marriage to Caonabó

Before Matunherí dwindles away, he allows Anacaona to make a marital pact with Maguana chief Caonabó. The betrothal begins with a supernatural state: from a cauldron, he serves a bitter pre-nuptial drink that numbs her into a trance. In a tingly state, the bride-to-be acquiesces to bathing in lucky herbs. After body painting, she receives gold jewelry and a fragrant ribbon before undergoing a temptation ceremony offering her fifteen appealing men. After she rejects rivals, her fiancé displays territorial body art and blackened teeth filed thin and inlaid with shells and stones. His subjects revel at the royal marriage and join in excessive gift-giving to their future queen, including Caonabó's beloved birds, an icon of his genial spirit and love of beauty. Reviewer Kyrah M. Daniels of Wesleyan University in Middletown, Connecticut, stated the author's purpose: "To contrast the gentle ways of the Native Americans with the greediness of European plunderers, Danticat instills a sense of caring and generosity in her characters" (Daniels, 2005, 163).

The author creates suspense by introducing the second stave as "1491," tantalizingly close to world change with the surge of the European Renaissance the following year. A post-wedding arrival at the village of Niti, Maguana, on the south-central portion of Hispaniola, introduces the reader to the foundation of San Juan, Dominican Republic. The burden of monarchy isolates Anacaona, who chooses to compose ballads, spin thread, design necklaces and carvings, and train with the spear to fill idle time. Her daughter Higuamota lightens the household atmosphere with infant demands on her nanny. Simultaneously, like her mythic grandmother, Anacaona continues preparing for war with a division of energies between mothering and combat suited to the coming invasion.

Dominance and Genocide

The onset of musket fire and thievery of gold objects clarify the intent of Columbus and his Spaniards, "cruel men who would not hesitate to harm an old woman or a child" (Danticat, 2005, 138). At the mines, the colonizers butcher enslaved press gangs, whose corpses litter the landscape. Edwidge differentiates between bold Maguana warriors and Chief Guacanagarí, the ruler of Marién who chooses to appease Columbus's interlopers with cotton and cassava bread.

In 1494, Caonabó's nighttime raid that subdues the Spaniards ends successfully with Anacaona's escape by canoe and a brief fête of victory.

Edwidge created a biography rich in female resistance to dominance and ethnic erasure. The narrative places in an authoritative role the warrior/wife, who continued protecting her people in widowhood and recording their pre-colonial struggles. The thriving population of 200,000 Taino declined to a few hundred. A quick summary of rebellion, chaining, and execution covers the capture of Caonabó and Manicaotex, genocide of the Taino, and the hanging of Anacaona. The symbolic female monarch and young mother fell victim to exploiter Nicholas Ovanda, a bloodthirsty invader characterized in an essay by Jamaica Kincaid. In an evaluation of the works of Botswanan painter Pamela Phatsimo Sunstrum for *Paris Review,* Edwidge ties pre–Columbian history to recovered spear points once traded by black navigators with islanders. The timing suggests that the Taino dealt peaceably and honorably with African arrivals and thrived in a multicultural milieu until Columbus and his Hispanic raiders suppressed Haitians via genocidal colonialism.

See also Colonialism, Death, Racism, Ritual.

Sources

Daniels, Kyrah M. "Review: *Anacaona,*" *Journal of Haitian Studies* 11:2 (2005): 163–164.

Danticat, Edwidge. *Anacaona: Golden Flower, Haiti, 1490.* New York: Scholastic, 2005.

_____. "Fanm Se Poto Mitan: Women are the Pillars of Society," *Women: A Celebration of Strength.* New York: Legal Momentum, 2007.

_____. "Pamela Phatsimo Sunstrum: New and Recent Paintings," *Paris Review* 232 (Spring 2020): 105–121.

_____. "We Are Ugly, But We Are Here," *Caribbean Writer* 10 (1996); *Women Writing Resistance.* Boston: Beacon, 2017, 21–26.

Duboin, Corinne. "*After the Dance* d'Edwidge Danticat," *Transatlantica* 2 (15 November 2007): 2.

Saunders, Nicholas J. *The Peoples of the Caribbean:*

An Encyclopedia of Archaeology and Traditional Culture. Santa Barbara, CA: ABC-Clio, 2005.

Smith, Katharine Capshaw. "Interview," *Children's Literature Association Quarterly* 30:2 (Summer, 2005): 194–205.

Anacaona's Genealogy

Like the author herself, Anacaona, a future Taino *cacica* (ruler), grows up under the fostering care of a maternal uncle, Matunherí, and his plural wives. Note that Edwidge compiled a family tree from historical figures as well as fictional.

The Taino ruler maintained esteem in subsequent Haitian culture. In *The Farming of Bones,* Valencia Duarte sees in her newborn daughter Rosalinda the profile of Anacaona.

SOURCES

Danticat, Edwidge. *Anacaona: Golden Flower, Haiti, 1490.* New York: Scholastic, 2005.

———. "Fanm Se Poto Mitan: Women are the Pillars of Society," *Women: A Celebration of Strength.* New York: Legal Momentum, 2007.

———. *The Farming of Bones.* New York: Penguin, 1998.

Saunders, Nicholas J. *The Peoples of the Caribbean: An Encyclopedia of Archaeology and Traditional Culture.* Santa Barbara, CA: ABC-Clio, 2005.

Smith, Katharine Capshaw. "Interview," *Children's Literature Association Quarterly* 30:2 (Summer, 2005): 194–205.

The Art of Death: Writing the Final Story

One of thirteen works from Greywolf Press surveying the author's craft, Edwidge's addition of a text on death

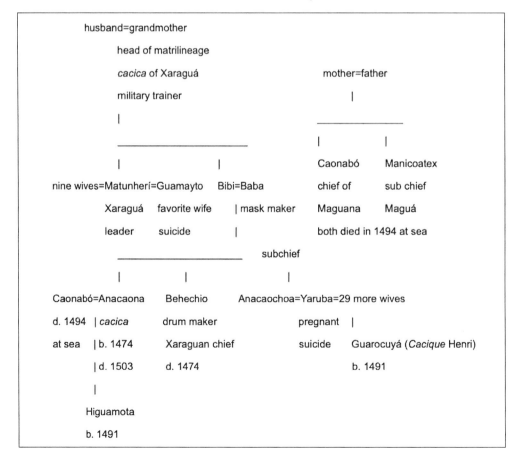

explores types of demise and their effects on the living. National Public Radio reviewer Michael Schaub characterized her topic as difficult for any author, "but Danticat has made them centerpieces of her fiction and nonfiction for more than twenty years" (Schaub, 2019). Her structured anthology merges memoir with exegesis to contribute to a list of essential themes—time, subtext, history, perspective, description, poetics, and syntax. Having witnessed a series of church funerals and burials in girlhood as foster daughter of the Rev. Joseph Nozius Dantica, she words a personal sensitivity to loss and its effect on others. Of her method, *Kirkus Reviews* lauded the slender collection for being "overarching and broad in scope" and for asking of death "if we really can describe it adequately at all" (*Kirkus Reviews,* 2017).

The writer grappled with fear by reading and writing literature, especially since the loss of parents nine years apart—André Mira Danticat on May 24, 2005, and Rose Souvenance Napoléon on October 2, 2014. For exempla, the author added works by some twenty-five masters—Michael Ondaatje, Susan Sontag, Albert Camus, Margaret Atwood, Dylan Thomas, Sigmund Freud, Langston Hughes, Anne Sexton, Michel de Montaigne, Leo Tolstoy, Zora Neale Hurston, Thornton Wilder, Alice Sebold, even James Barrie's classic escapist play *Peter Pan.* As always, Edwidge demonstrates Toni Morrison's worth as a Nobelist mentor with passages from the novels *Beloved* and *Sula.*

Living Dyingly

At age 78, Rose Souvenance Danticat recorded for her heritage cassettes on behavior, parenting, and planning a funeral. To daughter Edwidge, she urged independence, but banned open-toed shoes in church, a touch of motherly humor. The author meditates on the process of dying and its meaning to Rose, who chose to curtail chemotherapy. Warm, intimate recollections, according to Daniel Simon, editor of *World Literature Today,* "read like a love letter to Danticat's mother," who died under hospice care at Edwidge's Miami home in Little Haiti (Simon, 2018, 25). The author composed another version, "The Possibility of Heaven," for the February 2015 issue of *Sojourners.*

Ars Moriendi

An anonymous treatise marking the conclusion of the Middle Ages and the end of the Black Death in Europe, the original *Ars Moriendi* (The Art of Dying) surveys church rituals comforting the moribund. The mortality manual suggests practical ways of facing departure from earth and residence with God. The author speaks of literary last breath scenes and the shared sense of evanescence in witnesses of an "unparalleled experience" (Danticat, 2017, 29). The attempt to imagine expiring—a last heartbeat—causes her to report to Tante Rezia the nightly sexual assault by Cousin Joel, a predator who shared residence at her relatives' home for six weeks. In the pretense of searching for bedsheets, he fondled the young girls sharing a room. In the estimation of analyst Melanie Brooks, a writing teacher at Boston's Northeastern University, Edwidge succeeded in "unraveling the tragic string of circumstances" leading to an "unforeseen outcome" that left her vulnerable to extreme grief (Brooks, 2017, 121).

Dying Together

The Haitian search on January 12, 2010, for earthquake victims in Carrefour, Léogane, and Port-au-Prince involved Edwidge in a vigil shared with Caribbean relatives. She advised surveyors of disasters to concentrate on particulars and on the "clarity of focus and an attentiveness" to every minute of being, a focus of the doomed leapers from the World Trade Center on 9/11/2001 (*ibid.*, 51). Without details, the written version "might pale—or fail—in comparison to the news, documents, photographs, video, and, more recently, cell phone footage" (*ibid.*, 62). For the perspective on Dominican Generalissimo Rafael Trujillo's Guardia who engineered the October 2–8, 1937, massacre of black Haitians, the author relied on a single witness, the fictional domestic Amabelle Desír, an orphan recovering from skeletal injuries and loss of her lover, Sebastian Onius, in *The Farming of Bones.*

Wanting to Die

Edwidge insisted that solitude and suffering offered elusive benefits to the human journey and motifs for classic literature. She spoke forthrightly of choice, naming as examples Leo Tolstoy's classic suicide narrative *Anna Karenina* and Toni Morrison's mythic novel *Song of Solomon* and the self-annihilation of poet Anne Sexton by carbon monoxide poisoning. In personalized detail of the unknowable, she examined the despairing self-annihilator and the decision to embrace mortality rather than elongate pain and regret. According to critic Valerie Sayers, on staff at Notre Dame University, that wisdom reminds us "how little we can know" about the will to die (Sayers, 2017, 29).

Condemned to Die

In addition to judicial condemnation, the text covers the casual murders of blacks on risky U.S. streets. Edwidge highlights the infanticide at the heart of Toni Morrison's *Beloved*, a fictionalized version of the self-emancipation of Kentucky slave Margaret Garner in January 1856. The specifics cause readers to reflect on the novel and its lyrical scrutiny of infant slaughter motivated by a slave mother's fear of child bondage. Edwidge's summation of the shibboleth that sentenced black Dominican laborers to death in *The Farming of Bones* reduces condemnation to one word—*pe'sil* (parsley)—a test of lingual capacity among francophones who don't trill their r's (Jeremiah and Aule, 2019, 14). The term gave to the bloodletting the name "Parsley Massacre."

Close Calls

The collection of sparse memories illustrates how narrative educates and sustains the living, even though it offers no closure. Any unexpected brush with collision, such as husband Fedo Boyer's advance up a highway off ramp, creates both guilt and privilege, "an atmospheric bridge between life and death" (Danticat, 2017, 130). A tactful reminiscence of her own scary moments speaks with grace and power a personal view.

Circles and Circles of Sorrow

For models of meager holds on mortality, the author gains moral force from classic Greek myth. She cites the tenuous example of Poseidon's son Antaeus, the Libyan desert dweller who lived only so long as he touched earth. A more complex myth explains Persephone's seasonal death after her kidnap to the underworld. The cycle recurs annually when she retreats into the underworld to satisfy her mother Demeter's deal with Persephone's captor Hades, god of the dead. As a point of emotional uplift, the author verifies the body's need to smile *in extremis* because of release of dopamine and serotonin, "feel good" neurotransmitters that elevate mood. The incorporation of humor with universal leave-taking in the prayer "A New Sky" (which *PEN America* originally printed in September 2015 as "A Prayer before Dying") asserts Edwidge's awareness of her mother's humanity and fun-loving idiosyncrasies.

Feetfirst

Edwidge reprised the abstract "Without Her" from the April 25, 2015, issue of the *New York Times* as "Feetfirst." On seeing a hearse deliver Rose Danticat's remains to a Brooklyn funeral home, the author concluded, "My mother really is a body now … and only that" (*ibid.,* 170). Multiple experiences with relatives' demise amplify the author's wisdom and enable her to grow as kindred, witness, and writer. Authority Marilyn McEntyre, a professor of English at Westmont College in Santa Barbara, finds evidence of a spiritual bulwark—"faith that grows new shoots in sentences put down in dark hours," such as the author's musings on Cousin Marius Danticat's death from AIDS in "Flight" (McEntyre, 2018, 50).

Critical response to Edwidge's essays particularized the collection's strengths. Daniel Simon credited variety of source material: "Danticat weaves communal as well as literary response to death into her own private meditations on loss" (Simon, 2018, 25). For *Commonweal,* the essayist Valerie Sayers found the author's works thoughtful, principled, and controlled: "She neither exploits nor sentimentalizes" (Sayers, 2017, 29). From *Lancet Oncology* came analyst Caroline A. Kinsey's complaint that "The book's academic presentation reads like a string of quotes dryly pieced together, the author hopping to the next before digesting the last," a valid criticism (Kinsey, 2017, 1576). Kinsey also charges the author with omitting

"alternative or dissenting perspectives" (*ibid.*). Isabel B. Slone, a literary reviewer for the Toronto *Globe and Mail,* tempered her critique with an undeniable conclusion: "You are never doing more than peering inside a specifically carved peephole into the author's pain. It's objectively creepy, but the transgressive feeling that comes along is magnetically irresistible" (Slone, 2017).

Sources

Brooks, Melanie. *Writing Hard Stories: Celebrated Memoirists Who Shaped Art from Trauma.* Boston: Beacon, 2017.

Danticat, Edwidge. *The Art of Death: Writing the Final Story.* Minneapolis, MN: Graywolf Press, 2017.

_____. *The Farming of Bones.* New York: Penguin, 1998.

_____. "Flight," *New Yorker* 87:27 (5 September 2011): 32.

_____. "The Possibility of Heaven," *Sojourners* 44:2 (February 2015): 22–24.

_____. "Without Her," *New York Times Magazine* (23 April 2015).

Jeremiah, Methuselah, and Moses Aule. "Exploring Feminine Subjectivity in Caribbean History: A New Historicist Perspective in Edwidge Danticat's *The Farming to Bones,*" *Igwebuike* 4:2 (2019).

Kinsey, Caroline A. "Review: *The Art of Death,*" *Lancet Oncology* 18:12 (1 December 2017): 1576.

McEntyre, Marilyn. "Seeing Others Through: The Work of Witness," *Christian Scholar's Review* 48:1 (Fall, 2018): 45–50.

Mirakhor, Leah. "Review: *The Art of Death,*" *Los Angeles Times* (14 July 2017).

"Review: *The Art of Death,*" *Kirkus Reviews* (1 June 2017).

Sayers, Valerie. "Giving Grief Its Due," *Commonweal* 144:14 (8 September 2017): 29–30.

Schaub, Michael. "Coming to Terms with Loss and Grief in Gorgeous *Everything Inside,*" *NPR* (29 August 2019).

Simon, Daniel. "Review: *The Art of Death,*" *World Literature Today* 92:2 (March/April 2018): 25.

Slone, Isabel B. "Review: *The Art of Death,*" [Toronto] *Globe and Mail* (21 July 2017).

Behind the Mountains

Using the first-person voice of thirteen-year-old Haitian Céliane Espérance, *Behind the Mountains* profits from the gifts of observation, letter writing, and storytelling and details of Edwidge's relocation from Haiti to Brooklyn, New York. The progression of human experiences takes visual form in the proverb "Behind the mountains there's another mountain" (Lyons, 2003, 195). Dedicated to niece and nephew Nadira and Ezekiel, the children of Eliab and Karl Danticat, the author's first YA novel opens in Beau Jour southwest of Port-au-Prince in the Léogâne Mountains on October 18, 2000, with a diary, a gift to the narrator for top grades from teacher Madame Auguste. In an episode set in Port-au-Prince, the background depicts political forces and post-election street protests in November three and a half months before the restoration of Jean-Bertrand Aristide to the presidency on February 4, 2001.

Edwidge draws on names from her own family tree for the genealogy and incorporates the West Indian folk monster Galipot, the three-legged horse, which she referenced for the *New Yorker* in 2015 in "The Long Legacy of Occupation in Haiti." The scary cautionary tale parallels the death-dealing Jamaican duppy, a tripedal horse-zombie, and the three-legged Saharan camel of Mali, a terror image of Sudanese and Tanzanian lore, as well as West African funerary icons of the Hausa, Songhai, and Tuareg. The horse fable precedes chaos after a pipe bomb explodes under a bus in Carrefour, Haiti, on the Day of the Dead on November 2. Contributing anxiety, rescuers remove Céliane from the scene and treat her injuries at a Carrefour Dufort clinic 20 miles west of Port-au-Prince, apart from the hospital that admits her mother Aline. Like the banyan tree, Céliane is upended.

A common thread in developing countries, the folk grapevine spreads word of Aline and Céliane's recovery to the grandparents in Beau Jour. Random shootings and more bomb detonations heighten tensions that "wound our souls" (Danticat, 2002, 50). Retreat from the atmosphere to home comforts the Espérance clan. The gift of emigration to Brooklyn before Christmas introduces myriad New World sense impressions— walking on ice, watching snowflakes, shopping on Flatbush Avenue, neon lights, a family photo. In the crush of newness and excitement, the noisy tiff between Aline and Victor seems expected as she defends her island culinary style over diminution to the "sticks and rocks" of a Haitian fire-surround, the same cookery found among the peasantry in "Seven Stories" (*ibid.*, 97). Food prevails as a common denominator of balance and a New Year celebration and recalls Granmè's fragrant cook shed, a sensual matrilineal retreat for three generations.

Using a return from the first school day as a test of logic, Edwidge stresses Céliane's disappointment in needing the help of a kind pedestrian, an unspoken proof that New Yorkers can be compassionate to immigrants. Friends Faidherbe and Immacula enjoy scaring Céliane with cautionary stories about Jackie Robinson School, especially the gangs known as Bloods and Crips, black street terrorists formed in Los Angeles in the 1960s. Campus events include a shooting and police investigation of Gary, Céliane's classmate. He epitomizes the émigré deported to Haiti because he fails to adapt.

At home, the Espérance family undergoes months of disorder as Moy stakes out the parameters of manhood. Against the will of Papa, Moy resides with an older woman and paints a series of works that his sister entitles "Behind the Mountains." To commemorate moving upstairs to a larger apartment, Moy and Franck, Papa and Manman's employer, hang the paintings, which, step by step, illustrate the move from Haiti to the U.S.

Creativity in the Espérance children smooths over family animosities, in part from Céliane's letter to her father, which tempers the explosive words and silences that threaten family harmony. With a brief bio, the author indicates how the fictional newcomer weathers some of the discord incurred by the Danticat household after their 1981 reunion in Brooklyn.

SOURCES

Collins, Jo. "Novels of Transformation and Transplantation: The Postcolonial Bildungsroman and Haitian American Youth in Danticat's *Behind the Mountains* and *Breath, Eyes, Memory*," *Wasafiri* 27:4 (1 December 2012): 27–34.
Danticat, Edwidge. *Behind the Mountains: The Diary of Célianne Esperance*. New York: Orchard Books, 2002.
_____. *Everything Inside*. New York: Knopf, 2019.
_____. "The Long Legacy of Occupation in Haiti," *New Yorker* (28 July 2015).
Lyons, Bonnie. "Interview," *Contemporary Literature* 44:2 (Summer 2003): 182–198.
Paravisini-Geberrt, Lizabeth. *Literature of the Caribbean*. Santa Barbara, CA: Greenwood, 2008.
Smith, Katharine Capshaw. "Interview," *Children's Literature Association Quarterly* 30:2 (Summer, 2005): 194–205.

Behind the Mountains Genealogy

Essential to an understanding of immigration to New York City in Edwidge's first YA novel lie the clan adjustments that accompany new responsibilities and coming of age. Analyst Katharine Capshaw Smith described the author's "cultural liminality ... [and] exploration of working class Haitian subjectivity ... [and] new definitions of family

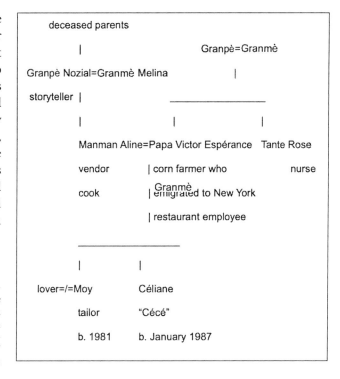

relationships" (Smith, 2005, 194, 195). For comfort and reassurance as she adapts to "interpretive training wheels," the narrator, Céliane Espérance, returns frequently two generations to Granpé Nozial's storytelling about the first experience with ice (Collins, 2020, 6).

By paralleling the hardships of girlfriend Thérèse in Haiti, the author illustrates Céliane's good fortune in finding helpful schoolmates and progressing in speaking, reading, and writing English. The period of alienation in nineteen-year-old Moy's first months in Brooklyn epitomizes the emergence of the immigrant artist after a traumatic period of personal testing and ambivalence.

SOURCES

Collins, Anastasia M. "Call and Response: Constructed Identity and Legible Experience in Danticat's Young Adult Novels," *Research on Diversity in Youth Literature* 2.2 (2020): 1–24.
Collins, Jo. "Novels of Transformation and Transplantation: The Postcolonial Bildungsroman and Haitian American Youth in Danticat's *Behind the Mountains* and *Breath, Eyes,*

Memory," *Wasafiri* 27:4 (1 December 2012): 27–34.

Danticat, Edwidge. *Behind the Mountains: The Diary of Célianne Esperance.* New York: Orchard Books, 2002.

Smith, Katharine Capshaw. "Interview," *Children's Literature Association Quarterly* 30:2 (Summer, 2005): 194–205.

Breath, Eyes, Memory

Edwidge completed her first novel in 1994 at age twenty-five with an intense scrutiny of angst in a manless household at Croix-de-Rosets (Cross of Roses), a town honoring Christian emblems. Covering four generations of a rural Haitian matrilineage, *Breath, Eyes, Memory* champions the imagination for rescuing immigrants from loneliness, low self-esteem, and deracination. The book appeared in French translation as *Le Cri de l'Oiseau Rouge* (The Cry of the Red Bird), a Vodou emblem of powerful turmoil in human lives. In *Create Dangerously,* she acknowledged the choice to write her first book in English, "this language that is not mine," rather than the more familiar Haitian Creole or French (Danticat, 2010, 14–15).

To grant autonomy and a sense of belonging to West Africa, the fictional women share song and narratives much as Afro-Caribbean slaves who clung to their motherland and its cultural and religious heritage. In an interview with Sandy Alexandre and Ravi Y. Howard for *Journal of Caribbean Literature,* Edwidge exulted that "Even people who are stripped of everything material still have something left when they have their memories" (Alexandre and Howard, 2007, 168). From the beginning, the Caco family's recollections include genealogies, shared harvests and burials, recipes for potluck dinners, pointed questions, and gossip about the Napoléon clan in Haiti and Henry's medical studies in Mexico.

Family Imbalance

The coming-of-age action opens before a daughter's flight from Haiti to her mother's home on Nostrand Avenue in south Brooklyn after nine years' separation. At a breakfast shared with Tante Atie, while listening to Atie's biography of her sister Martine, protagonist Sophie Caco inhales the aroma of cinnamon rice pudding, a sense impression redolent with affection and traditional Caribbean cookery. In evidence of devoted foster mothering, Atie sets out company utensils and a lace cloth for the meal. She clothes her departing niece in starched underwear and saffron dress embroidered with daffodils in her favorite shade of yellow. The spring bulb attests to the colonial importation of European flowers linked to Easter, the Christian holiday promoting redemption.

A violent form of patriarchy distorts gender perceptions. Inexact reflections on Sophie's siring by a Tonton Macoute rapist give no clear explanation of her paternal looks, which differ from Tante Atie, grandmother Ifé, and her 31-year-old mother Martine, who shared the age of the crucified Christ. On Martine's reunion with her daughter after a lengthy parting, Sophie refuses standard obeisance to her parent, a violation of social intercourse and blood kin protocol. Edwidge reprised the hostile meeting for a 1994 issue of *Seventeen* and the March 2000 issue of *Literary Cavalcade* in the vignette "A Rain of Daffodils."

Coping with Rejection

Mother and daughter share self-hatred of the body. Sophie's self-loathing takes the form of bulimia, an American scourge brought on by media standards of the appealingly slim female. For Martine, a former cane worker, according to reviewer Jennifer C. Rossi, a professor of African American studies at Saint John Fisher College in Rochester, New York, "A victim of sexual violence (trauma) can become emotionally separated (exiled) from her own body" (Rossi, 206, 203). American racial standards influence Martine to whiten her skin with cosmetic bleach.

A more serious form of self-abuse, Martine's rejection of a mid-life pregnancy sired by her lover, attorney Marc Chevalier, force her to stab herself seventeen times in the abdomen. Hungarian specialist Eva Federmayer described the target as "a monster-fetus as if she were carrying her own rapist inside" (Federmayer, 2015, 4). The seventeen plunges kill the fetus and herself symbolically with the exact number of years of Sophie's existence. The death scene suggests the mental residue of sex crimes and a repudiation of womanhood and involuntary maternity.

The plot focuses on the arbitrary defense of female virginity, a source of shame, trauma, and guilt in vulnerable girls. To stave off her mother's fears, Sophie makes up a fantasy boyfriend, Henry Napoléon, and his return to Haiti, a safe distance from her maidenhead. In New York, Sophie cultivates a true male/female relationship with an older man, Joseph Woods, a pseudo-father from New Orleans endowed with mature wisdom. The author's revelations angered some middle-class Haitian-American females for relating personal details of a shameful heritage: monitoring virginity by digital testing in the vagina. Analyst Newtona Johnson, a professor at Middle Tennessee State University and contributor to *Obsidian III*, declared that male subjugation impacted female psyches and women's relationships with female offspring, to whom the mothers become sexual predators.

See also Caco Genealogy Mothers, Virginity.

Sources

Alexandre, Sandy, and Ravi Y. Howard. "Interview," *Journal of Caribbean Literature* 4:3 (Spring 2007): 161–174.

Danticat, Edwidge. *Breath, Eyes, Memory*. New York: Soho Press, 1994.

_____. *Create Dangerously: The Immigrant Artist at Work*. New York: Vintage, 2010.

_____. "A Rain of Daffodils," *Literary Cavalcade* 52:6 (March 2000): 4–8.

Federmayer, Eva. "Violence and Embodied Subjectivities: Edwidge Danticat's Breath, Eyes, Memory," *Scholar Critic* 2:3 (December 2015): 1–17.

Johnson, Newtona. "Interview," *Obsidian III* 6/7:2/1 (Fall 2005–2006): 147–166, 264.

Pierre-Pierre, Garry. "At Home with Edwidge Danticat: Haitian Tales, Flatbush Scenes," *New York Times* (26 January 1995): C1.

Rossi, Jennifer C. "'Let the Words Bring Wings to Our Feet': Negotiating Exile and Trauma through Narrative in Danticat's *Breath, Eyes, Memory*," *Obsidian III* 6:2 (Fall/Winter, 2005): 203–220.

Brother, I'm Dying

A generational elegy, *Brother, I'm Dying* assesses through the nonlinear biography of siblings Joseph Nosius Dantica and André Mira Danticat the political backstory of immigration for black Haitians arriving in New York and Miami. The French translation carried the title *Adieu Mon Frère* (Farewell My Brother), a reminder of the religious source of *adieu* (to God). Joseph pursued Christian, underclass political ideals until the rise of Jean-Claude "Papa Doc" Duvalier on October 22, 1957. In place of support for populist labor leader Daniel Fignolé, Joseph invested self in Protestantism. He became a Baptist deacon and led an abstemious life at his new church, L'Eglise Chrétienne de la Redemption (the Christian Church of the Redemption).

After American doctors biopsied Joseph's cancerous larynx in 1978, at age 55, he traveled to New York for a laryngectomy and tracheotomy at Kings County Hospital in Brooklyn. The threat to communication for a preacher compounded the author's frustration at limited phone calls from her birth father in Brooklyn. To fill the gap, Edwidge dreamed of "smuggling … words" to flesh out scanty letters in French because Mira underestimated the power of correspondence to express his feelings about Joseph's muteness. In the verse "Postscript," disease further disempowers his speech with "each gluey breath" (Danticat, 2010, 410). Mira's near muteness from irreparable pulmonary fibrosis diminishes her faith in "herbs and ancient medicine," the natural basis of Haitian medicine.

Communicating Kinship

In the narration of the brothers' last months together, Edwidge resorted to a Danticat genealogy permeated with ancestral family stories and autobiography. Of her method of harvesting life-altering events, she disclosed how "grappling with memory is, I believe, one of many complicated Haitian obsessions" (Danticat, 2010, 63). Analyst Marie Sairsingh, an English professor at the College of the Bahamas, asserted the value of such clan narratives: "The ancestral folk stories function as trans-generational links that represent the distillation of ancestral wisdom from which the living can draw inspiration" (Sairsingh, 2013, 9). Cut off from tribal heritage, the author sank into despair.

For background, Edwidge concentrated on family resilience and her own first-person account of migrating at age twelve with ten-year-old brother Bob from Haiti and meeting brothers Kelly and Karl, ages seven and five, both born in the U.S. The gift of a Smith-Corona portable Corsair typewriter boded well for the budding author. Her skill with words in French, Creole, and English and her ability to read Uncle Joseph's lips empowered her to guard and guide him for ear, nose, and throat appointments. Technology upgraded sign language and lip reading: the use of a prosthetic larynx produced a miracle of sound. Joseph revived personal relationships along with ambitions for his church, school, and clinic.

A Hellish Departure

From uncompromising political clashes, corruption, and gang virulence in the late 1980s and 1990, the text advanced to a welcome to Haitian president Jean-Bertrand Aristide, who survived random blood-letting for seven months. After Mira's stay in a Brooklyn hospital, Edwidge imparted lengthy prayers and leave-taking. The melancholy scene contrasted the author's breathless description of a raid on October 24, 2004, at Joseph's church and public misperception about his alliance with police and U.N. peacekeepers. Suspense heightened as the old man negotiated alone with hoodlums and watched the looting and arson of his home, church, and school. After sequestering for the night with Anne, a parishioner, he pulled on a wig and feminine muumuu for a 3:30 a.m. escape from the gangsters who overran the Bel Air neighborhood. In the story "Ghosts," Edwidge later labeled the harrowing setting "the Baghdad of Haiti" (Danticat, 2008, 108).

In a hyperrealistic atmosphere, the family history took on energy and menace from repeated ruses to disguise Joseph's flight from pursuers. An anti-gang officer characterized the conflict as a war. Joseph's pilgrimage from bureau to bureau—civil police, United Nations task force, even Portuguese-speaking Brazilian officers, Royal Canadian Mounties, and National Coalition for Haitian Rights—mimicked the crazy quilt of alleys and courtyards in the poorest district. Joseph's 52-year-old son Maxo traversed the same labyrinth on his way to join the elderly pastor for their flight to Miami.

An Inhumane Welcome

In backtracking over Joseph and Maxo's interrogation by Miami immigration officials, Edwidge pieced together a betrayal and gross miscarriage of justice. The mistreatment of black immigrants impacted her speeches, interviews, and subsequent writings with the monitoring of a refugee camp to marginalize and subdue undocumented aliens. Of the American disdain for black Haitian newcomers, the author asserted that "Haitian asylum seekers find themselves at the very bottom and suffer the most inhumane treatment, in contrast, very sharp contrast to other asylum seekers" (Smiley, 2004). She distinguished the treatment of Hispanic Cuban arrivals, who, not being black, received preference based on lighter skin color.

While battling late pregnancy discomforts, Edwidge also had to report to Mira her uncle's incarceration at Krome Detention Center, a notoriously racist complex she exposed in the *Nation* article "Not Your Homeland." She later reported in a critical essay for the *Washington Post* the wasteful U.S. Immigration and Customs agency, which "detains about 400,000 men, women and children per year, most of whom pose no threat to the United States…. It costs taxpayers as much as $164 a day to detain [each]" as opposed to $14 daily for home supervision, curfews, and electronic monitoring for "broadly

defined classes of people" (Danticat, 2013, A13). A world literature specialist at the University of Washington, critic Wendy Knepper surmised, "Danticat's account of her pregnancy links the hopes and fears concerning the gestation of life to biopolitics: the miscarriages of justice, aborted hopes of sovereignty, and stillborn democracies that characterize Haitian history" (Knepper, 2012, 204).

Simultaneously, Mira anticipated good news from a pulmonology examination at Columbia Presbyterian near Manhattan's Riverside Drive while his brother spent the weekend at Krome minus his medication for hypertension and prostatitis. The last hours of Joseph's life stripped him of volition—confinement to a wheelchair, transport to a clinic, and admission to Jackson Memorial Hospital in shackles. A mass of institutional rules prevented his niece and son from speaking to him one last time. Joseph died on Wednesday, November 3, following "deplorable care," a regretted misdeed that continues to aggrieve the author (Danticat, 2007, 238).

Parting and Reunion

Edwidge constructs her memoir/testimonial as a humanitarian document attesting to sibling love and veneration of elders. She skirmished in print and speech with a bureaucracy under which "human rights have obviously been decoupled from their human context" (Bennett, 2008, 3). Reviewer Ian Bethel Bennett, a dean of liberal arts at the University of the Bahamas, summarized the Homeland Security cover-up of racial preference as "the profound fraud of a great deal of what people see as positive efforts to protect America's borders" (*ibid.*, 4). Simultaneous medical examination of Mira in Manhattan preceded Joseph's autopsy, two procedures that seemed cold and apathetic.

Contiguous obituaries assaulted the Danticats with loss of male heads of family. For Mira, a woebegone viewing of Joseph at his funeral removed all doubt that he and his older brother would not long be parted. Encumbered by an oxygen tank, Mira lamented beside Joseph's grave at Cyprus Hills in Queens, New York, that mutual yearning for a livable country found no fulfillment. Edwidge's shock and rage left unsettled the comforts two brothers took in an end to pain and reunion at burial plots under a shared headstone. As is often incorporated in thanatographies, the double demise concedes Danticat's inability to take consolation from witnessing and writing the facts. She confers a last blessing on her father by naming her first daughter Mira, a precious bond to the Danticat past.

Sources

Bennett, Ian Bethel. "Review: *Brother, I'm Dying*," *Anthurium* 6:1 (June 2008): 1–4.
Danticat, Edwidge. *Brother, I'm Dying*. New York: Vintage, 2007.
———. *Create Dangerously: The Immigrant Artist at Work*. New York: Vintage, 2010.
———. "Ghosts," *New Yorker* (24 November 2008): 108–113.
———. "Not Your Homeland," *Nation* 281:9 (26 September 2005): 24, 26.
———. "Postscript," *Callaloo* 33:2 (Spring, 2010): 410.
———. "U.S. Takes Wasteful Approach to Detaining Immigrants," *Washington Post* (15 March 2013).
Knepper, Wendy. "In/justice and Necro-natality in Edwidge Danticat's *Brother, I'm Dying*," *Journal of Commonwealth Literature* 47:2 (June 2012): 191–205.
Lipman, Jana K. "Immigrant and Black in Edwidge Danticat's *Brother, I'm Dying*," *Modern American History* 2:1 (March 2019): 71–75.
Sairsingh, Marie. "The Archeology of Memory: Ontological Reclamation in Danticat's *Brother, I'm Dying* and *The Farming of Bones*," *International Journal on Studies in English Language and Literature* 1:1 (March 2013): 6–10.
Smiley, Tavis. "Interview," *Tavis Smiley Show* (Los Angeles NPR) (6 November 2004).
Vitone, Elaine. "Interview," *Publishers Weekly* 254:30 (30 July 2007): 66.

Caco Genealogy

Essential to the Bildungsroman *Breath, Eyes, Memory*, the Caco family tree,

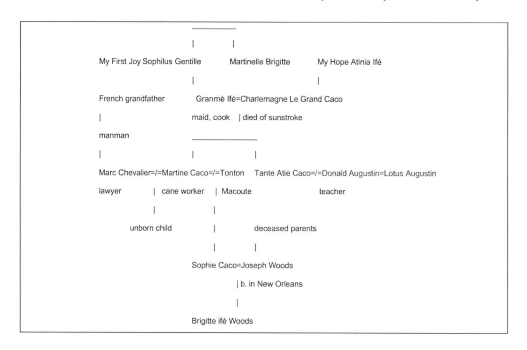

rooted in female strength, retains over five generations of exemplary courage and endeavor. Within a traditional androcentric society, Grandmè Ifé outlived her mate, a cane cutter resplendently named Charlemagne Le Grand Caco. While she toiled at maid service and cooking, he died of sunstroke, a symbolic contrast of domestic and agrarian labor. Martine, her daughter, labored in cane fields until felled and impregnated by an unidentified Tonton Macoute.

Subsequent models of womanhood tout Tante Atie for enduring a broken heart while rearing niece Sophie and ensuring her education. As interpreted by Hungarian expert Eva Federmayer, "Healing is configured in the narrative by transmuting violence through empathy, mutual recognition, and generosity" (Federmayer, 2015, 3). By breaking free of Martine's mental aberrations, Sophie finds inner powers to reclaim her marriage and rear Brigitte Ifé Woods as a normal daughter.

Sources

Danticat, Edwidge. *Breath, Eyes, Memory.* New York: Soho Press, 1994.
Federmayer, Eva. "Violence and Embodied Subjectivities: Edwidge Danticat's Breath, Eyes, Memory," *Scholar Critic* 2:3 (December 2015): 1–17.
Pierre-Pierre, Garry. "At Home with Edwidge Danticat: Haitian Tales, Flatbush Scenes," *New York Times* (26 January 1995): C1.
Rossi, Jennifer C. "'Let the Words Bring Wings to Our Feet': Negotiating Exile and Trauma through Narrative in Danticat's *Breath, Eyes, Memory,*" *Obsidian III* 6:2 (Fall/Winter, 2005): 203–220.

Cane

Edwidge ennobles sacred and essential foodstuffs to Haitians, especially fields of cane in the farmlands of *Célimène* and the cane syrup topping manioc cakes at the pre–Lenten carnival in *After the Dance.*

Following the revolution of 1804, Emperor Jean-Jacques Dessalines promoted sugar production without the use of slaves. In an interview with Bonnie Lyons for *Contemporary Literature,* the author characterized cane as the prime commodity of Léogâne, her family's homestead. Her interview "The Dominican Republic and Haiti: A Shared View from the Diaspora" with Richard André for *Americas Quarterly* emphasized a connection between President Woodrow Wilson's order of the U.S. invasion on July 28, 1915, and the burgeoning of political power among cane producers. Sugar magnates exacerbated a prejudicial caste system between the two races, black and Hispanic. In an article on the parsley massacre for *New Republic,* investigative reporter Harold Courlander revealed that black laborers earned twenty cents per day.

Edwidge incorporated elements of the sugar industry in memory stories: the widows sleeping on pallets of sugar sacks in "Caroline's Wedding," chateaus of planters gone to ruin in "Seven Stories," and, in "The Dew Breaker," the title character's breakfast of a smoke and three cups of kleren, a grassy-flavored rum micro-distilled from cane. Apart from nutrition and financial gain, the author enwreathes the prime crop in a cycle of poverty, criminality, bloodshed, and martyrdom exemplified by the collapse of cane cutter Charlemagne Le Grand Caco from sunstroke in *Breath, Eyes, Memory* and waterboarding with a sugar sack in "Dosas." In "Monkey Tails," the character Romain quotes Voltaire's aphorism about greedy Europeans raising the demand for Caribbean sugar. Romain adds that cane products marketed in Europe bear Haitian blood, a metaphoric vampirism by colonists. In creative activism, Edwidge voiced the 95-minute documentary *The Sugar Babies,* which appeared in French as *Les Enfants du Sucre.* Set in the Dominican Republic and written and directed by Amy Serrano for Siren Studios, the text protests the enrichment of sugar moguls since the colonial era by labor abuses, worker exploitation, and human trafficking, a crime worsened by the sale of organs for transplant.

Life with Sugar

Cane products haunt island lives. For the story "A Wall of Fire Rising," Big Guy muses on living in the shadow of a sugar mill and, in infancy, drinking sweet water tea boiled from pulp and flavored with salt. A significant obstacle in the myth of the flying African identifies salt as an element forcing the dreamer back to earth. Cane labor depletes workers, who sometimes must stand in the smoke of burning fields to drive out venomous snakes before the finish of harvest. Edwidge observed, "I saw people go off to the cane fields in the Dominican Republic and return ghosts of themselves," a testimonial to exhaustion, disease, machete accidents, snakebite, and poor nutrition (Lyons, 2003, 194). The significance of a profitable crop sets the pattern of railroads, which connects plantation towns to the Port-au-Prince refining mill and offers sweet snacks protruding from the cars to eager hands. The innocence of children relays in adulthood the cost of a sweet tooth.

The primary crop poses a colonial paradox—a source of jobs and one of the major tormentors and island destabilizers. The privations of agrarian labor in *Breath, Eyes, Memory* cause Tante Atie Caco to shield niece Sophie from an unpromising future that could result in death in the field as unforeseen as Atie's father Charlemagne's collapse. At the end of the burial service for Sophie's mother Martine Caco, the girl lashes out at a cane field, the place where a Tonton Macoute raped Martine and sired Sophie. The blow against chaff represents the futility of vengeance against nature in a place where economics and corrupt government doubly damn islanders.

In *The Farming of Bones,* translated into French with a pun, *La Récolte Douce des Larmes* (The Sweet Crop of Tears), Edwidge sets the plot in Alegría, the ironic Spanish word for "joy." She depicts heads shaved to avoid cane ticks. For victim Sebastien Onius, the heavy smell of sucrose "in his room, in his clothes, in the breeze, even in his hair" disrupts his sleep, his brief respite from labor (Danticat, 1998, 172). Sharp leaves slash eyes of cane cutters; rigid stalks rip faces of steely male laborers into "crisscrossed trails of furrowed scars" (*ibid.,* 1). Parturient women work up to the last minute and give birth in the shade of stalks, a symbolic prophecy that the next generation will endure the same persecutions as their parents.

During multiple harvests over a ten-year period, the grip on machetes covers palms in calluses, thickens nails, dismembers hands and feet, and wears away lifelines, a subtle glimpse of human erosion in service to the Hispanic landowner. An elderly female harvester at the cane mill bears a blade slice through her cheekbone, "the flesh healed because it had to but never sealed in the same way again" (*ibid.,* 222). Others lost fingers and an ear, a gradual whittling away of power and person and of value to the labor market. After his wife died, Old Kongo's son, laborer Joël Raymond Loner, earns a reputation for the strength to pull an ox cart, a skill that lowers him to bestial status. When landowners cause Joël's death by careless driving, Kongo returns to the cane fields as his last bastion, a pitiful asset from grueling employment.

Annihilating Blacks

In June 1996, *Granta* published Edwidge's story "The Revenant"—issued in fall 1996 in *Conjunctions* as "Condolences"—a spare exchange between Señor Pico and Dr. Berto, an authority figure. During the bloodbath of 30,000 peasants at the Massacre River of the Dominican Republic on October 2–8, 1937, Berto rescues Haitians fleeing the cane fields. His observation of "Haitians chopped up with machetes like they were meat to be shredded" parallels the degraded field workers with cane, a profitable crop hacked into sugar and distilled into molasses and rum (Danticat, 1996). The images return more powerfully in the author's historical novel *The Farming of Bones*. Traversing an agrarian hell, Amabelle Desír stirs up a hot, foul odor on the path, a suggestion of the postcolonial scourge of cane work.

Through a dream figure, Sugar Woman, in "The Revenant" and again in *The Farming of Bones,* the author relates a cruel aspect of the Haitian cane-cutter's management—a muzzle that prevents the worker from eating Dominican produce. Chains on ankles halt blacks from running away. A mordant image of darkness turns layered cane leaves into "a coffin under the ground with six feet of dirt piled over your face," a silencing of agricultural workers as final as the executions by which Generalissimo Rafael Trujillo annihilates blacks (Danticat, 157, 1998). He chooses to rid the country of nonwhite laborers in an act of racial cleansing cloaked as patriotism. He reasons that "They once came here only to cut sugarcane, but now there are more of them than there will ever be cane to cut…. How can a country be ours if we are in smaller numbers than the outsiders?" (*ibid.,* 260–261).

SOURCES

Courlander, Harold. "Not in the Cables," *New Republic* (24 November 1937): 67.

Danticat, Edwidge. *The Dew Breaker*. New York: Abacus, 2004.

———. "The Dominican Republic and Haiti: A Shared View from the Diaspora," *Americas Quarterly* 8:3 (Summer 2014): 28–35.

———. *The Farming of Bones*. New York: Penguin, 1998.

———. "The Revenant," *Granta* 54 115 (20 June 1996).

Derby, Lauren. "Film Review of *The Price of Sugar* and *The Sugar Babies*," *Caribbean Studies* 36:2 (July–December 2008): 250–265.

Harbawi, Semia. "Writing Memory: Edwidge Danticat's Limbo Inscriptions," *Journal of West Indian Literature* 16:1 (1 November 2007): 37–58.

Lyons, Bonnie. "Interview," *Contemporary Literature* 44:2 (Summer 2003): 182–198.

Carnival

With two publications—*After the Dance* and the shortened version *A Walk through Carnival*—Edwidge promotes carnival for its spirit of place, laughter, and fantasy. Details featured floats, bands, and historical costuming, including the "sequined thong and feathered headdress" preserved in the Carnival Museum in "Seven Stories" (Danticat, 209, 186). She characterized competition and fun time as essentials of Haitian life. In "Becoming Brazilian," a memoir for *Obsidian III,* she commented that "there are two things that islanders won't do without: soccer and carnival" (Danticat, 2006, 145).

In Jacmel on Haiti's south central shore, the writer advocated seasonal joy and spontaneous improvisation. She favored music that boosts spirituality and incites rebellion against government corruption. Her memoir *After the Dance* incorporates elements of gaiety, for example, the maypole ritual and Taino costumes for the children's parade that delight Rose Lavaud in *Claire of the Sea Light*. The disguise motif in "Seven" marks the meeting of a Haitian couple at the Tuesday finale during ritual weeping beside a bonfire that ends Lenten masking.

Parade Details

Critic Rebecca Dirksen's *After the Dance, the Drums Are Heavy: Carnival, Politics, and Musical Engagement*, a 2019 survey of the pre–Easter festival from Oxford Press, listed polyphonic, contrapuntal, and polyrhythmic elements that augment a seething chaos vilifying sociopolitical wrongs. She declared,

> The modus operandi is carnivalesque and the motor is music. It's at once silly, serious, sexy, violent, provoking, tension-diffusing, boisterous, solemn, exaggerated, confining, sprawling, claustrophobic, liberating, generative, destructive, healing, hyperbolic, understated, dynamic, profound—and certainly noisy [Dirksen, xxxi].

In an article for the *Toronto Star*, Edwidge detailed the allure of dance: "People come from near and far to Kanaval Jacmel, crowding the main thoroughfare, Barranquilla Avenue, following on foot, or dancing behind the packed floats of their favourite musical bands" (Danticat, 2013, T3). Among the sights, she enumerates cemeteries, remnants of the Moulin Price steam engine, a waterfall filling Bassin Bleu, and French colonial houses featuring wrought iron balconies like those in New Orleans, Savannah, and Charleston.

Edwidge returned to the Jacmel carnival before Easter on April 24, 2011, and composed an afterword for *After the Dance* in 2015. Critical response from experts in world literature and West Indian culture tended to be positive. In a review for *Journal of Haitian Studies*, analyst Nick Nesbitt of Miami University stressed "the presence of the departed among the living ... characteristic of all Danticat's work" (Nesbitt, 2004, 194). Daphne Lamothe, an Afro-Caribbean expert at Smith College, esteemed carnival season as "a dynamic cultural production that allows for an exploration of the practices and politics of belonging,"

a source of unity and Caribbean identity (Lamothe, 2012, 360). She noted alterations to the annual fête in 2012, when she declared that dances, songs, and languages during the festivities "have come to signify a dynamic multiculturalism" adapted to change, assimilation, universality, and worldliness (*Ibid.*).

Masking and Disguise

To *Callaloo* journalist and interviewer Michael S. Collins, Edwidge reflected on her frequent mention of masks, which she attached to Greek comedy-tragedy dissembling and pre–Columbian first peoples and their mimicry. Facial obscurity becomes a factor in the fifteenth-century Taino coming of age dance of the title figure in *Anacaona*. In *The Farming of Bones*, Edwidge returned to the issue of mask making after Old Kongo, a skilled carpenter, shapes a countenance similar to his dead son Joël Raymond Loner. An African tradition of culture and religion, masking followed blacks to the New World and entertained partiers at Jacmel, a UNESCO World Heritage site. As silent storytellers, they contained face and head coverings from papier-mâché and costumes from original design, two means of reenacting West Indian history and ancestry of heroes and martyrs.

In *Create Dangerously*, the author remarked on the connection between festival galas and government corruption by the Duvaliers' military police, the Tonton Macoute, fans of Orchestra Septentrional d'Haiti. During violent clubbing by the ungovernable death squad, "people who survived had to put on their masks" to reclaim cultural roots anonymously (Collins, 2007, 472). She compared the practice to gold Egyptian funerary masks on dead pharaohs, a suggestion of the background of "The Book of the Dead," a story of false surfaces covering past sins. On Tuesday night every Ash Wednesday, carnival merrymakers gather at the beach to burn masks and costumes and weep for the end of their Lenten holiday. The grief enacts redemption through an iconic letting go of ancient animosities and grudges.

Sources

Beard, David. "Seeing Haiti, When It Can Dance and Laugh," *Boston Globe* (5 September 2002): M7.

Collins, Michael S. "Interview," *Callaloo* 30:2 (Spring, 2007): 471–473, 674.

Danticat, Edwidge. *After the Dance: A Walk Through Carnival in Jacmel, Haiti.* New York: Vintage, 2002.

_____. "Becoming Brazilian," *Obsidian III* 6/7:2/1 (Fall 2005/2006): 139–145.

_____. *Create Dangerously: The Immigrant Artist at Work.* New York: Vintage, 2010.

_____. *Everything Inside.* New York: Knopf, 2019.

_____. "Haiti's Quiet Beauty Captivates in Jacmel," *Toronto Star* (28 December 2013): T3.

_____. "Seven," *New Yorker* (24 September 2001).

Dirksen, Rebecca. *After the Dance, the Drums Are Heavy: Carnival, Politics, and Musical Engagement in Haiti.* Oxford University Press, 2019.

Lamothe, Daphne. "Carnival in the Creole City: Place, Race, and Identity in the Age of Globalization," *Biography* 35:2 (Spring 2012): 360–374.

Murphy, Dwyer. "The Art of Not Belonging," *Guernica* (3 September 2013).

Nesbitt, Nick. "Review: *After the Dance*," *Journal of Haitian Studies* 10:1 (2004): 194–196.

Catholicism

Catholicism influences even the small details of Haitian life in Edwidge's works, especially the Sunday mass at Notre Dame Catholic Church in Miami's Little Haiti in "Dosas," the volunteerism of godparents in "Between the Pool and the Gardenias," the Vodou use of Guinea to name the spirit world in *Breath, Eyes, Memory*, and the threat of blood on a communion dress in "The Missing Peace." Callie Morrissete's singing of "Ave Maria" at a make-believe funeral in "Seven Stories" derives from her Catholic background and elementary school classes

taught by nuns. In "The Missing Peace," Lamort renames herself Mary Magdalene after her deceased mother. The name, doubled in the family tree, honors Jesus's female disciple and alleged wife.

Much of Edwidge's religious detail is personal. Inside Sainte Rose de Lima Cathedral, she glimpses stained glass and candles, traditional worship enhancements. She highlights the naming of Sor Rose (Sister Rose), a patroness of southern Haiti in the novel *Claire of the Sea Light* and the first person sanctified in the Western Hemisphere. In terror of the Duvalier regime, the story "The Journals of Water Days 1986" pictures terrified Haitians praying to the Holy Family, "Jesus, Marie, Joseph. Mother Jesus, look after us," an entreaty repeated in *Breath, Eyes, Memory* (Danticat, 1996, 376). Tradition highlights human visions of the Holy Family in the singing of "Silent Night" and "What Child Is This," standard parts of midnight mass liturgy echoing mystery and wonder.

The Last Mapou mentions the religious war on paganism that causes Catholics to authorize removal of the kapok tree, the site of Vodou nuptials and blessing of births. Mariology appears in Marie's recitation of the "Ave Maria" in "Between the Pool and the Gardenias," Junior's solo in the Sainte Trinité choir in *Eight Days,* and the funeral service with Hail Marys and a rosary for a female refugee drowned in transit to the U.S. in "Caroline's Wedding." The rosary recurs as a female talisman in "Monkey Tails" when Michel's mother prays for protection from vigilantes. In the 2020 *New Yorker* essay "Haiti Faces Difficult Questions Ten Years after a Devastating Earthquake," the author mourned anew the collapse of the Port-au-Prince landmark Notre Dame de l'Assomption Cathedral (Our Lady of the Assumption) and the demise of Archbishop Joseph Serge Miot, a Roman Catholic activist.

Women and Faith

In a patriarchal hegemony, Edwidge's female characters rely on womanly divinities. For Anne Bienaimé in *The Dew Breaker*, versions of the Holy Mother's generosity to children anticipate mercy for the beautician's drowned stepbrother. Divinity influences place names, as with Croix de Rosets (Cross of Roses) and La Nouvelle Dame Marie (the New Lady Mary). For respites from sexual damage and humiliation in *Breath, Eyes, Memory*, in the view of Yolanda Pierce, Dean of the Howard University School of Divinity, "Few of the characters in the novel find emotional peace or physical healing outside of death, as they navigate their brutal personal histories, full of both political and sexual violence" (Pierce, 2010). Instead of dogma and repentance, they turn to storytelling and icons from a syncretic Guinean, Yoruban, and Catholic cosmology.

For the Caco matriarchy, a merger of beliefs fleshes out forms of healing. While her mother Martine tests her hymen, Sophie Caco prays to the Virgin, the Catholic standard of female purity and obedience and intercessor to the troubled. For therapy to stem sexual dysfunction, she relies on a Santerian priestess who leads serenity prayers, incense and candle lighting, and libations to Afro-Caribbean divinities. Sophie leans especially on Erzulie, consoler of black women. On Christmas Eve, Tante Atie and Martine turn to a French colonial custom and attend Mass in Gothic surroundings. They contemplate crèches in the Champs de Mars (Plain of Mars) public park, a tableau created in a cave by St. Francis of Assisi in 1223 in Greccio, Italy, and recaptured at St. Jerome's Church in *Behind the Mountains*.

Catholic Imagery

References to church ritual appear in dreams in "Children of the Sea," in which a rebel radio broadcaster envisions mermaids dancing like priests during Mass, and in the artistry of a monument carver in *After the Dance* whose enwreathed crosses gave the name Croix-des-Bouquets (Cross of Garlands) to his town in western Haiti. For the speaker in "Between the Pool and the Gardenias," a sequence of miscarried fetuses requires naming and burial under blessed names: Jacqueline, a twelfth-century Roman saint who fed the poor; Josephine, a Sudanese saint who escaped enslavement; and Céliane (gracious), a gesture to the entire celestial panoply. Jesus's miracle turning water into wine enters Anne Bienaimé's fantasies in "The Book of Miracles." For friends Freda, Rézia, and Mariselle in "The Funeral Singer," work on General Educational Development (GED) classes inspires them to light candles to Saint Jude, the first-century CE patron of lost causes.

In *The Farming of Bones,* the maid Juana portrays fanaticism for Catholic saints and hagiology. For Amabelle Desír, a refugee recovering from the Haitian ordeal at the Massacre River, rootless wandering in Cap Haïtien ends with her entry to Our Lady of Assumption Cathedral on Rue 18, where she refuses communion and confession. Her worries for Father Jacques Romain and Father Vargas win the respect of Father Emil, who reports their survival of prison and Father Romain's residence with his sister across the Massacre River at the same Haitian town of Ouanaminthe. At a reunion with the priest in 1961, Amabelle discovers a violation of strict Catholic principle—Romain abandoned celibacy, married, and sired three sons, who helped him recover from derangement.

See also Erzulie, *Krik? Krak!* Genealogy, Music, Religion.

Sources

Danticat, Edwidge. *The Farming of Bones*. New York: Penguin, 1998.

_____. "The Journals of Water Days," *Callaloo* 19:2 (Spring, 1996): 376–380.

_____. *The Last Mapou.* Brooklyn: One Moore Book, 2013.

_____. "The Missing Peace," *Just a Moment* 4:1 (Winter, 1992–1993).

Pierce, Yolanda. "Restless Spirits: Syncretic Religion in Edwidge Danticat's *Breath, Eyes, Memory,*" *Journal of Pan African Studies* 3:5 (March 2010).

Samway, Patrick. "A Homeward Journey: Edwidge Danticat's Fictional Landscapes, Mindscapes, Genescapes, and Signscapes in *Breath, Eyes, Memory,*" *Mississippi Quarterly* 57:1 (1 December 2003): 75–84.

Célimène

Dedicated to daughters Mira and Leila Boyer, Edwidge's 64-page "conte de fées pour fille d'immigrante" (fairy tale for immigrant girls) for the orphaned Haitian takes its style, verse, and structure from "d'une vieille chanson folklorique haïtienne" (an old song from Haitian folklore) (Danticat, 2009, 5). The girl's name recalls Emperor Jean-Jacques Dessalines's attempt in 1805 to bind black Haitians to mulattos to create a peaceable transfer of inheritances and union of castes. He offered his eldest daughter, 16-year-old Marie Françoise Célimène Dessalines—to revolutionary Alexandre Sabès Pétion, a quadroon who rejected the arranged nuptial. The man-to-man plotting of a young girl's future illustrated the devaluation of female slaves and wives to elements of political strategy.

In the introduction to her faith tale, Edwidge describes the theme as suited to "cette jeune immigrante que j'étais à douze ans" (the young immigrant I was at age twelve) (*ibid., 5*). To her credit, Célimène possesses joie de vivre and a rapport with the villages, rivers, greenery, birds, and animals around her, which illustrator Mance Lanctôt characterizes in humble farm work and amid shady ferns. She and younger brother Mo farm and barter cacao and coffee for their daily peasant fare—corn, plantains, and yams. The absence of meat and fresh seafood is common among the poor.

From Maiden to Wife

Living at their fictional hometown of Pik Rose (rose peak), the curly haired, copper skinned, oval-faced protagonist surveys a blue sky and aqua mountains, the details of a tropical agrarian setting. With younger brother Mo, Célimène longs to leave home and "voler de ses propres ailes" (stretch her wings), a statement imbued with the meaning of her name, "heavenly strength" (*ibid.*). While the immature Mo annoys a bird with a branch, his sister sensibly builds a fire for cooking supper. In patriarchal tradition, the brother, endowed with his father's oversight, manages the choices of his female sibling. However, the risks fall to his sister to manage. To survive an adventurous marriage far from home, she learns to fend for herself and to build optimism, two female strengths that boost her spirits.

The gist of the story hinges on the brother's approval of a "mystérieux visiteur" (mysterious arrival). "Cadet Mo" governs the selection of a future husband for his beautiful older sister, who bears the physical appeal of their deceased mother (*ibid., 13*). Célimène, the idealist, reaches out to the stars while Mo fantasizes about becoming a hunter. She invites Zaken, the newcomer, to a breakfast of cornmeal porridge and smoked herring, a typical island repast. By imagining a more fulfilling life, she falls for him, but Mo demands more than a handsome face for his sister. Zaken offers abundant love and devotion to her for the rest of his life. Célimène identifies in Zaken "les qualités de tous ceux que j'ai aimés" (the traits of all those whom I have loved), a beneficent, if idealistic recommendation for a future mate (*ibid.,* 18).

A Fantasy Romance

The author embroiders the fairy tale with marvels alongside standard elements of romantic fantasy—a sleepy heroine dreaming of her handsome love, mapou leaves bathed in moonlight, and a man's voice entering the open window of her chamber. The details reflect two originals—"Rapunzel," an 1812 publication by the Brothers Grimm, and John Keats's "The Eve of St. Agnes," issued in 1819 in a gesture to St. Agnes, patron of girls and female purity. Zaken promises to share his wealth. To the practical-minded Mo, Zaken states confidently his marriage plans: "Elle laissera tout pour me suivre" (She will leave everything to go with me), a male expectation of the submissive female (*ibid.,* 19). A mystic voice from Liya, a 36-foot purple anaconda, conjures up an Adam and Eve scenario and a shapeshifter capable of deception by shedding its skin. Because of its immense jaws, it scared away Zaken's first ten wives, becoming a test of Célimène's adaptability to her new home.

Key to narrative revelations lie in what Pierre-Raymond Dumas and Augustin Chenald term "La mobilité (rupture, voyage, marriage, exile)" (mobility—the break with the past, travel, wedlock, and exile) (Dumas and Chenald, 2011). Zaken conceals from Célimène that he is a village chief, not a simple peasant. A bride blessed at Vodou rites by a Houngan, the village priest, and a lavish home, she encircles her new residence seven times by the light of one candle, a symbolic blessing of the seven-day week. She discovers alleys of palms and avenues bordered by "grandes maisons and de vastes parcs" (sumptuous houses and huge parks) (Danticat, 2009). Shady mapou trees and afternoon breezes symbolize the newness and promise of America that Edwidge found when she migrated to New York City to "une vie meilleure" (a better life) (*ibid.*).

See also Adaptation, Grotesque, Patriarchy.

SOURCES

Burnham, Thorald M. "'Everything They Hate': Michèle, Mildred, and Elite Haitian Marrying Strategies in Historical Perspective," *Journal of Family History* 31:1 (2006): 83–109.

Danticat, Edwidge. *Célimène—Fairy Tale for the Daughter of Immigrants.* Montreal: Memoire d'Encrier, 2009.

Dumas, Pierre-Raymond, and Augustin Chenald. "'Célimène' ou la problématique de l'exil au coeur du merveilleux," *Le Nouvelliste* (21 June 2011).

"La nouvelle collection 'L'Arbre du Voyager,'" *Le Nouvelliste* (3 November 2009).

"Review: *Célimène,*" *France-Antilles* (30 June 2010).

Children's Literature

A wave of post-colonial stories about Africa and the Caribbean received support from educators, teachers, parents, and writers. A favorite, Edwidge's diary introduction of *Anacaona,* a fifteenth-century Taino cacica (ruler), describes the exit from girlhood through a creative dance and masking. An introductory essay in *Children's Literature Association Quarterly* in 2005 promoted the use of children's narratives to shape self-awareness: "The rise of a culturally redemptive children's literature from Africa and the Caribbean signals a new approach to reconstituting Black identity, one that comments unreservedly on neocolonialism and the challenges it presents to Black experience" (MacCann and Smith, 2005, 137). The citation accounts for Edwidge's drive to recapture the ancient past and to honor the recent experiences of émigrés like her paternal uncle,

Joseph Nosius Dantica, and her parents, André Mira and Rose Souvenance Danticat.

Recalling specific crimes of imperialism, Edwidge assails the cultural disparity and inequities communicated by schools and textbook publishers. The YA novel *Untwine* depicts *Alice in Wonderland, Little Women,* and the 56 Nancy Drew mysteries as the stock myth of white society. For high school students in Miami's Little Haiti, Danielle, the teacher in "Reading Lessons," chooses to read Hans Christian Andersen's fairy tale "The Snow Queen." Because of Paul's aping of her face and mouth, Danielle turns into the story's troll and smacks him. A dramatic irony pictures Danielle's metamorphosis into the troll, who acts out the murder of her mother by a boy Paul's age. The chain of evil extends to another blow, Paul's mother's retaliation against Danielle, a clash between reader Louise George and parent Odile Desír, two authority figures adapted for *Claire of the Sea Light.*

Balancing Backstory

The chief breaker of black stigma, impersonal folklore reclaims the hidden events passed over and censored by white histories. Aphorism, legend, and fable in her works, such as Louise George's oral readings in school and fabulist Jean de la Fontaine's "The Sun and the Frogs" in *Claire of the Sea Light,* offer nonwhite youth the sustenance they need to endure eras of corruption and evil. From universal themes, such as the ageless hero in James Barrie's play *Peter Pan* named in *The Art of Death,* young islanders survive the ruptures of slavery, revolution, dislocation, climate change, Apartheid, and Caribbean dictatorships, notably those wielded by Generalissimo Rafael Trujillo and "Papa Doc" and "Baby Doc" Duvalier.

Edwidge's dynamic storytelling awakens children to the validity of Creole dialect, the Haitian motherland, and home culture, for example, in the workshop anecdotes the barber tells his son Junior in *Eight Days.* By respecting the young reader's instincts and intelligence, she exorcises the distress of past centuries and replaces gaps and distortions with the shared heritage of the Afro-Caribbean islander omitted from standard curricula. In reference to Haitian accomplishments, analyst Aitor Ibarrola-Armendáriz regretted that "Little is said in today's history books of the significance of the revolution and the achievements of the world's oldest black republic," which toppled colonial overlords in January 1804 under the leadership of General Jean Jacques Dessalines (Ibarrola-Armendáriz, 2011).

Stories for All

The author declared artificial the demarcation between adult and young adult reading. She added that, for island children, the shouldering of serious responsibilities in early youth offered a mature view of the world at a time when play should predominate. For either audience, she aimed "to tell a good story that's both fulfilling and entertaining" (Smith, 2005, 199). Many of her earliest characters and themes unite West Indians with important moments in American history. Her stories glorify Haitian-Americans, particularly Jean Baptiste Point du Sable and the founding of Chicago in 1790, and naturalist Jean James Audubon, painter of American wildlife, who issued *The Birds of America* in 1827.

Edwidge explained her motivation for replacing stock figures with personal encounters, the source of a poem on Sleeping Beauty in "All Geography Is Within Me." She emphasized that "I hope to change the way the reader defines Haiti as well as the way he or she defines

America, to let them know that indeed Haitian-Americans have earned themselves a place here" (Smith, 2005, 204). For the documentary *Girl Rising,* the author wrote the story of seven-year-old Wadley, a female resident of Port-au-Prince. Actor Cate Blanchett narrated how the family suffered loss of their home in the December 2010 earthquake.

See also *Célimène,* Storytelling.

Sources

Capshaw, Katharine. "The Limitless Vision of Edwidge Danticat's Work for Young People," *Research on Diversity in Youth Literature* 2:2 (2020): 2.

Danticat, Edwidge. "All Geography Is Within Me," *World Literature Today* 93:1 (Winter 2019): 58.

_____. *Anacaona: Golden Flower, Haiti, 1490.* New York: Scholastic, 2005.

_____. *Claire of the Sea Light.* New York: Vintage, 2013.

_____. *Untwine.* New York: Scholastic, 2015.

Ibarrola-Armendáriz, Aitor. "Broken Memories of a Traumatic Past and the Redemptive Power of Narrative in the Fiction of Edwidge Danticat," *Cross/Cultures* 136 (2011): 3–27, 248.

MacCann, Donnarae, and Katharine Capshaw Smith. "This Quest for Ourselves," *Children's Literature Association Quarterly* 30:2 (Summer, 2005): 137–139.

Smith, Katharine Capshaw. "Interview," *Children's Literature Association Quarterly* 30:2 (Summer, 2005): 194–205.

Claire of the Sea Light

Employing a complex fiction cycle, Edwidge summarizes the history of Ville Rose in terms of futility, yearnings, and the reciprocity of birth and death. She first mentioned the blighted coastal town in southeastern Haiti in the anthology *Krik? Krak!* and presented a segment of the novel in the Winter 2012–2013 issue of *Progressive* under the title "Giving and Receiving." Reviewer Christine Germain, a composition professor at the University of North Carolina at Charlotte, summarized the collection as outlining "the portrait of a town in peril, which can be read as a microcosm for life in Haiti," particularly the streets that imitate thorns (Germain, 2014, 215). A bit of homespun wisdom condenses efforts to survive in a single image—churning butter out of water, a typically agrarian moral for a marine fable featuring the sea's tentative gifts. The book appeared in French translation as *Pour l'Amour de Claire* (For the Love of Claire).

In each exemplum of what reviewer Deborah Sontag of the *New York Times* calls "a collision of fates," the victims are absent—the elder Claire Narcis Faustin, dead in childbirth; Caleb, a fisherman drowned at sea whom villages honor with a vigil; Laurent Lavaud, a shop owner shot before the radio station; and his daughter Rose killed in a motorcycle collision (Sontag, 2013). A returnee, Max Ardin, Jr., a potential suicide, is the father of an illegitimate son and the closeted lover of Bernard "Bè" Dorien, a dead journalist misidentified and avenged by rogue cops as a contract killer. From the decrepit Anthère Lighthouse, named for the pollinator in sexual plant production, Claire provides visual evidence of ongoing decline in Ville Rose and a panoramic view of the community efforts to save individuals. The circular narrative, according to an anonymous critique in *Publishers Weekly,* comprises "a story that feels as mysterious and magical as a folk tale and as effective and devastating as a newsreel" ("Review," *Publishers Weekly,* 2013).

In the ponderous analysis of Florida State University professor Maxine Lavon Montgomery for *CLA Journal,* the interlocking scenarios echo the legend of a matriarchal deity, Mami Wata (Mother Water). A diasporic pan–African saltwater sprite revered in Cameroon, Congo, Ivory Coast, Nigeria, Senegal, Togo, and Zambia, she controls a trickster sea "that does not keep secrets" (Zipp, 2013, 20). The siren or mermaid communes with the all-powerful creator and rewards the faithful with wealth. She protects women and children, the focus of Edwidge's characterization of Claire Limyè Lanmè Faustin, Rose Lavaud, and Pamaxime Voltaire. To lure Mami Wata to his aid, waterman Nozias Faustin travels his fishing route each day with a sack of trinkets—comb, mirror, conch shell—the kinds of treasures that entice a female water deity.

Claire of the Sea Light

In Part One, a menacing magical realism in the form of a twelve-foot tsunami inundating the Haitian coastline precedes a personal shock—fisherman Nozias Faustin's arrangement when he leaves Ville Rose to give away his seven-year-old daughter Claire to a better life of fostering by a prosperous shopkeeper. In Pythagoras's numerology, the number seven represents the pure and mystic elements of the spiritual world, a motif the author may have adopted from novelist Toni Morrison's *Beloved* and reprised in the wedding dance in "One Thing." The career Nozias follows on the Caribbean Sea declines rapidly from "silt and trash" and overfishing, common threats to the earth's seven seas (Danticat, 2013, 9). Because of the precarious nature of a fisherman's work, he fears he may die in the oceans, leaving his motherless daughter to fend for herself on the streets or in brothels selling sex, her only commodity. Each year, he dresses Claire in the same style outfit and leads a ritual procession to the elder Claire's plot at the graveyard, a mystic rededication of daughter to beloved wife.

Background fills in mother Claire Narcis's transcendent dive into a school of silvery fish. Already pregnant with Claire Faustin, the mother chooses a luminous name from the Anthère Lighthouse—Limyè Lanmè, "of the sea light," an upbeat description that yokes the daughter to the local beam to sea. Edwidge later observed in the memoir "House of Prayer and Dreams" that a town like Ville Rose "deserves places of healing and memory, beacons and lighthouses" (Danticat, 2013, 42). Like Mami Wata, the wife promises Nozias the wealth of nature that only the sea can provide. Prefacing the rearing of the younger Claire after his wife's death in labor, Nozias describes the ordeal of dressing a motherless newborn and finding a wet nurse. Coming to his aid, the fabric vendor, Gaëlle Cadet Lavaud, mother of three-year-old Rose, offers the first feeding.

At age seven, Claire learns that her foster mother will be Gaëlle, who has lost her husband to a shooting and her ten-year-old daughter to a motorcycle accident. The catastrophes occurred on Claire's birthday, a dominant motif. People on the shore depart at midnight after mourning the loss of Caleb to a giant wave, building a beacon fire, and comforting his mute widow Josephine. After Claire goes back to her cot to gather belongings, she disappears, leaving Nozias and Gaëlle to search for her. Suspense over her whereabouts fuses the next chapters into a single narrative featuring children in need of protection.

The Frogs

To express community interconnectedness, Edwidge gathers backstories of Ville Rose residents—of whom five percent are wealthy and the rest poor. During Gaëlle's pregnancy with Rose ten years earlier, biblical plagues engulf the town: the heat becomes relentless; local frogs explode. Gaëlle collects for burial the corpses of a green-horned variety, a brown dwarf jungle frog, and a scarlet koki tree frog. Her child-bearing discomfort abates after she swallows a koki, an African binder of gestation based on Heqet, an Egyptian fertility goddess nurtured by the annual Nile flood. Following the birth, the mother exults in her daughter's beauty. Unexpectedly, Laurent encounters gang violence and dies in front of Radio Zòrèy (Ear Radio), a token victim of a violent, vengeful society.

Ghosts

A revision of the story "Ghosts" from the November 24, 2008, issue of *New Yorker,* the third chapter renames Pascal, the main character, Bernard "Bè" Dorien and the "midlevel slum" Cité Pendue (the hanged city), an allusion to Dante's spiral path through hell in the *Inferno* (*ibid.*, 236). The Dorien family earns a living by supplying pigeons for a blood ritual of manhood, a graphic connection between late teen sexual stirrings and gang membership. Gangsters, called *chimè* (ghosts), exaggerate their ties to Nubia, the ancient civilization in the Nile Valley from 3500 BCE until its Christianization in 400 CE, by taking the names Tiye (kill) and Piye (pillage), objectives of felonious power wielders. Betrayed by Tiye, Bernard lodges in a police interrogation cell for allegedly shooting fabric dealer Laurent Lavaud outside the radio station.

Ego and ambition prove the young men's undoing. After Tiye poses as the big man for freeing Bernard, three bullets in the heart riddle Bernard's chest while he sleeps. Ironically, he had planned to submit to the station, the town's public forum, an article for broadcast about youthful criminals and their emergence from want. He proposed choosing street thugs who had lost limbs to underworld savagery, emblems of truncated souls. An announcement of his murder overturns his media report in meaning and inference after the news misidentifies him as "another bandit ... erased from the face of this earth" (*ibid.*, 83). The faulty comment illustrated Bernard's acute sense of need in Haiti for truth in media.

Home

In the analysis of Boston *Globe* journalist Laura Collins-Hughes, "The question of how to be a man pulses through the book" (Collins-Hughes, 2013, N13). A decade after Bernard's murder, his friend Maxime "Max" Ardin, Jr., returns from Miami to Ville Rose. Maxime, Sr., a pompous school principal, invites his son's paramour Flore Voltaire and her son Pamaxime to confront Max, Jr., for abandoning fatherly responsibility. On transporting the woman and child back to the slums from Ville Rose, Max traverses the same emblematic road to Dante's underworld edged in modern discards—foam food boxes, tires, and plastic juice bottles.

The chapter title raises issues of ambiguity in birth and belonging. Max, Jr., ponders the shooting of Bernard and the deaths of two gang leaders, Piye and Tiye, in a suspicious warehouse fire. At the beach, Max, Jr., joins mourners of Caleb and searches for Claire. His long absence from Ville Rose stirs self-incrimination and sends him fleeing from recompense for raping Flore. As in the Greek concept of *hamartia*, there is no escape from personal failings.

Starfish (2013)

Part two begins at the radio station with Louise George, a programmer who suffers from reverse menstruation, a bizarre condition that causes oral bleeding. For her lover, Maxime Ardin, Sr., she agrees to read aloud to children at his private school. Because a pupil, Henri Desír, mocks her and takes Claire Faustin's barrettes from her hair, Louise slaps him, a

Claire of the Sea Light

dramatic confrontation that the author introduced in the story "Reading Lessons." In a show of manly power, Maxime, Sr., forces Louise to attend a teacher conference, at which Henri's mother, Odile Desír, strikes the teacher in retaliation. Louise interprets the confrontation to be Max's patriarchal method of strengthening her.

Anniversary

Still grieving for husband Laurent and daughter Rose, Gaëlle Lavaud gains a reputation for cruising bars at night and coaxing men to her bed, even Yves Moulin, the driver responsible for her daughter's death. Gaëlle decides to restore the crumbling Anthère Lighthouse, which her grandfather built. The overlooking tower, a symbol of patriarchy and rigid social hierarchy, has lost its light fixture, the beam intended to secure lives at sea. The structure alludes to the French folk song "Au Claire de la Lune," in which Lubin, Pierrot's poet friend, regrets that he lacks candlelight and a pen. The story ends with female charity—a brunette who invites Lubin to share her quill and light, a reference to Gaëlle's sexual appetites.

Edwidge leaves the narrative with unspecified solutions for problems in Ville Rose, a city garnished by thorns. Joining Claire Faustin on the day of her disappearance, Gaëlle sits on Nozias's cot in anticipation of staying the night and transforming the girl into a *restavèk* (fosterling). As a replacement for Rose, Claire anticipates losing her individuality by becoming a duplicate for the dead girl.

Di Mwen, Tell Me

Teacher Louise George assumes the role of community storyteller, a reincarnation of the succubus, the seductive female bearing the vampiric urge to taste blood. According to a riveting on-air narrative,

during a hailstorm, Flore Voltaire lies in the maid's quarters of the Ardin house. She later confesses to the radio interviewer the nature of "one moment that changed [her] life" (*ibid.,* 172). Impregnated by rapist Max, Jr., she suffers a reenactment of the medieval atrocity *droit du seigneur,* the right of a feudal lord to deflower members of the serf class. The Romantic Fallacy connects the stormy night with a character disturbance that extends into the destiny of Pamaxime, whom Max and Flore conceived through violence.

Money offers an unsatisfactory solution for a common problem of sexual assault between an elite male and subservient female. In recompense for the attack, she accepts Maxime, Sr.'s, bribe of $2,000 in American bills. She spends the cash wisely on a prosperous beauty parlor, an encouragement to black women to empower themselves through physical allure, the work of Anne Bienaimé in *The Dew Breaker* and Mona in the story "Dosas." A decade later, Flore fears the Ardins may try to take Pamaxime from her and plots to migrate from Haiti with the boy and her mother, a standard matriarchal rescue.

Toronto *Globe and Mail* reviewer Donna Bailey Nurse credits the act of narrating Flore's life story as "a great equalizer, allowing the powerless to take revenge" (Nurse, 2013). While listening vicariously with Flore to Louise's radio interview, Max, Sr., encapsulates the task of rearing a boy. Although obviously disquieted by Max, Jr.'s, peccadilloes, the father concludes, "His son would always come first" and struggles to find an illustrative story exonerating him for sexual cruelty (*ibid.,* 185). At an unforeseen moment, friend Jessamine discloses Max, Jr.'s, love for Bernard Dorien. Of the parental reflections, Yvonne Zipp, a critic for *Christian Science Monitor,* credits the author with packing the story cycle with "aphorisms and quiet wisdom" based on adult solutions to family issues, both licit and illicit (Zipp, 2013, 20).

At the beach, Nozias Faustin, an underclass version of Max, Sr., passes to Gaëlle a packet of documents that include birth certificate and passport, evidence of her legitimate birth that islanders summarize as "papers." He adds a letter dictated to Caleb, the neighborhood scribe, explaining that Nozias did not sell his daughter. Like Max, Sr., the fisherman muses over Claire's maturity. He relives news of his wife's pregnancy while he visited her at the funeral parlor, where she lovingly washed and dressed corpses. The joyous news reflects the flash of silvery fish in Claire Narcis's dive into the glinting school, a message from nature of the Faustin family's hopes and the community's trust in the sea. A deeper allusion to Pierre-Auguste Vafflard's painting "Young et sa fille" (Young and His Daughter) pictures a loss as bitter as those encountered by Faustin and Gaëlle.

Claire de Lune

At the operatic end of the circular narrative, Claire wanders the market and cafe in a state of ambivalence, a perilous indecision influenced by the author's concerns for her two girls during the nefarious anti-immigrant presidency of Donald Trump. On Claire's seventh birthday, she retreats into solitude and inner confusion, an ephemeral state inconsistent with a name meaning clear and bright and with the perky violets Jessamine admires at the Ardin home. Reflection on Claire's birth triggers thoughts of herself and the elder Claire as twins. Lying partially submerged in the sea, the younger Claire pretends to immerse herself in amniotic fluid and to hear her mother's heartbeat in the thrum of waves, a reiteration of Amabelle Desír's reconnection with Massacre River in *The Farming of Bones*. While sitting

with Gaëlle, Claire longs for more information about her mother, a fabric store customer whom Gaëlle claims to have seen in spirit form at the cemetery. Claire walks toward the shack to gather belongings, then chooses to scramble up the hill to the Anthère Lighthouse, the guiding image of her flight from/toward home.

Of the reconnection with hopeful prospects in a single day, Spanish analyst Silvia Martinez-Falquina, an English professor at the University of Zaragoza, respects the cohesive mystery: "The stories of grief of each individual character are brought to the fore, images of isolation and open-endedness abound" (Martinez-Falquina, 2015, 848). In reference to Max, Jr.'s, near death, she adds "The search for connection is often frustrated. Healing does not seem to be so easy to achieve" (*ibid.*). Looking down on a rescue scene as residents struggle to rid Max's lungs of saltwater, Claire decides to turn back, an embrace of circularity that restores resolve and transforms her into the sea light predicted by her mother. In a reflection on the dilemmas of postcolonials, Martinez-Falquina defined the novel's theme as Claire's renewal from a traumatic life "fighting invisibility and oblivion" (*ibid.*, 834).

Shoreline bonding unites fisherfolk, the fabric vendor, and other members of Ville Rose society in forcing breath into Max. A collage of themes—renewing the lighthouse, community, a new song for Claire's circle games—threatens to overpower characterization. Like the town's rose petals enfolding the victim, Hector Tobar, a reviewer for the *Los Angeles Times,* acknowledges an enchantment both brilliant and sensational. In a critique for *Highbrow,* Kaitlyn Fajilan disclosed unity—"a gleaming tapestry of third-world fables, whose every thread is dyed with equal parts tribulation and triumph" (Fajilan, 2013).

Unlike Tobar, Fajilan, and Laura

Collins-Hughes of the *Boston Globe,* who described the author's style as dextrous, John Barron, book critic for the *Chicago Times,* pinpointed top-heaviness in Edwidge's conclusion: "Her findings are modestly intriguing, as are those throughout the novel, but none comes close to carrying the punch that the knockout opening scenes call for—or promise" (Barron, 2013, 14). In an interview with the *Minneapolis Star Tribune* writer Kristin Tillotson, Edwidge confided her own misgivings about the outcome: "I had written an alternate, sadder ending to Claire's story…. It's hard for me to write a hopeful ending because I want to be true to reality. And when reality is brutal, it's not an easy decision" (Tillotson, 2013, E1).

Sources

Barron, John. "Early Promise Falls Short: Danticat's Admirable Work Fails to Form a Substantive Whole," *Chicago Tribune* (7 September 2013): 14.

Collins-Hughes, Laura. "Town of Lost Souls," *Boston Globe* (25 August 2013): N13.

Danticat, Edwidge. "Claire of the Sea Light," *Haiti Noir.* Brooklyn: Akashic, 2010, 115–138.

_____. *Claire of the Sea Light.* New York: Vintage, 2013.

_____. "Ghosts," *New Yorker* (24 November 2008): 108–113.

_____. "Giving and Receiving," *Progressive* 76:12 (December 2012/January 2013): 19–20.

_____. "House of Prayer and Dreams," *Sojourners* 442:4 (April 2013): 38–39, 41–42.

_____. "Reading Lessons," *New Yorker* 80:42 (10 January 2005): 66–73.

Fajilan, Kaitlyn. "Getting Lost in the World of Edwidge Danticat," *Highbrow* (6 November 2013).

Gérazime, Roselyne E. "Lasirèn, Labalèn: L'abysse en migration dans *Claire of the Sea Light,*" *Journal of Haitian Studies* 25:1 (2019): 178–200.

Germain, Christine. "Review: *Claire of the Sea Light,*" *Palimpsest* 3:2 (2014): 214–215.

Martinez-Falquina, Silvia. "Postcolonial Trauma Theory in the Contact Zone: The Strategic Representation of Grief in Edwidge Danticat's *Claire of the Sea Light,*" *Humanities* 4:4 (2015): 834–860.

Montgomery, Maxine L. "A Lasiren Song for the Wonn: Edwidge Danticat's *Claire of the Sea Light* and the Legend of Mami Wata," *CLA Journal* 59:4 (June 2016): 316–329.

Nurse, Donna Bailey. "Edwidge Danticat Rescues Haiti from Its Western Labels," [Toronto] *Globe and Mail* (30 August 2013).

"Review: *Claire of the Sea Light,*" *Publisher's Weekly* (27 May 2014).

Robinette, Anne. "Bilingual and Bimodal Expression: The Creolization in Edwidge Danticat's Oeuvre," (thesis) Dickinson College, spring, 2017.

Sontag, Deborah. "Island Magic," *New York Times* (30 August 2013).

Tillotson, Kristin. "Daughter of Haiti," *Minneapolis Star Tribune* (8 September 2013): E1.

Zipp, Georg. "Selling Poverty: Junot Díaz's and Edwidge Danticat's Assessments of Picturesque Stereotypes of Poverty in the Caribbean," *Zeitschrift für Anglistik und Amerikanistik* 63:2 (2015): 229–246.

Zipp, Yvonne, "Review: *Claire of the Sea Light,*" *Christian Science Monitor* (26 August 2013): 20.

Claire of the Sea Light Genealogy (novel)

A carefully plotted Haitian village interrelated by marriage, social class, and sexual dalliances, Ville Rose produces

		grandparents	grandfather=businesswoman		grandfather=teacher		
aunt	|	|	engineer	|	|		
foster mother	|	father	mason	magistrate	potter, builder		
	|	|		|	|		mother
	|	Laurent "Lolo" Lavaud=Gaëlle Cadet Lavaud=/=Max Ardin, Sr.=/=Louise George				|	
Nozias Faustin=Claire		murdered	fabric vendor		|	|	
fisherman	|Narcis			|	Bernard=/=Maxime Ardin, Jr.=/=Flore		
	|mortuary worker		Rose	"Bo" Dorien	immigrant	| beautician	
	|		milk sister	shot	to Miami	|	
Claire Limyè Lanmè Faustin			killed in traffic			|	
					Pamaxime Voltaire		

children burdened by poverty, illiteracy, crime, prejudice, regret, and unforeseen termination.

SOURCES

Danticat, Edwidge. "Claire of the Sea Light," *Haiti Noir*. Brooklyn: Akashic, 2010, 115–138.
———. *Claire of the Sea Light*. New York: Vintage, 2013.

"Claire of the Sea Light" Genealogy (short story)

In the short story version issued three years before the novel, Claire Limyè Lanmè Faustin is the focus of a study on motherlessness. For solace, she retreats into imagination, the same haven that reassures Junior in *Eight Days* and a lover of nature in Edwidge's fairy tale *Célimène*. At her mother's gravesite in Ville Rose, Claire muses over superstitions about revenant children whose mothers died in childbirth.

The source of her quandary, a deceased parent becomes an impalpable presence lacking form and voice. In her place, Claire Faustin relies on a foster parent, her maternal aunt, one of the unnamed women in Haitian lore who serve as pillars of strength.

SOURCES

Danticat, Edwidge. "Claire of the Sea Light," *Haiti Noir*. Brooklyn: Akashic, 2010, 115–138.
———. *Claire of the Sea Light*. New York: Vintage, 2013.

Colonialism

The four-century colonial heritage of francophone islands mingles strands of Spanish, Dutch, Indian, and French language, philosophy, architecture, art, and governance, such as execution by hanging, which the title figure in *Anacaona* envisions for the first time at Marién to the northwest. *Claire of the Sea Light* incorporates the remains of Abitasyon Pauline, the castle on Mòn Initil (Useless Mountain) that Napoleon Bonaparte abandoned to nature at Carrefour in 1802. In "Seven Stories," set on an unidentified island, Edwidge pictures a national penitentiary as a tourist attraction. Beside it, a high-walled fort retains the looks of "a dungeon and torture chamber during colonial days" (Danticat, 2019, 186).

After despoliation of the Taino, a Native American tribe, tropical palms, food plants, and orange and red flowers like those artist Alix Delinois imagined for *Eight Days* disappeared from

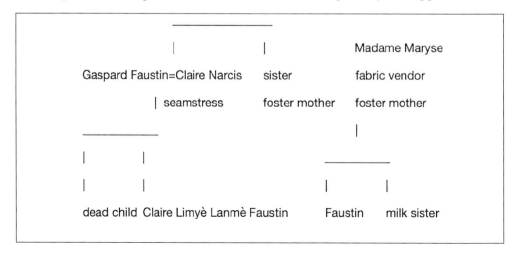

beaches and mountain slopes. Plantations yielded tobacco, coffee, and sugar to enrich French investors. The poor relied on black foodstuffs—pigeon peas, plantain, rice, cassava/manioc, yam—complemented by corn porridge, goat stew, cod patties, fried pork, and salted herring, menus featured in "A Wall of Fire Rising," "The Funeral Singer," *Célimène,* and "Caroline's Wedding." Formal landscaping incorporated European plants, notably, the spring daffodil, Sophie Caco's favorite Easter flower in *Breath, Eyes, Memory,* which she intends for Tante Atie, her foster mother.

Edwidge accounts for Haiti's uniqueness, which heaped wealth and privilege on enslavers, producers of 40 percent of global sugar reserves. Literature specialist Renee Shea of Maryland explained how islanders based core customs on West African deities, songs, dances, and rites: "After people were transported from Africa to different parts of the islands, they had to build their own habitats. A lot of the places where they stayed were very small and built in a way to be dark because these were really places just to sleep in" (Shea, 1996, 384). Adaptation caused black islanders to syncretize Vodou elements with Catholicism, a patriarchal faith dominated by the Holy Family, a male pope, and priests. The mythic rape of African slave Sor Rose (Sister Rose) by a French lord provided the basis of Haiti's Negroid population that exploiters left illiterate, alienated, and poor, the result of French racism, European education systems, and the demeaning of women like Tante Atie, whom illiteracy shames.

Thwarting Imperialism

Resistance flourished among Haitians. In the conclusion to the hurricane era essay "Dawn after the Caribbean Tempests," Edwidge cited Audre Lorde's assertion "We were not born to be your vassals," a defiance of Hispanic conquest, centuries of ownership, and exploitation by European outsiders (Danticat, 2017, TR5). The story "Seeing Things Simply" pictures Princesse and Catherine, a neophyte artist from the francophone island of Guadaloupe, tentatively shedding surface details to locate the innate female beauty just beginning to blossom in her body. By ignoring the faults of a colonial society—alcohol, random sex, gambling, idleness, perversity—she retrieves the intrinsic value that the French left behind in Haiti.

In an opposing view of colonial overlords, writers protest the remnants of bondage, deforestation, and land theft, the outgrowth of European annihilation of Indian and African heritage. In an essay on the island's history of pain, Aitor Ibarrola-Armendáriz, an expert in language from the University of Deusto, Spain, noted that world response yielded "centuries of invasion, blackmail, the robbery of Haiti's natural resources and the impoverishment of its people" (Ibarrola-Armendáriz, 2010, 25). Folk stories from Cap-Haïtien claimed that French cane magnates shared burial space with murdered slaves and casks of treasure. The paradoxical ghost tales accorded agency to black spirits, the guardians of ill-gotten fortunes.

Historic Landmarks

In an interview with author Junot Díaz, Edwidge asserted, "There are so many examples of [colonialism] all around us still. In our part of the world, we have not totally recovered" (Danticat, 2007, 90). She blamed living adjacent to the United States as the source of a "new brand" of imperialism (*ibid.*). From researching the island's French colonialism and the twelve-year war of independence begun in 1791, she incorporated in *After the Dance: A Walk Through Carnival in Jacmel, Haiti* facts from eighteenth-century history. She set the tour on the Rue de l'Eglise at the Hotel de la Place, a 30-acre estate of French colonial design gone to ruin near the shantytown of Carrefour 20 miles west of Port-au-Prince. Along the street, a Lenten procession bore images of good and evil that placed colonial power-wielders alongside demons and devils.

For the title figure in the novel *Claire of the Sea Light,* a birthday visit to Ville Rose's cemetery raises the specter of a Haitian caste system. Marking the grave of her mother Claire Narcis, dead with her fetus in childbirth, a simple carved cement cross contrasts the terra cotta shade of the earth. A poignant contrast between the red earth obscuring the mother's cross reflects the wealth of the privileged, who left a metal wreath with a gold sash and a handful of white roses for the Lavaud child, whose name seven-year-old Claire can't decipher. Commemorating prominent colonials—the Ardins, Boncys, Cadets, Lavauds, Marignans, Moulins, Vincents—marble mausoleums immortalize those who died before the Haitian Revolution drove out the world's most powerful colonial army.

See also Slavery, Vodou.

SOURCES

Danticat, Edwidge. "Claire of the Sea Light," *Haiti Noir.* Brooklyn: Akashic, 2010, 115–138.
_____. *Claire of the Sea Light.* New York: Vintage, 2013.
_____. "Dawn after the Caribbean Tempests," *New York Times* (6 November 2017): TR5.
_____. *Everything Inside.* New York: Knopf, 2019.
_____. "Junot Díaz," *BOMB* 101 (Fall 2007): 89–95.
Dayan, Joan. "Erzulie: A Women's History of Haiti," *Research in African Literatures Caribbean Literature* 25:2 (Summer, 1994): 5–31.
Ibarrola-Armendáriz, Aitor. "The Language of Wounds and Scars in Edwidge Danticat's 'The Dew Breaker.'" *Journal of English Studies* 8 (2010): 23–56.
Johnson, Newtona. "Challenging Internal Colonialism: Edwidge Danticat's Feminist Emancipatory Enterprise." *Obsidian III* (2005): 147–166.
Martinez-Falquina, Silvia. "Postcolonial Trauma Theory in the Contact Zone: The Strategic Representation of Grief in Edwidge Danticat's *Claire of the Sea Light,*" *Humanities* 4:4 (2015): 834–860.
Shea, Renee. "The Dangerous Job of Edwidge Danticat," *Callaloo* 19:2 (Spring, 1996): 382–389.

Colors

Edwidge favors visual beauty as an introit to theme, as with bright blues in the sky and mountains surrounding an orphaned brother and sister in *Célimène,* manman's bright red toenail polish in *Eight Days,* and the lime mountains in "A Taste of Coffee." For Tiye, the self-important gang leader in the third chapter of *Claire of the Sea Light,* the peacock shade of his shirt denotes underworld vanity. She accounted for sensitivity to tones in "Color Blocking," a 2013 interview for *Aquitectonica:* "There were really strong symbols attached to each color and you would offer something based on some emotion that you were trying to convey" (Danticat, 2013). To accentuate a rogue wave in *Claire of the Sea Light,* the author ends the opening paragraph with a phantasm. From the ocean bottom arises "a giant blue-green tongue" that aims to lick "a pink sky" (Danticat, 2013, 3). The hues imply a livid mouth menacing a delicate-toned overhead the color of tender flesh and of Claire's muslin birthday dress, an annual gift marking motherlessness and reverence.

Throughout her canon, the author specifies Negroid skin tones from penny-colored in "Sunrise, Sunset," bronze in the face of the title character in "Freda," and chestnut for Olivia, the alleged kidnap victim in "Dosas," to cinnamon, tawny, mahogany, russet, sepia, cocoa, sienna, and coffee. The gamut extends to onyx for Callie Morrissete and ocher for her husband, Prime Minister Greg Murray, in "Seven Stories" and ebony for fisherman Nozias Faustin and an endearing honey for Rose Lavaud, the fabric vendor's daughter in the opening chapter of *Claire of the Sea Light.* Complexion tones incorporate nut-brown on Claude in "Night Talkers" and sable for Darline in "Without Inspection." In "Tatiana, Mon Amour," the author finds humor in a black sorority differentiated into "nearly white, Afro-Asian, chestnut, ebony, tan, copper, butterscotch, mahogany, cafe-au lait, high yellow, mid-yellow, dark bronze-yellow, brown sugar, amber cream" (Danticat, 2004, 746). The shades indicate a diverse sisterhood that accepts all members, regardless of complexion.

Connotative Shades

Death requires a subjective palette in the essay "Mourning in Place," in which the Miami sky becomes "a colossal color-field painting, with layers upon layers of hues and shades, pigments and shapes, dipping into the horizon" (Danticat, 2020, 38). In the aftermath of Cousin Marius Dantica's demise from AIDS in Miami in *Create Dangerously*, the author sits by the sea in Haiti amid a shifting chiaroscuro of sun and shadow. Expecting Tante Zi to bewail the loss, Edwidge retreats into "the calm turquoise sea and bare brown mountains in the distance," a dyad of tone suggesting a pleasing life before interment in island soil as clouds cast gray over the day (Danticat, 2010, 93). In a finale of the January 12, 2010, earthquake, in the view of critic Valérie Loichot, a professor of Romance languages at Emory University in Atlanta, the author continued to isolate riveting, ironic colors, finding relevance in the painting of a chocolate angel on a refugee tent etched

against an indigo sky and "a pile of muddied corpses" (Loichot, 2020).

In the grim short fiction "Dream of the Butterflies" for the 1991 issue of *The Caribbean Writer,* the author used color to contrast nightly machine gun fire in an urban ghetto. To escape mayhem, Marie Micheline, the martyred single parent of two, revisits "a time when she had been living on a farm in the hills of Leogâne," a country getaway brightened with dewy mornings, cricket chirps, and a vast variety of butterflies (Danticat, 1991, 98). As though juxtaposing them against black and white print, the story numbers crimson, yellow, green, and orange wings, "a rainbow of colors" (*ibid.*). Through daydreams relieving menace, Marie teaches her son and daughter to escape in color imagery.

The Tones of Memory

Analyst Marsha Bianca Jean-Charles, a classroom assistant at Cornell and Columbia universities, summarizes Edwidge's methods: "naming the characters a surname of historical importance, narrating in the first person, weaving in folktales that offer insight into the protagonist's state of mind, and using colors as symbols" (Jean-Charles, 2011, 42). Edwidge specifies in *Anacaona* the Taino covering of a fifteenth-century future *cacica* (ruler) with crimson anatto paste crushed from seeds of the achiote tree. During treatment of patients, *bohiti* (healers) blacken their faces with wood ash. A suitor's prismatic headdress duplicates rainbow-hued hybridized birds, a token of Caonabó's marriage proposal to Anacaona. The birds return in a mystic circling of the kingdom of Maguana, a positive omen of celestial blessing. In the YA novel *Untwine,* recollections of a trip to Mexico renew Giselle Boyer's admiration for Guanajuato Cathedral, a classic Hispanic basilica shaped in massive stones to give the impression of a medieval fortress. In a mental fog after a car crash leaves her semi-comatose, the patient relives an illusion of benediction and healing—the gold glow resulting from natural light through stained glass.

A funereal consecration in *The Farming of Bones* reprises whirling tints "like a sky full of twisted rainbows," an upbeat farewell painted on the coffin of Rafael "Rafi" Duarte, a day-old twin of Rosalinda Teresa (Danticat, 1998, 90). Through hand painting, the sorrowing mother, Valencia Duarte, relieves heartache and expresses joy in the child's birth and blessing on his serene passing. For Man Denise, a contrasting grieving parent in Cap Haïtien, yellow coffee beans couple mother to children, Sebastien and Mimi Onius, for whom she threaded the yellow beans onto bracelets. After their slaughter face down in a courtyard, the tokens identify their remains. The choice of primary tones recaptures the individuality and promise of children who die before their time.

Reflecting the Tropics

Ethnic change in Haiti calls for African colors in an immigrant's gift dress in "New York Day Women," uplifting blue and gold slopes misted in grey fog in *Behind the Mountains,* and a proposal letter wrapped in pink and green and a pair of red panties to ward off spirits of dead men, the shades of romance and passion in "Caroline's Wedding." In *Breath, Eyes, Memory,* the color yellow engulfs Sophie Caco's dreams of her émigré mother Martine, a surreal figure wrapped in yellow bed linen and adorned with daffodils, a dazzling spring flower the author revisits in naming Claire Narcis Faustin in *Claire of the Sea Light.* The primary shade recurs in "The Missing Peace" to designate a guest house. In remembrance

of her deceased mother, the occupant, Emily Gallant, arranges on the floor symbolic purple squares, the Christian tone of repentance.

Edwidge recalls family events in terms of intense island colors. On her departure from Haiti in *Brother, I'm Dying,* she wears a lemony yellow dress like Sophie Caco's, a touch of sunshine to brighten the flight to New York City. When her Uncle Joseph Nosius Dantica arrives at the New York airport in fall 1983, she wears orange, another citrus shade tinged with sunlight. The hues serve a double purpose—revelry in the best of tropical life and fruit and welcoming family with choices that tinge reunion with happiness and contentment. In a foreword to *The African Lookbook,* Edwidge hails the looks of black people in a "range of beauty and elegance the world was otherwise telling us we could not possess" (Danticat, 2021, ii). *Booklist* praised the visual history for revealing African power and grace, evidence of resilience and resistance to racism.

Sources

Danticat, Edwidge. *The African Lookbook.* foreword. New York: Bloomsbury, 2021.

_____. *Claire of the Sea Light.* New York: Vintage, 2013.

_____. "Color Blocking," *Arquitectonica,* https://www.interiorsandsources.com/article-details/articleid/15929/title/color-blocking-edwidge-danticat (1 July 2013).

_____. *Create Dangerously: The Immigrant Artist at Work.* New York: Vintage, 2010.

_____. "Dream of the Butterflies," *Caribbean Writer* 5 (1991): 98–99.

_____. *The Farming of Bones.* New York: Penguin, 1998.

_____. "Freda," *Brown Sugar 4.* New York: Washington Square Press, 2005, 31–41.

_____. "Mourning in Place," *New York Review of Books* 67:14 (24 September 2020): 38.

_____. "Tatiana, Mon Amour," *Callaloo* 27:2 (2004): 439–453.

Jean-Charles, Marsha Bianca. "Of Griottes & Pantomimes: Dyaspora Love, Dreams, Memories, and Realities in the Works of Edwidge Danticat as they relate to Black Feminisms," thesis, Wesleyan University, 2011.

Loichot, Valérie. *Water Graves: The Art of the Unritual in the Greater Caribbean.* Charlottesville: University of Virginia Press, 2020.

Shea, Renee. "The Dangerous Job of Edwidge Danticat," *Callaloo* 19:2 (Spring, 1996): 382–389.

Coming of Age

Edwidge varies forms of maturation to each neophyte character, such as Mo's interviewing candidates for a husband for his sister in *Célimène,* Edwidge reintroducing herself to Great Aunt Ilyana in "A Taste of Coffee," and, in one of her wittier narratives, "Reading Lessons," Danielle rubbing crushed butterflies on her breasts to make them grow. The title figure in the historical biography *Anacaona* details a high-born Taino girl preparing for a coming-out ritual and receiving indigenous gifts of nature—sea stone, shark teeth, shells, and feathers. In Native American custom, she plaits her hair, reddens her skin with anatto paste, and costumes herself with a ritual outfit and mask. Her uncle completes the ritual cutting of her braid with an ax. The procedure impacts Haitian carnival, a Lenten festival enriched into the twenty-first century by historic parade figures like Anacaona as she emerges into woman of the house and motherhood. For strength, she leans on the guardian spirit of her grandmother, a mystic ruler who communicates intuitively to the third generation.

Edwidge views the sufferings of a multigenerational matriarchy in *Breath, Eyes, Memory,* a survey of females surviving sexual violence and motherly testing of virginity. Critic Jana Evans Braziel, the chair of intercultural studies at Miami University, summarized the novel's themes as "adolescent alienation, migration, traumatic uprooting from a childhood in the Caribbean ..., and the challenges of establishing new relations in the U.S." (Braziel, 2003, 110). For protagonist Sophie Caco, her mother Martine's regret at bearing the child of a Tonton Macoute rapist motivates self-loathing and mutilation in Sophie, who must weather her mother's suicide with wisdom and forgiveness. Rejoicing at release from anguish, according to Florence Ramond Jurney, a Romance language professor at Gettysburg College, Sophie is able to shout *"Ou libéré!"* in her escape from boundaries (Danticat, 1994, 233). For the author's first YA novel, *Behind the Mountains,* unfolding adulthood impinges on the adaptation of immigrants Cécé and Moy Espérance to New York City. New challenges from language and urbanism yields truculence and rebellion, standard evidence of confusion within teen boundaries. To learn from past generations, the siblings listen to memories of Granpé Nozial, a wise preserver of oral tradition.

Readying for the Future

Edwidge characterizes groundwork toward a female cultural pillar through Grann's storytelling in *The Last Mapou.* The unnamed granddaughter accepts a creation narrative for its approval of a single tree that survives island deforestation. By alerting her to extinction in nature, Grann readies her for a period of Haitian history that requires stout-hearted activism and a long-range view of the ecosystem. Similarly influenced by an older generation, the author takes the middle ground with Maxime, Sr., who deplores his son Max, Jr.'s, rape of the maid Fiore Voltaire, yet reverts to male preferences to exonerate his immigrant son. A more stirring view of mentoring, *Brother, I'm Dying* exemplifies Uncle Joseph Nosius Dantica, the Baptist minister who requires his niece to adhere to evangelical Christian standards of modesty. Ironically, he overlooks Joel, an in-house predator who fondles Edwidge and other girls in evening groping and intimidation. In *The Art of Death,* she divulges the crimes to Tante Rezia. As a result of a strict upbringing, Edwidge reaches her mid-thirties before she ventures to carnival, the rowdy, racy Lenten festival held in Jacmel in the travelogue *After the Dance.*

Maturation influences stories of failure and death, including the damaged career of sculptor Ka Bienaimé, daughter of a Haitian prison torturer in *The Dew Breaker,* and the separation of Gabrielle Boyer from twin Isabelle in *Untwine* following Isabelle's death in a car accident. The author's cousin, Marius Dantica, pays the price of dissolute living in *Create Dangerously* by dying of AIDS before he attains the self-control of manhood. For Bernard "Be" Dorien, the fictional nineteen-year-old news reporter for Radio Zòrèy (Radio Ear) in the short story "Ghosts," a lack of experience with criminals puts him in jeopardy on both sides of the issue—gangs and the police. A fearful growth story in *The Farming of Bones* involves the adoption of Amabelle Désir by a family of Hispanic Dominicans. For Valencia Duarte, the addition of Amabelle Desír to the household allays the grief of losing a baby brother in childbirth along with their mother, Rosalinda Teresa. Amabelle displays adulthood in aiding Valencia give birth to twins and to bury the stillborn boy, Rafael "Rafi" Duarte, whom sister Rosalinda survives. The siege of emotions revives in Amabelle the drowning deaths of her parents, herbalists Irelle Pradelle and Antoine Desír, a memory that haunts and dismays, yet prepares her for a tranquil death on return to Massacre River.

Diaspora and Teens

In an interview for *Journal of Caribbean Literature,* the author described immigration as a form of *Bildungsroman* in folklore and myth. Her narrations of the Haitian diaspora favor perspectives of the young and vulnerable, particularly two refugees—Claude, a youthful offender imprisoned for drug dealing and patricide in "Night Talkers," and Célianne, a fifteen-year-old impregnated by a militiaman in "From the Ocean Floor." The outcome contrasts gendered situations: Claude rids himself of guilt by narrating his offenses to Dany Dorméus. Célianne, burdened with a stillborn fetus, opts to jettison the child and drown herself in the sea. Critic Jo Collins at the University of Kent summarizes the teens' challenges as "language, loss, neo-colonialism, and diasporic identity" (Collins, 2012, 27). In both cases, they fail to balance the demands of growing into adulthood with the temptations, confusions, and threats of living under tyranny.

In "Monkey Tails," the hero worship of twelve-year-old Michel for eighteen-year-old Romain bares the anxieties and insecurities of fatherless sons during the vengeful chaos following "Papa Doc" Duvalier's 1986 flight from Haiti. In a token of friendship and togetherness, Michel later names his newborn son Romain. With the story "Children of the Sea," originally published in October 1993 in *Short Fiction by Women* as "From the Ocean Floor," the author differentiates island upbringing by gender. The member of the Radio Six who writes to the girl he leaves behind claims that boys are less domestic and more likely to protest and join underground groups who draw attention to the Duvaliers' crimes. Girls like the unnamed writer of daily letters grow up protected by anxious fathers and prepared by their mothers for a life of modesty and caution.

See also Adaptation, *Anacaona,* Doubles, Vulnerability.

SOURCES

Alexandre, Sandy, and Ravi Y. Howard. "Interview," *Journal of Caribbean Literature* 4:3 (Spring 2007): 161–174.

Braziel, Jana Evans. "Daffodils, Rhizomes, Migrations: Narrative Coming of Age in the Diasporic Writings of Edwidge Danticat and Jamaica Kincaid," *Meridians* 3:2 (2003): 110–131.

Collins, Jo. "Novels of Transformation and Transplantation: The Postcolonial Bildungsroman and Haitian American Youth in Danticat's *Behind the Mountains* and *Breath, Eyes, Memory*," *Wasafiri* 27:4 (1 December 2012): 27–34.

Danticat, Edwidge. *Anacaona: Golden Flower, Haiti, 1490*. New York: Scholastic, 2005.

_____. *Breath, Eyes, Memory*. New York: Soho Press, 1994.

_____. *The Dew Breaker*. New York: Abacus, 2004.

_____. *The Farming of Bones*. New York: Penguin, 1998.

_____. "From the Ocean Floor," *Short Fiction by Women* (October 1993).

_____. *The Last Mapou*. Brooklyn: One Moore Book, 2013.

_____. "Reading Lessons," *New Yorker* 80:42 (10 January 2005): 66–73.

_____. *A Walk Through Carnival*. New York: Vintage, 2016.

Jurney, Florence Ramond. "Exile and Relation to the Mother/Land in Edwidge Danticat's Breath Eyes Memory and The Farming of Bones," http://cai.sg.inter.edu/revista-ciscla/volume31/jurney.pdf.

Couples

To enhance study of human relationships and their effect on society, children, and the family, Edwidge creates uneven pairings as hopeless as ear nose and throat nurse Nadine Osnac with the telephone voice of Eric in "Water Child" and the failing marriage of David and Sylvie Boyer in the YA novel *Untwine*. For contrast, she backs the novel with long-married grandparents Régine and Marcus Boyer, an alternate source of support and wisdom for David and Sylvie. In *Create Dangerously,* she elevates a marriage exemplum, the devotion of activist Jean Léopold Dominique and Michèle Montas, the journalist wife who nurtured the legend of his sacrifice for truth. Alongside couples like Edwidge and Fedo Boyer in *After the Dance* and Denise and Joseph Nosius Dantica in *Brother, I'm Dying*, the insecurity, rocky rapport, and unrest in failing liaisons reflect greater threats to contentment from divided families and social fraying:

Title	Couple	Relationship
After the Dance	Edwidge/Fedo Boyer	a couple comfortable with each other during a visit to Jacmel
	Hadriana Siloed/Hector Danoze	mythic lovers approaching the marriage altar
Anacaona	Anacaona/Coanabó	royal newlyweds serving their tribes in wedlock
	Behechio/Yaruba	homesick wife who chooses suicide to marriage
	Baba/Bibi	contented older Taino couple
	Guamayto/Matunherí	grieving widow who kills herself with poison
The Art of Death	Denise/Joseph Dantica	pious couple who rear Edwidge and Bob
Behind the Mountains	Aline/Victor Espérance	parents separated by Victor's immigration to New York and reunited in restaurant work
	lover/Moy Espérance	clandestine lovers
	Melina/Nozial	grandparents who nurture children with storytelling
"Between the Pool and the Gardenias"	Marie/philanderer	a marriage lacking trust and loyalty
	Marie/pool cleaner	brief sexual encounter
"The Book of the Dead"	Anne Bienaimé/barber	a secretive couple who shoulder a guilty past
"The Book of Miracles"	Anne Bienaimé/barber	devoted wife who conceals her husband's murderous past from their daughter and neighbors
Breath, Eyes, Memory	Atie Caco/Donald Augustin	illicit couple who relieve Atie's solitude
	Charlemagne Le Grand Caco/Ifé	widow who retains memories of her husband
	Donald/Lotus Augustin	ordinary married couple

84 Couples

Title	Couple	Relationship
	Joseph Woods/Sophie	newlyweds impaired by Sophie's sexual dysfunction
	Marc Chevalier/Martine Caco	lovers who differ on the importance of a pregnancy
Brother, I'm Dying	André Danticat/Rose Souvenance Napóleon	immigrant factory worker with sickly mate
	Denise/Joseph Dantica	devout parents of needy children
	Edwidge/Fedo Boyer	eager and supportive parents-to-be
"Caroline's Wedding"	Carl Azil/Hermine	warm marriage ended by Carl's death from cancer
	Carl Azil/widow	phony marriage to ease Carl's immigration to New York
	Caroline/Eric Abrahams	exuberant bride-to-be and her Bahamian groom
Célimène	Célimène/Zaken	mysterious suitor and his idealistic bride
"Children of the Sea"	girlfriend/journalist	lovers parted by political corruption
Claire of the Sea Light	Bernard Dorian/Max Ardin, Jr.	a closeted homosexual who grieves Bernard's shooting death
	Claire Narcis/Nozias Faustin	an unwed couple who share their poverty
	Flore Voltaire/Max Ardin, Jr.	short-term lovers having no emotional bond
	Gaëlle Lavaud/Yves Moulin	pickups at a bar for a brief fling
	Laurent Lavaud/Gaëlle	loving couple torn apart by his murder
	Louise George/Max Ardin, Sr.	lovers lacking a strong trust
Create Dangerously	Jean Léopold Dominique/ Michèle Montas	devoted journalists who support each other's work and activism
"Dosas"	Blaise/Elsie	a wife blindsided by her husband's love for her best friend Olivia
	Blaise/Olivia	lovers who victimize his ex-wife Elsie
	Dédé/Elsie	unlikely rescuer who regrets not marrying her
Eight Days	barber/manman	frantic parents trying to rescue Junior from debris
The Farming of Bones	Amabelle Désír/Sebastien Onius	fearful lover searching for news of her mate
	Amabelle Désír/Yves Rapadou	survivors thrown together after a massacre into a sterile pairing
	Felice/Joël Raymond Loner	lovers kept apart by a disapproving father
	Pico/Valencia Duarte	unsteady relationship of new mother and army officer
"Ghosts"	Dorien	a hard-working couple who risk income and wealth by serving criminals at their restaurant
	teen boys/dates	youths prepare for deflowering girlfriends with a ritual involving pigeon blood
"The Gift"	Anika/Thomas	former lovers severed by losses from the 2010 earthquake
	Dina/Thomas	wife who learns before her death that Thomas is an adulterer
"In the Old Days"	Maurice Dejean/wives	relationships doomed by Maurice's idealism
Mama's Nightingale	Saya's mama/papa	devoted parents separated by Mama's jailing
"Monkey's Tail"	Regulus/wife	a self-destructive pair during the Duvalier regime
"Night Women"	clients/prostitute	a mother hiding immorality from her son in a small hut
"The Port-au-Prince Marriage Special"	Mélisande/men	a hotel maid who accepts intimacies with guests
"Quality Control"	Marlene Boyer/president	phony relationship to impress people

Title	Couple	Relationship
"Seven"	husband/wife	long separated immigrants attempting to reunite while concealing adulteries
"Seven Stories"	Callie Morrissete/Greg Murray	a political couple busy with entertaining
	Charles Morrissete/widow	couple separated by assassins
	"Finance"/"Olympic Runner"	nicknamed couple married on the beach
"Sunrise, Sunset"	Carole/Victor	a husband who tries to gloss over his wife's dementia
	James/Jeanne	young couple disturbed by postpartum depression
Untwine	David/Sylvie Boyer	couple contemplating divorce
	Marcus Boyer/Régine	stable older couple and consolers of granddaughter
"A Wall of Fire Rising"	Big Guy/Lili	a pair distracted by the husband's fantasies
"Water Child"	Eric/Nadine Osnac	lovers separated after Eric moves on
	Osnac parents	married couple united in their concern for an immigrant daughter
"Without Inspection"	Arnold/Darline	a pair of immigrants instantly willing to help each other
	Darline/husband	immigrants separated by husband's drowning

The variety of relationships illustrates the flexibility of love to suit myriad situations as ordinary as Carole and Victor's coping with aging in "Sunrise, Sunset" and as bizarre as Aunt Atie Caco's longing for Donald Augustin, a married neighbor in *Breath, Eyes, Memory,* and of sexual partnering of Gaëlle Lavaud with Yves Moulin, her daughter's killer, and immigrant Max, Jr.'s, closeted grief for Bernard "Be" Dorien, his undisclosed love in *Claire of the Sea Light*. For immigrants like Caroline Azil and Eric Abrahams, union presents a blending of identities. At the altar, according to Jamaican feminist Helen Pyne-Timothy, Caroline accepts a Bahamian husband and a new ethnicity of American, Caribbean, and West Indian. In the brief appearance of Jessamine in "Di Mwen, Tell Me," the suggests the author's choice of live and let live rather than catcalls and gossip.

See also Grandparents, Mothers.

Sources

Danticat, Edwidge. *A Walk Through Carnival.* New York: Vintage, 2016.

Feifer, Megan. "The Remembering of Bones," *Palimpsest* 9:1 (2020): 35–49.

Munro, Martin. "Writing Disaster: Trauma, Memory, and History in Edwidge Danticat's *The Farming of Bones*," *Ethnologies* 28:1 (2006): 81–98.

Pyne-Timothy, Helen. "Language, Theme and Tone in Edwidge Danticat's Work," *Journal of Haitian Studies* (1 October 2001): 128–137.

Strehle, Susan. "Global Fictions of Wreckage and Unsheltered Communities," *Contemporary Historical Fiction, Exceptionalism and Community.* London: Palgrave Macmillan, 2020, 189–199.

Create Dangerously: The Immigrant Artist at Work

In a twelve-part splicing of memoir with essay on bravery in the arts, Edwidge composed a polyphonic overview of witnessing, her term for first-person accounts of global events and conditions that refute injustice, inhumanity, and genocide. She pictured the most fearful "scribbling on prison walls" like Dickens characters in *A Tale of Two Cities,* and counting dates to execution (Danticat, 2010, 19). In the estimation of Hungarian-American studies expert Eva Federmayer, "Her work is inflected by the violence of the land, a dangerous place from which she also derives her inspiration" (Federmayer,

2015, 1). Emotions of fear, transplantation, and resistance remove borders and confer a universal citizenship on all artists and readers who dare to seek truth. Analyst Nadège T. Clitandre lauded the author for "exposing the lived experiences" of the Haitian diaspora and introducing readers to the transnationalization of immigrant identities (Clitandre, 2018).

Create Dangerously

In the opening chapter, the author dramatizes a major atrocity—the execution of Louis Drouin and Marcel Numa on November 12, 1964. She described the event as an historical touchstone and a "creation myth" that encouraged islanders to flee Haiti for new lives elsewhere. To Dwyer Murphy, an interviewer for *Guernica,* she explained her curiosity about the two Haitian-Americans who "ended up dead in the last openly state-sponsored public execution in Haiti" (Murphy, 2013). Murphy commended the author for keeping the execution before world readers to revere survival and "fight forgetfulness" (*ibid.*)

Edwidge compares the double assassination to the exile of Adam and Eve from Paradise for disobeying the creator. If the Almighty had chosen a firing squad, the author quips, there would not have been "another story told, no stories to pass on" or translated into Haitian Creole (Danticat, 2010, 6). She opts to devote her career to the type of writing that takes courage to read, to absorb, the purpose of exposing torturers in *The Dew Breaker* and immigrant camps in *Brother, I'm Dying.* A critical response to the chapter from journalism professor Amy Wilentz at the University of California Irvine raised questions of logic: "By the end of this section we are not sure what field we are in: Haitian history, personal memoir, anthropology, comp lit or religious studies" (Wilentz, 2010, BR-14). In a more affirming comment, Wilentz praises the author for maintaining the texture of Haitian realities, even though she left them behind at age twelve.

Essential to the author's theory of art lies an urge to elucidate past outrages for the uneducated and to lure readers into risking all for enlightenment, for the images that free the heart. She lists Haiti's ordeals—"deaths from hunger and executions and cataclysmic devastation at home, the deaths from paralyzing chagrin in exile, and the other small, daily deaths in between" (*ibid.,* 17). Of past saints and martyrs to the arts, she extols author Jacques Stephen Alexis and expat Dany Laferrière, an immigrant to Montreal. She honors Franketienne, a multitalented writer and abstract painter who targeted the Duvalier reign with the Vodou novel *Dézafi* (fires), the first fiction published in Haitian Creole. Of the artist's output, she treasured each as a substitute "for a life, a soul, a future" (*ibid.*, 20).

2. Walk Straight

The second chapter, a reprise of the story "A Taste of Coffee," issued in *Calabash* in summer 2001, contains the author's letter to a character, Sophie Caco Woods, from the novel *Breath, Eyes, Memory.* The text wishes individuality and uniqueness for Sophie and an easier parting from elderly relatives like Aunt Ilyana. The unforeseen death reminds Sophie to cherish family members and respect them while they live.

3. I Am Not a Journalist

With prose taken from 2003 anthology *The Butterfly's Way* and the article "Bonjour Jean" in a February 2001 issue of the *Nation,* Edwidge recounts the martyrdom of activist Jean Léopold Dominique in sight of his daughter Jan at a Radio Haiti-Inter station ambush. The author recalls meeting him at Ramapo College in New Jersey. A victim of political intrigue, Jean had incurred a military raid on his station. Nonetheless, he encouraged film goers to see Haitian-made movies such as *Anita, Masters of the Dew,* and *Night and Fog* to learn about socio-political corruption. Viewing for non-readers became the reason "why the visual arts have flourished in Haiti" (Danticat, 2010, 44).

The author details the creation of a legend about Jean Dominique, a city-based journalist from western Haiti who allegedly lived among poor farmers along the 320 km. (199 mile) riverside. At his martyrdom on April 3, 2000, residents of the Artibonite Valley imagined his frequent visits to their land to share their homes and join in planting and harvesting coffee. By the time his wife Michèle Montas had spread his ashes at the Artibonite River, the reporter had joined island romance. To sustain his activism, she reopened Radio Haiti on May 3, 2000, and joined demonstrations, rallies and pickets demanding the investigation of the killing within "a climate of impunity" (*ibid.,* 56). After two years, a would-be assassin instead shot Michèle's bodyguard on December 25, 2000.

4. Daughters of Memory

With thoughts from the foreword to *Memoir of an Amnesiac* and the introduction to *Love, Anger, Madness,* the author recalls the elitist curriculum of Haitian literature studies, taught by Miss Roy, the impetus for Edwidge's college major in French classics. She muses on the fault of Haitians for ignoring a full national chronicle, both honorable and dissolute. The result, she declared, was "a long history of setbacks and disillusionment, our constant roller-coaster ride between

saviors and dictators," perhaps her most apropos summation of Haitian malaise (*ibid.,* 64). Jean Dominique's daughter Jan admitted that viewing her father's assassination thwarted her writing career. Edwidge applauded Jan for bold authorship in the face of potential murder, a dilemma in the careers of the Radio Six and exiled novelist Marie Vieux-Chauvet.

5. I Speak Out

While producing a documentary about Haiti in Newark, New Jersey, Edwidge met Alèrte Bélance, a victim of abduction and maiming in the killing fields of Titanyen, site of mass graves for citizens martyred by the corrupt political system of General Raoul Cedras. She survived ear, arm, fingers, and tongue amputation and a machete chop to the cheek on October 16, 1993, by Emmanuel "Toto" Constant, a CIA informer and head of the Front pour l'Avancement et le Progrès Haitien (FRAPH, the Front for the Advancement and Progress of Haiti). Within three years, some 5,000 Haitians died.

When Alèrte's husband saw her in the hospital, she resembled "the chopped meat they sell at the market" (*ibid.,* 79). Because skillful doctors reattached her tongue, Alèrte was grateful to tell her ordeal on the *Phil Donahue Show* and to appear in the screen adaptation of Toni Morrison's *Beloved.* Her message rang clear and stark: "The devil has raped the confidence of the people" (*ibid.,* 85).

6. The Other Side of the Water

The death of Edwidge's cousin Marius Dantica from AIDS, which appeared in the Sunday *New York Times Book Review,* October 10, 2010, expressed islanders' ability to resist misfortune. With lines from the essay "Out of the

Shadows" in the June 2006 edition of *Progressive,* the understated study of family relations placed Edwidge in a writer's predicament—whether to admit to Tante Zi that the author plans to write about the demise of an illegal migrant far from home. The chapter stresses the frustration of collecting data about Marius's finances, his legal papers, and the preparation of his diseased remains for flying back to Haiti. With as little drama as possible, Zi favors a medical cause of death rather than drowning at sea.

7. Bicentennial

Of Haitian response to bondage at the onset of the Haitian Revolution in Bois Caiman on August 14, 1791, Edwidge demands, "Is there anything more timely and timeless than a public battle to control one's destiny" (*ibid.,* 104). The creation of the Haitian state by rebel slaves on January 1, 1804, compared unfavorably with the formation of the United States. Thomas Jefferson, a slave owner, declared Haitians "cannibals of the terrible republic" (*ibid.,* 98). According to the article "Thomas Jefferson: The Private War: Ignoring the Revolution Next Door" in the July 4, 2004, issue of *Time* and the introduction to *The Kingdom of This World,* Jefferson's contemporaries considered choosing Haiti as a penal colony or an offshore place to repatriate freedmen. He favored seizing Cuba as a foothold in the Caribbean.

8. Another Country

In an essay recycled from the April 2009 issue of the *Progressive,* the author contrasted response to tropical storm Jeanne, which struck Gonaïves, Haiti, on September 13, 2004, with the disorder and outlawry in New Orleans after Hurricane Katrina on August 22, 2005. She chided Americans for allowing squalor to flourish as a birthright. The uniting factor—destruction of the World Trade Center on 9/11/2001—caused her and other immigrants to embrace their new American citizenship. In one of the few derogatory critiques of her work, book analyst Steven Poole of the London *Guardian* rebuked the narrative for "[devolving] into a famous author's air-conditioned travelogue" (Poole, 2010, 8).

9. Flying Home

During many round trips to Haiti and book presentations in New York and Salt Lake City, Edwidge observed human dramas involving community effort in "On Borrowed Wings," an article for the October 2004 issue of *Telegraph India.* Her meditation on the death of Jamaican-American sculptor Michael Richards, who "chiseled himself as a dying man in agony, in pain," divulges eerie connections to his loss in the 9/11 World Trade Center collapse (*ibid.,* 125). For interpretation of Richards's existential sculpture "Tar Baby vs. Saint Sebastian," based on the Tuskegee Airmen, she looked to Ralph Waldo Emerson's promotion of verse for offering "better perception" of changes to come (*ibid.,* 124).

10. Welcoming Ghosts

The author reviews two Caribbean painters—Puerto Rican-Haitian neo-expressionist Jean-Michel Basquiat and Haitian surrealist Hector Hypolite, both phantoms of African culture and spirituality. A Vodou houngan (priest) and *sèvité* (devotee) of spiritual artistry, Hippolyte profited from merging African animism with European Catholicism. Basquiat credited cultural memory with endowing black islanders with visions of Africa and Vodou icons. He noted the spelling of Toussaint L'Ouverture (the way maker), the "Black Spartacus," as a tie to Legba, the Vodou gatekeeper and god of openings and intersections (*ibid.*, 133).

11. Acheiropoietos

Bearing a sixth-century CE term for miraculous holy icons, Edwidge's chapter ponders the provocative images of catastrophe and atrocity made by photojournalist Daniel Morel, a collector of images of brutalized Tonton Macoutes in 1986. She honored Morel for depicting people "already captured by the gods of painful circumstances" (*ibid.*, 146). Another viewer of skewed life portraits, Turks-Cuban photographer Jacqueline Charles, an Emmy- and Pulitzer-quality journalist for the *Miami Herald,* commemorated the flood-damaged corpse of an island child to halt "complete erasure" of a human life (*ibid.*, 147). Edwidge summarized the work as an example of "all impassioned creative endeavors" (*ibid.*, 148).

12. Our Guernica

Drawing on "A Little While," an article for *New Yorker* from February 1, 2010, the author meditates on islanders' love for Haiti, even after two centuries of political turmoil and a devastating 7.0 earthquake on January 12, 2010. Writing and speaking about disaster relieved some of the trauma and restored admiration for local people who dug friends out of the rubble without aid from world charities. To interviewer Kam Williams, a journalist for the Cleveland, Ohio, *Call & Post,* the author acknowledged she was pleased to find everybody in Haiti doing something to help others. With themes from "Aftershocks Bloodied, Shaken—and Beloved" for the January 17, 2010, issue of *Miami Herald,* Edwidge elevated the mission as "bearing witness" (*ibid.*, 161).

On arrival at Port-au-Prince on February 4, the author inventoried toppled buildings that included her childhood school, Christian murals at Saint Trinité, the Centre d'art, and the national cathedral. Interviewer Dwyer Murphy added another serious loss, art collector George Nader's gallery. She saw "piles of human remains freshly pulled from the rubble" and hugged family members to give them hope (*ibid.*, 165).

Months after the disaster, Edwidge published the essay "Flight" in the *New Yorker* on the sorrows of people trying to interpret the final moments of loved ones. Reviewer Marie-José Nzengou-Tayo, a lecturer at the University of the West Indies, credited her subtle prose for engaging readers in an *"empathie* bond" with past artists and their works (Nzengou-Tayo, 2012, 129). The author pondered suffering, final thoughts, and regrets about lives left behind. She later promoted the granting of protected states for Haitian survivors. For herself, she assigned a lifetime of discovery through memory: "The job of reconstructing lives belongs to the living, the memory keepers" (Danticat, 2011, 32).

Based on "A Year and a Day" from *New Yorker* January 17, 2011, Edwidge's essay added, "We all carry within ourselves our own private memorials of loss and an increasing fear of future ones" (*ibid.*). Josh Rosner, a book critic for the *Canberra Times,* admired the author's resolve to visit family graves and "console those whom fate saved" (Rosner, 2010, 29). For its comprehensive views on testimonial art, Wajdi Mouawad, a book critic for Paris *Le Monde,* considered the book "la victoire contra la violence" (a triumph over violence) (Mouawad, 2012, 8)

See also Earthquake, *Eight Days.*

SOURCES

Clitandre, Nadège T. *Edwidge Danticat: The Haitian Diasporic Imaginary.* Charlottesville: University of Virginia Press, 2018.

Danticat, Edwidge. *Create Dangerously: The Immigrant Artist at Work.* New York: Vintage, 2010.
_____. "Flight," *New Yorker* 87:27 (5 September 2011): 32.
Federmayer, Eva. "Violence and Embodied Subjectivities: Edwidge Danticat's Breath, Eyes, Memory," *Scholar Critic* 2:3 (December 2015): 1–17.
Mouawad, Wajdi. "Compter les morts en Haïti," *Le Monde* (29 June 2012): 8.
Murphy, Dwyer. "The Art of Not Belonging," *Guernica* (3 September 2013).
Nzengou-Tayo, Marie-José. "Review: Create Dangerously," *Caribbean Quarterly* 58:4 (December 2012): 127–133, 146.
Ortiz, Ricardo L. "Reiterating Performatives: The Writer, the Reader and the Risks of Literary Action," *Latinx Literature Now.* London: Palgrave Macmillan, 2019, 13–21.
Poole, Steven. "Review: *Create Dangerously,*" *Guardian* (6 November 2010): 8.
Rosner, Josh. "Smiling as Your Soul Aches," *Canberra Times* (13 November 2010): 29.
Wilentz, Amy. "The Other Wide of the Water," *New York Times Book Review* (10 October 2010): BR-14.
Williams, Kam. "CP2 Talks with Critically Acclaimed Author Edwidge Danticat," [Cleveland, OH] *Call & Post* (1 December 2010): CP2.

Creole

The author grew up in a Creole language milieu where fewer than 5 percent understood the standard French that undergirded commerce and government since 1804. Everyone—11 million—spoke hybrid French. No one wrote it, but many listened to investigative journalism in Creole on Radio Zorey (Radio Ears), the source of payback by Duvalier killers in "Children of the Sea" and *Claire of the Sea Light.* On a tour of a West Indian island in "Seven Stories," patois invigorated the haggling between buyers and food vendors. In an article for the Toronto *Globe and Mail,* journalist Ray Conlogue characterized the island lingo as "a mixture of the simplified French spoken by slaves together with bits of African languages" that emerged from colonial French of the 1700s and incorporated indigenous Taino and imported West African Kwa from half the slave population plus Spanish, Portuguese, and English (Conlogue, 2004, R3).

For Edwidge, the sounds became "another voice in your head," which she threads into English sentences to enrich dialogue (Danticat, 2004). At age eighteen, she wrote a mixed title for "A Haitian-American Christmas: Cremace and Creole Theatre." For Bee, the snoop in "The Secret Island," deciphering her parents' love letters requires consulting a Creole dictionary. The dialect had no grammar rules or standardized spelling, as with *alarive* (at the [river] bank), a term meaning "surprise" in *Eight Days; batey* (shanty town) in "The Dominican Republic's War on Haitian Workers"; *bohiti* (spiritual healers) in *Anacaona; pan de muerto* (break of death) in the poem "On the Day of the Dead"; and *Lambi,* the title of a Haitian political journal in *Create Dangerously* referring to the call of the conch shell.

Story Essentials

The novel *Claire of the Sea Light* expresses the impossibility of narrating Haitian life stories without including such unavoidable island terms as Claire Limyè Lanmè Faustin's bilingual jump rope rhyme and the circle game *wonn* (ronde), a palpable base that survives from ancient rites. The latter parallels "Ring around the Rosie," an English playground singing game from the late 1700s based on pagan circle dance. Reminded of the beginnings of a *revenen,* a child born after the mother's death, Claire treasures *vini* (come), the elder Claire's dying word to hurry the fetus along (Danticat, 2013, 219). The author valued Creole dialect for increasing the story's vigor, nuance, and immediacy.

By age eight, Edwidge became aware of anti-fascism plays translated into Haitian Creole and performed on neighborhood stages to protest the regime of Jean-Claude "Papa Doc" Duvalier. She came of age valuing "maxims and phrases [that] keep coming back, buried deep in memories by the rote recitation techniques that the Haitian school system had taught so well" (Danticat, 2010, 9). For "The Dating Game" broadcast in 2007 from the *New Yorker Out Loud*, she outlined the complexity of Haitian Creole for immigrants. She explained her own polyglot method: "A lot of us came into our creativity at the same time we came into this other language and [bilingual writing] is a product of it" (Danticat, 2007). Of the creation of Creole narratives, she declared in an interview with *Guernica's* Dwyer Murphy, "I'd rather have people writing in Creole who do it because they love it and are good at it and who think that it's the best tool for the story they are telling, rather than people who write badly in Creole, just to have things in Creole" (Murphy, 2013).

The author recalled age twelve in Brooklyn, where she began learning English, her "stepmother tongue" (Shea, 1995, 13). It became the first language she could both speak and write, a dual skill she shared with fictional Céliane Espérance in *Behind the Mountains*. Of the successful language choice, editor Martin Munro, an expert in francophone language at Florida State University, admired Edwidge for "[freeing] herself from the rigid language-identity equation that characterizes most literary traditions, and which has become an orthodoxy in much postcolonial theory" (Munro, 2007). Nonetheless, the author highlighted the innovation of Frankétienne, a multi-skilled fiction and stage writer and abstract painter who exposed corruption of the Duvalier reign with a Vodou novel, *Dézafi* (From the Fire), the first fiction published in Haitian Creole. Years after composing "A Wall of Fire Rising," she translated the story for radio into Creole. She explained that her method

awakened spirits: "I felt closer to how I felt the story as a child" by "using slivers of the second language" (Gleibermann, 2018, 30).

Grace Notes

Like musical grace notes, scattered models of Haitian Creole enlighten the reader to transposition of Parisian French into island dialect. Although critics accused her of exoticizing language, the inclusion taught the author "how not to censor myself" (Gleibermann, 2018). In *Behind the Mountains*, the French *Joyeaux Noel* (Merry Christmas) became *Jwaye Nowèl*, a makeshift spelling before the standardization of Creole orthography. In *Mama's Nightingale*, the protagonist, Saya, takes comfort during her mother's absence by listening to the answering machine repeat Mama's message: "Tanpri kite bon ti nouvèl pou nou" (Please leave good news for us), a suggestion of the Christian gospel (Danticat, 2015). Papa reduces a loving reassurance to one word—*anpil*, Creole for "very much" (*ibid.*).

As a writer, Edwidge frequently creates scenarios in which island language becomes prominent in personal relationships, as with the musical voice of a waitress in "Freda"; *rele* (call) and *melliza*, Spanish for twin in *Untwine; ayibobo*, both alleluia and amen in "Seeing Things Simply"; and *labouyi bannan*, spicy grated plantain porridge in the personal essay "Plantains, Please." In *Breath, Eyes, Memory*, Creole patterns include idioms such as "went to Guinea" (died), a reference to beliefs that deceased black Haitians return to West Africa as spirits (Dantica, 1994, 104). The author contrasted Sophie Caco's Haitian patois with that of Joseph Woods, a New Orleans native. On the cab ride home, the driver remarks on the Haitian-Americans who return thoroughly Americanized with no memory of Creole, the plight of Claude, the ex-con deported back to Haiti in "Night Talkers." To express his change of attitude, he must go through the English of immigrant Dany Dorméus, both originally Creole speakers.

SOURCES

Conlogue, Ray. "Haunted by Haiti's Ghosts," [Toronto] *Globe and Mail* (19 April 2004): R3.

Danticat, Edwidge. *Breath, Eyes, Memory.* New York: Soho Press, 1994.

_____. *Claire of the Sea Light.* New York: Vintage, 2013.

_____. *Create Dangerously: The Immigrant Artist at Work.* New York: Vintage, 2010.

_____. "The Dating Game," *New Yorker Out Loud* (11 June 2007).

_____. "Freda," *Brown Sugar 4.* New York: Washington Square Press, 2005, 31–41.

_____. *Mama's Nightingale.* New York: Dial, 2015.

_____. "Voices from Hispaniola," (contributor) *Meridians* 5:1 (2004): 68–91.

Fish, Amy. "'Leave Us Good News': Collective Narrations of Migration in *Mama's Nightingale*," *Research on Diversity in Youth Literature* 2:2 (January 2020): 1–17.

Gleibermann, Erik. "Inside the Bilingual Writer," *World Literature Today* 92:3 (May–June 2018): 30.

Lyons, Bonnie. "Interview," *Contemporary Literature* 44:2 (Summer 2003): 183–198.

Munro, Martin, ed. *Exile and Post-1946 Haitian Literature.* Liverpool, UK: Liverpool University Press, 2007.

Murphy, Dwyer. "The Art of Not Belonging," *Guernica* (3 September 2013).

Pierre, Jacques. "The Growth of Creole Language Studies," *Duke Today* (5 June 2014).

_____. "Jacques Pierre: Creole a Key to Haitian literacy," *Durham Herald-Sun* (5 September 2014).

_____. "Jacques Pierre: Help for Haiti Must Include Embracing Creole," [Raleigh] *News & Observer* (21 February 2014)

Robinette, Anne. "Bilingual and Bimodal Expression: The Creolization in Edwidge Danticat's Oeuvre," (thesis) Dickinson College, spring, 2017.

Shea, Renee. "The Dangerous Job of Edwidge Danticat," *Belles Lettres* 10:3 (Summer 1995): 12–15; *Callaloo* 19:2 (Spring, 1996): 382–389.

Death

Edwidge speaks repeatedly of death in Haiti, dramatizing the demise of Grann after an obvious illness in *The Last Mapou,* the orphaning of Mo and his sister, the title character in *Célimène,* and the street gang leaders Piye and Tiye who murder at will in the story "Ghosts." She pictures a variety of lethal situations—a highway wreck in Miami that kills Isabelle Boyer in *Untwine,* the slow demise of Marc in "In the Old Days," and the unforeseen disaster—the January 12, 2010, earthquake in the poem "On the Day of the Dead," a catastrophe that renders thousands homeless in *Tent Life* and also kills Oscar, a fictional child trapped in the rubble in *Eight Days.*

Cause	Victims	Work
abortion	Nadia's fetus	"Water Child"
AIDS	Marius Dantica	*Create Dangerously*
arson	Dany Dorméus's parents	"Night Talkers"
	Piye	"Home"
	Tiye	"Home"
automobile wreck	Isabelle Boyer	*Untwine*
	Joël Raymond Loner	*The Farming of Bones*
breast cancer	Audre Lorde	*The Art of Death*
childbirth	Clarie Narcis Faustin	*Claire of the Sea Light*
	Marie Magdalène	"The Missing Peace"
	Rosalinda	*The Farming of Bones*
conquest	Arawak	*After the Dance*
	Taino	*Anacaona*
decapitation	Madam Roger's son	"Children of the Sea"
disappearance	Caleb	*Claire of the Sea Light*
	Caonabó	*Anacaona*

Death   93

Cause	Victims	Work
	fat man's mother	*The Dew Breaker*
	Freda's father	"The Funeral Singer"
	Manicaotex	*Anacaona*
	Romain's mother	"Monkey Tails"
drowning	Amabelle Desír	*The Farming of Bones*
	Anne's stepbrother	*The Dew Breaker*
	Antoine Desír	*The Farming of Bones*
	Brother Timonie	"The Funeral Singer"
	Irelle Pradelle	*The Farming of Bones*
	Odette	*The Farming of Bones*
	Darline's husband	"Without Inspection"
	rebel radio announcer	"Children of the Sea"
earthquake	Dina	"The Gift"
	Joseph Serge Miot	"Anniversary Blues"
	Maxo Danticat	*The Art of Death*
	Maxo Danticat	"Flight"
	Nick Danticat	"Flight"
	Nick Danticat	*Create Dangerously*
	Oscar	*Eight Days*
	Qadine	"The Gift"
execution	indigent	"The Missing Peace"
	Louis Drouin	*Create Dangerously*
	Marcel Numa	*Create Dangerously*
	Mariselle's husband	"The Funeral Singer"
	Mimi Onius	*The Farming of Bones*
	Sebastian Onius	*The Farming of Bones*
grief	Michel's mother	"The Journals of Water Days 1986"
hanging	Anacaona	*Anacaona*
	Taino	*Anacaona*
heart attack	Michel's mother	"Monkey Tails"
hospice care	Marc	"In the Old Days"
infection	Jeanne	*Create Dangerously*
lung disease	André Mira Danticat	*The Art of Death*
	André Mira Danticat	*Brother, I'm Dying*
	André Mira Danticat	"Postscript"
	Matunherí	*Anacaona*
motorcycle wreck	Rose Lavaud	*Claire of the Sea Light*
murder	Aspril Aubin	*After the Dance*
	Celine Mellier	*After the Dance*
	Claude's Father	"Night Talkers"
	father	"Sawfish Soup"
	Fernand Mellier	*After the Dance*
	Isabelle	"The Missing Peace"
	Jacques Stephen Alexis	*After the Dance*
	Rose	"Between the Pool and the Gardenias"
	writers	"The Journals of Water Days 1986"
natural causes	François Duvalier	"Monkey's Tails"
old age	Aunt Ilyana	*After the Dance*
	Aunt Ilyana	"A Taste of Coffee,"
	Estina Estème	"Night Talkers"
	Grandma Sandrine	*Untwine*
	Taino Grandmother	*Anacaona*
ovarian cancer	Rose Danticat	*The Art of Death*
	Rose Danticat	"Feetfirst"

Death

Cause	Victims	Work
	Rose Danticat	"A New Sky"
	Rose Danticat	"The Possibility of Heaven"
	Rose Danticat	"Without Her"
pancreatitis	Joseph Nozius Dantica	*Brother, I'm Dying*
poison	Anne Sexton	*The Art of Death*
	Guamayto	*Anacaona*
	minister's wife	"The Dew Breaker"
prison	Toussaint Louverture	*The Farming of Bones*
prostate cancer	Carl Romélus Azile	"Caroline's Wedding"
shot	Bernard "Bè" Dorien	*Claire of the Sea Light*
	Jean Dominique	*The Art of Death*
	Jean-Jacques Dessalines	*The Farming of Bones*
	Laurent Lavaud	*Claire of the Sea Light*
	Marie Micheline	"Dream of the Butterflies"
	Mariselle's husband	"The Funeral Singer"
	Pascal Dorien	"Ghosts"
	preacher	"The Dew Breaker"
	Rafael Trujillo	*The Farming of Bones*
stillbirth	Célianne's infant	"Children of the Sea"
	Marie's three infants	"Between the Pool and the Gardenias"
	Rosalinda's son	*The Farming of Bones*
	Victoria Pico	"The Revenant"
stroke	Tante Rezia	*The Art of Death*
sudden death	Hadriana Siloed	*After the Dance*
	young girl	*After the Dance*
suicide	Célianne	"Children of the Sea"
	Freda's father	"The Funeral Singer"
	Guy	"A Rising Wall of Fire"
	Henri Christophe	*The Farming of Bones*
	Lili	"Between the Pool and the Gardenias"
	Martine Caco	*Breath, Eyes, Memory*
	Regulus	"Monkey Tails"
	Yaruba	*Anacaona*
sunstroke	Charlemagne Le Grand Caco	*Breath, Eyes, Memory*
torture	Vincent Ogé	*After the Dance*
truck wreck	passengers	*After the Dance*
unknown	Edner Toutebon	*After the Dance*
	Madam Roger	"Children of the Sea"
	Ray	"One Thing"
windstorm	Nahe	*Anacaona*
	Piragua	*Anacaona*
	Yaybona	*Anacaona*
work accident	Arnold	"Without Inspection"

In the bitter verse "A Despot Walks into a Killing Field," she dramatizes the destiny of citizens murdered under tyranny and "dumped/by earth movers/into mass graves" (Danticat, 2015, 37). With no more respect, victims of the earthquake receive the same send-off.

For Darline in "Without Inspection," the devastating drowning of her husband off the Miami shore and her son Paris's rescue precipitated another kind of death—the transformation of the old Darline at sea and the beginning of a seashore rescuer mission to inbound immigrants. According to Daniel Simon, editor of *World Literature Today*, Edwidge uses words to "circumnavigate the arc in between" living and dying (Simon, 2018, 15). Of honor to the deceased, she compares seven-place mausoleum protocols for Dany Dorméus's elderly Aunt Estina Estème in "Night Talkers"; seven-year-olds Callie Boyer and Kim Morrissete spend an afternoon playing just-pretend corpse and priest in "Seven Stories," an imaginary state derived from the shooting death of Prime Minister Charles Morrissete. *Create Dangerously* equates Haitian funereal spells with rituals of ancient Egyptians, the source of a father's fascination with judgment in the afterlife. The decision becomes a key facet of "The Book of the Dead," where "documentation of worthiness and acceptance" allowed admittance into the next world (Danticat, 2010, 19).

Customs and Liturgy

In a gesture to Haitian mourning traditions at burials, the author stated the importance of conch shell, marbles, empty jars, and the singing of gospel hymns at observances "In the Old Days"; the cutting of souvenir snippets from Aunt Estina Estéme's shroud in "Night Talkers"; and the slaughter of roosters in daily bouts of cockfighting, a gruesome view of destiny in "Seeing Things Simply." At the Lavaud mausoleum in the novel *Claire of the Sea Light,* handfuls of white roses complement a lavish marble exterior and gold name sash with a guilt offering from the driver who struck a motorcycle and killed Rose. For Aunt Ilyana in "A Taste of Coffee," it is crucial that she share the turquoise mausoleum of her daughter Marie Jeanne so they "can be together again in death as they had always been in life" (Danticat, 2001, 41). The contiguity of sites provides the family a melancholy reunion.

Edwidge repeats the mortal cycle in other stories. Looking back to the fifteenth-century Taino in *Anacaona*, the author contrasts the destruction of a family—Nahe, Piragua, and Yaybona—in a hurricane with the decline of Uncle Matunherí from respiratory distress. At a reception for family, the widow Guamayto looks forward to a reunion in the hereafter, a tradition eased by an oral dose of poison with which she ends her mourning. In a tableau of the afterlife, the title figure reveres Mácocael, the guardian stone of the dead, and observes the rhythmic thump of drums guiding spirits of deceased warriors among the Night Marchers to the Caribbean Sea. Lest they force her into the cortege before her time, the protagonist hurries home.

The author depicts the teen-age protagonist Anacaona as brave and insightful for her age. The island queen extends anticipation of her own mortality with the request, "Make sure the road is clear for us when our time comes," a mature acceptance of earthly limitations (Danticat, 2005, 107). The ritual double funeral for aunt and uncle involves Egyptian-style gifts—quartz beads, a turtle shell, amulets and effigies, ceremonial thrones and axes, pipes, and water and cassava bread, refreshments for the journey. At Guamayto's collapse, the family learns of Anacaona's pregnancy, a positive event to balance a period of woe.

Muddled Causes

"The Dew Breaker" poses a felonious death unveiling an anonymous murderer's character and regrets. The unanticipated scarring of the fat man's cheek results from a quick switch of control from his post as Tonton Macoute to prisoner. With the designation of "fat man," Edwidge implies the profits of ruthlessness under the Duvaliers and a layer of insidious wrongs that retirement can't assuage. The officer responds with rapid shots of his .38, but can't erase the fact that he violated orders to release the preacher. Within seconds, the martyred prisoner causes the title character's downfall and brands him forever with a mark of Cain, the scriptural murderer commemorated in Genesis 4:11–16. With more urgency, *Brother, I'm Dying* lists cadavers scattered among derelict cars and trash in Bel Air, a slum turned into no-man's land by police and a United Nations task force combatting gangs. The maiming and abandonment of bodies, such as the Haitian laborers butchered at the Massacre River and forced off cliffs of La Romana in *The Farming of Bones,* political mass graves at Titanyen in *Create Dangerously,* and the murdered father in the poem "Sawfish Soup," cheapens Haitian culture, making death the conqueror.

The writer's story "A Year and a Day" lists casualties to disasters, political violence, infection, humiliation, and broken hearts. She acclaimed those who endured and tried "in any way they could, to reclaim a shadow of their past lives" (Danticat, 2011). She identified death as a standard theme of oral culture, especially maternal or infant mortality in childbirth, such as the demise of infant Rafael "Rafi" Duarte in the opening scenario of *The Farming of Bones* and the failed births in "Children of the Sea" and "Between the Pond and the Gardenias." On the island among security guards and the president's entourage in the original version of "Quality Control," Jess can only watch the jettisoning of body bags into the sea and shudder at their contents. Farther afield, refugees anticipate drowning in "Children of the Sea" and a sequel, "Caroline's Wedding"; female journalists die by gun and bomb in "Quality Control."

Sources of Narrative

Of the author's experience with death, she noted, "What I fear most is the loss of loved ones," the focus of "Dream of the Butterflies" in which a mother shelters her son and daughter from machine gun fire in their dirt-floored hut while concealing a fatal wound (Brown, 2007, M2). Of the author's personal reaction to mortality, she mused, "Maybe [*Brother, I'm Dying*] was a rage against it…. It is always a shock" (*ibid.*). She incorporates death of the most vulnerable in her stories: two unnamed brothers killed in an apartment fire in "Westbury Court," an infant girl jettisoned alongside a sewer drain in "Between the Pool and the Gardenias," and Anne's three-year-old brother drowning in the sea in "The Book of Miracles." For Valencia Duarte in *The Farming of Bones,* the loss of her mother Rosalinda and infant brother in childbirth leaves a serious gap in self-identity. Valencia grieves, "I will never be a whole woman, for the absence of Mami's face" (Danticat, 1998, 102). Her servant, Amabelle Desír, prophesies that the shadow of Rafi, the dead twin, will always follow his sister Rosalinda. When Amabelle mulls over rumors of the death of her lover, Sebastien Onius, she feels an internal ache "in places I could neither name nor touch," a common visceral lament (*ibid.,* 243).

Edwidge's canon enriches the subject of mortality with a broad range of causes, for example, the willing of a spirit to comfort wife and son in "Without Inspection" and the touching farewell "Wild Is the Wind," the last words to Marie-Jeanne of her lover Ray in "One Thing" (Danticat, 2020, 72). As a model of destructive ambition, in "A Wall of Fire Rising," the writer pictures Big Guy, the malcontented father, stealing a hot air balloon and jumping to his death as it soars above a town. For "Dosas," while Gaspard dickers over a kidney transplant from daughter Mona, kidnappers allegedly murder Olivia and dump the corpse at her mother's door. In 2019, the writer contemplated the Covid pandemic and disruption of mourning rituals—"the home visits, the festive wakes, the funerals, and post-burial repasts," the subject of her essay "Mourning in Place" for the *New York Review of Books* (Danticat, 2020). She validated reminiscences of life for dignifying the deceased and solacing kin and neighbors.

See also Music, Noirism, Religion, Superstition, Tradition, Vodou.

Sources

Brown, DeNeen L. "Interview," *Washington Post* (14 October 2007): M2.

Danticat, Edwidge. *Anacaona: Golden Flower, Haiti, 1490.* New York: Scholastic, 2005.

_____. "A Despot Walks into a Killing Field," *Progressive* 76:5 (May 2012): 37.

_____. *The Farming of Bones.* New York: Penguin, 1998.

_____. *The Last Mapou.* Brooklyn: One Moore Book, 2013.

_____. "Mourning in Place," *New York Review of Books* (24 September 2020).

_____. "One Thing," *New York Times Magazine* (7 July 2020): 62–72.

_____. "A Taste of Coffee," *Calabash* 1:2 (Spring-Summer 2001): 39–48.

_____. "A Wall of Fire Rising," https://www.bisd303.org/cms/lib3/WA01001636/Centricity/Domain/1342/-A%20Wall%20of%20Fire%20Rising-.pdf.

_____. "A Year and a Day," *New Yorker* (9 January 2011).

Simon, Daniel. "Review: *The Art of Death*," *World Literature Today* 92:2 (March/April 2018): 25.

Sontag, Deborah. "Island Magic," *New York Times* (30 August 2013).

Details

The author's skillful positioning of minutiae activates insights that move her writing beyond the surface to contemplative values, such as the kind of gifts from home that a wife would pack in her suitcase in "Seven," repeat of the word "caves" in "One Thing," and Elsie's loss of a job in "Dosas." Specific sense impressions create mental images: Darline's list-making in "Without Inspection," the sounds of sawing in *The Last Mapou* that supplants views of tree removal, and a single annoying fly in the imagist poem "Trimester." Specifics rule in *Create Dangerously*, in which students discern teacher Miss Roy's citric scent of vetiver and her filed nails, spike heels, and forced Parisian accent in citations of classic French literature. Closer to her own experience, the author revered a parent's entertainment for a sick child in *My Mommy Medicine* and taped stories reassuring Saya during her mother's jailing in *Mama's Nightingale*. For an immigrant family in *Behind the Mountains,* Moy Espérance contributes a personal moving-day gift—drawings of his family's migration to New York, a tribute to their unity and spirit of adventure.

Specificity marks other narratives with items that form visual impressions as memorable as a name printed on Olivia's feet in "Dosas," flowers that Valencia paints on Rafael "Rafi" Duarte's coffin in *The Farming of Bones,* the menacing huge mouth of a twelve-meter purple anaconda in *Célimène,* and the pebble that commemorates the abortion of Nadine Osnac's baby in "Water Child." Examples yoke the name of Ville Rose to ovule, petals, thorns, and stem in the novel *Claire of the Sea Light* and the SOS sound of a conch shell and the interment of a dead rooster in "Seeing Things Simply." Physical impairment foregrounds Beatrice Saint Fort's bent back with years of sewing in "The Bridal Seamstress," the sacrifice of pigeons in "Ghosts," and the unveiling of a prosthetic arm in "Caroline's Wedding," an acknowledgment of Hermine Azil's manhandling by border guards during her pregnancy. In *Breath, Eyes, and Memory,* Tante Atie Caco explains how a special strain of bulbs produces daffodils, Sophie Caco's favorite flowers and the source of yellow in her Mother's Day card to Martine. Beneath the visual image lies a connection to European invaders, who introduced Sophie's favorite daffodil bulbs in the West Indies, a common subject in the anti-colonial writings of Jamaica Kincaid in *My Garden Book,* "Alien Oil in the Garden," and *Among Flowers: A Walk in the Himalayas.*

Character Specifics

The insanity of the title figure's father in the short story "The Dew Breaker," after the tyrant Papa Doc Duvalier's seizure of peasant land, yields an irony that places the future torturer in the category of victim. The implication, that injustice in a boy's life can yield barbarity in his strike against society. For the short fiction "Dream of the Butterflies," in the 1991 issue of *The Caribbean Writer,* the author poses contrasting specifics for Marie Micheline. A young mother of a son and daughter, she huddles on a clay floor to safeguard the trio from urban gunfire. Amid bullet showers, she fixates on a Haitian mountain retreat in Léogâne steeped in sensual delights. For sanity, she recalls phenomena of color, light, and sound—comets against inky skies, cricket and animal sounds, and the beauties of fireflies and myriad colored butterflies, the upward-tending rewards of residing far from urban disorder.

A masterly summation of fear and physical debility, Giselle Boyer's fear of losing herself after her twin Isabelle dies in the YA novel *Untwine* melds the themes of coming of age and sibling affection. Giselle's mental lockdown forces her to control unresponsive toes and senses and to figure out family problems—who would feed Dessalines the cat during her hospitalization and whether her twin Isabelle has truly gone. Edwidge compounds the mental fugue with sudden deafness and Isabelle's numinous visit with her sister to say goodbye. A simple blunder, the first walk in Isabelle's slippers, repeats the medical error of identifying Giselle as Isabelle and arranging a funeral for the survivor, who is silenced from identifying herself correctly. The particulars trace the sudden parting of Sylvie Boyer's one-egg twins and the memories and regrets that contribute to survivor guilt, the burden that follows Giselle to the spreading of her sister's ashes at their grandparents' home in Haiti. Bits of mortal matter return Isabelle to nature in a place both girls revered for its beauty and peace.

Recounting Loss

Laden with specifics of menus, herbal healing, ritual body paint, therapeutic sweats in a manatee hide, and customary betrothal temptations, the fifteenth-century biography *Anacaona* rallies the history of First People long vanished from Haiti after Christopher Columbus's 1493 invasion. Description leaves open to speculation whether the author researched Taino minutiae or fictionalized them. In contrast to the peril caused by pale-skinned Spanish insurgents in armor in November 1493 and nightly street warfare that terrorizes Marie Micheline in "Dream of the Butterflies," the bold gunning, arson, and looting caused by Bel Air thugs in *Brother, I'm Dying* stipulates deaths from lists of martial debris—"empty tear gas canisters, hollowed grenades, spent cartridge and bullet shells"—that litter a Port-au-Prince neighborhood in October 2004 (Danticat, 2007, 194). The surreptitious dumping of body bags in "Quality Control" hints at a dodgy means of scrapping cadavers murdered by political vice, the gathering storm in "Seven Stories."

In a reverse of stark realism, in *Eight Days*, Edwidge pictures the results of the January 12, 2010, earthquake on fictional Junior, who retreats into his imagination to replace terror and collapsing debris with fantasy games, exercise, and amusements. Even though pal Oscar dies in the cataclysm, Junior refuses to yield to despair. A media interview with the boy involves cameras and microphones, evidence of serious concern for his ordeal. The author reflected on additional encounters with violence in the essay "Flight" and the poems "Sawfish Soup" and "On the Day of the Dead." She stated in *The Art of Death* that precise writing makes sense of bereavement, reduces personal haunting, and transforms ghosts and absence into language that facilitates recovery. Scholar Martin Munro, an expert on Francophone studies at Florida State University, added that, by reading the words, "we seek some disavowed salvation ourselves" (Munro, 2007, 207).

See also Color, Earthquake, Nature, Violence.

Sources

Danticat, Edwidge. *The Art of Death: Writing the Final Story.* Minneapolis, MN: Graywolf Press, 2017.
_____. *Brother, I'm Dying.* New York: Vintage, 2007.
_____. "Dream of the Butterflies," *Caribbean Writer* 5 (1991): 98–99.
_____. *Everything Inside.* New York: Knopf, 2019.
Meacham, Cherie. "Traumatic Realism in the Fiction of Edwidge Danticat," *Journal of Haitian Studies* (1 April 2005): 122–139.
Munro, Martin. *Exile and Post-1946 Haitian Literature: Alexis, Depestre, Ollivier, Laferrière, Danticat.* Liverpool, UK: Liverpool University Press, 2007.
Simon, Daniel. "Review: *The Art of Death*," *World Literature Today* 92:2 (March/April 2018): 25.

The Dew Breaker

Edwidge solidified her critical acclaim with the novel *The Dew Breaker,* a loosely allied set of nine stories and vignettes about the title character. The former Tonton Macoute officer, identified as "the fat man" and "the barber," earns infamy for his government-sanctioned evildoing. The author called the anthology a "collage of real events" emerging from the Papa Doc and Baby Doc Duvalier regimes, which she treated as a research project. The work earned a Story Prize and a nomination for the PEN/Faulkner Award (Rousmaniere, 2004). In 2005, she issued it in French as *Le Briseur de Rosée.*

Interviewer Jill Krementz, a noted author and journalist, admired *The Dew Breaker* for its rhythmic lilt and compelling themes—moral choice, complicity, and redemption. *New York Times* book critic Michiko Kakutani called the "looping structure of overlapping stories" a "philosophical meditation" on renewed lives, a repeat of the resolve of journalist Aline Cajuste in "The Bridal Seamstress" and Claude in "Night Talkers" to focus on privy heartaches that feed mental agony. The motif of an investigative reporter anticipating a hidden story returned to Edwidge's fiction with Jess, a magazine writer in "Quality Control" and its rewrite, "Seven Stories," with magazine writer Kimberly "Kim" Boyer. The author gave both journalists gender-ambiguous names, a reflection of the female challenge of a man's job.

The Book of the Dead

An intriguing, suspenseful father-daughter narrative, Edwidge's opening stave in *The Dew Breaker* introduces Egyptian culture in the life of a museum goer. Ka Bienaimé, a young sculptor, envisions her beloved Papa in a static pose, which she shapes in mahogany for a client. Named "well-loved spirit" for her impact on him, she influences his departure from prison employment in Haiti to a career in barbering. Both he and his wife Anne, a hairdresser, withdraw from society after settling in East Flatbush, Brooklyn, he to quiet meditation about Egyptian death ritual and repentance and she to work as a hairdresser and attendance at daily

Catholic mass, a contemplative retreat from trauma.

By orchestrating a major cataclysm in the Bienaimé home, the author pictures Ka at a threshold of awareness that she grew up in free-floating secrecy and guilt about her father's atrocities committed under an assumed surname. Significantly, fearful recall—the father's nemesis—stalks him day and night, smudging the line between torturer and tortured. Without knowing the events in her family's past, Ka intuits too much about personal and island history in her art. To texturize the work, she leaves raw places on the surface, an indication of truths too damaging to stay hidden, but too deep to expose. In an interview, the author affirmed the anatomical harm caused by uncertainty: "The body was attacked as well as the soul" (Layne and Goran, 2005, 16).

Coming-of-age anguish places Ka in inner turmoil over her adored father's vicious biography. Papa's jettisoning of the portrait statue into a manmade lake in Lakeland, Florida, allows him a respite from concealing employment as a prison torturer—a hunter of prey—during Haiti's heinous Duvalier regime. His scarred face, nightmares, and lies about his birthplace symbolize the blight on his character that the "good angels" of his conscience can't cancel. A tenuous conclusion affirms a father uplifted by the scent of lemongrass while his daughter prepares for the long road ahead of bearing the family secrets. The drive from Florida to New York mimics the long passage of Egyptian souls toward judgment.

Seven

A sketchy reunion of an unnamed husband and wife after seven years apart, "Seven" first appeared in *New Yorker* in October 2001. The story uncovers insubstantial emotional bearings for an immigrant couple separated at Post-au-Prince immediately after marrying. Like the seven-year punishments of Jacob, the biblical patriarch in Genesis 29:18–30, the vignette outlines a punitive security check at JFK Airport and the destruction of Haitian gifts. The wife shares a Brooklyn flat with roomers Dany and Michel during the riots after the March 16, 2000, police shooting death of Patrick Dorismund in Manhattan. In the background, the three roomers suppress discussion of the August 9, 1997, brutalizing and sodomizing of Haitian-American security guard Abner Louima, a racial atrocity committed by New York City police.

In a respite from bleak environs, on the weekend, the wife takes an all-day bus ride with her husband to familiarize herself with the neighborhood, a tour that separates her from involvement in urban scenery. On the way home from Prospect Park, she fantasizes cross-dressing in a Carnival disguise with bridal attire amid the expressionless faces of New Yorkers. The idea of costuming as a cover for an unsatisfactory relationship and past dalliances enlarges on the common ambiguities of immigrants who reunite after years apart. The story also pairs with "The Book of the Dead," Egyptian scripture compiled by priests around 1550 BCE and suggests by the husband's age that these events follow the siring of a child by Eric with ear, nose, and throat nurse Nadine Osnac in "Water Child."

Water Child

Seven months after aborting an eight-week fetus, ENT nurse Nadine Osnac gains a reputation for extreme privacy and lack of enthusiasm for conversation or fun, two forms of social glue that could allay her psychic pain. Making a dysfunctional ritual of reading letters from home, at lunch in the Brooklyn hospital cafeteria, she dines over a tuna melt, an abstract reflection of the title fetus before its demise. After much mental struggle, she delays phoning her parents, whom she assists with half her salary to repay the cost of a nursing degree. Unexpressed, the longing for affection increases her alienation.

Clues begin to draw together the loose edges of the puzzle. At a condo in Canarsie, New York, Nadine uses the TV for white noise and makes a rite of collecting voicemail tapes from Eric, her ex-boyfriend and possibly the roomer in "Seven," who also works at Medgar Evers College. To commemorate their child's conception, she enshrines a rock in a glass of water, a palpable token of an unfulfilled pregnancy and a burden to the heart. Too late, the telephone interface with Eric ends with an unlisted number, a silent break with a potential outlet for grief.

An epiphany emerges from a mute patient's outburst. Unlike Ms. Hinds, a classroom teacher and cancer survivor coping with a laryngectomy and anger at muteness, Nadine chooses self-silencing. As though glimpsing an unrecognizable specter, she stares at a blurred reflection in the elevator door. Like the water child, she becomes the stony blob in the water glass. Like Ms. Hinds, she is forever halted from talking to her baby or its father.

The Book of Miracles

On the family drive from Westchester, New York, Ka Bienaimé travels with her parents to Christmas Eve mass through lighted neighborhoods. Anne Bienaimé secretly observes December 24 with paper straw for the Christ Child's manger and a drape of mistletoe, a Druidic symbol of reconciliation and forgiveness. In the midst of Holy Communion, she looks into a congregant's face that

resembles Emmanuel "Toto" Constant, a satanic leader of a Haitian death squad from 1991 to 1994. The false epiphany overshadows Anne's search for a yuletide miracle and introduces an anticlimactic departure from Saint Thérèse Church into the cold night, an appropriate atmosphere for a dysfunctional home.

Details contrast Anne's religious fantasies with seasonal urban tastelessness, symbolized by a plastic reindeer. Fragmented sense impressions—Ka's smart-mouth rejoinders, incense, pats on little boys' heads, Anne's epilepsy, faded flyers on lampposts—jockey between ineffable and mundane specifics, which critic Ray Conlogue of the Toronto *Globe and Mail* calls "Kafka-esque" (Conlogue, 2004, R3). At the heart of narrative emotion, she hovers on the brink of hysteria that someone will recognize her husband, the former prison torturer. A three-word reminder—"I wasn't there"—separates the family into two survivors of the Duvalier regime and their daughter Ka, a U.S.–born Haitian-American who has only after-memory of atrocities. Like children of Holocaust survivors who lack recollection of genocide, she internalizes island outrage from stories, the sources of Edwidge's canon.

Night Talkers

Edwidge's "return of the native" narrative allies 31-year-old Dany Dorméus and Claude, both island ex-pats with complicated past lives in Beau Jour, a mountain village in Haiti. At Dany's arrival, Old Zo recounts much of the region's interconnection:

Contrasting ex-con Claude's lack of gratitude for rescue by "backward-ass peasants," Dany's respect for his elderly aunt/foster mother Estina Estème and Haitian folk customs ennobles him (Danticat, 2004, 102). His subconscious

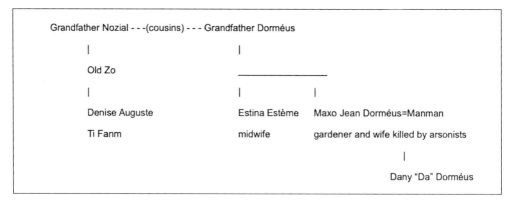

struggles to identify nightmares, the phantasms of a boyhood crisis. At a climactic point, Dany recounts events at age six when a shooter killed his parents, threatened him with a gun, and blinded Tante Estina by setting fire to the house. Dany later recognized the murderer in a New York barbershop, a direct tie to the title figure, the Dew Breaker.

Coincidence unites "Night Talkers" with Anne Bienaimé's fears in the previous stave of someone recognizing her husband as a mass killer like Emmanuel "Toto" Constant, orchestrator of the Raboteau Massacre on April 22, 1994, killing supporters of Jean-Bertrand Aristide. The nighttime incursion raises the question of "why one single person had been given the power to destroy," an allusion to the treachery of Papa Doc Duvalier and his murderous son Baby Doc (*ibid.*, 107). To counterbalance the gunman's intimidation of island peasants, the story poses Estina Estéme's charisma to draw Dany Dorméus home from New York to settle questions of his parents' murder. To express love and respect, Dany sends a blue dress, the color of the Virgin Mary's cloak, an iconic hue of devotion suited to his foster mom.

The redirection of narrative from identifying a murderer toward a beneficent wake exalts Estina Estéme, whose name suggests "esteemed little star." In her quiet offering of neighborliness and healing, she raised Dany after his orphaning. Selflessly, she encouraged his migration to New York to escape a vicious dictatorship especially hard on teenage boys. She helps to acclimate Claude to village customs after his checkered years as drug user and dealer, murderer, and prisoner. Storytelling by neighbors at Beau Jour fills in her past deeds guiding mothers through difficult births and soothing the night talkers, troubled souls "who spoke their nightmares out loud," a symptom of mental and spiritual misgivings (*ibid.*, 120).

Estina returns to the subject of nightmares and weeping in "A Taste of Coffee," in which she identifies herself and her Aunt Ilyana as fellow sufferers. At Estina's unexpected demise after hearing Dany's confrontation with the sleeping barber, his story remains unrepeated, a silence that ends the cycle of terrorism and requital. The setting on a seven-place mausoleum underscores the common end for all people and the post-death narration of biographical stories that encompass character, wisdom, and experience. Like the reading of a will, the oral tradition passes treasures to the next generation.

The Bridal Seamstress

An off-kilter interview between a producer of bespoke wedding dresses and Aline Cajuste, a journalist from the

Haitian American Weekly, the story illuminates a survivor of island death squads. Beatrice Saint Fort suffers paranoia over a former prison guard reputedly living on the corner in Far Rockaway, Queens, an island town that the Mohegan Indians called "lonely place." A haunted woman in her late fifties working toward retirement, she remains unmarried, childless, and resolved to escape detection by a mental ghost. Loving and maternal, she asks her clients to call their mothers, a parental safeguard for young brides veiled by ignorance. She changes addresses often to avoid the dew breaker, who she fears is stalking her. The phantom that haunts her memories of Haiti once invited her to a dance, then tortured her with blows to her feet, a suggestion of preventing physical escape without maiming her physical beauty.

Both characters bear cogent names: Beatrice Saint Fort, a combination denoting blessed holy strength, and Aline, a straight—A-line—connection to Haiti's matrilineal past. (The surname recurs in "The Secret Island" as an English teacher.) Aline's surname, Cajuste, denotes an ability to defend women like the seamstress. The interaction between Aline and Beatrice alerts the interviewer to her true calling—politically oppositional journalism honoring "men and women chasing fragments of themselves long lost to others" (Danticat, 2004, 137–138). Aline observes the plastic on the couch and Beatrice's plopping a thimble on each finger, a crusader's armor protecting her from "tremendous agonies [that] filled every blank space" (*ibid.*, 137). The two women observe the delicate drop of ash tree leaves tumbling slowly to the ground, a metaphor for Beatrice's declining years bearing corrosive memories from Haiti's past. Like Yggdrasil, the magic tree of North mythology, the sturdy trunk balances the earth on its axis.

Monkey Tails

An allegory of father figures and hero worship, twelve-year-old Michel's pairing with eighteen-year-old Romain contrasts views of political chaos and its effects on evolving manhood. Opening on February 7, 1986, Michel's narrative reprises the extremes of rage and reprisal during the ouster of dictator Jean-Claude "Baby Doc" Duvalier and his wife Michèle Bennett Duvalier. In the upheaval following Duvalier's departure, cathedral bells, car horns, banners, and mock funeral processions express local excitement at freedom from tyranny. Michel observes a furor of water stealing at the tap station of Monsieur Christophe, Michel's unacknowledged father, who bears the name of Haiti's first president, Henri/Henry Christophe. The character recurs in Edwidge's 1996 story "The Journals of Water Days." The boy notes "how people with means can make the less fortunate feel special by putting them to work," a reflection on the arbitrary allotment of supremacy under the Duvaliers and their paramilitary (*ibid.*, 147–148). Like Christophe's water pouring into the street, the cleansing flood unleashes in islanders a rush of joy and inspires requitals at former Tonton Macoutes.

The story emphasizes the precarious coming of age of two Haitian males during unpredictable changes and suggests a similarly traumatic growing up of Baby Doc, a trickster figure who assumed his father's place as the long-tailed monkey at age nineteen. The memoir ends in 2004 as Michel, an émigré to New York like Dany Dorméus in "Night Talkers," tapes his autobiography—the "monkey's tale"—while awaiting the birth of his son. His reflections attest to his mother's death from grief and the abandonment of Romain's home because his mother never returned from Curaçao. Romain disappears after his father Regulus shoots himself in the head, leaving Michel to miss a fellow orphan.

The Funeral Singer

While studying for a General Educational Development diploma in basic education coursework in New York, three Haitian women battle post-traumatic stress disorder by meeting to "parcel out our sorrows" (Danticat, 2004, 170). Their sisterhood illustrates the value of the Greek φιλία (philia), a sharing of background, youth, political ideals, and diaspora. They support each other with humor and memories of home, including the detention center at the Casernes Dessalines barracks, the locus of dire persecutions and murder mentioned in the last stave, "The Dew Breaker." Their recall appeases formidable images and events of the Duvalier reign, a contrast to the silence and avoidance of camaraderie in nurse Nadine Osnac's story, "Water Child."

Freda, the 22-year-old title figure, can't escape a poignant undertow—the self-destructive fate of her father, a fisherman whom authorities question and break out his teeth, a reduction to powerlessness. After his suicide at sea, she becomes the funeral singer by performing "Brother Timonie," a maritime dirge for a boat pilot. Anticipating her own death if she returns to Haiti to join the militia, she sings the song once more to entertain restaurateur Rézia and Mariselle, a widow whose artist husband is executed for painting the truth about Haiti's persecutors. More singing unites the trio in escaping past horrors and looking ahead to new roles, the source of success for sculptor Ka Bienaimé and actor Gabrielle Fonteneau in "The Book of the Dead."

The Dew Breaker

Edwidge's fragmented novel bears the efforts of a native Haitian at interpreting an historical morass. Spanish critic Aitor Ibarrola-Armendáriz, an expert in modern languages at the University of Deusto, calls the author's fiction "constructing a collective past from the shards of a vase that has been repeatedly shattered into a thousand pieces" (Ibarrola-Armendáriz, 2010, 33). She begins the finale with edgy immediacy—a Baptist preacher's awareness that he will soon be martyred by the Tonton Macoute, who previously murdered his wife with poisoned candy. The arrest in l'Eglise Baptiste des Anges (the angels' Baptist church) takes him from the Bel Air slum by truck to Casernes Dessalines barracks, a death dungeon conveniently located alongside a graveyard.

After the 29-year-old fat man in charge releases the preacher from his cell, the prisoner muses on "the kindness of his cellmates, men of different skin tones and social classes all thrown together in this living hell ... man-angels" (Danticat, 2004, 225–226). When the fat man violates macoute orders by shooting the preacher, he recognizes in his brutal enforcement of the Duvalier regime that strength and control of the peasantry is actually an illusion. Bearing the mark of Cain, he vomits in the street, an emesis of the atrocities that formed his ten-year career as a corrupt law officer. The gush offers a sliver of hope for his rehabilitation.

Details of the officer's delayed healing enmesh his life with Anne, a frenzied fanatic on the subject of miracles and a balance to his unspeakable criminality. Her removal of splinters from his wound reflects the emotional shrapnel that pierces Haitian tormenters. The mixing of an herbal and honey infusion to heal him precedes a personal miracle—flight the next day to New York with her new husband, whom she loves and shields from exposure for being a Haitian death squad officer. Her disjunction with daughter Ka by phone fails to relieve the family's secrets and private hurts. Like the splinters in the fat man's face, tiny reminders of complicity add up to torture of a household.

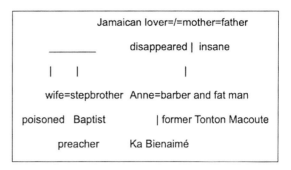

along with the vivid daily recriminations of her father, a failed member of the Duvalier Tonton Macoute. On the maternal side, Ka loses an aunt to poisoning.

Ka bears a significant name, an Egyptian designation for "soul" that epitomizes mortal wrongs and their repentance. Without direct knowledge of Haiti and its onerous past, she enjoys the benefits of a Haitian-American birth, but lacks the details of suffering and crimes that haunt Anne and the barber.

Sources

Danticat, Edwidge. *The Dew Breaker*. New York: Abacus, 2004.
Raab, Josef. "Liberation and Lingering Trauma: U.S. Present and Haitian Past in Edwidge Danticat's *The Dew Breaker*," *Politics and Cultures of Liberation* 7 (3 April 2018): 265–284.

Doubles

Edwidge examines human match-ups with varied strategies, for example, girlfriends and fellow citizenship students Freda, Rézia, and Mariselle in "The Funeral Singer" and Michel and Romain, pals in "Monkey Tails." For Caonabó and his Taino brother Manicoatex, who team-up in *Anacaona* for hunting, fishing, and Maguana-style mock combat, capture brings characters together for the last time, resulting in the brothers' disappearance in the custody of conquistadors. Other examples demonstrate bifurcation,

Sources

Bellamy, Maria Rice. "More Than Hunter or Prey: Duality and Traumatic Memory in Edwidge Danticat's *The Dew Breaker*," *MELUS* 37:1 (Spring 2012).
Conlogue, Ray. "Haunted by Haiti's Ghosts," [Toronto] *Globe and Mail* (19 April 2004): R3.
Danticat, Edwidge. *The Dew Breaker*. New York: Abacus, 2004.
———. "The Journals of Water Days," *Callaloo* 19:2 (Spring, 1996): 376–380.
Ibarrola-Armendáriz, Aitor. "The Language of Wounds and Scars in Edwidge Danticat's 'The Dew Breaker,'" *Journal of English Studies* 8 (2010): 23–56.
Kakutani, Michiko. "Hiding from a Brutal Past Spent Shattering Lives in Haiti," *New York Times* (10 March 2004).
Krementz, Jill. "Interview," *The Writer* 117:12 (December 2004): 66.
Layne, Prudence, and Lester Goran. "Haiti: History, Voice, Empowerment," *Sargasso* 2 (2004–2005): 3–17.
Raab, Josef. "Liberation and Lingering Trauma: U.S. Present and Haitian Past in Edwidge Danticat's *The Dew Breaker*," *Politics and Cultures of Liberation* 7 (3 April 2018): 265–284.
Rousmaniere, Dana. "Grappling with Haiti's Beasts," *Atlantic* (June 2004).
Valbrun, Marjorie. "Haiti's Eloquent Daughter," *Black Issues Book Review* 6:4 (July/August 2004): 42.

The Dew Breaker Genealogy

Like a tattered spiderweb, the Bienaimé family tree delineates a caustic irony—strands of broken trust, distress, and breakdown through three generations. Ka, a budding sculptor, inherits the background of an adulterous paternal grandmother and insane grandfather the fates of Claude and Dany Dorméus in "Night Talkers" while they mourn Aunt Estina Estéme; the dual stripping of life from mind and body in *The Art of Death;* and the boyhood of Oscar and Junior, the pals in *Eight Days* who incur a realistic game of hide and seek after Haiti's January 12, 2010, earthquake that kills Oscar. From a female perspective in "Dosas," Olivia forms the *dosa* (untwinned) third member of a trio of friends, a triad overbalanced by marriage between the first two members, Elsie and Blaise, and criminality in the overlapping second pair, Blaise and Olivia. The entrance of Dédé, an unlikely suitor, extends doubling for Elsie, who seems trapped in faulty pairing by her inability to differentiate between users and friends.

Birthing gone awry in the novel *Claire of the Sea Light* relates a gendered superstition that daughters who survive after their mothers succumb during labor attest to a pair struggling for primacy. The younger Claire Limyè Lanmè Faustin looks and walks like her mother. In a model of cooperation, she dances a ring game with girlfriends on the beach. By age seven, she anticipates becoming for Gaëlle Lavaud a replacement for daughter Rose Lavaud. In duplication, Claire faces personal erasure to alleviate Gaëlle's grief for Rose.

In a similar theme of attrition, Grann's rephrasing of human death with the demise of a kapok tree in *The Last Mapou* speaks indirectly to a young granddaughter who is ill-prepared to lose her granny, but eager to protect nature. Fortunately for Haiti, the oral transmission of optimism thrusts the girl into the role of spokesperson for the ecosphere, an extension of Grann's oral tradition. Similarly at one with the outdoors, the author travels into the hill country above Jacmel in *After the Dance* to visit cemeteries and enjoy forested areas with her fiancé, Fedherbe

"Fedo" G. Boyer. The two take comfort at a night in an inn and a return ride to the shore, an expedition that pairs lovers and merges mountains with sea.

Sinister freakishness at birth involves babies meant to be twins. In the fifth chapter of *Create Dangerously,* the author contrasts medical views on missing limbs in newborns with the Vodou-Santeria belief that such infants were twins *in vitro.* Because one fetus has died, it "put a visible mark on the living twin," a supernatural explanation of the author's brother Kelly, born without a forearm (Danticat, 2010, 75). Science counters folklore with the theory that the missing anatomical part dissolves in the uterus before birth. Edwidge recreates the anomaly in "Caroline's Wedding," in which a prosthesis takes the place of Caroline's malformed arm, a token of American ambitions for a new citizen.

United Spirits

In 1996, *Granta* issued Edwidge's story "The Revenant"—published in the Fall 1996 *Conjunctions* as "Condolences"—which opens on the death of Victoria Pico, infant twin of Rafael. For the historical novel *The Farming of Bones,* the author reverses the two, with one-day-old Rafael "Rafi" Duarte's sister Rosalinda Teresa surviving after his demise. Vodou treasure holy twins or marasas, identical lovers who share physical and spiritual parts of their lives. The benefits of doubling encourage Ka Bienamé's father in "The Book of the Dead" to name her Ka for the compassionate element of human life, a feature missing from his early days as a Tonton Macoute. Unfortunately for Ka, gracing her with an altruistic name obligates her to seek the cause of her father's need for blessing.

In *Breath, Eyes, Memory,* doubling causes Martine Caco to share unity and anguish with her daughter. To avoid the trauma of marital coitus with husband Joseph Woods, Sophie Caco allows her mind to become Martine's double, a defender against repeated nightmares of rape by the Tonton Macoute, Sophie's sire. Simultaneously, Martine cultivates a dual existence as survivor and mental defective fearful of asylums. After her suicide from stab wounds to the abdomen, Sophie dresses her mother as a duplicate of Erzulie, the clotheshorse and stimulant to female self-adornment and womanly pride.

Virginity permeates creation myth with the magical emergence of Haitians from the trunks of kapok trees in *The Last Mapou* and the receding of Sophie Caco into a mental retreat. Purity testing causes her to withdraw into a second self, an imaginary double who experiences the humiliation of Martine's little finger probing her vagina. Sophie discusses with Grandmè Ifé Caco the three-generation tradition of assaulting a daughter's privacy to ensure that she remains pure and marriageable, a trait destroyed by Martine's rape. Pressures on Sophie induce her to imagine the Vodou concept of *marasa* (twins) or split personality, with one being at a distance from pain and humiliation. The two unhealthy psyches seek release in opposite refuges—Sophie in the mothering of Brigitte Ifé Woods and Martine in self-destruction and an annihilation of maternity.

The mother-daughter discordance derives from the dichotomy of the self-absorbed goddess Erzulie, a divine mother, sexual plaything, and sensual temptress. The contradictions destroy Martine, the anguished dual annihilator who stabs herself to end personal suffering, nightmares, and the potential psychic harm of bearing another child. The narrative redeems Martine through death. To turn the insensate corpse into the active side of Erzulie, Sophie breaks funeral tradition and dresses her mother in a Jezebel-red suit, an icon of sexuality and agency over male tormentors.

Twinning and Doubling

Edwidge's YA novel *Untwine* builds drama and angst from the closeness of sixteen-year-old Giselle and Isabelle Boyer, identical Haitian-American one-egg twins. Born clasping hands, the two reenact their birthing in a car crash that kills Isabelle and leaves Giselle unconscious for five days. The action creates irony out of their paired birthmarks on opposite sides of their heads and the opposing views of the Miami highway, where only Isabelle can see the red minivan approaching. The clarifier of a false identity, Sylvie Boyer knows her girls so intimately that she immediately recognizes Giselle and enables her to prepare for a lifetime of untwining. More female intervention from Grandma Régine and Aunt Leslie solaces the survivor and enables her to escape regret and survivor's guilt.

In the art critique of Botswanan painter Pamela Phatsimo Sunstrum for *Paris Review,* the author emphasized the presence of Vodou orisha Yemayá, the Yoruban controller of waters. Repeated images of doubling and tripling figures identify fluid imagery as the reflector of mirror doublets, "the kind they might find staring back at them from a river or stream" (Danticat, 2020, 108). The mythic likenesses unite humans in the paintings "Kwame" and "All This Wringing and Clutching" into "a community of the seen and the unseen, the present and the past," the controlling themes of *Anacaona* and *Claire of the Sea Light* (ibid.). *Untwine* surveys a more terrifying doublet—Giselle staring at a coffin bearing her physical likeness in Isabelle's corpse. To shed the liability of a lost self, Giselle collects differing details in the girls' lives, including bedroom slippers and strawberry body wash. The survivor distributes her sister's ashes over water in Haiti, a return of the deceased to Yemayá, the shielder of women, conception, infant safety, healing, and survivors of wreckage.

SOURCES

Clitandre, Nadège T. *Edwidge Danticat: The Haitian Diasporic Imaginary.* Charlottesville: University of Virginia Press, 2018.

Danticat, Edwidge. *Breath, Eyes, Memory.* New York: Soho Press, 1994.

_____. "Pamela Phatsimo Sunstrum: New and Recent Paintings," *Paris Review* 232 (Spring 2020): 105–121.

_____. "The Revenant," *Granta 54* 115 (20 June 1996).

_____. *Untwine.* New York: Scholastic, 2015.

Munro, Martin. *Exile and Post-1946 Haitian Literature.* Liverpool, UK: Liverpool University Press, 2007.

Shea, Renee. "The Dangerous Job of Edwidge Danticat," *Callaloo* 19:2 (Spring, 1996): 382–389.

Dreams

Edwidge values elegiac Haitian art for its recording of dreams acknowledging life and visualizing death, the complex of meanings for Ray for his soon-to-be widow in "One Thing," and daydreams of a handsome husband in *Célimène*. The author put dream women cut from toothpaste boxes to good purpose in *The Art of Death*. The fantasy women took Edwidge's place during nightly sexual violation by Cousin Joel. She recalled, "These cut-out images would come fully alive while my body was being violated" (Danticat, 2017, 43). Duality enabled her to pity her paper aliases while shielding her immature mind from a fondling pervert.

Illusory replacements, such as Emilie Gallant's night visitations in the story "The Missing Peace," allow a spiritual respite. The pun on peace/piece refers to Emilie's unsettled mind about the common burial pit for political victims. In an uplifting moment in "The Secret Island," Bee's mom erases in dreams her husband's jailing and deportation to Haiti. Her vision places him on the opposite shore of a Japanese pond in the Brooklyn Botanic Gardens. His wave informs his wife "you're going to be seeing someone very soon," a snatch of wishful thinking (Danticat, 2006, 11). Continuing her nap, she uses "dreams to be closer to Papa" (*ibid.*). Her daughter Bee chooses pretense as a more accessible way to imagine Papa still in New York.

Dreaming with Purpose

To encourage female artists at Howard University, Edwidge lectured on the passage of dreams from West African abductees in shackles to the twenty-first-century inheritor. She accords respect for night apparitions, especially the ominous Sugar Woman in ankle chains and muzzle who haunts Amabelle Dérsir's late visions in *The Farming of Bones*. Of the mixture of dream and real chapters, Chitra Divakaruni, a journalist for the *Los Angeles Weekly* and creative writing teacher at the University of Houston, applauds "images that create the unique texture of the book: images of children carrying their dead parents home and dead sons laid naked in the earth, of masks for remembrance and beaded bracelets for protection, of bitter oranges and basil to heal" (Divakaruni, 1998). For Amabelle, the waterfall unites reveries of love for Sebastian Onius in a mythic memory that fills her dreams.

Multicolored butterflies in the mountain setting of Léogâne flutter a mental getaway for Marie Micheline, the martyred victim of urban machine gun spurts in the short story "Dream of the Butterflies." At a startling moment in the YA novel *Untwine*, the author embodies the ghost of Isabelle Boyer, who visits twin Giselle in the hospital to say goodbye. Of the girls' closeness, Giselle states, "We were tourists in each other's heads," both imagining a Niagara Falls disaster, skiing in an avalanche, and a hot-air balloon view of earthquake damage in Port-au-Prince (Danticat, 2015, 147).

Wisps of Prophecy

Elevating prophetic mind escapes, the author fictionalizes predictive dreams of a fifteenth-century Taino *cacica* (ruler) and diarist of *Anacaona.* The text foreshadows subsequent calamities in Chief Caonabó's troubled dreams in the year 1491, precognitions of the arrival of Genoa navigator Christopher Columbus from Spanish regents Ferdinand II and Isabella of Castile. The biographical Taino queen foresees death and destruction in a tsunami engulfing Xaraguá and in her husband Caonabó's drowning at sea while in custody of conquistadors. Fear of a serpent choking her neck finds reality in Marién, where a travel party first views tribal victims hanged in trees, the early outcome of colonial overreaching. Entangling dreamscapes accurately depict Haiti's future under European colonizers.

In retrospect to personal experience, the author explained that she kept notes on her vivid night imagery. She viewed the topsy-turvy, sometimes terrifying dreams of characters, particularly Gracina Azule in "Caroline's Wedding," who tries to reunite with the spirit of her deceased father Carl; Michel, the erotic dreamer in "Monkey Tails"; and Célianne "Cécé" Espérance in *Behind the Mountains,* who depends on Papa's reassurance that "many things like Galipòt," the monster horse, exist only in dreams, not in real life (Danticat, 2002, 55). On a more positive note, in "The Dew Breaker," the fat man sleeps during recovery from a slash to the cheek and dreams of gardening again in boyhood with his mother among fruit plants, herbs, and healthful weeds. The most propitious mindscape, Junior's playtime visions in *Eight Days* maintain his sanity until earthquake rescuers can extract him from debris and juxtaposition by his dead pal Oscar.

To visualize the relationship between godmother Amabelle Desír and the spirit of Victoria, a twin dead in infancy, Edwidge's "The Revenant"—printed in the Fall 1996 *Conjunctions* under the title "Condolences"—pictures the two rejoined in a cosmic visitation. The author intends the dream to alert Amabelle to the enslavement of Haitian cane workers in Dominican fields. The subject of her dreams returns in *The Farming of Bones,* in which genocide at the Massacre River reminds her that she witnessed the drowning of her parents, herbalists Irelle Pradelle and Antoine Desír. For Sophie Caco, protagonist of *Breath, Eyes, Memory,* dreams of leaving Haiti to reunite with her mother Martine Caco in New York City bear the tone of nightmares. Sophie, too, relives her mother's rape by a Tonton Macoute and recalls a muscular felony—"pounding alive into a helpless young girl" (Danticat, 1994, 193). The atmospheric phantasms torment Martine and cause her to bite her flesh and rip bedsheets, symptoms of hysteria. The mania proves prophetic of suicide, Martine's release from a mental purgatory.

SOURCES

Danticat, Edwidge. *The Art of Death: Writing the Final Story.* Minneapolis, MN: Graywolf Press, 2017.

_____. *Behind the Mountains: The Diary of Célianne Esperance.* New York: Orchard Books, 2002.

_____. *Breath, Eyes, Memory.* New York: Soho Press, 1994.

_____. "Dream of the Butterflies," *Caribbean Writer* 5 (1991): 98–99.

_____. "The Revenant," *Granta* 54 115 (20 June 1996).

_____. "The Secret Island," *Colorlines* 9:4 (November/December 2006): 9–14.

_____. *Untwine*. New York: Scholastic, 2015.

Divakaruni, Chitra. "Dreaming in Haitian," *Los Angeles Weekly* (26 August 1998).

Lyons, Bonnie. "Interview," *Contemporary Literature* 44:2 (Summer 2003): 183–198.

Murphy, Dwyer. "The Art of Not Belonging," *Guernica* (3 September 2013).

Duvaliers

Edwidge relived Haiti's "thirty-year father-son dictatorship" in stories, such as memories of military violence in Jacmel in *A Walk Through Carnival,* and, for "In the Old Days," the urge of a husband to open a school for the poor of Port-au-Prince (Danticat, 2019, 41). The poem "A Despot Walks into a Killing Field" contains an ironic gibe that "life was better/because rice was cheaper/under the despot's reign," a version of "he made the trains run on time" from the Mussolini era (Danticat, 2012, 37). In "The Secret Island," the love letters hidden in a suitcase instruct Bee on the miseries of island life before her parents migrated to New York. Bee's father encapsulates for his child a simple truth of good vs. evil: "The bad people have more power" (Danticat, 2006, 14). In the introduction to *Love, Anger, Madness,* the author specified the year 1967, when the regime "was becoming more and more severe, enrolling the poor as henchmen and women, killing them to reduce their number, and persecuting intellectuals for their ideas and artists for their creations" (Danticat, 2010, xiv).

The author explained the source of François "Papa Doc" Duvalier's perverted nationalism—he equated it with nourishment, the reason for killing or exiling mulatto professionals, intellectuals, and business leaders from Haiti, including novelist Dany Leferrière, who migrated to Montreal in 1976. She reflected on her parents' flight to New York "in the middle of a thirty-year dictatorship during which most people were being terrorized" and women and girls ravished (Danticat, 2017, 43). In "Does it Work?," a 2006 op-ed piece for the *Washington Post,* she recorded threats against the innocent "to drown them, dismember them and set them on fire" (Danticat, 2006, B1). She witnessed the results of broken teeth, lopped ears, gouged eyes, scars, and tremors still evident as "a darkness that would always surround them" (*ibid.*).

Massive Intimidation

In *Create Dangerously,* the author characterizes graft and corruption as a power that "[threatened] to bury all that is Haitian," including Afro-Caribbean art and music (Danticat, 2010, 144). Hungarian expert on American studies Eva Federmayer explains that "this highly orchestrated and spectacularized ordeal of postcolonial tyranny … [grounds] her artistic creed" (Federmayer, 2015, 2). The text portrays the execution of immigrants Louis Drouin and Marcel Numa, guerrilla fighters shot by firing squad as an object lesson to schoolchildren. The dire situation involved punishment of "strings of words that, uttered, written, or read, could cause a person's death" (Danticat, 2010, 9). The paranoia rampant in Port-au-Prince derives from stringent laws making it "a crime to pick up a bloodied body on the street," the gory scene in the poem "Sawfish Soup" (*ibid.*).

Of oppression, Edwidge remarked on her belief that tyrants compete with writers to make themselves into supermen, a character flaw the Duvaliers shared with Generalissimo Rafael Trujillo as "crucial to their reign" (Danticat, 2007, 95). Sounds in "The Journals of Water Days 1986" identify "military trucks [that] roared up and down the narrow spaces between the shanties" and gunshots that filled the air with wood slivers and the odor of gunpowder (Danticat, 1996, 376). She charged the elder Duvalier with a mania to wipe out commentators: "No writer of his time was left alive long enough to be as prolific as Francois 'Papa Doc' Duvalier" (*ibid.*, 92). In a 2007 interview with novelist Junot Díaz, she suggested a cause for the mass slaughter: "Dictators want to silence writers because they want to be the only ones speaking" (*ibid.*). She added a truism about martyrdom—by extinguishing creative voices, Duvalier made them more noteworthy in death. The author cited her mother's superstition that a strong wind encircled the earth when Papa Doc Duvalier died. Rose credited the meteorological anomaly to "a protest in hell" at having to accommodate so vile a soul (Danticat, 2007, 93).

Peripheral Damage

The author's short fiction sketches shades of disruption in witnesses, particularly Jeanne, who sees her aunt beaten and her father bolt for Cuba in "Sunrise, Sunset." Her mother Carole regrets a "world where it is normal to be unhappy, to be hungry, to work non-stop and earn next to nothing, and to suffer the whims of … tyrants" (Danticat, 2017). In a rumination on fatherhood, fictional Max Ardin, Sr., a wealthy citizen of Ville Rose in *Claire of the Sea Light,* calls the Duvalier era tragic for a generation of children. Because of his son Max, Jr.'s, savage rape of housemaid Flore Voltaire, he blames unkept promises and casual murders. Max, Sr., concludes that "idealists had been killed to make room for gangsters … life had become so cheap that you could give anyone a few dollars to snuff it out" (Danticat, 2013, 186). The implied comparison of human existence to a candle flame reflects

the same despair as Macbeth's "tomorrow and tomorrow" speech, which reduces one life to a "walking shadow" (*Macbeth*, V:v, 23).

The chaos of living under daily intimidation and random killings made its mark on female sanity, such as Anne's rescue of the fat man from pursuit in "The Dew Breaker," the taunting of Madam Roger with her son's decapitated head in "Children of the Sea," and the mother fearful of removing her husband's corpse from the street in the 1991 poem "Sawfish Soup." In "Caroline's Wedding," the narrator recalls her father's joke about God refusing to rise in honor of Papa Doc lest the elder Duvalier steal the heavenly throne. For the story "Between the Pool and the Gardenias," the author pictures a fictional servant named Marie mimicking motherhood. Innocently, she retrieves an infant corpse from the street and attempts to halt its putrefaction with cleansing and deodorizers, a symbolic purification that did nothing to stanch the reek of Duvalier corruption. Analyst Raquel D. Kennon exonerated Marie for her mental flight of fancy to "mentally [distance herself] from the carnage by which they are surrounded, including the often horrendous quotidian realities of life under dictatorship" (Kennon, 2017, 163).

See also The Dew Breaker, Tonton Macoute, Violence.

Sources

Adisa, Opal Palmer. "Up Close and Personal," *African American Review* 43:2–3 (Summer/Fall 2009): 345–355.

Danticat, Edwidge. *The Art of Death: Writing the Final Story.* Minneapolis, MN: Graywolf Press, 2017.

_____. *Claire of the Sea Light.* New York: Vintage, 2013.

_____. *Create Dangerously: The Immigrant Artist at Work.* New York: Vintage, 2010.

_____. "A Despot Walks into a Killing Field," *Progressive* 76:5 (May 2012): 37.

_____. "Does It Work?," *Washington Post* (24 September 2006): B1.

_____. *Everything Inside.* New York: Knopf, 2019.

_____. "The Journals of Water Days," *Callaloo* 19:2 (Spring, 1996): 376–380.

_____. "Junot Díaz," *BOMB* 101 (Fall 2007): 89–95.

_____. *Love Anger Madness: A Haitian Triptych.* introduction. New York: Modern Library, 2010, xi–xviii.

_____. "Sawfish Soup," *Caribbean Writer* 5 (1991): 10–11.

_____. "The Secret Island," *Colorlines* 9:4 (November/December 2006): 9–14.

_____. "Sunrise, Sunset," *New Yorker* (18 September 2017).

_____. *A Walk Through Carnival.* New York: Vintage, 2016.

Federmayer, Eva. "Violence and Embodied Subjectivities: Edwidge Danticat's Breath, Eyes, Memory," *Scholar Critic* 2:3 (December 2015): 1–17.

Kennon, Raquel D. "'We Know People by Their Stores': Madness, Babies, and Dolls in Edwidge Danticat's *Krik? Krak!," Madness in Black Women's Diasporic Fictions.* New York: Springer, 2017, 163–197.

Earthquake

In "Haiti: Bloodied, Shaken—and Beloved," "Flight," "A Little While," and "Haiti Faces Difficult Questions," personal essays for the *New Yorker* and *Miami Herald,* Edwidge described her visions of the 7.0 earthquake and 52 aftershocks that struck Léogâne near Port-au-Prince on January 12, 2010. The disaster injured 300,000 and killed 316,000 Haitians. Although she did not witness the rumble, she compared the cataclysm to the Apocalypse—the end of time—and the biblical sufferings of Job, but credited the mass loss of lives and structures to a geological fault line and to the building of houses on inclines in Port-au-Prince. On her first post-disaster visit to the island, she found mothers trying to keep infants dry in temporary tents inundated with rain and mud. Positioning of skeletons left rescuers wondering about "an individual's final instinct during his or her last moments on earth" (Danticat, 2011, 32).

In the article "Living and Loving Through Tragedy," the writer praised islanders for relocating out of harm. The Haitians intently digging with bare hands, keeping watch on those trapped in the rubble, and the raising of a tent city by locals and neighbors gave her pride and hope. She envisioned the "Gran Met," Vodou's grand master of creation, overseeing all actions. A year after the great quake, she issued in *Good Housekeeping* the article "Turning the Page on Disaster." On a human level, she stated in *Tent Life* "what Haiti has always offered: spontaneous and lasting community as well as cooperation" (Danticat, 2011, 9). The struggle against strife, she commented, demands representation in writing and the arts.

In Flesh and Blood

In 2013, the author disclosed the plunge of the 63-year-old Roman Catholic archbishop Joseph Serge Miot from a papal balcony and the reduction to rubble of Notre Dame de l'Assomption Cathedral (Our Lady of the Assumption), which had served Port-au-Prince as Catholic landmark and lighthouse since 1884. In retrospect of ordinary anxieties, she commiserated with those "shielding their heads from the rain, closing their eyes, covering their ears, to shut out the sounds of military 'aid' helicopters" (Danticat, 2010, 18). A decade after the calamity, she noted, "Sorrowful anniversaries magnify absence" (Danticat, 2020). To NPR interviewer Audie Cornish, she recalled the native islander's dread during a news lag: "So it's very—it's terrifying. It's—it's as if you have your heart being ripped out imagining what the condition could be, especially since it hasn't been fully assessed, and we don't know how many people have died" (Cornish, 2016).

Edwidge made mature farewells to earthquake victims such as the fictional

Oscar. He didn't fare so well as Junior in *Eight Days,* who diverted himself with imaginary play, or Justine, who escaped unhurt. In the poem "On the Day of the Dead," the author compared the annual November 2 Catholic ritual for the past twelve months of obituaries with the unexpected losses from the earthquake, including her cousin Maxo. She regretted that people in the path of the vast tremor had no chance to summon La Flaca, lady of the dead, or Le Bawon (Barron Samedi), the graveyard protector. In contrast to a somber reminder of mortality, Alix Delinois of Harlem, New York, the illustrator of *Eight Days,* dedicated pastel, collage, and acrylic drawings to the originality and optimism of survivors.

Global Response

Like a driver too mesmerized by a traffic accident to turn aside, the writer returned to the subject of earthquake fatalities in *The Art of Death.* From eyewitnesses on CNN, she learned that "entire neighborhoods had slid down hills. Churches, schools, and hospitals had crumbled, killing and burying countless people" (Danticat, 2017, 46). Increasing the terror of the moment, aftershocks jolted the living with fear of more tremors and a possible tsunami. Deprived of shelter, sanitation, food, and water, according to the essay "Anniversary Blues," they had only "their dignity left intact" (Danticat, 2012, 21). Contributing to sorrow, according to her memoir "Look at Me" for the December 2013 issue of *Harper's* magazine, traditional funeral photographs disappeared in the cleanup.

Edwidge agreed to visit CNN's *Anderson Cooper 360°* to speak of "one of the darkest nights in our history" (Danticat, 2017, 27). She reported in an interview for *Arquitectonica* the survival of only 10–20 percent of *Léogâne,* which lay near the epicenter. Gradually, news reached her about the death of Cousin Maxo Dantica and his ten-year-old son Nozial and the entrapment of three other children in the family home. To ensure her own safety after flying to Haiti on February 4, she slept on a relative's roof amid the husks of recovered corpses. The world, meanwhile, pledged $9.9 billion in aid. Perhaps through "donor fatigue," the good-hearted followed through with less than ten percent of the amount to "people who are eager to get a foothold" (Danticat, 2012, 22).

See also Eight Days.

SOURCES

Cornish, Audie. "Award-Winning Author Recalls Past Experiences with Hurricanes in Native Haiti," *NPR Weekend Edition* (7 October 2016).

Danticat, Edwidge. "Anniversary Blues," *Progressive* 76:2 (10 January 2012): 20–22.

_____. *The Art of Death: Writing the Final Story.* Minneapolis, MN: Graywolf Press, 2017.

_____. "Color Blocking," *Arquitectonica,* https://www.interiorsandsources.com/article-details/articleid/15929/title/color-blocking-edwidge-danticat (1 July 2013).

_____. *Create Dangerously: The Immigrant Artist at Work.* New York: Vintage, 2010.

_____. "Flight," *New Yorker* 87:27 (5 September 2011): 32.

_____. *Haiti after the Earthquake* (audio). co-narrator. Prince Frederick, MD: HighBridge, 2011.

_____. "Haiti: Bloodied, Shaken—and Beloved," *Miami Herald* (17 January 2010).

_____. "Haiti Faces Difficult Questions Ten Years after a Devastating Earthquake," *New Yorker* (11 January 2020).

_____. "House of Prayer and Dreams," *Sojourners* 442:4 (April 2013): 38–39, 41–42.

_____. "In Flesh and Bone," *Tent Life: Haiti.* Brooklyn: Umbrage, 2011, 8–9.

_____. "Living and Loving through Tragedy," *Sojourners* 39:3 (March 2010): 10–11.

_____. "Look at Me," *Harper's* 327:1963 (December 2013): 64.

_____. "Turning the Page on Disaster," *Good Housekeeping* (January 2011).

_____. "We Have Stumbled, But We Will Not Fall," *Essence* 41:1 (May 2010): 100.

Mika, Kasia. "New Beginnings without New Heroes? 1791–1804 Haitian Revolution and the 2010 Earthquake in Nick Lake's *In Darkness* (2012)," *Karib–Nordic Journal for Caribbean Studies* 4:1 (1 November 2018).

Eight Days: A Story of Haiti

A miracle tale of resilience and courage, Edwidge's *Eight Days* pays tribute to qualities in island people, particularly the normal sharing of fun in the barber's household that instills character in their seven-year-old boy Junior, his younger sister Justine, and their playmate Oscar. The opening scene, a media interview with the protagonist, discloses in the boy's words an ability to grieve for his parents and sister, to cry for Oscar, and to set his mind free from a home collapsed by earthquake. The author stated on *NPR Morning Edition* her delight in basing creativity on memory as a source of world improvement.

Her invention shapes a potential tragedy into a glimpse of boyhood enthusiasm for life. In the style of Genesis 1 through 2:3, day by day, Junior escapes mentally to shoot marbles, play hide and seek, race bikes, and fly a kite. To his credit, he sings a solo with the Sainte Trinité children's choir, an outlet of an Episcopal music school, the oldest on the island, opened in Port-au-Prince in 1956. After the eight-day mindscape keeps Junior alive, the illustration pictures an ordinary barefoot boy facing a clutch of fourteen news reporters.

Realism in Play

Foreshadowing tragedy, Edwidge pictures Junior's pal Oscar joining an imaginary soccer game and dying suddenly, an omen on day five that some islanders cannot survive the impact. Junior allows himself an appropriate period of grief before returning to survival mode. Sibling joy on a rainy day unites Junior with sister Justine in splashing in puddles and catching drops in their mouths. In town on the Plain of Mars Plaza before the National Palace, the two bike around Belgian-trained sculptor Albert Mangonés's bronze statue of an unnamed maroon, a 1968 balletic icon of the Africans who fled bondage under French colonists. Alongside the powerful black liberator, the illustration pictures Justine on a bike with training wheels racing her older brother, who lets her win. A sweet mango on the seventh day anticipates the sweetness of liberation on the eighth.

By suggesting the transformation of real sense impressions into creative images, the author appears to rid Junior of debilitating fears. His agile inventiveness converts sounds of falling timbers and burning buildings, which he equates with the sparking and crackling of burning barbershop debris. To relieve him of hunger and thirst, Edwidge suggests memories of catching rain in an open mouth and eating pulpy fruit. The ennui of the house wreckage on his body for six days gives place to a bike adventure through the Port-au-Prince plaza, a familiar and reassuring playground that encourages him to stretch weary muscles in normal competition.

Kudos for the Author

Critical opinion backed the author's choice of topic. *The Routledge Handbook to the Culture and Media of the Americas* lauded Edwidge for creating a narrative format manifesting complicated feelings of the very young. *Kirkus* appreciated the affirmative tone, an asset for children trapped in natural misfortunes. In 2013, the author returned to social issues in her memoir "House of Prayer and Dreams" for *Sojourners*. Like Oscar and Junior, she had grown up in the squalor of Bel Air. Of "bittersweet years," she stated, "We children were experts in creating places of refuge in our imaginations, even when the world around us seemed to be falling apart" (Danticat, 2013, 41). To reprise memories of Haitian strife in her early years, she acknowledged coordinating the painful and funny with the dreamlike.

The child's version of terror, according to Sean P. Connors of the University of Arkansas and essayist Anna O. Sotter, proves that "literature for adolescents might be stylistically complex, that it might withstand rigorous critical scrutiny, and that it might set forth thoughtful social and political commentaries" on crisis and conflict, such as jailing and assassination at the core of *Mama's Nightingale, The Dew Breaker,* "Nineteen Thirty-Seven," and "Seven Stories" (Sotter & Connors, 2009, 63–64). Additional approval of Patricia A. Crawford at the University of Pittsburgh and Sherron Killingsworth Roberts, a professor at the University of Central Florida, cites aid in perception and coping with challenge as dual rationales for assigning literature about adversity.

See also Earthquake.

Sources

Crawford, Patricia A., and Sherron Killingsworth Roberts. "Literature as Support: Using Picture Books to Assist Young Children in Coping with Natural Disasters and Human Crises," *Assisting Young Children Caught in Disasters.* New York: Springer, 2018, 171–180.

Danticat, Edwidge. *The Dew Breaker. New York: Abacus, 2004.*

_____. *Eight Days: A Story of Haiti.* New York: Orchard Books, 2010.

_____. "House of Prayer and Dreams," *Sojourners* 442:4 (April 2013): 38–39, 41–42.

_____. "On the Day of the Dead," http://carboninnovations.net/node/3411, (6 September 2011).

Lee, Felicia. "Dark Tales Illuminate Haiti, Before and After Quake," *New York Times* (9 January 2011).

"Review: *Eight Days,*" *NPR Morning Edition* (9 September 2010).

Sotter, Anna O., and Sean P. Connors. "Beyond Relevance to Literary Merit: Young Adult Literature as 'Literature,'" *ALAN Review* 37 (Fall 2009): 62–67.

Erzulie

Still influenced by the Haitian Vodou panoply of her childhood, Edwidge stated curiosity and some envy of Erzulie. Literature romanticized the love goddess as a mulatto loa or deity of erotic intimacy, revenge, and resistance. She modeled the stereotype of womanly frippery derived from the self-important French colonists, who turned fashion into a global commodity. In lieu of a living mother, the tender/obdurate Venus figure protects Claire Narcis in the novel *Claire of the Sea Light,* a woman who gives her life for maternity. The loss echoes the depredations of slavery—of captive women forced to choose between motherhood and sexual bondage to a master.

A hybrid divinity, Erzulie Balianne (whale), a commander of the in-between, figures in the younger Claire Limyè Lanmè Faustin's round dance, a circle game that directs little girls' steps counterclockwise over the Atlantic toward the West African motherland. The children's chant honors Mami Wata (mother water), an Afro-Caribbean sea sprite who seizes swimmers and boaters and drowns them. In Haiti and Sierra Leone, the cross-bred godhead exalts immigrants who brave the sea, particularly slaves crossing the Atlantic over the Middle Passage and modern-day refugees like the radio announcer in "Children of the Sea" and Arnold, Paris, and Darline in "Without Inspection."

The Paradoxical Virgin

In earlier fiction, the author examines the dynamics of sexual demons in her contribution to Caribbean gothic. Sophie Caco Woods's household in *Breath, Eyes, Memory* maintains confidence in Erzulie. A transcendent counterpart to the loving, healing, maternal Virgin Mary of Roman Catholicism, Erzulie arrived in Hispaniola in 1517 with the first West African slaves, who revered her through sacrament and oral tradition. During sexual phobia group meetings, a Santerian priestess helps Sophie release her fears of coitus through transformative ritual. Sophie presents the statue of Erzulie that Grandmè Ifé Caco gave her in Haiti, a reunion of the protagonist with a maternal champion capable of playful passion, nurturing, and wonder. The figurine epitomizes the desirability and courage of a love goddess who spans all races, all ethnicities.

In girlhood, Sophie envisions the Virgin Mother as lavishly dressed, wise, and orthodox, but lacking the broad backstory of the independent Vodou all-healer and cosmic all-mother. She ponders the story of Erzulie's intervention in a woman's spontaneous bleeding and the mythic metamorphosis of a human female into a butterfly, a symbol of escape from pain and sorrow. Infatuated with the goddess Erzulie and her restorative powers, Sophie celebrates divine presence: "Even though she was far away, she was always with me. I could always count on her like one counts on the sun coming out at dawn" (Danticat, 1994, 59). As a vision of earth cycles, Erzulie takes on the mystique of Mother Nature and pairs with Martine Caco's corpse in a lavish display of burial clothes.

Female Disparities

Less legitimate, less pious than Jesus's ever-virgin mother, Erzulie embodies a fluid West African belief system that syncretizes libido and reproductive function. In *Create Dangerously,* the author characterized the heart-shaped *vèvè* emblem outlined on bare ground with cornmeal that summons Erzulie Fréda (cold-hearted Erzulie). Self-absorbed and alluring, she adheres to fewer moral dicta of innocence, virginity, purity, and submission, the themes of Edwidge's first book. From an African perspective, the love goddess exudes luxury, seduction, and jurisdiction over patriarchal males, who are often the progenitors of female miseries.

Unlike the gentle, long-haired Lasirèn, receiver of fishermen who die at sea in the novel *Claire of the Sea Light,* Erzulie possesses all avatars of womanhood. She is in one body a youthful beauty, haggard crone, and fertile darling—displaying none of the claustrophobic ideals and dry sexlessness of the Catholic virgin. From research at Loyola University, Raffaela N. Wilson contended, the triad's "relationship to one another is more reflective of the contentious relationships involved in Haiti's struggle for independence—Spanish/French, Europe/Africa, Catholic/Vodou and poor/elite" (Wilson, 2009, 23).

See also Vodou, Women.

Sources

Adisa, Opal Palmer. "Up Close and Personal," *African American Review* 43:2–3 (Summer/Fall 2009): 345–355.

Danticat, Edwidge. *Breath, Eyes, Memory.* New York: Soho Press, 1994.

_____. *Create Dangerously: The Immigrant Artist at Work.* New York: Vintage, 2010.

Dayan, Joan. "Erzulie: A Women's History of Haiti," *Research in African Literatures* 25:2 (Summer, 1994): 5–31.

Lyons, Bonnie. "Interview," *Contemporary Literature* 44:2 (Summer 2003): 182–198.

Montgomery, Maxine L. "A Lasiren Song for the Wonn: Edwidge Danticat's *Claire of the Sea Light* and the Legend of Mami Wata," *CLA Journal* 59:4 (June 2016): 316–329.

Wilson, Raffaela N. "Black Women and the Search for Spiritual Liberation," a graduate thesis submitted at the University of Georgia, 2009.

Everything Inside

Issued in Edwidge's fiftieth year, the third short fiction collection seasons small worlds with insight and grit. Radiating from one of her best titles, miniature scenarios expose startling, at times disturbing glimpses of volatility, heartbreak, and tragedy generated by secrecy and betrayal. According to author Achy Obejas, the writer examines these extremes with "a fierce forgiveness" of "our capacity to fall into the temptations of violence, of selfishness, of irrationality, and still, somehow, also be able to nourish and love" (Obejas, 2019, 67). Rather than chide humankind for faults, her stories urge readers to identify with needy souls and "to consider our own capacity for the unforgivable" (*ibid.*) The result is compassion and boundless forbearance.

In the essay "Love, Our Only True Adventure," the author celebrates short fiction anthologies for "the accumulation of encounters," the type of human gatherings that Geoffrey Chaucer, the father of the English language, introduced to Middle English in 1385 in the pilgrimage that shaped *The Canterbury Tales* (Danticat, 2020). For maximum profit from so diverse a compendium, she advised readers to "find rays of hope" in narratives by savoring them individually and bringing a personal perspective to the collection. Of the essence of short fiction, Marilou Sorensen, a reviewer of an anthology for *Deseret News,* values "particles of the characters and settings [that] remain in the reader's mind" (Sorensen, 1996).

Reviewers—*Booklist, Boston Globe, Esquire, Kirkus, Ms., New York Times Book Review, Oprah Magazine, Publishers Weekly*—admired the eight stories for their love triangles, soulful choices, unyielding dysfunction, and intuitive flashes of wisdom. Journalist Colette Bancroft of the *Tampa Bay Times* attributed success to the author's leaping into action with energized first sentences. NPR's Michael Schaub stressed the urgency, candor, and economy of diction. Humanist

Joanie Conwell reported for the *Los Angeles Review of Books* the existential solitude of people "exiled in their own suffering," a sequestering that echoes with anguish and bewilderment (Conwell, 2019). Bancroft took a more optimistic view: "Danticat's luckiest wanderers find their heart's home, wherever it may be" (Bancroft, 2019).

Dosas (2006)

Previously printed in the January 2006 issue of *Callaloo* as "Elsie" and, a year later, in *Sable,* the short story recurred in two collections—*One World Two* and *Tales of Two Americas.* The action sums up a rip-off that profanes character loyalties and trust—Elsie's distraction from Miami Shores home health duties by the phone demands of ex-husband Blaise for ransom funds to rescue his two-timing girlfriend Olivia. Mona, Elsie's employer, complains "about how much time you spend on the phone," a symbolic halving of attention between renal-failure patient Gaspard and an alleged kidnap victim in Haiti (Danticat, 2019, 30). Stowing everything inside, beneath a network of lies, a miscommunication that further muddies a two-nation crisis, Elsie cloaks her regret that Olivia has upended the triangle and stolen Blaise along with Elsie's savings.

Analysts hold no hope for the concluding dyad of Elsie and Dédé, a lackluster musician on the lookout for available sex. In a review for *Ploughshares,* critic Bailey Trela describes the original off-kilter threesome as a relationship further doomed by circumstance and betrayal. Aminatta Forna, in a critique for the *New York Times,* charged Elsie herself for extending compassion to two contemptible users. Forna blames "the unreliability of the human heart" for Elsie's effortless fall for Dédé, another fraud (Forna, 2019). Critic Renée Graham, a reviewer for the *Boston Globe*, highlights how the author "measures the fallibility of grace and … the myriad ways people disappoint" (Graham 2019, N10).

In the Old Days (2012)

A Haitian-American household severed by immigration after the 1986 fall of the 29-year Papa Doc and Baby Doc Duvalier regime, Nadia's family exists in splinters. Out of sight, Maurice Dejean, her dying father, ignores his 25-year-old daughter. As featured in the spring 2012 issue of *Callaloo* and the anthology *So Spoke the Earth: The Haiti I Knew, the Haiti I Know, the Haiti I Want to Know*, the New York high school English as a Second Language teacher oscillates between concern for an unknown parent and the nostalgic reminder of funereal traditions that conclude with a libation of rum, a sorrow dance, and the keening of family and friends.

Contributing paradox, the intervening introduction of Nadia to family friends and a meal of bread soup appear to waste the final moments of Maurice's life. Her complex leave-taking from an unknown "Papa" captures the enigma of obligation to a corpse (Danticat, 2019, 60). Surrounded by supportive friends, Nadia envies a second wife who experiences real heartache, symbolized by jingling bangles. When the story first appeared in *Callaloo,* it earned serious critical regard for depicting a messy mourning period fraught with regret.

The Port-au-Prince Marriage Special (2008)

A hard-edged face-off between cruelty and gullibility, the story of a mortally ill domestic gained fans when it appeared in *Conjunctions,* the October 2013 issue of *Ms,* and the anthology *Haiti Noir 2.* The narrative highlights life's end for Mélisande, an AIDS-riddled victim of a one-night stand, and exposes multiple frauds, beginning with a "fat, white nongovernmental-organization-affiliated" guest and a white Canadian quack (Danticat, 2019, 58). At a crux in her care, the foreign snake oil salesman takes the hotel worker's money for worthless pills.

Plenty of fault lies at hand. Aminatta Forna, a journalist for the *New York Times Book Review,* linked the double-dealing with "the actions of some foreign aid workers who added to the country's miseries after the earthquake" (Forna, 2019, 10). A more cutting hurt, the cook Babette's inability to sympathize with daughter Mélisande epitomizes reliance of Haitians on outsiders, who finance the bogus medical treatment. The plot failed to win applause from Joanie Conwell of the *Los Angeles Review of Books* for lacking intimacy and immediacy.

The Gift (2011)

A post-earthquake rendezvous in Miami, "The Gift" retitles the story "Bastille Day" from the June 2011 issue of *Caribbean Writer.* Alex Correia directed the stage version of *Bastille Day* at Purchase College in Harrison, New York, on September 27–October 5, 2019. In a sultry bar overlooking Biscayne Bay, the action mismatches the wealthy Thomas, a right-legged amputee, with his former mistress. He originally connected with the portrait artist and decorator Anika, a protagonist suitably called by a Scandinavian name meaning "grace," a gift you don't have to deserve.

Unliberated on the Fourth of July, Anika guilts herself for the affair with a married man who lost wife Dina and daughter Qadine in the cataclysm and for miscarrying Thomas's love child. As a gift after seven months of grief, she paints for Thomas a representation of his family as humanized birds. His rejection of the "crazy shit" symbolist painting over dinner turns her to solitude and wine (Danticat, 2019, 105). Her reflective mood evokes a chant honoring people lost in the 2010 earthquake and a child never born.

Hot-Air Balloons (1996)

The title *Everything Inside* proves its prophetic worth for Neah, daughter of a prestigious anthropologist from Trinidad, an intriguing protagonist introduced in the original story as Polly Sherlon for the June 19, 1996, *Granta,* and two anthologies—*The F Word, Contemporary UK Feminism* and *Immigrant Voices: 21st Century Stories.* In a post-journey meeting at a Miami college, Neah gains insight into Haitian have-nots from roommate Lucy, the light-bringer, who knows from an agrarian background the struggle of the island poor. Her parents labored as harvest pickers to aid Lucy's immigration in the U.S.

The key to Edwidge's story is extreme contrast—the wealthy and privileged college professor vs. Lucy's parents, field workers. In an "aha" moment, Neah, bearing a form of "new" as her name, gains from Lucy a greater appreciation of privilege and the self-indulgent volunteering for Leve (lift), a nonprofit rape crisis center. The story illustrates Edwidge's suppression of action for the sake of character development and the theme of nature vs. nurture.

Sunrise, Sunset (2017)

A fitful narrative from the September 2017 *New Yorker* and repeated the next month in "The Writer's Voice" overflows with tri-generational identities. Edwidge's touching story juxtaposes two women beset by mental strain. An infant baptism contrasts Carole and daughter Jeanne with the reactions of husbands Victor and James, seven-month-old Jude, pastor Paul, childhood friend Jeanne, sister-in-law Zoe, mother-in-law Grace, and godfather Marcos. The fulsome cast enhances a climactic scene in which hands reach for Carole and rescue the grandson she threatens to drop from a balcony. In the resolution, her retreat into mental fog illustrates the blur of senility that precedes her custody in an institution cut off from family. The unavoidable end to reason and agency suggests the dependence of Blanche Dubois in Tennessee Williams's play *A Streetcar Named Desire* on the "kindness of strangers." Ironically for Carole, her family already seem like aliens.

Seven Stories (2014)

An allegorical story-within-a-story of hidden sacrifice at Maafa, a coastal Caribbean village named for the African Holocaust, the best of Edwidge's entries carefully delineates the parameters of the "bubble," the protagonist's term for the privileged life (Danticat, 2019, 183). The narrative recounts an elite wedding between the drolly named "Finance" and "Olympic Runner" that elicits high-flown oratory by Gregory Murray, a West Indian prime minister. Edwidge chose alternate names—Jess and Marlene Boyer—for characters from the original story, "Quality Control," issued in the *Washington Post Magazine* November 5, 2014.

Companions in Brooklyn at age seven, Callie Morrissete and magazine author Kimberly Boyer stir memories of an underworld cabal causing an assassin to gun down Callie's father, Prime Minister Charles Morrissete. In her adult friendship with Kim, Callie divulges that her morally complex mother paid for the family's exile in the United States by granting sexual favors to border officials. The secret poisons household relations, causing the prime minister's widow to recede into the background. Jeopardizing the next generation and possibly sabotaging her marriage to Greg Murray, Callie resolves to remain childless.

Kimberly draws inferences from a collection of Arawak, Carib, and Taino huts and from the "glass-shard-capped walls" separating villas and palacios from tin shacks in shantytown (*ibid.*, 170). Bits of description add capitalistic interest in the copper, gold, and silver that enrich the terrain. Callie's pristine collection of "taffeta, chiffon, brocade, damask, and gingham" ribbons, like snippets of the past, betoken elements of a life never fully enjoyed (*ibid.*, 190). She describes living in a "castle" as existing with "grown-ups with guns" securing the family's safety (*ibid.*, 168). Paradoxically, a security guard killed Callie's father. The story brings out of the shadows the widow, Mrs. Morrissete, who shrinks away from false rumors that Callie shared her sexual martyrdom.

Without Inspection (2018)

A mythic tragedy on a par with Ovid's "Daedalus and Icarus," the final short story focuses on the ambiguities of diaspora, especially for low-wage laborers who perform dangerous work with slipshod safety devices. In 2009, Edwidge published the poem "Plunging" in *Caribbean Writer* and the story "Without Inspection" in the May 2018 *New Yorker* and the September/October 2019 edition of *Poets & Writers*. She based the visceral image of a laborer's plummet into wet cement at Bal Harbour, one of Florida's chic enclaves outside North Miami. The media account listed his wallet contents—photos of a daughter and two one-dollar bills. She issued the poem

with woodcuts by Gaylord Shanilec looking out a high-rise window at the sea, the ambiguous source of refuge and death for immigrants.

The story gained attention for its slo-mo style when it appeared in the *New Yorker.* Lacking suspense as to the cause of the refugee Arnold's death, the narrative relies on irony. For Arnold, a preference for freedom from affluence precedes his unexpected loosening from safety gear that had kept him safe on scaffolding surrounding a forty-eight-floor luxury hotel. By contrasting the sirens of police and coast guardians arriving to take him to Krome incarceration center, Edwidge develops the quick rescue that saves Arnold from helicopters, cop cars, and police dogs.

Darline, the volunteer refugee salvager, connects with Arnold verbally by relating her own experience of arriving in Miami by sea and choosing to save son Paris from drowning rather than to rescue her husband. In the final 6.5 seconds of consciousness down the 500-foot tumble, Arnold exults in freedom, but recoils from death. He relives her frequent singing of "Latibonit O," a tune honoring sundown in the style of the Neapolitan folk tune "O Sole Mio," and wills his spirit to communicate with Darline and Paris. His unselfish farewell to earth hopes for the best for all victims, especially those who make it to the beach.

With homage to the author who "[lays] waste to readers' hearts," novelist Jenny Shank, book critic for the Minneapolis *Star Tribune,* credits tenderhearted characters with being "relentlessly all-in" (Shank, 2019). Made worthy by their bold risk taking, each resonates with unexceptional foibles, all common to humankind, from self-doubt in "Sunrise, Sunset" to credulity in "Dosas." Negative reviews listed heavy-handed realism and despair as downers for narratives that tend to illuminate characters in the act of making imprudent choices. A more damning complaint, the replication of Edwidge's stories published elsewhere as early as 1996 leave open to question the author's reason for repeats of published works and changes to names and plots. Despite some reader disappointment and confusion about narrative resolutions, critics vary on choosing their favorites among the eight stories, some listing the very titles others disliked.

SOURCES

Bancroft, Colette. "Review: *Everything Inside*," *Tampa Bay Times* (28 August 2019).

Chen, Karissa. "Edwidge Danticat Wants More Haitian Storytellers" (30 September 2019): *electricliterature.com/edwidge-danticat-wants-more-haitian-storytellers/*

Conwell, Joanie. "Sunrise over Maafa: On Edwidge Danticat's *Everything Inside*," *Los Angeles Review of Books* (18 September 2019).

Danticat, Edwidge. *Everything Inside*. New York: Knopf, 2019.

_____. "Love, Our Only True Adventure," (1 August 2020): https://hello-sunshine.com/post/love-our-only-true-adventure.

_____. "Plunging," *Caribbean Writer* 23 (2009); St. Paul, MN: Midnight Paper Sales, 2009.

Forna, Aminatta. "Review: *Everything Inside*," *New York Times* (27 August 2019).

_____. "Motherland," *New York Times Book Review* (15 September 2019): 10.

Graham, Renée. "Danticat's New Stories Are Not," *Boston Globe* (1 September 2019): N10.

Obejas, Achy. "Bearing the Unforgivable," *World Literature Today* 93:1 (Winter 2019); 66–67.

Schaub, Michael. "Coming to Terms with Loss and Grief in Gorgeous *Everything Inside*," *NPR* (29 August 2019).

Shank, Jenny. "Review: *Everything Inside*," [Minneapolis] *Star Tribune* (29 August 2019): E8.

Sorensen, Marilou. "Book Crackles with Haiti's Flavor, Tradition," *Deseret News* (20 February 1996).

Wells, Leslie. "Edwidge Danticat in Conversation at Purchase College," *Riverdale Press* (27 September 2019).

The Farming of Bones

An historical novel set during the Spanish Civil War of 1936–1939, Edwidge's Caribbean fiction *The Farming of Bones* focuses on archival silence on a bloodbath in the Caribbean. She protests an act of nationalistic ethnic cleansing known as the "parsley massacre," which histories of the Dominican Republic omit. Her counter-archive exposes the racism and xenophobia of Dominican Generalissimo Rafael Leonidas Trujillo Molina's slaughter on October 2, 1937, of 30,000 black Haitian peasants by carbine, club, bayonet, and machete. According to *el jefe's* rationale, the mass murder ostensibly retaliated against blacks for farm thievery and cattle rustling. Days of nonstop killing forced the Massacre River's current to "engulf hundreds and hundreds of corpses" and created what the author later called "a river filled with ghosts" (Danticat, 2005, 8, 7). Ironically, Trujillo had to deceive biographers about his black grandmother.

The novel appeared in French translation under the title *La Récolte Douce des Larmes* (The Sweet Crop of Tears), a reference to the importance of Haitian laborers to the cane harvest and the aggrandizing of European parvenus on the profitable sugar market and its byproducts, molasses and rum. Cane farming began in 1493 after Christopher Columbus introduced the profitable plant on Hispaniola. The author returned to the event in a 2014 interview with Dominican-American author Junot Díaz, "The Dominican Republic and Haiti: A Shared View from the Diaspora." She asserted that Trujillo killed Haitians and "wiped out several generations of Dominican families" because of their dark skin (Danticat, 2014, 31). Those who survived the death squads Edwidge esteemed as "the spiritual children of the river" (Danticat, 2005, 9).

The Cover-Up

Inspired by Adolf Hitler's racism as expressed in his memoir *Mein Kampf*,

Trujillo corroborated with Nazi claims that "All who are not of a good race are chaff" (Hitler, 1998, 17). The generalissimo attempted to shift blame for his *antihatianismo* to Dominican farmers by beginning the Guardia's murders with machetes, a laborer's tool, rather than military Krag rifles. Resolute in his ultranationalism to exterminate black contaminants from the populace, he remained in power with his henchmen until his assassination on May 30, 1961. Researcher Amy Novak, an English professor at the University of California, contended a disturbing erasure of fact: "No documentation with direct references to the massacre—before, during, or after it—has been found in Dominican archives" (Novak, 2006, 96).

The mysterious act of mass murder that targeted even dark-skinned Hispanic Dominicans earned for the eastern half of the island the name "country of death" (Danticat, 1998, 236). Devastation of black lives prompted no outcry from the U.S., Dominican Republic, or Haiti. Only a few publications—*Collier's, Nation, New Republic*—reported the butchery. Anthropologist Harold Courlander and lecturer Henry C. Wolfe made the only expert report in "Not in the Cables: Massacre in Santo Domingo," issued in *New Republic* on November 24, 1937. The article stated that volunteers aided deputies in rounding up Haitians at Dajabon and killed them "without respect to sex or age" and tossed fifty more into the sea at Monte Christi (Courlander, 1937, 67). Some 400 lay buried in a trench. Nearly two decades later, *Life* magazine conducted an investigation for its February 24, 1957, issue. However, individual reshaping of lives and voices relating heinous truths helped the fictional refugees to recover and aid society in reclaiming order and human rights. Edwidge won an American Book Award for candor and kudos from *Newsweek, Nation, New Yorker, Wall Street Journal, New York Times, Publishers Weekly,* and the *Boston Globe*.

Preview of Catastrophe

The novel opens in fictional Alegría on August 30, 1937, with the birth of a twin boy and girl to Valencia and Pico Duarte, a maternal dynamic that sets the tone and atmosphere for the post-traumatic rebirth in the conclusion. At the unexpected demise of neonate Rafael "Rafi" Duarte, Valencia insists on painting a whorl of rainbow colors on his infant coffin, a use of her anguish for creative purpose. Rather than welcome new life, Pico buries the child's layette, a futile means of ridding the parents of grief. The loss of a day-old boy intersects with a traffic accident that kills a mill worker, Joël Raymond Loner, son of the mask maker Old Kongo. An interpolated incident describes the drowning of herbalists Antoine and Irelle Pradelle Desír, a nightly phantasm that disturbs Amabelle's sleep. To her lover, cane laborer Sebastien Onius, the couple seems like voyageurs (wayfarers), a designation that proves prophetic during the coming pogrom.

A rumor of the eradication of Haitians circulates among cane workers, who sip coffee offered by Valencia's staff. Amid bone-shaped cane, armed laborers form a night brigade and post sentries, an ineffectual black police force organized too late to halt carnage. At the Duarte house, Pico seems anxious about his next military assignment, which begins with boarding a truck convoy of Guardia (police). Dr. Javier confirms a radio broadcast of the Generalissimo's orders to annihilate Haitians, a bold act that Amabelle interprets as one of the "grand fantasies of presidents wanting the whole island to themselves" (Danticat, 1998, 138). Sebastien rebukes her for trusting the Hispanic upper class, especially Valencia, who lives the lie that her husband is merely obeying military duties, one of the veils that Germans drew over SS atrocities at Auschwitz and Buchenwald.

Depiction of domestic placidity, which precedes military action in *Anacaona* and *Brother, I'm Dying,* balances the home life of *The Farming of Bones* with unspeakable bloodletting and nightmares in the last half. Suspense and literary conflict heighten as military trucks speed by the Duarte residence and characters determine their next moves. When Pico's troops arrive and hold the rebel Unèl's forces at gunpoint, Doña Eva begs for mercy for her son, Dr. Javier. The maid Juana describes the situation as "losing our country to madmen," a frequent descriptor of the island's chaotic history under the Duvaliers and Trujillo (*ibid.,* 153). Contributing to the peasant reaction is the nonsense that "the Generalissimo has not said that he caused the killing, but he agreed to give money to affected persons," a recompense to laborers earning twenty cents per day impeded by bureaucratic fraud (*ibid.,* 231).

Shared Terror

While uniformed terminators spread over the killing field, victim dependence on rumor lessens the accuracy of reported atrocities, the torching of workers' homes, and the sheltering of black Haitians at sugar mills. As the American South discovered before the Civil War, masters waver in their reliance on black staff, who may have switched allegiance from white households to rebellious peons. In search of Sebastien, Amabelle follows friend Yves Rapadou into the mountains and hears fellow escapee Tibon's account of cliff murders six at a time at La Romana, where he manages to dive into the Atlantic Ocean and hide in an underwater cave.

For Amabelle, the collapse and explosion of falling stars results in darkness, the fate of Haitians ensnared by Trujillo's Guardia and their civilian volunteers. In a positive trope, the text hails strangers who form *ad hoc* fugitive communities, organize a night watch, and protect sleepers during a brief hiatus in terror. In *The Art of Death,* Edwidge confided how one fictional voice carried the whole load of history: "I had to count on Amabelle's singular tale, her microscopic truth, to tell a much larger story" (Danticat, 2017, 75).

The breakup of on-the-road camaraderie separates Haitians from two Dominican sisters, who could pass the linguistic test of pronouncing *perejil* (parsley) with a distinctive Spanish rolled r. Like the use of the Hebrew term shibboleth (corn or stream) in Judges 12:6 as a password to identify Ephraimite insurgents from the west into Gilead northeast of the Jordan River, the 1937 Dominican genocide hinged on survivors saying *perejil,* a one-word determiner of workers' future. Beyond the perils of crossing the watery border into Haiti, Amabelle must combat a legal obstacle—the folk methods of judging land ownership and birthrights in a place where deeds and birth certificates are rare. The absence of corroborative papers leaves in limbo a chronicle of Trujillo's barbarity.

Recapping the Unspeakable

Urgency overtakes Edwidge's narrative after Amabelle and her companions view the remains of twelve Haitian traders hanged from bullwhips. In Dajabón near the northeastern Haitian border, the runaways witness gleeful Hispanic persecution of black cane workers with machete slices, kicks to the mouth and torso, and parsley stuffed into Haitian mouths to suffocate victims. A heavy irony accompanies the shooting of Wilner and drowning of Odette, Amabelle and Yves's saviors. The rapid turnaround, like sunrise, retrieves the protagonists from the dark and places them in healing hands in tent hospitals treating burns, fevers, hysteria, and wrenched bones. Amabelle imagines the wraith of her mother, Irelle Pradelle, a loving comforter. Reveling in life, the survivors look back on regrets and anticipate the best to come—hugs from relatives and lovers, domino competitions, and cockfights, a bloody scrimmage of poultry for amusement.

In homage to the enduring human voice, Edwidge's historical novel acclaims eyewitnesses and their panicky scraps of story about kin and unknown casualties. The text exposes villainies as random as the shooting of mounts on a horse farm, the execution of seven hundred souls lying prone in a courtyard, hovering vultures scenting death, and the drowning of two hundred Haitians off the pier at Monte Cristi, a sea town named for God's son. Dialogue, rich in aphorism, credits patriotic speakers for their thanks to historic heroes—Toussaint L'Ouverture, Jean Jacques Dessalines, and Henri Christophe—and cites their panic that liberty bears no guarantees. Among Haitians north of Cap Haïtien, the *rescapés* (returning émigrés) stand out as "*those* people, the nearly dead," whom the upper class scorns (Danticat, 1998, 218).

The Aftermath

While residing in Cap Haïtien, returnees anticipate enrichment from Trujillo's offer of a settlement of $525,000 in cash. After graft usurps the funds, Amabelle struggles to profit from communal commemoration, a ritual of mourning that replaces the flimsy investigation of Trujillo. In recall of her parents' death, she seems to float in memory, "grieving for who I was, and even more for

what I've become" (Danticat 1998, 2). Like poet Randall Jarrell's narrator in "The Woman at the Washington Zoo," Amabelle seems to beg, "You know what I was, you see what I am: change me, change me!" (Jarrell, 2007, 72). The lack of compensation suggests that money, however ample, would make little difference in the rehabilitation of *rescapés* like Amabelle and Yves.

Amabelle's distraught spirit symbolizes the river, dividing country from country and the living from the dead. She copes with anatomical evidence of aging—traumatic crippling in her knee, side, lip and jaws, buzzing ears, and rabid dreams that connote a living hell from wounds she can't acknowledge. In the analysis of Heather Hewett, a gender specialist at the State University of New York, the "experience of living in a changed body" inhibits her moving beyond the past (Hewett, 2006, 128). Her anguished spirit must revisit the site of massacre, which her mind has never eluded. Identifying with the dead and berating herself for Odette's drowning, Amabelle searches for Sebastien Onius and learns of his execution-style murder along with sister Mimi in a courtyard during Trujillo's *el corte* (the cutting), a euphemism for race extermination.

Corrosive Memories

The author indicates that words appear ineffectual against visual and auditory memories. While she and Yves contemplate the profits from selling beans and sewing, a symbol of reuniting a fragmented life, she declares anxiety a permanent facet of her existence—"I couldn't trust time or money to make me forget" (*ibid.*, 244). She longs to cleanse herself of the past through repetition of sterile routines that blot out regrets. The author inserts a Trujillan mantra forced on

Father Jacques Romain in prison exonerating Dominicans from eradicating black Haitians. The priest intones the words of brainwashing: "We, as Dominicans, must have our separate traditions and our own ways of living," a preposterous pretext for genocide (*ibid.,* 259).

After Trujillo's death on May 30, 1961, nearly a quarter century after the massacre, Haitians dance in the streets and invite the fictional Amabelle to state late-in-life testimonials. The narrative involves her first in sewing projects and develops into a pilgrimage back to Alegría via an illicit courier in a jeep, a subtle jab at the U.S. and its 1965 marine invasion. At Valencia Duarte's new residence, the two share their memories of powerlessness during the massacre, when Pico's wife hid vulnerable Haitians while he perpetrated official depravity. Central to her marriage is falsifying Pico's role in genocide, especially the roundup of Dr. Javier and the Duartes' household staff. On return to the Massacre River, Amabelle halts to float in the warm current, a recreation of her flight from death by merging with water like a fetus in amniotic fluid awaiting birth.

The author epitomized memory and information in her own family destroying racial myth and lies. In a 2015 interview with journalist Dana De Greff of the *Miami New Times,* Edwidge charged the Dominican government with "trying to erase this whole segment of history and population ... even before they had this huge recruitment of people to work on the sugarcane fields" (De Greff, 2015). The labor market wanted "your blood and sweat for our business, for our construction, for our sugarcane, but we just don't want you to live among us" (*ibid.*). Critic Megan Feifer, a specialist in women's issues at Medaille College in Buffalo, New York, endorsed Edwidge's effort to examine an historic cataclysm and to summarize how survivors "begin ... coming to terms with the aftereffects of history" through personal recuperation (Feifer, 2020, 35).

See also Fear, Mothers, Music, Noirism, Violence.

Sources

Clitandre, Nadège T. *Edwidge Danticat: The Haitian Diasporic Imaginary.* Charlottesville: University of Virginia Press, 2018.

Courlander, Harold, and Herbert David Croly. "Not in the Cables," *New Republic* (24 November 1937): 67.

Danticat, Edwidge. *The Art of Death: Writing the Final Story.* Minneapolis, MN: Graywolf Press, 2017.

_____. "The Dominican Republic and Haiti: A Shared View from the Diaspora," *Americas Quarterly* 8:3 (Summer 2014): 28–35.

_____. *The Farming of Bones.* New York: Penguin, 1998.

_____. *Massacre River.* preface. New York: New Directions, 2005, 7–10.

De Greff, Dana. "Author Edwidge Danticat on the Dominican Republic: 'Government Is Trying to Erase a Whole Segment of History,'" *Miami New Times* (12 October 2015).

Feifer, Megan. "The Remembering of Bones," *Palimpsest* 9:1 (2020): 35–49.

Hewett, Heather. "At the Crossroads: Disability and Trauma in *The Farming of Bones,*" *MELUS* 31 (Fall 2006): 123–145.

Hitler, Adolf. *Mein Kampf.* Boston: Houghton Mifflin, 1998.

Jarrell, Randall. *Selected Poems.* New York: Farrar, Straus and Giroux, 2007.

Mirabal, Nancy Raquel. "Dyasporic Appetites and Longings," *Callaloo* 30:1 (Winter 2007): 26–39, 410.

Novak, Amy. "'A Marred Testament': Cultural Trauma and Narrative in Danticat's *The Farming of Bones,*" *Arizona Quarterly* 62:4 (2006): 93–120.

Wucker, Michele. "Race & Massacre in Hispaniola," *Tikkun* 13:6 (November/December 1998): 61–63.

The Farming of Bones Genealogy

Multiple ethnic and clan lines crisscross *The Farming of Bones* with conflicting loyalties and disintegrating safety nets. In the upper class compound, Pico

Duarte responds to dictator Rafael Leonidas Trujillo's annihilation plan while Papi, Pico's benign father-in-law, listens to radio broadcasts about the Spanish Civil War and relives his irredeemable part in slaughter:

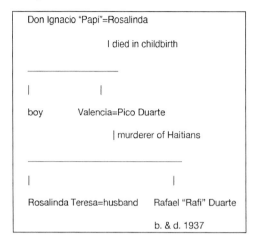

In conjunction with the family sorrow at losing a male heir of the Duarte family, workers respond to the heartless death and abandonment of Joël Raymond Loner, a black cane worker: His father's name—Kongo—epitomizes the West African identity of peons living apart from Hispanic society in the Dominican Republic:

```
      Grandfather      Grandfather
      mask    |              |
      maker   |              |
              |              |
      Joël Raymond Loner=/=Félice
```

From two generations in the past, Old Kongo discredits Joel's lover Félice as the granddaughter of a chicken thief, a trivial crime that keeps the aged father from prizing her as a consoler during his mourning. With the iconic name "Loner," Joël lies buried in an undisclosed spot that Kongo chooses. The protagonist's family tree associates her with two mother figures, both of whom personify the rigors of sorrow

During Amabelle Desír's futile search for her lover, she seeks strength and reassurance from two parents, Man Rapadou, the widow of a murdered man, and Sebastien's mother Man Denise. Paradoxically, Amabelle returns to Valencia, her Hispanic mistress, to clarify events and rid herself of grief. Of the indifference of the island elite, historian Elizabeth Abbott, dean of women at the University of Toronto, referred to the aftermath as "a shame too great to dwell on" (Abbott, 2011, 67).

Sources

Abbott, Elizabeth. *Haiti: A Shattered Nation*. New York: Overlook, 2011.
Clitandre, Nadège T. *Edwidge Danticat: The Haitian Diasporic Imaginary*. Charlottesville: University of Virginia Press, 2018.
Danticat, Edwidge. *The Farming of Bones*. New York: Penguin, 1998.
Feifer, Megan. "The Remembering of Bones," *Palimpsest* 9:1 (2020): 35–49.

Fear

In Edwidge's stories, terrified people flee their fears through physical liberation as well as through dreams, insanity, sexuality, storytelling, and imaginary self-liberation, the retreat of Junior in *Eight Days* and the playacting of Callie Morrissete, wife and hostess of Prime Minister Gregory Murray in "Seven Stories." Of personal terrors, she exposed in *The Art of Death* a literary method of grasping loss: "I want to both better understand death and offload my fear of it, and I believe reading and writing can help" (Danticat, 2017, 7). Two contrasting escape plans in *Claire of the Sea Light* depict traumas of the Haitian underclass. Fisherman Nozias Faustin must find more lucrative employment outside Ville Rose and settle seven-year-old Claire Limyè Lanmè Faustin with a foster mother before he can leave. At the same time, beautician Flore Voltaire, the mother of Pamaxime, illegitimate son of Max Ardin, Jr., receives enough bribe money from the boy's wealthy Ardin grandfather to migrate along with her mother and son. She intends a secret getaway, a means of conquering jitters of Pamaxime's capture by the rapist's father. Spanish reviewer Silvia Martinez-Falquina, a Romance language lecturer at the University of Zaragoza, described the shackling of characters in hurtful and terrorizing recall, causing them to "[remain] frozen and separated from 'normal' memories," the main reason for Max, Jr.'s, attempted suicide and Claire's flight toward the Anthère lighthouse (Martinez-Falquina, 2015, 837). The final glimpse of the Ville Rose seaside community implies that unity among residents eases dread.

For aristocratic wife Valencia Duarte, calming husband Pico's fear for her safety alone at home in *The Farming of the Bones* involves rifle practice with calabashes as targets, a foreshadowing of the Trujillo massacre plot. The contrast with Amabelle Desír's hellish retreat over the Massacre River elevates the persecuted Haitian maidservant for banding with other black refugees and successfully fording the boundary against a swift current. Because of her love for Sebastien Onius, anxiety strikes most heavily when she questions others about his whereabouts. Edwidge pictures the courageous house servant sinking into tears or sleep, her only escapes from worry for her lover. In contrast, Sebastien's friend Yves finds no respite for his inability to escape fright and save Sebastien, Mimi, Dr. Javier, and two priests. Yves speaks an existential truth—that the more slaughter he views, the more he wants to survive, a telling

self-awareness of someone who barely reaches Haiti alive.

Mind over Panic

The author epitomizes the role of the mind in mitigating terror, a retreat for Romain's mother in "Monkey Tails," for investigative reporter Jean Léopold Dominique in *The Art of Death,* and for the cornered minister and his attacker in "The Dew Breaker." For the girl in *The Last Mapou,* unease about Grann is not surprising in a child who realizes the fragility of old people. Rather than obsess over a limited time on earth, Grann involves her granddaughter in a creation myth that aggrandizes *mapou* (kapok) trees. By allying the loss of a dying mapou with valuable sources of wood, medicines, seeds, and habitats for bats and honeybees, Grann suggests a beneficial halt to deforestation, a modern crisis in Haiti. By turning the girl into the next crop of storytellers, Grann's narration reshapes fear of death into activism on behalf of nature.

Other fictional characters rely on strength of mind in times of imminent death. In the young adult novel *Untwine,* the mental transport of sixteen-year-old Giselle Boyer eases her trauma of misidentification during a semi-coma. To channel energy toward self-reclamation, she directs mental powers toward wiggling her toes. Similarly ephemeral, in the short story "Dream of the Butterflies," the flights of many-hued wings relieve a mother's panic at random urban gunfire against her frail hut. For Oscar and Junior, earthquake victims in *Eight Days,* retreat into imaginary playtime keeps Junior alive until rescue. For a coming of age ritual in *Anacaona,* the title figure combats fear of swollen legs and dwindling strength by fasting while soaking in herbal dressings. The combined efforts restore her vigor for a unique dance to impress prestigious visitors. The tenuous moment in her maturation precedes an ethnic horror in the development of the Western Hemisphere—the genocide of island Taino in 1493 by Genoan navigator Christopher Columbus and his Spanish conquistadors.

Looming Perils

In *Brother, I'm Dying*, a twenty-first-century terror dominates the narrative of Uncle Joseph Nosius Dantica's imprisonment in Miami in October 2004. Incarceration follows days of stumbling through bullet-ridden neighborhoods in Bel Air, a Post-au-Prince slum, to elude murderous gangs. Upon his death in U.S immigration custody, the authorities agree to let his son Maxo view Joseph's body at the morgue, but urge Edwidge to respect the fragility of her unborn fetus by avoiding a grisly sight. She stated her opinion on seeing a corpse: "Of the many ways that death might transform the love that the living had experienced, one of them should not be fear" (Danticat, 2007, 249). Against advice, she surveyed the results of electroshock and autopsy on Joseph and summarized the changes in his expression as suffering "a horrible nightmare," an image of callous treatment in a public institution (*ibid.,* 250).

Courageously, Joseph's niece speaks truth to power. Of U.S. President Donald Trump's executive order of January 25, 2017, on deporting immigrants and expanding the list of individuals affected, for the first time, she observed anxiety in Miami's Little Haiti. Cowering from newly tripled U.S. Immigration and Customs Enforcement (ICE) patrols like the one that entraps Saya's mom, a fictional restaurant worker in *Mama's Nightingale,* the author professed: "I've never seen people so afraid since the election.

They're afraid they're going to be picked up on their way to work" (Ukani, 2017). Edwidge characterized the president's language as hostile to black immigrant females and disruptive to small countries in the Caribbean and Central and South America. The day before the election of Joe Biden, she issued in the *Miami Herald* "Be the Vote for Immigrant Families under Threat by the Trump Administration."

SOURCES

Alexandre, Sandy, and Ravi Y. Howard. "Interview," *Journal of Caribbean Literature* 4:3 (Spring 2007): 161–174.

Danticat, Edwidge. *The Art of Death: Writing the Final Story.* Minneapolis, MN: Graywolf Press, 2017.

_____. "Be the Vote for Immigrant Families under Threat by the Trump Administration," *Miami Herald* (1 November 2020).

_____. *Brother, I'm Dying.* New York: Vintage, 2007.

_____. *Claire of the Sea Light.* New York: Vintage, 2013.

Martinez-Falquina, Silvia. "Postcolonial Trauma Theory in the Contact Zone: The Strategic Representation of Grief in Edwidge Danticat's *Claire of the Sea Light,*" *Humanities* 4:4 (2015): 834–860.

Ukani, Alisha. "Language and Activism," *Harvard Political Review* (26 March 2017).

Folklore

The reverence of Edwidge's characters toward inherited fable and peasant lore elevates a network of ritual narratives, notably, the naming of Gaëlle Lavaud's baby girl after the folkloric Sor Rose, black mother of Haiti in *Claire of the Sea Light;* the singing of "Latibonit O," a folksong about sickness and death in "Without Inspection"; and the union of couples and the burying of umbilical cords under the kapok tree in *The Last Mapou.* In *Create Dangerously,* the wearing of red bras by nursing mothers keeps deceased infants from trying to suckle. An historic event, the burning at the stake in January 1758 in Cap-Français of the Maroon hero Makandal, concludes in a phantasm after he shapeshifts into "a million fireflies," a mystic foreshadowing of revolution to come (Danticat, 2010, 16). In her evaluation of writing about mortality, the author also developed the family tree of Baron Samedi with his wife, Gran Brigit, a Haitian death loa syncretized from Irish myth. A local tale of a disembodied voice from a soursop tree transformed Brigit into a manifestation of charity toward the underclass.

The author's canon incorporates ancient oral narratives about specters and visions with recent catastrophes. A retrospect on 9/11/2001 reviewed the death of Jamaican-Costa Rican sculptor Michael Rolando Richards in the collapse of Tower One of the World Trade Center. The author pondered Richards's art works and their entwined themes of flight and death. She wondered whether precognition warned the artist of disaster and alerted him to exit "his earthly body" and fly away like the Africans in myth (*ibid.*, 124). Her curiosity suggests a mind receptive to the supernatural, especially images of flight.

The violation of time and place in mystic stories suggests acceptance of the abstruse in service to human emotion. In the aftermath of the murder of activist Jean Léopold Dominique at a radio station ambush, family spread his ashes from a calabash onto the river at the Artibonite Valley in western Haiti. Peasants reported a myth that he had visited them at the river and at the coffee plantations in the high country. Out of devotion, they revered his sharing their homes, planting, and harvesting, even though he was in Port-au-Prince at the time and could not have toured the region. Nonetheless, "he had already become a legend," evidence of delusions of a hero honoring farmers (Danticat, 2010, 52).

Storied Lore

Fragments of oral narrative impact the essay "Plantains, Please," in which the fruit appeared in Indu legend as Eden's forbidden fruit. Anne Bienaimé, a fanatical Catholic in "The Book of Miracles," spends Christmas Eve fantasizing about kneeling animals, pealing bells, heavenly gates, and flames blinking like Bethlehem's star. Giselle Boyer, the sixteen-year-old twin survivor of a car crash in *Untwine*, hears the Russian tale of the Slavic firebird ringing in her head as she ponders the rejuvenating water of life and her sister Isabelle's demise. Memories of a sixteenth birthday at a nature preserve in Mexico reprise an Aztec belief that monarch butterflies host the souls of deceased children fluttering back to life. The legend consoles parents that their children have hope of resurrection with wings. In each instance, Edwidge exonerates the believer for swallowing occult motifs to satisfy human need.

Of such oral culture, the author declared, "Stories, whether within the family of folktales, or just spirituality and rituals, are so important to survival, to continuity" and to human connections (Gleibermann, 2019, 68). Inscrutable blends of religion with superstition explain sun showers as the devil beating his wife and marrying his daughter and, in "Seven Stories," accounts for gifts to children on Three Kings' Day, the acts of an angel who refused to accompany the magi. One tale in *After the Dance* describes Sejourne Cave, a 127-meter root cellar in Jacmel, as a passageway to anywhere in Haiti. A melancholy island story identifies the *sabliye* palmetto with forgetting the past, a mental purge forced on African slaves who walk in its shade. Another places Jesus's mother at his burial place, where her tears formed "flowers on the crown of the Virgin Mary," vines covering tombstones (Danticat, 2002, 29). The sentimental connection between Joseph's wife and weeping reminds the devout of the parent/son connection of a holy martyr—God's son—to an earthly mother, a common subject in fresco, sculpture, and painting.

Haitian Lore

Just as stories of Jesus's crucifixion reiterated the end of his human existence, the writer promoted storytelling for preparing audiences to expect inevitable changes, particularly the coming of age of a Taino *cacica* (ruler) in *Anacaona* and the maturing of the title figure in the French fairy tale *Célimène*. In the fable "Travelling" for the *UN Chronicle,* Edwidge recounted a cautionary tale from storyteller Diane Wolkstein's collection "The Magic Orange Tree." The open-ended narrative tells of the migration of a turtle and birds from a hostile environment. She reformulated the standard moral to view the destruction of natural habitats and depleted resources from the ecosystem, a theme that dominates *The Last Mapou* and Edwidge's survey of the pine forest in *After the Dance.*

A resilient city, "The Cap" (Cap-Haïtien) recovered so many times from fire that folk tales connected to its history. French colonial planters reputedly lay buried alongside boxes of treasure and the slaves they had killed. The French believed that black souls guarded their stash. Henri Christophe fortified the Cap and its grand residences to keep colonial generals from returning to dig up cemeteries. Children anticipated finding gold coins and silver antiques "which the ground would vomit up when it rained," an evocative emesis of Haiti's racist past (Danticat, 1998, 217).

See also Music, Rape, Religion, Storytelling.

SOURCES

Danticat, Edwidge. *After the Dance: A Walk Through Carnival in Jacmel, Haiti.* New York: Vintage, 2002.
_____. *Célimène—Fairy Tale for the Daughter of Immigrants.* Montreal: Memoire d'Encrier, 2009.
_____. *Everything Inside.* New York: Knopf, 2019.
_____. *The Farming of Bones.* New York: Penguin, 1998.
_____. "Travelling," *UN Chronicle* 46:3/4 (2009): 23.
Duffey, Carolyn. "In Flight from the Borderlines: Roses, Rivers, and Missing Haitian History in Marie Chauvet's 'Colère' and Edwidge Danticat's 'Krik? Krak!' and 'The Farming of Bones,'" *Journal of Caribbean Literatures* 3:1 (Summer, 2001): 77–91.
Gleibermann, Erik. "The Story Will Be There When You Need It," *World Literature Today* 93:1 (Winter 2019): 68–74.

Food

Food overshadows Haitian women's work—making coffee, roasting cassava cakes over charcoal, tossing purple corn to chickens, raising pumpkins, sun-drying mushrooms, pulverizing millet with pestle and mortar, and frying pigeon meat, a restaurant specialty in the story "Ghosts." In reference to coming of age, Edwidge acknowledged to interviewer Renée Shea a gender divide at home in Brooklyn, where "I had to be in the kitchen with my mother, learning how to cook" (Shea, 1995, 13). At Jacmel's pre–Lenten carnival in *After the Dance,* street cooks offer her and other fair goers traditional fare—boiled corn, *taso* (fried goat), and manioc cakes with cane syrup, a reminder of the centrality of sugar to islanders. The author incorporates food into essential scenarios, such as holy guava, profitable yucca wine and bread, cassareep (cassava root) flavoring, communal betrothal platters, a shaved iced fresko street treat, condensed milk blended with beet juice, and, in *Anacaona,* a serving of pineapple and salt fish, a fifteenth-century restorer of strength for the future Haitian Taino *cacica* (ruler).

Bartering for produce like the title figure in *Célimène* assures fresh vegetables and fruit for peasant meals but reduces Nozias and seven-year-old daughter in *Claire of the Sea Light* to cornmeal and eggs, for which they exchange fresh fish. In the biography *Anacaona,* baskets of gift foods offer turtle, iguana, fish and manatee from island waters and agricultural harvest of yams, pepper, bananas, guavas, and papayas. Fresh viands grilled together over the *barbacoa* before consumption by guests typify sharing intended to heighten tribal accord in southwestern Haiti. In *Untwine,* Giselle Boyer pictures heaven as a reunion of her splintered family over heritage favorites—beans and rice, pumpkin soup, and *griyo,* fatty pork bites marinated in sour orange juice and fried.

Special Occasions

At a reception for tiny Rosalinda Teresa Duarte and wake for her deceased twin Rafi in *The Farming of Bones,* Valencia's servants offer guests cafecito, a thumb-size cup of espresso coffee sweetened with brown sugar, a product of the Dominican cane fields. For the traditional corn feast, islanders limit consumption to raw, roasted, boiled, powdered, and meal shaped into cornbread. After the narrative turns from family matters to the *trujillato*—Trujillo's three-decade rule—and the genocide of Haitian field workers in October 1937, nuns distribute simple meals of black beans over corn mush and slices of avocado, a plate offering nourishment along with the upbeat colors of Africa—yellow, black, and green. Safe in Cap Haïtien, refugee Yves Rapadou receives a celebratory feast of corn mush, black beans, goat meat with eggplant, and codfish sauce over watercress, a folk purgative of a fatty liver. For the wealthy Ardins in *Claire of*

the Sea Light, a party for returnee Maxime, Jr., features cod patties, which welcome the immigrant back home from Miami.

In 1999, the author spoke candidly of her love for plantains in the personal essay "Plantains, Please" for *The Caribbean Writer.* To express their multiple uses, she cited plantain recipes suited to breakfast, lunch, or dinner. She introduced a leather and wood kitchen device for flattening the fibrous fruit and described eating plantains ripe and sweet, creamed into spiced porridge with evaporated milk, fried into fritters seasoned with nutmeg and cinnamon, or boiled and smothered in herring, tomato, and onion sauce. Her memorable cuisine lauded plantains for their flexibility in meals for rich or poor and for anchoring memories of home cuisine.

Varied Menus

Distinct menus mark the U.S. ambassador's stash of grilled cashew nuts and molasses in "Becoming Brazilian," a chicken and mango salad at Prime Minister Gregory Murray's residence in "Seven Stories," and an avocado, cashew, and palm heart salad for Owen Tiggs, a patient ill with pulmonary fibrosis in the story "Elsie," which the author retitled in *Everything Inside* as "Dosas." For less prosperous gatherings, Edwidge creates a family dinner of herring and cornmeal mush spread on banana leaves in "A Wall of Fire Rising" and a breakfast of kleren rum for the title figure in "The Dew Breaker." In *Breath, Eyes,* Memory, characters consume cinnamon rice pudding, cassava (manioc) sandwiches, and coffee for breakfast; coconuts, boiled eggs, biscuits, and bananas for a snack; boudin (sausage), soursop, beans and maize with avocado, and watermelon juice for dinner; and sweet potato pudding for a satisfying potluck. The dominance of plant food indicates households too poor to buy seafood or raise goats for meat.

To Nancy Raquel Mirabal, a journalist for *Callaloo,* Edwidge defined memorable eating of tom-tom, plantain with pickled pepper, and the January 1 celebratory joumou, a beef and pumpkin soup that Giselle Boyer savors in *Untwine*: "We're nostalgic about food because food sustains us ... anchors us to a place" (Mirabal, 2007, 410). The meal returned in fiction after the Espérance family reunited in New York in *Behind the Mountains,* in which food eases emigration from Haiti to Brooklyn. Edwidge recalled hiding simple meals of cornmeal mush or rice from outsiders, who ridiculed poor diets as evidence of low-class people. "I remember eating kalalou as a child. It was a very special Sunday dish for us ...with crabs" (Mirabal, 2007, 39). In stories of New York City, the author created a contrast with frankfurters, canned soda, and hot chestnuts sold on the street and egg salad sandwiches from a deli.

Eating Culture

Overtones of West African descent accompany the baking of coconut and peanuts into two types of candy in *Behind the Mountains* and the growing of Congo beans or pigeon peas (*Cajanus cajan*), a common source of protein in India and former slave colonies. For three GED students in "The Funeral Singer," peas accompany a meal of fried plantain, rice, and goat stew. For wellness, Hermine Azile, the mother in "Caroline's Wedding," boils cow bones into bone soup, a source of strength from the iron in marrow. She begins the day of her two daughters, Gracina and Caroline, with a breakfast of dried herring in a thick omelet and blesses Caroline's wedding shower with patties of cod and ground beef, an American commodity replacing the lower class goat meat from Haiti.

Gift foods grace visits and leave taking, particularly hen soup, eggs, and nutmeg for a new mother in *The Farming of Bones* and Anika's *akra*—malaga (coco) fritters fried for Thomas views with elegant entrees at a Biscayne Bay restaurant in "The Gift." At Edwidge's departure to Miami in *Brother, I'm Dying,* she carries an overnight bag of cod patties, fried snapper, cassava bread, plantain chips, and sweet potato cake. In the story "Nineteen Thirty-Seven," the main character chooses a favorite snack—fried pork and plantains sprinkled with spiced cabbage—as a gift for her mother Défilé, a prison inmate. The story "Seven" catalogs gifts packed in a woman's suitcase—coconut candy, coffee beans, and citrus peel preserves. More information about grapefruit peel appears in "New York Day Women," in which an intrusive Haitian-American daughter adds cinnamon bark as a flavoring. Visitors enjoyed *diri ak pwa* (rice and beans), the national Haitian dish from slave times. According to Nancy Raquel Mirabal's essay "Dyasporic Appetites and Longings" in *Callaloo,* native Haitians relished the combination for its sentimental value: "One could easily return home, simply by lifting a fork to one's lips" (Danticat, 2007, 259).

See also Women.

Sources

Danticat, Edwidge. "Becoming Brazilian," *Obsidian III* 6/7:2/1 (Fall 2005/2006): 139–145.

_____. *Brother, I'm Dying.* New York: Vintage, 2007.

_____. *Everything Inside.* New York: Knopf, 2019.

_____. "Nineteen Thirty-Seven," *Oxford Book of Caribbean Short Stories.* Oxford, UK: Oxford University Press, 2001: 447–456.

_____. "Plantains, Please," *Caribbean Writer* 13 (1999): 179–180.

Mirabal, Nancy Raquel. "Dyasporic Appetites and Longings," *Callaloo* 30:1 (Winter 2007): 26–39, 410.

Shea, Renée. "The Dangerous Job of Edwidge Danticat," *Belles Lettres* 10:3 (Summer 1995): 12–15.

Freedom

The concept of liberty underlies a majority of Edwidge's themes and settings, for example, the émigré's destination and the afterlife of the dead in "The Other Side of the Water," release from enclosure in a leaky boat in "Children of the Sea," and nurse Nadine Osnac's reprieve from loneliness for Haitian parents in "Water Child." In *Krik? Krak!,* the writer accentuates movement with "travel from Haiti to America, travel from the ground to the sky, from land to the sea, and from reality to dreamland," similar in fantasy to the Chinese depiction of the gold mountain (Alexandre & Howard, 2007, 161). Some travel terrorizes because it is "physically perilous" and journeyers not "greeted with open arms. They are imprisoned or turned back" (*Ibid.*). Haitian history warns of the self-liberating struggle in the parting works of General Toussaint Louverture, who defended the "tree of liberty" and its deep roots (Abbott, 1988, viii).

The author surveyed fearful escape as models of courage and daring, descriptors of Callie Morrissete, wife of Prime Minister Gregory Murray in "Seven Stories." To Sophie Caco Woods in *Breath, Eyes, Memory*, Tante Atie's literacy has set her free from anti-woman traditions. By splitting her hymen with a pestle, Sophie escapes weekly parental probing to investigate her private sexual activity. In an interview with journalist Tyler Cowen for *Urban Fusion,* Edwidge asserted a libertarian truism: "La liberté est quelque chose que nous devons toujours surveiller" (Freedom is something we should guard) (Cowen, 2020). According to refugees from Generalissimo Rafael Trujillo's massacre of black Haitians in October 1937, in *The Farming of Bones,* liberation is an ephemeral state that demands constant restoration.

Individual examples like Amabelle Desír's recreation of birthing in the Massacre River in *The Farming of the Bones* produce unusual actions, such as Gabrielle's spreading of Isabelle's ashes in *Untwine* to rid her of being a twin and Anne Bienaimé's shedding of guilt through prayer and worship in *The Dew Breaker*. Murder, beatings, and lethal tortures release prisoners in death in two stories, "Dream of the Butterflies" and "Nineteen Thirty-Seven." Mrs. Morrissete, the widow of a Caribbean prime minister in "Seven Stories," self-sequesters at a former residence to strip her daily life of sorrow. Arnold, the tragic laborer in "Without Inspection," requires a firm hand on possessions—a closet stuffed with clothes and shoes and a car that demands monthly payments, all evidence of his unrestricted residency in the U.S. For Saya, the protagonist of *Mama's Nightingale*, the bird's call represents a redeeming melody on her idealized rainbow trail to freedom.

Sounds of Autonomy

Other voices corroborate character concepts of deliverance and empowerment, such as Little Guy's performance of Boukman Dutty's speech in "A Wall of Fire Rising" defying French colonialism and a parade of celebrants waving flags and blowing horns in "Monkey Tails" to mark the ouster on February 7, 1986, of Jean-Claude "Baby Doc" Duvalier. In *Brother, I'm Dying,* Uncle Joseph Nozius Dantica's definition of Negro spirituals depicts the object of black sorrow songs as departure to Africa, Heaven, or independence. For ex-con Claude, the father-killer in "Night Talkers," self-empowerment through migration overturns his notion of escaping Haiti permanently. After a term in prison and deportation, he has little choice but to repatriate to his birth home and try once more to grow into an adult.

Ironically, the sharing of anecdotes with Dany Dorméus opens valuable routes to self-esteem and a reevaluation of their motherland, epitomized by a deceased midwife, Aunt Estina Estème.

Edwidge is careful not to oversimplify the cost of freedom. For the interwoven characters in *Claire of the Sea Light,* the author sets the coastal fable in contested space: the turbulent town of Ville Rose and a rigid social hierarchy that impacts all homes, top to bottom. Residences face the Caribbean Sea, an idyllic home to fishermen and a promised land to immigrants from the U.S. like Max Ardin, Jr., who eludes the shame of homosexuality by returning from Miami. The unreliable destiny of watermen quickly extinguishes Caleb in the opening chapter when nature engulfs him in a tsunami. In search of his remains, shore people collaborate in a water and beach scan for some news of his fate or that of his fishing boat. The hopeless rescue attempt ironically alleviates community members of social alienation.

Relief of Conscience

Simultaneous with Caleb's disappearance in a gargantuan wave, Max, Jr., the Miami immigrant, longs to free himself from homosexual yearning for Bernard "Bè" Dorien by ending his life in the waves along Ville Rose. At the novel's resolution, people of all social levels combine energy and revival techniques to wrest Max from a death sentence, a form of voluntary migration like that of slaves escaping the Middle Passage by leaping overboard. In the background, Flore Voltaire, the domestic servant he raped, also turns to the ocean as a path to a new life with her illegitimate son named Pamaxime (not Maxime). Her departure defies the rapist and embraces single motherhood, which she shares with Darline and Oula in "Without Inspection" and the sex worker in "Night Women," who hides from her son how she earns a living. Like slaves before her, Flore conceals her destination, expecting secrecy to protect Pamaxime from forced return to the prominent Ardins. The narrative salutes courageous women willing to risk all for a freer life.

A simpler statement of freedom extends to national treasuries in Edwidge's *New Yorker* essay "Demonstrators in Haiti Are Fighting for an Uncertain Future." The two-paragraph statement, issued in the *New Yorker* on October 20, 2019, demanded rights for the rural and urban poor to equality, inclusion, justice, and respect. In view of Haiti's past, the author adds an assurance of female rights—"freedom from government and privately funded gangs, who routinely rape women and girls" (Danticat, 2019). In a nation where a felonious elite misdirect or purloin Petrocaribe funds, she includes accountability, an eyeball-to-eyeball honesty with hands lying open on the table.

See also Slavery.

Sources

Abbott, Elizabeth. *Haiti: An Insider's History of the Rise and Fall of the Duvaliers.* New York: Simon & Schuster, 1988.

Alexandre, Sandy, and Ravi Y. Howard. "Interview," *Journal of Caribbean Literature* 4:3 (Spring 2007): 161–174.

Chen, Wilson C. "Narrating Diaspora in Edwidge Danticat's Short-Story Cycle *The Dew Breaker,*" *Literature Interpretation Theory* 25:3 (2014): 220–241.

Cowen, Tyler. "Ma conversation avec Edwidge Danticat," *Urban Fusion* (5 November 2020).

Danticat, Edwidge. *Claire of the Sea Light.* New York: Vintage, 2013.

_____. "Demonstrators in Haiti Are Fighting for an Uncertain Future," *New Yorker* (10 October 2019).

_____. *Everything Inside.* New York: Knopf, 2019.

Johnson, Newtona. "Interview," *Obsidian III* 6/7:2/1 (Fall 2005–2006): 147–166, 264.

Moïse, Myriam. "Borderless Spaces and Alternative Subjectivities," *Border Transgression and Reconfiguration of Caribbean Spaces.* London: Palgrave Macmillan, 2020, 193–217.

Montgomery, Maxine L. "A Lasiren Song for the Wonn: Edwidge Danticat's *Claire of the Sea Light* and the Legend of Mami Wata," *CLA Journal* 59:4 (June 2016): 316–329.

Grandparents

The subject of previous generations in Edwidge's writing projects a warmth and acceptance, as with Mira's concern for Grandma Issa Boyer, a survivor of the January 12, 2010, earthquake in *Eight Days;* a mournful period following the death of Grandma Sandrine in *Untwine;* and the gift of Maxime Ardin, Sr., in *Claire of the Sea Light,* who offers cash to aid Flore Voltaire in rearing his illegitimate grandson, Pamaxime. From the author's childhood, she recalled the photo of her dead grandmother, the kind of mantelpiece commemoration common in Haiti, and a flag from the days of her grandfather Nozial's warfare against U.S. Marine insurgents. To Interviewer Erik Gleibermann of *World Literature Today,* she asserted, "You are who you are" because of your grandparents, who pass along face, posture, gestures, and idiosyncrasies (Gleibermann, 2019, 71).

Edwidge referred to a funeral photo as her grandmother's "watchful gaze," as though a living spirit surveyed and guided her (Danticat, 2013). Living grandparents armed her with recipes, herbal therapies, anecdotes, and tales, the kind of memories that linked her to the past. In "Women Like Us," she added that five generations of females shared "the natural bonds of family resemblance as well as resilience" (Putnam, 2003, 52). One grandmother told inventive call-and-response narratives: "If the audience seemed bored, the story would speed up, and if they were participating, a song would go in. The whole interaction was exciting to me. These cross-generational exchanges didn't happen often" (Charters 1998, 42). When they did, they imparted such valuable lore as the philosophical anecdote "The Angel of Death and Father God."

Grandparents' Skills

Fictional Sophie Caco, one of the author's most successful characters, demonstrates the give and take among female generations. She esteems her matrilineage in *Breath, Eyes, Memory* by naming her baby Brigitte Ifé after her maternal grandmother and great aunt Martinelle Brigitte. For Sophie's benefit, her maternal grandmother imparts nuggets of wisdom in aphorism and stresses that mothers are their children's first friends. Aged character traits remind her that elderly woman taught her women's fiber work skills—knitting and sewing. At a climactic break with Haiti, travel to New York tears Sophie from the security of Tante Atie and Grandmè Ifé Caco, the anchors of a motherless existence.

Additional breaks between generations intrude on Edwidge's stable characters. The creation lore of Grann's storytelling in *The Last Mapou* diverts a granddaughter from sadness for her elderly relative's depleted health. Narrative convinces the girl that attrition is a natural part of life, from the beginning of Haiti's history to the ecological threats that loom from deforestation. A focus of the story "Sunrise, Sunset," grandparents like Carole represent fragile, short-term family members who can easily slip away, a reminder of mortality to the young. For Edwidge, memories of Rose Danticat begin with the shared named Rose. In *Brother, I'm Dying,* she recalls advice on pregnancy before the birth of the first Danticat grandchild, named Mira for the author's father. Rose's decline from cancer and her death in Miami, as described in "Without Her" and "Feetfirst," retain a salving grace—death among three generations of supportive women.

The writer often reclaims the storytelling of elders such as Granpé Nozial in *Behind the Mountains* and the lifestyle, healing, cookery, and domestic labor of grandmothers as skillful as Granmè Melina. For the Taino diarist in *Anacaona,* the guardian spirit of an unnamed grandmother ruler models strength of character and dedication to soldiery. At focal moments in the title figure's coming of age and engagement to Caonabó, she exemplifies redoubtable strength and readiness for matrimony and motherhood. In "The Indigo Girl," Melina "beat rocks on her clothes in the river in Léogâne," an image of dogged incorruptibility (Danticat, 2004, 28). Costume and fiber work link the older generation with the tying of the tignon, a self-fashioning West African head wrap of proud, hard-laboring Afro-Caribbean girls in *Breath, Eyes, Memory.* A colonial relic of the tignon sumptuary laws identifying female slaves in public places, it began in 1786 as Governor Estevan Miro's suppression of black slaves and freedwomen in New Orleans and developed into a snazzy element of resistance.

Parental Surrogates

Similarly, Valencia Duarte, mother of twins in *The Farming of Bones,* draws fortitude from memories of her mother Rosalinda and preserves her name for daughter Rosalinda Teresa. According to the essay "Nature Has No Memory," the author got the idea for the book from artist Ernst Prophète, who commemorated his grandmother in art for surviving Generalissimo Rafael Trujillo's massacre of black Haitians in October 1937. Another elder alerted Edwidge to the power of oral tradition: "The best way to commemorate the horrors of the past … is to stop the injustices of the present" (Danticat, 2013). The author incorporated stories of the massacre, which forms dual empowerment: verbal history "anchors it for me; it's keeping them alive by retelling" (Jaggi, 2004, 20). From the stories of her grandfather, she learned "things … not written anywhere. Sitting with an older person tells you another side" (*ibid.*). Crucial to timing is awareness that these touchstones are aging rapidly, taking with them untold aspects of the past.

Elderly relatives frequently become family substitutes. They may replace disabled or deceased parents, Lamort's situation with her grandmother in the story "The Missing Peace" and the rearing of Dany Dorméus by Aunt Estina Estème, a blind foster mother and respected midwife in Beau Jour in the story "Night Talkers." For Giselle Boyer in *Untwine,* stout-hearted paternal grandma Régine Boyer sustains the nearly comatose sixteen-year-old with hospital visits and helps her cope with losing twin sister Isabelle. The choice of "queen" for the elder woman's name suggests dignity as well as a commanding presence. In the matrilineage of resilient females, mother Sylvie retrieves her daughter from misidentification as Isabelle. At the grandparents' mountain home in Haiti, mother and daughter, both content in the company of the older generation, enjoy a peaceful respite from sorrow and loss as they sprinkle Isabelle's ashes over the sea.

Sources

Charters, Mallay. "Edwidge Danticat: A Bitter Legacy Revisited," *Publishers Weekly* 245:33 (17 August 1998): 42, 43.

Danticat, Edwidge. "The Indigo Girl: Between Haiti and the Streets of Brooklyn," *Sojourners* (December 2004): 28–31.

_____. *The Last Mapou.* Brooklyn: One Moore Book, 2013.

_____. "Look at Me," *Harper's* 327:1963 (December 2013): 65–73.

_____. "Nature Has No Memory," https://www.borderoflights.org/edwidge-danticat, 2013.

_____. "Sunrise, Sunset," *New Yorker* (18 September 2017).

Gleibermann, Erik. "The Story Will Be There When You Need It," *World Literature Today* 93:1 (Winter 2019): 68–74.

Jaggi, Maya. "Island Memories," *Guardian* (19 November 2004): 20.

Putnam, Amanda. "Braiding Memories: Resistant Storytelling within Mother-Daughter Communities in Edwidge Danticat's *Krik? Krik!*," *Journal of Haitian Studies* 9:1 (Spring 2003): 52–65.

Grotesque

Much of Edwidge's work fabricates straightforward prose with shocking scenarios, for example, a priest forced to drink urine and a freakish man born with both legs in his back in *The Farming of Bones,* where defiling of laborers' bodies replicates the intrusion of bondage on the individual. The author dramatizes the splattering of "blood and brain matter" on eyeglasses at the execution of anti–Duvalier guerrilla warriors Louis Drouin and Marcel Numa in *Create Dangerously,* and a ball game played with a decapitated head in *Brother, I'm Dying* (Danticat, 2010, 5). Alongside abstract theatricals of the AIDS virus, floats, marching units, and costumed clowns in *After the Dance* blend the carnivalesque with erotic dance and risible parody to mock the Tonton Macoute and evil civil officials. The Gothic poem "A Despot Walks into a Killing Field" reflects on raped women "pregnant with the children they stabbed inside of us" and the severance of human parts—teeth, eyes, ears, fingers—after dehumanizing interrogations (Danticat, 2012, 37).

Depravity demonizes Edwidge's anti-heroes. For Maria, the domestic fantasizing motherhood in "Between the Pool and the Gardenias," preserving the rotting remains of an infant requires methods of concealing the odor. The tossing of babies as air targets in "A Crime to Dream" depicts the Tonton Macoute's barbarities against all citizens, particularly the very young and helpless. A contrasting story of revenge, "The Journals of Water Days" portrays a fisherman pouring kerosene into the mouth of a militiaman. After carving into the man's chest, the angry retaliator finds no heart, a symbolic absence similar in tone to the beast sacrificed by augurs in Act II, scene 2 of William Shakespeare's *Julius Caesar.* Nearby, blood spurts from bullet holes in a pig, a preposterous contrast between heartless shooter and swine.

Ominous Anomalies

Edwidge sets the mood for disturbing narration with enduring details, such as the burning alive of Dany Dorméus's parents in "Night Talkers." Before the birth of Rose, Gaëlle and Laurent Lavaud's first child in *Claire of the Sea Light,* a sonogram discloses a cyst along her chest and spine, a portent that disappears at her birth. Subsequent aberrant scenarios in "Ghosts" place Bernard "Bè" Dorien in police custody, where he soils himself with vomit. Another exotic eruption, radio programmer Louise George suffers from reverse menstruation, which causes blood to flow from her mouth. A surprising source of distortion and mystique, illustrator Edouard Duval-Carrié shapes *The Last Mapou,* a generational fable, with serpentine tree roots and limbs and unidentifiable human shapes on an embroidered cushion, which appears to include two hanging victims.

For the French fairy tale *Célimène*, Edwidge creates conflict with a mystic reptile—a twelve-meter purple anaconda called Liya. The Hebrew name links it with God's presence, a belief that dates to ancient Greek and Roman temple herpetologists, including Olympias, mother of Alexander the Great. Liya's prominent feature—an outsized head "large enough to swallow an adult in one bite"—caused the defection of Zaken's first ten wives (Danticat, 2009). The gaping mouth represents a risk that the peasant girl takes in trusting Zaken, whom she marries and follows to his village. The test of Célimène's courage reflects motifs of other fairy tale brides from the folk classics *Arabian Nights,* "Beauty and the Beast," and French fabulist Charles Perrault's "Bluebeard," a tale of perverse love and patriarchal possession.

Repulsive Imagery

The author's detailed view of pre–Columbian Quisqueya (Hispaniola) unfolds a violent, unpredictable Taino culture beset by Caribe enemies, the focus of the YA biography *Anacaona.* Two suicides, one of Yaruba, an expectant mother and wife of a chief, testify to deep yearnings for her birth home and honor. At the title figure's post-nuptial welcome to the village of Niti, Maguana, a ball player stabs his chest with a poisoned arrow to signify his grief at losing a game. For the sake of decorum before the bride, attendants bear the corpse away. Anacaona departs the nuptial reception to look at central Hispaniola, an upbeat tour to follow the omen of unexpected martyrdom.

In details of cruelty to women, "Hot-Air Balloons" unearths women selling their children into prostitution and rapists who bite off women's tongues, a monstrous gesture toward female silencing. Prison torment includes removing fingernails with pliers in "The Book of the Dead" and mass murderer Emmanuel "Toto" Constant's method of scalping faces of corpses in "The Book of Miracles" to prevent police identification of the remains. In a side episode of "Children of the Sea," the Tonton Macoute present a mother, Madam Roger, with the cranium of her son, a member of the rebellious Radio Six. The paramilitary enlarges on suffering by ridiculing her and suggesting that she cannibalize the head for dinner. When the squad returns to glean information on the traitors, Edwidge limits their torture of Madam Roger to sounds of their rifles pounding her skull and then to silence.

SOURCES

Danticat, Edwidge. *Célimène—Fairy Tale for the Daughter of Immigrants.* Montreal: Memoire d'Encrier, 2009.
_____. "A Crime to Dream," *Nation* 280:17 (2 May 2005): 13–15.
_____. "A Despot Walks into a Killing Field," *Progressive* 76:5 (May 2012): 37.
_____. "The Journals of Water Days," *Callaloo* 19:2 (Spring, 1996): 376–380.
Duboin, Corinne. *"After the Dance* d'Edwidge Danticat: visions carnavalesques de l'espace haïtien," *Transatlantica* 2 (15 November 2007).
Dumas, Pierre-Raymond, and Augustin Chenald. "'Célimène' ou la problématique de l'exil au coeur du merveilleux," *Le Nouvelliste* (21 June 2011).
Putnam, Amanda. "Braiding Memories: Resistant Storytelling within Mother-Daughter Communities in Edwidge Danticat's *Krik? Krik!," Journal of Haitian Studies* 9:1 (Spring 2003): 52–65.
Spears, Crystal. "Removing the Masks of Lady Liberty: The Grotesque in the Literatures of the Defeated Americas," *CEA Critic* 75:3 (2013): 235–242.
Sylvain, Patrick. "Textual Pleasures and Violent Memories in Edwidge Danticat *Farming of the Bones," International Journal* 2:3 (2014): 1–19.

Haiti

Edwidge stated in 2004, "There is no one Haiti … but several" (Danticat, 2004, vi). She has produced a panoply of Haitian history, from creation and pre–Columbian times at Quisqueya to the twenty-first century. In the essay "Edwidge Danticat's Haiti: Bloodied, Shaken—and Beloved" for the *Miami Herald,* she quotes a common comparison: "Haiti is *tè glise,* slippery ground … stable one moment, then crumbling the next" from centuries of colonialism, slavery, tyranny, and overwhelming poverty (Danticat, 2010). To the nation's detriment, according to Michael Harris, a reviewer for the *Los Angeles Times,* the media "has reinforced our idea of the place as a sink of violence, poverty, and hopelessness," themes incorporated in child memories in the poem "Sawfish Soup," photojournalism in *Tent Life,* and the story "Night Women" (Harris, 2002, R7). Facts prove otherwise, as do land-based folklore in *The Last Mapou,* the fairy tale *Célimène,* and the YA and children's books *Untwine, Behind the Mountain,* and *My Mommy Medicine.*

The author, according to Macy Halford, a journalist for the *New Yorker,* succeeds at crushing borders that divide ethnicities. Edwidge accounts for "a continuous need for expression that an environment like Haiti demands" (Lee, 2011, C1). She expresses admiration for prehistoric trade with African navigators in "Pamela Phatsimo Sunstrum: New and Recent Paintings," an art critique for *Paris Review,* and, in *Anacaona,* the fifteenth-century Taino heritage of storytelling, masking, body painting, ritual dance, traditional courtship, and canoe travel. At hurricane warnings, builders gum palm fronds to roofs of huts thatched from local materials. The pre–Columbian outlook of the Taino *cacica* (ruler) treasures the Caribbean isle after she receives feathers, dye, shark teeth, shells, clay, and sea rocks, all indigenous coming of age gifts.

Cycles of History

Historic cycles have seesawed with advances and losses, a nadir represented in Heart-of-Darkness stereotypes in the media that Edwidge covered in "The Dominican Republic and Haiti: A Shared View from the Diaspora." In the French colonial era preceding the 1791 revolution, according to *The Black Jacobins,* by Trinidadian historian Cyril Lionel Robert James, "Haiti was the wealthiest and most flourishing of the slave colonies in the Caribbean, the pride of France and the envy of every other imperialist nation" (James, 1989, 1). At its height, it produced 40 percent of the world's sugar. From prosperity came spare cash to pay for lavish fashions, house slaves, concubines, and sexual adventuring. Black orphans fell between the levels of island children and domestic robots, the dilemma of Rosie, a house slave in "Monkey Tails," and Arnold, the refugee who escapes penury in "Without Inspection." Ultimately, the author exults in Napoleon's defeat: Haitians "wrenched their liberty from the grip of the world's most powerful army of their time" (Danticat, 2004, viii).

In 1805, President Henri Christophe began a fifteen-year construction of Citadelle Laferrière, a fort on a mountaintop called the Bonnet à l'Evêque (the bishop's cap), a place where Amabelle Desír played in childhood in *The Farming of Bones* and imagined protection. At the novel's opening in October 1937, she flees a calculated bloodbath of Haitians by Spanish Guardia and summarizes the fearful divide as "two different people trying to share one tiny piece of land" (Danticat, 1998, 145). On the bus ride away from a temporary field hospital, refugees take in the beauty of mountains, trees, and birds, the visual handholds of home.

Without broadcasting Haiti's postrevolution miseries, Edwidge avoided criticism of what reviewer Aitor Ibarrola-Armendáriz, a Romance language expert in Deusto, Spain, terms a "fast succession of emperors, kings, revolutionaries, dictators, and for-life presidents who have misruled the land for over five hundred years" (Ibarrola-Armendáriz, 2010, 26). One survivor's recall of hero François Toussaint Louverture rephrased the general's parting words before his exile from Hispaniola to

France on May 22, 1802: "In overthrowing me you have cut down in Saint Domingue only the trunk of the tree of liberty; it will spring up again from the roots, for they are numerous and they are deep" (Abbott, 1988, viii). Similar in imagery to Thomas Jefferson's 1787 regard for the tree of liberty, Louverture heartened his followers before the final surge of libertarianism freed the island on January 1, 1804.

Historic Lows

Before American flight from the Duvalier regime, the cultural savor and texture graced the outflow of the Harlem Renaissance in Langston Hughes's autobiography *I Wonder as I Wander,* poem "Danse Africaine," and travelogue for the *New York Amsterdam News* and in Zora Neale Huston's anthropological research in *Tell My Horse.* After the launch of a 29-year despotism described in "Children of the Sea" and "The Dew Breaker," fictional islanders chafed at strictures on the lowest caste and wished to elevate their daughters to promising marriages with professional men, the source of Callie's social elevation in "Seven Stories." Less a matter of snobbery than survival, the advancement offers women's protection from the vicious paramilitary. Edwidge depicted the execution of immigrant rebels Louis Drouin and Marcel Number by François "Papa Doc" Duvalier's firing squad in *Create Dangerously.* A more plaintive survey in *Brother, I'm Dying* summarized bribery and random slaughter leaving naked and maimed corpses in the Port-au-Prince slums. To allegorize a pitiful situation, Tante Denise, depleted by stroke, tells Edwidge a story of a contest between God and the death angel. Because death strikes all people equally and without prejudice, God comes out second by comparison.

In the twenty-first century, Edwidge lapses into soulful concern for fellow Haitians, whether still there or part of the outflow, the source of ex-con Claude's unrest in "Night Talkers." As climate change became more prominent, she regretted deforestation of her modern island home in the travelogue *After the Dance* and the children's story *The Last Mapou.* In the memoir "Travelling" for the *UN Chronicle,* she feared the island climate is "getting hotter and hotter all the time and people and livestock cannot possibly survive extreme temperatures" (Danticat, 2009, 23). She predicted that the upheaval of ecosystems "leave an already vulnerable land open to further catastrophic disasters" (*ibid.*). The prophecy proved true in 2010, the year of a devastating earthquake, hurricane, mudslides, and outbreak of cholera imported by a UN rescue team.

Instead of hurling political screeds, the writer examined individual choices and the character strengths that keep Haitians alive and optimistic. In *Brother, I'm Dying,* she championed Uncle Joseph Nosius Dantica, an elderly mute and bishop of a slum church who remained at his evangelistic mission until gangs burned his residence, sanctuary, and school in October 2004. Additional inbred Caribbean grit marks a launderer in "The Indigo Girl," midwife Estina Estème in "Night Talkers," farm laborer Ovid in *After the Dance,* the Radio Six in *Create Dangerously,* and immigrant sculptor Ka Bienaimé and actor Gabrielle Fonteneau in "The Book of the Dead." In the essay "Dawn after the Caribbean Tempests," she echoed the affirmation of Carmen Yulín Cruz Soto, Mayor of San Juan, Puerto Rico, who declared, "We're a people, damn it" (Danticat, 2017, TR5).

An Ongoing Struggle

To contrast a dismal New York dusk, the nostalgic trickster tale "Je Voudrais

Etre Riche" indulged in warm memories of "a palm tree-fringed ray of sunshine" (Danticat, 2004, 187). To Edwidge, the image exemplified "resort Haiti," an island ideal that ignored unforeseen shortages and sudden downfalls, such as the flooding, tremors, and species collapse the author mentioned in *Claire of the Sea Light* and "Port-au-Prince, City of Survivors: Voices from Haiti" (Danticat, 2020, 149). The essay "Machandiz (Merchandise)" explained how the Petrocaribe deal for Venezuelan oil resulted in embezzlement and high prices out of reach of the underclass, who lived on $1.50–$3.00 a day. Less idyllic, the Associated Press announcement in May 2012 of copper, gold, and silver in Haiti raised new fears of exploitation and nickel and dime wages for poor employees arriving barefoot to properties run by foreign capitalists. In "House of Prayer and Dreams," she censured the conflicted history of do-gooders in the post–Columbian era: "Many who have come to conquer and kill since the time of Christopher Columbus have carried a Bible and a cross and have used God's name to justify evil deeds" (Danticat, 2013, 39).

After the 2010 disasters, Edwidge chose the Greek king Sisyphus of Corinth as "a great metaphor for Haiti" for persevering in rolling boulders up a hill (Harvey, 2011). While tent camps struggled with foul water and mud inundations, women continue to groom themselves and bathe their children. She reported in an interview for *Arquitectonica,* "They saw them as a kind of refuge because even when you'd lost everything, you could still present a beautiful place to the world" (Danticat, 2013). In an interview for *Journal of Caribbean Literature*, she noted the rosy memories of the older generation and variances in collective recall.

Edwidge and other island writers anticipated the disapproval of their parents for publishing harsh truths about the motherland, especially the testing of virginity in young girls in *Breath, Eyes, Memory*. In a foreword to *Fault Lines*, she summarized Haiti's diminution among the powerful: "There is rarely a representative of grassroots urban or rural sections in the international commissions and panels that will decide the future of this country" (Danticat, 2013, xiv). The overlook of home-grown character bypasses worthy citizens, particularly the stout-hearted women of "A Taste of Coffee," "Nineteen Thirty-Seven," and *Behind the Mountains*.

See also Carnival, Nature, Poverty.

Sources

Abbott, Elizabeth. *Haiti: An Insider's History of the Rise and Fall of the Duvaliers*. New York: Simon & Schuster, 1988.

Alexandre, Sandy, and Ravi Y. Howard. "Interview," *Journal of Caribbean Literature* 4:3 (Spring 2007): 161–174.

Danticat, Edwidge. "Color Blocking," *Arquitectonica*, https://www.interiorsandsources.com/article-details/articleid/15929/title/color-blocking-edwidge-danticat (1 July 2013).

_____. *Create Dangerously: The Immigrant Artist at Work*. New York: Vintage, 2010.

_____. "Dawn after the Caribbean Tempests," *New York Times* (6 November 2017): TR5.

_____. "The Dominican Republic and Haiti: A Shared View from the Diaspora," *Americas Quarterly* 8:3 (Summer 2014): 28–35.

_____. "Edwidge Danticat's Haiti: Bloodied, Shaken—and Beloved," *Miami Herald* (17 January 2010).

_____. *The Farming of Bones*. New York: Penguin, 1998.

_____. *Fault Lines: Views across Haiti's Divide*. Ithaca, NY: Cornell University, 2013, xi–xiv.

_____. "House of Prayer and Dreams," *Sojourners* 442:4 (April 2013): 38–39, 41–42.

_____. "Je Voudrais Etre Riche: A Trickster Tale," *Caribbean Writer* 18 (2004): 187–193.

_____. *The Last Mapou*. Brooklyn: One Moore Book, 2013.

_____. "Machandiz," *Tales of Two Planets: Stories of Climate Change and Inequality in a Divided World*. New York: Penguin, 2020, 149–158.

_____. "A Portal Moment for Portal Writers and Scholars," *CLA Journal* 56:4 (June 2013): 290.

_____. "Port-au-Prince, City of Survivors: Voices from Haiti," *Salon* (12 January 2020).

_____. *Research in African Literatures* (preface) 35:2 (Summer, 2004): iii–viii.

_____. "So Brutal a Death," *New Yorker* 96:17 (22 June 2020).

_____. "Travelling," *UN Chronicle* 46:3/4 (2009): 23.

_____. *Untwine*. New York: Scholastic, 2015.

Freeman, John. "Introduction," *Tales of Two Planets: Stories of Climate Change and Inequality in a Divided World*. New York: Penguin, 2020, xi–xxv.

Halford, Macy. "Edwidge Danticat's Dangerous Creation," *New Yorker* (6 January 2011).

Harris, Michael. "Review: *After the Dance*," *Los Angeles Times* (11 August 2002): R7.

Harvey, Charlotte Bruce. "Haiti's Storyteller," *Brown Alumni Magazine* (January/February 2011).

Ibarrola-Armendáriz, Aitor. "The Language of Wounds and Scars in Edwidge Danticat's *The Dew Breaker*," *Journal of English Studies* 8 (2010): 23–56.

James, C.L.R. *The Black Jacobins*. New York: Vintage, 1989.

Lee, Felicia. "Dark Tales Illuminate Haiti, Before and After Quake," *New York Times* (10 January 2011): C1.

Health

Wellness or its absence dominates character studies in Edwidge's writings, such as medicines distilled from kapok sap in *The Last Mapou*, Mona's worry over her father Gaspard's treatment for renal failure in "Dosas," Uncle Joseph Nozius Dantica's loss of speech to a laryngectomy in *Brother, I'm Dying*, and Thomas's post-earthquake therapy in a psychiatric hospital in "The Gift." Aunt Leslie, a pediatrician, prescribes Benadryl for hives caused by her nieces' allergy to butterflies in *Untwine* and medical advice on recovering from cranial damage for Giselle, the survivor of a car crash. During a tour of a West Indian island in "Seven Stories," Kim Boyer, a magazine writer, flees the staged hospital visit to view real peasant care. In a crowded triage, those chosen for immediate treatment lie on "bedsheets or pieces of cardboard," the amenities shared by the poor (Danticat, 2019, 187). Others less lucky stand in line and, like bus riders, await numbered tickets.

Specifics follow with hot guanabana tea for sleep, lemon halves for bleeding, and aloe compresses for fever and carbuncles in *The Farming of Bones*; and the treatment of throat pain, hypertension, stroke, and diabetes in *Brother, I'm Dying*, with traditional herbalism and soothing Granmè Melina's arthritis with camphor and castor oil rubs. A deadlier destabilizer of health, according to Robert H. McCormick, a reviewer at Franklin College in Switzerland, "unresponsive bureaucracy" caused Uncle Nozias Dantica to die in shackles at Miami's Krome Detention Center from untreated acute pancreatitis (McCormick, 2008, 74). In *Anacaona*, superstition combats tungiasis, the infected bite of the *nigua* (sand flea) with the power of an amulet to ward off insects. A Taino healer of the late 1400s prescribes an herbal purge to cleanse internal poisons, similar in purpose to the massage, manatee hide sweats, cooling swings in a hammock, and charcoal paste fed to Matunherí to cure pulmonary distress.

The story "Elsie," which the author retitled as "Dosas" in *Everything Inside*, refers to an untreatable ailment—pulmonary fibrosis, the lung disorder that killed André Mira Danticat in *Brother I'm Dying*. She acknowledges emotional causes of abdominal pain and a tea antidote as well as poultices for burns in "Night Talkers" and the dangers of stroke and dementia in Carole, the failing grandmother in "Sunrise, Sunset" who experiences "that now familiar sensation of herself waning" despite doses of coconut oil and omega-3 (Danticat, 2017). Lacking Carole's grace, daughter Jeanne refuses breastfeeding her infant and teas of aniseed and fennel for afterbirth disorders. Perhaps the most damning for Haitians, Marius Dantica's death in Miami in summer 1996 from AIDS in *Create Dangerously* resurrects the scurrilous

Health 143

charge against islanders for causing a virus spread by dissolute sexual behavior. The international shuffling of identity papers and passports requires eight days, all because the public perceives AIDS as morally reprehensible.

Natural Remedies

The pervasive use of Haitian herbs for healing and cooking marks the lives of islanders living close to the soil, for example, Bernard "Bè" Dorien's nerve-soothing cup of verbena tea and Claire Narcis's cooking herbs in rum to help her conceive in the novel *Claire of the Sea Light* and, in "Reading Lessons," Danielle's selection of butterflies to squash on her breasts to make them grow. In "The Dew Breaker," Anne Bienaimé spends five gourdes (about $4.50) for ginger, honey, and yerba buena, a citrusy mint, as an infusion to reduce swelling on the fat man's maimed face. A tea of ginger for Manman Aline and Céli-anne's rubdown with castor oil in *Behind the Mountains* become antidotes for aching bones and head caused by anemia and a pipe bomb explosion under a bus. For Little Guy in "A Wall of Fire Rising," a famine meal of boiled cane pulp produces "sweet water tea," a carminative and vermifuge (Danticat, 1995, 49). With a pinch of salt, it allegedly holds off hunger pangs until Lili and Big Guy can earn money for food.

In *Break, Eyes, Memory,* a Haitian matrilineage shares tumors as symptoms of ingrown social quandaries inflicted on women. For Grandmother Ifé, chagrin (loss) is a treatable disease lessened with tea, but no panacea removes the pineapple-sized hump on her back. Martine Caco turns to vervain, verbena, and quinine to end her first pregnancy and mammectomy to remove cancerous breasts. Tante Atie treats edema in her calf with leeches, which suck out the "bad blood" (*ibid.,* 149). For Sophie Caco, bathing in "catnip, senna, sarsaparilla, *corrosol* (soursop) ... red hibiscus, forget-me-nots, and daffodils" refreshes (Danticat, 1994, 112).

Edwidge described the constant danger of drowning, the cause of Freda's father's suicide at sea in "The Funeral Singer," Anne's stepbrother's death in *The Dew Breaker,* and Caleb's disappearance in a giant wave in *Claire of the Sea Light.* To alter the sport of swimming to a therapy of salt water, in *The Farming of Bones,* wise aunts toast oranges black, then rub joints with the juicy pulp before taking a restorative dip in salt water, a cure for body aches and cuts. The folk treatment returned as a kindness from a Cap Haïtien vendor to Amabelle Desír and Yves Rapadou, émigrés from Haitian slaughter in the Dominican Republic in October 1937. Whatever its value, the skin rub fails to restore her youthful complexion, now a "map of scars and bruises, a marred testament" (Danticat, 1998, 225). An anguished scene pictures the watery self-annihilation of Amabelle Desír after her return to Alegría.

Dramatic Demise

The author uses ailments in "Hot-Air Balloons" and *Claire of the Sea Light* as evidence of faulty character—a gall bladder that shoots stones into the kidneys, lungs, and heart as though firing a catapult and, in the latter novel, Louise George's reverse menstruation, which causes bleeding from the mouth. For Anne Bienaimé, the fanatic Catholic of "The Book of Miracles," epilepsy marks a troubled life with Freudian seizures, as though her mind fights the truth about her husband's violent past as an officer of the Tonton Macoute. A more predictable end of life, Grandmother Carole's dementia in "Sunrise, Sunset" and midwife

Estina Estème's death in sleep in "Night Talkers" preface the decline of beloved and dependable family pillars.

Lethal contagion with cholera and tuberculosis is more dismaying, causing Haitians to accept imminent demise as their future. The story "The Port-au-Prince Marriage Special" depicts the fate of Mélisande, an AIDS victim who waits too late for a diagnosis. Her only hope, retroviral drugs, cost ten dollars per pill. The departure of the Canadian doctor to conceal his selling of a fraudulent placebo strands the patient without alternatives. Publication of the story and *The Art of Death* preceded Edwidge's composition for *Sojourners* of "The Possibility of Heaven," a memoir of her mother's symptoms of ovarian cancer and the chemotherapy that caused her midriff to balloon. In "Without Her" and "Feetfirst," the author takes comfort in Rose Danticat's favorite beatitude—Matthew 5:4, which promises solace for the bereaved.

See also Brother, I'm Dying, Death.

Sources

Danticat, Edwidge. "The Book of Miracles," *The Story Prize*. New York: Strong Winds, 2019.
_____. *Breath, Eyes, Memory.* New York: Soho Press, 1994.
_____. "Elsie," *Callaloo* 29:1 (January 2006): 22–29.
_____. *Everything Inside.* New York: Knopf, 2019.
_____. "Hot-Air Balloons," *Granta* 115 (20 June 1996).
_____. *Krik? Krak!* New York: Soho Press, 1995.
_____. *The Last Mapou.* Brooklyn: One Moore Book, 2013.
_____. "The Port-au-Prince Marriage Special," *Ms.* 23:4 (Fall, 2013): 50–55.
_____. "The Possibility of Heaven," *Sojourners* 44:2 (February 2015): 22–24.
_____. "Reading Lessons," *New Yorker* 80:42 (10 January 2005): 66–73.
_____. "Sunrise, Sunset," *New Yorker* 93:28 (18 September 2017): 54–60.
McCormick, Robert H. "Review: Brother, I'm Dying," *World Literature Today* 82:1 (2008): 74.
Simon, Daniel. "Review: The Art of Death," *World Literature Today* 92:2 (March/April 2018): 25.
Sontag, Deborah. "Island Magic," *New York Times* (30 August 2013).

Humor

Edwidge lightens the serious side of characters with keen wit and impromptu sallies, such as the selection of butterflies to rub on breasts to make them grow in "Reading Lessons" and the snake in *Célimène* that can squeeze life from a victim "comme le jus d'une orange pressée" (like juice from an orange crush) (Danticat, 2009). The parody of English as a second language in *The Dew Breaker* shares a misreading of Lincoln's Gettysburg Address as "four scones and seven tears ago, our fathers blew up this condiment" (Danticat, 2004, 165). In the satiric "Tatiana, Mon Amour," Sophie makes snide reference to the nearness of insanity to genius in Abena Yooku, who "Didn't have even that far to travel" (Danticat, 2004, 442).

For the novel *Claire of the Sea Light,* in the opinion of Benjy Caplan, journalist for the *Miami New Times,* Edwidge's quips are sly and disarming, such as an anecdote about dressing her aunt for burial. Fisherman Nozias Faustin's flight from a vasectomy contrasts the noir humor of Mayor Albert Vincent's chortle that "some executioners cross themselves before they shoot their victims," a smirky connection between killers and mechanical Catholic rituals (Danticat, 2013, 89). Professional funnies emerge from the jest "our having to punch a clock" and labor to give birth in *Create Dangerously* for Adam and Eve's violation of God's commands. Another birthing gibe recalls Aunt Denise Dantica's production of son Maxo in 1948 by a three-day ordeal "pushing him out of my eyes" (Danticat, 2010, 153).

Easing Tension

Other scenarios lessen fearful events with colorful, off-the-cuff drollery. For "A New Sky," a prayer aiding Edwidge to mourn her mother in *The Art of Death,* the lines mix sense impressions of the universe with the prosaic—a tin can of cash secreted in the freezer and a blender that needs a new blade. On the way to a Vodou gathering, novelist Lyonel Trouillot eavesdropped on a group playing dominoes. By moonlight, they used the occasion to mourn islanders killed in the 2010 earthquake and to titter at foibles of the dead. A chilling blend of funny and grievous, the true identity of the surviving twin in *Untwine* enlightens Giselle's Aunt Leslie and Uncle Patrick on a life-and-death mistake. When her mother Sylvie Boyer points out the black birthmark behind her daughter's right ear, Giselle imagines a drum roll, a media indication of melodrama.

In an October 2020 interview with children's author Laura Pegram for the Kweli International Literary Festival, sponsored by the *New York Times,* Edwidge explained how the pairing of the hilarious with the noir ensures balance, such as the exaggeration of earthquake survivor Junior "in the entire country, in the entire world" in *Eight Days* and Man Rapadou's story of the prisoner fed on bread and water in *The Farming of Bones* who returns home and dies of gorging (Danticat, 2010, n.p.). The noirish anecdote quiets Rapadou's guests who appreciate her ability to "laugh out of sadness" (Danticat, 1998, 222).

At a suspenseful pass in *Anacaona,* the Taino diary writer anticipates Chief Caonabó's message with circling birds and muses secretly that he may be "short a few feathers himself" for his fascination with winged creatures (Danticat, 2005, 76). Much of the author's humor in *After the Dance* bears a waggish edge, as with the papering of shacks with pictures of celebrities such as Brigitte Bardot, whom a barefoot peasant gouges in the eyes with his toenails. To entertain

Sophie Caco and fill in stories of relatives in *Breath, Eyes, Memory,* Tante Atie relates the doomed effort of Grandmè Ifé to command snakes to return to their lair, a reflection of the mystic aura of reptiles.

The forming of family in *Brother, I'm Dying* makes light of Bob's fluid imagination, which he evolves from reading comic books with cousin Nick. The claim of outer space equipment in his head inspires Kelly to threaten cranial surgery with a butter knife. To cinch sibling relationships, Bob's reversal of the offer awards Kelly and Karl the same sci-fi amusements that Bob and Edwidge bring from Haiti. Receiving rather than taking, Kelly acclimates to having an older sister and brother and to sharing their hard-wired brain power. The author valued the imaginary brain surgery for "[starting] us on our way to becoming a family," a settlement of differences without rancor (Danticat, 2007, 118).

Everyday Gibes

Untwine imparts human foibles in members of the Boyer family, as with the twins' April Fool's pranks and Aunt Leslie's medical pun "We just have to be patient" (Danticat, 2015, 121). Giselle dubs Dr. Emmanuel Aidoo, the attending physician from Accra, Ghana, "duck doctor" and his students "ducklings" for following in a line behind him during rounds. At Isabelle's viewing in her "girly" coffin, Giselle imagines her family squabbling over the painted hibiscus, a four-language uproar "like fights at the United Nations" (*ibid.,* 161, 160). Grandpa Marcus Boyer likes lugubrious jokes, such as the condemned man who refuses a last cigarette because it would be bad for his health. The gentle touch of grandparent banter follows Giselle to Haiti for a farewell to her twin's ashes.

Perhaps because of the hurtful subject of *Untwine,* Edwidge generously larded heavy thoughts with lighter ones. In a restoration of normality after a car crash, the narrative discloses the high school courtship letters in French between David Boyer and Sylvie, who dressed for class in virginal white blouse and long navy skirt. The flirting of two top students weakens David's academic concentration and causes him to lose weight. Decades later, the correspondence conveys to their twin daughters, Giselle and Isabelle, the clichés of lovers that expressed a teen crush similar to their own coming of age romances. In an interview with Jessica Horn for *Meridian,* Edwidge acknowledged that shielding children from adult topics is futile: "It was a kind of illusion, a veil, that we were being protected from information 'too strong for our ears,' things that because they seemed forbidden, we became very curious about and we discovered anyway" (Horn, 2001, 20).

Sources

Danticat, Edwidge. *Anacaona: Golden Flower, Haiti, 1490.* New York: Scholastic, 2005.
_____. *Brother, I'm Dying.* New York: Vintage, 2007.
_____. *Célimène—Fairy Tale for the Daughter of Immigrants.* Montreal: Memoire d'Encrier, 2009.
_____. *Create Dangerously: The Immigrant Artist at Work.* New York: Vintage, 2010.
_____. *The Dew Breaker.* New York: Abacus, 2004.
_____. *Eight Days: A Story of Haiti.* New York: Orchard Books, 2010.
_____. *The Farming of Bones.* New York: Penguin, 1998.
_____. "Reading Lessons," *New Yorker* 80:42 (10 January 2005): 66–73.
_____. "Tatiana, Mon Amour," *Callaloo* 27:2 (2004): 439–453.
Beard, David. "Seeing Haiti, When It Can Dance and Laugh," *Boston Globe* (5 September 2002): M7.
Caplan, Benjy. "Miami's Literary Genius," *Miami New Times* (29 August 2013): 28.
Horn, Jessica. "Edwidge Danticat: An Intimate Reader," *Meridians* 1:2 (Spring 2001): 19–25.
Pegram, Laura. "A Sense of Rupture," *Kweli Journal* (17 October 2014).

Immigration

Separations trouble Edwidge, the survivor of losses by death, estrangement, and diaspora. In the essay "New York Was Our City on the Hill" for the *New York Times,* she explained how severances made the term "home … more abstract, less reachable, less tangible" (Danticat, 2004, CY10). She stated to Dwyer Murphy, an interviewer for *Guernica,* the significance of risk—"how much people sacrifice to be here, to make it here," the background of the 2005 *Nation* article "Not Your Homeland" (Murphy, 2013). She deepened issues of flight from Haiti with examples of jailing of her Uncle Joseph Dantica in *Brother, I'm Dying,* stillbirth and a mother's suicide in "Children of the Sea," a worksite death in the poem "Plunging," and a father's drowning in the short story "Without Inspection." To enhance pathos in the latter narrative, the mother, Darline, names her boy Paris, the father's dream city.

The incarcerated women in "A Crime to Dream" and "No Greater Shame" lived isolated in places such as West Miami's Comfort Suites Hotel in view of plazas off limits to their children and patrolled by armed guards. In an essay for *Nation,* Edwidge asserted that their treatment violated "the kinds of ideals that this country stands for" (Danticat, 2005, 14). For fictional beautician Flore Voltaire, Maxime Ardin, Jr.'s, abandoned rape victim in *Claire of the Sea Light,* migration from Haiti offers relief from an oppressive rich household who threaten to seize her son Pamaxime. Because Max, Jr., sired the boy, Flore accepted money from the elder Maxime and intended to take him out of the country with her mother, a typical female-headed household like that of Hermine Azile in "Caroline's Wedding" or Darline and Paris in "Without Inspection."

Witnessing for Them

To fictionalize the emotional rift of migration, the writer composed a fairy tale, *Célimène,* about the challenge of leaving home for a new life. In an interview for *Essence* with islander singers called the Fugees, the author's essay on "Hanging with the Fugees" quoted the Haitian spirit of unity: "As people of African descent, we are all refugees. Everyone came to this Country on a boat at one time or another" (Danticat, 1996, 86). In a model of disjunction, she created the Haitian Espérance family in *Behind the Mountains.* The father communicates from New York by audiocassette. Before mailing him a letter, daughter Célianne combats common fears: "Maybe he has changed. Maybe I have changed," a normal ambivalence as teens exit childhood and reliance on adults (Danticat, 2002, 16).

Edwidge particularized the grim details of life in the margins for migrants. In the true vignette "Celia," the author personalized the terror of a mother struggling to breathe while trapped in a metal container on the way from Guatemala to Brownsville, Texas. She observed, "Raging, seemingly impassable seas have not stopped migrants from leaving places that … won't let them stay" (Danticat, 2019, xiii). To DeNeen Brown, a journalist at the *Washington Post,* the author mused, "Someone is always left behind…. The hardest, the most tragic ones, are people who are never reunited, who never reconnect, who lose a parent, who lose a child through migration," the destiny of Célianne's stillborn infant in "Children of the Sea" and of Cousin Marius Dantica's remains after death from AIDS in Miami in *Create Dangerously* (Brown, 2007, M2). She characterized writing as a source of memory, "of gathering pieces of myself that I lost during those years" of separation from the Danticat household and from relatives left behind in Haiti (*ibid.*)

A Global Concern

In a conversation with journalist Nancy Raquel Mirabal for *Callaloo,* Edwidge noted the size of the Haitian diaspora, which more than equaled the island population, and the economic ties, which, in 2007, returned $800 million to families in Haiti. She identified the persecutions that turned islanders into expatriates and declared, "U.S. policies have created the conditions that force people to flee Haiti in the first place" (Berger, 2008, 35). Once they reach the U.S., in a post–9/11 paranoia, they "live with the double threat of being both possible victims and suspects, often with deadly consequences," her conclusion in the article "Death by Asylum" in *Sojourners* magazine (Danticat, 2005, xi). Taunting among students in *Breath, Eyes, Memory* varied from "boat people" and "stinking Haitians" to "the Frenchies" (Danticat, 1994, 66). In "Seven Stories," an elderly apologist for anti-immigration policy justified his preference for "people who offer more" as new citizens (Danticat, 2019, 175). Because of the openly hostile Trump presidency, the writer issued an election eve 2020 op-ed piece urging, "Be the Vote for Immigrant Families under Threat by the Trump Administration."

The writer charged U.S. border entry policies with worsening fears that North America will be overcrowded with nonwhites, Muslims, and impoverished black and brown "boat people," whom Americans label "disposable" (Mirabal, 2007, 33). For the *New York Times,* she dubbed the obdurate, sometimes capricious immigration officials "the all-powerful gatekeepers," the initiators of face-to-face conflicts and first impressions (Danticat,

148 Immigration

2004, CY10). Upon entry, "Haitians have a very low rate of being granted asylum because we are black and poor" (Berger, 2008, 36). Once received into a detention center, she stated in the foreword to *The Penguin Book of Migration Literature,* refugees become invisible and "live in the shadows; they become slowly erased and their voices become muffled or go unheard" (Danticat, 2019, xii). The shadow figures became her focus, as she stated in *Everything Inside,* because "Fiction brings us under the skin of the people we're reading about" (Danticat, 2019).

Finding a Home

The writer stated to an interviewer at the University of Miami the difference in experience depending on the generation. Older ex-pats avoided the struggle of traveling to the Dominican Republic or France. Even though they risked imprisonment and infantilism by their need for interpreters and legal advisers, they preferred South Florida, where climate and the nearness of Little Haiti and the Bahamas suited tastes and needs. A parade float in the Jacmel carnival, depicted in *After the Dance,* featured American Coast Guard officers on a cutter that preceded a small refugee craft surrounded by sharks. At the festival viewing stand, the masquerading U.S. shore patrol forced refugees to leap overboard, a fate awaiting untold numbers of the 38,000 escapees in 1991 after the ouster of Aristide.

Overall, the exodus left transients vulnerable to inequities that treated Haitians unjustly, inhumanely, a parallel to West African abductees arriving over the Middle Passage on slave ships to auction blocks. To U.S. citizens, Edwidge condemned a system that elicited "wails of the more recently arrived migrant children who were separated from their parents at the U.S.-Mexico border and have been kept in cages, and iceboxes, some never to see their parents again" under the draconian Trump regime (Danticat, 2020). Analyst Valerie Kaussen, a literature specialist at the University of Missouri at Columbia, described the constant dangers in having to "cross and re-cross borders that are policed by coast guards, border patrols, and other institutions of surveillance" (Kaussen, 2015, 25). At a refugee's funeral in "Caroline's Wedding," the priest honors past struggles: "In the shackles of the old Africans … to the quarters of the New World, we came. Transients, Nomads" (Danticat, 1995, 147). Analyst Newtona Johnson of *Obsidian III* summarized the multiple liabilities of immigration as "the loss of roots, the loss of a sense of belonging, the loss of power, and even the loss of an 'authentic' cultural identity" (Johnson, 2005–2006, 153).

See also Vulnerability.

Sources

Alexandre, Sandy, and Ravi Y. Howard. "Interview," *Journal of Caribbean Literature* 4:3 (Spring 2007): 161–174.

Berger, Rose Marie. "Death by Asylum," *Sojourners* 37:4 (April 2008): 32–36.

Brown, DeNeen L. "Interview," *Washington Post* (14 October 2007): M2.

Danticat, Edwidge. *Behind the Mountains: The Diary of Célianne Espérance.* New York: Orchard Books, 2002.

_____. "Be the Vote for Immigrant Families under Threat by the Trump Administration," *Miami Herald* (1 November 2020).

_____. *Breath, Eyes, Memory.* New York: Soho Press, 1994.

_____. "A Crime to Dream," *Nation* 280:17 (2 May 2005): 13–15.

_____. *Everything Inside.* New York: Knopf, 2019.

_____. "Hanging with the Fugees," *Essence* 27:4 (1 August 1996): 85–86.

_____. *Krik? Krak!* New York: Soho Press, 1995.

_____. "New York Was Our City on the Hill," *New York Times* (21 November 2004): CY1.

_____. "Not Your Homeland," *Nation* 281:9 (26 September 2005): 24, 26.

_____. *The Penguin Book of Migration Literature.* Foreword. New York: Penguin, 2019, xi-xiv.

_____. "Voices from Hispaniola" (contributor), *Meridians* 5:1 (2004): 68–91.

_____. *We Are All Suspects Now: Untold Stories from Immigrant Communities after 9/11.* foreword. Boston: Beacon Press, 2005, vii-xi.

_____, and Lucrèce Louisdhon-Louinis. "Interview," *MediaSpace* (25 August 2013).

Johnson, Newtona. "Interview," *Obsidian III* 6/7:2/1 (Fall 2005–2006): 147–166, 264.

Kaussen, Valerie, "Migration, Exclusion, and 'Home' in Edwidge Danticat's Narratives of Return," *Identity, Diaspora and Return in American Literature.* New York: Routledge, 2015.

Mirabal, Nancy Raquel. "Dyasporic Appetites and Longings," *Callaloo* 30:1 (Winter 2007): 26–39, 410.

Murphy, Dwyer. "The Art of Not Belonging," *Guernica* (3 September 2013).

Introductions

A graphic author of human dilemmas and tragedies, in anecdotes, short stories, and longer narratives, Edwidge seizes readers with title and first sentence as revealing as Nathaniel Hawthorne's *The Scarlet Letter,* as stark as Chapter One, "The Prison Door." As early as 1991, she grappled with street murder in the pun "Sawfish Soup," a poem for *Caribbean Writer,* airing her affection for orphaned children and for victims of raw urban crime with the serrated edge of a sawfish. The concept of vulnerability continued to lace stories of the young and naive— *Anacaona, Eight Days,* "Dream of the Butterflies," "The Revenant," and "Hot-Air Balloons," a story of terrible truths confronted by uninitiated aid workers.

In a first novel, *Breath, Eyes, Memory,* Edwidge stated a manifesto, a reference to sources of plots from storytelling, witnessing, and recollection. The simplification of method acknowledges past information from oral tradition and contrasts it with the author's present. In memory, stories like the matrilineage of former maid and cook Granmè Ifé Caco, daughters Atie and Martine Caco, granddaughter Sophie Caco Woods, and great granddaughter Brigitte Woods outpace straightforward biography by viewing successive generations and their emotional and cultural baggage. The author's opening sentence poses a paradox— Sophie's celebration of Mother's Day with a card and wilted daffodil intended for Aunt Atie, her foster mother. The final exchange between Sophie and her grandma indicates that, after the terrible death of Martine and her unborn child, Sophie has gained insight into a relationship with a complex single parent, the victim of rape by the Tonton Macoute. The perception enables Sophie to answer the question "Are you free?" (Danticat, 1995, 204).

Short Fiction

For the anthology *Krik? Krak!,* the author chooses a Creole summons to hearers interested in call and response oral stories, a common Haitian pastime. The ten narratives form staves of a single theme, the struggle of Haitians during fearful times. "Children of the Sea" refers both to naive attempts at crossing the Atlantic Ocean to the U.S. and of a failed jaunt that ends in a stillbirth and the young mother Célianne's suicide. The title recurred in a 1997 play version at the Rites and Reasons Theater in Providence, Rhode Island, and in the French adaptation at Chappelle du Verbe Incarné in Avignon, France.

Extending the pathetic destiny of Célianne, the story leads into dire events begun in "Nineteen Thirty-Seven," the year that tyrant Generalissimo Rafael Trujillo organized the slaughter of 30,000 black laborers to rid the Dominican Republic of nonwhite residents. With an historic citation beginning "A Wall of Fire Rising" and the title "Between the Pool and the Gardenias," Edwidge fleshes out the matrilineage of Josephine, granddaughter of Eveline, drowned in the

Massacre River on the day that daughter Défilé gave birth to Josephine. Taken as a triad, the stories expose female suffering during overlapping eras of terror, which cause Josephine to ally with Jacqueline and other victims of genocide and sorrow. The suggestion of the Jacquerie, a coterie of French rebels, elevates the atmosphere to agency and direction against government corruption. A hint from "Night Women" implies that infant corpses in the gutter like Marie's baby Rose are conceived by the wretched work of prostitutes, who have no commodity to sell other than sex to support their families. The tune in the background—the Creole version of "Are you sleeping?"—imparts a reminder to "Brother John" (the indolent U.S.) that poverty diminishes lives as close as Haiti (Danticat, 1995, 174).

The pun in "The Missing Peace/ Piece" reflects mother hunger in women who grow up without maternal affection and guidance. By picturing the formation of a quilt from fabric scraps, like the Grandma Baby's death wrap in Toni Morrison's historical novel *Beloved,* the author introduces a major feminist motif: the merger of everyday shreds into something colorful, warming, and practical. Juxtaposed with "Seeing Things Simply," the stories extol the female mentor, who guides young searchers toward their inner truths and strengths. The final two stories, "New York Day Women" and "Caroline's Wedding" move north to immigrant females who patch together frayed marriages and lives in a foreign country. The former story implies insight in the first-person narrator, who declares, "I see my mother," an aha moment that reevaluates an older woman (*ibid.*, 127). With a witty riddle, the second work, a novella, points to the satisfaction of answered questions.

Edwidge's skill at introducing her works reached an important peak with *The Farming of Bones.* The title poses a complex metaphor for unconscionable agribusiness in the Dominican Republic that profits from sugar production by black Haitian laborers. Chapter One opens on the sexual escapism of Amabelle Desír during love sessions with Sebastian Onius, a muscular harvester of cane. The author reverted to strict history for *Kreyòl* with the article "A Brief Reflection on the Massacre River," a designation from colonial days, when murder at the river banks prefaced Trujillo's genocide of October 1937.

Adult Regrets

Before completing *The Dew Breaker,* her third novel, in 1999, Edwidge issued in *New Yorker* the opening stave, "The Book of the Dead," a bravura study of an emerging sculptor named Ka, the Egyptian term for "spirit." Her father, a searcher for forgiveness, gained discernment by taking his daughter to the Brooklyn Museum to peruse Egyptian navigation of a river of fire to divine judgment in the afterlife. The opening line, "My father is gone," introduces a girl who adores her father and the paradox of her portrait in mahogany, which forces him to see "the dew breaker," one of the marauding Tonton Macoute of the Duvalier era (Danticat, 2004, 1). After he jettisons the sculpture in a Florida lake, his wife, Anne Bienaimé, reflects on the death of her stepbrother "in the prison yard at dawn, leaving behind no corpse to bury, no trace of himself at all," a multifaceted trope for the fat man, a prison torturer—under the alias Bienaimé (well-loved)—who tries to elude his heinous past (Danticat, 2004, 242).

Between the novel's introit and finis, characters troubled by past sins and losses act out the stories "Seven," a regret of adultery, and "Water Child," Nadine Osnac's loss of a fetus to abortion, which she commemorates with a watery shrine. "The Book of Miracles," a return to the Bienaimé family, dramatizes a scary moment when Ka thinks she recognizes a Haitian killer at Catholic mass. Memories seize the next four stories, the ghostly replays that trouble "Night Talkers," people who reveal secrets in their sleep, and establishing the case of terror in "The Bridal Seamstress," a pairing of journalist Aline Cajuste with a maker of bespoke wedding dresses who flees flashbacks to an attack by the Tonton Macoute. In the last of the four stories, tokens of recall honor a newborn in "Monkey Tails" and Freda's performances of dirges in "The Funeral Singer."

SOURCES

Danticat, Edwidge. *The Dew Breaker*. New York: Abacus, 2004.
_____. *Krik? Krak!* New York: Soho Press, 1995.
Martinez-Falquina, Silvia. "Postcolonial Trauma Theory in the Contact Zone: The Strategic Representation of Grief in Edwidge Danticat's *Claire of the Sea Light*," *Humanities* 4:4 (2015): 834–860.
Misrahi-Barak, Judith. "'My Mouth Is the Keeper of Both Speech and Silence ...' or The Vocalisation of Silence in Caribbean Short Stories by Edwidge Danticat," *Journal of the Short Story in English* 47 (1 December 2006): 155–166.

Krik? Krak!

With the anthology *Krik? Krak!*, Edwidge creates a kaleidoscope of human emotions in eleven stories conjoined by matrilineage, suffering, and frequent references to butterflies, emblems of beauty and effortless motion. Book critic Joanne Omang at the *Washington Post* lauded the author's skill at weaving "the sad with the funny, the unspeakable with the glorious, the wild horror and deep love that is Haiti today" (Omang, 1995). The anthology won a nomination for the National Book Award for its detailed examination of the bloodthirsty Tonton Macoute. According to Gabrielle Bellot, a fiction critic for *Publishers Weekly,* the paramilitary "[acts] with the impunity of their belief that Vodou protects them" while they victimize "ordinary people just trying to get by" (Bellot, 2019).

The protocol of storytelling, introduced in Chapter 18 of *Breath, Eyes, Memory*, places Grandmother Ifé Caco in charge of nightly narrative, for which she chooses a fool tale based on male-female seduction. Edwidge varied ordinary themes with her style of what children's author Amanda Putnam, on staff at Roosevelt University in Chicago, called "resistant storytelling" (Putnam, 2003, 52). For the sake of regime change, the author views the direct and peripheral anguish wrought on islanders by the Duvaliers.

Children of the Sea (1993)

With the austere motif of journalist-fiction writer Stephen Crane's classic narrative "The Open Boat," Edwidge introduces the collection with an epistolary tribute to the six brave young souls who anchored protest radio against Haitian tyrants. After the shooting of the six outside Fort Dimanche Prison on April 3, 2000, protesters demanded their bodies. The topic returns in "The Funeral Singers," "Ghosts," and the essay "All Geography Is Within Me." In the latter, she acknowledges the whims of fate: "Some people's potential new beginnings can also lead to their end" (Danticat, 2019, 58). The author dedicated the story to a cousin, Marie Micheline Marole, who drowned at sea with her daughters and granddaughters in April 1989. For bold reportage, Evelyn Hawthorne, a professor at Howard University in Washington, D.C., named Edwidge "the fitting carrier of denied histories" (Hawthorne, 2004, 42)

In the original plot published as "From the Ocean Floor" in the October

1993 issue of *Short Fiction by Women,* one of the Radio Six leaves his Haitian girlfriend behind and travels by sea toward Miami. Before he departs the island, the unnamed girlfriend takes out her terror and sadness on her father, who charges her with sluttish behavior. On the way, the lovers record daily events in their diaries. Sense impressions manifest the rigors of sun, thirst, filth, and nightly cold on migrants, one of whom is pregnant. Storytelling and song relieve nausea, but nothing quells the peril of a leaky, sinking boat.

The natural boundaries—land, sky, sea—take on metaphoric effect. To the Radio Six activist traveling north, the endlessness of the waves suggests a boundless love for his girlfriend. Overwhelming hope, the day-by-day sail becomes a death sentence that only a Coast Guard rescue can stem. When fifteen-year-old Célianne goes into labor with a child sired by a Tonton Macoute rapist, the activist ponders another mouth to feed as supplies come to an end. The reference to breastfeeding a newborn recalls the stunning conclusion to John Steinbeck's *Grapes of Wrath,* in which Rose of Sharon Joad bears a stillborn infant and offers mammary feeding to a starving old man. The value of breast milk elevates in stature women who have little to give but lactation.

Inhuman choices reflect the author's paring existence down to stark biological elements—pilgrims sharing the last scraps of food for sustenance and hurling excrement into the sea. In the final words, the rebel throws his notebook in the water and drowns off the Bahamas, leaving his girlfriend disquieted by black butterflies, the messengers of death. The drama meshes with "Caroline's Wedding" and the drowning of a mother who tosses her dead infant into the waves, an echo of West African martyrdom during the Middle Passage. Imagery contrasts water as the means of flight and the source of death.

Nineteen Thirty-Seven

The visit to a prison built by U.S. Marine occupation forces in the 1920s introduces unnerving government structures that enslave and persecute vulnerable Haitian women for sorcery. The bogus accusation to stymy female rebel factions recalls the targeting of Massachusetts women by the Salem Witch Trials from February 1692 to May 1693. Josephine, daughter of the inmate Défilé and granddaughter of a victim of the October 1937 Dominican slaughter at the Massacre River, carries a female treasure, a statue of the Madonna produced in slave days. An icon of the grieving mother of Christ, the figurine resonates with female inmates and survivors of the carnage to 30,000 Haitians by Generalissimo Rafael Trujillo's Guardia. The idol's tactile surface uplifts Josephine's mother, despite malnutrition, deteriorating skin, beatings, and the onset of tuberculosis.

Through a jumble of cataclysmic details, Josephine perceives her place in Haitian female history, which, fed by martyrs' blood, flows like the Massacre River toward liberty. Because of her birth within hours of her grandmother's murder and her mother's flight to safety through a bloody morass, she gains respect for a matrilineage dating to great-great-great-grandmother Défilé, whom the author revisits in the story "Between the Pool and the Gardenias." Out of veneration for sisterhood, Josephine allies with Jacqueline and women still incarcerated. Jacqueline's name suggests the French Jacquerie, a peasant uprising in 1358 that returns to prominence in Charles Dickens's classic history novel *A Tale of Two Cities.*

In addition to commemorating the

holy mother, the fractured narration of female roles in the 1804 Haitian Revolution retrieves the example of Marie Sainte Dédée Bazile. A raving subversive, she followed Emperor Jean-Jacques Dessalines to his demise—gunned down at Pont Larnage on October 17, 1806, and his corpse ripped apart by street mobs in the Port-au-Prince plaza. The remaining prisoners grasp the mother's belongings, including a pillow stuffed with her hair, an icon of martyrdom softening the way for future defiers of tyranny. All cling to the myth of female flight to liberty, the ritual of river daughters, and a subsequent generation filled with joy.

A Wall of Fire Rising (1991)

A cautionary tale of unfulfilled yearning, Edwidge's outtake from the Ibo myth of the flying Nigerians revisits black resistance to captivity and grueling labor that confers neither dignity nor a living wage far from the motherland. Her glimpse of a three-member peasant family, originally published in the summer 1991 issue of *Cymbals* as "A Wall of Fire," contrasts the resilient mother Lili with her devoted son Little Guy and fantasy-obsessed husband, Big Guy. Simultaneously with Little Guy flaunting his stage role as Dutty Boukman, "one of the forefathers of Haitian independence," Big Guy longs to fly the Assad family's hot air balloon, a petty juvenile ambition (Danticat, 1995, 48). He regrets having so little seniority on sugar mill employment lists and cringes at the thought of passing on his job of latrine cleaner to Little Guy. He regrets advancing less than his own father achieved. His suicide by leaping from the purloined balloon seems a relevant end to a life of scrubbing toilets.

The author separates genders in her characterization, picturing Lili as a stoic mom who places future hopes on her son, but who offers few intimacies to heighten Big Guy's marital satisfaction. The backstory associates Haitian men with the rebellious males of 1791. Just as past legends focus on men, Big Buy is the family's most important adult. In his shadow, Lili accepts the formidable task of searching out sustenance for her endangered family and encouraging her son's education in speech and history.

Ignoring the affluence of the Assads, owners of a sugar mill, Lili sticks to grim responsibilities, beginning each morning with filling a recycled gasoline container with water to balance on her head and searching for food for dinner, which she serves in calabashes on banana leaves. Close monitoring of Big Guy's dreams and self-pity informs Lili that yearning to fly is more than a vagary of fleeing entrapment, but she fails to read into his comment about a dead man's reputation a hint of self-destruction. The story concludes somberly on a battered corpse with open eyes still trained on the sky—his ideal of success—and not on his hardy widow or fatherless boy.

Night Women (1993)

A dreamy vignette originally published in *Caribbean Writer* in summer 1993 and the next year in *Clerestory* as "Voices in a Dream," Edwidge's fourth narrative hovers on the edge of one night's anxiety and a mother's guardianship of innocence and decency. Storytelling protects a small boy from the truth of a threadbare lineage as the son of an unwed prostitute and her anonymous customer. The pairing of profitable copulation with her alleviation of the boy's insecurities creates a dual view of flesh and love. The fantasy of night visits from angels and ghosts protects the child from the reality of a squalid existence in a one-room shack provided by profits from a lone commodity, the mother's body.

The issue of control obligates the woman with a daily bedtime ritual based on childhood's familiarity with imagination and storytelling. The cyclical narratives shield her son from the omnipresent trauma within single parenthood among the poor. In the background, the boy hums the crucial question: "Are you sleeping," a line from Jean-Philippe Rameau's Baroque round "Frère Jacques (Brother John)," composed in the early 1700s. A lone curtain epitomizes the thin tissue of lies that the boy will soon interpret for himself. The author nudges the reader with reminders of "sleeping" in the outside world, which ignores third world misery.

Between the Pool and the Gardenias (1993)

The despairing narrator Marie experiences a mystic transformation after finding a dead baby girl. The text, reprised from the summer 1993 issue of *Caribbean Writer: Best of the Small Presses* and the 1994 Heinemann anthology *Monologues by Women,* suggests a biblical influence. For gravitas, Edwidge juxtaposes pool fish, emblems of Moses on the Nile and of Christ with his Galilean fishermen disciples, and gardenias, a fragrant bush flower and bridal adornment representing a gentle chastity similar in incorruptibility to the Virgin Mary. The pairing echoes stereotypical extremes of squalor and purity in male versions of women's history.

In the anthology's fifth stave, background weds the protagonist to an historic matrilineage: Great Grandma Eveline's murder at the Massacre River in early October 1937 and Grandma Défilé's martyrdom among allegedly red-winged female prison inmates from the story "Nineteen Thirty-Seven." Following "A Wall of Fire Rising," Godmother Lili's suicide in widowhood occurs after her grown son Guy migrates to Miami. Marie communes with female spirits and adds a surreal daughter to the family tree by claiming the corpse of Rose, one of the abandoned offspring of "Night Women."

Sense impressions enrich Marie's delusions of motherhood, a relief from the loss in the first trimester of three pregnancies sired by her philandering husband. The detailed dressing, cleansing, and perfuming of a decaying baby amid her employers' luxuries recalls the odor of rotting pig guts, a Port-au-Prince sewer, and the dung heap that the Dominican pool man cites to describe his sexual encounter with Marie. The noir imagery suggests the underrated state of the island's domestic caste under the Duvalier regime. The make-believe holy family—Marie, Rose, and the Dominican laborer—collapses with his repudiation of a one-time sex partner. Just as his call for gendarmes eclipses Marie's dreamscape, Haiti falls into fascism and repression under the Duvaliers.

The Missing Peace (1992)

The ironic fable of an encounter between fourteen-year-old Lamort and an American visitor, Emilie Gallant, bases the theme of mother hunger on parental deaths and daughters left motherless. The narrative, recycled from the 1992 literary anthology *Just a Moment,* a 1994 issue of *Caribbean Writer,* and the 1996 collection *Feminism 3: The Third Generation in Fiction,* reprises a common feminist fiber image—the collection of oddments for patching into a quilt. Piecework epitomizes the fragmented memories that burden Lamort and the task of reconstructing the self.

Even though Lamort can't read "Le Petit Écolier" (The Little Scholar), a French textbook issued in 1959, Emilie recognizes a paradoxical wisdom in her island guide. Lamort has an instinct for deep, mature truths, but too easily accepts islanders' beliefs, including her grandmother's disapproval of a fetus born to a dying mother. On the way to a cemetery, Emilie and Lamort encounter Toto, a hostile guard who buries mass shooting victims at night, and Raymond, Lamort's admirer and victim of Toto's shooting. Because "peace" is no longer the password, Lamort leads Emilie back to her residence and guards her overnight.

The meaning of names—Lamort (death), Emilie (compete) Gallant (exuberant), Toto (Swahili for "child"), and Raymond (protector)—outlines the basics of the episode. To the initial flirtation on a dust heap, a past episode recounts Raymond's bullet wound on February 7, 1986, when violence erupted from the ouster of Baby Doc Duvalier. Emilie dreams of her mother and requires Lamort to lead her to the common grave of political victims. She insists that Lamort give up so dire a name and reclaim her mother's names, Marie Magdalène, a disciple of Jesus that specious history calls his wife. The upswing in Lamort's self-esteem gives her the courage to rebuke a pushy grandmother and to demand renaming.

Seeing Things Simply

In a gendered coming of age story similar in tone and style to "The Missing Peace," Princesse, a receptive, intelligent student, accepts the casual mentorship of Catherine. The 27-year-old francophone painter from Guadeloupe, a hint at the Renaissance mystic Catherine of Siena, teaches by example. By isolating the two during daily art work, the narrative pictures the child stripping her body and mind of dross to ponder the visual and

philosophical wisdom of a more mature female.

On the walk to studio sessions, Princesse passes iconic distractions common to the islands—rum, bestial gambling, and flirting. To an aging male scholar, she represents a point of luck in an otherwise unimpressive day. The pairing reprises the standard graybeard educating the youngster, the motif undergirding mentoring of Samuel by the high priest Eli at Shiloh in I Samuel 2:35, the guidance of Arthur Pendragon by Merlin in Mary Stewart's *The Crystal Cave* and *The Hollow Hills,* and the training of Luke Skywalker by Obi-wan Kenobi in *Star Wars.*

A touch of suspense during Catherine's absence to acknowledge a death gives Princesse an opportunity to do her own mulling of shapes and natural phenomena. Drops of blood on her white shirt suggest the sacrifices that artists make for their work. Because Catherine rewards her with a sip of rum and an insightful review of her modeling, Princesse begins internalizing the daily influences, symbolic traces of French artistry on island life and self-image. Her first drawing captures the female side of Haitian domesticity in the likeness of a devalued peasant wife who models erect posture while bearing household burdens. The passage of luck in the cockfights and the loss of roosters contrasts the lasting effects of the mentorship, an investment of youth and time in a possible art career for Princesse.

New York Day Women

Edwidge's semi-autobiographical story describes a mother from Brooklyn on her stroll through the Manhattan business district, passing Carnegie Hall and the Plaza Hotel on the way to Central Park. Her daughter Suzette, a worker on lunch break from an advertising agency, plays the voyeur by shadowing the mother. She observes the mother's childcare for a little boy with a Big Bird comic book and canned soda, questionable elements of modern American education and nutrition. The author applies counterpoint to Suzette's suppositions about her immigrant mother and the reality of a fifty-nine-year-old woman who feels comfortable in a cosmopolitan setting. Citations of maternal wisdom, like recorded announcements, illustrate how the older woman imparts guidance, such as kindness toward people who need seats on the subway.

Strands of Caribbean culture detail what the mother has left behind by migrating to New York. She sends clothing to relatives and avoids patriarchal criticism of females who straighten their hair, a self-important male intrusion on female liberties. In contrast to the jogger mom who leaves her blond boy with the sitter, Suzette has a mother who makes Raggedy Ann dolls to satisfy a longing for grandchildren. To balance career with femininity in Suzette's life, the mother adds lace collars to her daughter's softball shirts and discourages excessive thinness, an obsession in style-conscious Manhattanites. The conclusion, an image of heavy salt bags, suggests unshed tears that characterize an island parent's concerns as Suzette assumes more big city traits. A clue to Suzette's values, work in advertising, hints at capitalism's phony bait to sell fads.

Caroline's Wedding

The ninth stave of *Krik? Krak!* advances views of mothers and daughters and their naturalization to American citizenship in the 1990s. The introduction reprises the tragedy of fifteen-year-old Célianne and her infant sired by a Duvalier secret policeman, a resetting of the myth of Sor Rose (Sister Rose), Haiti's

symbolic mother. The Azile women—Caroline, Gracina, and their mother, Hermine Françoise Génie Azile—live with constant grief for Caroline's father, Carl Romélus Azile, who died of prostate cancer. Hermine's dislike of Eric Abrahams, Caroline's Bahamian groom increases household tensions. The modern obstacle, a courthouse wedding, jeopardizes the stock of legends and superstitions that Hermine repeats to ensure a Haitian background for her nubile daughters. To make herself more American and less Haitian, the most adapted daughter, Caroline, experiments with hair dye and a prosthetic forearm.

Spiritual detachment threatens family peace with reminders that Papa married a widow to legitimize his passage to America. Hermine realized a loss of intimacy during their years of separation. The drugging of Hermine during pregnancy by an immigration guard causes a birth defect, Caroline's truncated forearm. The giver of unconditional love to the household, the older sister Gracina heals the fractured female circle as best she can, soothing Caroline by concealing from their mother her forbidden nights with Eric. The American Zoetrope Screenplay Contest featured the cinema version of Edwidge's story, winner of the summer 2017 grand prize of $5,000 for scenarists France-Luce Benson, Darcy Miller, and Easmanie Michel, a cinema major at New York University.

Epilogue:
Women Like Us (1996)

In an extended metaphor structured like a conversation with self, Edwidge compares the black writer's task with hair braiding—the union of strands long and short, dark and light to recreate women's lives. The feminine vignette first appeared in *Essence* in May 1996. The speaker's devotion to composition at first dismays the mother, who fears that domestic labors go unappreciated by an artsy daughter. Unable to quiet the female voices whispering in her subconscious, the young writer remains stoic in a time when storytellers and radio journalists suffer under tyrants like Papa Doc and Baby Doc Duvalier. Trusting an instinctive network of long-dead women, she resurrects historic ancestors from the afterlife and their collective.

In the Old Days (2012)

The twentieth anniversary edition of *Krik? Krak!* incorporated a story from a 2012 issue of *Callaloo*. The narrative views distance between daughter Nadia, an English as a Second Language teacher, and father Marc, who abandoned his wife before knowing he had sired a daughter. On arrival from New York to Miami, she comes too late to meet him. Following a social gathering with her stepmother and friends over lemonade, Nadia realizes that they conceal Marc's death. She makes an impersonal farewell over his body. The differences in memories reflect the unsettled relationships of daughter and father and of Marc and his two wives. The vivid closure elucidates unfinished business, the type of family debacle that refuses completion.

See also Grotesque, Slavery.

Sources

Anker, Elizabeth S. "Embodying the People in Edwidge Danticat's *Krik? Krak!*," *Novel* 47:1 (Spring, 2014): 149–166.
Bellot, Gabrielle. "Edwidge Danticat Returns to Haiti in New Stories," *Publishers Weekly* (21 June 2019).
Danticat, Edwidge. "All Geography Is Within Me," *World Literature Today* 93:1 (Winter 2019): 58.
_____. "From the Ocean Floor," *Short Fiction by Women* (October 1993).
_____. *Krik? Krak!* New York: Soho Press, 1995.
_____. "The Missing Peace," *Just a Moment* 4:1 (Winter, 1992–1993).
_____. "A Wall of Fire," *Cymbals* (Summer 1991).
Hawthorne, Evelyn. "Sites/Sights of Difference," *MaComère* (2004): 40–48.
Kennon, Raquel D. "'We Know People by Their Stories': Madness, Babies, and Dolls in Edwidge Danticat's *Krik? Krak!*," *Madness in Black Women's Diasporic Fictions*. New York: Springer, 2017, 163–197.
Michel, Easmanie. "Interview," www.youtube.com/watch?v=OMpv2OzcDKQ, 3 October 2014.
Omang, Joanne. "Review: *Krik? Krak!*," *Washington Post* (14 May 1995).
Putnam, Amanda. "Braiding Memories: Resistant Storytelling within Mother-Daughter Communities in Edwidge Danticat's *Krik? Krak!*," *Journal of Haitian Studies* 9:1(Spring 2003): 52–65.
Young, Jason R. "All God's Children Had Wings: The Flying African in History," *Journal of Africana Religions* 5:1 (2017): 50–70.

Krik? Krak! Genealogy

Scattered links between fictional families increase the cohesion of Edwidge's narratives, a strategy perfected by Mississippi writer William Faulkner. The stories "Nineteen Thirty-Seven," "A Wall of Fire Rising," and "Between the Pool and the Gardenias" introduce the backbone of a single matriarchy:

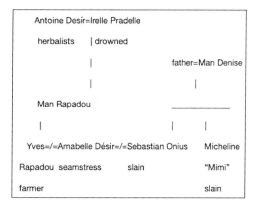

By allying women in a loosely framed family tree, the author illustrates the value of Haitian women to households and society, including women like sex workers who leave dead infants in the street. Lili's volunteer parenting as a Catholic sponsor attests to the willingness of friends to influence spiritual formation and provided legal guardianship under the sixth-century CE canonical code of the Emperor Justinian. The chain of tragic deaths indicates the price of parenthood and citizenship in a nation tyrannized first by Dominican Republic Generalissimo Rafael Trujillo and Haiti's dual despotism of the Duvaliers.

Sources

Anker, Elizabeth S. "Embodying the People in Edwidge Danticat's *Krik? Krak!*," *Novel* 47:1 (Spring, 2014): 149–166.

Danticat, Edwidge. "All Geography Is Within Me," *World Literature Today* 93:1 (Winter 2019): 58.

_____. *Krik? Krak!* New York: Soho Press, 1995.

_____. "A Wall of Fire," *Cymbals* (Summer 1991).

Hawthorne, Evelyn. "Sites/Sights of Difference," *MaComère* (2004): 40–48.

Omang, Joanne. "Review: *Krik? Krak!*," *Washington Post* (14 May 1995).

Putnam, Amanda. "Braiding Memories: Resistant Storytelling within Mother-Daughter Communities in Edwidge Danticat's *Krik? Krak!*," *Journal of Haitian Studies* 9:1 (Spring 2003): 52–65.

Language

Edwidge speaks in interviews about the advantages of being multi-lingual in Creole, French, and English and her ability to "[transfer] an image in my head onto a page" (Danticat, 2004, 68). She commends the value of lingual facility to fictional and real characters and events, such as Arnold's pretense to be the Cuban-Hispanic laborer Ernesto in "Without Inspection" and the gadget relieving the muteness of her uncle Joseph Nosius Dantica, silenced by laryngeal cancer in *Brother, I'm Dying*. For refugees in "Children of the Sea," according to Judith Misrahi-Barak, a specialist on postcolonialism at Paul-Valéry University, Montpellier, "Speech is the only refuge available to the boat refugees, providing a tenuous but organic link between people" (Misrahi-Barak, 2006, 162). One of the ironies of the island diaspora, standard Parisian French rises in importance to Haitian intellectuals. To insure respect from bank tellers, Joseph urges his niece to conduct business in textbook French.

In reflections on first-generation Haitian-Americans, Edwidge lamented the dearth of written memories in the U.S. compared with writings in French by Haitian-Canadians. To Ray Conlogue, an interviewer for the Toronto *Globe and Mail*, she regretted the lapse in Creole, the birth language, which immigrants shared with North American slaves, especially in New Orleans: "Language is a vessel of intimacy, and that generation did not possess such a vessel" (Conlogue, 2004, R3). To further the pride of island children in history, her story "A Wall of Fire Rising" depicts Little Guy memorizing the maroon rebel Dutty Boukman's resounding speech that asserts a sanguine future: "In the ashes, I see the bones of my people," an allusion to the Egyptian myth of the Phoenix bird and its rise from total destruction (Danticat, 1995, 48).

Government Brainwashing

Edwidge accentuates the danger of data manipulation, a trademark sin of the Trump administration. In *Create Dangerously,* she vilifies François "Papa Doc" Duvalier, the circulator of fascist news and pamphlets and banner of books. He capitalized on the firing squad execution of guerrilla warriors Louis Drouin and Marcel Numa on November 12, 1964. He twisted the horror show into a noir form of visual learning by requiring school children to watch. In the fifth chapter, the author admires resistance to the Duvalier propaganda machine by Haitian-American filmmaker-scenarist Patricia Benoit, an exile from the corrupt system. Skilled in Island languages, she varied intonation of Creole, French, and

English to suit the audience and increase listener receptivity. The control of vocal timbre won Benoit the 2012 Tribeca Film Festival Best New Narrative Director for *Stones in the Sun,* a cinema correcting faulty Haitian history which starred Edwidge in the part of Yannick, a teacher and activist who risks all to stay in her homeland.

For similar purpose of enlightening the public, Pascal Dorien, the naive news reporter for Radio Zòrèy (ear radio) in the short story "Ghosts," fantasizes that he may one day disclose lifestyle in "the *geto* from the inside" (Danticat, 2008, 111). Critic Kaitlyn Fajilan, a reviewer for *Highbrow,* notes the author's affinity for media: "Danticat all but anthropomorphizes the radio, allowing it to function as a kind of mouthpiece for the Haitian people, its profusion of stories and songs echoing the plurality of voices" (Fajilan, 2013). Pascal's facility with translating daily slum news from Bel Air into vernacular Creole enables him to characterize Tiye (kill), a one-armed capo surrounded by three vicious lieutenants. Pascal imagines that his tell-all program will draw thousands of listeners "daily, weekly, monthly" with "a kind of sick voyeurism" for the crime gripping degenerate neighborhoods (*ibid.*). Contributing to the draw, he supports the hour-long program of Max Ardin, Jr., a DJ who promotes "Kreyòl rap—hip-hop from the slums—[which] was just beginning to make it to the airwaves" (*ibid.*). For both boys, language encourages them to escape poverty and tap into the ready cash of capitalism.

Settling In

The author's writing in *Homelands* sparkles with insights into the nature of metamorphic language and linguistic homelessness. She called immigrants "urban nomads … ambient voyagers" with "a wanderer's heart" cutting them off from the music, custom, routine, religion, and patois of their motherland (Danticat, 2006, 11, 12). In the foreword to *The Penguin Book of Migration Literature,* she personalized bilingualism: "Some of us are born speaking one language and will die speaking another. We are seeds in one soil and weeds in another," a hint at American revulsion at the sounds of Creolized French (Danticat, 2019, xii).

The author pictured the two languages residing side by side in the brain. The Haitian diaspora altered children so drastically by the new language that they couldn't converse with grandparents. She exonerated younger Haitian-Americans for being "up against strong forces of race, place, and time, a mosaic of cultures … that demand immediate absorption" (Danticat, 2006, 9). To seize the future, they leave their lingual heritage behind, the choice of Claude in "Night Talkers."

To *Miami New Times* journalist Alexandra Martinez, the author spoke of a lingual transformation: "Our parents had to reinvent themselves, they had to learn new languages, and we're the inheritors of that beauty" (Martinez, 2016). To disclose selection of a new home language, the author avoided writing in Creole or French and chose English, "her stepmother tongue," as a neutral and most pragmatic vehicle (Munro, 2007, 215). Indigenists lambasted her stories for excluding the intonation, accent, inflection, and rhythm of authentic island folk talk. British analyst Martin Munro challenged disparagers of her writing by reminding readers that literature "must be able to travel, to impose on itself and find a worthy place among others…. What counts is the human color of the work," a clear-cut description of Edwidge's talent (Munro, 2007, 142).

See also Creole, Names.

SOURCES

Conlogue, Ray. "Haunted by Haiti's Ghosts," [Toronto] *Globe and Mail* (19 April 2004): R3.

Danticat, Edwidge. *Create Dangerously: The Immigrant Artist at Work.* New York: Vintage, 2010.

_____. *Ghosts, New Yorker* (24 November 2008): 108–113.

_____. *Homelands: Women's Journeys Across Race, Place, and Time.* foreword. Emeryville, CA: Seal Press, 2006, 8–12.

_____. *Krik? Krak!* New York: Soho Press, 1995.

_____. *The Penguin Book of Migration Literature.* foreword. New York: Penguin, 2019, xi–xiv.

_____. "Voices from Hispaniola" (contributor) *Meridians* 5:1 (2004): 68–91.

DeGraff, Michel. "Boston Public School Partner Explains Haitian Creole Program," *BNN News* (25 September 2017).

Fajilan, Kaitlyn. "Getting Lost in the World of Edwidge Danticat," *Highbrow* (6 November 2013).

Holden, Stephen. "The Old Country Never Goes Away," *New York Times* (20 November 2014).

Lyons, Bonnie. "Interview," *Contemporary Literature* 44:2 (Summer 2003): 181–198.

Martinez, Alexandra. "Edwidge Danticat Discusses Memoir and Immigration at Little Haiti Cultural Center," *Miami New Times* (30 March 2016).

Matza, Michael. "Interview," *Philadelphia Inquirer* (6 February 2012): A2.

Mirabal, Nancy Raquel. "Dyasporic Appetites and Longings," *Callaloo* 30:1 (Winter 2007): 26–39, 410.

Misrahi-Barak, Judith. "'My Mouth Is the Keeper of Both Speech and Silence …' or The Vocalisation of Silence in Caribbean Short Stories by Edwidge Danticat," *Journal of the Short Story in English* 47 (1 December 2006): 155–166.

Munro, Martin. *Exile and Post-1946 Haitian Literature.* Liverpool, UK: Liverpool University Press, 2007.

The Last Mapou

A first-person picture book illustrated in bursts of color by Haitian-American artist Edouard Duval-Carrié, the author's nature story *The Last Mapou* adheres to the publisher's mission to stimulate readers by presenting a national icon. The setting favors children in low literacy populations by coordinating learning with subjects relevant to the milieu. An enlightening scenario portrays a girl and grandmother on a morning walk through the garden past a mapou, a tree as revered as the Norse Yggdrasil, a cosmological touchstone in the Old Norse Edda. The narrative juxtaposes food plants—almond, avocado, and mango—among colorful lycoris lilies, oleander, and hibiscus. The gift of a red blossom illustrates the ability of islanders to adorn themselves simply with one flower behind the ear.

A heritage tree, a 200-year-old mapou (also known as silk cotton or kapok), stands so grand and elegant that its honey-hued wood dominates the back garden and shades the welcoming benches below. A relative of the grapevine and African baobab tree, Grann's mapou once housed bats until it began to dry. As leaves and bark declined, its roots lost their grip on the soil. Without going into detail, Grann indicated a dilemma—rescue the tree or remove it before it collapsed on her house or on her. The speaker compared the dwindling of a tree to pain and labored breath, signs of ill health in Grann. On a positive note, the mapou in folklore connected earth to heaven.

Stories as Myth

Like the Grandmother Carole in "Sunrise, Sunset," Tante Atie in *Breath, Eyes, Memory,* and the mother in *My Mommy Medicine,* Grann has experience entertaining a granddaughter each Saturday. While rocking on the porch, Grann teaches her to carve self-portraits in wood from the coastal mapou and to embroider toy figures and place mats. The origination tale of human birth from a tree enables Grann to justify the importance of the tree to the first islanders, who lived inside the trunks. The tree became a staff of life, giving soft wood for housing, seed fiber for bedding, and trunks for hollowing into sea transportation. With mobility came the necessity to migrate from the high country and live closer to the shore.

The mapou developed into a giver of fertilizer, soap, and oil as well as sap for treating illnesses. Tree blossoms adorned residences and sheltered bees, which drew hives to the branches as a source of honey. The mapou dominated culture as an ancestral blessing—an altar for weddings and a sacred repository for infant umbilical cords. As population increased, demands on the tree threatened its survival. To preserve the past, Grann stuffed a story-cushion with silky fiber and embroidered the top with nine images of humankind emerging from the trunks and building civilization. Eventually, only Grann's tree survived when pruning saws lopped its dying branches. As a token of both life and death, the illustrator turned the roots into a snaky tangle and the tree into a tomb bearing a future island amid an umbilical mesh.

Strong as a Tree

As a foil to mortality, Grann leaves her grandchild a portrait doll shortly before the old lady sickens and dies. Like the heritage of storytelling families, Grann's nature tale becomes the girl's oral legacy. For the author as well, the life history of an outstanding tree ignites a concern for deforestation, which Catholicism encouraged to halt the use of the mapou for Vodou ritual. Edwidge warns that clear-cutting Haiti's native forests for building purposes and making charcoal threatens not only the ecosystem, but also the spiritual and ancestral underpinnings.

In post-publication reflection of her reverence for the mapou, Edwidge offered a salute to the species. To an interviewer for *Urban Fusions*, she elevated the plant to "une sorte d'arbre sacré, et c'est aussi un grand arbre qui dure pour toujours. C'est une institution royale, un mapou" (a type of sacred tree, and it is also a great tree that always endures. It's a royal institution, the mapou.) (Cowen, 2020). For bilingual storytellers and speakers of Haitian Creole, Texas Christian University sponsored *Dènye Pye Mapou,* a translation by Creolist Michel DeGraff, a professor at the Massachusetts Institute of Technology, and Jacques Pierre, a lecturer at Duke University, and distributed 1,000 copies to students.

SOURCES

Cowen, Tyler. "Ma conversation avec Edwidge Danticat," *Urban Fusions* (5 November 2020).
Danticat, Edwidge. *Dènye Pye Mapou.* Brooklyn: One Moore Book, 2013.
_____. *The Last Mapou.* Brooklyn: One Moore Book, 2013.
Joffre, Ruth. "It Wants to Be Told," *Kenyon Review* (10 October 2019).
Pierre, Jacques. "The Growth of Creole Language Studies," *Duke Today* (5 June 2014).
_____. "Jacques Pierre: Creole a Key to Haitian literacy," *Durham Herald-Sun* (5 September 2014).
_____. "Jacques Pierre: Help for Haiti Must Include Embracing Creole," [Raleigh] *News & Observer* (21 February 2014).

The Last Mapou Genealogy

The family tree in *The Last Mapou* extends Edwidge's interest in matriarchy and its benefits to the younger generations as a soul force. The line of descent reduces genealogy to a nameless schematic, beginning four generations previous to the plot.

The designations attest to a genealogical pattern—the tendency of a trait to skip a generation before recurring in grandchildren. Perhaps Grann develops oral tradition in her granddaughter because Manman shops every Saturday, leaving her child in capable hands.

See also Fear.

SOURCES

Danticat, Edwidge. *Dènye Pye Mapou.* Brooklyn: One Moore Book, 2013.

```
Grandmother Eveline

drowned in the Massacre River

October 1936

|

Défilé

a prison martyr to

allegations of red-winged

shapeshifting

|

Josephine - - - - - - - - - - - - - - godmother Lili= Big Guy

  b. October 1937              suicide    | toilet janitor

                                          | suicide

                                          |

                              Little Guy

                              immigrant to Miami
```

_____. *The Last Mapou*. Brooklyn: One Moore Book, 2013.

Joffre, Ruth. "It Wants to Be Told," *Kenyon Review* (10 October 2019).

Literacy

Edwidge surveys language obstacles for Haitians and immigrants, for example, the use of oral creation myths to replace academic schooling in *The Last Mapou* and Grandma Rose's storytelling to bolster Kim Boyer and Callie Morrissete's training at a nun school in "Seven Stories." In the novel *Claire of the Sea Light,* Odile Desír identifies herself with an X on official documents in token of illiteracy. At a birthday visit to the cemetery, seven-year-old Claire Limyè Lanmè Faustin is limited to reading her first name, which she shares with deceased mother Claire Narcis. Her father, fisherman Nozias Faustin, recognizes even less of the alphabet than those six letters. Ironically, strips of the newspaper *La Rosette* cover walls of his seacoast shack, but remain unread.

More pressing, the fisherman's meager income, ecological depletion, shore pollution, and the dangers of a marine occupation threaten his growing child's future. As stated by Valérie Loichot, a Romance language specialist at Emory University in Atlanta, "hunger and illiteracy are irremediably linked" (Loichot, 2004, 92). Faustin's lack of schooling underlies the conflict—a need to locate a foster parent to educate his seven-year-old daughter Claire. Without the burden of a girl to support, he can hunt construction jobs elsewhere, perhaps in the Dominican Republic, where the government recruits Haitians for building sites and cane fields.

As a contrast to the underclass, the author boasts in the *Newsweek* essay "Edwidge Danticat Returns to Haiti and Finds Resilience and Regeneration" of thousands of islanders gathering at a defunct cane plantation. They assemble for the annual Fête Dieu Livres en Folie (the Feast of God Mad Books), a celebration of literacy led by 135 island authors. In fiction, she develops the background of Maxime Ardin, Sr., who hints at lines from *Macbeth* and cites French poet Arthur Rimbaud and the title of Nathaniel Hawthorne's *Scarlet Letter* while he muses over the hardships endured by the generation that grew up under the Duvaliers (Danticat, 2013, 187). The casual mention of classic literature attests to Ardin's success as opposed to Nozias's poverty and his need for Caleb, a Ville Rose scribe, to write a letter to daughter Claire. Even without knowledge of letters, Nozias can understand the manual sign language of Josephine, Caleb's wife, a mute who makes up her own cyphers.

A National Peril

The author stated in an interview for *Journal of Caribbean Literature* the problem of illiteracy in 70 percent of islanders, an obstacle to formation of a true democracy. In *Create Dangerously,* efforts to improve education emanate from the *centre d'étude* (community center), an informal clubhouse. The single agency supplies fully equipped learning labs for children who live in homes lacking electricity. It also funds the Ciné Club that introduces controversial movies "essential to the majority of Haitians" who can't read, notably *Poto Mitan: Haitian Women, Pillars of the Global Community, Girl Rising,* and *Courage and Pain* (Danticat, 2010, 44). An expanded definition of narratology admits collections of recipes from silenced women, which the author validates as food writing in "Plantains, Please" for *The Caribbean Writer* for granting basic learning to the most debased citizens.

Edwidge regrets the endeavors among her extended family of readers, intellectuals, and artists who had to "attend a decrepit village school as children" (Danticat, 2010, 14). Others of the Danticat family "were so weather-beaten, terror-stricken and maimed that they were stifled" (*Ibid.*). She valued comic books that introduced brother Bob and cousin Nick to sci-fi and childhood stories that Granmè Melina and other relatives told rather than read. She viewed textbook alternatives as spurs to the imagination and promoted the return of literate Haitians from the diaspora to teach their countrymen, the fictional Marc's decision at the core of the story "In the Old Days."

Making the Effort

In the essay "An Accident of Literacy," Edwidge commiserated with parents spending 15 percent of their income to educate one child, who was typically the oldest male. The acquisition of reading occurs in the story "New York Day Women," in which the daughter Suzette admires her mother for learning to read from her brothers' school books. For Caroline Azile in "Caroline's Wedding," a job teaching English as a Second Language introduces the main character to her Bahamian fiancé, Eric Abrahams. A different slant in *The Farming of Bones* questions Hispanic translations of Haitian stories, which undergo rephrasing "in words you do not understand, in a language that is theirs, and not yours" (Danticat, 1998, 244).

In Edwidge's first novel, *Breath, Eyes, Memory,* the text opens on the illiteracy of Tante Atie Caco, who performs agrarian work rather than attend school because she is embarrassed to be unschooled in old age. To prevent illiteracy in the next generation, she insists that niece Sophie Caco get an education, which seems to her niece like an elite privilege. Martine Caco, Sophie's mother, nurtures dreams of their matriarchy "becoming important women … the first women doctors from my mother's village," which epitomize the fantasies of illiterate peasant girls (Danticat, 1994, 43). In the following generation, Martine anticipates Sophie's success as a triumph for all three women—aunt, niece, and mother. On rejoining Atie in Haiti, Sophie congratulates her aunt's elementary reading skills.

The daily struggle for schooling continues in "A Wall of Fire Rising" with the need for kerosene for lamps to brighten a hut. For Little Guy, a failed lamp requires him to join neighborhood pupils in sitting under streetlights for illumination.

For those who learn neither French nor English, such as the art student Lamort in "The Missing Peace," absence of education is humiliating. A more dangerous situation, the indenturing of little girls as domestics in exchange for schooling leaves Rosie, the indentured domestic in "Monkey Tails," hopeless and women like Tante Rose in *Behind the Mountains* unprotected and powerless to ward off sexual predators. Rosie wisely finds work at an orphanage and completes school out of reach of her former master. Rose's thirteen-year-old niece Céliane "Cécé" Espérance pities "thousands of girls who end up alone in the city with nothing" (Danticat, 2002, 124).

See also Storytelling.

SOURCES

Adisa, Opal Palmer. "Up Close and Personal," *African American Review* 43:2–3 (Summer/Fall 2009): 345–355.

Alexandre, Sandy, and Ravi Y. Howard. "Interview," *Journal of Caribbean Literature* 4:3 (Spring 2007): 161–174.

Danticat, Edwidge. "An Accident of Literacy," https://www.buildon.org/2012/09/an-accident-of-literacy-guest-blog-by-edwidge-danticat/, 8 September 2012.

_____. *Behind the Mountains: The Diary of Célianne Espérance*. New York: Orchard Books, 2002.

_____. *Breath, Eyes, Memory*. New York: Soho Press, 1994.

_____. *Claire of the Sea Light*. New York: Vintage, 2013.

_____. *Create Dangerously: The Immigrant Artist at Work*. New York: Vintage, 2010.

_____. "Edwidge Danticat Returns to Haiti and Finds Resilience and Regeneration," *Newsweek* 158:7 (15 August 2011).

_____. *The Farming of Bones*. New York: Penguin, 1998.

_____. *The Last Mapou*. Brooklyn: One Moore Book, 2013.

_____. "New York Day Women," *New York Stories*. Mineola, NY: Dover, 2016, 150–155.

_____. "Plantains, Please," *Caribbean Writer* 13 (1999): 179–180.

Loichot, Valérie. "Edwidge Danticat's Kitchen History," *Meridians* 5:1 (2004): 92–116.

Phillips, Delores B. "Recipes for Reading Recipes? Culinary Writing and the Stakes of Multiethnic Pseudonarrative," *Narrative Culture* 7:1 (Spring, 2020): 79–97.

Mama's Nightingale

A story of creativity and advocacy for justice, Edwidge's *Mama's Nightingale* depicts Saya battling a parent's isolation and jailing, government hindrances to family unity. The episode rang true to the author, whose "grandpa was deported back to Haiti because he didn't have the right papers," a vague grouping of documents, passports, visas, and birth certificates (Solomon, 2017, B1). In boldly colorful pages dominated by New Orleans artist Leslie Staub's sky blue and Caribbean pink, the text pictures Saya in blue footed pajamas, a mark of little girl snuggling. Staub chooses as icons of communication blue birds and overlapping green leaves, positive images of Mama's unfailing nurturance. Like the lyric night bird, her voice penetrates a blank spot in Saya's life and makes it sparkle with affection.

The accidental erasure of Mama's taped voice on the answering machine deepens Saya's pain at Mama's incarceration. The name Sunshine Correctional lampoons bureaucratic detention after an ICE (U.S. Immigration and Customs Enforcement) raid nabs Mama at the restaurant where she works. The situation mirrors the arrest of Rose Danticat after a factory raid. Creole enabled Edwidge to retell the event for a hypothetical reader, her Tante Ilyana. A starred critique in *Kirkus Reviews* lauded the combination of words and images for warmth and fervor and awarded Edwidge a Best Books of 2015 citation.

Breaking Silence

Communication, a controlling theme, depicts Papa writing letters to the media, the mayor and congresswoman, and the judges who confine aliens who lack documentation. Sense impressions heighten the pathos of weekly jail visits, where Saya absorbs Mama's fragrant coconut hair dressing and tender touch, her humming of the nightingale's call, and her search for the rainbow trail to freedom. The storytelling that boosts mother-daughter rapport derives from their mutual enjoyment of Haitian songs and nursery rhymes of the Ti Zwazo (little bird), a popular motif among francophone children in Guadeloupe, Haiti, Martinique, and Réunion. A petite source of rescue, the bird diverts witches from devouring children, a folk rendition of the U.S. immigration system. Reunion dreams ease the tension that causes abdominal pain, a common complaint from worried youngsters. *Horn Book* credited the children's work for offering comfort to splintered families.

The value of technology as substitute communicator for a live storyteller relieves Saya's sorrow by relaying Mama's bedtime narrative in a "wind-chime voice," an image of absence (Danticat, 2015). Mama's tale of a mother bird separated from her baby duplicates sense impressions of bedtime protocol. From a comforting fable, Saya develops self-control, a necessary restraint to ease departures from the jail and reproachful glares from guards, public servants who have little background in child displacement. In folk art style, Leslie Staub creates a microcosm of well-being in images of winged hearts, dolphins, mermaids, and fish, which outnumber the one sad heart holding keys to a padlock reflecting Haiti's history of slavery.

Speaking Truth to Power

Edwidge depicts Saya developing lingual facility and discovering the transformative magic of storytelling. Through communication with Mama, her singular triumph opens the padlock. Staub implies the potency of child agency by patterning Saya's dress with keys, the sunderer of legal barriers to diaspora. The *New York Times* and *Booklist* praised an outcome

rich in illumination that combines Creole phrases with evocative island folk art. Analyst Amy Fish, on staff at Concordia University in Montreal, credits the author with intensifying "young people's visibility at the center of immigration discourse" on paper, on tape, on TV news, and before a judge (Fish, 2020, 2).

Media intervention alerts a female jurist to the family's isolation and need for homecoming, an impasse in the U.S. shared by more than 70,000 parents. Gender components imply that women on the bench tend to empathize with dire situations disconnecting little ones from home. The resolution credits the oral tradition with opening the metaphoric cage and freeing the mother nightingale. Staub's pictorial epilogue conveys homecoming with a blue streamer held in the mother bird's beak, a visual ensign of hope. *Publisher's Weekly* and *School Library Journal* honored the book for its serious, honest message and ray of solace to immigrant populations. Creators Syndicate in Los Angeles chose *Mama's Nightingale* as a book celebrating Black History Month.

Sources

Danticat, Edwidge. *Mama's Nightingale*. New York: Dial, 2015.

Fish, Amy. "'Leave Us Good News': Collective Narrations of Migration in *Mama's Nightingale*," *Research on Diversity in Youth Literature* 2:2 (January 2020): 1–17.

Henderson, Jane. "Edwidge Danticat, St. Louis Literary Award Winner, Says She's Gained Nuance, Deeper Meaning," *Chicago* (18 October 2019).

Solomon, Lois K. "Noted Novelist Offers Writing Tips to Fourth Graders for State Exams," *South Florida Sun-Sentinel* (27 January 2017): B1.

Verbrugge, Jennifer. "Review: *Mama's Nightingale*," *School Library Journal* 62:5 (May 2016): 61.

Memory

As a buttress against rootlessness and loss, Edwidge stores up the history of her homeland in writing, particularly

Eight Days and The Farming of Bones. In reference to memory's impact on act, she delighted in its ability to "reinterpret and re-create and hopefully dream a better world" ("Review," 2010). In varied genres, Haiti's past foregrounds the Native American biography Anacaona, a grandmother's fable The Last Mapou, the essay "Look at Me" for Harper's, and the compendium The African Lookbook, which treasures native gestures and poses. Like her idol, Nobelist Toni Morrison, Edwidge embraces "rememory," the conversational anecdotes that fortify family gatherings. Personal reminiscence in funeral chats in "Night Talkers" and in Mira and Joseph's boyhood stories in Brother, I'm Dying evaluates background realistically and finds strength and courage to persevere. Reflection is an offshoot of sisterhood and vocal performance in "The Funeral Singer" and of recovery from Prime Minister Charles Morrissete's assassination in "Seven Stories." Survivors' ruminations salve acute hurt and numbness and facilitate reordering of events into a beneficial letting go.

Of the loss of both parents, in the personal essay "Love, Our Only True Adventure," the writer cherished the solace of sketches: "All we are left with are the stories: funny stories, odd stories, tales of woe as well as joy," particularly imitative retellings that involve voicing and body language (Danticat, 2020, n.p.). For the essay "Flight" in the New Yorker, Edwidge assigned the living the task of internalizing personal losses from the collapse of the World Trade Center on 9/11 and of performing rituals and acts of memorialization that keep the victim alive in the heart. To regain vitality and optimism, fanatic Catholic Anne Bienaimé in "The Book of Miracles" regularly attends mass and Christmas Eve services, rituals steeped in medieval liturgy and song. Lacking Anne's recall of escape from Haitian violence, her American daughter Ka in "The Book of the Dead" expresses ambivalence toward family secrets by sculpting mahogany into an idealized likeness of her father. The two views maintain falsehoods—Anne's surface rejection of her husband's criminal past and Ka's incognizance of it.

Edwidge taints some recall with irreversible sins, such as dual adulteries in "Seven," suicide in The Art of Death, and Louise George's assault on a student in Claire of the Sea Light. Reiteration of past felonies offers a tutorial to Claude, a patricidal teen and ex-con in "Night Talkers." Parallel to his recollection of growing up the hard way through crime and punishment, the story he tells Dany Dorméus extols Aunt Estina Estème, his redeemer. The beloved elder midwife in Beau Jour recovers from blinding and rears Dany, her orphaned nephew, whom she rescues from fire. For Dany, approaching his aunt's home stirs inklings of a generous woman who encouraged his emigration to New York City to escape the onslaught of the Tonton Macoute, the Duvalier secret police who killed his parents. A new path enables Dany to grasp opportunities in a less toxic environment.

Recall of Trauma

Social disruption invokes more prosperous times, as with uncommunicative ENT nurse Nadine Osnac in "Water Child," Pascal Dorien's intent to introduce his radio audience to the milieu of gang leaders in "Ghosts," and Beatrice Saint Fort's reciprocal friendship with young brides in "The Bridal Seamstress." Marie Micheline, mother of two in "Dream of the Butterflies," liberates herself and her son and daughter from constant machine gun fire by training her thoughts on summers at Léogâne, where she once contemplated many-tinted wings and cricket chirps. By banishing her own story, Marie condemns herself to "longing for something we are not even sure we ever had," one of the handicaps of losing touch with reality (Danticat, 2010, 65).

Uplifting reminiscence enables sixteen-year-old Giselle Boyer in *Untwine* to edge beyond a semi-coma and paralysis in a Miami hospital and overcome fear for her twin Isabelle and parents, whom a teen driver injured in a car crash. As details of the accident slip away from her damaged brain, the perceptions alter in form and value to Giselle after she returns home to Isabelle's empty room and strawberry-scented body wash. For relief from mourning, she listens to anecdotes about the two girls' closeness from grandparents Marcus and Régine Boyer, Aunt Leslie and Uncle Patrick, and school friends Tina and Jean-Michel. Ritual dispersal of Isabelle's ashes in Haiti releases Giselle from crisis mode with a display of sibling affection, one of the benefits of cremation.

Memory as Release

Of her method of harvesting epiphanies in *Breath, Eyes, Memory,* Edwidge disclosed how "grappling with memory is, I believe, one of many complicated Haitian obsessions" (Danticat, 2010, 63). Islanders honor folklore as old as Taino place names in *Anacaona* predating the arrival of Christopher Columbus on December 5, 1492. The Gallicized name Ouanaminthe, a town on the Massacre River in *The Farming of Bones,* distinguishes its Native American roots. The purpose of witnessing and recalling, according to the author, is to preserve events for the identity of a people, a benefit to orphans Mo and the title character in *Célimène*. Donna Bailey Nurse, a book critic for the Toronto *Globe and Mail,* states the corollary: "Having no one to remember you is like never having lived at all" (Nurse, 1998, D12).

The author's success in *Create Dangerously* earned kudos from Wajdi Mouawad, a book analyst for *Le Monde,* for producing "un livre de mémoire, un livre d'amour, un livre de courage" (a book of memory, a book of love, a book of courage) (Mouawad, 2012, 8).

To Opal Palmer Adisa, an interviewer from *African American Review,* the author stated respect for the ancestral past. She writes of a heritage left by earlier generations such as the statue of an unidentified maroon in *Eight Days,* parade costumes and masking in *After the Dance,* and relating true stories as a relief of pain, the purpose of a survivor friendship in *The Farming of Bones* and news to the grandparents in Beau Jour of Aline and Céliane Espérance's recovery from a pipe bomb under a bus in *Behind the Mountains*. Images of miscarriages in "Between the Pool and the Gardenias" haunt the speaker, who gravitates toward a sweet infant lying in the gutter, a metaphor for Haiti's loss and betrayal of its young. A major issue in *Brother, I'm Dying,* "Children of the Sea," and *Claire of the Sea Light,* the absence of the dead enables Haitians to reflect on enslaved forebears and the myriad disappearances of West Africans on the Middle Passage.

While seeking news on the January 12, 2010, earthquake in "Living and Loving through Tragedy," Edwidge exerts her flair for sheltering needy children. She responds like a substitute parent to a child named Kiki, a smiling survivor. The experience inspired the writing of *Eight Days,* a dreamscape of Junior's endurance through imagination and play that he once shared with Manman. In the story "New York Day Women," a Haitian mother exemplifies courtesy and patience for her Haitian-American daughter Suzette, for whom she sews female frippery onto garments. To journalist Bonnie Lyons of *Contemporary Literature,*

Edwidge described her own mothering during the eight-year absence of Rose Souvenance Danticat, "who may have been there in fragments, who was first a wonderful memory that represents absence" (Lyons, 2003, 195).

See also Death, *The Farming of Bones*, Tradition.

Sources

Adisa, Opal Palmer. "Up Close and Personal," *African American Review* 43:2–3 (Summer/Fall 2009): 345–355.

Danticat, Edwidge. *Brother, I'm Dying*. New York: Vintage, 2007.

_____. *Create Dangerously: The Immigrant Artist at Work*. New York: Vintage, 2010.

_____. "Flight," *New Yorker* 87:27 (5 September 2011): 32.

_____. "Look at Me," *Harper's* 327:1963 (December 2013): 64.

_____. "Love, Our Only True Adventure," (1 August 2020): https://hello-sunshine.com/post/love-our-only-true-adventure.

Lyons, Bonnie. "Interview," *Contemporary Literature* 44:2 (Summer 2003): 182–198.

Martinez-Falquina, Silvia. "Postcolonial Trauma Theory in the Contact Zone: The Strategic Representation of Grief in Edwidge Danticat's *Claire of the Sea Light*," *Humanities* 4:4 (2015): 834–860.

Mouawad, Wajdi. "Compter les morts en Haïti," *Le Monde* (29 June 2012): 8.

Nurse, Donna Bailey. "Edwidge Danticat Rescues Haiti from Its Western Labels," [Toronto] *Globe and Mail* (30 August 2013): D12.

"Review: *Eight Days*," *NPR Morning Edition* (9 September 2010).

Mothers

From the birth of royal Taino princess Higuemota in *Anacaona* to a maternal aunt's foster mothering of a niece in "Claire of the Sea Light" and Rose Danticat's instructions to Edwidge on prenatal care in *Brother, I'm Dying*, the author magnifies the role of Haitian females as the mainstays of society. From personal experience, she credits maternity with making women more humane and intuitive, the title figure's strengths in *Célimène* and Carole's redeeming traits in

"Sunrise, Sunset." In "Seven Stories," the author exalts with brief mention Callie Morrisete's mother, who seduces a border authority to expedite escape from Prime Minister Carl's assassination. For Darline in "Without Inspection," devotion to a child causes her to abandon her husband in the sea and save son Paris from drowning. The expenditure of self continues at the restaurant in Little Haiti, where stirring pots in a steamy kitchen drains her of fluids. In recognition of close ties with mothers, Edwidge makes frequent use of the name "Rose" for characters, reflecting ancient Roman symbolism of beauty overlapping the shortness of human life. Her story "The Missing Peace" pictures Emily changing her name out of regard for her mother, Mary Magdalène, the mythic weeper at the foot of the cross whose tears spawned a blooming red rose bush.

Maternity in Edwidge's stories clings to an innate spirituality. One fictional fisherman, Nozias Faustin in the novel *Claire of the Sea Light,* confesses his doubt that he can rear daughter Claire. He harbors self-defeat: "What did he know about raising a little girl? … There were so many things that could go wrong," a clear demarcation of gender differences imparted by a widower who relies on a sister-in-law as foster parent (Danticat, 2013, 15). At the novel's climax, Max Ardin, Sr., summarizes the task that awaits Flore Voltaire, mother of Pamaxime, Max's illegitimate grandson. The lengthy passage outlines step-by-step aspects of upbringing from childhood, verifying the grandfather's misgivings about his own son, a child of divorce. In both instances, caring seems to spring from the female body and womanly acceptance of all children as worthy of affection and care.

Models of successful and neglectful parenting, discipline, wisdom, and love infuse passages throughout the author's canon:

Mothers 169

Source	Mother	Children	Relationship
Anacaona	Anacaona	Higuemota	spoiler of beloved infant
	Bibi	Anacaona	humble Taino parent
	grandmother	Matunherí	family matriarch and soldier
	Yaruba	fetus	suicide
Behind the Mountains	Manman Aline	Moy, Céliane	maker of decisions
	Espérance	"Cécé" Espérance	
"Between the Pool and the Gardenias"	Marie	dead infant	tender caretaker of a rotting infant corpse she names Rose
"The Book of Miracles"	Anne Bienaimé	Ka Bienaimé	a religious fanatic lost in fantasy
Breath, Eyes, Memory	Grandmè Ifé	Atie, Martine	Caco family matriarch
	Maman Brigitte	Caco clan	an island presence who shields members from black magic
	Martine Caco	Sophie Caco, fetus	unstable rape victim and mother-to-be
	Sophie Caco	Brigitte Woods	positive role model
	Tante Atie Caco	Sophie Caco	foster mother and educator
Brother, I'm Dying	Denise Dantica	Edwidge, Bob, Marie Micheline, Maxo	mother, foster mother, and storyteller to children separated from parents
	Edwidge	fetus	attentive mother-to-be
	Rose Danticat	Edwidge, Bob, Kelly, Karl	immigrant mother reuniting older children with younger
"Caroline's Wedding"	Hermine Azile	Gracina and Caroline Azile	widowed family mediator and cook
Célimène	mother	Célimène, Mo	a presence who exists only in memories
"Children of the Sea"	Célianne	dead infant	drowns herself after burying her child in the sea
	Madam Roger	rebel son	a martyr forced to accept her boy's skull from mockers
"Claire of the Sea Light"	maternal aunt	Claire Faustin	a foster mother who rescues a motherless niece
Claire of the Sea Light	Claire Narcis	Claire Limyè Lanmè Faustin	imaginary parent after death in childbirth
	Flore Voltaire	Pamaxime	a vengeful mother who plots migration from Haiti
	Gaëlle Lavaud	Rose	a grieving mother and widow
Create Dangerously	Tante Zi	Marius Dantica	advises Edwidge on how to write about Zi's dead son
"The Dew Breaker"	mother	fat man	teacher of gardening
The Dew Breaker	Anne Bienaimé	Ka Bienaimé	concealer of the murderous past in Haiti
"Dream of the Butterflies"	Marie Micheline	son, daughter	protector from urban violence
Eight Days	manman	Justine, Junior	a clever, spirited parent who joins family play
The Farming of Bones	Rosalinda	Valencia Duarte	treasured parent who died in childbirth
	Doña Eva	Javier, Beatriz	pleader for her son's safety
	Iradelle Pradelle	Amabelle Desír	dollmaker and ghostly consoler of refugee
	Man Denise	Sebastian, Mimi	griever for children massacred in the Dominican Republic
	Man Rapadou	Yves Rapadou	welcomer of a refugee son and his friend
	Valencia Duarte	Rosalinda, Rafi	painter of Rafi's coffin with flowers

Source	Mother	Children	Relationship
"Living and Loving through Tragedy"	Edwidge	Kiki	substitute parent and comforter
Mama's Nightingale	Saya's mom	Saya	jailed storyteller on tape
"The Missing Peace"	Marie Magdalène	Emily Gallant	a dead parent recaptured in art
My Mommy Medicine	mother	daughter	soother of illness
"New York Day Women"	immigrant mom	Suzette	dealmaker and modeler of female independence
"Night Talkers"	Aunt Estina	Dany Dorméus Estéme	foster mom and rescuer
"Night Women"	sex worker	son	deceiver of boy about his mother's work
"Nineteen Thirty-Seven"	Défilé	Josephine	loving inmate beaten to death for sorcery
"The Port-au-Prince Marriage Special"	Babette	Mélisande	financially strapped mother who loses compassion for a dying child
"Reading Lessons"	mother	Danielle	an element missing from Danielle's life
"The Secret Island"	Ma	Betty "Bee"	a resilient mom who misses her deported husband
"Seven Stories"	Mrs. Morrissete	Callie Morrissete	sexual martyr to Callie's safety from assassins
"Sunrise, Sunset"	Carole	Jeanne	an aging mother concerned for her daughter's postpartum depression
Untwine	Grandma Régine	Sylvie, Giselle	a dependable source of love and encouragement for daughter and granddaughter
	Sylvie Boyer	Giselle, Isabelle	identifier of the surviving twin
"A Wall of Fire Rising"	Lili	Little Guy	encourager of a school assignment on Haitian history
"Water Child"	Nadine Osnac	fetus	aborter of fatherless child
"Without Inspection"	Darline	Paris	defender of shy son

Her children's books—*Mama's Nightingale* and *My Mommy Medicine*—present Saya's mom as a teller of stories from a jail cell by audio tape that captures the timbre and lilt of her voice. *My Mommy Medicine poses* a more hands-on mother relieving the tedium and anxiety of sick days with an array of imaginative activities that include pirate disguises. The YA novel *Untwine* celebrates another ever-present parent, Sylvie Boyer, the kind of woman who surrounds her twin daughters with opportunities as diverse as birthday sleepovers, flute training, travel, worship, and designing invitations.

Murderous Times

In an historical novel fraught with unthinkable crime, *The Farming of Bones* highlights motherhood with poignant scenarios, both domestic and nationalistic. For Valencia, a new mother of twins, her deceased mother Rosalinda becomes a beneficent presence in the birthing chamber. In gratitude for the spirit's lingering during labor and delivery, Valencia declares, "I never felt alone" (Danticat, 1998, 26). Valencia blesses her mother by naming the female twin Rosalinda Teresa. Juana, the maid, reflects on the help of St. Monica, benevolent mother of St. Augustine. The maternal motif recurs in the awakening of Amabelle Desír, a recumbent evacuee from Dominican persecution. Her mother's ghost consoles and cheers with "You, my eternity" (Danticat, 1998, 206). In both relationships, memory retrieves the parent from the afterlife with a spiritual presence.

The latter half of *The Farming of Bones* extends comforts both real and spectral. An enveloping hug and examination of son Yves's scalp in Cap Haïtien presents his mother, Man Rapadou, in ecstatic welcome because he survived dictator Rafael Trujillo's mass slaughter of black cane workers. Her probing takes on greater dimensions with hand-shaped palmetto branches shading her prodigal. To soothe his orphaned friend Amabelle, whose teeth are too damaged for chewing goat meat, Man Rapadou tenderly spoons pumpkin soup into her mouth "as though I were a sick, bedridden child" (*ibid.*, 223). The maternal comfort is particularly restorative to Amabelle, who worries about unfinished business with her parents, herbalists Antoine Désir and Irelle Pradelle, after they drowned.

The author favors the ministrations of penniless but adoring moms as devoted as Aunt Estina Estème, Dany Dorméus's foster mother in "Night Talkers." Following her burial, Dany and Claude revisit tales of her kindness to the community as local midwife. In the story "A Wall of Fire Rising," Lili devotes herself to family and supports son Guy during a period of verbal development. From a less promising relationship, the mother in "Night Women" fabricates imaginative stories of angels and stars to shield the boy from her sex work. In a poignant view of Marie Micheline, a mother warding off machine gun bullets of the Tonton Macoutes in "Dream of the Butterflies," Edwidge pictures a thin maternal body in the corner of a tin-sheathed hut. The vignette focuses on the life of her son and daughter in a "violence-plagued, poverty-scourged ghetto" (Danticat, 1995, 16). A long way from Marie's childhood mountain home with its crickets, fireflies, shooting stars, and butterflies, an emblem of fragility and escape, she rocks her children and promises treats from the market. With her dying breath, she reminds them of beauty and hope, the only heritage a pauper has to pass on.

Uneven Memories

The fragmentation of family accounts for the rise of women to decision makers for themselves and their children, for example, new mother Marie in "Children of the Sea"; Manman Aline, the parent of a Haitian son and daughter, Moy and Célianne in *Behind the Mountains* while Papa lives in New York; and the author and her brother Bob's separation from Rose Danticat in *Brother, I'm Dying*. To *Miami New Times* interviewer Alexandra Martinez, Edwidge outlined the fears of mixed-status households "where you have U.S.-born children who might be terrified that one of their parents might be deported, and then parents who have legal status but children are in detention" (Martinez, 2016). The concern accounts for the author's defaming of the Trump regime, which legitimized separation of Hispanic infants and children from their parents and lodging them in concentration camps. On the eve of the November 2020 election, in response to the 545 child inmates lacking parents, she submitted to the *Miami Herald* the op-ed piece "Be the Vote for Immigrant Families under Threat by the Trump Administration." Neither Hispanic nor a victim in a cage, she spoke from the heart a mother's concern for any child imperiled by brutality.

Anxiety and mental instability mark the outer rim of fictional tolerance for hurt and insecurity as insidious as the U.S. caging of alien children. In the story "Water Child," the action depicts the decision of Nadine Osnac, a Haitian-American ENT nurse, to abort a fetus. To give it personhood, she collects treasures to place on a commemorative altar. The absence of the child's father

Eric causes her to value a cassette recording of the words of "the near father of her nearly born child" (Danticat, 2000, 84). In a less tolerable condition, Marie, a servant in "Between the Pool and the Gardenias," nurtures an illusion of motherhood by tending an infant corpse left in a gutter. One critic, Raquel D. Kennon, a professor of African-American studies at California State University, justifies the mental aberration as "some measure of creative control over the trauma … through the process of (re)fabrication," a playacting of motherhood that fills the void left by three stillbirths (Kennon, 2017, 163).

See also Grandparents, Patriarchy, Women.

SOURCES

Alexander, Simone A. James. "M/othering the Nation: Women's Bodies as Nationalist Trope in Edwidge Danticat's 'Breath, Eyes, Memory.'" *African American Review* 44:3 (Fall, 2011): 373–390.

Danticat, Edwidge. *Behind the Mountains: The Diary of Célianne Espérance.* New York: Orchard Books, 2002.

_____. "Be the Vote for Immigrant Families under Threat by the Trump Administration," *Miami Herald* (1 November 2020).

_____. "Claire of the Sea Light," *Haiti Noir.* Brooklyn: Akashic, 2010, 115–138.

_____. "Dream of the Butterflies," *Belles Lettres* 10:3 (Summer, 1995): 16.

_____. *The Farming of Bones.* New York: Penguin, 1998.

_____. "Living and Loving through Tragedy," *Sojourners* 39:3 (March 2010): 10–11.

_____. "The Missing Peace," *Just a Moment,* 4:1 (Winter, 1992–1993).

_____. "Water Child," *New Yorker* (11 September 2000): 84.

Kennon, Raquel D. "'We Know People by Their Stories': Madness, Babies, and Dolls in Edwidge Danticat's *Krik? Krak!,*" *Madness in Black Women's Diasporic Fictions.* New York: Springer, 2017, 163–197.

Lyons, Bonnie. "Interview," *Contemporary Literature* 44:2 (Summer 2003): 182–198.

Martinez, Alexandra. "Edwidge Danticat Discusses Memoir and Immigration at Little Haiti Cultural Center," *Miami New Times* (30 March 2016).

Patterson, Christina. "Interview" (London) *Independent* (13 March 1999): 14.

Shea, Renee. "The Dangerous Job of Edwidge Danticat," *Callaloo* 19:2 (Spring, 1996): 382–389.

Music

Edwidge integrates melody and rhythm in an array of human actions, feelings, and aims: the singing of work ditties during evening cooking over boulders and celebrating a life at a wake in "Night Talkers," wooers' calls to young girls in *Célimène,* Darline's absent-minded phrasing of the folk tune "Latibonit O" in "Without Inspection," jubilance with maracas and tambourines at the dictator's death in *The Farming of Bones,* and Blaise's ill-defined band career, an unrealistic ambition he shares with Dédé in "Dosas." At a just-pretend funeral in "Seven Stories," seven-year-old Callie Morrissete sings "Ave Maria," Franz Schubert's classic prayer to the Virgin Mary based on the annunciation in Luke 1:28–33 (Danticat, 2019, 165). The gentle, tranquil hymn contrasts Callie's superficial adult life in a palace surrounded by grand celebration of a state wedding. After an embarrassing anti–Haitian gaffe by a guest during Kimberly "Kim" Boyer's visit to Callie's residence, Prime Minister Greg Murray has the band play "Haitian Fight Song," composed by double bassist Charles Mingus, an advocate for civil rights. The eight-minute jazz classic features a complex brass and piano obbligato fraught with disturbing trumpet riffs, a brassy recreation of Haiti's troubled history.

Performances fill significant spots in political resistance, an essential unifier in Caribbean culture. Less picturesque in Edwidge's anti-racism essay "So Brutal a Death" for the June 22, 2020, *New Yorker* are the insistent songs, drums, and "political hip-hop blasting from cars trailing the crowds" at protests (Danticat, 2020, 72). In Jacmel during Carnival, music coalesces the street scene into a polyglot tumult of marching units and floats that the author observes in *After the Dance.* Experiencing the pre–Lenten holidays for the first time, she writes of an explosion of the senses—"the ear-splitting music and the unbridled dancing amid a large group of people, whose inhibitions were sometimes veiled by costumes and masks" (Danticat, 2002, 15–16). In the essay "Port-au-Prince, City of Survivors: Voices from Haiti," the author reflects on konpa from trucks and lotto booths and product ditties from vendors, who sing their products' praises like the Charleston street sellers in George and Ira Gershwin and DuBose Heyward's American opera *Porgy and Bess*. As forms of advertisement, the jingles stir a positive response to Haitian commerce.

The draw of popular music in *Create Dangerously* justifies photojournalist Daniel Morel's romance with the Orchestra Septentrional d'Haiti. The oldest urban outlet for island rhythm since its formation on July 28, 1948, it belongs to a populist front that helped crush government corruption. Because the group counted the Tonton Macoute among fans, the musicians became "a big part of the political landscape" with hit tunes "La Boule de Feu" (Ball of Fire), "Gitana" (Gypsy), "Seul dans la Nuit" (Alone in the Night), and "Joujou" (Toy) (Danticat, 2010, 144). The 20-piece band, an archetype of persistence for over 70 years, has kept belting out West Indian syncopation through occupation, liberation, and tyranny.

Concerning the orchestral merengue "Compadre Pedro Juan," which became dictator Rafael Trujillo's theme song in *The Farming of Bones*, Dwyer Murphy, an interviewer for *Guernica*, noted the impact of musical groups on political unrest and protest. At a stirring moment in city violence outside the Dajabón cathedral, the dictator's orchestra halts for a twenty-one gun salvo as he exits the sanctuary. In the furor, Dominicans cheer, sound sirens, stomp feet, and belt out "Quisqueyanos valientes" (stout-hearted Hispaniolans) the national anthem, which Olivia renders as a solo in the story "Dosas." The opening phrase used an indigenous identification of Spanish islanders for examples of strength (Danticat, 1998, 192). The familiar "banana republic" scenario satirized the bloodthirsty mob who vented hatred on blacks while showering love on their leader.

Musical Folklore

From childhood, island children incorporated Afro-Haitian rhymes and skipping songs as mnemonics during playacting. Young girls holding hands for the two-language *Wonn* (ronde) game in *Claire of the Sea Light* move counter clockwise around the "it" girl in the center. Like clock hands, they shift through 360 degrees, voicing their joy and mimicking the counterpoint of Mami Wata (Mother Water) lore. An enigmatic deity among animistic Afro-West Indian people, the shapeshifting Vodou goddess transcends division between the living and dead, including Caleb, the drowned fisherman, and Max Ardin, Jr., who survives suicide with the help of beach volunteers. For Claire's introit to a closed female society, the *wonn* song that she chooses incorporates oral verse and music with a water divinity who empowers females. The understory ennobles the elder Claire Narcis as the invisible spirit and a symbol of West Africa, the ethnic birth home as inaccessible to postcolonial black nations as is mothering to Claire Faustin.

In *Anacaona*, the author establishes a folk backstory through the drumming of Night Marchers and a healer's singing of curative ballads to an island beat. Maracas, flutes, drums, and conch shells summon curative Vodou spirits. Additional examples from the author's time incorporate loud pro-election intoning of carnival hymns throughout Port-au-Prince in *Behind the Mountains* and Joseph Woods's gravitation to spirituals, slave sorrow songs, works by Charlie Bird Parker and Miles Davis, and Latin American music in *Breath, Eyes, Memory*. Recordings of conch shell and drum tunes disclose his African-American roots and mark ritual passages in fifteenth-century Taino coming of age. In Woods's courtship of Sophie Caco, he serenades on a keyboard New Orleans style from next door. At her mother Martine Caco's funeral, the addition of gourd rattles, conch shells, and cow horns to the talking drum complete a folk send-off at the gravesite. The ritual esteems exuberance for life, a fervor epitomized by her red dress.

Life Cycles in Tune

The author illustrates the traditions that introduced newcomers to Haiti, pervading airport arrivals with drum, tambourines, and conch shells in the tourist story "Quality Control." Complex thoughts about tyrannic torture cycles contrast the Christmas Eve carols "What Child Is This?" and "Silent Night," the focus of Catholic liturgy in "The Book of Miracles." On entering Clara Barton High School, Edwidge's teacher, Mr. Dusseck, taught English as a Second Language with the words to "Lift Ev'ry Voice and Sing," the Negro national anthem. On February 12, 1900, John Rosamond Johnson set his brother James Weldon's Johnson's poem to music for a Lincoln's birthday observance in Jacksonville, Florida. The National Association for the Advancement of Colored People adopted the song as an official theme and added it to youth culture and collections of West Indian island ballads.

Music boosts intrinsic worth and

authenticity to the media and everyday esthetics. On the ocean pilgrimage to Miami in "Children of the Sea," characters sing poet Othello Bayard's "Haiti Chérie" (Beloved Haiti) and tell stories to ease constant nausea and sunburn. The song returns by radio in "Caroline's Wedding." An illegitimate boy in "Night Women" hums the Baroque round "Frère Jacques," written in the early 1700s by Jean-Philippe Rameau, a French composer of opera, ballet, and harpsichord music. A more arcane allusion in "Anniversary," dredges up the dismal cry of Lubin in "Au Claire de la Lune," a bereft writer in need of a pen and light, which he receives from a compassionate brunette.

A fanfare of musical genres, like the author's splash of literary types, expresses confidence in island culture and its forbearance. At the demise of Maurice Dejean in "In the Old Days," a small home gathering processes to drumming and joins in "Shall We Gather at the River," a gospel metaphor for the flow of life into eternity. For mourners in *Untwine*, music and art reverence grief as a never-ending process. In the essay "Mourning in Place" for the *New York Review of Books*, Edwidge detailed a lavish pre–Covid birthday celebration featuring "different types of music—hip-hop, Haitian konpa, gospel," a lavish selection before disease precipitated "too much death in our realm, and too few opportunities to celebrate the lives the dead had lived" (Danticat, 2020).

SOURCES

Danticat, Edwidge. *After the Dance: A Walk Through Carnival in Jacmel, Haiti*. New York: Vintage, 2002.
_____. "All Geography Is Within Me," *World Literature Today* 93:1 (Winter 2019): 58.
_____. *Anacaona: Golden Flower, Haiti, 1490*. New York: Scholastic, 2005.
_____. "The Book of Miracles," *The Story Prize*. New York: Strong Winds, 2019.
_____. *Create Dangerously: The Immigrant Artist at Work*. New York: Vintage, 2010.
_____. *Everything Inside*. New York: Knopf, 2019.

_____. *The Farming of Bones.* New York: Penguin, 1998.

_____. "Mourning in Place," *New York Review of Books* (24 September 2020).

_____. "One Thing," *New York Times Magazine* (7 July 2020): 62–72.

_____. "Port-au-Prince, City of Survivors: Voices from Haiti," *Salon* (12 January 2020).

_____. "Quality Control," *Washington Post* (16 November 2014): 25.

_____. "So Brutal a Death," *New Yorker* 96:17 (22 June 2020): 18–19.

Montgomery, Maxine L. "A Lasiren Song for the Wonn: Edwidge Danticat's *Claire of the Sea Light* and the Legend of Mami Wata," *CLA Journal* 59:4 (June 2016): 316–329.

Murphy, Dwyer. "The Art of Not Belonging," *Guernica* (3 September 2013).

Wilson, Betty. "Literature and Activism, Literature as Activism," *Caribbean Quarterly* 66:3 (2020): 405–424.

My Mommy Medicine

The most recent of Edwidge's children's works, *My Mommy Medicine* parallels the themes and tone of Amy Hest's *Don't You Feel Well, Sam,* a fond survey of the mother-as-nurse scenario. The text applauds the parent who embraces, tends, and relishes her young, a devotion exemplified by Valencia Duarte for her lost son Rafi in *The Farming of Bones* and by Manman, Saya's jailed parent in *Mama's Nightingale.* Enhanced by illustrator Shannon Wright's drawings of a mirror image daughter with mother, the author's picture book bubbles with anticipation of feel-good amusement and unending togetherness on an otherwise gloomy day.

Edwidge's vignettes thrive on such specifics as a rubdown with menthol, squash soup, and competitions at Uno, dominoes, jack rocks, and indoor horseshoes. References to melody and finger-and-hand games—"Itsy Bitsy Spider," the lullaby "You Are My Sunshine," and popular round "Frère Jacques"—stimulate fantasy with mental pictures. Pirate stories encourage dress-up in outfits usually reserved for boys. Creative ideas—cardboard castles, door bulletin boards, sofa cushion playacting, poufy scrubbers for bubble baths, and reflective stars on the ceiling—engage parents in hands-on projects that relieve sick-day doldrums.

Reflecting on her own daughters, Mira and Leila, the author highlights tactile occasions for "soothing, reassuring, and somewhat healing" (Danticat, 2019). A list of caregivers—mother, aunt, dad, grandma, grandpa, guardian, or caretaker—broadens the occasions of assuagement from an adult to a child. The obligatory dose of cough syrup reminds readers that cures sometimes require real drugstore medicine. Reviewers highlighted the book's strengths: *Publisher's Weekly* noted the importance to a child of being the center of concern. *School Library Journal* applauded the value of caregivers to healing. *Booklist* found a cozy antidote effective on anxiety or sickness, especially when administered by a single parent, Darline's method of soothing son Paris's trauma in "Without Inspection" and the cause of Marie's martyrdom in "Dream of the Butterflies."

Less energetic, dramatic, and colorful than *Mama's Nightingale,* the later picture book contributes a few assets of its own, particularly scrutiny of a healthy mother-daughter relationship and the glow of being cherished. The characters share facial structure and mounds of springy curls. For a round of sunshine songs, artist Shannon Wright brightens the lemony yellow blanket that transforms into a sea captain's cape. The mother exhibits snuggly curves rather than fashion model bones and flashes alert, expressive eyes to heighten card game suspense. The vivid parental image, according to *Publishers Weekly,* seems "more like an adult's recollection than a child's impression" ("Review," 2018, 83). Least appealing in artwork, the characters' costumes remain plain and ineffective from beginning to end. The work won a Parent's Choice Recommended Award for 2019.

SOURCE

Chambers, Kia. "Review: *My Mommy Medicine,*" https://comewagalong.com/book-review-my-mommy-medicine-by-edwidge-danticat/ (12 May 20219).

Danticat, Edwidge. *My Mommy Medicine.* New York: Roaring Brook, 2019.

Gonzalez, Fernando. "Little Haiti Book Festival Has Many Stories to Tell," *Miami Herald* (5 May 2019): NE14.

Henricks, Clara. "Review: *My Mommy Medicine,*" *School Library Journal* (1 March 2019).

Nix, Kemmie. "Review: *My Mommy Medicine,*" https://www.parentschoice.org/product/my-mommy-medicine/2019.

"Review: *My Mommy Medicine,*" *Kirkus Reviews* (15 December 2018).

"Review: *My Mommy Medicine,*" (London) *Daily Mail,* https://shop.dailymail.co.uk/readerlink/my-mommy-medicine-by-edwidge-danticat-hardcover-0da018a536c549fba55516b2dbee679c-p.html.

"Review: *My Mommy Medicine,*" *Publisher's Weekly* 265:43 (22 October 2018): 83.

Names

Nuanced character, landmark, and place names elucidate Edwidge's themes, as with the slum Cité Pendue (the Hanged City), the Anthère Lighthouse, the boy Pamaxime ("pas Maxime" or not Max's) in *Claire of the Sea Light,* and Ka Bienaimé (well loved spirit), the daughter of Anne, who bears the name of Jesus's paternal grandmother in "The Book of the Dead." Similar distinguishing by a Christian name mark Mélisande (strong worker), the dying nanny in "The Port-au-Prince Marriage Special," and Aunt Estina Estème (esteemed little star), the rural midwife in "Night Talkers" whose wake elicits respectful anecdotes from Claude and Dany Dorméus about her goodness. In *The Farming of Bones,* a mother's ghostly comfort makes a pun out of her daughter's name, "ma belle, Amabelle"

(my beauty, lovable) (Danticat, 1998, 206). A cruel irony attaches to the cane town of Alegría (joy), a target of Dominican Republic dictator Rafael Trujillo's slaughter of Haitian laborers. On a more positive note, Marie Micheline (like God) in "Dream of the Butterflies" martyrs herself to shield her son and daughter from machine gun bursts.

Edwidge reveres the role of history and legend in character names, such as Pastor Ben (son of my right hand) in *Untwine* and the onomatopoetic sound of laughter in Kiki, a character in "Living and Loving through Tragedy." The surname of Sophie (wisdom) Caco, a college student who searches for an appropriate career in *Breath, Eyes, Memory,* commemorates the *cacos,* black Haitians like her great grandfather, who rebelled against white American invaders. Her grandmother Ifé Caco bears the first name of a mythic Yoruban town in Nigeria revered as the birthplace of humankind. Her storytelling nurtures younger generations with adages from the fount of African wisdom lore. Edwidge recycles the name Sophie/wisdom in the satiric "Tatiana, Mon Amour," featuring the Russian for "princess." Other character lists bear concealed commentary on action, place, and person:

- Assad (lion), wealthy Muslim sugar planters in "A Wall of Fire Rising"
- Beatrice Saint Fort (blessed holy strength), a haunted survivor of the Tonton Macoute in "The Bridal Seamstress"
- Bernard (brave bear), the ambitious radio journalist in *Claire of the Sea Light*
- Blaise (stutterer), the duplicitous ex-husband in "Dosas"
- Brigitte (exalted strong woman), the most recent addition to the Caco matrilineage in *Breath, Eyes,*

Names 177

Memory and a namesake of Maman Brigitte, an island deity who wards off black magic

- Caleb (bold heart), a fisherman and scribe overwhelmed by unexpected wave action in *Claire of the Sea Light*
- Caonabo (golden one), patriarchal cacique of the Taino in *Anacaona*
- Céliane Espérance (heavenly hope), a name suited to a refugee from a pipe bomb blast in Carrefour Dufort (square of the fort), Haiti, in *Behind the Mountains*
- Clio (glory), the Greek muse of history in "Hot-Air Balloons," in which Guy seeks to ennoble himself in a self-destructive act
- Défilé (damaged), an insane woman in "Nineteen Thirty-Seven" who anchors the matrilineage of granddaughter Josephine (may God increase)
- Doña Eva (lady woman), Dominican protector of her son and daughter Javier (bright) and Beatriz (blessed) in *The Farming of Bones*
- Emilie (compete) Gallant (exuberant), the name of an American artist in Haiti in "The Missing Peace"
- Emmanuel (God is with us) Constant, a mass murderer of Haitians in *The DewBreaker*, and the name of Emmanuel Aidoo (Ghanian Fante for "ten"), the neurologist who treats Giselle Boyer for brain damage in *Untwine*
- Eric (sole ruler) Abrahams (father of nations), future husband of Caroline Azile in "Caroline's Wedding"
- Eveline (woman), victim of the October 1937 Parsley Massacre in "Between the Pool and the Gardenias"
- Faustin (ditch), a meaningful name for Nozias, a poverty-stricken fisherman who tries to improve his humble life in *Claire of the Sea Light*
- Franck (free), Papa Victor Espérance's generous sponsor in New York in *Behind the Mountains*
- Iradelle (watchful) Pradelle (meadow), the ghostly presence in *The Farming of Bones* who solaces refugees
- Jacqueline (replacement), the friend of Josephine's mother, inmate Défilé, who dies of prison beatings in "Nineteen Thirty-Seven" and recalls the French Jacquerie, a coterie of peasant rebels in Charles Dickens's *A Tale of Two Cities*
- Javier, named for St. Xavier, one of the original Jesuits, an intellectual Christly brotherhood in *The Farming of Bones*
- Jonas (dove), a vicious child kidnapper in "Please Translate" who bears a harmless given name
- Ka (spirit) Bienaimé (well loved), a sculptor, receives from her father in "Book of the Dead" the Egyptian designation for a body companion to "dead hearts being placed on scales and souls traveling aimlessly down fiery underground rivers" (Danticat, 2004, 17).
- Kimberly (king's fort meadow) Boyer (bow maker), a journalist visiting the prime minister Charles Morrissete's widow and daughter Callie (beautiful) in "Seven Stories"
- Loner (laborer), a suitable surname for a cane cutter like Joël (Jehovah is God) Raymond (protector), the son of Old Kongo in *The Farming of Bones*
- Nadine (messenger) Osnac (hope), the grieving mother of an aborted fetus in "Water Child"; similarly named, Nadia, an English as a Second Language teacher in "In the Old Days," suffers from unfinished family business with her father Marc

178   Names

- Nounoune (silly girl), the name of a bride in *The Farming of Bones* who wakes up screaming in her husband's bed
- Old Kongo (mountains), a Dominican mill worker and mask maker bearing a name from West Africa in *The Farming of Bones*
- Oscar (warrior spear), a strong friend of the protagonist Junior (younger) in *Eight Days*
- Oula (resolved), a protective mother in "Without Inspection"
- Pico (beak) Duarte (wealthy), a vicious Guardia officer and husband of Valencia in *The Farming of Bones*
- Yves (yew) Rapadou (unrefined cane sugar), a cane worker in *The Farming of Bones*
- Suzette (lily), daughter of a devoted immigrant mother in "New York Day Women"
- Vaval (renewal), the Carnival King martyred annually for the redemption of society in *After the Dance*
- Xavier (new house), innkeeper in Port-au-Prince and assistant to Melisande (hearty worker), an AIDS patient in "The Port-au-Prince Marriage Special"
- Zaken (wise elder), a patriarchal element in the relationship of Zaken with his wife, title character in *Célimène* (heavenly strength)

Edwidge notes the frequent use of classical names in Haiti, as with Junior (younger), the hero of *Eight Days,* and Princesse in "Seeing Things Simply," a feminized Roman designation of the *princeps* (chief citizen). For *After the Dance*, Ovid, an agricultural worker, reflects the classic literature of the Roman author of *Metamorphoses* (Changes). A similar line of Greco-Roman first names attaches to

characters in *Untwine:* Grandma Régine (queen), Grandpa Marcus (of the god Mars), Uncle Patrick (noble) and Aunt Alejandra (defender), and Sylvie (woodsy) Boyer. Others include:

- Albert (noble) Vincent (conquering), winner of the mayor's race in *Claire of the Sea Light*
- Anisi (unusual), Dieula (admirable), and Lina (light) Espérance (hope) in "A Place of Refuge" share identities crediting their value to the Bel Air slum
- Caroline (man), the independent daughter of Hermine and Carl (freeman) Azile in "Caroline's Wedding"
- Claude (stuttering), an immigrant damaged by drugs and imprisonment for murder in "Night Talkers"
- Denise (lover of Dionysus), the strict, pious wife of Joseph Nozias Dantica in *Brother, I'm Dying*
- Dolores/Doloritas (grieving), the name of two refugees from the October 1937 genocide of Haitians at the Massacre River in *The Farming of Bones*
- Ernesto (sincere), ironic fake name of Arnold in "Without Inspection"
- Flore (flower) Voltaire (determined) exemplifies a mother who uses profits from her beauty shop to rescue her fatherless son Pamaxine (not Maxime) from the wealthy Ardin family
- Gracina (thanks) ameliorates sad memories and difficult passes in family life in "Caroline's Wedding"
- Hermine (traveler) Azil (Xhosa for "arrived"), immigrant mother of the sisters Gracina and Caroline and widow of Carl in "Caroline's Wedding"
- Don Ignacio (fire-forged), the

Dominican immersed in accounts of the Spanish Civil War in *The Farming of Bones*

- Gregory (alert) Murray (sea town), an ironic name for the prime minister in "Seven Stories"
- Immacula (unspotted), a mischievous schoolmate of Céliane Espérance in *Behind the Mountains*
- Jesula (Jesus is here), a tent camp dweller fearful of rape in "A Place of Refuge"
- Jude (praised), the baby and focus of family concern in "Sunrise, Sunset,"
- Justine (fair), a loving little sister of Junior in *Eight Days*
- Lamort (death), the given name of a child born to Marie Magdalène, a dead mother in "The Missing Peace"
- Lucy (light), a roommate who enlightens the do-gooder Neah (new) in "Hot-Air Balloons"
- Marc (Mars), an idealistic father named for the Roman god of war in "In the Old Days"
- Marie-Jeanne (Maria, God is merciful) Lamartiniere (Mars, Roman god of war), the wife of a dying man in "One Thing"
- Max (greatest) Ardin, Jr. (fiery), a radio DJ in "Ghosts" and returnee from Miami in *Claire of the Sea Light*
- Mo (dark skin), the name of a dominating orphaned brother in *Célimène*
- Paris (wallet), Darline's fatherless son in "Without Inspection"
- Pascal (Easter) Dorien (gift), a naive radio journalist in "Ghosts"
- Princesse (chief), an art student in "Seeing Things Simply"
- Regulus (little king), a self-important member of the Tonton Macoutes in "Ghosts"

- Rose (flower), a dead infant in "Between the Pool and the Gardenias"; the child of the Lavauds (valleys) in *Claire of the Sea Light;* Rose Souvenance (remembrance) Napóleon (new town) bears the given name in *Brother, I'm Dying,* "Feetfirst," "Without Her," and *The Art of Dying*
- Sebastien (venerable), a Haitian son in *The Farming of Bones* named for a Roman martyr who had two deaths
- Teresa (hunter), the strident identification of the surviving Duarte twin in *The Farming of Bones*
- Valencia (being strong) Duarte (Wealthy), a mother of twins Rosalinda (beautiful rose) Teresa and Rafael (God heals) and wife of Pico, a Trujillo henchman in *The Farming of Bones*
- Victor (winner), an immigrant from Haiti living in New York in "Seven"
- Victoria (triumph), the twin who dies in infancy in "The Revenant" and "Condolences"

Significant intersections of names occur in "One Thing" with the blend of Roman and Hebrew in Marie-Jeanne and, in *Behind the Mountain,* when Mr. Casimir teaches Céliane Espérance about the Siege of Savannah from September 17, 1779, to October 18, 1779, during which Polish-American hero Casimir Pulaski died while leading patriot cavalry against the British. For "Children of the Sea," a Brooklyn priest blesses the remains of an unknown drowning victim; for Arnold in "Without Inspection," registration under the Spanish name Ernesto causes his remains to be misidentified, a parallel to the misnaming of Isabelle, Giselle Boyer's twin killed in *Untwine*. The author's father, André Miras Danticat in *Brother,*

I'm Dying, bears Greek and Latin given names meaning "warrior" and "wonder." His surname is unknown.

See also Catholicism.

Sources

Alexander, Simone A. James. "M/othering the Nation: Women's Bodies as Nationalist Trope in Edwidge Danticat's 'Breath, Eyes, Memory.'" *African American Review* 44:3 (2011): 373–390.

Chase, George Davis. "The Origin of Roman Praenomina," *Harvard Studies in Classical Philology* 8 (1897), 103–184.

Danticat, Edwidge. *The Dew Breaker.* New York: Abacus, 2004.

_____. *The Farming of Bones.* New York: Penguin, 1998.

Misrahi-Barak, Judith. "'My Mouth Is the Keeper of Both Speech and Silence …' or The Vocalisation of Silence in Caribbean Short Stories by Edwidge Danticat," *Journal of the Short Story in English* 47 (1 December 2006).

Nature

Edwidge identifies Caribbean topography by its vivid colors and terrain and the relationship between animals, peasants, and their habitats. In the interview "Color Blocking" for *Arquitectonica,* she justified her thinking: "You're sort of in collaboration with nature—you have to be, it's what's giving you the signs" (Danticat, 2013). A tropical forest of coconut palms depicts the West Indies in the art accompanying "Without Inspection." Seafood features in a death poem, the 1991 street drama "Sawfish Soup," a species dying out in much of the world. A society wedding in "Seven Stories" achieves oneness with the shore, where dunes outline the ceremony and stars and lightning out to sea preserve sky glories above the wedding bonfire. Mysticism in *Claire of the Sea Light* enshrouds the school of silvery fish and connects the frogs that disappear because of volcanic activity and the hailstorm that smells scorched like lightning. Beyond those, sound carries "the echoes of swelling waves meeting the seashore," a reflection on the oneness of sand with seawater (Danticat, 2013, 169). Into the air, farmers twirl their glinting hoes in respect to "maitre soleil" (master sun), a proof that Haitian customs derive from Africa (Kaussen, 2004).

Of the author's shifting views of saltwater, analyst Magdalena Cohen characterized it as "an all-knowing god-like presence that has the power to hurt, to heal, to grant life and to take life away" (Cohen, 2004, 201). Human intrusions on the shore begin a destabilizing process threatening life forms and the livelihood of fishermen like Caleb and Nozias Faustin. In the personal essay "Machandiz (Merchandise)," the author reported on a summer visit to her mother-in-law's property, where a red tide of toxic algae combined with foam and plastic detritus "made it impossible to even approach the beach, much less swim" (Danticat, 2020, 150). At fault, the ecological imbalance aroused by pollutants, flooding, soil erosion and overfishing attests to "cosmic unrest owing to some form of transgressive human behavior" (Montgomery, 2016, 323). Social disjuncture motivates gang crime and the willful destruction of the Anthère Lighthouse, an emblem of direction and guidance.

Edwidge experiences the setting from first-hand interaction with Haiti. She reflects in "Voices from Hispaniola," a personal essay for *Meridians,* on her hesitance to recreate the home island "because I am overwhelmed by sensation" (Danticat, 2004). Visible elements identify the uniqueness of Haiti with garden edibles, bats, bees, and flowers in *The Last Mapou.* Above, the "swirls of cirrus, cumulus, and alto stratus clouds" in muted colors appear vivified at sunset in the essay "Mourning in Place" (Danticat, 2020). The writer rejoices that "the world is still very much alive," but regrets

Haiti's susceptibility to abuse, such as the vanishing of tall mapou trees "into charcoal" and the erosion of mountain topsoil into the sea in *After the Dance* (Danticat, 2020; 2008, 109). In a television interview, the author emphasized the confusion in children born to Haitian-American immigrants, who color their childhood memories with mountain and beach scenarios that belie lurid images on CNN (Conlogue 2004, R3).

The Haitian mountains recur regularly in the author's canon, particularly as a setting for seasonal flash floods and mudslides in *Claire of the Sea Light* and the animistic rituals of the Taino in the biography *Anacaona*. Without stating the obvious—that colonialism despoiled the Native American heritage—Edwidge concludes the heroine's life story without detailing the avarice of Hispanic conquistadors. As though returning to a fifteenth-century Eden, the innocence of a rainy day in *Eight Days* pictures a two-page spread by illustrator Alix Delinois of palms, underbrush, and touches of red and orange flowers against a mountainous backdrop in purples and blues. The panoply of tropical colors and life forms contrasts the ruin in *Tent Life* generated in 2010 by an earthquake. By retreating into memories of the outdoors, Junior, a seven-year-old survivor, preserves the freedom he enjoys in the high country, which enables him to escape the terror of an eight-day entrapment under a collapsing building.

Because islanders live in close contact with agrarian rhythms of planting and growing, their stories intertwine. The respect and hero worship of peasant farmers for activist Jean Léopold Dominique, martyred on April 3, 2000, by unknown gunmen outside his Radio Haiti-Inter station, caused local people to invent folklore about his devotion to the poor. Before the family scattered his ashes on the Artibonite River, local myth had already incorporated his bold support of Haiti's rural peasantry into the folklore of the fertile countryside, the "heart of the Country's breadbasket" (Danticat, 2010, 52). Their illusions pictured him helping with the planting and harvesting of coffee.

Impersonal Nature

An early appreciator of vanishing nature, Edwidge spoke in "Dream of the Butterflies," a melodramatic short story for the 1991 *Caribbean Writer,* of changes to Léogâne, the mountainous retreat southwest of Port-au-Prince that she loved in childhood. Through the characterization of Marie Micheline, she acknowledges that "The green mountains had begun to fade into gigantic ivory-shaded rocks" and that vanishing verdure and animal life was an old story for islanders (Danticat, 1991, 98). The text itemizes childhood's delight in dew, crickets, sunset, fireflies, comets, and butterflies ranging from white and yellow to dark as night. After moving to an urban slum, Marie regrets the loss of nature's gentle sounds, which criminals replace with gunfire, the dominant sensation in *Brother, I'm Dying.*

In a 2004 interview, the author referred to the Haitian islander's awareness of the sea and human vulnerability, as depicted by the drowning of Anne Bienaimé's brother in *The Dew Breaker* and a rogue wave in the short story "Claire of the Sea Light" which overwhelms a man in a dinghy. In the novel version, the wave sinks the cutter *Fifine* and drowns Caleb, a fisherman ironically named in Hebrew "bold heart." The image calls to mind the folkloric prayer "O Lord, your sea is so great and my boat is so small." The stripping of salable fish by fishermen reduces Nozias Faustin to worry about destroying young conches and egg-filled lobsters rather than "let the sea replenish itself" (Danticat, 2013, 9). His unease at the status of sea life contrasts the ebullience of his pregnant wife Claire Narcis, who swims in a school of silvery ocean fish, a token of the being she carries in her uterus.

A metaphoric water menace engulfs Amabelle Desír in *The Farming of Bones* at her return to the Massacre River on an inky night after escaping mass murder by Guardia of black Haitian cane harvesters. On a warm October morning, she slips naked into the shallows, where pebbles score her back and the current rides rough above her. In search of gentleness, softness, she awaits dawn, an existential promise of a better future. By reliving her flight from certain death, she hopes to gain "a clearer sense of the moment, a stronger memory" to replace the phantasms of the Parsley Massacre (Danticat, 1998, 307). The search for sanity proves futile because nature lacks memory to restore peace, reflection, and optimism. All that awaits her is oblivion, the extinction of all sensation.

For *After the Dance,* Edwidge contrasts secular entertainment at the pre-Lenten Jacmel festival with a side trip into the high country enriched along the understory with fern, bracken, and cactus around caves, cascades, and grottoes. In a pine forest, she views boulders split over time. Called *kraze dan* (breaking teeth) in Creole, the jagged contours remind her of the earth's timespan. She muses on "a living entity, the oceans and rivers her blood, the soil her skin, and the stones, her bones" (Danticat, 2002, 104). The text envelops her in cool air, dark night, and "a loud thundering rain ... like a million hands clapping" (*ibid.,* 105). Seeking other responses to the terrain, Edwidge visits local cemeteries and reads an anonymous farewell in the inn's guest book, "I left a bit of my soul in these impenetrable mountains" (*ibid.*)

Treasured Beauty

The author elevates nature's quiet as a contrast to manmade ruination. She embeds in a fairy tale the title figure of *Célimène,* the sweet-natured country girl who resides at peace in a peasant environment "en harmonie avec" (in harmony with) plants, animals, and rivers—an ecological Eden (Dumas and Chenald, 2011). Edwidge revisits other nature lovers in *Untwine,* in which Isabelle Boyer and her twin Giselle view monarch butterflies in Mexico and learn that the winged insects represent the souls of deceased children stirring to life. Isabelle befriends Ron Johnson, a fellow outdoor type who likes birds, pilot whales, and rock climbing. She and twin Giselle aid a burrowing owl, an endangered species that requires treatment at a wildlife rehabilitation center. The rescue creates irony from Isabelle's death in a Miami highway accident, a detour from beauty in a lover of art, orchestral music, and strawberries.

Nature transcends the grim family tragedy in *Untwine.* For the twins' sixteenth birthday, their Aunt Leslie sends them to a butterfly sanctuary in central Mexico, where buzzing insects cause them to sneeze. Allergies disrupt the twins' sleep and raise hives, which Leslie treats with Benadryl, a common antihistamine. A later reverie reminds Giselle of her grandparents' silk cotton tree and the corona of cosmic gases that forms around the sun on rainy days. The radiant halo suggests Isabelle's death and return to her twin as a spirit. Appropriately, Isabelle lies in a coffin painted with hibiscus and covered in birds of paradise and camellias, blossoms of home.

Sources

Cohen, Magdalena. "The Ability of Water to Heal and Unify in Edwidge Danticat's *The Farming of Bones* and 'Children of the Sea,'" *Caribbean Writer* 18 (2004): 201.

Conlogue, Ray. "Haunted by Haiti's Ghosts," [Toronto] *Globe and Mail* (19 April 2004): R3.

Danticat, Edwidge. *After the Dance: A Walk Through Carnival in Jacmel, Haiti.* New York: Vintage, 2002.

_____. *Célimène—Fairy Tale for the Daughter of Immigrants.* Montreal: Memoire d'Encrier, 2009.

_____. "Claire of the Sea Light," *Haiti Noir.* Brooklyn: Akashic, 2010, 115–138.

_____. *Claire of the Sea Light.* New York: Vintage, 2013.

_____. "Color Blocking," *Arquitectonica,* https://www.interiorsandsources.com/article-details/articleid/15529/title/color-blocking-edwidge-danticat (1 July 2013).

_____. *Create Dangerously: The Immigrant Artist at Work.* New York: Vintage, 2010.

_____. "Dawn after the Caribbean Tempests," *New York Times* (6 November 2017): TR5.

_____. "Dream of the Butterflies," *Caribbean Writer* 5 (1991): 98–99.

_____. *Everything Inside.* New York: Knopf, 2019.

_____. *The Farming of Bones.* New York: Penguin, 1998.

_____. "Ghosts," *New Yorker* (24 November 2008): 108–113.

_____. *The Last Mapou.* Brooklyn: One Moore Book, 2013.

_____. "Machandiz," *Tales of Two Planets: Stories of Climate Change and Inequality in a Divided World.* New York: Penguin, 2020, 149–158.

_____. "Mourning in Place," *New York Review of Books* (24 September 2020).

_____. "Sawfish Soup," *Caribbean Writer* 5 (1991): 10–11.

_____. *Untwine.* New York: Scholastic, 2015.

_____. "Voices from Hispaniola" (contributor) *Meridians* 5:1 (2004): 68–91.

Dumas, Pierre-Raymond, and Augustin Chenald. "'Célimène' ou la problématique de l'exil au coeur du merveilleux," *Le Nouvelliste* (21 June 2011).

"Interview," *BookBrowse* (2004), https://www.bookbrowse.com/author_interviews/full/index.cfm/author_number/1022/edwidge-danticat.

Kaussen Valerie. "Slaves, Viejos, and the Internationale," *Research in African Literature* 35:4 (Winter 2004).

Montgomery, Maxine L. "A Lasiren Song for the Wonn: Edwidge Danticat's *Claire of the Sea Light* and the Legend of Mami Wata," *CLA Journal* 59:4 (June 2016): 316–329.

fiction. She accounted to interviewer Kevin Nance of *Poets & Writers* for a unique West Indian milieu: "The truth is somewhere in the middle—it's part noir, part light-complicated and complex, the way people are" (Nance, 2011, 13). For her skill at 43 emails in "Please Translate," the London *Times* lists the story of kidnapping among the best crime fiction of 2020. She labeled redemptive the gory details of machete torture of Alèrte Bélance, a maimed activist in *Create Dangerously* who lost an ear, forearm, fingers, and half her tongue. "Quality Control" offers a visual tease, the unobtrusive atmospheric control, a wry euphemism for dumping of body bags in the sea under the constant surveillance of armed guards. In the foreground, guests at an A-list society wedding enjoy the best of entertaining, feasting, and safe residence at a palatial manse encircled by razor wire and walls topped with glass shards, like shark teeth rising from the sea.

In a convoluted fable of destiny and death, *Claire of the Sea Light* conjoins residents of Ville Rose, a town of 11,000 laid out like a blossom with thorns. The author makes a grim joke of the idyllic visuals by picturing the election of a mayor, Albert Vincent, who owns the funeral home and employs the protagonist's mother, Claire Narcis, as corpse washer throughout her pregnancy with Claire Limyè Lanmè Faustin. Instead of bearing a rose-like fragrance, she smells like embalming chemicals, a looming prefiguration of death in stillbirth. By salting in grisly details here and there amid upbeat sense impressions, the author controls noirism, stopping short of gothic overkill.

Noirism

Pride in black culture, especially among women, sparks ambiguous contrasts, Edwidge's contributions to noir

Caste Victims

For the story "Ghosts," Edwidge merged pathos with vengeance, stressing the haphazard retaliation of special forces officers against Tiye, a gangster named "kill" whom thugs drill with bullets in the back of his skull during sleep. He and other young males grow up homeless and unsupervised and become "unrecognizable to anyone but one another" (Danticat, 2008, 110). A gang leader, Tiye epitomizes street life with his bald head and steel and plastic arm, a prosthesis equipped with hooks for holding his beer as well as gripping prey. Pascal Darien, a young reporter, enters "a box of a room" under the torture of senses—a hot interrogation cell within the odor of vomit, the flicker of fluorescent lights, the chafing of cuffs against his wrists, and taunts from prison officers who throw freezing water on his face (Danticat, 2008, 112). The involvement of authorities with the same viciousness as gangsters suggests an environment layered top to bottom with brutality.

The writer indulged in a grotesque demise with the art poem "Plunging," which details the final thoughts of a construction worker who falls into a cement mixer at Bar Harbour, Florida, the site of Arnold's grotesque death in "Without Inspection." The prospect of asphyxiation and silencing in wet concrete increases the noir value of an immigrant's story in which Arnold poses under the Cuban-Hispanic identity of Ernesto. The setting among the overtly wealthy enhances his sacrifice in service to white society. Edwidge repeated the pairing in "The Dew Breaker," a face-off between a Tonton Macoute torturer and the prisoner who slices his cheek. The scar gives ironic evidence of a career soaked in the blood of innocents until a chance power shift afflicts the torturer. The unpredictability of a criminal life reminds perpetrators of the likelihood of payback, both anticipated and unplanned.

The author exonerated herself for choosing dark stories and verse for *Haiti*

Noir 2 by selecting timeless works. Carolina Villalba, a reviewer at the University of Miami, cites how Edwidge "[blurs] the lines between what is noir and what is singularly Haitian worship of West African spirits" (Villalba, 2014, 4). She highlights misused models of Vodou that yield "a more nuanced and complex presentation of Haitian lives" than outsiders gained, particularly perceptions of the love goddess Erzulie (Danticat, 2014, 16). The poem "On the Day of the Dead," the photo essay *Tent Life,* and the essay "Living and Loving through Tragedy" pitied victims of the Haitian earthquake on January 12, 2010, who died without an opportunity to commune with La Flaca (bones), a deity of the departed, or Le Bawon (the Baron), protector of cemeteries. The chancy alliance of earthquake victims with Vodou devotion further challenges outsiders to estimate the value of so dour a theology.

Unimaginable Evil

For *Krik? Krak!,* Edwidge fabricated a sinister view of child murder in the superstition against Défilé, a prisoner incriminated for witchcraft in "Nineteen Thirty-Seven," the year of the Parsley Massacre. Cellblock guards exonerated themselves by citing the elderly peasant for removing her skin from a starved body each night and by claiming to have beaten her to death to rectify her violation of humanity. For *Conjunctions,* the author contributed "Please Translate," a suspenseful revelation to a mother of an ex-lover's drowning of a baby, Jimmy. Tone and atmosphere bob and weave as the speaker wheedles and threatens Jonas, the man who kills Jimmy and steals her car. The author also swerved from reality by stressing the servant Marie's attempts at imaginary motherhood in "Between the Pool and the Gardenias." As she dresses and tends a rotting infant corpse, the odor requires increasing amounts of fumigation to keep baby Rose from smelling like pig guts, a vile reminder of visceral decay.

The Farming of Bones recaps Haitian horrors during dictator Rafael Trujillo's ethnic cleansing of the Dominican Republic in October 1937, which leaves bodies cleft with machete blows and twelve Haitian traders dangling from bullwhips in a tree. The genre, according to critic Villalba, chooses the conventions of West Indian corruption and crime and "contributes to the ways it has been scripted as a dark, unknowable space" (Villalba, 2014, 1). A reverse image of ghoulish burial among corpses and vultures in the historical novel revives a refugee, who wakes up smiling in memory of his wife Nounoune's screams on her first night in his bed. The episode recurs in his nightmares, nullifying the original meaning of Nounoune as "silly girl." In the same narrative, a family chuckle at Man Rapadou's anecdote about the starved ex-con who died face-first in a plate of food illustrates the juxtaposition of a witty tragedy, one that Man Rapadou wants to spare her refugee son Yves. Protagonist Amabelle Desír recalls her father's aphorism about such misfortune: "Misery won't touch you gentle. It always leaves its thumbprints," whether public or hidden from the world (Danticat, 1998, 222).

Sources

Adisa, Opal Palmer. "Up Close and Personal," *African American Review* 43:2–3 (Summer/Fall 2009): 345–355.

Danticat, Edwidge. "Ghosts," *New Yorker* (24 November 2008): 108–113.

_____. *Haiti Noir 2.* Brooklyn: Akashic, 2014, 15–19.

_____. "Please Translate," *Conjunctions* 63 (Fall, 2014): 36–40.

_____. *Plunging* (verse) St. Paul, MN: Midnight Paper Sales, 2009.

_____. "Quality Control," *Washington Post* (16 November 2014): 25.

Nance, Kevin. "Haiti Noir, Haiti Light," *Poets & Writers* 39:1 (January/February 2011): 12–13.

Villalba, Carolina. "A Newer Noir: Bringing a Classic Genre to the Caribbean," *Anthurium* 11:1 (2014): 1–4.

Patriarchy

Patriarchy on a grand scale infests Haiti, the Dominican Republic, and other parts of the West Indies through a cycle of male dominance:

- Behechio and the last Taino caciques
- the Genoan navigator Columbus and his Hispanic conquistadors
- Napoleon's French Code diminishing the power of women and children
- the androcentric Catholic church and its shame-inducing priests
- racism, genocide, and despotism under Generalissimo Rafael Trujillo
- the Duvaliers, Papa Doc and Baby Doc, and their torture squad, the Tonton Macoute
- the indenture of orphans like Rosie, a house slave in "Monkey Tails," and fiber workers like "The Indigo Girl"

Indirectly, the wielders of control influenced Danticat's characters by setting examples of male suppression and diminution of females:

Title	Character	Faults
Anacaona	Behechio	Anacaona's dominating brother
	Matunherí	male decision maker for Anacaona
"Anniversary"	Yves Moulin	cruiser of bars for womanizing
The Art of Death	Cousin Joel	a violator of helpless young girls
Behind the Mountains	Papa Espérance	stubborn, argumentative head of household
"Between the Pool and the	philandering husband	abandoner of Marie

Patriarchy

Title	Character	Faults
Gardenias"	Dominican pool man	womanizer who incriminates Marie
"The Book of Miracles"	Bienaimé	paterfamilias of a shamed family
Breath, Eyes, Memory	Catholicism	prescribed gender roles for women
"The Bridal Seamstress"	Tonton Macoute	tortured Beatrice Saint Fort's feet
Brother, I'm Dying	Joseph Nosius Dantica	a pulpit minister who governs his niece
Célimène	Zaken	controlling husband
	Mo	brother who chooses a mate for his sister
"Children of the Sea"	Tonton Macoute	terrorizer of Madam Roger
"Claire de Lune"	Anthère Lighthouse	the guardian light named "Pollinator"
Claire of the Sea Light	Max Ardin, Jr.	rapist and reluctant sire of Pamaxime
	Nozias Faustin	decider of Claire's future and selector of her dresses and foster mother
	Piye	gangster and backer of urban thugs
	Tiye	one-armed gangster and terrorist
The Dew Breaker	Bienaimé	the "fat man" who controls his wife and daughter to conceal a terrorist's secrets
"Dosas"	Blaise	facilitator of fraud against ex-wife Elsie
	Dédé	user of Elsie for sex
"Dream of the Butterflies"	Tonton Macoute	despoilers of Marie's home and terrorizers of her son and daughter
"Eight Days"	barber	role model for Junior of a male trade
The Farming of Bones	Javier	self-important physician
	Pico Duarte	a dominator of wife Valencia and an officer assigned to murder black Haitians
	Rafael Trujillo	racial supremacist and demagogue
	Yves Rapadou	farmer and dominator of Amabelle Desír
"Ghosts"	Tiye	a one-armed gang leader reliant on blackmail
"The Gift"	Thomas	callous widower of Dina
"Hot-Air Balloons"	Sherlon	user of women
"In the Old Days"	Maurice DeJean	abandoner of wife for idealistic interests
"The Journals of Water Days"	fisherman	wielder of vengeance against militia
	Tonton Macoute	despoilers and terrorizers of citizens
"Mama's Nightingale"	Papa	writer of letters to authorities
"Monkey Tails"	Monsieur Christophe	master of Michel, the hireling who is his unacknowledged son
"Night Talkers"	Claude	an out-of-control murderer and swaggerer
	Dany Dorméus	tracker of his parents' killers
"Night Women"	clients	patrons of a sex worker
"Nineteen Thirty-Seven"	prison guards	officials who beat Défilé to death
"The Port-au-Prince Marriage Special"	jeweler	man who tricks Mélisande with a phony ring
	womanizer	infector of Mélisande with AIDS
"The Possibility of Heaven"	medical elite	decision makers for Rose Danticat
"Quality Control"	soldiers	men who threaten women with weapons fire
"The Secret Island"	Papa	an immigrant who marries a widow to acquire papers
"Seeing Things Simply"	village men	controllers of wives
"Seven Stories"	assassins	men who terrorize Callie Morrissete
	prime minister	head of household
"Starfish'"	Maxime Ardin, Sr.	manipulator of his lover, Louise George
Untwine	David Boyer	Army veteran and attorney
"A Wall of Fire Rising"	Big Guy	self-important head of household

Donette A. Francis, on staff at the University of Miami, accounted for the debasing influence of slave, colonial, imperial, and patriarchal eras. For decades, political coups and sabotaged elections subordinated women's experiences of poverty and trauma, the fate of sex workers in "Night Women" and of Lili, submissive wife of the self-absorbed dreamer Big Guy in "A Wall of Fire Rising." Featured in the story "The Journals of Water Days," the French legacy elevated male chauvinism that placed men as heroes and black females at the nadir of social worth. On the positive side of international exodus, displacement from male control offered female refugees as determined as Flore Voltaire, a hairdresser in *Claire of the Sea Light,* new opportunities to overcome gender bias.

Grand displays of supremacy squandered the country's wealth, the backstory of Generalissimo Rafael Trujillo in *The Farming of Bones;* silenced Anne Bienaimé in *The Dew Breaker;* erased a wife in "Seeing Things Simply"; and legitimized Henri Christophe's building of a monument to himself in *Claire of the Sea Light.* In the fairy tale *Célimène,* the title figure learns the hard way that husband Zaken demands departure from home in Pik Rose and a break with her girlhood. The poem "A Despot Walks into a Killing Field" revisits ceremonial receptions where "mighty-seeming people" bow their heads and stand to shake a tyrant's hand "as if/the despot were holy" (Danticat, 2012, 37).

Rediscovering Women

As presented in the essay "We Are Ugly but We Are Here," the diminution of females derives from a restatement of Celie's assertion in Alice Walker's novel *The Color Purple.* The concept dominates Edwidge's stories of women's courage

from pre–Columbian time. For the future Taino Queen in *Anacaona,* the prestige of her brother Behechio, Uncle Matunherí, father Baba, and husband Caonabó outpaces her importance. Even though Anacaona holds a powerful slot in the royal line, she recedes from court decisions to tend her toddler, the standard expectation for a young mother. After Christopher Columbus's seizure of Hispaniola in 1493, Catholicism further forced female citizens into extremes— submissive madonnas or soiled whores, an identification with property and its exchange value that perpetuates women's worth as sexual amusements. Benedetta Faedi, a law professor at Golden Gate University, outlined the criminality that radiates from the adulation of males:

> Poverty, poor governance, and armed violence further exacerbate strong patriarchal values, cultural patterns of a power-imbalance between men and women, a gender-specific sexual asymmetry, which ultimately foster the widespread and systematic rape of girls and women [Faedi, 2008, 176].

Despotism under the Duvaliers extended social paralysis by setting undisciplined Tonton Macoute militia over villages, where they focused their rapacity on girls and women. Compared to Valencia Duarte in *The Farming of Bones,* maidservant Amabelle Desír displays more resolve than the wife of the self-aggrandizing Pico Duarte, a Guardia leader of a 1937 death squad killing black Haitians.

Female beautification embodies male expectation of elegance and charm in their women, including those who straighten their hair in "New York Day Women" and the bride's experiments with hair dye in "Caroline's Wedding." For Anisi, Dieula, and Lina Espérance, the seamstresses in "A Place of Refuge," glamorous outfits and shiny shoes set off braids and wigs that mark their attempts to rise in the Bel Air slum, a goal of Tante Denise, a self-important preacher's wife in *Brother, I'm Dying*. In *Claire of the Sea Light*, Flore Voltaire, a twentieth-century mother, determines to accept hush money from Max Ardin, Sr., for his son's siring of Flore's boy Pamaxime through rape. With cash in hand, she operates a prosperous beauty parlor and plots an escape from the wealthy Ardin family. The story illustrates the importance of women's financial enabling in a largely misogynistic society.

Revaluing Women

Denial of education diminishes strong women because of their poor language skills, the plight of Lili in "A Wall of Fire Rising," the sex worker in "Night Women," Lamort in "The Missing Peace," and cane laborer Tante Atie Caco in *Breath, Eyes, Memory*. While males thrive in citizenship, women cower on the periphery under protection by fathers, husbands, and outsiders like Neah in "Hot-Air Balloons" and conceal female sexuality, evidence of agency and self-assertion. Catholicism promotes patriarchy by undergirding strict control of female bodies and offspring with an imprisoning domestic milieu. Illiterate women earn paltry sums as sex workers, farm workers, and market vendors, inadequate substitutes for respected professions paying salaries large enough to support a family and secure a home. Journalist Christina Patterson of the London *Independent* justified the motivation of mothers like Martine Caco testing their daughters' virginity "to ensure the continuation of their one salable commodity," a euphemism for a profitable marriage (Patterson, 1999, 14).

Androcentrism continues in the present day to displace women. In *Breath, Eyes, Memory*, they hang a light to announce the birth of a boy baby, but extinguish lights to note the arrival of a girl, who becomes less cherished because of her gender. Edwidge brings down the stage light on female birth: "There will be no lamps, no candles, no more light" (Danticat, 1994, 146). Analyst Renee Latchman observes, "Darkness ... will follow her for the rest of her life because she is female" (Latchman, 2014, 61). For Sophie Caco, rearing daughter Brigitte Woods involves freeing mother and daughter from anti-woman ritual. The author's promotion of literacy and education for girls attests to the weakening of traditional male control by fathers, brothers, husbands, and lovers, the specter that stalks Beatrice Saint Fort, "The Bridal Seamstress," into the diaspora. See also Duvaliers, Rape, Tonton Macoute, Virginity, Women.

Sources

Conwell, Joan. "Papa's Masks: Roles of the Father in Danticat's 'The Dew Breaker,'" *Obsidian III* (2005): 221–239.

Danticat, Edwidge. *Breath, Eyes, Memory*. New York: Soho Press, 1994.

_____. "A Despot Walks into a Killing Field," *Progressive* 76:5 (May 2012): 37.

_____. "The Journals of Water Days," *Callaloo* 19:2 (Spring, 1996): 376–380.

_____. "We Are Ugly, But We Are Here," *Caribbean Writer* 10 (1996): n.p.

Faedi, Benedetta. "The Double Weakness of Girls: Discrimination of Sexual Violence in Haiti," *Stanford Journal of International Law* 44 (2008): 147–204.

Francis, Donette A. "'Silences Too Horrific to Disturb': Writing Sexual Histories in Edwidge Danticat's *Breath, Eyes, Memory*," *Research in African Literatures* (July 2004): 75–90.

Johnson, Newtona. "Challenging Internal Colonialism: Edwidge Danticat's Feminist Emancipatory Enterprise." *Obsidian III* (2005): 147–166.

Latchman, Renee. "Edwidge Danticat's *Breath, Eyes, Memory*: A Critique on the Tradition of 'Testing,'" *African Youth in Contemporary Literature and Popular Culture*. New York: Routledge, 2014, 65–74.

Mahase, Radica. "The Terror and the Time: Banal Violence and Trauma in Caribbean Discourse," *Nieuwe West—Indische Gids* 92:1/2 (2018): 156–157.

Patterson, Christina. "Interview," (London) *Independent* (13 March 1999): 14.

Poverty

The author fills her works with compassionate views of Haiti's destitute—the elderly couples, homeless, and widowed and parturient women awaiting food distribution. Her canon particularizes individual destitution of fishermen Caleb and Nozias Faustin in *Claire of the Sea Light* who "pull fish out of the sea that were so small that in the old days they would have been thrown back" (Danticat, 2013, 9). She commiserates with children such as the son of the sex worker in a cramped hut in "Night Women," babies sleeping on dirt floors in *Tent Life*, and the graveless lying under mass burials, a visual image of destitution in the poem "A Despot Walks into a Killing Field." Expert analyst Valérie Loichot, a Romance language specialist at Emory University in Atlanta, compared the danger of hunger to that of illiteracy, the second "disabling void" of third world characters (Loichot, 2004, 92).

Edwidge stresses coping by making do, as with the bright housing tints in the slum town of Jalousie. In "Color Blocking," an interview for *Arquitectonica,* she characterized bright walls and public transportation "as sort of a way to keep back the other dark things, the hunger and political strife ... weaved into the symbolism of daily life" (Danticat, 2013). To conceal their shame, mass goers at the Port-au-Prince cathedral on Christmas Eve lie to tourists about going to universities and residing in affluent homes. Campers at Pak Kado (Gift Park) shelter under lean-tos formed from sheets draped over cardboard. To entertain themselves, children thumb rocks like marbles and crease plastic bags into kites. The memoir "New York Was Our City on the Hill" for the *New York Times* declared her parents' departure north from Haitian squalor a flight to an imaginary Eden free of tyranny's impoverishment. Under a "Faustian bargain," they fled layered injustice of "brutal regimes ... and extreme poverty caused by the Duvaliers' mismanagement and excesses" (Danticat, 2004, CY1).

In the introduction to *Love, Anger, Madness,* Edwidge charged Haiti's tyrants with enlisting the underclass in terrorist acts. Bloodthirsty harvesters reduced the population by slaughtering the poor and selling their organs in the industrialized world. To age twelve, she regretted being left behind at age four in Bel Air, "an impoverished and politically volatile neighborhood" in Port-au-Prince where "the future was not a given" (*ibid.*). Meanwhile, Mira and Rose Danticat "were likely to be working more hours than anyone else, for less money, and with few if any benefits," a coercion exacerbated by "intermittent layoffs and humiliating immigration raids" (*ibid.*). In the story "Hot-Air Balloons," the author contrasted the immigrant factory worker with the field picker in Georgia and Florida. In the idealized "New World," migrant workers pictured in "Not Your Homeland" for *Nation* slept at depleted motels in dirt-floored barracks, and adjacent to animal stalls, a reminder of Jesus's lowly birth to the Holy Family in Bethlehem.

History's Misfortunes

The island underclass are most affected by random crime and by disasters, such as the January 12, 2010, earthquake and landslides; a cholera epidemic imported in October 2010 by United Nations relief workers, the subject of the *New Yorker* account "A Year and a Day"; and the manic wave that sweeps away Caleb, a fictional fisherman sitting in his boat in the novel *Claire of the Sea Light.* Reflecting on literary motifs, Edwidge declared it unlikely that Haitians would write a Romeo-and-Juliet story. Because the caste system thoroughly separates elitists from the underclass, according to Ray Conlogue, a writer for the Toronto *Globe and Mail,* the wealthy disdain "throngs of the poor" (Conlogue, 2004, R3). The vast divide prohibits the privileged from "[forsaking] their class for love," but not from accessing village women for casual sex (*ibid.*).

Of the armchair voyeurism available in literature, critic George Zipp, author of *Poverty in Contemporary Literature,* in an essay for *Zeitschrift für Anglistik und Amerikanistik,* declared that "Poverty is not just part of the geographical landscape but also an important social and cultural faultline in the entire region" that takes shape in a range of causes and consequences (Zipp, 234). Perusal of humble coastal housing pictures the one-room shack of Nozias and Claire Limyè Lanmè Faustin, a tin or thatched roof, and the newsprint glued to the walls with manioc gum, a pathetic excuse for wallpaper for an illiterate fisherman. Even more dismaying, Nozias trades fresh-caught fish for cornmeal and eggs, the family's supplies for a meatless dinner contributing to soul-crushing scurvy and endemic malnutrition.

Making Do

Details enlarge scenes of trauma and hunger, such as the post-massacre tent clinic treating survivors in *The Farming of Bones,* babies covered in flies at a public hospital in the memoir "Becoming Brazilian," and the pathetic belongings of the dead laborer in "Without Inspection." For Arnold, the doomed laborer, destitution in boyhood forced him to dig in the trash for pieces of paper for making airplanes, his only toys. In an interview with Opal Palmer Adisa, a writer for *African American Review,* Edwidge regretted reports of Haitians defeating hunger by eating clay cookies. She empathized with the have-nots in "A Wall of Fire Rising" in which Lili feeds her family simple meals on banana-leaf plates, the title figure in *Célimène* barters for island vegetables, and in "Nineteen Thirty-Seven," where friends value a pillow stuffed with a prisoner's hair, evidence of simple recycling.

Cassandra Spratling, in a summary for the *Detroit Free Press,* imparted a two-edged compliment: "Like a straight shot of hard liquor, Danticat is not for the faint of heart" (Spratling, 2002, C1). Edwidge noted the hierarchy that left the poor neglected and despised by neighbors as the burnt crust on the pot bottom. Chapter three of *Claire of the Sea Light* speaks through teen journalist Bernard "Bè" Dorien the plight of slum dwellers in Cité Pendue: "They were used, then abandoned, because they were out of choices, because they were poor" (Danticat, 2013, 82). The plight of women fuels a demand for evidence of chic fashion, a philosophy that Anne Bienaimé adheres to in *The Dew Breaker.* Cosmetologist Flore Voltaire goes into the beauty shop business because "even in their misery … the poorest and unhappiest of women could fight heartache with beauty"—scarves, braids, hats, wigs, and tignons, the dignified head wrap of black women since slave times (*Ibid.,* 178, 177).

Sources

Adisa, Opal Palmer. "Up Close and Personal," *African American Review* 43:2–3 (Summer/Fall 2009): 345–355.

Conlogue, Ray. "Haunted by Haiti's Ghosts," [Toronto] *Globe and Mail* (19 April 2004): R3.

Danticat, Edwidge. "Becoming Brazilian," *Obsidian III* 6/7:2/1 (Fall 2005/2006): 139–145.

_____. *Claire of the Sea Light.* New York: Vintage, 2013.

_____. "Color Blocking," Arquitectonica, https://www.interiorsandsources.com/article-details/articleid/15929/title/color-blocking-edwidge-danticat (1 July 2013).

_____. "A Despot Walks into a Killing Field," *Progressive* 76:5 (May 2012): 37.

_____. *Love Anger Madness: A Haitian Triptych.* introduction. New York: Modern Library, 2010, xi–xviii.

_____. "Message to My Daughters," *The Fire This Time: A New Generation Speaks about Race.* New York: Scribner, 2017, 205–216.

_____. "New York Was Our City on the Hill," *New York Times* (21 November 2004): CY1.

_____. "Not Your Homeland," *Nation* 281:9 (26 September 2005): 24–26.

Loichot, Valérie. "Edwidge Danticat's Kitchen History," *Meridians* 5:1 (2004): 92–116.

Spratling, Cassandra. "Haitian Heritage Author Edwidge Danticat Treats Poverty and Oppression in Plain Words," *Detroit Free Press* (1 April 2002); C1.

Zipp, Georg. "Selling Poverty: Junot Díaz's and Edwidge Danticat's Assessments of Picturesque Stereotypes of Poverty in the Caribbean," *Zeitschrift für Anglistik und Amerikanistik* 63:2 (2015): 229–246.

Racism

Edwidge related her despair that Americans reject Afro-Haitians, but not Hispanic Cubans. According to her interview in "The Dominican Republic and Haiti: A Shared View from the Diaspora," colorism emerged from U.S. Marines, particularly those from the segregated South. After the July 28, 1915, occupation, ingrained hatred of blacks "[rewarded] any kind of proximity to whiteness, pushing us beyond colorism to a version of the U.S. Jim Crow system" (Danticat, 2014, 31). The outgrowth—color-based hierarchies—set a pattern of exclusion among races and classes on both sides of the island "where light skin color is a kind of currency … a kind of class of its own" (*ibid.*). In the conclusion to the November 2013 essay "Suddenly Stateless" for the *Los Angeles Times,* she asked what Americans have learned about "institutionalized racism" from experiences in the Balkans, Germany, and South Africa (Danticat, 2013, A24).

In "AHA!," a 1997 speech to the Inter-American Development Bank Cultural Center, the writer regretted the bigotry barrier, a central issue in the collection *Becoming American: Personal Essays by First Generation Immigrant Women.* She cited the rancor spewed by white American kids chanting "Get back on your banana boats, you dirty Haitians," a spite echoed by a respected dinner guest in "Seven Stories" (Chen, 2014, 220). Extending bias, the slurs alienated people with black skin on a par with boat people and other undesirables: homosexuals, drug addicts, hemophiliacs, and AIDS carriers. The vituperation inhibited newcomers from thinking of themselves as Americans.

A Colored Woman

The caste, physique, and skin color of people living in Haiti and the Dominican Republic take on critical value in the author's writing, for example, the tricking of Xavier, the white hotel owner in "The Port-au-Prince Marriage Special" by a white Canadian quack, the charge that black women have broad buttocks in the author's interview with Junot Díaz for *BOMB,* and the "African mask of a face" on Jessamine in *Claire of the Sea Light* (Danticat, 2013, 182). In a 2007 interview with Díaz, she pondered a *Miami Herald* charge that Dominican clubs refuse entry to black American embassy staff and Marines. Their reasoning was personal: so citizens of the Dominican Republic will "not be considered or called black" (Danticat, 2007, 95).

As Edwidge's daughters, Mira and Leila Boyer, came of age, her essay "I Still Have a Dream" for *Progressive* reclaimed the higher ground that Martin Luther King established on August 28, 1963, before a quarter million Americans assembled at the Lincoln Memorial. She deduced it was time to "at least alert them to the potentially life altering, or even life ending, challenges they might face as not just young women, but young black women in the United States"

(Danticat, 2015, 16). She believed it "hard to forgive ... racial supremacy ... because it has wounded us so deeply in the past" (*ibid.*), an indirect reference to slavery and to Dominican Generalissimo Rafael Trujillo's slaughter of 30,000 black cane workers on October 2–8, 1937, at the Massacre River. The worries of a devoted mom set the tone of writings about vulnerable young girls, particularly the title figure in *Claire of the Sea Light* and Lili in "Hot-Air Balloons."

Battling Injustice

In a blast at Afro-phobia, the author quotes poet Felix Morisseau Leroy's first-person poem "Tourist," a dramatic moment in the life of an islander who is too shamed by poverty and negritude to pose for a photo. He fears being "misread, mis-seen, and misunderstood ... out of context" (Danticat, 2010, 145). For the discrediting of guerrilla rebels Louis Drouin and Marcel Numa in *Create Dangerously,* dictator François "Papa Doc" Duvalier had proclaimed them *blan* (white) foreigners. The misrepresentation of ethnicity stripped them of value as migrants who had returned from the United States to rid Haiti of a vicious tyrant. Edwidge took a stronger stand for human rights after her 81-year-old uncle Joseph Nosius Dantica's wrongful five-day incarceration at Miami's Krome Detention Center and his death on November 2, 2004, in shackles from untreated pancreatitis. She speaks through magazine writer Kimberly "Kim" Boyer in "Seven Stories" a resentment of overt prejudice, especially an honored guest in the home of the prime minister and his wife. Like the snake in Eden, the insidious hiss echoed the European stereotypes that have slithered through history and surfaced during the Trump administration.

Prejudice settles in on the youngest of Edwidge's characters. At the birth of a fictional twin boy and girl to Pico and Valencia Duarte in the opening of *The Farming of Bones,* Grandfather Don Ignacio refutes Doctor Javier's description of charcoal coloring on baby Rosalinda Teresa. The don's negrophobia legitimizes the racial purity of his Dominican household. Not only "pure Spanish blood" on both sides, the mother claims lineage from conquistadors, specifically El Almirante, the Genoan Cristobal Colón (the admiral, Christopher Columbus), an ironic lionizing of the despoilers of Hispaniola and slayers of the Taino First Peoples (Danticat, 1998, 18).

Additional mantras of partiality arose in other island professionals. The Trujillian philosophy of de-mongrelization revisits the narrative in the brainwashed alert of Father Jacques Romain, who warns of the "tainting" of Hispanic blood if black Haitian cane workers continue to live and propagate in the Dominican Republic (*ibid.,* 259). Rafael Trujillo's Guardia become so bloodthirsty that they slaughter dark-skinned Hispanics along with Afro-Haitians to ensure a lighter complexion across the populace. In homage to the victims, Edwidge composed "Poem 2" in the anthology *Standing Tall.* The concluding lines repeat the claim, "Their blood, Bondye (good God), flows in me" (Danticat, 2010, n.p.).

Sources

Chen, Wilson C. "Narrating Diaspora in Edwidge Danticat's Short-Story Cycle *The Dew Breaker,*" *Literature Interpretation Theory* 25:3 (2014): 220–241.

Danticat, Edwidge. "Aha" (speech) Inter-American Development Bank Cultural Center, 1997.

_____. *Create Dangerously: The Immigrant Artist at Work.* New York: Vintage, 2010.

_____. "The Dominican Republic and Haiti: A Shared View from the Diaspora," *Americas Quarterly* 8:3 (Summer 2014): 28–35.

_____. *The Farming of Bones.* New York: Penguin, 1998.

_____. "I Still Have a Dream," *Progressive* 79:2 (February 2015): 15–17.

_____. "Junot Díaz," *BOMB* 101 (Fall 2007): 89–95.

_____. "Poems," *Standing Tall: Portraits of the Haitian Community in Miami, 2003–2010.* Miami: Museum of Contemporary Art, 2010, n.p.

_____. "So Brutal a Death," *New Yorker* 96:17 (22 June 2020): 18–19.

_____. "Suddenly Stateless" (contributor) *Los Angeles Times* (10 November 2013): A24.

Murphy, Dwyer. "The Art of Not Belonging," *Guernica* (3 September 2013).

Rape

In interviews, Edwidge speaks out on sexual exploitation of women and girls and the influence of rape on mother-daughter relationships. A carnal transaction at the airport avoided a secret peril to Callie Morrissete and her mother, who bargained with sex in "Seven Stories" to save them both from assassins. The choice became "the price for getting on the plane" (Danticat, 2019, 195). Eva Federmayer, a Hungarian specialist in American studies, substantiated the crime as pivotal to the author's themes: "It embodies the structural violence that fleshes out the political body of Haitian dictatorships" (Federmayer, 2015, 5). Of the earthquake on January 12, 2010, the author reported rising rape counts in displacement camps. She epitomized the fears of slum dwellers in "A Place of Refuge," a story in the May 2011 issue of *Allure,* in which the refugee Jesula, the author's cousin, goes to bed in a displacement camp with her jeans on to impede rapists. The cautious sleeper adds a warning to plain women: "Being ugly doesn't protect you either" (Danticat, 2011).

In *The Art of Death,* the writer narrates her own targeting for cyclical sex crime—a nightly groping by Cousin Joel on four girls sleeping in one room at the home of Denise and Joseph Nozius Dantica. She concealed from her pious aunt and uncle that shielding her from the predations of the Tonton Macoute did nothing to end nightly loathing of fondling and terror of being murdered in her cot. Fortunately, Joel departed the family after six weeks. The irony turns the anecdote into a cautionary tale about the predations that girls and women suffer in silence within their own residence. Years later, a burst of sobbing opened the way for confession to Tante Rezia, André Mira's youngest sister, about the episodes, which to Edwidge "represented another kind of death, the death of innocence for little girls" (Danticat, 2017, 44).

Innocence Devastated

For Haiti's mythic past, the writer returns to the symbolic story of Sor Rose (Sister Rose), the island's historic black mother and rape victim. A black slave, Sister Rose conceived a child during an assault by a French colonial, an iconic explanation of the ethnic caste system at the island's founding. Explained by Joan Dayan, a culture specialist at Vanderbilt University, the "refined images of white women depended upon the violation and ravaging of black women" whom Catholic society left "excluded from marriage, threatened by poverty, and often abandoned" (Dayan, 1994, 9). The nation she bore recurs in the author's stories in *Krik? Krak!* in the melancholy tale of a mother drowning herself after tossing her baby's corpse into the Caribbean Sea in "Children of the Sea." For "Caroline's Wedding," the mother's violation by a jailer with a drug results in Caroline's birth without a forearm, a token of female disempowerment. The daughter hallows her mother's sacrifice with the delivery of red roses, a gesture to Sor Rose, an incarnation of the daringly carnal Erzulie, Vodou deity of all females.

The color resounds in the story collection with the abandoned baby Rose in "Between the Pool and the Gardenias," and in the novels *Céliméne* and *Claire of the Sea Light* in the towns Pik Rose (Rose Peak) and Ville Rose. In the latter, the blossoming sexuality of a privileged boy precipitates the vicious rape of maidservant Flore Voltaire by Maxime Ardin, Jr., a closeted homosexual seeking to prove vigorous heterosexuality. In a radio call-in confessional to talk-show host Louise George, Flore refers to the crime as the moment that changed her life. The understatement omits the mental struggles of Max, Sr., grandfather of Flore's illegitimate boy Pamaxime, a name formed from his birth father's name and the adverb *pas* (not). Illustrating the result of a child born of violence, Pamaxime draws a father figure with an empty O for features, a child's representation of absent fatherhood.

Machiavellian Sex

The author recovers indelible memories on characters who survive rape, such as Alice Sebold's victim in *The Lovely Bones,* a novel that Edwidge reviews in *The Art of Death*; Défilé, the aptly named prize of a prison guard in "Nineteen Thirty-Seven"; the likelihood of rape in *Tent Life;* and restaurateur Rèzia's memories of violation in "The Funeral Singer." The latter assault occurred in an aunt's brothel, when a uniformed man demanded her niece. The Taino diary narrator in *Anacaona* reviles the Kalina (Carib), insurgents from South America who steal yucca, men, and women. The impregnating of Taino females restates the rape of the Sabines in Roman legend from 750 BCE, which the historian Livy wrote about in *Ab Urbe Condita* (From the city's founding). Gang kidnap resulted in the enlargement of Italian tribes through coercive sex with captive brides, a predictable basis of the city Rome and its choice of Mars as a patron god.

No less martial, the Duvalier paramilitary established a reputation for violating island women, the motivation for the poem "A Despot Walks into a Killing Field," a false identification of Emmanuel "Toto" Constant in "The Book of Miracles"; and the rape crisis center Leve (lift) in "Hot-Air Balloons." Martine Caco's first glimpse of her daughter in New York in *Breath, Eyes, Memory* recalls the face of the Tonton Macoute rapist, Sophie Caco's unknown father, and the end to virginity testing for Martine by Grandmè Ifé. After following in the tradition of superintending maidenhood, Martine regrets complicity with the island protocol of checking the hymen of her own daughter. In New York, the rape recurs in nightmares "like getting raped every night" (Danticat, 1994, 190). The violation reflects the myth of Haiti's birth to Sor Rose and a Frenchman. To beat back phallic abuse, Sophie runs through a cane field punishing the stalks and yanking them up from the roots, a symbolic assault on patriarchal control of women. The legend infiltrates Edwidge's short fiction collection, *Krik? Krak!,* in the tragic birthing of Célianne's baby girl in "Children of the Sea" and the vaginal images permeating rose symbols in "Between the Pool and the Gardenias" and "Caroline's Wedding," and motivates the pro-woman essay "Demonstrators in Haiti Are Fighting for an Uncertain Future."

See also Patriarchy, Violence.

Sources

Adisa, Opal Palmer. "Up Close and Personal," *African American Review* 43:2–3 (Summer/Fall 2009): 345–355.

Danticat, Edwidge. *The Art of Death: Writing the Final Story.* Minneapolis, MN: Graywolf Press, 2017.

_____. *Breath, Eyes, Memory.* New York: Soho Press, 1994.

_____. "Color Blocking," Arquitectonica, https://www.interiorsandsources.com/article-details/articleid/15929/title/color-blocking-edwidge-danticat (1 July 2013).

_____. "Edwidge Danticat," *Nation* 296:4 (28 January 2013): 18.

_____. "A Place of Refuge," *Allure* 21:3 (March 2011).

Dayan, Joan. "Erzulie: A Women's History of Haiti," *Research in African Literatures Caribbean Literature* 25:2 (Summer, 1994): 5–31.

Federmayer, Eva. "Violence and Embodied Subjectivities: Edwidge Danticat's Breath, Eyes, Memory," *Scholar Critic* 2:3 (December 2015): 1–17.

Martinez-Falquina, Silvia. "Postcolonial Trauma Theory in the Contact Zone: The Strategic Representation of Grief in Edwidge Danticat's *Claire of the Sea Light*," *Humanities* 4:4 (2015): 834–860.

Wilson, Raffaela N. "Black Women and the Search for Spiritual Liberation," a graduate thesis submitted at the University of Georgia, 2009.

Religion

Edwidge learned from Haitian society the island's variety of faiths and ethnicities, which mothers practice with silent prayer in "Seven Stories" while waiting in line for obstetrical or pediatric care. For the devout, celebration of Three Kings' Day or Epiphany on January 6 ended the yule season with gifts for children, priestly blessings, and the *galette des rois* (king cake) and a propitious baby Jesus doll tucked inside. Emphasizing the centrality of belief systems, mothers and daughters bear the name Prudence and Mercy in "Nineteen Thirty-Seven"; girls wear communion dresses to hospital triage. Examples convey some animosity between Catholicism and Vodou in *The Last Mapou*, in which the church condemns a tree for serving as a setting of weddings and births. Insouciance marks the story "Ghosts" alongside "a few Protestant and Catholic churches, Vodou temples, restaurants, bakeries, and dry cleaners, even Internet cafes" (Danticat, 2008, 108). For a campus send-up in "Tatiana, Mon Amour," the author turns college fealties into drollery with a weekly gathering at the "First Daughters of Sheba Church," where a female sisterhood aged eighteen to seventy feels at home with an Ethiopian queen.

From fifteenth-century history, Edwidge revered Attabeira, the water deity in *Anacaona* who takes possession of villagers Yaybona, Piragua, and Nahe, victims of a freak windstorm. On the premarital isolation of Anacaona, a period of prayer and meditation in Uncle Matunherí's temple pleads for ancestral guidance and clears her mind for wifely duties. Like cutting the umbilical cord, extensive reflection distances the Taino cacica (ruler) for giving up home and taking up residence with husband Caonabó, the Maguana chief. The assignment, worded by Guamayto, Matunherí's favorite wife, delineates the obedient fiancée from suicidal sister-in-law Yaruba, who chooses death by poisoning rather than live away from her childhood milieu.

Words to God

Updated prayers and liturgy designate the female street evangelists in multiple capacities: preachers of asceticism to carnival goers in *After the Dance*, liturgist at an immigrant funeral in "Caroline's Wedding," and comforter of Josephine, the mute widow of Caleb in the novel *Claire of the Sea Light*. In "The Missing Peace," a grandmother reduces the relationship of the devout to the world as "God's regime," a replacement of island dictators with the Almighty (Danticat, 1995, 93). The term describes the fanaticism of Anne Bienaimé, who seeks relief of guilt and shame in *The Dew Breaker*. For her husband's past crimes on behalf of the Tonton Macoute, she attends daily mass, Christmas Eve services, and religious retreats, but faithful Catholicism fails to lighten her burden.

In shantytown, Middle Eastern Haitians of the Assad clan earned the stereotyped designation of "Arabs." Amid the West African diaspora, a few Muslims share the mythos and ritual of varied Christian denominations and of Vodou and Santerian followers. For sixteen-year-old Giselle Boyer, the severed twin in *Untwine,* a lethal car crash leaves her wondering whether to pray. Her thoughts turn to family and the overwhelming value of music, art, career, and Haitian New Year's foods and the prayers of Pastor Ben. An agnostic given to wishful thinking, she envisions heaven as "all the places you love" or the ones you want to experience, a summation of the resting place for Isabelle's ashes off the property of her grandparents, Marcus and Régine Boyer (Danticat, 2015, 11).

Haiti's Religious History

At a glimpse of the Haitian diaspora in *Behind the Mountains,* the author voices through narrator Céliane Espérance a closeness to the St. Jerome's Church congregation:

> At Saint Jerome's, Haiti did not seem so far away. I felt that if I reached out and touched anyone at the mass, I could be back in Haiti again, as though every person there was carrying a piece of Haiti with them in the warmth of their skin, beneath their winter coats [Danticat, 2002, 95].

For servants in *The Farming of Bones,* thanks and requests to martyred third century BCE. Carthaginian saints Perpetua and Felicity; St. Monica, the fifth-century CE Algerian mother of St. Augustine; St. Agnes, the third-century CE Roman patron of chastity; and Anne, Jesus's first-century BCE. Jewish maternal grandmother from Galilee, enlist female powers to protect the twin babies of mistress Valencia Duarte.

At the announcement of Haitian genocide on the Dominican Republic border, Father Romain and Father Vargas conceal a concerted rescue of islanders under cover of a mass for St. Thérèse of Lisieux, the popular nineteenth-century French "Little Flower of Jesus" and protector of the human body. Old Kongo turns to St. Christopher, the third-century CE Canaanite patron of travelers, an appropriate shielder of an elderly African. On Amabelle Desír's flight into the mountains toward Dajabón in the north of the Massacre River, she observes a three-person procession in a trance state bearing a statue of the Virgin Mary and chanting rosaries. Amabelle observes "accord between desperate women," a shared fear for family, lovers, and the sick (Danticat, 1998, 167). The subject of saints returns in Cap Haïtien, where Man Rapadou explains why she named her son Sebastien after the Roman soldier martyred by the Emperor Diocletian in 288 CE. Martin Munro, an expert in francophone literature at the University of Aberdeen, related the motivation for ties to persecution: "Haiti may be a political and social catastrophe, but it has a glorious, epic history, and an endlessly creative culture, which to some extent counterbalance or compensate for daily indignities and ongoing suffering" (Munro, 2007, i).

Personal Experience

From childhood to adulthood, the author prayed twice daily, early and late, and valued her words to God as private and urgent. In the philosophical essay collection *The Art of Death,* she respected prayer as an intensely personal experience with God. When food was scarce, her uncle Joseph Nosius Danticat urged her to pray and have faith, the situation in the *New Yorker* personal essay "Crabs." Weekdays, her school class attended mass at the landmark cathedral Notre Dame de l'Assomption (Our Lady of the Assumption), marking the empowerment of the Virgin Mary. Edwidge passed the sanctuary daily

Religion 197

on her walk down Rue Pavée to class and valued the structure as a haven in a chaotic city. She also walked by Notre Dame du Perpetual Secours (Our Lady of Constant Help), patron of Haiti. After the churches collapsed in the January 12, 2010, earthquake, she recalled their influence as sounds: "The chimes of these churches' bells guided the routines of my day" (Danticat, 2013, 41). The essay "Edwidge Danticat Returns to Haiti and Finds Resilience and Regeneration" acknowledges a childlike wonder in hymn singing on Corpus Christi Day, a testimonial to Jesus's humanity and divinity. Simultaneously, "altar boys in flowing white robes and girls in communion dresses weave rosary beads through their fingers" to facilitate prayer (Danticat, 2011).

After Edwidge moved to Miami, she continued attending a Protestant church and joined in the monthly foot-washing ritual, which she described in the personal essay "Sole Mates" for *O Magazine.* She characterized her island religious heritage as West African animism and mysticism melded with Roman Catholicism. She viewed the African posture and white blouse and plaid skirt uniform of a parochial student in the vignette "The Indigo Girl." In "Message to My Daughters," she credited nuns and priests with distributing food to refugees from the Dominican Republic. The combination of ancient African lore with contemporary Catholic mercy enabled her to envision hope that transcended obstacles. In response to her beliefs, she writes about people who face brutality and prejudice. To seize the advantage over tormentors, in 1981, the author and other Haitian children brandished red handkerchiefs, muttered a mantra, and pretended to wield a Vodou spell, causing enemies to flee.

Scripture confirmed the author's faith, especially during the sharing of supplies and water in lean-to cities after the earthquake. In the collection *Tent Life,* Haitians lived up to Jesus's command to "Love thy neighbor," as recorded in the gospel of Matthew 22:39 (Danticat, 2010, 11). While Rose Danticat received cancer treatment in Miami, Edwidge escorted her to a small evangelical assembly of some four families to sing and read the bible. Rose took comfort in the lyric beauty of the Beatitudes and Psalm 23. In mourning, her daughter read Revelation and composed a suitable call on God in which Rose anticipates the glory of union with the eternal and expects ongoing blessings on the family.

See also Catholicism, Earthquake, Ritual, Vodou.

SOURCES

Danticat, Edwidge. *Behind the Mountains.* New York: Orchard Books, 2002.

_____. "Edwidge Danticat Returns to Haiti and Finds Resilience and Regeneration," *Newsweek* 158:7 (15 August 2011).

_____. *Everything Inside.* New York: Knopf, 2019.

_____. *The Farming of Bones.* New York: Penguin, 1998.

_____. "Ghosts," *New Yorker* (24 November 2008): 108–113.

_____. "Haiti: A Bi-Cultural Experience" (lecture). Washington, D.C.: IDB Cultural Center (7 December 1995): 1–9.

_____. "House of Prayer and Dreams," *Sojourners* 442:4 (April 2013): 38–39, 41–42.

_____. "The Indigo Girl: Between Haiti and the Streets of Brooklyn," *Sojourners* (December 2004): 28.

_____. *Krik? Krak!* New York: Soho Press, 1995.

_____. *The Last Mapou.* Brooklyn: One Moore Book, 2013.

_____. "Living and Loving through Tragedy," *Sojourners* 39:3 (March 2010): 10–11.

_____. "Prayer before Dying," *PEN America 19* (18 September 2017): 34–36.

_____. "Sole Mates," *Oprah Magazine* (April 2008).

_____. *Untwine.* New York: Scholastic, 2015.

_____. "A Voice from Heaven," *The Good Book: Writers Reflect on Favorite Bible Passages.* New York: Simon & Schuster, 2015, 263–269.

Munro, Martin. *Exile and Post-1946 Haitian Literature.* Liverpool, UK: Liverpool University Press, 2007.

Smith, Katharine Capshaw. "Interview," *Children's Literature Association Quarterly* 30:2 (Summer, 2005): 194–205.

Tillotson, Kristin. "Daughter of Haiti," *Minneapolis Star Tribune* (8 September 2013): E1.

Ritual

Edwidge acknowledges various cultic rituals for their value to real and fictional characters, for example, the marrying of the earth's first couples and the blessing of their offspring under the kapok tree in *The Last Mapou,* the rebirth of baptized spirits in "A Year and a Day," and the christening of baby Jude, Carole's grandson in "Sunrise, Sunset." The author concentrated on symbolic clothing to mark occasions. For Martine Caco in *Breath, Eyes, Memory,* burial in a red dress redeemed her from a life of suffering. For Edwidge, ritual detailed stages of loss in *Brother, I'm Dying,* concluding with the burial of sibling with sibling in a New York graveyard. At the merger of spirits in the washing of feet biblical style in "Sole Mates," she declared the rite a way to "[know] each other in a slightly different way than we had before" (Danticat, 2008). Rose Danticat's adoption of black at her mother's demise acknowledged the grim mourning period in *The Art of Death.* Because the passage of days eased the burden of sorrow, clothing lightened in color and tone to signal the end of sadness and the dawning of acceptance.

After discovery in rubble of her cousin, Maxi Dantica, in *Create Dangerously,* the author noted the absence of funerals for victims buried in mass graves after the January 12, 2010, earthquake. She promoted honoring departed spirits in the poem "On the Day of the Dead," a seven-stage circling of home for newlyweds in *Célimène* to represent days of the week, and, in "Ghosts," the bleeding of pigeons into Carnation condensed milk and Malta, a fizzy malt beverage, to make a drink suited to the deflowering of a virgin teenage male. For the title character in *Claire of the Sea Light,* a pilgrimage on her birthday to her mother's grave unites celebration of a new dress with sorrow that Claire never met her parent. In each example, actions, gestures, songs, processions, and prayers consecrate some vital stage of humankind from birth to burial.

Indigenous Customs

Haitian ritual dates to the island's First Peoples. In the historical biography *Anacaona,* Uncle Matunherí swings a ceremonial ax to cut a virgin's braid, a token of fifteenth-century BCE Taino girlhood. Near his life's end, tribesmen lift torches to lure ancestral shamans to ease Matunherí's chest pains and gasping for breath. More detailed, Anacaona's nuptials involve body paint with Maguanan icons on the groom Caonabó, who released prize birds to honor his beloved. Uncle Matunherí opened the ceremony with a puff of tobacco smoke to the four directions, a standard recreation of the sacred circle in First Peoples protocols. After drumming and blessings, the simple wedding ends. Festivities take the allied family members into the high country to leave food offerings to the yucca god Yúcahu and the water goddess Attabeira, a deity who also superintends fertility, an appropriate domain for a wedding.

Twentieth-century tokens of events color the acts at nurse Nadine Osnac's altar commemorating an aborted fetus in "Water Child," Anne Bienaimé's secret Christmas decorations in "The Book of Miracles," and Giselle Boyer's memories of sharing a church pew with her sister and parents in *Untwine.* In "Caroline's Wedding," Hermine Azile joins other Haitian-American women in attending funeral services for refugees drowned off the Miami shore. Woeful cries punctuate the priest's reading of names of 129 victims in the catastrophe, causing Hermine to reflect on the slaves who died during the Middle Passage. Célianne, the suicide in "Children of the Sea" who drowned after jettisoning her dead infant, represents victimization of Haitians by the Duvalier regime and the extensive harm to families by the vicious Tonton Macoute. Those fleeing possible murder arrive in New York to the home of André Mira Danticat in *Brother, I'm Dying,* in which he welcomes newcomers with familiar Haitian meals. Critic Nancy Raquel Mirabal, a specialist in American Studies at the University of Maryland, justified the feast for "[recognizing] the healing power of food, of its ability to immediately connect us to our roots through taste, smell, memory," by the simple act of "raising a fork to our lips" (Mirabal, 2007, 26).

Rites and Traditions

Ritual in Edwidge's canon represents sustaining actions for positive and negative events as repetitive as Papi's reliving of the Spanish Civil War on radio in *The Farming of Bones,* Anika's reframing of two deaths in surreal art in "The Gift," and Callie's expectation of hair ribbons in "Seven Stories" on Three Kings Eve preceding Epiphany. For the story "In the Old Days," the author mentions the great-hearted invitations of patrons of the Rendez Vous (Come back) restaurant "to join christening and baptism parties, communion and wedding lunches, graduation dinners, wakes and funeral receptions" (Danticat, 2012, 357). The constant gatherings and departures account for the restaurant's name, which anticipates frequent family-style returns.

The shared loss in Haiti's earthquake turned digging for remains in wreckage into its own ceremony, the preface to Junior's recovery in *Eight Days* and the theme of Edwidge's personal essays "Living and Loving through Tragedy" for *Sojourners* and "Mourning in Place" for *New York Review of Books.* Because so many lay in common graves, Edwidge

regretted that "Everyone is being robbed of rituals," such as family meals in *Tent Life,* celebrating Isabelle Boyer's life with a bath in strawberry body wash in *Untwine,* and covering the door in purple cloth, cleaning mausoleums, and sharing anecdotes like the mourners of Aunt Estina Estème in "Night Talkers" (Danticat, 2010, 11). At the funeral of Martine Caco in *Breath, Eyes, Memory,* daughter Sophie takes comfort from her mother's suicide with the village processional, sorrow songs, and the clack of gourd rattles and talking drums. She joins a women's group to free herself by supporting other troubled women. Reflecting on her assessment of customs, the author stated, "Rituals are part of continuity" (Shamsie, 2020).

See also Religion, Tradition; Vodou.

Sources

Danticat, Edwidge. *"Ghosts," New Yorker* (24 November 2008): 108–113.
_____. "In the Old Days," *Callaloo* 35:2 (2012): 355–363, 562.
_____. *The Last Mapou.* Brooklyn: One Moore Book, 2013.
_____. "Living and Loving through Tragedy," *Sojourners* 39:3 (March 2010): 10–11.
_____. "Mourning in Place," *New York Review of Books* 67:14 (24 September 2020): 38.
_____. "Sole Mates," *Oprah Magazine* (April 2008).
Mirabal, Nancy Raquel. "Dyasporic Appetites and Longings," *Callaloo* 30:1 (Winter 2007): 26–39, 410.
Murriel, Maria. "Read This Book About Writing. About Death," *World* (14 July 2017).
Shamsie, Kamila. "Memory, Ritual and Migration," *Edinburgh International Book Festival* (interview) (15 August 2020), https://www.edbookfest.co.uk/press-release/memory-ritual-and-migration-discussed-by-edwidge-danticat-and-kamila-shamsie.

Slavery

Bondage dominated the West Indies after 1493, when British sugar planters staffed Barbados and Jamaica with press gangs, and Hispanics coerced Mexico and Hispaniola's Taino mineworkers into gold prospecting. After much oppression of laborers and kidnap of natives to Spain, Indian culture dwindled with seven million deaths, a majority from malnutrition, measles, mumps, chickenpox, smallpox, diphtheria, influenza, pneumonia, whooping cough, plague, yellow fever, typhoid, and malaria. When conquistadors changed the ethnicity of chattel in Haiti in 1517, black slavery replaced the dwindling aboriginal Taino stock with slaves abducted by white profiteers from West Africa. By 1535, the Taino culture disappeared.

The Colonial Ordinance introduced dominance as an organizing principle. Known as the Code Noir of 1685, initiated by market reformer Jean-Baptiste Colbert of Rheims, it epitomized slaves as movable possessions who reproduced their own kind as a profit for investors. The work beasts in French colonies produced cane sugar. In the narrative "Seven Stories," frescoes revisit a slave port, where European traders in human lives wield whips over African boys and women, most of them Dahomey, Fula, Ibo, and Nago. Afro-Caribbeans preserved that heritage in narratives, place names, liturgy, clothing and hair styles, and songs of their birth country.

Bestial Capitalism

The era of New World exploitation, according to culture expert Joan Dayan of Vanderbilt University, "ushered in unbridled appetites and unheard-of cruelties" based on worldly indulgence, perversity, and greed (Dayan, 1994, 9). In sympathy with the tortured and oppressed under what Thomas Jefferson called "unremitting despotism," Edwidge respected Ginen (or Guinea), ancestral home of black Atlantic coast natives south of the Sahara from the 700s, as a haven for souls in the afterlife (*ibid.*). Icons of heritage picture Africa's beginnings in a people blessed with exuberance, probity, and gravitas, a stark opposite to captives reduced to chains and abject servitude. She charged islanders in *Create Dangerously* for paradisiacal paintings of the outback's verdure, "but never the Middle Passage," the dire expanse of saltwater prefacing suicide, auction blocks, and exhaustive labors (Danticat, 2010, 64). In "Poem 2" of the anthology *Standing Tall,* she declared, "Their blood, Bondye (good God), could fill the sea" (Danticat, 2010, n.p.).

In an introit to *Poetry of Haitian Independence,* the writer commends the cause and purpose of the New Year's Day 1804 Haitian Revolution of black bondsmen against French colonialism, which she characterized as "a bloody twelve-year slave uprising, the only time in the history of the world that bond servants successfully overthrew their masters and formed their own state" (*ibid.,* 97). Unfortunately, black lords rose to savagery equal to that of white slavers. By citing both the French original and the English translation of the Haitian national anthem, "Hymne Haytienne," she captured the desperation of a people too long held in bondage, an image she reprised with Olivia's solo version of the hymn in "Dosas." The rebuke to leisured poets reminds nationalists that winning freedom begins with liberation, but does not guarantee it, a concept integral to the historical novel *Anacaona.*

History in Legends

The resilience of chattel slavery survives in 1986 in "Monkey Tails" with the domestic chores of Rosie, a relative of a mistress who forces her to do menial work, and Michel, assistant to water magnate Monsieur Christophe, his unacknowledged father. The slag of incarceration and homesickness recurs in *After the Dance,* in which the legend of the *sabliye* tree (sabal palm) recalls African abductees forced to walk in its shade to forget their homeland and quell desires to repatriate to West Africa. For residents of Ville Rose in *Claire of the Sea Light,* fears of spectral maroons haunting *Mòn Initil* (Useless Mountain) evolve from bones still found on its slopes. After fleeing placement with Gaëlle Lavaud, a potential foster mother, seven-year-old Claire Limyè Lanmè Faustin fantasizes the life of a maroon in the safety of caves near the Anthère Lighthouse, once a beacon of hope. As though reprising African culture, she dances ring games counter clockwise, a return trip to the motherland in song.

For Junior and his little sister Justine in *Eight Days,* the sight of a 1968 tribute to maroons in the Champs de Mars Plaza emphasizes the muscularity, bare chest, and jubilant note on a conch shell. The player is the *Marron Inconnu* (unknown maroon), sculpted by architect and human rights advocate Albert Mangonès of Martissant. The heroic pose before the National Palace pictures the blast announcing abolition of bondage, a symbolic gesture asserted by a broken chain on his ankle and a machete.

The harvest tool became a weapon, the standard threat by which African islanders rid themselves of French exploiters who militarized press gangs.

Mythic and Real

At the birth of the aristocratic Duarte twins, Rosalinda Teresa and Rafi at Alegría, Dominican Republic, in *The Farming of Bones,* the maid Juana praises saints Felicity and Perpetua, a pregnant slave and a new mother martyred in 203 BCE in Carthage (Tunisia) under the Roman emperor Septimius Severus. House worker Amabelle Désir dreams of Sugar Woman, an iconic shade of the drudge era who wears ankle chains and a muzzle to prevent her from eating the master's crop. Comparing the status of immigrant workers to slaves, Tibon, a refugee from wholesale murder on the escarpment at La Romana, describes the hopeless status of Haitians sold into labor squads "so our own country can be free of them" (Danticat, 1998, 176). He clings to a memory of thrashing a Dominican boy to make him admit "we're the same, me and him, flesh like flesh, blood like blood," a victory in miniature (*ibid.,* 180).

An unbearable caste system separated a citified, Catholic, francophone elite from the peasantry. In Edwidge's canon, the underclass lives in a "quasi-apartheid" of Vodou, Creole, and African culture (Kaussen, 2015, 26). In "Children of the Sea," the opening drama of *Krik? Krak!,* a young media rebel who escapes perpetual peonage before arrest and imprisonment writes a daily missive to his island-bound girlfriend. His thoughts about crossing the Caribbean Sea to Miami mirror the Middle Passage, a segment of triangular slave trade that carried West African abductees forever westward or southward across the Caribbean into Central and South America. Those commemorated in "Seven Stories" for leaping from slave decks "were seduced by the dream of an eternal freedom," a specious myth of heaven on earth (Danticat, 2019, 182).

Over four centuries from 1500 to 1900, captives from the Bight of Benin and the Gold Coast traveled west as much as six months in slave ship holds before reaching land. Of the six million marketed in the west, some 900,000 died of disease, malnutrition, torture, and terror before completing the Middle Passage. Some killed themselves. In *The Art of Death,* Edwidge ennobles the choice as "transitions, spiritual journeys to places from their past, homes that had become idealized—in their minds ... the most effective way of nullifying their designation as property" (Danticat, 2017, 79). Rather than erasure, suicide "[affirmed] their humanity" as residents of an undersea society glorified in August Wilson's play *Gem of the Ocean* (*ibid.*).

Burdens of the Past

Slave era lore of Africans who drowned themselves on the way to the New World sanctifies a spot where the dead reunite on the Atlantic Ocean floor. In a funeral tale from *Brother, I'm Dying,* a storyteller retains the mystique of the Atlantic crossing by referring to the afterlife as "the land beneath the waves," the sacred burial ground of black ancestors (Danticat, 2007, 266). Survivors and their offspring make up 80 percent of Haiti's black population, most suffering pervasive malnutrition. The connection between bondsmen and refugees fleeing Haiti by ship returns in Arnold's death under the false name Ernesto in "Without Inspection" and in "Caroline's Wedding," where Hermine Azile mourns 129 victims of drowning off Miami.

The author hallows matrilineage in "Nineteen Thirty-Seven," a story based on dictator Rafael Trujillo's 1937 slaughter of 30,000 Haitian cane workers at the Massacre River on the Dominican Republic's western border. As a female heritage, the main character, Josephine, treasures a statue of the Madonna owned by Défilé, a subjugated forebear five generations removed. For the immigrant Danticats arriving in Brooklyn in *Brother, I'm Dying*, welcoming dishes of *diri ak pwa* (rice and beans) replicate the standard meal for slaves, becoming Haiti's national dish. By partaking of folkloric foods grown from island soil, newcomers share an element of home that had nurtured their shackled ancestors. Still subjugated by racism, the author's essay "I Still Have

a Dream" depicted Haitian exiles "trying to survive by demanding that one's subjugators change their visions and their laws, and by constantly trying to prove one's humanity" (Danticat, 2015, 16).

See also Erzulie.

SOURCES

Danticat, Edwidge. *The Art of Death: Writing the Final Story.* Minneapolis, MN: Graywolf Press, 2017.
_____. *Brother, I'm Dying.* New York: Vintage, 2007.
_____. *Create Dangerously: The Immigrant Artist at Work.* New York: Vintage, 2010.
_____. *Everything Inside.* New York: Knopf, 2019.
_____. *The Farming of Bones.* New York: Penguin, 1998.
_____. "I Still Have a Dream," *Progressive* 79:2 (February 2015): 15–17.
_____. "The Journals of Water Days," *Callaloo* 19:2 (Spring, 1996): 376–380.
_____. "Nineteen Thirty-Seven," *Oxford Book of Caribbean Short Stories.* Oxford, UK: Oxford University Press, 2001: 447–456.
_____. "Poems," *Standing Tall: Portraits of the Haitian Community in Miami, 2003–2010.* Miami: Museum of Contemporary Art, 2010, n.p.
_____. *Poetry of Haitian Independence.* foreword. New Haven, CT: Yale University, 2015, xi–xviii.
Dayan, Joan. "Erzulie: A Women's History of Haiti," *Research in African Literatures Caribbean Literature* 25:2 (Summer, 1994): 5–31.
Kaussen, Valerie, "Migration, Exclusion, and 'Home' in Edwidge Danticat's Narratives of Return," *Identity, Diaspora and Return in American Literature.* New York: Routledge, 2015.

Storytelling

Edwidge Danticat values narrative as a form of keeping people and their legacies alive in memory and of reviving the spirit with the woman's anecdotes to her ailing mate Ray in "One Thing" to "give him a reason to come back to us" (Danticat, 2020). Stories aid illiterates in crafting their own autobiographies, a source of radio narratives for programmers Pascal Dorien in "Ghosts" and Louise George in "Di Mwen, Tell Me." Oral narrative became a token of normal daily life after the January 12, 2010, earthquake in *Eight Days* and *Tent Life* and during Grann's cultural education of her granddaughter in *The Last Mapou*. Without jests, personal anecdotes, and travelogues, humankind risks "de-storification," a lack of narrative, according to Julia Ferrante, on staff at Middlebury College, Vermont. The loss reduces human significance and understanding of others (Ferrante, 2011). By joining voices, tellers comfort listeners with a chain of tales, one eliciting another, fanning out in a lifeline of related subjects.

Remembrance offers a source of the creation myth of Adam and Eve, who would have expunged all stories if God had chosen to execute them like the two rebels in *Create Dangerously*. In the text, the author values a posthumous biography of her cousin, AIDS victim Marius Dantica, "in death fragments of a life that had swirled in hidden stories" concealing his homosexuality (Danticat, 2010, 94). Customary anecdotes about the midwife and foster mother Estina Estème in "Night Talkers" fill in returnees Dany Dorméus and Claude from diaspora on her altruistic life. In similar fashion, gossip about Marius demeans a young man's ungovernable antics in Miami, far from his mother, Tante Zi, in Haiti. Out of shame for her intent to compose an essay about Marius, Edwidge hangs her head.

For the indigenous children of the corn who became Taino in the historical novel *Anacaona,* the Indian queen's epic of the Maguana battle against Spaniards at Marién on November 19, 1493, records verbally and in carvings a tale of hope that the Taino will survive invasion. In modern times, after days of seasickness in "Children of the Sea," the rescue of memory in a grandfather's story of the first ice yields comfort and inspiration. Out of love in the YA novel *Untwine*, the Boyer family relies on "remember when" stories to allay a frazzled day following Isabelle's funeral (Danticat, 2015, 200). Affection for the cat Dessalines enables them to dredge up anecdotes both funny and sad, a normative union of contrasting emotions.

First-Person Witness

Horror stories grip readers of *The Farming of Bones* with images of lopped heads and limbs carried away by the Massacre River. For a wandering cortege of refugees, the eyewitness Tibon awakens them to the extent of danger ahead: he summarizes a merciless execution of black Haitian workers. Under orders by dictator Rafael Leonidas Trujillo Molina, Guardia soldiers force black laborers from the seaside cliffs at La Romana, a coastal town in southeastern Dominican Republic. In the October 1937 genocide, blacks died six at a time leaping to the boulders below. The moral of Tibon's story spells out the plight of the undesirables of African blood.

Carnage at the Massacre River pushes survivors to the nth degree of vigor and endurance. Arriving on the safe side at a perilous crossing, they force out individual scenes and episodes affirming life, "the haste in their voices sometimes blurring the words, for greater than their desire to be heard was the hunger to tell" (Danticat, 1998, 207). One of the author's most poignant ovations to personal narrative, the exchange of details arouses and emboldens refugees. Recall carries shock that Dominicans long familiar to the persecuted Haitians "went at them with … machete, first my son, then my father, then my sister" (*ibid.*). The butchery stymies logic, as does the erasure of facts from Dominican archives. In her elevation of personal accounts, the author eschews maps, documents, DNA remains, and print and electronic data in favor of a teller's orality and gestures, the ephemera of performance narrative.

Yearnings and Losses

Twenty-first-century anecdotes reprise nights of concealing the sex worker's toil from her little boy in "Night Women" and years of siblings missing Carl Azile, the deceased father of Gracina and Caroline in "Caroline's Wedding." Narrative relieves fatherlessness in "Monkey's Tail" and insomnia in *Breath, Eyes, Memory* and reclaims self, the motivation for the trickster tale "Je Voudrais Etre Riche" (I would be rich). From "a wanderer's heart," Edwidge stated an urge to share memories of Haiti, "my home beyond exile, the motherland within myself" (Danticat, 2006, 12, 11). In the reunion of sisters Martine and Tante Atie Caco, they gaze at the sky and retell stories about stars. Atie asserts that young women "should be allowed to keep their pleasant stories," a folkloric hope chest of remembrance (Danticat, 1994, 165).

To DeNeen L. Brown, a book analyst for the *Washington Post,* the author credited her dreams with filling in missing events and motivations, especially of Ka Bienaimé, a post–Baby Doc Duvalier survivor in "The Book of Miracles." For personal and clan validation, *Brother, I Am Dying* esteems her Uncle Joseph Nosius Dantica's Christian mission. She rejected academic notions that culture-based writing equated with social studies or anthropology. Rather, she applied the storytelling art to insight into universal questions about mysteries of mortality and self, the tutorial purpose of Michel's tape recorded memoir in "Monkey Tails." To Charlotte Bruce Harvey, a Brown University interviewer, Edwidge declared narrative a human eternal: "Stories go back to the beginning of time. People have always told each other stories: stories told on cave walls, stories recited over the campfire, stories about the quest for bread. They need the story of who they are" (Harvey, 2011).

Gifts from the Past

Of Edwidge's childhood introduction to oral journeys and vignettes, she remarked, "I was told a lot of stories as a child and I saw how orality—tone, pitch—can make a story different each time," an appreciation for voice she shares with Laguna Pueblo author and raconteur Leslie Marmon Silko (Misra, 2018). From her Uncle Joseph, cautionary tales about Carnival in Jacmel embroidered the truth of street revelry with libidinous males groping young girls and militia clouting heads with rifle butts. Recall of aunts and grandmothers filled in times when the electricity failed or when someone braided the author's hair or eased heartache at wakes. She referred to the females at intimate storytelling gatherings as "kitchen poets," an appropriate term for Grandmè Melina, who turns a Rapunzel plot into a parable of infirmity and illness borne by a death serpent (Danticat, 2019, 58).

Much as Michel educates his unborn son in "Monkey Tails," the author feels an obligation to pass along the gift stories, such as human emergence from the kapok tree in *The Last Mapou,* Taino creation lore of the birth of the seas in *Anacaona,* and the onomatopoetic tale of the three-legged horse Galipòt in *Behind the Mountains.* Of her career, in 2019, Edwidge stated, "I see all genres in writing as being storytelling," including myth, legend, vignette, fantasy, fool and cautionary tales, anecdote, scripture, and history (Joffre, 2019). She advocated sharing stories to enhance comprehension of war and ruthlessness. For facts about Generalissimo Rafael Trujillo's inhumanity toward black cane workers in *The Farming of Bones,* she read Albert C. Hicks's "Blood in the Streets: The Life and Times of a Caribbean Dictator" in *Collier's,* perused historic places, and interviewed survivors.

The oral history invigorated a catastrophe long carried in the heart.

See also Breath, Eyes, Memory, Erzulie.

Sources

Brown, DeNeen L. "Interview," *Washington Post* (14 October 2007): M2.

Danticat, Edwidge. "All Geography Is Within Me," *World Literature Today* 93:1 (Winter 2019): 58.

_____. *Breath, Eyes, Memory*. New York: Soho Press, 1994.

_____. *Create Dangerously: The Immigrant Artist at Work*. New York: Vintage, 2010.

_____. *The Farming of Bones*. New York: Penguin, 1998.

_____. *Homelands: Women's Journeys Across Race, Place, and Time*. Emeryville, CA: Seal Press, 2006, 8–12.

_____. *Krik? Krak!* New York: Soho Press, 1995.

_____. *The Last Mapou*. Brooklyn: One Moore Book, 2013.

_____. "Love, Our Only True Adventure," (1 August 2020): https://hello-sunshine.com/post/love-our-only-true-adventure.

_____. "One Thing," *New York Times* (7 July 2020): 62–72.

_____. *Untwine*. New York: Scholastic, 2015.

Feifer, Megan. "The Remembering of Bones," *Palimpsest* 9:1 (2020): 35–49.

Ferrante, Julia. "Storytelling Keeps Memory, Tradition Alive, Author Edwidge Danticat Says," *Targeted News Service* (13 April 2011).

Gleibermann, Erik. "The Story Will Be There When You Need It," *World Literature Today* 93:1 (Winter 2019): 68–74.

Harvey, Charlotte Bruce. "Haiti's Storyteller," *Brown Alumni Magazine* (January/February 2011).

Joffre, Ruth. "It Wants to Be Told," *Kenyon Review* (10 October 2019).

Misra, Jivin. "Interview," *Brooklyn Review* (18 June 2018).

Superstition

Edwidge blends realism with the surreal, a factor in the rubbing of live butterflies on breasts to make them grow in "Reading Lessons," the wearing of red panties in "Caroline's Wedding" to dissuade violation by spirits, and suspicions of children born to dying mothers in "The Missing Peace." In the last thoughts of laborer Arnold in "Without Inspection," while his life leaks into a cement mixer, he imagines becoming a spirit visiting his lover Darline and her son Paris through sense impressions like wind or breeze. He ponders causing glass to break, his favorite song to play, or a shadow or odor of work sweat announcing a ghostly presence. Additional signs—itchy palms, fluttering kisses, dream appearances—broaden his avenues of reconnecting with the living, a hopeful belief that death is not the end.

Extended reality offers a token accolade to West African tales and Haitian Vodou, such as the creation of the first human couple from the trunk of a kapok tree (or silk cotton tree) in *The Last Mapou* and the tying of a corpse's ankle with ribbon or rope to stop its wandering and the rescue of a zombie from living death by ingesting salt, two folk beliefs in *The Art of Death*. In the novel *Claire of the Sea Light,* Edwidge divulges Haitians' fear that *Mòn Initil* (useless mountain) is home to the spirits of runaway slaves. From the same narrative, she warns that sleeping on the back causes bad dreams and that revenants—motherless children like Claire Limyè Lanmè Faustin—could slip away to join their parents in the afterlife. According to the elder Claire Narcis, who dresses corpses in Albert's funeral parlor, a fear of body snatching by zombies causes some islanders to bury their dead secretly beneath a coffin filled with cement. The outlandish scenarios added a note of the outré to books and films about Haiti.

Writing the Irrational

In *Create Dangerously,* the author attaches the execution of immigrant rebels Louis Drouin and Marcel Numa before a firing squad to unsubstantiated beliefs about eyes. Haitian killers practiced eye gouging on their victims to remove an incriminatory imprint from corneas, evidence like photographic negatives that could return guilty verdicts in court. The grisly glimpse of Drouin and Numa riveted twelve-year-old eyewitness Daniel Morel, who chose to become a photojournalist for the Associated Press reporting calamities and massacres. His specialty articles appeared in *Vanity Fair, BBC News, World Press, Atlantic, Wall Street Journal, ABC News,* and *New York Times.*

The author's models of irrationality vary in depth and significance—Karl's assumption that the Angel of Death hovers over his father in "Papi," Lili's doubts about Big Guy's angular hairline in "A Wall of Fire Rising," and, in "Between the Pool and the Gardenias," Marie's belief in perusing the mirror on the November 2 Day of the Dead to see reflections of ancestors. For twins Giselle and Isabelle Boyer in *Untwine*, gifts of bracelets on their twelfth birthday teach them the Islamic reverence for the Hand of Fatima, a protective token warding off the evil eye. Fifteenth-century Taino elders in *Anacaona* tell of spirits lacking navels, rainbow snakes that bite fingers, shapeshifting into guavas and nightingales, destroying the cannibalistic Kalina (Carib) from South America, and joining Night Marchers on a pilgrimage to the Caribbean Sea. The future *cacica* (ruler) feels the guidance of her grandmother's spirit, who was already a shade before Anacaona was born. Uncle Matunherí's reading of star patterns before her marriage illustrates a link between philosophy and constellations dating to earth's beginnings.

In other works, mystical happenings seem less ominous than the betrothal of Anacaona to Caonabó, for example, the gift of protective dog teeth to the newborn Duarte twins, Rosalinda Teresa and Rafi, and the wearing of yellow coffee bean bracelets by Man Denise's children, Mimi and Sebastien, in *The Farming of Bones.* The albino lottery agent Chabin in *Breath, Eyes, Memory* can tell fortunes and turn himself into a snake. Tante Atie Caco draws peasant conclusions about red blood forming from red foods, watermelon and beets. After a Tonton Macoute squad kills the emperor Jean Jacques Dessalines on October 17, 1806, Grandmè Ifé fears that the man's ghost threatens her grandbaby Brigitte.

Wandering specters impact the serenity of other Haitian islanders. In the story "A Year and a Day," the writer explains the emergence of spirits from waterways and their occupation in whispering trees and echoing caves, an auditory assurance of tribal concern for family. Rather than terrify, the voices console the living with junctures to progenitors. Défilé, a woman imprisoned for life on charges of flying with red wings in "Nineteen Thirty-Seven," represents the surreal escape of a pregnant woman by swimming the Massacre River. In her honor, a revered female treasure, the Virgin Mary's statue, patron of mothers, weeps tears of blessing on the mother-to-be.

The Presence of Death

In memories of island storytelling, the author frequently connects metaphysical omens with death. In "The Dew Breaker," the title character recalls his mother's belief that two people speaking the same word at the same time would die on the same day. Edwidge's narratives recalled "lejann" (legend) about three-legged horses and women with flaming wings, a lethal charge against imprisoned sorcerers in "Nineteen Thirty-Five." Songs of supernatural females emerge from singers in the cane fields, where men revive myths of the *platonnade* (platoons), sirens who seduced males before drowning them. Slave era lore of Africans who kill themselves on the Middle Passage to the New World sanctifies a spot where the dead assemble on the ocean floor, the motif of August Wilson's play *Gem of the Ocean*. In an interview with Deborah Treisman, a *New Yorker* staffer, Edwidge explained, "Many of our ancestors saw flying, both real and imagined, as an escape from the unbearable circumstances of the Middle Passage, slavery, and some of what came after" (Treisman, 2018).

In *Breath, Eyes, Memory*, Edwidge speaks through protagonist Sophie Caco, who pictures the use of sacred hymns and prayers to save the soul from conjuror Chabin, the lottery agent. In hopes of the hereafter, she weds the Catholic heaven to African faith in Guinea, the spirit's destination and meeting place with past family. During her group treatment for sexual trauma, she receives advice and guidance from a Santerian priestess who seeks serenity in prayer and worship over fumes rising from incense and candles. From sessions with other survivors of violence, Sophie learns to value herself as daughter, mother, and sexually attractive female. Unlike the Semite woman in Luke 48:43–50 who secures healing from loathsome bleeding by touching the hem of Jesus's cloak, Sophie takes mythic and artistic succor from Grandmè Ifé's stories and a gift statue of Erzulie, the island goddess who offers freedom through transformation into a butterfly. For religious sustenance, Sophie seeks Afro-Southern hymnography, the prayer-like spirituals that marchers intone in *After the Dance* and that Grandma Baby offers to assuage diasporic transients in Toni Morrison's *Beloved* through unified breathing, rhythm, and harmony.

See also Erzulie, Vodou.

Sources

Danticat, Edwidge. "All Geography Is Within Me," *World Literature Today* 93:1 (Winter 2019): 58.

———. "Junot Díaz," *BOMB* 101 (Fall 2007): 89–95.

———. *The Last Mapou.* Brooklyn: One Moore Book, 2013.

———. "Nineteen Thirty-Seven," *Oxford Book of Caribbean Short Stories.* Oxford, UK: Oxford University Press, 2001: 447–456.

———. "Reading Lessons," *New Yorker* 80:42 (10 January 2005): 66–73.

———. "A Year and a Day," *New Yorker* (9 January 2011).

Pierce, Yolanda. "Restless Spirits: Syncretic Religion in Edwidge Danticat's *Breath, Eyes, Memory,*" *Journal of Pan African Studies* 3:5 (March 2010).

Tobar, Hector. "Review: *Claire of the Sea Light*," *Los Angeles Times* (25 August 2013): E4.

Treisman, Deborah. "Edwidge Danticat on her Caribbean Immigrant Experience," *New Yorker* (7 May 2018).

Tonton Macoute

The legacy of Haiti's state-supported mass murderers began in 1959 and kept up daily mental and psychic maiming until dissolution of the Duvaliers' private militia in February 1986. Historian Paula Morgan, author of *The Terror and the Time,* stated the purpose of continued crisis—"[buttressing] the multigenerational rule of the Duvaliers" (Mahase, 2018, iii). She added the exemption of squads "from prosecution for any acts of violence carried out during the performance of this duty" (*Ibid.*). By 1976, the dictatorship quelled all resistance except in hirelings for the private police force. In the abbreviated memoir *A Walk Through Carnival,* Edwidge reported on the militia's exhibitionism at Lenten carnival in Jacmel. Self-important Tonton Macoutes "[clubbed] people over the head with sticks or rifle butts," sadistic behaviors that gave Haiti a reputation for out-of-control violence and random murders (Danticat, 2016, 1). Post-traumatic stress disorder from the atrocities reached across the Caribbean to collective diaspora in the entire Western Hemisphere.

Accusing special forces officers,

Edwidge began her literary backtalk in 1991 with the poem "Sawfish Soup," which intensifies the shooting of a father on his way to the store to buy juice. She spotlights arson that destroys a gang warehouse in *Claire of the Sea Light* and the execution of Bernard "Bè" Dorien and immigrant rebels Marcel Numa and Louis Drouin on November 12, 1964, in *Create Dangerously*. Tonton Macoutes—"denim-clad killers, henchmen, and henchwomen"—superintend the execution allegedly for the edification of school children: "Thus the legend of the Tontons Macoutes, bogeymen who come to take disobedient children away in a knapsack" (Danticat, 2010, 63). Her summation of the career of photojournalist Daniel Morel hails the street battery of former Tontons Macoutes, whose cadavers added to wire news services a macabre realism as startling as the assaults and shooting of viewers at an Orchestra Septentrional d'Haiti concert.

Fearful Villainy

The author commemorates the dramatic lawlessness of the Duvalier regime with clubbing by uniformed thugs in *After the Dance* and in her screen role as Yannick, star of *Stones in the Sun*. Shot in Brooklyn by Syncopated Films with Patricia Benoit directing, the action defined the post–Duvalier lives of Haitian immigrants in Brooklyn and the residue of bestiality against women perpetrated by the Duvalier death phalanx. In the story "Monkey Tails," she creates the burning, lynching, and stoning of the fictional Regulus, a Tonton Macoute who commits suicide. The marriage of Marie Micheline in *Brother, I'm Dying* to loutish Pressoir Marol places the mother and fatherless infant Ruth in the hands of a vicious Duvalier henchman and wife abuser who had impregnated many girls. The author

underscores the absence of checks and balances to prevent Tonton Macoute extremes of sexual violence on adults and children.

Terror permeates personal memories and nightmares of Minister Edner Day, the savage representative from Port-au-Prince in *Create Dangerously* who ordered murders of Bel Air residents in February 1986, and the casual nature of violence with pistol grips and Uzis against unarmed peasants in *Breath, Eyes, Memory,* which horrifies shoppers at the market. Carrying doleful memories into a new life, "fat man," a fictional guilt-ridden Tonton Macoute in Brooklyn in "The Book of the Dead," faces a zombie existence as the undead. A witness, Dany Dorméus in "Night Talkers," incurs orphaning at age six as a result of the paramilitary's mistaken identity of his parents. By getting a closer view of a Brooklyn barber, he relives his parents' wrongful victimizing and his aunt's blinding in a house fire set by the militia. Dany relives the sufferings of victims choked until their eyes bulged, a symbolic overload of ghastly torments.

Legendary Bloodshed

In mythic style, island parents used cannibalistic Tonton Macoute stories to frighten children of "Uncle Gunnysack," who kidnaps and devours the vulnerable. Analyst Newtona Johnson, an English professor at Middle Tennessee State University, outlined in *Obsidian III* how the tyrannic police force persecuted females by raping mothers and daughters. They intimidated whole families by arranging sexual perversions involving women coupling with sons, brothers, and fathers. Folklore promoted woman-as-object thinking through jokes, fables, and tales of male superiority over cringing, silenced females.

Trapping Haitians in a lurid nihilism

predisposed them to depression, sleep interruptions, substance abuse, psychosomatic illness, abortions, and suicide. In *The Dew Breaker,* seamstress Beatrice Saint Fort gives the book its title by identifying men who would "come before dawn, as the dew was settling on the leaves, and they'd take you away," a counterpoint of innocent nature trampled by booted assassins (Danticat, 2004, 131). The torture of her feet in "The Bridal Seamstress" precedes greater barbarities when the post–Tonton Macoute mob in "Monkey Tails" force-feeds a militiaman gasoline and sets him aflame. The atrocity illustrates the spiraling outrages caused by grudges and vengeance.

See also The Dew Breaker, Duvaliers.

SOURCES

Danticat, Edwidge. "Becoming Brazilian," *Obsidian III* 6/7:2/1 (Fall 2005/2006): 139–145.

_____. *Create Dangerously: The Immigrant Artist at Work.* New York: Vintage, 2010.

_____. *The Dew Breaker.* New York: Abacus, 2004.

_____. "Sawfish Soup," *Caribbean Writer* 5 (1991): 10–11.

_____. *A Walk Through Carnival.* New York: Vintage, 2016.

Johnson, Newtona. "Interview," *Obsidian III* 6/7:2/1 (Fall 2005–2006): 147–166, 264.

Kaussen, Valerie, "Migration, Exclusion, and 'Home' in Edwidge Danticat's Narratives of Return," *Identity, Diaspora and Return in American Literature.* New York: Routledge, 2015.

Mahase, Radica. "The Terror and the Time: Banal Violence and Trauma in Caribbean Discourse," *Nieuwe West—Indische Gids* 92:1/2 (2018): 156–157.

Tradition

In speeches and interviews, Edwidge can't stop talking about home, whether mourning her deceased Uncle Joseph or anticipating standard New Year's soup on January first. In the critique of Renee H. Shea, a book reviewer for *Belles Lettres,* "To read Danticat is to learn about Haiti— the folklore and myth, the traditions, and the history," the subject of the YA biography *Anacaona* and the island history of despotism and slaughter in *The Dew Breaker* (Shea, 1995, 13). For Nadia, a confused adult daughter in "In the Old Days," the covering of framed pictures with black bedsheets follows the expiration of Maurice Dejean. Nadia learns from her stepmother that any reflection could halt the departing spirit in its journey to the land of the dead, a belief dating to the slave era.

The foreword to Diane Wolkstein's collection *The Magic Orange Tree* praises the vibrant oral tradition of black Africans. Edwidge extols the tales that survived wholesale migrations—from West Africa in slave ships bound for the West Indies and from Haiti to North, South, and Central America and the world beyond. An interview for *Callaloo* revealed a constant state of flux among immigrants. To retain a sense of home, traditions are "constantly being redefined as people find more and more ways to be a community, to be a family," whether among refugees in New York, Florida, France, or the Bahamas (Mirabal, 2007, 31).

Repeated Details

The author interweaves memorable details in her stories, such as the private burial of children after their parents depart the cemetery in *Untwine,* the submission of unwed girls to judgmental male relatives in *Célimène,* and the tiny gourd rattles on a baby's grave in "The Funeral Singer." For "Seven Stories," a West Indian people build a wedding bonfire on the beach and wind through the streets by candlelight on New Year's Eve to shed "all the awful things that have happened … in the previous year" (Danticat, 2019, 181). In a description of peaceful courtyard life in Cap Haïtien for *The Farming of Bones*, the author pictures a commune where residents share "their caresses and arguments, their gossip, and the cries of their restless children" (Danticat, 1998, 224). Sources from family talk yielded narrative, "Fables and metaphors, whose similes and soliloquies, whose diction and *je ne sais quoi* daily slip into your survival soup" (Shea, 1995, 15).

To Garry Pierre-Pierre, a journalist at the *New York Times,* Edwidge explained that islanders value folk medicine—herbs, salves, tonics, and teas—as curatives, such as a body rub with parsley to ward off insects in *The Farming of Bones,* aloe poultices for burns in "Night Talkers," and Grandmè Ifé Caco's tea to combat chagrin in *Breath, Eyes, Memory.* A more intrinsic custom, the retention of one child into adulthood to tend elderly parents explains Tante Atie Caco's devotion of her mother Ifé. The coupling of mother to daughter explains the author's tending of Rose Danticat before and after death, the subject of the memoirs "Without Her." The reminiscence proved so endearing to Edwidge that she reprised it in *The Art of Death* under the abrupt title "Feetfirst."

Personalized Tradition

In *Breath, Eyes, Memory,* Martine Caco clings to customary funeral rituals where survivors superintend obsequies while the dead remain at home until burial on the second day. In the resolution of *Brother, I'm Dying,* a grieving daughter violates tradition by demanding no wake for her father. Under the guidance of an old woman familiar with the undersea land of the dead, the daughter accepts a standard wake as a form of honor, rejoicing, and life celebration. To transcend sorrow, she demands feasting, singing, dancing, and storytelling, "For it is not our way to let our grief silence us" (Danticat, 2007, 267).

Edwidge returned to funereal customs in *Create Dangerously* with the capturing of deaths in photos during a flood. Photojournalist Jacqueline Charles, on staff at the *Miami Herald,* allowed a sorrowing father to wash and dress a drowned child for a keepsake picture, a lugubrious souvenir that Edwidge reprised in the memoir "Look at Me" for *Harper's.* The author explained that funereal portraits became heirlooms, "calling cards to generations yet unborn" (Danticat, 2013, 65). For her family, pictures offered "a way of keeping them with us, and at the same time allowing his loved one's face to stand for many" (Danticat, 2010, 147). In the essay "All Geography Is Within Me," she honored such preservations of a life in "the words we have spoken, the songs we have sung, the ways that we have moved our bodies through these dances that have come to us," the gifts of ancestral recall and respect (Danticat, 2019, 58). In the poem "Bajou/Dawn," she summons family from the hill country to share mourning, cradling, singing, and comfort, the traditions that unite them like an umbilical cord.

See also After the Dance, Carnival, Food, Memory, Vodou.

Sources

Danticat, Edwidge. "All Geography Is Within Me," *World Literature Today* 93:1 (Winter 2019): 58.
_____. "Bajou/Dawn," *Afro-Hispanic Review* 32:2 (Fall, 2013): 149–150, 156.
_____. *Create Dangerously: The Immigrant Artist at Work.* New York: Vintage, 2010.
_____. *Everything Inside.* New York: Knopf, 2019.
_____. "Look at Me," *Harper's* 327:1963 (December 2013): 65–73.
_____. "Without Her," *New York Times Magazine* (23 April 2015).
Mirabal, Nancy Raquel. "Dyasporic Appetites and Longings," *Callaloo* 30:1 (Winter 2007): 26–39, 410.
Pierre-Pierre, Garry. "At Home with Edwidge Danticat: Haitian Tales, Flatbush Scenes," *New York Times* (26 January 1995): C1.
Shea, Renee. "The Dangerous Job of Edwidge Danticat," *Belles Lettres* 10:3 (Summer 1995): 12–15.

Untwine

Edwidge based her YA novel *Untwine* on ancient Greek mythic pairs such as Apollo and Artemis; Leda and Zeus and their twin girls, Helen and Clytemnestra, and sons Castor and Polydeuces; and the founders of Rome, Romulus and Remus. From Marasa, the Vodou tradition of revering twins and superstitions about their power and/or blessing, the author initiated a story idea in graduate school. While her mother, Rose Souvenance Danticat, suffered from ovarian cancer, Edwidge returned to the story while sitting quietly by the hospital bed and shared last moments with her dying parent, a somber scenario that influenced the novel's tone and atmosphere.

The story begins with an intimate oneness of Haitian-American sisters seen through a one-person narration. Clutching hands in stalled traffic, sixteen-year-old one-egg twins Giselle and Isabelle Boyer, students at Morrison High, incur a deadly car accident just as they had entered life, hand in hand ninety seconds apart. The surprise collision reprises the sufferings of thirteen-year-old Haitian pipe bomb victim Céliane Espérance in *Behind the Mountains* and the tenderness of *My Mommy Medicine,* a female legacy of treatment for ills or melancholy.

A Dawning Truth

Fearing lateness to a spring concert, Isabelle speaks regret that echoes in Giselle's mind with a line from the 1951 Disney movie *Alice in Wonderland,* Lewis Carroll's classic tale of dislocation and confusion. The atmospheric children's story prefaces Giselle's severance from Isabelle and parents David and Sylvie Boyer and a hazy ambulance ride on a back board and in neck brace and oxygen mask. Medical acronyms of EMTs report the concussive damage to her head. In a hospital room, where she finds hands tied down, a tube in her mouth, and broken teeth, she continues to see herself as the fictional Alice in a constant fall to an unknown stop. In *A Poetics of Relation: Caribbean Women Writing at the Millennium,* Odile Ferly, an expert in francophone studies at Clark University in Worcester, Massachusetts, describes the dire plunge as redefined identity.

The visual collage stresses sense impressions or the lack of them during Giselle's nearly comatose state that allows her few distractions from medical treatment and terror for the family. The narrative derives strength from counterpoint—a brain injured twin left in a precarious state in Miami's pediatric wing of Jackson Hospital for five days and recovering parents on the brim of divorce in the same institution. The backstory imparts some previous experience with death in the passing of maternal Grandma Sandrine.

The confusion of twin identities contributes a surreal atmosphere to Giselle, who once communicated telepathically with her sister Isabelle. Suspense builds as Giselle unravels the mystery—Aunt Leslie calls her Isabelle, who died of head and neck injuries. A bizarre possibility troubles Giselle: "What if I am Isabelle and don't realize it," an intrusion into "the windows to my soul" (Danticat, 2015, 64, 150). Watching a police badge glow gold and lustrous, she fears that waking up will split her forever from her sister until Isabelle's spirit delivers a parting word. Edwidge elevates the power of language to ease their severance.

Losing a Part of Self

Still unsolved in Giselle's mind lie two conundrums: police suspicion of a deliberate assault on the Boyer family and the needs of Dessalines, the family cat who corresponds to Alice's pet Dinah in *Alice in Wonderland.* In both situations, an endearing feline builds courage and hope for the future in a girl sundered from the nuclear family. In unvoiced thoughts about Isabelle's death, Giselle ponders Dessalines' grief, "How will he react when she doesn't come home?" (Danticat, 2015, 63). By projecting the question on a domestic animal, she avoids asking herself the same thing, a fearful descent into self-analysis. She concludes, "Every day from now on will be a day without Isabelle," a mature acknowledgment of a life-altering absence (*ibid.,* 96).

Within Giselle's alternating real and surreal mind travels, the narrative contrasts multiple cataclysms—Dad's four-week deployment to Iraq in Operation Desert Storm the previous January 1991, the Boyers' divorce, car crash, and Isabelle's death, leaving "a glory-less world" (*ibid.,* 110). Simultaneous with great leaps in maturity, the twins had anticipated getting driver's licenses and developing boy-girl relationships, two major advances for sixteen-year-olds. After sense impressions regress with deafness, Giselle surveys a silent family vigil. She focuses on moving a little toe and describes her paralyzed self as "I'm in here somewhere," an existential assertion of being like the amputee's mental awakening in the Karl Shapiro's poem "The Leg" (*ibid.,* 122).

Just as death took Isabelle, Giselle's thoughts turn to the stagy magic trick of sawing a girl in half, a grotesque image of permanent separation. In a powerful bedside moment, Sylvie recognizes the misidentification of her living daughter. To convince the family, she substantiates Giselle's survival by locating the birthmark on her head. Survivor's guilt, like that suffered by Amabelle Desír in

The Farming of Bones, takes the form of Giselle's regret for being late to depart for the school symphony concert and, by extension, for causing Isabelle's loss.

Becoming One

At a height of pain, Giselle journeys to the funeral home with parents and paternal grandparents, Marcus and Régine Boyer, her support system. She wears sunglasses like armor to shield her eyes during Isabelle's viewing, which seems "like looking at me" (*ibid.,* 162). At home again, friends Tina and Jean-Michel and acquaintances from school and the neighborhood struggle for something consoling to say. Differences in the twins comfort Giselle, who bathes in Isabelle's strawberry body wash and lounges on her sister's bed. She discovers in herself the best of Isabelle. With Sylvie and David Boyer, she profits from filling gaps in their memories, but continues to feel split apart, a reenactment of the double fetus in a one-egg conception.

Edwidge loses steam in the last quarter of the novel, the progress of Giselle's untwining/untwining when the family visits her Boyer grandparents' home in Haiti to scatter Isabelle's ashes. In search of justice, Giselle focuses on the police perp search for Gloria Carlton, the driver of the other car. The fake name turns out to be the alias of Janice Hill, a foster child from Gainesville. In an unremarkable resolution, according to Deborah Stevenson, editor of *Bulletin of the Center for Children's Books,* Giselle's gradual return to normal teen relationships restores her sociability with Jean-Michel and Tina.

Of the need to tell tragic death stories, the author explained, "Writers will never stop writing them, because, alone or en masse, people will continue to die, and though it happens every day, when it hits close to home, we will always be caught off guard," an emotion the novel shares with Robert Frost's poem "Out, Out—" and James Agee's Southern American novel *A Death in the Family* (Danticat, 2002, 2). For *Untwine,* Edwidge chooses sense impressions, children's literature and film, classical music, and visual art to translate sorrow into a manageable whole. Her experience with cognitive haunting yields "some unknown insights" that help her cope with sorrow and enable her to accept a life sentence of emptiness (*ibid.,* 6). Critic Jim Higgins of the Portland, Maine, *Press Herald* credits the author with satisfying standard teen yearnings—"the idea of hearing what everyone says about you, the secret communications of twins, even the fantasy of attending your own funeral" (Higgins, 2015, E5).

See also Doubles, Mothers.

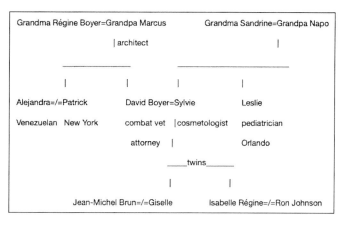

Sources

Danticat, Edwidge. *Untwine.* New York: Scholastic, 2015.
Ellis, Alicia E. "The Art of Death: Grief and Loss in Edwidge Danticat's *Untwine,*" *Research on Diversity in Youth Literature* 2:2 (January 2020): 1–20.
Ferly, Odile. *A Poetics of Relation: Caribbean Women Writing at the Millennium.* New York: Palgrave Macmillan, 2012.
Gleibermann, Erik. "The Story Will Be There When You Need It," *World Literature Today* 93:1 (Winter 2019): 68–74.
Stevenson, Deborah, ed. "Review: *Untwine,*" *Bulletin of the Center for Children's Books* 69:4 (December 2015): 192.

Untwine Genealogy

Essential to Edwidge's YA novel *Untwine,* the family structure pulls together varied sources of empathy and strength to mourn Isabelle's passing and restore her sister Giselle Boyer's well being. Sharing maternal aunt Leslie's expertise in pediatrics reassures the Boyers that Giselle will recover mental faculties and learn to live untwinned. David Boyer, an army veteran and attorney, applies a lawyer's thought processes to solving the mystery of a crash caused by another Morrison High student.

A significant soother of Giselle's shredded thoughts, a visit to her grandparents' home in Haiti rebuilds trust in nature to boost and gladden family spirits.

Sources

Danticat, Edwidge. *Untwine.* New York: Scholastic, 2015.
Higgins, Jim. "Uncommon Sadness, Uncommon Beauty," [Portland, ME] *Press Herald* (4 October 2015): E5.

Violence

The Caribbean's long history of mayhem and massacre empowers regional art because, according to Edwidge, "All the strife inspires all the writers we have" (Lee, 2011, C1). Violence permeates her writing with a surprisingly impersonal calm, such as the dead baby girl at a city drain in "Between the Pool and the Gardenias" and the fresco in "Seven Stories" displaying the history of a slave port operated by European traders armed with whips. The recent past breeds fear in Callie Morrissete, the prime minister's daughter, that "a lot of people wanted me and [my mother] dead" (Danticat, 2019, 171). The author pictures in "Reading Lessons" the shooting of Danielle's mother by a teenage boy. After becoming a high school teacher in Miami's Little Hairi, Danielle internalizes the murder as memory, which takes shape symbolically in a chestnut-size lump on her breast. The author writes, "She had become a teacher … to find these types of boys early, to detect and save them," a messianic hope limited by classroom parameters (Danticat, 2006, 67).

For the poignant 1991 poem "Sawfish Soup," the writer speaks from a child's perspective the grief caused by the random shooting of "papa," who ventured out to buy juice for a child's dinner (Danticat, 1991, 10). Creating a pun from the knowledge that "someone saw," the poet exhibits the position of the corpse in the street, where it incurs spitting of passing soldiers, a reference to the Tonton Macoute (*ibid.*). She builds irony out of a case of mistaken identity and the uneaten dinner that waits on the table, a preventable loss like the murders of immigrant Dany Dorméus's parents in "Night Talkers." The images of the toothy sawfish enhance the horror of a chainsaw nose that strikes its prey in turbid water, a symbol of the island's squalid politics under the Duvaliers. More conflict followed in the author's canon with the police pistol whipping of a girl at the airport in the novel *Breath, Eyes, Memory* and the seven bullets in *Create Dangerously* awaiting martyred activist Jean Léopold Dominique as he arrived at Radio Haiti Inter on April 3, 2000.

Inland Retreats

In the short fiction of "Dream of the Butterflies," the bursts of machine gun fire in an urban ghetto alarm Marie Micheline, who forces her mind to envision the dewy hillsides and multihued butterflies of Léogâne. Through force of love and tender regard, she ensures the safety of her children, giving her own life in the process. Vulnerable islanders wonder, "Who knows when we might have to die?" (Danticat, 2010, 63). In an appearance on a TV talk show, Danticat dropped a reminder to viewers that the Haitian army "was created by the Americans" (Conlogue, 2004, R3). Ironically, Arnold, a refugee by boat from Port-de-Paix to Miami in the story "Without Inspection," discovers that Haiti shares with the U.S. the deaths of children "randomly gunned down by the police or by one another, in schools, in their homes, while walking in the street, or playing in city parks" (Danticat, 2019). Enhancing the irony, Arnold dies anonymously under the assumed Cuban-American name Ernesto, a Germanic term for "serious."

The 1964 guerrilla war in Haiti's mountains fomented by young rebels resulted in suicides, imprisonments, and hundreds of murders. Papa Doc Duvalier made a public spectacle out of the firing squad that executed rebels Marcel Numa and Louis Drouin, an event that opened the author's nonfiction. A less criminal assault, the car accident that kills sixteen-year-old flutist Isabelle Boyer and cripples her parents and twin Giselle in the YA novel *Untwine* teeters on the edge of felony until police learn the driver's identity and purpose in fleeing a foster home. Actually, the violence against Giselle robs her of a twin and leaves her the Boyer family's only child, a sundering that demands concentrated effort to rebalance body and mind.

For an encounter of refugees in the mountains near Dajabón in *The Farming of Bones,* Tibon, a cane laborer, describes the murders of Haitians orchestrated at La Romana in rows of six. In the background, the Guardia advises civilian volunteers in October 1937 on the genocide of field workers. The tutorial indicates where to strike the neck with a machete at the clavicle for easy decapitation. Over a disturbing fictional scene of escapees sleeping by the roadside, the author wafts the rancid smell of a corpse bonfire. When the action moves into a holiday spirit at Dajabón, a mountainous market town above the Massacre River, Generalissimo Rafael Trujillo's theme song "Compadre Pedro Juan" blares over acts of persecution with handfuls of peppered parsley forced into the jaws of Haitians. At the nadir of strength, Amabelle Desír, a servant to the Duarte household, concludes, "What was the use of fighting?" (Danticat, 1998, 192).

Literary Motifs

The author applies both distance and up-close observations of malevolence, for example, young urban toughs forming *chimès* (ghosts), a street term for gangs and drug dealers in the story "Ghosts" (Danticat, 2008, 110). She adds by way of social commentary that members tended to be lawless street Arabs reared parentless after the Duvalier regime murdered their families. In the novel *Claire of the Sea Light*, young gangsters shudder at the thought of victims arrested in Cité Pendue (hanging city), a slum eight miles north of Ville Rose, and "disappeared" in Port-au-Prince, the capital in west central Haiti (Danticat, 2013, 80). In the preface to *Massacre River* in 2008, the author views peaceful bathing along a stretch where Dominican soldiers previously slew and decapitated 30,000 Haitians with machetes.

In "The Book of Miracles," Edwidge places an Emmanuel "Toto" Constant look-alike in a New York church on Christmas Eve. With the support of the Front for the Advancement and Progress of Haiti, organized with CIA funds, the militia leader's face appears on a poster alongside the list "torture, rape, murder of 5,000 people" (Danticat, 2019, 78). Hovering over the mass are the lyrics of a carol demanding existential answers to "What Child Is This?" The holiday hymn inquires into the source of ferocity in someone who began life like the innocent baby Jesus.

Central to the issue of parenting in a tyrannic regime, Edwidge stresses the pattern of mothers testing their daughters' hymens, Martine Caco's violation of daughter Sophie's modesty in *Breath, Eyes, Memory*. Digital probing extends state violation of women's rights and the daily rapes by the Tonton Macoute paramilitary, the cause of Sophie's siring. Women's rebellion against misogyny reaches the extreme in Sophie's ripping of her hymen with a pestle and the suicide of the fictional Martine, a living zombie who seeks liberation from pregnancy in death. *After the Dance* treats as carnival masks the famed Haitian zombie. When several living zombies return to community life, the author's Aunt Denise Dantica declares them former political prisoners "so mentally damaged by dictatorship-sponsored torture that they had become either crazy or slow" (Danticat, 2002, 70).

See also Death, Duvalier, Tonton Macoute.

Sources

Conlogue, Ray. "Haunted by Haiti's Ghosts," [Toronto] *Globe and Mail* (19 April 2004): R3.

Danticat, Edwidge. *After the Dance: A Walk Through Carnival in Jacmel, Haiti*. New York: Vintage, 2002.

_____. "The Book of Miracles," *The Story Prize*. New York: Strong Winds, 2019.

_____. *Claire of the Sea Light*. New York: Vintage, 2013.

_____. *Create Dangerously: The Immigrant Artist at Work*. New York: Vintage, 2010.

_____. "Dream of the Butterflies," *Caribbean Writer* 5 (1991): 98–99.

_____. *Everything Inside*. New York: Knopf, 2019.

_____. "Ghosts," *New Yorker* (24 November 2008): 108–113.

_____. *Massacre River* (preface). New York: New Directions, 2008, 7–10.

_____. "Reading Lessons," *New Yorker* 80:42 (10 January 2005): 66–73.

_____. "Sawfish Soup," *Caribbean Writer* 5 (1991): 10–11.

Lee, Felicia. "Dark Tales Illuminate Haiti, Before and After Quake," *New York Times* (10 Jan 2011): C1.

Savaiano, Peter. "Review: 'Reading Lessons,'" https://iiereadingcircle.wordpress.com/2013/02/17/reading-lessons-by-edwidge-danticat/ 17 February 2013).

Virginity

The concept of female purity overwhelms Haitian girls with traditional hymns and liturgy to the Virgin Mary, the Catholic exemplum of obedience and chastity in "The Book of Miracles." In oral training, families circulate folk tales of wedding night bleeding and restrict unchaperoned visits to town and dates with young village men. In *After the Dance,* a tourist tale credits Jesus's mother with magic tears that produce flowers from the "crown of the Virgin Mary" (Danticat, 2002, 29). The vines enwreathe tombstones with fragrant reminders of the virgin's immaculate conception and protection of mothers. Another relic of Mariology, the statue that Défilé bequeaths her family in "Nineteen Thirty-Seven" retains the mystic tale of tears that benefit parturient women.

In the essay "We Are Ugly but We Are Here," Edwidge asserts that, amid constant turmoil in Haiti, "The women's stories never manage to make the front page. However, they do exist" (Danticat, 2017, 21). The depths of depravity against women terrifies Neah, a young volunteer in the story "Hot-Air Balloons." Her visceral exchanges with survivors for the Leve agency attempts to "lift" victims, but, ironically, threatens her coping with the grotesque details of personal narratives. She recoils from tongues bitten in half, a symbolic silencing of female victims in a patriarchal society. As a result of pro-woman activism, the author promoted inclusion of rape as a global war crime and a motivation for seeking political asylum from human rights violations.

Misplaced Scrutiny

Analyst Renee Latchman, an English professor at Howard University, explains that "Danticat recounts generations of women who pass down a tradition that damages women, although it is meant to uplift them" (Latchman, 2014, 53). Instead of preparing them for life and marriage, the sacrosanctity of the *virgo intacta* preserves family honor by forcing young females to think of themselves as merchandise, producing what Myriam J.A. Chancy, a scholar at Scripps College, calls a "Virginity cult" based solely on control of women (Chancy, 1997, 121). In *Breath, Eyes, Memory,* Sophie Caco lives a lie—a fabricated boyfriend, Henry Napoleon. His ironic last name requires a second lie, distancing in Haiti too far to be a threat to Sophie's hymen.

Edwidge's writing on *Breath, Eyes, Memory* in 1994 reflects on the Duvalier police state and the Haitian obsession with female docility. The flirtations after Christmas Eve Mass attest to sisters Tante Atie and Martine Caco's normal girlish silliness, as do pretended dates, which they break. Forced into maternity by a Tonton Macoute rapist, the fictional mother Martine takes a punitive attitude toward her daughter Sophie. Snide and sour, Martine turns the weekly vaginal testing into torture, a woman-on-woman violation that Sophie counters with prayer to the Virgin Mary. The psychological torment of the abstinence cult causes Sophie to take small steps, urinate quietly, and avoid acrobatic splits, bicycles, and horses, all folkloric endangerments of maidenhood. In adulthood, she suffers coital pain and reluctance to make love with husband Joseph Woods.

Women's Rights

Edwidge enlarges on victimization of virgins with Sophie Caco's friendships in a sexual phobia group, led by a Vodou priestess and female Santerian who base their devotions on the divinity of Erzulie. Buki, a survivor of female genital mutilation, expresses in a letter to her deceased grandmother Taiwo the ongoing hell of genital removal and a closed vaginal access. Buki sees victims as defenseless children beset by authority figures who themselves had suffered the same laceration of their vulva and clitoris. To halt the chain of woman-on-girl wounding that involved Grandmè Ifé, Tante Atie, and Martine Caco, Sophie vows to leave her daughter Brigitte untested, the beginning of the end for unthinkable child abuse for nubile girls.

The equivocal concept of female virginity makes inroads in unlikely places, including the cutting of the virgin's braid in *Anacaona*, Callie Morrissete's singing of "Ave Maria" in "Seven Stories," and human perfection in Edwidge's ecology picture book *The Last Mapou*. In Haitian creation myth, the emergence of unsullied first people from a kapok trunk maintains by inference the subsequent belief that only females had to remain sexually uninitiated. For the story "Night Talkers," Dany Dorméus rewards his aunt/foster mother Estina Estème, for rescuing him from fire. She sends her a blue dress from New York the color of the Virgin Mary's cloak, epitomizing her spotlessness, nurturance, and healing. To the unwary in "The Port-au-Prince Marriage Special," a knock-off engagement ring available from street venders advances the hoaxes of female despoilers. As a result of contracting AIDS from a one-night stand, Mélisande loses the respect of her mother Babette. Like traditional island parents, Babette views her daughter's chastity as an investment for the future, now ended with an inescapable death by a sexually transmitted disease.

See also Erzulie, Patriarchy.

SOURCES

Bergner, Gwen. "Danticat's Vodou Vernacular of Women's Human Rights," *American Literary History* 29:3 (Fall, 2017): 521–545.

Braziel, Jana Evans. "Daffodils, Rhizomes, Migrations: Narrative Coming of Age in the Diasporic Writings of Edwidge Danticat and Jamaica Kincaid," *Meridians* 3:2 (2003): 110–131.

Chancy, Myriam J.A. *Framing Silence: Revolutionary Novels by Haitian Women.* Piscataway, NJ: Rutgers University Press, 1997.

Danticat, Edwidge. *After the Dance: A Walk Through Carnival in Jacmel, Haiti.* New York: Vintage, 2002.

_____. *Breath, Eyes, Memory.* New York: Soho Press, 1994.

_____. "Hot-Air Balloons," *Granta* 115 (20 June 1996).

_____. "We Are Ugly, But We Are Here," *Women Writing Resistance.* Boston: Beacon, 2017, 21–26.

Francis, Donette A. "'Silences Too Horrific to Disturb': Writing Sexual Histories in Edwidge Danticat's *Breath, Eyes, Memory*," *Research in African Literatures* 35:2 (Summer, 2004): 75–90.

Latchman, Renee. "Edwidge Danticat's *Breath, Eyes, Memory*: A Critique on the Tradition of 'Testing,'" *African Youth in Contemporary Literature and Popular Culture.* New York: Routledge, 2014, 65–74.

Vodou

Fragments of belief in West African animism permeate Edwidge's writing with mystic loas (*lwas* or spirits) and traditional Yoruban ritual. In her vision of island peasantry, the Vodou holy world views spirits at work in the visible world. Madison Smartt Bell, a reviewer for *Washington Post,* charged the author with omitting from *After the Dance* the Vodou concept of *voye pwen* (send a point), an unleashing of magic through song, dance, words, or gestures. The absence suggests that Edwidge chose not to develop supernatural elements of a Lenten parade rich in political resistance. Analyst Joan Dayan, a specialist in Haitian culture at Vanderbilt University, accounted for the need for "traces of African religion" among the colonized:

These folk or local religions not only gave collective strength, but preserved the histories ignored, denigrated, or exorcized by the standard 'imperial' histories [which] … provided continuity for the dispossessed [Dayan, 1994, 5].

The *quid pro quo* enabled believers to rise above bondage and colonialism as they rewarded themselves with benevolent, omnipresent divinities.

Essential to reverence, through a trance state, a mortal becomes a *chwal* (holy equestrian), a vessel bearing the words of the divine. At a temple in Ville Rose in the novel *Claire of the Sea Light*, wall art communicates the multiple meanings of Catholic saints who double as loas. A syncretic image of the Virgin Mary poses as Mater Dolorosa (the grieving mother) opposite a sword. The point at her heart illustrates a Marian prophecy by St. Bernard of Clairvaux, the graphic positioning of a blade depicting the cause of sorrow in Mary, Our Lady of Sorrows. The three render her the intercessor for humankind.

A Humanized Cosmology

The author identifies in *Create Dangerously* and *vèvè*, Vodou cornmeal drawings to summon spirits, the centrality to *sèvités* (devotees) of a pantheon of gods:

- death gods Baron Samedi (Baron Saturday) and generous wife Gran Brigit, the only deity originating in Ireland
- Legba, the guide at the crossroads and intermediary to the afterlife
- Erzulie Freda (Lady Erzulie), a biracial icon of unending love
- Ogoun, the Haitian war god, a blacksmith who makes rum
- the Gede, a uniquely Yoruba-Haitian clan of merrymakers
- Azaka, the post-emancipation spirit of harvest for newly freed slaves.

In the story "Freda" for *Brown Sugar,* the character views the Gede family, keepers of the dead, as "our raunchiest spirits" for their phallic stunts (Danticat, 2005, 36). Iconic Vodou art summarizes the realms of each in a cross-topped tombstone and black cock for Samedi, Legba's intersection road sign, Erzulie's heart, and merged squares in the shape of a warrior's shield to represent Ogoun. At the night sacrifice of a pig to Ogoun, at Bois Caiman on August 13–14, 1791, folk hero Boukman Dutty, aided by mambo (priestess) Cécile Fatiman, launched the Haitian revolution with smears of porcine blood. Confusion arose from rebel attempts to compose a proclamation, which preliterate islanders were unable to write.

Out of reverence for Haiti's liberators and their African gods, the author revered Ginen, ancestral home of black Africans before slave times, and the union of couples and blessing the newborn under the kapok tree, a national soul force in *The Last Mapou*. In the island fairy tale *Célimène*, a houngan (spiritual adviser) conducts the nuptials of Célimène and Zaken. During the seven tours of their new home, the newlyweds carry "une bougie à la main, et allumèrent ensemble leur premier feu, symbole de leur avenir étincelant de bonheur" (a candle in their hands to kindle their first fire, a symbol of the spark of their happiness) (Danticat, 2009). Other examples range from the ibeji, an icon of birth twins of the Nigerian Yoruba referenced in *Untwine,* and "Gran Met," grand master of creation in *Tent Life,* to Le Bawon (The Baron), shielder of cemeteries and La Flaca (bony), the "grim reaper" of the departed in the poem "On the Day of the Dead."

Artist Representation

In a critique of works by Botswanan art mythographer Pamedla Phatsimo Sunstrum for *Paris Review*, the author found the influence of water Orisha Yemayá, Mother of All, the ruler of motherhood and emergent life from wind, lakes, and oceans. Sunstrum's pervasive blue implied the tonal identity of the Virgin Mary in Renaissance art. For the paintings "Buffalo" and "The Incense Burner," the color united seascape and sky, reminding viewers "that nature is part of us…. The water brought us here. The water will take us away" (Danticat, 2020, 107, 108). Edwidge concluded that Sunstrum pictured humankind as "transient travelers, itinerants of space and time," a repeated concept in the author's writings on diaspora (*ibid.,* 108).

For the pilgrims traveling by boat to Miami in "Children of the Sea," the jettisoning of personal effects includes pocket change given to Agwé, the marine spirit of oceans and husband of the beautiful and powerful Erzulie. At the gate of Casernes, the infamous barracks and interrogation center in Port-au-Prince, staff jokingly calls the gatekeeper Legba after the Vodou spirit who speaks for humans at the intersection between earth and the afterlife. The loa returns to interest in *After the Dance* in Edwidge's views of artists in Jacmel, where a collection of antique doors reprises Legba's guardianship of passageways. Of the mystic nature of divinity, "Poem 3" in the collection *Standing Tall* poses a rhetorical question about ephemeral divinity—"Are the lwas like the wind" (Danticat, 2010, n.p.).

During the author's tour of an historic graveyard in Jacmel, she interpreted Lucifer masks as Ogun, the Vodou blacksmith and "light bringer." She viewed crosses on mausoleums as syncretic Christian and Vodou icons honoring Baron Samedi (Baron Saturday), patron of cemeteries and grand honoree on the Day of the Dead each November 2, the holiday following All Saints' Day on November 1. She mused on the costuming of dictator François "Papa Doc" Duvalier in dark coattails and black hat, the visual accouterments of Baron Samedi. In *Behind the Mountains,* Tante Rose honors her deceased parents, the spirits who watch over the family. At pre–Lenten carnival Jacmel in *After the Dance,* Azaka, the harvest loa of Labor Day (May 1), processes in the entourage in farm costume and shakes a rattle, a symbol of the vigor imbuing St. Isidro, the Spanish plowman.

Hadriana's Myth

A Gothic tale recounted in *After the Dance*, the death of an erotically charged French bride, Hadriana "Nana" Siloé, extols a shapeshifter who lived at Manoir Hadriana, now a haunted hotel. Her death during carnival season on January 29, 1938, occurred at the altar of St. Philippe and St. Jacques Cathedral, built on Rue de L'Eglise in Jacmel in 1852. While she awaited marriage to a black Haitian, the handsome pilot Hector Danoze, Hadriana, an embodiment of Erzulie, fell dead. Witnesses declared the stunning demise the result of premarital passion, transformation into a giant butterfly, a symbol of continuance, and an omen of the Duvalier regime. By torchlight, a Vodou ritualist accompanied Hadriana's remains to the grave.

The following Sunday, Hadriana's body disappeared in the form of the divine serpent Simbi Lasous, a fresh water loa who migrated with a boatload of émigrés to Jamaica. A Jacmel prefect declared Hadriana a zombie transformed into a beautiful black female by spiritual poisoning, a trope for African bondage and the black arts. Her life-in-death state abetted constant roving in the Caribbean Sea. Novelist René Depestre immortalized the vanishing bride in the folkloric fiction *Hadriana dans tous les rêves* (Hadriana in All My Dreams, 1988).

See also Erzulie, *Untwine.*

Sources
Bell, Madison Smartt. "Distant Drums," *Washington Post* (18 August 2002).

Danticat, Edwidge. *After the Dance: A Walk Through Carnival in Jacmel, Haiti*. New York: Vintage, 2002.

_____. *Célimène—Fairy Tale for the Daughter of Immigrants*. Montreal: Memoire d'Encrier, 2009.

_____. *Create Dangerously: The Immigrant Artist at Work*. New York: Vintage, 2010.

_____. "Freda," *Brown Sugar 4*. New York: Washington Square Press, 2005, 31–41.

_____. *The Last Mapou*. Brooklyn: One Moore Book, 2013.

_____. "Pamela Phatsimo Sunstrum: New and Recent Paintings," *Paris Review* 232 (Spring 2020): 105–121.

_____. "Poems," *Standing Tall: Portraits of the Haitian Community in Miami, 2003–2010*. Miami: Museum of Contemporary Art, 2010, n.p.

Dayan, Joan. "Erzulie: A Women's History of Haiti," *Research in African Literatures Caribbean Literature* 25:2 (Summer, 1994): 5–31.

Dumas, Pierre-Raymond, and Augustin Chenald. "'Célimène' ou la problématique de l'exil au coeur du merveilleux," *Le Nouvelliste* (21 June 2011).

Gérazime, Roselyne E. "Lasirèn, Labalèn: L'abysse en migration dans *Claire of the Sea Light*," *Journal of Haitian Studies* 25:1 (2019): 178–200.

Vulnerability

Edwidge identifies in communities and individuals the foibles and weaknesses that threaten collapse, as with Junior's day of sadness after Oscar's death following the January 12, 2010, earthquake in *Eight Days,* Paris's reaction to his father's drowning in the Atlantic Ocean in "Without Inspection," and Beatrice Saint Fort's fear of a phantom pursuer in "The Bridal Seamstress." A variety of character flaws particularizes responses, such as the sorrow of the servant Amabelle Desír, a transitory phantom fleeing ethnic cleansing in *The Farming of Bones.* Her mourning for drowned parents, herbalists Antoine Desír and Irelle Pradelle, and neediness for her lover Sebastien Onius refuse to give her peace. Other fictional persons bear unique situations, the cause of removal of Grann's historic kapok tree in *The Last Mapou*, of Anika and Thomas's dual remorse for adultery and the loss of his wife and daughter Dina and Qadine in "The Gift," and of terror in sixteen-year-old Giselle Boyer after her twin sister Isabelle's death in *Untwine*. The revelation of sensitivity and defenselessness awards each character humanity and arouses reader compassion:

Title	Character	Weakness
Anacaona	Anacaona	willingness to cede power to brother Behechio; fear of Night Marchers
	Caonabó	a Taino chief who is inexperienced with Conquistador treachery
	Higuemota	an orphan raised by an old woman
	Yaruba	homesickness for tribe and family and willingness to die
Behind the Mountains	Gary	inability to adapt to migration
"Between the Pool and the Gardenias"	Marie	dependence on delusions of motherhood
"The Book of Miracles"	Ka Bienaimé	lack of enthusiasm for home life and religion
"The Book of the Dead"	the fat man, Ka's father	a guilt-ridden terrorist who lives a lie
"The Bridal Seamstress"	Aline Cajuste	a career journalist unsure of her focus
	Beatrice Saint Fort	delusional survivor who imagines a stalker
Brother, I'm Dying	André Mira Danticat	a victim of terminal pulmonary fibrosis
	Joseph Nosius Dantica	a pulpit minister silenced by a laryngectomy
Célimène	Célimène	idealistic orphan and obedient wife
"Children of the Sea"	Marie, other refugees	dependence on a small leaky boat and on Coast Guard rescue
"Claire of the Sea Light"	Claire Faustin	fear of losing her father Nosias and fostering with a new mother, Gaëlle Lavaud
Claire of the Sea Light	Flore Voltaire	single mother seeking safety for her family

Vulnerability
221

Title	Character	Weakness
	Maxine Ardin, Jr.	closeted homosexual grieving for Bernard
	Maxine Ardin, Sr.	grandfather eager for a grandson
	Nozias Faustin	suicidal thoughts for himself and his child
	Pamaxime	fatherless boy eager for a male parent
	Tiye	dependent on gang solidarity
Create Dangerously	Alèrte Bélance	a seriously maimed advocate for Haiti
	Tante Zi Dantica	a grieving mother laden with regret for her immigrant son Marius, killed by AIDS
The Dew Breaker	Anne Bienaimé	a Catholic fanatic unable to relieve guilt
	Ka Bienaimé	a daughter shielded from her father's guilty secrets
"Dosas"	Elsie	a naive nurse's aide faithful to unworthy friends
"Dream of the Butterflies"	Marie Micheline	daydreams of past delights of nature in the mountains of Léogâne
Eight Days	Oscar	a child trapped in earthquake ruins
The Farming of Bones	Amabelle Desír Onius	need to reunite with her lover Sebastian
	Valencia Duarte	failure to see her husband Pico's willingness to murder black Haitians
"Ghosts"	Pascal Dorien	a radio journalist naive about the nature of crime and corruption
	Tiye	a one-armed gang leader reliant on blackmail
"The Gift"	Anika	a lover who conceals the miscarriage of a child
	Thomas	an amputee who regrets betraying wife Dina
"Hot-Air Balloons"	Neah	a privileged aid worker uninformed about human need
"In the Old Days"	Nadia	a daughter left fatherless by Maurice Dejean, an idealist
The Last Mapou	Grann	acceptance of end-of-life symptoms and the passage of storytelling to her granddaughter
"The Missing Peace"	Lamort	illiterate and browbeaten by a grandmother
"Monkey Tails"	Michel, Rosie	children indentured as *rèstavèks*
"New York Day Women"	Suzette	devaluer of a working mom
"Night Talkers"	Claude	loser of self-control during a drug argument
	Dany Dorméus	incomplete knowledge of his parents' murder
"Night Women"	son	a boy too young to realize the cost of his mother's sex work
"Nineteen Thirty-Seven"	Josephine	lack of knowledge of her family's past
"The Port-au-Prince Marriage Special"	Mélisande	dreams of a lover and a cure for AIDS
	Xavier and wife	innkeepers tricked by reliance on a white Canadian physician
"The Possibility of Heaven"	Rose Danticat	slow demise from ovarian cancer
"Quality Control"	female journalists	no shelter from weapons fire
"Sawfish Soup"	son	a child alone on streets terrorized by Tonton Macoute
"Seeing Things Simply"	Princesse	a receptive talent awaiting instruction
"Seven"	husband and wife	mutual concealers of past liaisons
"Seven Stories"	Callie Morrissete	danger of being assassinated like her father
	widow	survivor dogged by memories of escape
"Sunrise, Sunset"	Carole	dementia from aging
	Jeanne	postpartum depression
Tent Life	female survivors	potential victims of rapists
Untwine	Giselle Boyer	a twin dependent on sister Isabelle
	Sylvia Boyer	a wife contemplating divorce
"A Wall of Fire Rising"	Lili	mom with a diminished role in the family
"Water Child"	Ms. Hinds	loser of speech from surgery
	Nadine Osnac	nurse who can't relax and socialize

Title	Character	Weakness
"Westbury Court"	two brothers	unsupervised children during a fire
"Without Inspection"	Darline	carries guilt for son Paris's mental handicap
	Paris	shy after his father's drowning
"A Year and a Day"	earthquake victims	polluted water and air

According to Valerie Kaussen, a professor at University Missouri Columbia, by concentrating on migrants, exiles, and their families, Edwidge's stories "meditate upon the meaning of home and homeland as both a psychic and geographic process which entails the crossing of borders that are at once legal, emotional, ideological, and cultural" (Kaussen, 2015, 25). Bouts of violence and proofs of legitimacy, such as those faced by Pascal Dorien and Tiye in "Ghosts" and Arnold posing as Ernesto in "Without Inspection," reinforce power structures based on forcing the poor and uneducated into a state of "social death" (Oliver-Rodger, 2015, 26).

After a stream of writings about the underclass, Edwidge manages to turn her best story into sympathy for the elite. In "Seven Stories," the prime minister's wife Callie Morrissete exists in a hazardous political state, the same peril that killed her father, Prime Minister Charles Morrissete. While the villagers of Maafa struggle with poverty and inadequate housing, the official residence welcomes A-list guests to a frivolous beach wedding. Callie dresses and hobnobs according to the demands of the official's wife. Elegance layers the occasion in subterfuge to conceal the nation's privations among the poor, the source of the next rebellion.

The undertone of insecurity requires armed guards, fences, and walls topped with broken glass, a mouthlike metaphor of jagged teeth menacing island government for failure to uplift the poor. Kim Boyer, a keen journalist, visits her old friend Callie after decades apart and observes class disparities. A racist comment spoils the occasion and reminds her that black people are not welcome. The explosive situation, cloaked in music, dance, chic fashion, and feasting suggests a coming storm virulent enough to cause another assassination. She stated to interviewer Gabrielle Bellot of *Publishers Weekly,* "Sometimes people know our most vulnerable places. Because of that, we do things we know we shouldn't do— things that have tragic outcomes. This is the kind of conflict that I'm drawn to" (Bellot, 2019). The meticulous contrast of character perspectives creates the author's best narrative and sets up parameters for a future novel to exorcise past secrets and socioeconomic angst.

See also Death, Immigrants, Nature.

Sources

Bellot, Gabrielle. "Edwidge Danticat Returns to Haiti in New Stories," *Publishers Weekly* (21 June 2019).

Danticat, Edwidge. *Everything Inside.* New York: Knopf, 2019.

Oliver-Rotger, Maria Antonia, ed. *Identity, Diaspora and Return in American Literature.* New York: Routledge, 2015.

Rubio-Zepeda, José. "Transitory Ghosts: Haitians and Dominico-Haitians in Santo Domingo," *Portal* 11 (2016): 30–32.

Women

Edwidge views West Indian women as defiers of victimhood and models of unique black beauty, the focus of the author's foreword to *The African Lookbook.* She describes the grotesque punishments of an asylum seeker in "A Crime to Dream," an essay for the *Nation* in which immigration remands the prisoner for "months without a haircut, comb or a change of underclothes" (Danticat, 2005, 14). Survivors determine to outpace social and political adversity, the intent of revolutionary war heroine Marie-Jeanne Lamartiniére in "One Thing"; Flore Voltaire, a Haitian beautician and single mother in *Claire of the Sea Light;* and Mona, a beautician, and Elsie and Olivia, Haitian-American nurse's assistants, in "Dosas." For Darline, the surviving parent of Paris in "Without Inspection," staying solvent in Miami's Little Haiti requires sweaty toil over boiling pots of island foods and little time for primping. In the epilogue of *Krik? Krak!,* the author reunites lone mothers like Darline and Elsie with otherworldly traditions—"We are never any farther than the sweat on your brows," a promise from the spiritual realm (Danticat, 1995, 194).

In Haitian folklore, people identified flying females as lougarous (werewolves); in Africa, the soaring women became crows and soul eaters. The author's writing plucks Haitian females out of myth and sets them in a myriad of domestic tasks—"Mothering, Boiling, Loving, Baking, Nursing, Frying, Healing, Washing, Ironing, Scrubbing"—and selling fresh water or sex when there is nothing else to sell (Danticat, 1994, 151). In "Hot-Air Balloons," a brochure pictures Haitian females "carrying heavy buckets of water on their heads while walking narrow dirt paths in the countryside, others sitting on riverbanks washing clothes, a few selling fly-covered meat in an open market" (Danticat, 2019, 114). For the future *cacica* (ruler) of Xaraguá in the Taino historical fiction *Anacaona*, preparing for the throne causes the title figure to insist on equality with her brother, Chief Behechio, who conducts secret talks with their uncle Matunherí. After a disastrous windstorm, Anacaona yields to a marriage omen of circling birds and, without complaint, mentally cedes to Behechio the

rule of Xaraguá. For Anacaona, like the devoted mothers in "Night Women" and "Dreams of the Butterflies," tending her toddler daughter Higuamota outweighs tribal duties in importance.

The author reprises the devotion of moms, aunts, and grandmoms in the YA novel *Untwine* and *My Mommy Medicine,* a picture book detailing the forms of play and entertainment that keep a sick child occupied. In the story "Sunrise, Sunset," Jeanne, a victim of postpartum depression, asks the rhetorical question "How do you become a good mother?," a skill her mother Carole seems to practice despite old age and dementia (Danticat, 2017). For Saya in *Mama's Nightingale,* although the parent resides in jail, she mails tapes of her voice telling bedtime stories, a verbal soother of anxiety. For the title figure in *Célimène,* harvesting cacao and coffee to barter for vegetables enables an orphaned peasant girl to feed herself and younger brother Mo. To satisfy longings for a better life, she agrees to marry Zaken, a stranger who promises a lifetime of devotion. By accepting risk, she binds herself to a residence far from her hometown of Pik Rose (Rose Peak) and to a grand lifestyle altogether different from the past.

Female islanders like Célimène move through early girlhood in the rhythms of everyday labor, beginning with carrying water on their heads from public fountains like Lili in "A Wall of Fire Rising" and the devalued wife in "Seeing Things Simply," laundering clothes like "The Indigo Girl," and sweeping the bare yards of leaves and branches, Sophie Caco's task in *Breath, Eyes, Memory*. Constant toil isolates them in the home among children or in distant places as "women without nests," a euphemism for unmarried or childless females like Tante Atie Caco (Danticat, 1995, 38). When politics and socioeconomic adversity plunder the boundary of home in *The Farming of Bones,* Valencia Duarte and her maid-servants Juana and Amabelle Desír incur more anxiety and suffering, especially for children and elders threatened by the Guardia's bloodletting. In the author's overview of female labors in *Tent Life,* she reports how a crisis like the January 12, 2010, earthquake belittles female efforts under tarp roofs and bedsheet walls to upgrade the least viable forms of sanitation and home order, especially warding off rapists from themselves and their little girls.

Fashion and Chic

Attire and hairdressing illustrate the need for self-respect and personal cleanliness, two difficult demands on poor and disadvantaged wives and daughters that reflect the influence of Erzulie, the Vodou goddess of beauty and passion. "Poem 4" in the collection *Standing Tall* speaks of moods elevated by "flowered dresses/ And lip-gloss clutching hands" (Danticat, 2010, n.p.). For Gaëlle Lavaud, the childless widow in *Claire of the Sea Light,* selling dress fabric placed her elegance and color sense in most homes in Ville Rose. The story "A Place of Refuge" for *Allure* magazine pictures Anisi, Dieula, and Lina Espérance in group work adorning glamorous dresses with beads and sequins. To counter the effects of living in the Bel Air slum of Port-au-Prince, the trio beautify themselves

> with bright or muted kerchiefs, head wraps or hats, relaxed or braided hair, wigs and talcum-powdered neck, impeccably pressed clothes, and shoes that were religiously polished and shined before they walked in the mud a few steps away. [Danticat, 2011].

The contrast enhances women's determination to make personal presentation count in a squalid environment that they can't change.

The writer extols females for being the ever-faithful disseminators of culture from one generation to the next, the gentrification that Tante Denise furthers in *Brother, I'm Dying* with elegant hats, wigs, and gloves. Unlike the males who write war stories, women speak of birth as the female equivalent of combat, a concept developed by French novelist Simone de Beauvoir. For Edwidge and her mother Rose Souvenance, endurance marks the post-conflict years of women surviving the Duvalier regime. Edwidge locates pride and self-determination in the story "The Artists of Maténwa," featuring makers of silk scarves for sale in the U.S. In an epilogue, "Women Like Us," she extols females for mustering "an army of women watching over you…. We are always with you" (Danticat, 1995, 194). The mantra illustrates the intimacy of female support groups like that attended by Sophie Caco in *Breath, Eyes, Memory* and the fervor of volunteerism like Neah's work with rape victims for Leve (Lift) in "Hot-Air Balloons" and Edwidge in "Living and Loving through Tragedy."

Females in Lore

The author deliberately scrutinizes women in *Everything Inside* to "show all the layers" (Bellot, 2019). Her canon sets island women apart from males for the ballads sung about mystic flying women, the amazons of ancient Africa and the source of the Vodou faith. Culture specialist Joan Dayan at Vanderbilt University charges Christianity with founding the "cult of mystification—the familiar splitting of women into objects to be desired or abhorred," the desexualized saint and the forbidden *cocotte* (bedroom slave) (Dayan, 1994, 8). Silencing and battery by men and androcentric institutions keep females invisible amid intimidation and assault, the sources of religious frenzy in Anne Bienaimé in "The Book of Miracles" and muteness in Défilé, the prisoner of "Nineteen Thirty-Seven." The latter narrative builds strength from a six-generation matrilineage and a female heirloom—a Madonna statue that Défilé received from her French slave master five generations earlier. At the story's climax, a teardrop "traveled down her white porcelain face," a reminder that Catholic iconography favors starkly Caucasian traits (Danticat, 2001: 454). For the title figure in "The Dew Breaker," winged females in shades from cinnamon and honey to jet flock above Papa Doc Duvalier's palace and hiss at his five-hour self-glorifying speech. Like the monstrously clawed female harpies in Hyginus's fables and Virgil's epic verse, the verbal rebuke magnifies women for refusing to be silenced and for constricting words to a scolding sibilance.

Of her education in all-male French literati featuring philosopher Voltaire, poet Arthur Rimbaud, and novelist Victor Hugo, the author internalized the gendered boundary: "Writing almost felt like it was a forbidden activity. Being poor and being female, it was unheard of to write books. It was a double transgression" (Lyons, 2003, 192). In *Claire of the Sea Light*, she alludes cleverly to "Au Clair de la Lune," a French folk song that awards a charitable brunette with the company of Lubin, a penniless poet in need of a light and quill, a phallic suggestion of womanly ministrations. Breaking free from misogyny with *Breath, Eyes, Memory,* a matriarchal novel, Edwidge surveyed family values and agency in a manless house, where unity among Grandmè Ife, Tante Atie Cao, Martine Caco, and daughter Sophie salved insecurity and doubt. Strength in the household's past enabled Sophie to exceed traditional strictures on women and rear daughter Brigitte Woods with hope for a beneficial mother-daughter relationship.

See also Mothers, Patriarchy, Vulnerability.

Sources

Alexandre, Sandy, and Ravi Y. Howard. "Interview," *Journal of Caribbean Literature* 4:3 (Spring 2007): 161–174.

Bellot, Gabrielle. "Edwidge Danticat Returns to Haiti in New Stories," *Publishers Weekly* (21 June 2019).

Danticat, Edwidge. *The African Lookbook.* foreword. New York: Bloomsbury, 2021.

_____. *Breath, Eyes, Memory.* New York: Soho Press, 1994.

_____. "A Crime to Dream," *Nation* 280:17 (2 May 2005): 13–15.

_____. *Everything Inside.* New York: Knopf, 2019.

_____. "Fanm Se Poto Mitan: Women are the Pillars of Society," *Women: A Celebration of Strength.* New York: Legal Momentum, 2007.

_____. "Introduction," *Vale of Tears.* Bethesda, MD: Ibex, 2005, 6–7.

_____. *Krik? Krak!* New York: Soho Press, 1995.

_____. "Nineteen Thirty-Seven," *Oxford Book of Caribbean Short Stories.* Oxford, UK: Oxford University Press, 2001: 447–456.

_____. "A Place of Refuge," *Allure* 21:3 (March 2011).

_____. "Poems," *Standing Tall: Portraits of the Haitian Community in Miami, 2003–2010.* Miami: Museum of Contemporary Art, 2010, n.p.

_____. "Sunrise, Sunset," *New Yorker* 93:28 (18 September 2017): 54–60.

Dayan, Joan. "Erzulie: A Women's History of Haiti," *Research in African Literatures Caribbean Literature* 25:2 (Summer, 1994): 5–31.

Germain, Christine. "Review: *Claire of the Sea Light,*" *Palimpsest* 3:2 (2014): 214–215.

Lyons, Bonnie. "Interview," *Contemporary Literature* 44:2 (Summer 2003): 182–198.

Munro, Martin. *Exile and Post-1946 Haitian Literature.* Liverpool, UK: Liverpool University Press, 2007.

Glossary

achitekti pèpè pepper architecture (*Claire of the Sea Light*, 2013, 48)

acronym terms shortened to letters, as in ETA and BP for "estimated time of arrival" and "blood pressure" (*Untwine*, 2015, 10)

Adiós, bebé Goodbye, baby (*The Farming of Bones*, 1998, 31)

Adventist a protestant faith anticipating the immediate return of Christ (*Breath, Eyes, Memory*, 1994, 65)

adye goodbye (*The Farming of Bones*, 1998, 265)

affranchis freed (*After the Dance*, 2002, 45)

Almirante Admiral (*The Farming of Bones*, 1998, 18)

angelitos small dead children ("On the Day of the Dead," 2011, n.p.)

ane years (*Brother, I'm Dying*, 2007, 139)

ankh Egyptian symbol of human life in ancient hieroglyphs (*Create Courageously*, 2010, 133)

anthère plant pollinator (*Claire of the Sea Light*, 2013, 10)

ashram religious retreat ("Hot-Air Balloons," 2019, 126)

Atis Fanm Matenwa Morning Women Artists ("Artists of Maténwa," 2004, 25)

auberge inn (*After the Dance*, 2002, 104)

au courant with the times (*Untwine*, 2015, 215)

au revoir goodbye (*Breath, Eyes, Memory*, 1994, 228)

aux moins at least ("The Port-au-Prince Marriage Special," 2014, 164)

ave hail (*The Dew Breaker*, 2004, 214)

ayibobo alleluia, amen ("Seeing Things Simply," 1995, 115)

BAC baccalauréat ("Monkey Tails," 2004, 152)

bagay yo things ("Claire of the Sea Light," 2010, 134)

Bajan from Barbados ("Dosas," 2017, 8)

balaclava knit face mask ("Ghosts," 2008, 111)

banbòch fun ("Water Child," 2004, 59)

banyan a fig tree that sends roots upward to form additional trunks ("Children of the Sea," 1995, 19)

Barbancourt rum Haitian rum ("On the Day of the Dead," 2011, n.p.)

batey shanty town ("The Dominican Republic's War on Haitian Workers," 1999, A13)

békéké cripple (*The Farming of Bones*, 1998, 260)

Berlitz a foreign language school begun in Providence, Rhode Island (*Brother, I'm Dying*, 2007, 62)

beton concrete (*Create Dangerously*, 2010, 53)

bezique a card game based on taking tricks (*The Dew Breaker*, 2004, 198)

bienvenue welcome ("Seven," 2001, n.p.)

blan a white Haitian (*Create Dangerously*, 2010, 7)

blokis traffic jams (*Behind the Mountains*, 2002, 27)

bohiti Taino spiritual healers (*Anacaona*, 2007, 55)

bolero slow lyrical music ("Caroline's Wedding," 1995, 171)

bòlèt lottery (*Breath, Eyes Memory*, 1994, 5)

Bondye good God (*Standing Tall*, 2010, n.p.)

bòn fèt happy birthday (*Claire of the Sea Light*, 2013, 225)

bonjou good morning ("Night Talkers," 2004, 89)

bonne chance good luck (*The Dew Breaker*, 2004, 221)

Glossary

bonsoir good evening (*Claire of the Sea Light*, 2013, 157)

bon voyage farewell (*Breath, Eyes, Memory*, 1994, 228)

boudin sausage (*Breath, Eyes, Memory*, 1994, 55)

bouki sucker ("Dosas," 2019, 30)

Boukman an Akan Vodou leader from Gambia who initiated the Haitian Revolution in August 1791 ("A Wall of Fire Rising," 1995, 46)

bourreau executioner (*The Dew Breaker*, 2004, 198)

boutilye bottler (*After the Dance*, 2002, 108)

bouzen whore ("Reading Lessons," 2004, 70)

bracero seasonal worker (*The Farming of Bones*, 1998, 38)

bread-and-circus a temporary soothing of the citizenry (*After the Dance*, 2002, 118)

bwa chèch dry wood (*Breath, Eyes, Memory*, 1994, 123)

cafecito espresso coffee sweetened with brown sugar (*The Farming of Bones*, 1998, 93)

caja cage ("Celia," 2007, 92)

calabash gourd (*Breath, Eyes, Memory*, 1994, 102)

calenda folk dance ("Revenant," 1996, n.p.)

calmate, hombre settle down, man (*The Farming of Bones*, 1998, 215)

calme-toi calm yourself (*Breath, Eyes, Memory*, 1994, 223)

camion bus ("Water Child," 2004, 63)

camionette van (*Brother, I'm Dying*, 2007, 207)

carrion carriage ("Night Talkers," 2002, 107)

caryatid a pillar or support shaped like a woman (*The Dew Breaker*, 2004, 193)

cassareep a cassava flavoring and antiseptic (*Anacoana*, 2007, 36)

caul birth tissue ("Revenant," 1996, n.p.)

Ca va byen? Are things going well? (*Breath, Eyes, Memory*, 1994, 212)

centime 1/100th of a gourde ("Monkey Tails," 2004, 145)

C'est comme une poupée She is like a doll (*Breath, Eyes, Memory*, 1994, 178)

Chaloska Charles Oscar (*After the Dance*, 2002, 67)

chany shoeshiner (*Brother, I'm Dying*, 2007, 139)

charismatic evangelical emotional religion revealing the Holy Spirit (*Claire of the Sea Light*, 2013, 29)

chatelaine key chain ("The Bridal Seamstress," 2004, 131)

chéri dear ("Ghosts," 2008, 112)

cherimoya sweet Latin American fruit ("Seven," 2004, 42)

Chez Moy Moy's place and a pun on chez moi (my house) (*Untwine*, 2015, 114)

chiktay smoked herring (*Haiti Noir 2*, 2014, 19)

chine spine (*The Farming of Bones*, 1998, 3)

chocolat-au-lait chocolate milk (*The Farming of Bones*, 1998, 203)

choukèt lawoze dew breaker or torturer ("The Bridal Seamstress," 2004, 131)

cinephile movie fan (*Create Dangerously*, 2010, 43)

clostra-block cement blocks mounted into a facade ("Ghosts," 2008, 109)

cocoplum the bland fruit of a Caribbean shrub (*The Farming of Bones*, 1998, 16)

comme il faut as one must to be socially correct (*Create Dangerously*, 2010, 21)

¿Como esta, mi amor? How are you, my love? (*Untwine*, 2015, 156)

conked straightened ("Dosas," 2017, 42)

coup de grace death blow (*Create Dangerously*, 2010, 4)

coup d'état rebellion ("Quality Control," 2014, n.p.)

craniopagus conjoined skulls (*Untwine*, 2015, 88)

Cremace Christmas ("Haitian-American Christmas," *New Youth Connections*, 1987)

Croix des Rosets Rosette Cross (*Breath, Eyes, Memory*, 1994, 19)

croque madame a toasted ham and cheese sandwich topped with a fried egg (*Untwine*, 2015, 39)

cryogenics the low-temperature storage of a corpse to preserve tissue (*The Art of Death*, 2017, 140)

cutter small coastal speedboat (*Claire of the Sea Light*, 2013, 3)

dactylo typist (*Breath, Eyes, Memory*, 1994, 56, 99)

degi plus (*Claire of the Sea Light*, 2013, 53)

demijohn jug (*Breath, Eyes, Memory*, 1994, 150)

Glossary

dengue fever a mosquito-borne fever that can cause a fatal drop in blood pressure (*Claire of the Sea Light*, 2013, 17)

desounen apathy ("Year and a Day," 2011, 298)

dezòd fractious (*Claire of the Sea Light*, 2013, 25)

dictator fils son of the dictator ("Monkey Tails," 2004, 150)

Dies diem docet The day teaches the day, meaning to learn something each day to carry over in subsequent days (*The Farming of Bones*, 1998, 147)

dieu si bon God so good (*Breath, Eyes, Memory*, 1994, 94)

dios mio my God ("Celia," 2007, 91)

djakout bag ("Haiti: A Bi-Cultural Experience," 1995, 8)

DKW German motorcycle (*The Dew Breaker*, 2004, 183)

dous sweets (*Behind the Mountains,* 2002, 7)

droit du seigneur a medieval privilege that allows aristocrats sexual rights to lower cast people (*Claire of the Sea Light*, 2013, 185)

duho Taino ceremonial chair (*Anacaona*, 2005, 134)

Dutty Boukman an enslaved rebel during the 1791 revolt against the French on Hispaniola ("A Wall of Fire Rising," 1995, 47)

dyasporas immigrants ("The Port-au-Prince Marriage Special," 2014, 168)

edema swelling (*Untwine*, 2015, 13)

elephantiasis gross swelling of limbs or genitals (*Claire of the Sea Light*, 2013, 38–39)

El Jefe the chief (Trujillo) (*The Farming of Bones*, 1998, 147)

En Attendant Godot Waiting for Godot (*The Dew Breaker*, 2004, 204)

en chair et en os in flesh and blood (*Claire of the Sea Light*, 2013, 95)

engagé busy ("Westbury Court," 2000, 80)

epaulets shoulder fringe (*The Farming of Bones*, 1998, 42)

epilogue conclusion ("Women Like Us," 1995, 189)

Étonnants Voyageurs astonishing travelers (*Create Dangerously*, 2010, 160)

Eucharist sacramental communion (*The Farming of Bones*, 1998, 250)

extreme unction a ritual comforting the dying (*Create Dangerously*, 2010, 4)

facteur postman (*Breath, Eyes, Memory*, 1994, 12)

fèy wònt shame leaf (*The Dew Breaker*, 2004, 235)

fini the end (*Claire of the Sea Light*, 2013, 80)

fizi rifle ("Dosas," 2019, 14)

flamboyant tree the *Delonix regia,* a tree covered in red flowers (*Breath, Eyes, Memory*, 1994, 97)

flanneur strolling flirt (*Breath, Eyes, Memory*, 1994, 165)

fontanel soft spot on an infant's head (*The Farming of Bones*, 1998, 284)

fortaleza fortress (*The Farming of Bones*, 1998, 156)

fredi cold ("No Greater Shame," 2003, 170)

frè m my brother (*Brother, I'm Dying*, 2007, 90)

Frère Jacques Brother John (*Untwine*, 2015, 123)

frisson ripple in a crowd ("Quality Control," 2014, 26)

gemelita twin (*Untwine*, 2015, 80)

gendarmes police ("Between the Pool and the Gardenias," 1995, 86)

gourde Haitian currency ("The Port-au-Prince Marriage Special," 2014, 166)

grade à Dieu thanks to God ("Water Child," 2004, 53)

grange farm building (*The Farming of Bones*, 1998, 253)

gran met grand master (*Breath, Eyes, Memory,* 1994, 116)

granmoun adult (*Brother, I'm Dying*, 2007, 89)

guanabana soursop (*The Farming of Bones*, 1998, 43)

guanin an alloy of copper, gold, and silver valued among the First Peoples of Central America and the Caribbean ("Pamela Phatsimo Sunstrum: New and Recent Paintings," 2020, 105)

guapa beautiful (*The Butterfly's Way*, 2001, xvii)

guardia police (*The Farming of Bones*, 1998, 20)

guayabera shirt traditional Cuban men's shirt with vertical columns of pleats (*Untwine*, 2015, 39)

hermanas sisters (*The Farming of Bones*, 1998, 293)

hog banana short, tangy tropical fruit (*The Farming of Bones*, 1998, 167)

hola hello (*The Farming of Bones*, 1998, 39)

honneur greetings (*Breath, Eyes, Memory*, 1994, 5), 103

houngan Vodou priest (*Create Dangerously*, 2010, 128)

hydrocephalus water on the brain ("Hot-Air Balloons," 1996, n.p.)

hyen cyanide poisoning from cassava (*Anacaona*, 2007, 42)

in medias res Latin for "in the middle of things" (*The Art of Death,* 2017, 19)

Jean-Michel Basquiat Haitian-Puerto Rican expressionist painter who overdosed on heroin in New York City at age 27 (*Untwine*, 2015, 91)

Je ne sais quoi I don't know what (*Breath, Eyes, Memory*, 1994, 79)

Je suis désolée I am sorry (*Untwine*, 2015, 224)

Je t'aime I love you ("Dosas," 2017, 8)

Je t'aime de tout mon coeur I love you with all my heart (*Breath, Eyes, Memory*, 1994, 27)

Je t'en prie I beg you (*Breath, Eyes, Memory*, 1994, 222)

jeter le masque throw off the mask (*After the Dance*, 2002, 16)

jeunesse étudiante young student (*The Dew Breaker*, 2004, 205)

Je Voudrais Etre Riche I would be rich (title, 2004, 187)

jouvenceaux youths (*After the Dance*, 2002, 117)

J'ouvert dawn (*After the Dance*, 2002, 143)

jumper pullover sweater (*Claire of the Sea Light*, 2013, 17)

ka Egyptian for "spirit" ("The Book of the Dead," 2004, 13)

kajou cashew ("Dosas," 2017, 4)

kaka Spanish for "excrement" ("The Book of the Dead," 2004, 16)

kalanda a Haitian dance derived from African warriors (*The Farming of Bones*, 1998, 130)

Kalina the Carib of Brazil, French Guiana, Guyana, and Suriname (*Anacaona,* 2007, 42)

karst limestone ("One Thing," 2020, 9)

kash kash liben shadows, shadows, nothingness (*Untwine*, 2015, 40)

keloid thick scar ("No Greater Shame," 2003, 171)

kente banded Ghanian fabric featuring the colors of Africa—yellow, green, black, blue (*Breath, Eyes, Memory*, 1994, 81)

kremis Christmas (*Behind the Mountains*, 2002, 71)

ki lè who? ("Dosas," 2017, 26)

ki sa What is that? (*Breath, Eyes, Memory*, 1994, 99)

kite'm leave me alone (*The Farming of Bones*, 1998, 107)

kleren beverage (*Claire of the Sea Light*, 2010, 129)

Knecht Ruprecht Servant Rupert, a German farm laborer reared by Saint Nicholas and a disciplinarian of children (*After the Dance*, 2002, 55)

kòm si like this (*Breath, Eyes, Memory*, 1994, 153)

konbit community (*Breath, Eyes, Memory*, 1994, 1, 54)

kondoleyans condolences ("Mourning in Place," 2020, 38)

konpa a dance similar to the calenda ("Dosas," 2017, 28)

konpe friend ("Children of the Sea," 1995, 22)

konplo scheme (*Claire of the Sea Light*, 2013, 142)

kounye ya now, yes? (*Claire of the Sea Light*, 2013, 96)

kòt a kòt side by side (*The Farming of Bones*, 1998, 143)

Krag bolt-action rifle (*Brother, I'm Dying*, 2007, 32)

Krik? Krak! traditional call and response (title, 1995, 197)

kriz crisis ("Children of the Sea," 1995, 19)

krizokal phony ("The Port-au-Prince Marriage Special," 2014, 175)

labouyi bannan spicy grated plantain porridge ("Plantains, Please," 1999, 179)

lakou shared courtyard (*After the Dance*, 2002, 33)

lambi conch (*Create Dangerously*, 2010, 6)

langaj secret vodou language ("Hadriana," 2017, ii)

La Vierge Virgin Mary (*The Farming of Bones*, 1998, 250)

leaf doctor herbalist ("The Port-au-Prince Marriage Special," 2014, 172)

Glossary

lechon piglet (*The Farming of Bones*, 1998, 181)

Legba the Vodou spirit who defends humans at the intersection between earth and the afterlife (*The Dew Breaker*, 2004, 230)

Le Monde a French newspaper, "The World" (*The Dew Breaker*, 2004, 195)

Le Nouvelliste a French-language daily newspaper published in Port-au-Prince (*After the Dance*, 2002, 94)

les filles girls (*Untwine*, 2015, 104)

Liautaud Haitian artist George Liautaud (*After the Dance*, 2002, 31)

libéte freedom ("The Missing Peace," 1995, 96)

li menm himself (*Claire of the Sea Light*, 2013, 176)

lingua franca a language shared by communicants (*The Art of Death*, 2017, 14)

li palé vwa mwin he spoke my voice (*Breath, Eyes, Memory*, 1994, 134)

llorada crying ("On the Day of the Dead," 2011, n.p.)

lòt bò dlo another river bank ("The Funeral Singer," 2004, 173)

lòt kote a the other side (*Untwine*, 2015, 6)

lougawou werewolf ("Nineteen Thirty-Seven," 1995, 34)

Lumière light (*The Dew Breaker*, 2004, 184)

lwa/loa spirit (*Claire of the Sea Light*, 2010, 121)

lycée elementary school ("A Wall of Fire Rising," 1995, 45)

maafa Swahili for "great disaster" ("Seven Stories," 2019, 196)

macadam paved (*The Farming of Bones*, 1998, 186)

maché market (*Breath, Eyes, Memory*, 1994, 120)

ma chère my dear ("Water Child," 2004, 53)

Madan Sara vendor (*Breath, Eyes, Memory*, 1994, 177)

madrassa a strictly Islamic religious school (*Create Dangerously*, 2010, 112)

madrigal a late Renaissance song sung with vernacular text ("Night Women," 1995, 74)

magic realism a blending of dream and fantasy with real details ("Hot-Air Balloons," 1996, n.p.)

main droite absente right hand missing (*Brother, I'm Dying*, 2007, 139)

mai sauvage wild May (*After the Dance*, 2002, 87)

maîtresse de la maison mistress of the house (*Breath, Eyes, Memory*, 1994, 196)

malfetè evildoer ("Dosas," 2017, 7)

malpròp dirty (*Breath, Eyes, Memory*, 1994, 217)

mamit container (*Breath, Eyes, Memory*, 1994, 116)

manbo Vodou priestess ("Between the Pool and the Gardenias," 1995, 83)

manzè mademoiselle ("Claire of the Sea Light," 2010, 121)

maquette scale model ("Seven Stories," 2019, 180)

maroon a runaway African slave (*The Farming of Bones*, 1998, 188)

maryaj pou dis marriage for ten [minutes] (*After the Dance*, 2002, 88)

mas o menos more or less (*Untwine*, 2015, 156)

matènèl nursery school (*Claire of the Sea Light*, 2013, 186)

mater dolorosa grieving mother ("Claire of the Sea Light," 2010, 121)

mayi moulen cornmeal porridge ("A Taste of Coffee," 2001, 42)

m'bwè pwa I don't know ("The Funeral Singer," 2004, 171)

mèg thin (*Breath, Eyes, Memory*, 1994, 100)

me gustan I like them (*Untwine*, 2015, 156)

melliza twin (*Untwine*, 2015, 80)

merci thank you (*Breath, Eyes, Memory*, 1994, 228)

merengue Haitian national dance ("Between the Pool and the Gardenias," 1995, 86)

mes belles my beauties (*Breath, Eyes, Memory*, 1994, 5)

mèsi anpil thanks very much (*After the Dance*, 2002, 163)

mèsi mil fwa thanks a thousand times (*Breath, Eyes, Memory*, 1994, 131)

mesye mister ("Claire of the Sea Light," 2010, 121)

métisse mixed culture (*Create Dangerously*, 2010, 68)

military de facto a military regime that overrules democracy (*After the Dance*, 2002, 117)

min my (*Breath, Eyes, Memory*, 1994, 158)

MINUSTAH plis ampil police A United

Glossary

Nations peace mission added more police (*Brother, I'm Dying*, 2007, 171)

mòde soufle blow style (*Brother, I'm Dying*, 2007, 204)

mon pè my father (*The Farming of Bones*, 1998, 269)

moral relativism cultural differences in opinion of right and wrong ("Hot-Air Balloons," 1996, n.p.)

M pa können I don't know ("Night Talkers," 2004, 109)

m'renmen romance (*The Farming of Bones*, 1998, 105)

m'se I am (*The Farming of Bones*, 1998, 171)

msye mister (*Claire of the Sea Light*, 2013, 8)

mujahideen Islamic guerrilla warrior (*Create Dangerously*, 2010, 112)

mulâtresse bicultural, biracial woman (*Breath, Eyes, Memory*, 1994, 52)

mwin me (*Breath, Eyes, Memory*, 1994, 70)

mwin relé I am called (*Breath, Eyes, Memory*, 1994, 98)

Mwin pa kapab enkò I can never again (*Breath, Eyes, Memory*, 1994, 224)

naboría laborer (*Anacaona*, 2005, 47)

naif primitive (*After the Dance*, 2002, 93)

Napoleonic code a patriarchal system of law that diminishes women's rights ("In the Old Days," 2012, 12)

Negro yams Jamaican root vegetables (*Breath, Eyes, Memory*, 1994, 10)

Nietzsche a German philosopher and composer (*Untwine*, 2015, 165)

nigua sand flea (*Anacaona*, 2007, 24)

nitaino Taino nobles (*Anacaona*, 2005, 13)

no mas no more (*The Farming of Bones*, 1998, 134)

non? isn't it? (*Breath, Eyes, Memory*, 1994, 7)

nou la we're here (*Claire of the Sea Light*, 2013, 179)

nouris sickened (*Claire of the Sea Light*, 2013, 162)

nou se moun mòn We are mountain people (*Brother, I'm Dying*, 2007, 35)

nouveau fou the new crazy (*Tent Life*, 2011, 8).

nouvelliste short story writer (*After the Dance*, 2002, 94)

novena prayers offered over nine consecutive days (*The Farming of Bones*, 1998, 167)

nue naked (*Brother, I'm Dying*, 2007, 139)

O bon dye Oh, good god (*Brother, I'm Dying*, 2007, 183)

oslè bones (*The Farming of Bones*, 1998, 43)

ou grangou Are you hungry? ("Without Inspection," 2019, 209)

ou sonje you are bleeding ("The Port-au-Prince Marriage Special," 2014, 169)

Pak Kado Gift Park ("Message to My Daughters," 2017, 205)

pan de muerto bread of death ("On the Day of the Dead," 2011, n.p.)

papa shango a voodoo practitioner (*Breath, Eyes, Memory*, 1994, 160)

parabasis a choral ode summarizing a dramatic theme (*After the Dance*, 2002, 144)

passing watermelons straining (*Breath, Eyes, Memory*, 1994, 100)

pastè pastor (*Claire of the Sea Light*, 2013, 29)

patois common substandard vernacular ("Women Like Us," 1995, 194)

pa vre Isn't it true? (*Breath, Eyes, Memory*, 1994, 94)

pax peace (*Claire of the Sea Light*, 2013, 30)

pè father (*Claire of the Sea Light*, 2013, 21)

pen patat sweet potato bread ("On the Day of the Dead," 2011, n.p.)

pensées thoughts (*Behind the Mountains*, 2002, 2)

Pentecostal a fervid Protestant faith (*Breath, Eyes, Memory*, 1994, 227)

pentimento an art term describing the evidence of an earlier painting beneath a more recent one ("Pamela Phatsimo Sunstrum: New and Recent Paintings," 2020, 107).

père, le premier, senior … fils, deux, junior father, the first, senior … son, two, junior (*Claire of the Sea Light*, 2013, 142)

perlite volcanic glass added to potting soil (*Claire of the Sea Light*, 2013, 190)

pesi parsley (*The Farming of Bones*, 1998, 201)

phenotype a species marked by environmental traits ("Junot Díaz," 2007, 95)

pholourie ball split pea snacks similar to hushpuppies ("Hot-Air Balloons," 1996, n.p.)

pietà a common pose of the Virgin Mary holding her crucified son (*The Art of Death*, 2017, 169)

pinez pine (*The Dew Breaker*, 2004, 224)

placenta a filter between a mother and an unborn fetus (*Brother, I'm Dying*, 2007, 165)

Glossary

pobrecita poor little thing (*The Farming of Bones*, 1998, 23)

poto mitan middle pillar (*Poto Mitan*, film, 2009)

prodwi a cosmetic bleach (*Breath, Eyes, Memory*, 1994, 160)

pwatrinè tubercular (*Claire of the Sea Light*, 2013, 123)

pwofesè professor (*The Farming of Bones*, 1998, 283)

quédate Spanish for "wait" ("Without Inspection," 2019, 212)

que diga amor which says love (*The Farming of Bones*, 1998, 201)

quince fifteenth birthday (*The Farming of Bones*, 1998, 291)

Quisqueya the pre–Columbian name for Hispaniola ("Voices from Hispaniola," 2004, 72)

Rara a pre–Easter Vodou musical festival ("Monkey Tails," 2004, 146)

rasin folkloric rock & roll (*Haiti Noir 2*, 2014, 19)

ras la fini end of the race ("Miras," 2010, 409)

redondo Spanish for "round tomb" (*After the Dance*, 2002, 32)

reken be careful ("Claire of the Sea Light," 2010, 132)

rele call (*Untwine*, 2015, 100)

repas meal (*Brother, I'm Dying*, 2007, 114)

répondeur answering machine ("Water Child," 2004, 58)

rèstavèk a foster child who lives like an in-home servant (*Breath, Eyes, Memory*, 1994, 139)

sabila aloe vera (*The Farming of Bones*, 1998, 125)

Sa k genyen What's wrong? ("Without Inspection," 2019, 215)

sak passé What's happening? (*Breath, Eyes, Memory*, 1994, 51)

salsify an oyster-flavored root vegetable (*The Farming of Bones*, 1998, 11)

salve greetings (*The Farming of Bones*, 1998, 39)

samba poet (*The Farming of Bones*, 1998, 169)

sancocho stew (*The Farming of Bones*, 1998, 58)

santé to your health ("The Gift," 2019, 89)

Santeria a Yoruban religion incorporating Catholic rituals and beliefs (*Breath, Eyes, Memory*, 1994, 206)

schist grainy shale rock ("The Book of the Dead," 2004, 13)

se it's ("Water Child," 2004, 66)

sea hearts sea bean pods (*Claire of the Sea Light*, 2013, 158)

second line parade volunteer dancers following a procession (*Untwine*, 2015, 119)

sè m he's mine ("Dosas," 2017, 6)

seren drizzle (*Create Dangerously*, 2010, 81)

se sa that's it (*Untwine*, 2015, 155)

se vre It's true. ("No Greater Shame," 2003, 170)

sezi startled ("Water Child," 2004, 55)

shawabti funerary figurine ("The Book of the Dead," 2004, 13)

Shepard Fairey American graphic artist famous for painting heavily shadowed faces of celebrities (*Untwine*, 2015, 117)

sirèt candy (*After the Dance*, 2002, 129)

soka calypso music (*Breath, Eyes, Memory*, 1994, 94)

sou de chèz completely (*Claire of the Sea Light*, 2013, 52)

speakeasy illegal liquor store (*Claire of the Sea Light*, 2013, 27)

swa dizan allegation ("In the Old Days," 2012, 358)

syèl heaven ("A Voice from Heaven," 2015, 264)

tableau vivant a silent scenario composed of living actors ("In the Old Days," 2019, 46)

tafia distilled molasses (*Breath, Eyes, Memory*, 1994, 119)

talking drum a two-headed column shaped like an hourglass and played with a curved stick (*Breath, Eyes, Memory*, 1994, 232)

tandé listen (*Breath, Eyes, Memory*, 1994, 152)

tap tap common transportation (*Breath, Eyes, Memory*, 1994, 32)

tcha tcha mimosa tree (*Breath, Eyes, Memory*, 1994, 109)

teledyòl grapevine (*Claire of the Sea Light*, 2013, 124)

t'es en retard you're late (*Untwine*, 2015, 69)

tèt koupe head cut off ("Caroline's Wedding," 1995, 155)

Ti Alice Little Alice (*Breath, Eyes, Memory*, 1994, 153)

ti lezanj cherub ("On the Day of the Dead," 2011, n.p.)

Ti Mache little market ("Sunrise, Sunset," 2019, 142)

ti moun little people (*Brother, I'm Dying*, 2007, 240)

tim tim riddles (*Breath, Eyes, Memory*, 1994, 123)

tintin crap (*Breath, Eyes, Memory*, 1994, 217)

toa female head of a matrilineage (*Anacoana*, 2007, 34)

tololo a celebratory chant (*Breath, Eyes, Memory*, 1994, 158)

Tonton Macoute vicious Haitian paramilitary (*Breath, Eyes, Memory*, 1994, 97)

touché you are right ("Hot-Air Balloons," 2019, 123)

très very (*Breath, Eyes, Memory*, 1994, 38)

trese riban braided ribbon (*After the Dance*, 2002, 87)

trompe d'oeils optical illusions ("In the Old Days," 2012, 356)

tulle a thin, gauzy dress fabric ("Without Inspection," 2019, 214)

uzi submachine gun (*Brother, I'm Dying*, 2007, 147)

Valenciennes lace eighteenth-century bobbin lace from Belgium and France (*The Farming of Bones*, 1998, 90)

vertigo dizziness (*The Farming of Bones*, 1998, 8)

vetiver an herbal fragrance like citronella ("A Taste of Coffee," 2001, 40)

vini come (*Brother, I'm Dying*, 2007, 85)

Virgencita Little Virgin Mary (*The Farming of Bones*, 1998, 8)

visage mutilée mutilated face (*Brother, I'm Dying*, 2007, 139)

wanga trance music, costumes, masking, and circle dance based on Vodou sorcery ("Children of the Sea," 1995, 6)

washi Japanese paper made from mulberry bark (*Untwine*, 2015, 112)

wi yes ("Dosas," 2017, 28)

wonn round (*Claire of the Sea Light*, 2013, 28)

zafra seasonal harvest (*The Farming of Bones*, 1998, 53)

Zemi a deity or ancestral spirit housed in a Taino sculpture or amulet (*Anacaona*, 2007, 26)

zenglendo glass shards (*Create Dangerously*, 2010, 78)

zóréy ears ("Ghosts," 2008, 111)

zumba exercise timed to the rhythm of Latin American music (*Untwine*, 2015, 115)

Appendix A:
Aphorisms in Danticat's Writing

Alone we are weak, together we are a flood. ("The Missing Peace," 1995, 101)

As long as you're breathing you can be hurt. ("Dosas," 2019, 38)

Blood calls blood. ("Night Talkers," 2004, 112)

A closed mouth doesn't catch flies. (*The Dew Breaker*, 2004, 197)

Crabs don't make papayas. (*Breath, Eyes, Memory*, 1994, 28)

Freedom is a passing thing. (*The Farming of Bones*, 1998, 210)

Home is not always a place you have trouble leaving. ("Ghosts," 2008, 211)

Hope is like a transient treasure that must be discovered again and again. (*Walking on Fire*, 2001, x)

How can some people not fully understand their ability to shatter hearts? (*Claire of the Sea Light*, 2013, 192)

Isn't death always solitary? (*Brother, I'm Dying*, 2007, 167)

It's harder for trouble to find you under your bed. ("Monkey Tails," 2004, 141)

It's so easy to love somebody ... when there's nothing else around. ("Between the Pond and the Gardenias," 1995, 84)

Life is never lost, another one always comes up to replace the last. ("The Book of Miracles," 2001, 456)

Love is only pleasure; honor is duty. (*The Farming of Bones*, 1998, 275)

L'union fait la force (Unity makes strength). (*The Farming of Bones*, 1998, 211)

Misery is living in a place that everyone calls a slum but you call home. (*After the Dance*, 2002, 58)

Misery won't touch you gentle. It always leaves its thumbprints. (*The Farming of Bones*, 1998, 222)

No story is ever complete. ("Seven Stories," 2019, 195)

Only dogs like bones. ("New York Day Women," 2016, 131)

Our stories are the bastard children of everything that we have ever experienced and read. (*Create Dangerously*, 2010, 62)

People with means can make the less fortunate feel special by putting them to work. ("Monkey Tails," 2004, 147–148)

Sisters before dudes. (*Untwine*, 2015, 77)

Sometimes you take detours to get where you need to go. ("Dosas," 2019, 37)

There are loves that outlive lovers. ("Without Inspection," 2019, 219)

Those who carry the scars must remember. ("The Book of the Dead," 1999, 194)

Thought servants never rule, rulers must serve. (*Anacaona*, 2007, 39)

We must graze where we are tied. (*Breath, Eyes, Memory*, 1994, 136)

When you're thirsty,... nothing ever tastes like the first drop. (*The Farming of Bones*, 1998, 183)

With patience, you can see the navel of an ant. ("Caroline's Wedding," 1995, 152)

Words have wings. Words have feet. Let the words bring wings to your feet. ("Does Your Face Light Up?," *Kweli Journal,* 2016)

You are who you love. (*Claire of the Sea Light*, 2013, 198)

You cannot chew before you have teeth. (*Behind the Mountains*, 2002, 3)

Appendix B: Historical References

1550 BCE	The Egyptian *Book of the Dead* enabled individuals to traverse the dangerous underworld.
1200 BCE	The Arawak, a branch of the Taino language group, migrated from South America to Haiti.
37 CE	The emperor Caligula began making a public display of love for his sister, Julia Drusilla.
December 5, 1492	Christopher Columbus became the first European to reach Haiti, named Hispaniola.
December 25, 1492	After the *Santa Maria* sank off Marién, Hispaniola, Chief Guacanagarí appeased the conquistadors with gifts.
August 15, 1493	Christopher Columbus established La Navidad settlement on Hispaniola's north central coast with timbers from the *Santa Maria* and forced the Arawak to mine gold in the mountains.
November 19, 1493	From Guadalupe, Columbus and explorer Alonso de Ojeda returned to La Navidad with 1,700 Spaniards, who captured Caonabó and Manicaotex for exhibition to the Spanish monarchs, Isabella I of Castile and Ferdinand II of Aragon.
1494	After failing at a nighttime raid on the Spaniards, Caonabó and Manicaotex died on a prison ship at sea.
August 5, 1496	Spanish investor Bartholomew, younger sibling of Christopher Columbus, established Santo Domingo, the first European settlement in the Western Hemisphere.
January 1497	Bartholomew Columbus reached Xaragua in southwestern Hispaniola.
1503	The Spanish governor Nicolas de Ovando ordered the hanging of Anacaona, the Taino who replaced her brother Behechio as cacique of Xaragua in southwestern Hispaniola.
1517	To improve efficiency, Hispanics replaced Taino mine slaves with the first African imports.
1536	French town builder Captain Jacques de Melo gave his name to Jacmel.
1541	Milanese painter Girolamo Benzoni began exploring the Caribbean and composing a history of the New World.
1625	French pirates controlled marine use of the Island of Tortuga.
September 1633	French planters imported African slaves to Haitian sugar and tobacco plantations.
September 20, 1697	By treaty, the French took control of western Hispaniola and named it Saint-Domingue.
1698	Jacmel became the capital of the French colony Saint-Domingue.
1728	Spanish settlers of Saint-Domingue killed 30 French pirates rustling cattle at the Massacre River.
February 1775	Haitians fought in the American Revolution.
September 16, 1779	Henri Christophe, Haiti's only monarch and a subsequent president, fought at the Siege of Savannah, Georgia, among 4,000 French troops and Polish cavalry officer Casimir Pulaski.

Appendix B: Historical References

April 26, 1785	Famed naturalist Jean James Audubon was born in Les Cayes, Haiti.
1790	African immigrant Jean Baptiste Point du Sable and his Native American wife Kitiwaha founded Chicago.
August 7, 1791	Pierre Pinchinat led a mulatto movement demanding equal rights for biracial islanders.
August 14, 1791	Boukman Dutty launched the Haitian revolution at a Bois Caiman Vodou sacrifice of a pig to Ogoun, the war god.
December 1791	François Toussaint L'Ouverture negotiated with the French for Haitian lives.
January 1, 1801	On Haitian Independence Day, Toussaint-L'Ouverture seized the republic of Haiti and freed slaves.
March 4–24, 1802	Female combat soldier Marie-Jeanne Lamartiniere fought in the Battle of Crête-à-Pierrot in the Artibonite valley of Haiti.
May 22, 1802	Boarding the frigate *Creole* for exile in France, Toussaint-L'Ouverture delivered an uplifting salute to Haitian liberty.
November 8, 1802	Pauline Bonaparte departed for Paris from Saint-Domingue.
March 1803	Naturalist Jean James Audubon immigrated from Haiti to New York City.
January 1, 1804	Under Jean Jacques Dessalines, Haiti led the Caribbean's first colony to independence and defeated Europe's largest invasion force.
January 21, 1804	Louis Boisrond-Tonnerre, Dessalines's secretary, composed the Haitian Declaration of Independence.
October, 1804	Dessalines built Fort Ogé, named for Vincent Ogé, a martyr to human rights for mulattos.
1805	The Haitian citadel, a fifteen-year project of Henri Christophe, commanded a mountaintop vantage point.
October 17, 1806	Black islanders seized northern Haiti, leaving the south to mulattos, while assassins killed Dessalines outside Port-au-Prince.
March 9, 1807	Militia commander Alexandre Sabès Pétion assumed Haiti's first presidency.
February 12, 1809	Abraham Lincoln was born in Hodgenville, Kentucky.
April 19, 1810	Caracas-born statesman Simon Bolivar liberated Venezuela from the Spanish.
December 15, 1815	Simon Bolivar stayed six months in Haiti during his battle against Spanish colonialism.
1816	Haiti's oldest school, Lycée Pétion in Port-au-Prince, carried the name of Alexandre Sabès Pétion.
1818	English entrepreneur Hannibal Price brought the Watt steam engine to Haiti, but did not use it.
February 9, 1822	The Dominican Republic split from Haiti after the Haitian army invaded, freed slaves, and promoted settlement by U.S. blacks.
June 28, 1841	Théophile Gautier's romantic ghost story *Giselle* debuted at the Paris Opera Ballet.
February 27, 1844	The Dominican Republic, led by Pablo Duarte, proclaimed independence from Haiti.
July 12, 1862	President Abraham Lincoln chose Benjamin F. Whidden as the first U.S. ambassador to Haiti.
April 23, 1876	Politician Pierre Boisrand-Canal began a provisional presidency of Haiti.
June 26, 1889	President Benjamin Harrison named orator Frederick Douglass as ambassador to Haiti and charge d'affairs for Santo Domingo.
January 2, 1893	Haitian National Day of Independence and Heroes coincided with the dedication of the Haitian Pavilion.
Summer 1895	Bolognese electrical engineer Guglielmo Marconi invented wireless radio telegraphy.
November 25, 1897	U.S. Marines arrived in Puerto Rico during the Spanish-American War.
July 1, 1898	The Battle of El Caney, Cuba, cost 85 percent of Cuban and Spanish lives because of the effective use of a ten-barrel Gatling gun. The Battle of San Juan Hill gave the U.S. a pyrrhic victory costing 258 lives.

238 Appendix B: Historical References

April 1, 1907	Publisher Clement Magloire founded *Le Matin* (morning), Haiti's newspaper.
June 25, 1910	Igor Stravinsky composed *The Firebird* as music for a Paris ballet.
1912	Dominican sugar producers restricted the number of blacks entering the country as cheap mill labor.
July 27, 1915	Police Chief Charles Oscar Etienne slaughtered 200 political prisoners in Port-au-Prince.
July 28, 1915	President Woodrow Wilson ordered the Yanki occupation, a U.S. Marine incursion in Haiti.
1925	Jacmel became the first Caribbean city to install electricity.
1928	Builders completed Notre Dame de l'Assomption Cathedral in Port-au-Prince.
December 6, 1929	U.S. Marines killed twelve Haitians during the Cayes massacre.
September 3, 1930	San Zenon, a tropical cyclone, killed 8,000 Santo Domingans.
1932	Theologian and ethicist Reinhold Niebuhr composed the one-sentence serenity prayer.
June 15, 1933	In Chicago, Florence Beatrice Price debuted a symphony, the first by a black female composer.
August 1, 1934	U.S. occupation forces left Haiti.
March 9, 1936	The U.S. supervised the drawing of a boundary between Haiti and the Dominican Republic.
July 17, 1936	The Spanish Civil War began when General Francisco Franco launched a coup at Melilla in Spanish Morocco.
September 18, 1936	Women served in the International Brigades, a Communist force during the Spanish Civil War.
October 1, 1937	Spanish Republican forces captured and destroyed Belchite south of the Pyrenees Mountains in Zaragoza, Spain.
October 2–8, 1937	Dominican Guardia under Rafael Trujillo massacred some 30,000 Haitian cane workers fleeing across the Massacre River and drowned 17,000 more at Montecristi, Dominican Republic. Haitian president Sténio Vincent, a proponent of Trujillo, made no outcry.
August 16, 1946	Haitians elected Léon Dumarsais Estimé as president.
January 1, 1947	Newspaperman Daniel Fignolé assembled the Haitian Peasant Worker Movement.
July 26, 1951	Disney's film version of *Alice in Wonderland* opened in London.
February 22, 1954	Paul Magloire appeared on a *Time* magazine cover displaying his Haitian military uniform.
December 12, 1956	President Paul Magloire abandoned Haiti.
May 25, 1957	Daniel Fignolé replaced Magloire as president.
October 22, 1957	After deposing President Daniel Fignole and exiling opponent Louis Déjoie to Cuba, Haitians named François "Papa Doc" Duvalier president.
July 29, 1958	François "Papa Doc" Duvalier's troops killed eight rebels, including investigative radio reporter Philippe Dominique, an exile to Miami.
October 2, 1958	Guinea became Africa's first French colony to gain freedom.
April 22, 1961	The Tonton Macoute captured Haitian novelist Jacques Stephen Alexis for torture and imprisonment, from which he never returned.
May 30, 1961	Assassins shot Rafael Trujillo outside Santiago, Dominican Republic.
October 2, 1963	Hurricane Flora struck Haiti with a Category 4 storm and killed 5,000 in flooding and mudslides.
June 14, 1964	François "Papa Doc" Duvalier declared himself Haiti's president for life.
November 12, 1964	Rebels Marcel Numa and Louis Drouin died under a firing squad at the order of François Duvalier.
1965	U.S. Marines invaded Santo Domingo.
April 22, 1971	After his father's death, nineteen-year-old Jean-Claude "Baby Doc" Duvalier became president.
1978	The U.S. Food and Drug Administration ordered Haitian pigs killed to halt African swine fever.

Appendix B: Historical References 239

November 28, 1980	The election of Ronald Reagan emboldened Jean-Claude Duvalier to exile Jean Dominique by ordering him killed on sight.
1983	Jean-Claude Duvalier protected a 7,400-acre pine forest above Jacmel. Dominican president Joaquin Balaguer warned of Haitian intent to populate the island with black citizens.
May 18, 1985	Tonton Macoutes marched on the national palace grounds.
February 7, 1986	After Haitians ousted Baby Doc Duvalier to exile in France, citizens of Boston, Miami, and New York celebrated his exit with street parades. General Henri Namphy governed for two years.
March 5, 1986	Jean Dominique and his wife, Michèle Montas, returned to Haiti from exile in Venezuela.
November 29, 1987	Grenades and bullets interrupted Haiti's elections and struck radio stations.
1988	René Depestre immortalized the zombie tale of Hadriana Siloed in the surreal novel *Hadriana in All My Dreams*.
February 7, 1988	Leslie Manigat became president of Haiti.
June 20, 1988	General Henri Namphy thrust Manigat from office.
September 17, 1988	General Prosper Avril ousted General Namphy.
April 17, 1989	Former Tonton Macoutes challenged Prosper Avril in a failed coup. Marie Micheline died in a Port-au-Prince shootout.
March 10, 1990	General Prosper Avril resigned the Haitian presidency.
January 17, 1991	Coalition bombardment until March 1 drove Iraqi insurgents from Kuwait.
February 7, 1991	Jean-Bertrand Aristide, a Catholic priest, became Haiti's first democratically elected president.
September 29, 1991	General Raoul Cédras led a coup that banished Aristide to Caracas, Venezuela, and closed the radio station of Jean Dominique and wife Michèle Montas, who fled to New York.
June 1993	Emmanuel "Toto" Constant organized a military death squad in Haiti.
June 15, 1993	Jean-Bertrand Aristide returned from Caracas to Haiti's presidency.
October 16, 1993	A political militia attacked Alèrte Bélance, a rice merchant in Port-au-Prince, and amputated her ear, fingers, forearm, and tongue.
October 12, 1994	Accompanied by 20,000 U.S. soldiers, Jean Bertrand Aristide repatriated from exile in Venezuela and Washington.
March 1995	Torturer Emmanuel "Toto" Constant sought asylum in Queens, New York.
March 31, 1995	The U.S. began withdrawing troops from Haiti, leaving U.N. soldiers in place.
August 9, 1997	Brooklyn police brutalized and sodomized Haitian-American security guard Abner Louima.
February 4, 1999	Four Bronx policemen shot and killed Amadou Diallo, an unarmed Guinean immigrant at Wheeler Avenue three blocks from the Bronx River.
January 12, 2000	Jacmel assassins murdered Fernand Mellier and his eighteen-year-old daughter Céline as well as their driver, Aspril Aubin.
March 16, 2000	New Yorkers raised issues of racism in the police shooting death of Patrick Dorismond at the corner of Eighth Avenue and West 37th Street in midtown Manhattan.
May 3, 2000	At Petionville in south central Port-au-Prince, Michèle Montas reopened Radio Haiti-Inter, the nation's first independent and first Creole language station.
April 3, 2000	Outside Fort Dimanche Prison, an assassin shot and killed investigative reporter and activist Jean Léopold Dominique, owner of Radio Haiti-Inter and subject of a documentary co-produced by Edwidge Danticat and Jonathan Demme.
November 30, 2000	Jean-Bertrand Aristide won the popular election for Haiti's presidency.
December 9, 2000	George W. Bush defeated Al Gore for the U.S. presidency after the Supreme Court overruled a Florida court decision.
January 18, 2001	At the University of Virginia, President Bill Clinton delivered his farewell address.

240 Appendix B: Historical References

January 20, 2001	At his Washington, D.C., inauguration, President George W. Bush made a speech about American ideals.
February 4, 2001	After René Garcia Préval left office, Jean-Bertrand Aristide began his last presidency of Haiti.
September 11, 2001	The terrorist attack on 9/11 at the World Trade Center in Manhattan caused immigrants to embrace their American citizenship.
December 25, 2002	Outside Port-au-Prince, a shooter murdered Michèle Montas's bodyguard, Maxime Séide at the Dominique home in Petionville.
March 2003	Before entering exile in New York, Michèle Montas closed Radio Haiti.
May 3, 2004	The documentary *The Agronomist* debuted at the United Nations headquarters in New York City.
February 28, 2004	Jean-Bertrand Aristide flew by American plane to the Central African Republic before settling in South Africa.
September 13, 2004	Tropical storm Jeanne struck Gonaïves, Haiti, killing 5,000 and uprooting 250,000.
September 8, 2006	The persecution of Haitian security guard Abner Louima by New York police aroused racial animosities at police headquarters.
Late October 2007	A research report tied the spread of AIDS to a migrant from Haiti.
January 12, 2010	An earthquake overwhelmed Haiti, killing 20,000 and destroying the Port-au-Prince cathedral. Jacmel became a UNESCO Heritage Site.
May 2010	The Associated Press announced the discovery of copper, gold, and silver in the Haitian hills.
September 2013	The Dominican Republic expelled 400,000 residents of Haitian ancestry and voided their citizenship.
September 18, 2017	Hurricane Maria devastated Dominica.

SOURCE

Danticat, Edwidge. *Tent Life: Haiti*. Brooklyn: Umbrage, 2011, 10–11.

Appendix C: A Guide to Places

Alegría a fictional section of central Dominican Republic known for sugar production on prosperous plantations staffed by black Haitians whom dictator Rafael Trujillo targets for extermination (*The Farming of Bones*, 1998, 16).

Beauséjour a high getaway southwest of Port-au-Prince in the Léogâne Mountains, the home of Joseph Nozius Dantica and great aunt Ilyana, whom Edwidge visited in summer 1999 ("Edwidge Danticat on the Luxury of Creating Art," 2020, PRS.org).

Bel Air a hilly slum in south central Port-au-Prince and center of gang warfare, random crime, and the church missions of Uncle Joseph Nozius and Aunt Denise Dantica ("Ghosts," 2008, 108).

Bois Caiman at Alligator Woods in Morne Rouge, southwest of Cap Haïtien, Boukman Dutty, a Vodou priest, and biracial priestess Cécile Fatiman presided over a nighttime oath ceremony and pig sacrifice to Ogoun on August 13–14, 1791 (*Krik? Krak!*, 1995, 44). The week-long effort launched the Haitian Revolution, leveled 1,800 plantations, and killed 1,000 slave owners.

Cap, The, a commune rich in history. Cap-Haïtien headed Saint-Domingue's governmental and artistic centers from 1503 until 1770, when Port-au-Prince became the new capital. The north-coastal city suffered repeated fires. (*The Farming of* Bones, 1998, 135).

Cap Haïtien *SEE* The Cap.

Carrefour Dufort a crossroads and bus connection 20 miles west of Port-au-Prince that bears the remains of the Hotel de la Place, a 30-acre manor featuring colonial French architecture. The town suffered street violence during 2001 protests and damage and loss of life from the January 12, 2010, earthquake (*Everything Inside,* 2019, 186).

Casernes Dessalines Barracks an army residence for Haitian soldiers built in Port-au-Prince in 1913, the barracks advanced from detention center to interrogation site from February 1986–April 1989, when guards subdued up to a dozen manacled prisoners daily with pepper spray, injections, and beatings with a wet towel (*The Dew Breaker*, 2004, 174).

Citadelle Laferrière a fortress that the revolutionary Henri Christophe constructed in 1820 via press gang on the Bonnet à l'Evèque, a peak in Nord, Haiti, to ward off invaders arriving via the Atlantic Ocean ("The Port-au-Prince Marriage Special," 2019, 67).

Cité Pendue a gang-ridden slum eight miles north of Ville Rose, a Haitian beach famous for tourism (*Claire of the Sea Light,* 2013, 63).

Dajabón a mountainous market town in the Dominican Republic above the banks of the Massacre River, a site of mass murder by Generalissimo Rafael Trujillo's Guardia in October 1937 (*The Farming of Bones,* 1998, 163).

Fort Dimanche a French colonial prison at La Saline in Port-au-Prince. During the Duvalier regime, the decrepit facility earned notoriety as Fort Death, the holding pen for victims of the Tonton Macoute, who tortured and murdered Haitians living in cramped cells ("Children of the Sea," 1996, 6).

Fort Ogé built in 1804 by Jean-Jacques Dessalines in the beach town of Jacmel, the protective battlements warded off French invaders for 200 years under the name of

242   Appendix C: A Guide to Places

Vincent Ogé, an Afro-French rebel executed on the wheel at The Cap on February 6, 1791 (*After the Dance*, 2002, 45).

Ginen a dual identity: Guinea or the Congo in West Africa and a surreal destination in the afterlife ("Children of the Sea," 1996, 12).

Gonaïves a Taino seaside capital established in 1422 at Artibonite in northwestern Haiti, the location of the January 1, 1804, declaration of independence from France by Jean-Jacques Dessalines ("The Port-au-Prince Marriage Special," 2019, 67).

Guanajuato a famed cathedral city in south central Mexico east of Guadalajara known for impassable alleys and stairs and underground avenues and plazas (*Untwine*, 2015, 46).

Jacmel the seaside locale of the Lenten Carnival parade, which earned the town the name "Riviera of Haiti" ("The Port-au-Prince Marriage Special," 2019, 67).

Jérémie a seaside town in far western Haiti and the home of rebels Marcel Numa and Louis Drouin, whom François "Papa Doc" Duvalier executed on November 12, 1964 (*Create Dangerously*, 2010, 1).

Krome a detention center in Miami, Florida, where U.S. Homeland Security completes the removal of immigrants by U.S. Immigration and Customs Enforcement and adjudication of each illegal border breach ("Without Inspection," 2019, 204).

La Romana a coastal getaway in southeastern Dominican Republic where soldiers forced Haitians off cliffs in the October 1937 genocide ordered by Generalissimo Rafael Trujillo (*The Farming of Bones*, 1998, 173).

Latibonit one of Haiti's ten departments, a rice-rich state in the north central area called "Artibonite" in English ("Without Inspection," 2019, 213, 215).

Léogâne a coastal mountain district 19 miles southwest of Port-au-Prince and home of the mythic Taino ruler Anacaona, whom conquistadors hanged in 1503. The author recast the town as Ville Rose and described cane as its prime commodity ("Haiti Faces Difficult Questions Ten Years after a Devastating Earthquake," 2020, n.p.).

Les Cayes the birthplace of John James Audubon in southwest Haiti, a significant harbor and departure point for coffee, cane, vetiver, timber, and bananas ("The Long Legacy of Occupation in Haiti," 2015, n.p.).

Marién a northwestern chiefdom from Taino times governed by a cacique until Spanish conquistadors under Genoan navigator Christopher Columbus landed on December 5, 1492. As Spanish investors migrated to more lucrative gold and silver lodes in Central and South America, in the 1520s, they left the colony to French, English, and Dutch pirates (*Anacaona*, 2005, 5).

Massacre River an historic site of the Hispanic murder of French pirates and the dividing line between Haiti and the Dominican Republic, where Generalissimo Rafael Trujillo orchestrated the genocide of black Haitian plantation workers in October 1937 (*The Farming of Bones*, 1998, 91).

Miami Shores north of Miami, Florida, the elite bedroom community known as the "American Mediterranean," features plazas, hotels, and verdure intended to lure tourists and full or part-time whites such as Gaspard, the patient in "Dosas" (*Everything Inside*, 2019, 5).

MUPANAH (the Musée du Panthéon National Haïtien) a landmark culture and history center on Avenue de la République in Port-au-Prince featuring Taino, Spanish, and French contributors alongside relics of slavery and the *Santa Maria*, Christopher Columbus's flagship ("The Port-au-Prince Marriage Special," 2019, *77*).

Palais Sans Souci residence at Milot near Cap Haïtien on the north shores of the island, where, in 1810, the builder, President Henri Christophe, named it "worry-free palace" (*The Farming of Bones*, 1998, 276).

Pont Larnage the site of the ambush that killed Emperor Jean-Jacques Dessalines, Haiti's founding father, on October 27, 1806, north of Port-au-Prince, later named Pont-Rouge (Red Bridge).

Port-au-Prince a hub of history in west central Haiti for its cathedrals, national cemetery, commerce, and Casernes Prison and for the street protests preceding Jean-Bertrand Aristide's restoration to the presidency on February 4, 2001 (*Claire of the Sea Light*, 2014, 23).

Port-de-Paix a coastal port in northwestern Haiti from which Arnold departs by raft

Appendix C: A Guide to Places

for Miami ("Without Inspection," 2019, 205).

Saint-Marc a coastal town northwest of Port-au-Prince, Haiti, the birthplace of Jean Baptiste Point du Sable, founder of Chicago (*Eight Days*, 2010, n.p.).

St. Thérèse of Avila Church a Catholic landmark six blocks from Brooklyn's Prospect park, the structure took shape in 1926 to serve a growing Haitian-American population around Sterling Place with counsel and scripture in French (*The Dew Breaker*, 2004, 75).

San Juan a major city of the Dominican Republic on the south-central region of Hispaniola and the location of the Taino village of Niti, Maguana, the home of newlyweds Anacaona and Caonabó (*Anacaona*, 2005, 137).

Santiago the second largest city in the northwest of Dominican Republic profits from the export of cigars, rum, and fabrics, it was originally called Santiago de los Caballeros (Santiago of the Knights), a reference to settlers who branched out from La Isabela, North America's first Hispanic town (*The Farming of Bones*, 1998, 210).

Titanyen sparsely populated town north of Port-au-Prince, site of the Valley of death— the historic location of political killings and of mass graves for 2010 earthquake victims (*Create Dangerously*, 2010, 77).

Turks and Caicos forty islands of an archipelago due north of Port-de-Paix, Haiti, at the western end of the Bahamas chain (*Everything Inside*, 2019, 207).

Ville Rose a Haitian city near Les Cayes on the southwestern extreme twenty miles south of Port-au-Prince on an unpredictable shore (*Claire of the Sea Light*, 2013, 46).

Appendix D: A Guide to Writing, Art and Research Topics

1. Describe the effectiveness of the following rhetorical and linguistic devices:

- *personification* nature … is as marvelous a carver as she is a destroyer (*Anacaona*)
- *simile* to be strong as mountains (*Breath, Eyes, Memory*)
- *apostrophe* "Latibonit O" ("Without Inspection")
- *alliteration* milk mother (*Claire of the Sea Light*)
- *epic hero* We have all come to think of him as heroically invincible (*Create Dangerously*)
- *cliché* "In the Old Days" (*Everything Inside*)
- *noir* the tone and atmosphere of the story "Please Translate"
- *magical realism* a giant blue-green tongue (*Claire of the Sea Light*)
- *creole* ankouraje (have courage) (*After the Dance*)
- *onomatopoeia* little frogs cry out "*toa, toa*" (*Anacaona*)
- *parallelism* Flabbergast me. Delight me. Amaze me. (*Untwine*)
- *history* a pudgy thirty-four-year-old man ("Monkey Tails")
- *hypothetical question* Was something wrong? (*Brother, I'm Dying*)
- *paradox* How can an amnesiac remember? (*Create Dangerously*)
- *juxtaposition* Her daughter chose that exact moment to mumble

something to her father ("The Book of Miracles")
- *sibilance* "Seeing Things Simply" (*Krik? Krak!*)
- *juvenile overstatement* in the entire country, in the entire world (*Eight Days*)
- *fantasy* an elixir against fading memories, a panacea to evoke images of spaces lost to us ("A Taste of Coffee")
- *rhyme* Not Jean Do! (*Create Dangerously*)
- *run-on* I mean, coming out of New York … ("Night Talkers")
- *romanticism* our little dwarf star who will soon join us (*Anacaona*)
- *historical allusion* Medgar Evers College ("Seven")
- *biblical allusion* Eight Days (title)
- *repetition* the near father of her nearly born child ("Water Child")
- *allusion* Welcome to Roach Motel ("No Greater Shame")
- *hyperbole* as conspicuous as a palm tree on Mars (*After the Dance*)
- *details* swinging batons and nightsticks (*After the Dance*)
- *humor* Four scones and seven tears ago ("The Funeral Singer")
- *pun* "The Missing Peace" (*Krik? Krak!*)
- *rhetorical question* What will we do with *our* beast? ("The Dew Breaker")

Appendix D: A Guide to Writing, Art and Research Topics

- *euphemism* born out of the petals of roses (*Breath, Eyes, Memory*)
- *metaphor The Farming of Bones* (title)
- *neologism* Anacaonabó (*Anacaona*)
- *generalization* A child out of wedlock always looks like its father. (*Breath, Eyes, Memory*)

2. Account for the significance of two secondary characters and the impact on plot and theme, especially these:

> Grandmè Ife
> Eric Abrahams
> Madame Augustin
> Victorio Pico
> Romain
> Marc
> Madam Roger
> Josette
> Jackie Kennedy
> Ti Fanm
> Marjorie Voltaire
> Christophe
> Ronald Mevs
> Marie Micheline
> court judge
> Kongo
> Oscar
> Jean Dominique
> Mayor Albert Vincent
> Paris

How do these characters influence significant action? emotions? memories? dialogue? Which secondary cast member would you omit? What role would you create for yourself as a secondary character in Haiti, New York, Dominican Republic, or Miami?

3. Contrast the settings and sources of melodrama, satire, or humor in two of these situations:

> burning cane fields
> avoiding Papi on his visit to Haiti
> dyeing hair copper
> receiving a son's decapitated head
> a negative confession

> reading labels in a mailbox
> touring Christmas lights
> hiding under a cot amid dust balls
> playing telephone with cans
> attending carnival in Salvador de Bahia
> listening to a taped story
> letting Justine win the bike race
> washing corpses
> spreading Isabelle's ashes

Which scenes provide visual effects for film or stage? Which suit oral story-telling, radio, mural, anime, cartooning, or shadow puppets?

4. Characterize the importance of setting to the historical and socio-economic drama in these scenes:

> working in a car wash
> murders on the Dominican border with Haiti
> looking for the Coast Guard
> a funeral for drowned refugees
> crowds punishing Tonton Macoutes
> taping a memoir for an unborn son
> cooking on three stones
> photographing graveyards
> training amid pepper smoke
> recording notes on corpses
> promoting the Ciné Club
> climbing Anthère Lighthouse

5. Compose an annotated map featuring these landmarks and settings in Edwidge's writings:

> Beauséjour
> Port-au-Prince
> Krome center
> Miami
> Jacmel
> Brooklyn
> Lakeland
> Carnival
> Prospect Park
> Far Rockaway
> St. Thérèse

Appendix D: A Guide to Writing, Art and Research Topics

Champs de Mars
Curaçao
Manhattan
Salvador de Bahia
Carrefour
Seguin
Xaragua
Cap Haïtien
Unknown Maroon
Titanyen
Port-de-Paix
Tampa
Brooklyn Museum

List locations of fun and relaxation on free days and holidays in New York, Florida, or Haiti.

6. Account for the significance of three of the following terms to the action of Edwidge's works:

ka
peasant
Boukman
matriarchy
magic realism
potluck
notebook
gourde
Lent
Tonton Macoute
refugee
tap station
tap tap
petroglyph
poverty Olympics
zombie
Hadriana
pine forest
surreal
wind chime voice
cacique
Carib
exile
tremor
prosthetic arm
martyr
diaspora

revenen
Krome
dew breaker

7. Locate three examples of destinations for visits and journeys as symbols of ambition, escape, loyalty, worship, and patriotism, particularly these:

car service
Pentecostal church
Christmas mass
banyan tree
Lakeland
Far Rockaway
Westchester
mausoleum
Duvalier Airport
La Sensation Hotel
GED class
court
Massacre River
pine forest
media interview
Lakeland

8. Debate the wisdom of two of the following choices and explain the characters' motivation:

driving a gypsy cab
settling among fellow Haitian-
    Americans
broadcasting on radio
marrying a Bahamian
sculpting mahogany
eating alone in the hospital cafeteria
taping an interview
throwing coins from a shiny black
    car
looking for Regulus
painting Jackie Kennedy
visiting Valencia Duarte
joining a *wonn* on the beach

9. Discuss the role of history in two of Edwidge's scenarios. Include background facts about these:

Appendix D: A Guide to Writing, Art and Research Topics 247

arrival of Christopher Columbus
Rafael Trujillo's Haitian genocide
Sor Rose
Boukman Dutty
ouster of Baby Doc Duvalier
Jacmel's French colonial section
a postponed election
Sgt. Sam Makanani
Carib attacks on Taino
detaining immigrant parents
playing near the National Palace
coastal pollution and erosion

10. Discuss the pervasive motif of women's accomplishments in three of Edwidge's works, especially these:

delivering a baby in a boat
stitching on sequins
escaping Pico
operating a beauty salon
Estina's rescue of Dany from fire
writing for a Haitian newspaper
selling art in a gallery
treating a facial wound
locating a lost daughter
telling about the death angel
painting with toenail polish
rescuing a child from drowning or
    kidnap

How do elderly or weak characters make themselves indispensable? Explain why the author values collaboration as well as self-liberation or self-rescue from poverty, illness, and danger.

11. Survey the rewards and recriminations of revering Vodou loas in two of Edwidge characters. Consider these:

sharing Erzulie's statue with sexual
    trauma survivors
donating coins to Agwé
parading and dancing to Para
    bands
luring Lasìren with a comb, mirror,
    and conch shell
dressing like Baron Samedi

a bride shapeshifting into Simbi
    Lassous

Contrast Catholic dogma and ritual with island faith from West Africa.

12. Summarize two of the following quandaries as themes in Edwidge's stories and longer works:

ethnic cleansing
supporting Dessalines
concealing guilt
predicting an earthquake
rescuing a neighbor
aborting a fetus
disobeying Tonton Macoutes
cutting trees
homesickness
refusing to leave home
raiding a restaurant
frog deaths
exile to Miami
hiring rogue police
killing field

13. Contrast two close relationships from Edwidge's writings. Choose from these examples:

the revenant/Amabelle
Céliane/dead baby
Hermine/Carl Azule
Nadine/water child
Estina/newborn triplets
Romain/Michel
Anne/the fat man
Anacaona/Behechio
Edwidge/Uncle Joseph
Amabelle/Yves Rapanou
Junior/the barber
Tiye/Pascal Dorien
Max, Jr./Bernard Dorien
"Ernesto"/Paris
Célimène/Mo

What endears one person to another? Why are some relationships unwise or threatening?

248   Appendix D: A Guide to Writing, Art and Research Topics

14. Describe how Edwidge presents two fearful issues in stories or novels, such as these:

> street gangs
> lougarous
> ICE patrols
> paramilitary
> crowded jails
> Fort Dimanche
> a facial scar
> drug dealing
> three-legged horse
> mob vengeance
> carnival crowds
> pipe bombs
> bribery
> surly jail guards
> ambush
> rogue wave

15. Arrange a literature seminar to introduce students to Caribbean lore in Edwidge's *Krik? Krak!* or *The Dew Breaker*. Conclude discussion of historical fiction with proposals for cover art, a collection of lore or ballads, musical instruments, church and Vodou ritual, oral interpretation, genealogies, chronologies, maps, costume or banquet sketches, candle lighting, or holiday illustrations for carnival, Christmas Eve, or Day of the Dead.

16. Give the meaning and motivation for three of Edwidge's autographies, stories, documentaries, or novels. Choose from these:

> "Papi"
> *Girl Rising*
> "Clair de Lune"
> "A Crime to Dream"
> "Feetfirst"
> "Sawfish Soup"
> "A New Sky"
> "Plantains Please"
> "Indigo Girl"
> "Seven Stories"

> "Anniversary Blues"
> "Becoming Brazilian"

Suggest more personalized titles for "Elsie," "Monkey Tails," "Seven," and *Breath, Eyes, Memory*.

17. What does Edwidge's application of daydreams, travel, anecdotes, feasting, dance, recitation, superstition, worship, letter-writing, memoir, masking, and song as antidotes to despair have in common with forms of escapism in one of these works:

> Jamaica Kincaid's "Ovando"
> Toni Morrison's *The Bluest Eye*
> Rita Dove's "Parsley"
> Julia Alvarez's *In the Time of the Butterflies*
> Gish Jen's "Who's Irish?"
> August Wilson's *Gem of the Ocean*
> Leslie Marmon Silko's "Lullaby"
> Barbara Kingsolver's *The Bean Trees*
> Amy Tan's "Fish Cheeks"
> Mariano Azuela's *The Underdogs*
> Rudolfo Anaya's *Bless Me, Ultima*
> Isabel Allende's *House of the Spirits*
> Walter Dean Myers's "The Treasure of Lemon Brown"

Which of Edwidge's protagonists embrace storytelling as a refuge and outlet for confusion, pain, loss, sorrow, and rage? How do ordered events in narrative, diary, dreamscape, or song restore mental and spiritual harmony?

18. Summarize the wisdom of worship, menus, songs, ritual, or oral narrative in three of these works:

> "Nineteen Thirty-Seven"
> *Behind the Mountains*
> "Night Talkers"
> "All Geography Is Within Me"
> *Mama's Nightingale*
> "Dosas"
> "Crabs"

Appendix D: A Guide to Writing, Art and Research Topics   **249**

"Sunrise, Sunset"
"Without Her"

19. Characterize the motivation and purpose of daring and self-endangerment in Edwidge's works.

- How does the cab driver extort double fees?
- What does the author photograph in the pine forest?
- Why does Moy accompany Tante Rose to vote?
- How does a return to Alegría change Amabelle?
- What can Pascal or Max, Jr., gain by interviewing felons on radio?
- How does André protect Papi from a pursuer?
- Why does Michel seek news of Romain in "Monkey Tails"?
- How do drugs influence Claude's shooting of his father?
- Why does Madam Roger scold the Tonton Macoute?
- Why does Odile Desír rebuke Louise George with a slap?

20. Analyze the elements of sibling relationships on two of these pairs from Edwidge's novels and stories:

Tante Atie/Martine
Gracina/Caroline
bridal seamstresses
Anne/preacher
Céliane/Moy
Tante Rose/Aline
Edwidge/Karl
Kelly/Bob
Junior/Justine
Pascal/Jules Darien Claire Narcis/ sister
Boyer twins

21. Summarize the significance of three of these details in Edwidge's novels and stories:

dressing a corpse in red
writing in a notebook
braiding hair
smelling lemongrass
cleaning a mausoleum
watching leaves fall
viewing a sleeping landlord
stealing water
Christmas shopping
collecting old doors
revering ancestors
seeing Night Marchers
painting a baby's coffin
Homme à Homme
hiring a jeep driver
seeing the statue of a maroon
signing to Josephine
killing pigeons

22. Propose the choice of one of Edwidge's works as a community read. Suggest an annotated ballad or character web, table readings, improvised dialogue, addition of a secondary character or characters, and new or untried methods of immigration. Make a dramatic character web to express periods of exhilaration or expectation in island lives, such as these:

- climbing Anthère Lighthouse in *Claire of the Sea Light*
- attending an orchestra concert in *Untwine*
- receiving an audio tape in *Behind the Mountains* or *Mama's Nightingale*
- the retirement of a dressmaker in "The Bridal Seamstress"
- the freeing of a youthful murderer from jail in "Night Talkers"
- reunion of a married couple in "Seven"
- being married on a beach

23. Compare aloud the variance of political, religious, and socio-economic opinions in Edwidge's short stories.

Why do police imply that the Boyers' car accident was intentional?

250 Appendix D: A Guide to Writing, Art and Research Topics

What do the Taino intend to learn
from a Kalina captive?
How do Haitian-American women
celebrate citizenship? holidays?
births?
Why does Anne Bienaimé attend
daily mass in "The Book of
Miracles"?
What does Uncle Joseph Nozius
Dantica gain by staying in Bel Air?
How does Old Kongo honor his
African ancestry?
How do pain and treachery threaten
Claire Limyè Lanmè and
Manman Aline?
Why do fathers in "Children of the
Sea" want daughters to marry well?
How does Toto Constant earn a bad
reputation?

Include adaptations to women's
rights, worship, and personal relationships.

24. Account for two different types
of confrontations in Edwidge's writing.
Choose from these:

a cab driver's report of murder to
police
selling a daughter's virginity
refusing Eric's cooking
reporting a missing father at the
hotel
hearing a murderer's story
revealing Michel's parentage
turning into a zombie
rejecting an older brother
awakening in a pit of corpses
identifying a hospitalized daughter
revealing a scandal on the radio
attending a parent-teacher
conference
shaking a despot's hand
skinning a victim's face

25. Contrast types of collaboration
and resistance in several of Edwidge's
works. Include the following models:

saving to leave Haiti
demanding corpses from prison
chanting at Carnival
refusing to go dancing with a Tonton
Macoute
painting a picture of torture
blocking streets during an election
learning to rule Xaraguá
dressing in a wig and muumuu
sharing survival stories
imagining a game of marbles with
Oscar
exiling "Papa Doc" Duvalier
describing child rape in a brothel

26. Compare the daring and contributions of decisive women in Edwidge's
works. Chose two of these:

Anacaona
Louise
Céliane
Gabrielle
Anne Bienaimé
Manman Aline
Marielle
Aline Cajuste
Ka
Estina Estème
Guamayto
Saya
Sylvie Boyer
Jessamine
Darline

27. List types of creativity in "Papi,"
After the Dance, Eight Days, "Seven,"
Anacaona, "Starfish," and *The Art of Death,*
such as painting a tap tap or carving views
of harvesting guava, a sacred fruit. How
do protagonists achieve great satisfaction
from love letters and tapes? from imagination? from romance? from solitude? from
collaboration? from cooking? from travel?
from success?

28. Summarize Edwidge's views on
immigration, especially the support of

Appendix D: A Guide to Writing, Art and Research Topics   251

people left behind in "Water Child" and *Behind the Mountains* and fearful memories of Tonton Macoute torture in "The Bridal Seamstress" and "Monkey Tails." Outline a radio interview with questions about her family experiences and changes in the system after the election of anti-immigration president Donald Trump and the onset of the covid epidemic.

29. Outline sources of pride in Edwidge's *Create Dangerously*, "The Bridal Seamstress," *My Mommy Medicine,* "Ghosts," "A Grain of Comfort," or *After the Dance.*

30. Account for humor in difficult times, such as Gracina Azile's lies to cover for Caroline's overnight absence in "Caroline's Wedding," pretending to lose a bike race in *Eight Days,* electing an undertaker as mayor in *Claire of the Sea Light,* and male May queens and the cross-dressing bride and groom at Carnival in "Seven."

31. Compare the training of Haitian girls in various skills both on the island and in the U.S.:

pounding corn
cooking
shopping
using a mortar
washing a corpse
braiding hair
diagnosing
changing bandages
selling drinks on a corner
sweeping
mixing herbs
selling corn flour
shelling peas
making candy
sewing
grating coconut
massaging arthritic joints
carving wood

embroidery
telling stories

32. Account for separation in the lives of four of these characters:

Rose
Grandmè Ifé
Céliane's infant
Claude
the barber
the fat man
Thérèse
Hector Danoze
Bibi
Pessoir Marol
Sebastien
Laurent Lavaud
David Boyer
Max Ardin, Jr.
Lamort
Marie Micheline

33. Select contrasting scenes from Edwidge's writings and describe their pictorial qualities, for example:

swaying revelers in Jacmel
proselyting in "House of Prayer and Dreams"
teaching Brigitte to say mama
urinating overboard in "Children of the Sea"
buying Caroline's wedding dress
wearing ankle bells for a hospice patient
teaching Nahe to swim
changing radio batteries during the election
splashing in puddles in *Eight Days*
using an artificial arm as a weapon
folding paper into boats
buying juice before dinner

34. Discuss the sources of affection or distancing or both between one of these pairs:

Martine/Marc
Edwidge/Papi

252 Appendix D: A Guide to Writing, Art and Research Topics

Madam Roger/son
Carl/Hermine
Tobin/Michel
niece/Uncle Joseph
Dany/Estina Estème
Nadine/parents
Aline/Marjorie Voltaire
Félice/Joël Loner
Saya/Mama
Céliane/Madame Auguste
Tina/Giselle Boyer
Flore/Pamaxime
Arnold/Darline

In which relationships have emotions stabilized? What outside forces alter affection? Why do characters treasure letters and other keepsakes?

35. Contrast flaws and strengths in two of these secondary characters from Edwidge's stories and novels:

Tante Atie
boat captain
Radio Six
Rosalie
Ms. Hinds
Old Zo
Granpè Nozial
Tante Rose
Charles Oscar
Azaka
Marahay
Odette
Suzette
Odile Desír
Man Denise
Jean Dominique

Which characters recognize their own weaknesses? talents? inescapable memories? needs for control, vengeance, rest or medical treatment, and camaraderie?

36. Write an extended definition of *womanhood* using as an example two of these stories:

"New York Day Women"
"The Indigo Girl"
"Hot-Air Balloons"
"The Possibility of Heaven"
"Sunrise, Sunset"
"The Port-au-Prince Marriage Special"
"Water Child"
"Dream of the Butterflies"
"Please Translate"
"Sole Mates"
"Message to My Daughters"
"A Place of Refuge"
"The Artists of Maténwa"
"Reading Lessons"

Incorporate changes in characters from failures to triumph as "poto mitan."

37. List types of comfort in these scenes. Explain why the characters are in need of treatment, food, reassurance, warmth, or solace:

meeting someone at the airport
burying Martine in a red dress
locating islanders lost in an
    earthquake
identifying with Guinean ancestors
bathing under the banyan tree
teaching high school ESL
checking out of the ENT hospital
confessing to imprisonment for
    patricide
winning Miss Carnival Queen
vomiting at Krome immigration
    center
hearing "Leave us good news"
holding a teacher conference

38. Compose letters to characters offering support for their troubles and advice in difficult situations, especially these:

Martine in New York
Celia in a metal container
a seamstress's retirement
water leaking from Christophe's
    station

Appendix D: A Guide to Writing, Art and Research Topics

Romain's mother in Curaçao
ENT patients in Kings Country
    Hospital
refugees in Cap Haïtien
high school orchestra members
Junior's parents and sister
Flore in a radio interview

39. Cite occasions for computation in Edwidge's works. Name the particulars of each situation, such as these:

driving from Port-au-Prince to
    Seguin
sailing from western Haiti to Miami
gaining documents of land
    ownership
burying 129 drowning victims

distance from Haiti to Nostrand
    Avenue
making a coffin for Estina Estème
traveling to Curaçao from Haiti
tailoring wedding dresses
measuring shadows of two trees
grating coconut for candy
keeping a calendar of Mama's
    absence
comparing AIDS data by nation
length of Massacre River
identifying Jean Dominique
selling pigeons for sacrifice
measuring concrete from a mixer

40. Determine the length of each of Christopher Columbus's voyages.

Bibliography

Primary Works by Edwidge Danticat

Novels and Prose Works

After the Dance: A Walk Through Carnival in Jacmel, Haiti. New York: Vintage, 2002.

The Art of Death: Writing the Final Story. Minneapolis, MN: Graywolf Press, 2017.

Beginnings, Endings, and Salt: Essays on a Journey through Writing and Literature. Grand Cayman, W.I.: Books & Books Press, 2021.

Breath, Eyes, Memory. New York: Soho Press, 1994.

Brother, I'm Dying. New York: Vintage, 2007.

Claire of the Sea Light. New York: Vintage, 2013.

Create Dangerously: The Immigrant Artist at Work. New York: Vintage, 2010.

The Dew Breaker. New York: Abacus, 2004.

Everything Inside. New York: Knopf, 2019.

The Farming of Bones. New York: Penguin, 1998.

Krik? Krak! New York: Soho Press, 1995.

Children's and Young Adult Works

Anacaona: Golden Flower, Haiti, 1490. New York: Scholastic, 2005.

Behind the Mountains: The Diary of Célianne Espérance. New York: Orchard Books, 2002.

Célimène—Fairy Tale for the Daughter of Immigrants. Montreal: Memoire d'Encrier, 2009.

Dènye Pye Mapou. Brooklyn: One Moore Book, 2013.

Eight Days: A Story of Haiti. New York: Orchard Books, 2010.

The Last Mapou. Brooklyn: One Moore Book, 2013.

Mama's Nightingale. New York: Dial, 2015.

My Mommy Medicine. New York: Roaring Brook, 2019.

Untwine. New York: Scholastic, 2015.

A Walk Through Carnival. New York: Vintage, 2016.

Plays

Bastille Day. Purchase College, State University of New York (4 October 2019).

Children of the Sea. Roxbury Community College. Boston, 1997.

The Creation of Adam. Rites and Reasons Theater. Providence, Rhode Island, 1992.

Dreams Like Me. Brown University New Plays Festival. Providence, Rhode Island, 1993.

Les Enfants de la Mer (Children of the Sea) (adaptation). Chapelle du Verbe Incarné, Avignon, France, July 2004.

Verse

"Bajou/Dawn," *Afro-Hispanic Review* 32:2 (Fall, 2013): 149–150, 156.

"A Despot Walks into a Killing Field," *Progressive* 76:5 (May 2012): 37.

Haiti/Little Haiti. North Miami, Fl: Museum of Contemporary Art, 2010. "Miras," *Callaloo* 33:2 (April, 2010): 409.

"On the Day of the Dead," http://carbon innovations.net/node/3411, 6 September 2011.

"Plunging," *Caribbean Writer* 23 (2009); St. Paul, MN: Midnight Paper Sales, 2009.

"Poems," *Standing Tall: Portraits of the Haitian Community in Miami, 2003–2010.* Miami: Museum of Contemporary Art, 2010, n.p.

"Postscript," *Callaloo* 33:2 (April, 2010): 410.

"Sawfish Soup," *Caribbean Writer* 5 (1991): 10–11.

"Trimester," *Callaloo* 33:2 (April, 2010): 411.

Film

The Agronomist (co-producer). New York: ThinkFilm, Inc., 2003; translated into French, *L'Agronome*, ThinkFilm, 2004.

Beloved (actor). New York: Harpo Films, 1998.

Caroline's Wedding (author). New York: Women in Film & Television, 2017.

Courage and Pain (co-producer). New York: Clinica Estetico, 1996.

The Foreigner's Home (scenarist), Ice Lens Pictures, Cleveland, Ohio, 2018.

Girl Rising (scenarist). New York: Girl Rising, 2013.

Hotel Haiti (actor). Montreal: Alma Barkey, 2011.

The Manchurian Candidate (actor). New York: Paramount, 2004.

Nou Bouke (We're Tired) (narrator). New York: PBS, 2011.

Poto Mitan: Haitian Women, Pillars of the Global Community (writer, narrator). New York: Documentary Educational Resources, 2009.

Stones in the Sun (actor) *Des Pierres au Soleil.* New York: Syncopated Films, 2012.

Bibliography

The Sugar Babies (voiceover) *Les Enfants du Sucre.* New York: Siren Studios, 2007.

Short Works

"An Accident of Literacy," https://www.buildon. org/2012/09/an-accident-of-literacy-guest-blog-by-edwidge-danticat/, 8 September 2012.

The African Lookbook. foreword. New York: Bloomsbury, 2021.

"After the Collapse," *New Yorker* (24 January 2010).

"AHA!," (speech) Inter-American Development Bank Cultural Center, 1997; *Becoming American: Personal Essays by First Generation Immigrant Women.* New York: Hyperion, 2000, 44.

"All Geography Is Within Me," *World Literature Today* 93:1 (Winter 2019): 58.

"All the Home You've Got," *Best American Essays 2018.* New York: Best American Paper, 2018, 37–42.

"The Ancestral Blessings of Toni Morrison and Paule Marshall," *New Yorker* (17 August 2019).

"Anniversary Blues," *Progressive* 76:2 (10 January 2012): 20–22.

"Another Country," *Progressive* 69:11 (2005): 24–26.

"Appreciating a Winner," *Gainesville Sun* (23 July 2009).

"An Appreciation of Nobel-Winner Wole Soyinka at 75," *Progressive* (14 July 2009).

"The Armchair Traveler," (Toronto) *Globe and Mail* (9 October 2002): T4.

"The Art of Death," *Poets & Writers Magazine* 45:4 (July-August 2017): 25–29.

"The Artist as Activist" (speech), Case Western Reserve, Cleveland, Ohio (20 March 2016): https://www.anisfield-wolf.org/2016/03/the-artist-as-activist-author-edwidge-danticat-in-cleveland/.

"The Artists of Maténwa," *Ms.* 14:3 (Fall 2004): 25–26.

At Home in the World: Women Writers, Public Lives. Princeton, NJ: Princeton University Press, 2017.

Aunt Résia and the Spirits and Other Stories. foreword. Charlottesville: University of Virginia Press, 2010.

"Bastille Day," *Caribbean Writer* 25 (June 2011).

"Be the Vote for Immigrant Families under Threat by the Trump Administration," *Miami Herald* (1 November 2020).

"Be Unafraid," *Why We Write about Ourselves.* New York: Plume, 2016, 62–72.

Beacon Best of 2000: Great Writing by Women and Men of All Colors and Cultures. editor. Boston: Beacon Press, 2000.

"Becoming Brazilian," *Obsidian III* 6/7:2/1 (Fall/ Winter, 2005/2006): 139–145.

Best American Essays 2011. editor. New York: Mariner, 2011.

The Best Teen Writing of 2012. foreword. New York: Scholastic, 2012.

"Between the Pool and the Gardenias," *The Caribbean Writer* 7 (Summer, 1993): 66–70; *Best of the Small Presses.* Wainscott, NY: Pushcart Press, 1994; *Monologues by Women.* Portsmouth, NH: Heinemann, 1994.

"Black Bodies in Motion and in Pain," *New Yorker* (22 June 2015).

"Bonjour Jean," *Nation* 272:7 (19 February 2001): 20–22.

"The Book of Miracles," *The Story Prize.* New York: Strong Winds, 2019.

"The Book of the Dead," *New Yorker* (21 June 1999): 194–199.

"Brave New Worlds," *Essence* 31:1 (May 2000): 169–170.

Breath, Eyes, Memory. introduction. New York: Soho Press, 2015.

"A Brief Reflection on the Massacre River," *Kreyòl 5* 2:17 (19 May 1999).

Brown Girl Brownstones. foreword. New York: Feminist Press, 2006.

The Butterfly's Way: Voices from the Haitian Diaspora in the United States, ed. introduction. New York: Soho Press, 2001, ix-xvii.

"A Caribbean Island of One's Own," *International New York Times* (9 November 2013): 23.

The Caribbean Writer 24. editor. Kingshill, St. Croix, W.I., 2010.

Caribbeanness as a Global Phenomenon. co-author. Tempe, AZ: Bilingual Press, 2014.

"Carnivalia," *Transition* 12:3 (2002): 40–49.

"Caroline's Wedding," *Short Stories for Students.* vol. 25. Detroit: Gale, 2007.

"Celia," *A Memory, a Monologue, a Rant, and a Prayer: Writings in Stop Violence against Women and Girls.* New York: Villard, 2007, 91–93.

Children of the Sea (story). *Short Stories for Students.* vol. 1. Detroit: Gale, 1997; *Imagining America: Stories from the Promised Land.* New York: Persea Books, 2003.

"Claire of the Sea Light," *Haiti Noir.* Brooklyn: Akashic, 2010, 115–138.

"Color Blocking," *Arquitectonica,* https://www.interiorsandsources.com/article-details/articleid/15929/title/color-blocking-edwidge-danticat (1 July 2013).

A Community of Equals. foreword. Boston: Beacon, 1999.

"Compliments," *Washington Post* (5 May 2013): B4.

"Condolences," *Conjunction* 27 (Fall 1996).

"Connecting the Political and Personal," *Connecting Histories: Francophone Caribbean Writers Interrogating Their Past.* Jackson: University Press of Mississippi, 2017, 100–119.

"Crabs: Praying for Food in Haiti," *New Yorker* (9 June 2008): 78–79.

"Create Dangerously," *Black Ink: Literary Legends on the Peril, Power, and Pleasure of Reading and Writing.* New York: Atria, 2018, 173–186.

"Create Dangerously" (excerpt), *New York Times* (8 October 2010).

"A Crime to Dream," *Nation* 280:17 (2 May 2005): 13–15.

"DACA, Hurricane Irma, and Young Americans'

Bibliography

257

Dreams Deferred," *New Yorker* (6 September 2017).

"Dangerous Unselfishness," *Plough* 16 (21 January 2019): 18–25.

"The Dating Game," *New Yorker Out Loud* (11 June 2007).

"Dawn after the Caribbean Tempests," *New York Times* (12 November 2017): TR5; *New Daughters of Africa*. New York: Amistad, 2019, 359.

"Demonstrators in Haiti Are Fighting for an Uncertain Future," *New Yorker* (10 October 2019).

Derby, Lauren. "Film Review of *The Price of Sugar* and *The Sugar Babies*," *Caribbean Studies* 36:2 (July-December 2008): 250–265.

"Detained Immigrants Deserve Humane Treatment," *Washington Post* (15 March 2013).

"Detention Is No Holiday," *New York Times* (28 May 2012): A27.

"The Dew Breaker," *Gumbo: A Celebration of African American Writers*. New York: Broadway Books, 2002, 3–12; *Literary Cavalcade* 57:2 (October 2004): 12–16.

"Dies Irae," *Conjunctions* 34 (Spring, 2000): 128–136.

"Diskou Edwidge Danticat" (lecture) https://www.dloc.com/results/?t=danticat (29 October 1998).

"Does It Work?," *Washington Post* (24 September 2006): B1.

"Does Your Face Light Up?" (keynote speech) *Kweli Journal* (9 April 2016), http://www.kwelijournal.org/video/2016/6/28/does-your-face-light-up-keynote-by-edwidge-danticat.

"The Dominican Republic and Haiti: A Shared View from the Diaspora," *Americas Quarterly* 8:3 (Summer 2014): 28–35.

"The Dominican Republic's War on Haitian Workers" (contributor) *New York Times* (20 November 1999): A13.

"Don't Let AIDS Study Scapegoat the Haitians," *Gainesville Sun* (5 November 2007).

"Dosas," *Sable,* Spring 2007; *One World Two*. Oxford, UK: New International, 2016, 238–250; *Tales of Two Americas*. New York: Penguin, 2017, 26–53.

"Dream of the Butterflies," *Caribbean Writer* 5 (1991): 98–99; *Belles Lettres* 10:3 (Summer, 1995): 16.

"Edwidge Danticat," *American Visions* 10:3 (June/July 1995): 38.

"Edwidge Danticat," *Nation* 296:4 (28 January 2013): 18.

"Edwidge Danticat Returns to Haiti and Finds Resilience and Regeneration," *Newsweek* 158:7 (15 August 2011); "Fête Dieu—Feast of Corpus Christi," *Haiti Bonjou* (30 May 2013).

"Edwidge Danticat Speaks on Mac McClellan Essay," *Essence* (9 July 2011).

"Edwidge Danticat's Haiti: Bloodied, Shaken—and Beloved," *Miami Herald* (17 January 2010).

"Elsie," *Callaloo* 29:1 (January 2006): 22–29, 238.

"Enough Is Enough," *New Yorker* (26 November 2014).

"Evelyne Trouillot," *BOMB* 90 (Winter 2004/2005): 49–53.

"Fanm Se Poto Mitan: Women Are the Pillars of

Society," *Women: A Celebration of Strength* foreword. New York: Legal Momentum, 2007.

"The Farming of Bones," *Newsweek* 132:10 (7 September 1998): 69; *Time* 152:12 (21 September 1998): 73–74; (Toronto) *Globe and Mail* (24 October 1998): D12; *Calgary Herald* (7 November 1998); K9; *Americas* 52:3 (May/June 2000): 64.

Fault Lines: Views across Haiti's Divide. foreword. Ithaca, NY: Cornell University, 2013, xi-xiv.

"Fear of Deportation in the Dominican Republic," *New Yorker* (17 June 2015).

"Flight," *New Yorker* 87:27 (5 September 2011): 32.

"For Toni Morrison" (coauthor) *Brick* 105 (Summer 2020): 70. "A Fountain of Peace," *On the Wings of Peace in the Memory of Hiroshima and Nagasaki*. New York: Clarion, 1995.

"Freda," *Brown Sugar 4*. New York: Washington Square Press, 2005, 31–41.

"Freedom Soup," *The Artists' and Writers' Cookbook: A Collection of Stories with Recipes*. Alexandria, VA: Powerhouse, 2016.

"From the Ocean Floor," *Short Fiction by Women* (October 1993); *Rhythm and Revolt*. New York: Plume. 1995.

"The Future in My Arms," *Essence* (May 2000).

"Gabriel Garcia Marquez: An Appreciation," *New Yorker* (18 April 2014).

"Ghosts," *New Yorker* (24 November 2008): 108–113.

"Ghosts of the 1915 U.S. Invasion Still Haunt Haiti's People," *Miami Herald* (25 July 2005).

"Giving and Receiving," *Progressive* 76/77:12 (December 2012/January 2013): 19–20.

Go Tell It on the Mountain. introduction. New York: Everyman's Library, 2016.

"Graduation," *Caribbean Writer* 5 (1991): 100–103.

"A Grain of Comfort," *O Magazine* 7:5 (May 2006): 147–148, 150; *Eat Joy: Stories & Comfort Food from 31 Celebrated Writers*. New York: Black Balloon, 2019.

Hadriana in All My Dreams. foreword. Brooklyn: Akashic, 2017.

Haiti: A Bi-Cultural Experience (lecture). Washington, D.C.: IDB Cultural Center (7 December 1995): 1–9.

Haiti: A Slave Revolution: 200 Years after 1804. co-author. New York: World View Forum, 2010.

Haiti after the Earthquake (audio). co-narrator. Prince Frederick, MD: HighBridge, 2011.

"Haiti: Bloodied, Shaken—and Beloved," *Miami Herald* (17 January 2010); *How to Write an Earthquake*. Iowa City, IA: Autumn Hill Books, 2011, 74–76.

"Haiti: The Poetry Behind the Bloodshed," *Providence Journal* (10 November 1991): D15.

"Haiti, 1804–2004: Literature, Culture, and Art," *Research in African Literatures* 35:2 (Summer, 2004); vii-viii.

"Haiti Faces Difficult Questions Ten Years after a Devastating Earthquake," *New Yorker* (11 January 2020).

"Haiti Needs Your Help," *The Progressive* (17 September 2008).

Haiti Uncovered: A Regional Adventure Into the Art

of Haitian Cuisine. foreword. New York: Nadege Fleurimond, 2014.

"Haitian-American Christmas: Cremace and Creole Theatre," *New Youth Connections,* 1987.

"Haitians Are Used to Insults," *Miami Herald* (12 January 2018).

"Haitians Need Help Now," *Atlanta Journal-Constitution* (23 September 2008): A11.

"Haitians Want to Know What the Government Has Done with Missing Oil Money," *New Yorker* (19 October 2018).

"Haiti's People Have Strong Will to Rebuild," *CNN* (13 January 2010).

"Haiti's Quiet Beauty Captivates in Jacmel," *Toronto Star* (28 December 2013): T3.

"Hanging with the Fugees," *Essence* 27:4 (1 August 1996): 85–86.

"A Harrowing Turning Point for Haitian Immigrants," *New Yorker* (12 May 2017).

"Homage to a Creative Elder," *Nation* (9 January 2013).

Homelands: Women's Journeys Across Race, Place, and Time. foreword. Emeryville, CA: Seal Press, 2006, 8–12.

"Hot-Air Balloons," *Granta* 115 (20 June 1996); *The F Word, Contemporary UK Feminism,* 2011; *Immigrant Voices: 21st Century Stories.* Chicago: Great Books Foundation, 2014.

"House of Prayer and Dreams," *Sojourners* 442:4 (April 2013): 38–39, 41–42.

"Hurricane Matthew's Devastating Toll in Haiti," *New Yorker* (6 October 2016).

"I Pass On," *Essence* 32:1 (May 2001): 160.

"I Still Have a Dream," *Progressive* 79:2 (February 2015): 15–17.

"Ignoring the Revolution Next Door," *Time* 164:1 (5 July 2004): 61.

"Impounded Fathers," *New York Times* (17 June 2007): 4, 12.

"In Flesh and Bone," *Tent Life: Haiti.* Brooklyn: Umbrage, 2011, 8–9.

In the Flicker of an Eyelid, co-translator and afterword. Charlottesville: University of Virginia Press, 2002.

"In the Old Days," *So Spoke the Earth: The Haiti I Knew, the Haiti I Know, the Haiti I Want to Know.* co-author. South Florida, FL: Women Writers of Haitian Descent, 2012; *Callaloo* 35:2 (Spring, 2012): 355–363, 562.

"The Indigo Girl: Between Haiti and the Streets of Brooklyn," *Sojourners* 33:12 (December 2004): 28–31.

The Infamous Rosalie. foreword. Lincoln: University of Nebraska Press, 2013.

"The Inspiration of Toni Morrison," *Progressive* (8 October 2008).

"Introduction," *Haiti Noir.* Brooklyn: Akashic, 2010, 115–138.

Island on Fire: Passionate Visions of Haiti from the Collection of Jonathan Demme. editor. Nyack, NY: Kaliko Press, 1997.

"James Baldwin's Hypothetical Country," *New Yorker* (25 February 2016).

"Je Voudrais Etre Riche: A Trickster Tale," *Caribbean Writer* 18 (2004): 187–193; *Southampton Review* 8:1 (Spring 2014).

"The Journals of Water Days 1986," *Callaloo* 19:2 (Spring, 1996): 376–380; *Callaloo* 24:2 (Spring, 2001): 427–431.

"Junot Díaz," *BOMB* 101 (Fall 2007): 89–95.

Kazal: The Memories of Kazal, a Photographic Approach. co-author. Roquevaire, France: Andre Frere, 2019.

"Kettly Mars Interview," *Granta* (19 June 2013).

The Kingdom of This World. introduction. New York: Knopf, 2006.

"Kite m Viv," *Let Haiti Live: Unjust U.S. Policies Towards Its Oldest Neighbor.* Brooklyn: EducaVision, 2004, 13–15.

La récolte douce des larmes. co-author. France: Loisirs, 2000.

Lee, Felicia. "Dark Tales Illuminate Haiti, Before and After Quake," *New York Times* (9 January 2011).

"Less Than Human," *Progressive* 73:4 (April 2009): 124.

"Let My People Stay," *Essence* 25:3 (July 1994): 124.

"Letter to Miami," WLRN Radio (July 2011).

"Li, Li, Li," *Good Housekeeping* 252:1 (January 2011): 99; *Guardian* (28 November 2012).

"Lifestyle Travel: South Africa Today," *Essence* 33:6 (October 2002): 204–208.

Like the Dew That Waters the Grass (foreword). Washington, D.C.: EPICA 1999.

"A Little While," *New Yorker* 85:47 (25 January 2010): 19–20.

"Living and Loving through Tragedy," *Sojourners* 39:3 (March 2010): 10–11.

"Living Dyingly," *Poets & Writers* (July/August 2017).

"The Long Legacy of Occupation in Haiti," *New Yorker* (28 July 2015).

"Look at Me," *Harper's* 327:1963 (December 2013): 65–73.

Lost and Found (afterword). Montreal: CICIHCA, 2009.

"Lost Shadows and Stick Figures," *Caribbean Writer* 6 (1992): 104–105.

Love Anger Madness: A Haitian Triptych. introduction. New York: Modern Library, 2010, xi–xviii.

"Love, Our Only True Adventure" (1 August 2020): https://hello-sunshine.com/post/love-our-only-true-adventure.

"Machandiz," *Tales of Two Planets: Stories of Climate Change and Inequality in a Divided World.* New York: Penguin, 2020, 149–158.

The Magic Orange Tree and Other Haitian Tales. foreword. New York: Knopf, 1997.

"Marie Micheline," *New Yorker* (11 June 2007): 96–103; (18 June 2007).

Massacre River. preface. New York: New Directions, 2005, 7–10.

Me Dying Trial. introduction. Boston: Beacon, 2003.

"Memories of a Duvalier Massacre, 50 Years Later," *Progressive* (25 April 2013). "Message to My

Bibliography

Daughters," *The Fire This Time: A New Generation Speaks about Race*. New York: Scribner's, 2017, 205–216.

"Miami," *Harper's* 335:2009 (October 2017): 34–35.

Miss Muriel and Other Stories. introduction. New York: Dafina, 2008.

"The Missing Peace," *Just a Moment*, 4:1 (Winter, 1992–1993); *Caribbean Writer* 8 (July 1994): 104–112; *Feminism 3: The Third Generation in Fiction*. Boulder, CO: Westview, 1996.

"Mississippi Burning," *Oprah Magazine* (October 2017).

"Mr. Robinson," *New York* 42:9 (23 March 2009): 34.

"The Most Meaningful Moment of My Day," *Real Simple* 10:11 (November 2009).

"Mourning in Place," *New York Review of Books* 67:14 (24 September 2020): 38.

"My Father Once Chased Rainbows," *Essence* 24:7 (November, 1993): 48.

"My Honorary Degree and the Factory Forewoman," *Brown Reader*. New York: Simon & Schuster, 2014.

"My New York," *New York* 33:49 (2000): 96.

"My Own Island" (contributor) *New York Times* (10 November 2013): TR8.

"My Personal Journey," *Behind the Mountains*. New York: Orchard Books, 2002.

"The Mysterious Power of Near-Death Experiences," *New Yorker* (10 July 2017).

"Nature Has No Memory," https://www.borderoflights.org/edwidge-danticat, 2013.

"A New Chapter for the Disastrous United Nations Mission in Haiti," *New Yorker* (19 October 2017).

"A New World Full of Strangers," *New Youth Connections*, 1987.

"New York Day Women," *New York Stories*. Mineola, NY: Dover, 2016, 150–155.

"New York Was Our City on the Hill," *New York Times* (21 November 2004): CY1; *The Place Where We Dwell*. Dubuque, IA: Kendall Hunt (2005): 68–72; *More New York Stories*. New York: New York University Press, 2010: 72–76.

"Night Talkers," *Callaloo* 25:4 (Fall 2002): 1007–1020; *Best American Short Stories*. Boston: Houghton Mifflin 2003.

"Nineteen Thirty-Seven," *Oxford Book of Caribbean Short Stories*. Oxford, UK: Oxford University Press, 2001: 447–456.

"No Greater Shame," *The Boston Haitian Reporter* (May 2003); *Haiti, a Slave Revolution*. New York: International Action Center, 2004, 168–172.

"No Refuge," *Essence* 34:2 (June 2003): 36.

"Not Your Homeland," *Nation* 281:9 (26 September 2005): 24–26.

"Obama Yes," *Progressive* 5 (17 September 2008).

Odilon Pierre, Artist of Haiti. coauthor. Nyack, NY: Kaliko Press, 1998.

"On Borrowed Wings," *Telegraph India* (October 2004).

"One Thing," *New York Times Magazine* (7 July 2020): 62–72; *The Decameron Project*. New York: Simon & Schuster, 2020.

The Other Side of the Sea. foreword. Charlottesville: University of Virginia Press, 2014.

"The Other Side of the Water," *New York Times Sunday Book Review* (10 October 2010): 14; *Haiti after the Earthquake*. New York: Perseus, 2011, 261–270.

"Our Maya," *Essence* 45:4 (August 2014).

"Our Story, Ourselves" (lecture), Howard University (28 February 2013).

"Out of the Shadows," *The Progressive* 70:6 (23 May 2006): 12–13.

"Pamela Phatsimo Sunstrum: New and Recent Paintings," *Paris Review* 232 (Spring 2020): 105–121.

"Papi," *Family: American Writers Remember Their Own*. Collingdale, PA: Diane, 2000.

"Passion Flowers," *Essence* (May 2001).

The Penguin Book of Migration Literature. foreword. New York: Penguin, 2019, xi-xiv.

"A Place of Refuge," *Allure* 21:3 (March 2011).

Plantains, Please. Caribbean Writer 13 (1999): 179–180.

"Please Translate," *Conjunctions* 63 (Fall, 2014): 36–40; *Cutting Edge: New Stories of Mystery and Crime by Women Writers*. Brooklyn: Akashic, 2019.

"Poetry in a Time of Protest," *New Yorker* (31 January 2017).

Poetry of Haitian Independence. foreword. New Haven, CT: Yale University, 2015, xi- xviii.

"Port-au-Prince, City of Survivors: Voices from Haiti," *Salon* (12 January 2020).

"The Port-au-Prince Marriage Special," *Conjunctions* 50 (March, 2008): 11–21; *Ms.* 23:4 (Fall, 2013): 50–55; *Haiti Noir 2*. Brooklyn: Akashic, 2014, 160–174.

"A Portal Moment for Portal Writers and Scholars," *CLA Journal* 56:4 (June 2013): 290.

"The Possibility of Heaven," *Sojourners* 44:2 (February 2015): 22–24.

"Prayer before Dying," *PEN America* 19 (18 September 2017): 34–36.

"The Price of Sugar," *Creativetime*, https://creativetimereports.org/2014/05/05/edwidge-danticat-the-price-of-sugar/

"The Prize," *Caribbean Writer* 18 (2004).

"Quality Control," *Washington Post Magazine* (5 November 2014): 25.

"A Rain of Daffodils," *Seventeen* 53:4 (1 April 1994): 152; *Literary Cavalcade* 52:6 (March 2000): 4–8.

"Reading Lessons," *New Yorker* 80:42 (10 January 2005): 66–73.

"Remembering the Earthquake in Haiti Seven Years Ago," *Miami Herald* (12 January 2017).

"Resistance and Loss in the Age of COVID-19," NPR (19 June 2020).

"The Revenant," *Granta* 54 115 (20 June 1996); *The Best Young American Novelists* (20 June 1996).

"Revenge of a Stigma," *Progressive* 72:2 (February 2008): 16.

"Ripple Effects," *New Yorker* 96:8 (13 April 2020).

"Rose-Anne Auguste, Haiti's Freedom Fighter," *Essence* 26:2 (June 1995): 50.

"The Secret Island," *Colorlines* 9:4 (November/ December 2006): 9–14; *La Prensa San Diego* 33:2 (12 January 2007).

"September 11th: Ten Years," *New Yorker* (5 September 2011).

"Seven," *New Yorker* 77:29 (24 September 2001): 88–97; *Best American Short Stories.* Boston: Houghton Mifflin, 2002; *O'Henry Prize Stories.* Boston: Anchor, 2002.

"Significant Others," *Sojourners* 38:10 (November 2009): 36–40.

"So Brutal a Death," *New Yorker* 96:17 (22 June 2020): 18–19.

"Sole Mates," *Oprah Magazine* (April 2008).

"Some of My Favorite Haitian Meals," *Let's Speak Haitian Food.* New York: CSJ Media, 2017, 73.

"The Soul of Little Haiti," *Miami Herald* (29 September 2019).

"South Africa Today," *Essence* (October 2002)

Starting with "I": Personal Essays by Teenagers. afterword. New York: Persea, 1997.

"Stateless in the Dominican Republic," (contributor) *Providence Journal* (16 November 2013): 1.

"Stop Deportations to Haiti," *Miami Herald* (18 February 2015).

"Storybook Ending," *Oprah Magazine* (May 2006): 147–150. "Suddenly Stateless" (contributor) *Los Angeles Times* (10 November 2013): A 24.

"Sunrise, Sunset," *New Yorker* 93:28 (18 September 2017): 54–60; (audio) "The Writer's Voice," *WNYC* (17 October 2017).

"Sweet Micky and the Sad Deja Vu of Haiti's Presidential Elections," *New Yorker* (3 December 2015).

"A Taste of Coffee," *Calabash* 1:2 (May 2001): 39–48.

"Tatiana, Mon Amour," *Callaloo* 27:2 (2004): 439–453; *Stories from Blue Latitudes* Emeryville, CA: Seal Press, 2006, 70–93.

"Tell Our Stories" (lecture) https://www.dloc.com/ results/?t=danticat (10 July 2013).

"Testimonial," *BOMB* 50 (Winter 1995).

Their Eyes Were Watching God. foreword. New York: Harper Perennial, 2006.

"This Is My Body," *Plough* 20 (19 March 2019).

"This Too Shall Pass? Hope and Community amid Disaster," *Plough* (21 April 2020).

"A Torturer in Full," (Toronto) *Globe and Mail* (27 March 2004): D20.

"Travel Dust and the Magical Tracks of Zora Neale Hurston," *Zora Magazine* (January 2016).

"Travelling," *UN Chronicle* 46:3/4 (2009): 23.

"Trump Reopens an Old Wound for Haitians," *New Yorker* (29 December 2017).

"Turning the Page on Disaster," *Good Housekeeping* 252:1 (January 2011): 99–103.

"U.S. Deportations to Haiti during Coronavirus Pandemic Are 'Unconscionable,'" *Miami Herald* (10 May 2020).

"U.S. Takes Wasteful Approach to Detaining Immigrants," *Washington Post* (15 March 2013).

Vale of Tears. introduction. Bethesda, MD: Ibex, 2005, 6–7.

"A Very Haitian Story," *New York Times* (24 November 2004): A23.

"A Voice from Heaven," *The Good Book: Writers Reflect on Favorite Bible Passages.* New York: Simon & Schuster, 2015, 263–269.

"Voices from Hispaniola" (contributor) *Meridians* 5:1 (2004): 68–91.

"Voices in a Dream," *Caribbean Writer* 7 (Summer, 1993); *Clerestory* (July, 1994).

Walking on Fire: Haitian Women's Stories of Survival and Resistance. foreword. Ithaca, NY: Cornell University Press, 2001, ix–xii.

"A Wall of Fire," *Cymbals* (Summer 1991).

"A Wasteful Approach to Detention," *Washington Post* (5 March 2013): A13.

"Wasting Money, Lives Through the Detention of Immigrants," *Washington Post* (14 March 2013): A13.

"Water Child," *New Yorker* 76:26 (11 September 2000): 84–91.

We Are All Suspects Now: Untold Stories from Immigrant Communities after 9/11. foreword. Boston: Beacon Press, 2005, vii–xi.

"We Are Ugly, But We Are Here," *Caribbean Writer* 10 (1996): n.p.; *Women Writing Resistance.* Boston: Beacon, 2017, 21–26.

"We Have Stumbled, But We Will Not Fall," *Essence* 41:1 (May 2010): 100.

"We Must Not Forget Detained Migrant Children," *New Yorker* (26 June 2018).

"Westbury Court," *Best American Essays 2000.* Boston: Houghton Mifflin, 2000, 77–81.

"When Home Hurts," *Transnational Narratives from the Caribbean.* New York: Routledge, 2019, 27–42.

"Why I Support Obama," *Progressive* 72:5 (May 2008): 12–13.

Wide Sargasso Sea. introduction. New York: Penguin, 2016, vii–xiii.

"With Our Very Last Breath" (contributor) University of California Television, Santa Barbara, 2011.

"Without Her," *New York Times Magazine* (23 April 2015).

"Without Inspection," *New Yorker* 94:13 (14 May 2018): 76–83; *Poets & Writers* (September/October 2019): 1.

"Women Like Us," *Essence* (May 1996); *Step into a World.* New York: Wiley, 2000.

"World Refugee Day," *The Progressive* (20 June 2013).

"Writing Tragedy, Writing Hope," (lecture) Duke University (9 February 2011).

"A Year and a Day," *New Yorker* 86:44 (9 January 2011): 19–20.

Secondary Sources

Books

Abbott, Elizabeth. *Haiti: A Shattered Nation.* New York: Overlook, 2011.

Brooks, Melanie. *Writing Hard Stories: Celebrated Memoirists Who Shaped Art from Trauma.* Boston: Beacon, 2017.

Chancy, Myriam J.A. *Framing Silence: Revolutionary Novels by Haitian Women.* Piscataway, NJ: Rutgers University Press, 1997.

Clitandre, Nadège T. *Edwidge Danticat: The Haitian Diasporic Imaginary.* Charlottesville: University of Virginia Press, 2018.

Davies, Carole Boyce. *Caribbean Spaces: Escapes from Twilight Zone.* Urbana: University of Illinois Press, 2013.

Dirksen, Rebecca. *After the Dance, the Drums Are Heavy: Carnival, Politics, and Musical Engagement in Haiti.* Oxford, UK: Oxford University Press, 2019.

Ferly, Odile. *A Poetics of Relation: Caribbean Women Writing at the Millennium.* New York: Palgrave Macmillan, 2012.

Hitler, Adolf. *Mein Kampf.* Boston: Houghton Mifflin, 1998.

James, C.I.R. *The Black Jacobins.* New York: Vintage, 1989.

Jarrell, Randall. *Selected Poems.* New York: Farrar, Straus and Giroux, 2007.

Larrier, Renée. *Autofiction and Advocacy in the Francophone Caribbean.* Gainesville, Universe Press of Florida, 2006.

Loichot, Valérie. *Water Graves: The Art of the Unritual in the Greater Caribbean.* Charlottesville: University of Virginia Press, 2020.

Munro, Martin. *Edwidge Danticat: A Reader's Guide.* Charlottesville: University of Virginia Press, 2010.

_____. *Exile and Post-1946 Haitian Literature.* Liverpool, UK: Liverpool University Press, 2007.

_____. "Writing Disaster: Trauma, Memory, and History in Edwidge Danticat's *The Farming of Bones*," *Ethnologies* 28:1 (2006): 81–98.

_____. *Writing on the Fault Line: Haitian Literature and the Earthquake of 2010.* Liverpool, UK: Liverpool University Press, 2014.

Oliver-Rotger, Maria Antonia, ed. *Identity, Diaspora and Return in American Literature.* New York: Routledge, 2015.

Paravisini-Geberrt, Lizabeth. *Literature of the Caribbean.* Santa Barbara, CA: Greenwood, 2008.

Saunders, Nicholas J. *The Peoples of the Caribbean: An Encyclopedia of Archaeology and Traditional Culture.* Santa Barbara, CA: ABC-Clio, 2005.

Articles, Chapters, and Theses

Abate, Heran. "A Joint Emotional World" (interview) (20 March 2020), https:// publicseminar.org/essays/a-joint-emotional-world/

Abbott, Jeff. "The Other Americans: Trump Is Spreading the Virus," *Progressive* (14 May 2020).

Adisa, Opal Palmer. "Up Close and Personal," *African American Review* 43:2–3 (Summer/Fall 2009): 345–355.

Alexander, Simone A. James. "M/othering the Nation: Women's Bodies as Nationalist Trope in Edwidge Danticat's *Breath, Eyes, Memory*," *African American Review* 44:3 (Fall, 2011): 373–390.

Alexandre, Sandy, and Ravi Y. Howard. "Interview," *Journal of Caribbean Literature* 4:3 (Spring 2007): 161–174.

Allfrey, Ella. "Interview," *Granta* (4 July 2011).

Anker, Elizabeth S. "Embodying the People in Edwidge Danticat's *Krik? Krak!*," *Novel* 47:1 (Spring, 2014): 149–166.

"Author Edwidge Danticat Wins $20,000 Story Prize," *AP* (26 February 2020).

Bancroft, Colette. "Review: *Everything Inside*," *Tampa Bay Times* (28 August 2019).

Barron, John. "Early Promise Falls Short: Danticat's Admirable Work Fails to Form a Substantive Whole," *Chicago Tribune* (7 September 2013): 14.

Barsamian, David. "Interview," *Progressive* (1 October 2003).

Beard, David. "Seeing Haiti, When It Can Dance and Laugh," *Boston Globe* (5 September 2002): M7.

Bell, Madison Smartt. "Distant Drums," *Washington Post* (18 August 2002).

Bellamy, Maria Rice. "More Than Hunter or Prey: Duality and Traumatic Memory in Edwidge Danticat's *The Dew Breaker*," *MELUS* 37:1 (Spring 2012).

Bellot, Gabrielle. "Edwidge Danticat Returns to Haiti in New Stories," *Publishers Weekly* (21 June 2019).

Bennett, Ian Bethel. "Review: *Brother, I'm Dying*," *Anthurium* 6:1 (June, 2008): 1–4.

Berger, Rose Marie. "Death by Asylum," *Sojourners* 37:4 (April 2008): 32–36.

Bergner, Gwen. "Danticat's Vodou Vernacular of Women's Human Rights," *American Literary History* 29:3 (Fall, 2017): 521–545.

Birnbaum, Robert. "Interview," *The Morning News* (20 April 2004).

Braziel, Jana Evans. "Daffodils, Rhizomes, Migrations: Narrative Coming of Age in the Diasporic Writings of Edwidge Danticat and Jamaica Kincaid," *Meridians* 3:2 (2003): 110–131.

Brown, DeNeen L. "Interview," *Washington Post* (14 October 2007): M2.

Brown, Jeffrey. "Edwidge Danticat on the Luxury of Creating Art" (interview) *PBS News Hours* (21 October 2020), https://www.pbs.org/newshour/show/edwidge-danticat-on-the-luxury-of-creating-art.

Burnham, Thorald M. "'Everything They Hate': Michèle, Mildred, and Elite Haitian Marrying Strategies in Historical Perspective," *Journal of Family History* 31:1 (2006): 83–109.

Butler, Maia L., and Megan Feifer. "Edwidge Danticat's Elegaic Project," *Revisiting the Elegy in the Black Lives Matter Era.* New York: Routledge, 2020, 200–215.

Cadogan, Garnette. "Interview," *BOMB* (4 November 2014).

Caplan, Benjy. "Miami's Literary Genius," *Miami New Times* (29 August 2013): 28.

Capshaw, Katharine. "The Limitless Vision of Edwidge Danticat's Work for Young People," *Research on Diversity in Youth Literature* 2:2 (2020): 2.

Charters, Mallay. "Edwidge Danticat: A Bitter

Legacy Revisited," *Publishers Weekly* 245:33 (17 August 1998): 42, 43.

Chase, George Davis. "The Origin of Roman Praenomina," *Harvard Studies in Classical Philology* 8 (1897), 103–184.

Chen, Wilson C. "Narrating Diaspora in Edwidge Danticat's Short-Story Cycle *The Dew Breaker*," *Literature Interpretation Theory* 25:3 (2014): 220–241.

Clark, VeVe A. "Developing Diaspora Literacy and Marasa Consciousness," *Theater Survey* 50:1 (2009): 9–18.

Cohen, Magdalena. "The Ability of Water to Heal and Unify in Edwidge Danticat's *The Farming of Bones* and 'Children of the Sea,'" *Caribbean Writer* 18 (2004): 201.

Collins, Anastasia M. "Call and Response: Constructed Identity and Legible Experience in Danticat's Young Adult Novels," *Research on Diversity in Youth Literature* 2:2 (2020): 1–24.

Collins, Jo. "Novels of Transformation and Transplantation: The Postcolonial Bildungsroman and Haitian American Youth in Danticat's *Behind the Mountains* and *Breath, Eyes, Memory*," *Wasafiri* 27:4 (1 December 2012): 27–34.

Collins, Michael S. "Interview," *Callaloo* 30:2 (Spring, 2007): 471–473, 674.

Collins-Hughes, Laura. "Town of Lost Souls," *Boston Globe* (25 August 2013): N13.

Conlogue, Ray. "Haunted by Haiti's Ghosts," (Toronto) *Globe and Mail* (19 April 2004): R3.

Conwell, Joan. "Papa's Masks: Roles of the Father in Danticat's 'The Dew Breaker,'" *Obsidian III* (2005): 221–239.

Conwell, Joanie. "Sunrise over Maafa: On Edwidge Danticat's *Everything Inside*," *Los Angeles Review of Books* (18 September 2019).

Cornish, Audie. "Award-Winning Author Recalls Past Experiences with Hurricanes in Native Haiti," *NPR Weekend Edition* (7 October 2016).

———. "Marking the Events," *NPR Weekend Edition* (11 September 2011).

Courlander, Harold, and Herbert David Croly. "Not in the Cables," *New Republic* (24 November 1937): 67.

Cowen, Tyler. "Ma conversation avec Edwidge Danticat," *Urban Fusion* (5 November 2020).

Crawford, Patricia A., and Sherron Killingsworth Roberts. "Literature as Support: Using Picture Books to Assist Young Children in Coping with Natural Disasters and Human Crises," *Assisting Young Children Caught in Disasters*. New York: Springer, 2018, 171–180.

Daniels, Kyrah M. "Review: *Anacaona*," *Journal of Haitian Studies* 11:2 (2005): 163–164.

"Dark Tales Illuminate Haiti, Before and After Quake," *New York Times* (9 January 2011).

Davis, Rocio G. "Oral Narrative as Short Story Cycle: Forging Community in Edwidge Danticat's *Krik? Krak!*," *MELUS* 26:2 (Summer 2001): 65.

Dayan, Joan. "Erzulie: A Women's History of Haiti," *Research in African Literatures Caribbean Literature* 25:2 (Summer, 1994): 5–31.

DeGraff, Michel. "Boston Public School Partner Explains Haitian Creole Program," *BNN News* (25 September 2017).

De Greff, Dana. "Author Edwidge Danticat on the Dominican Republic: 'Government Is Trying to Erase a Whole Segment of History,'" *Miami New Times* (12 October 2015).

Divakaruni, Chitra. "Dreaming in Haitian," *Los Angeles Weekly* (26 August 1998).

Dorfman, Ariel. "Songs of Loss and Reinvention," *New York Review* (3 December 2020).

Duboin, Corinne. "*After the Dance* d'Edwidge Danticat," *Transatlantica* 2 (15 November 2007): 2.

Duffey, Carolyn. "In Flight from the Borderlines: Roses, Rivers, and Missing Haitian History in Marie Chauvet's 'Colère' and Edwidge Danticat's 'Krik?Krak!' and 'The Farming of Bones,'" *Journal of Caribbean Literatures* 3:1 (Summer, 2001): 77–91.

Dumas, Pierre-Raymond, and Augustin Chenald. "'Célimène' ou la problématique de l'exil au coeur du merveilleux," *Le Nouvelliste* (21 June 2011).

Dyer, Erv. "Interview," *New Pittsburgh Courier* (20 September 2017): A9.

"Edwidge Danticat on Art in the Aftermath of the Quake" (interview) *Boston Haitian Reporter* (2010).

Ellis, Alicia E. "The Art of Death: Grief and Loss in Edwidge Danticat's *Untwine*," *Research on Diversity in Youth Literature* 2:2 (January 2020): 1–20.

Faedi, Benedetta. "The Double Weakness of Girls: Discrimination of Sexual Violence in Haiti," *Stanford Journal of International Law* 44 (2008): 147–204.

Fajilan, Kaitlyn. "Getting Lost in the World of Edwidge Danticat," *Highbrow* (6 November 2013).

Fassler, Joe. "All Immigrants Are Artists," *Atlantic* (27 August 2013).

Federmayer, Eva. "Violence and Embodied Subjectivities: Edwidge Danticat's Breath, Eyes, Memory," *Scholar Critic* 2:3 (December 2015): 1–17.

Feifer, Megan. "The Remembering of Bones," *Palimpsest* 9:1 (2020): 35–49.

Ferrante, Julia. "Storytelling Keeps Memory, Tradition Alive, Author Edwidge Danticat Says," *Targeted News Service* (13 April 2011).

Fichtner, Margaria. "Author Edwidge Danticat Writes about Being Young, Black, Haitian, and Female," *Contemporary Literary Criticism* 139. Detroit: Gale, 2001.

Fish, Amy. "'Leave Us Good News': Collective Narrations of Migration in *Mama's Nightingale*," *Research on Diversity in Youth Literature* 2:2 (January 2020): 1–17.

Flora, Carlin. "Interview," *Psychology Today* 40:6 (November-December 2007).

Forna, Aminatta. "Motherland," *New York Times Book Review* (15 September 2019): 10.

———. "Review: *Everything Inside*," *New York Times* (27 August 2019).

Bibliography

263

Francis, Donette A. "'Silences Too Horrific to Disturb': Writing Sexual Histories in Edwidge Danticat's *Breath, Eyes, Memory*," *Research in African Literatures* 35:2 (Summer, 2004): 75–90.

Freeman, John. "Interview," *St. Petersburg Times* (21 March, 2004).

_____. "Introduction," *Tales of Two Planets: Stories of Climate Change and Inequality in a Divided World*. New York: Penguin, 2020, xi-xxv.

Fürst, Saskia. "Palimpsests of Ancestral Memories: Black Women's Collective Identity Development in Short Stories by Edwidge Danticat and Dionne Brand," *English Academy Review* 34:2 (2017): 66–75.

Gérazime, Roselyne E. "Lasirèn, Labalèn: L'abysse en migration dans *Claire of the Sea Light*," *Journal of Haitian Studies* 25:1 (2019): 178–200.

Germain, Christine. "Review: *Claire of the Sea Light*," *Palimpsest* 3:2 (2014): 214–215.

Gleibermann, Erik. "Inside the Bilingual Writer," *World Literature Today* 92:3 (May-June 2018): 30.

_____. "The Story Will Be There When You Need It," *World Literature Today* 93:1 (Winter 2019): 68–74.

Gonzalez, Fernando. "Little Haiti Book Festival Has Many Stories to Tell," *Miami Herald* (5 May 2019): NE14.

Graham, Renée. "Moving beyond the Divide: People Are Disappointing; Edwidge Danticat's New Stories Are Not," *Boston Globe* (1 September 2019): N10.

Halford, Macy. "Edwidge Danticat's Dangerous Creation," *New Yorker* (6 January 2011).

Handal, Nathalie. "We Are All Going to Die," *Guernica* (15 January 2011).

Harbawi, Semia. "Writing Memory: Edwidge Danticat's Limbo Inscriptions," *Journal of West Indian Literature* 16:1 (1 November 2007): 37–58.

Harris, Michael. "Review: *After the Dance*," *Los Angeles Times* (11 August 2002): R7.

Harvey, Charlotte Bruce. "Haiti's Storyteller," *Brown Alumni Magazine* (January/ February 2011).

Hawthorne, Evelyn. "Sites/Sights of Difference," *MaComère* (2004): 40–48.

Henderson, Jane. "Edwidge Danticat, St. Louis Literary Award Winner, Says She's Gained Nuance, Deeper Meaning," *Chicago* (18 October 2019).

Henricks, Clara. "Review: *My Mommy Medicine*," *School Library Journal* (1 March 2019).

Hewett, Heather. "At the Crossroads: Disability and Trauma in *The Farming of Bones*," *MELUS* 31 (Fall 2006): 123–145.

Higgins, Jim. "Uncommon Sadness, Uncommon Beauty," (Portland, ME) *Press Herald* (4 October 2015): E5.

Holden, Stephen. "The Old Country Never Goes Away," *New York Times* (20 November 2014).

Horn, Jessica. "Edwidge Danticat: An Intimate Reader," *Meridians* 1:2 (Spring 2001): 19–25.

Ibarrola-Armendáriz, Aitor. "Broken Memories of a Traumatic Past and the Redemptive Power of Narrative in the Fiction of Edwidge Danticat," *Cross/Cultures* 136 (2011): 3–27, 248.

_____. "The Language of Wounds and Scars in Edwidge Danticat's 'The Dew Breaker,'" *Journal of English Studies* 8 (2010): 23–56.

Inskeep, Steve. "Whether or Not We Belong Is Not Defined by Us," *NPR* (30 August 2019).

Irwin, Demetria. "Barnard College Honors Edwidge Danticat," *Amsterdam News* (3 November 2011): 25.

Jaggi, Maya. "Island Memories," *Guardian* (19 November 2004): 20.

Jean-Charles, Marsha Bianca. "Of Griottes & Pantomimes: Dyaspora Love, Dreams, Memories, and Realities in the Works of Edwidge Danticat as they relate to Black Feminisms," thesis, Wesleyan University, 2011.

Jeremiah, Methuselah, and Moses Aule. "Exploring Feminine Subjectivity in Caribbean History: A New Historicist Perspective in Edwidge Danticat's *The Farming to Bones*," *Igwebuike* 4:2 (2019).

Joffre, Ruth. "It Wants to Be Told," *Kenyon Review* (10 October 2019).

Johnson, Newtona. "Challenging Internal Colonialism: Edwidge Danticat's Feminist Emancipatory Enterprise," *Obsidian III* (2005): 147–166.

_____. "Interview," *Obsidian III* 6/7:2/1 (Fall 2005–2006): 147–166, 264.

Kakutani, Michiko. "Hiding from a Brutal Past Spent Shattering Lives in Haiti," *New York Times* (10 March, 2004).

Kaussen Valerie. "Slaves, Viejos, and the Internationale," *Research in African Literature* 35:4 (Winter 2004).

Kennon, Raquel D. "'We Know People by Their Stories': Madness, Babies, and Dolls in Edwidge Danticat's *Krik? Krak!*," *Madness in Black Women's Diasporic Fictions*. New York: Springer, 2017, 163–197.

Kerlee, Ime. "Interview," https://scholarblogs.emory.edu/postcolonialstudies/2014/06/10/danticat-edwidge/, May 2017.

Kinsey, Caroline A. "Review: *The Art of Death*," *Lancet Oncology* 18:12 (1 December 2017): 1576,

Knepper, Wendy. "In/justice and Necro-natality in Edwidge Danticat's *Brother, I'm Dying*," *Journal of Commonwealth Literature* 47:2 (June, 2012): 191–205.

Kopchik, Kathryn. "Bucknell Forum: Haitian-American Edwidge Danticat to Speak April 12," *Targeted News Service* (7 March 2011).

Krementz, Jill. "Interview," *The Writer* 117:12 (December 2004): 66.

Krug, Julie. "The Spectacular KICK," *The Writer* 128:11 (November 2015): 24–29.

"La nouvelle collection 'L'Arbre du Voyager,'" *Le Nouvelliste* (3 November 2009).

Lamothe, Daphne. "Carnival in the Creole City: Place, Race, and Identity in the Age of Globalization," *Biography* 35:2 (Spring 2012): 360–374.

Latchman, Renee. "Edwidge Danticat's *Breath, Eyes, Memory*: A Critique on the Tradition of 'Testing,'" *African Youth in Contemporary Literature and Popular Culture*. New York: Routledge, 2014, 65–74.

Layne, Prudence, and Lester Goran. "Haiti: History, Voice, Empowerment," *Sargasso 2* (2004–2005): 3–17.

Lee, Felicia. Lewis-Brown, Alscess. "Bearing Witness," *Caribbean Writer* 28 (2014): 208.

Lipman, Jana K. "Immigrant and Black in Edwidge Danticat's *Brother, I'm Dying*," *Modern American History* 2:1 (March, 2019): 71–75.

Loichot, Valérie. 'Edwidge Danticat's Kitchen History," *Meridians* 5:1 (2004): 92–116.

Louisdhon-Louinis, Lucrèce. "Interview," *MediaSpace* (25 August 2013).

Lyden, Jacki. "Edwidge Danticat, Dealing with Birth and Death," *NPR Fresh Air* (26 September 2007.

Lyons, Bonnie. "Interview," *Contemporary Literature* 44:2 (Summer 2003): 181–198.

MacCann, Donnarae, and Katharine Capshaw Smith. "This Quest for Ourselves," *Children's Literature Association Quarterly* 30:2 (Summer 2005): 137–139.

Mahase, Radica. "The Terror and the Time: Banal Violence and Trauma in Caribbean Discourse," *Nieuwe West—Indische Gids* 92:1/2 (2018): 156–157.

Manzella, Abby. "Danticat's Love Stories Can't Escape Politics in 'Everything Inside,'" *St. Louis Post-Dispatch* (15 September 2019): B8.

Martin, Janelle. "Wandering Bodies: The Disruption of Identities in Jamaica Kincaid's Lucy and Edwidge Danticat's *The Farming of Bones*" (dissertation) Wake Forest University, 2015.

Martinez, Alexandra. "Edwidge Danticat Discusses Memoir and Immigration at Little Haiti Cultural Center," *Miami New Times* (30 March 2016).

Martinez-Falquina, Silvia. "Postcolonial Trauma Theory in the Contact Zone: The Strategic Representation of Grief in Edwidge Danticat's *Claire of the Sea Light*," *Humanities* 4:4 (2015): 834–860.

Matza, Michael. "Interview," *Philadelphia Inquirer* (6 February 2012): A2.

McCormick, Robert H. "Review: *Brother, I'm Dying*," *World Literature Today* 82:1 (2008): 74.

McEntyre, Marilyn. "Seeing Others Through: The Work of Witness," *Christian Scholar's Review* 48:1 (Fall, 2018): 45–50.

Meacham, Cherie. "Traumatic Realism in the Fiction of Edwidge Danticat," *Journal of Haitian Studies* (1 April 2005): 122–139.

Mika, Kasia. "New Beginnings without New Heroes? 1791–1804 Haitian Revolution and the 2010 Earthquake in Nick Lake's *In Darkness* (2012)," *Karib–Nordic Journal for Caribbean Studies* 4:1 (1 November 2018).

Miller, E. Ethelbert. "Interview," *Foreign Policy in Focus* (16 October 2007).

Mirabal, Nancy Raquel. "Dyasporic Appetites and Longings," *Callaloo* 30:1 (Winter 2007): 26–39, 410.

Mirakhor, Leah. "Review: *The Art of Death*," *Los Angeles Times* (14 July 2017).

Misra, Jivin. "Interview," *Brooklyn Review* (18 June 2018).

Misrahi-Barak, Judith. "'My Mouth Is the Keeper of Both Speech and Silence. .' or The Vocalisation of Silence in Caribbean Short Stories by Edwige Danticat," *Journal of the Short Story in English* 47 (1 December 2006): 155–166.

Moïse, Myriam. "Borderless Spaces and Alternative Subjectivities," *Border Transgression and Reconfiguration of Caribbean Spaces*. London: Palgrave Macmillan, 2020, 193–217.f

Montgomery, Maxine L. "A Lasiren Song for the *Wonn*: Edwidge Danticat's *Claire of the Sea Light* and the Legend of Mami Wata," *CLA Journal* 59:4 (June 2016): 316–329.

Mouawad, Wajdi. "Compter les morts en Haïti," *Le Monde* (29 June 2012): 8.

Murphy, Dwyer. "The Art of Not Belonging," *Guernica* (3 September 2013).

Murriel, Maria. "Read This Book About Writing. About Death," *World* (14 July 2017).

Nance, Kevin. "Haiti Noir, Haiti Light," *Poets & Writers* 39:1 (January/February 2011): 12–13.

Navarro, Xavier. "Primal Scream? Rebel Yell! Correlations Between Death and Nostalgia and the Preservation of History in the Haitian Storytelling Tradition: *Krik? Krak!*," *Caribbean without Borders*. Cambridge: Cambridge Scholars, 2015.

Nesbitt, Nick. "Review: *After the Dance*," *Journal of Haitian Studies* 10:1 (2004): 194–196.

Norris, Michele. "Interview," *NPR* (15 March 2004).

Novak, Amy. "'A Marred Testament': Cultural Trauma and Narrative in Danticat's *The Farming of Bones*," *Arizona Quarterly* 62:4 (2006): 93–120.

Nurse, Donna Bailey. "Edwidge Danticat Rescues Haiti from Its Western Labels," (Toronto) *Globe and Mail* (30 August 2013): D12.

Nzengou-Tayo, Marie-José. "Review: Create Dangerously," *Caribbean Quarterly* 58:4 (December 2012): 127–133, 146.

Obejas, Achy. "Bearing the Unforgivable," *World Literature Today* 93:1 (Winter 2019): 66–67.

Omang, Joanne. "Review: *Krik? Krak!*," *Washington Post* (14 May 1995).

Ortiz, Ricardo L. "Reiterating Performatives: The Writer, the Reader and the Risks of Literary Action," *Latinx Literature Now*. London: Palgrave Macmillan, 2019, 13–21.

Patterson, Christina. "Interview," (London) *Independent* (13 March 1999): 14.

Pegram, Laura. "A Sense of Rupture," *Kweli Journal* (17 October 2014).

Phillips, Delores B. "Recipes for Reading Recipes? Culinary Writing and the Stakes of Multiethnic Pseudonarrative," *Narrative Culture* 7:1 (Spring, 2020): 79–97.

Pierce, Yolanda. "Restless Spirits: Syncretic Religion in Edwidge Danticat's *Breath, Eyes, Memory*," *Journal of Pan African Studies* 3:5 (March 2010).

Pierre, Jacques. "The Growth of Creole Language Studies," *Duke Today* (5 June 2014).

———. "Jacques Pierre: Creole a Key to Haitian Literacy," *Durham Herald-Sun* (5 September 2014).

———. "Jacques Pierre: Help for Haiti Must

Include Embracing Creole," (Raleigh) *News & Observer* (21 February 2014).

Pierre-Pierre, Garry. "At Home with Edwidge Danticat: Haitian Tales, Flatbush Scenes," *New York Times* (26 January 1995): C1.

Poole, Steven. "Review: *Create Dangerously*," *Guardian* (6 November 2010): 8.

Postigo, Daniela. "Author Danticat MFA '93 Returns to Campus for Reading," *Brown Daily Herald* (21 September 2007).

Pulitano, Elvira. "An Immigrant Artist at Work" (interview), *Small Axe* 15:3 (1 November 2011): 39–61.

Putnam, Amanda. "Braiding Memories: Resistant Storytelling within Mother-Daughter Communities in Edwidge Danticat's *Krik? Krik!*," *Journal of Haitian Studies* 9:1 (Spring 2003): 52–65.

Pyne-Timothy, Helen. "Language, Theme and Tone in Edwidge Danticat's Work," *Journal of Haitian Studies* (1 October 2001): 128–137.

Raab, Josef. "Liberation and Lingering Trauma: U.S. Present and Haitian Past in Edwidge Danticat's *The Dew Breaker*," *Politics and Cultures of Liberation* 7 (3 April 2018): 265–284.

"Review: *The Art of Death*," *Kirkus Reviews* (1 June 2017).

"Review: *Célimène*," *France-Antilles* (30 June 2010).

"Review: *Claire of the Sea Light*," *Publisher's Weekly* (27 May 2014).

"Review: *Eight 'Days*,'" NPR Morning Edition (9 September 2010).

"Review: *My Mommy Medicine*," *Kirkus Reviews* (15 December 2018).

"Review: *My Mommy Medicine*," *Publisher's Weekly* 265:43 (22 October 2018): 83.

Robinette, Anne. "Bilingual and Bimodal Expression: The Creolization in Edwidge Danticat's Oeuvre," (thesis) Dickinson College, spring, 2017.

Rockett, Darcel. "Interview," *Chicago Tribune* (8 May 2019).

Rosner, Josh. "Smiling as Your Soul Aches," *Canberra Times* (13 November 2010): 29.

Rossi, Jennifer C. "'Let the Words Bring Wings to Our Feet': Negotiating Exile and Trauma through Narrative in Danticat's *Breath, Eyes, Memory*," *Obsidian III* 6:2 (Fall/Winter, 2005): 203–220.

Rousmaniere, Dana. "Grappling with Haiti's Beasts," *Atlantic* (June 2004).

Rubio-Zepeda, José. "Transitory Ghosts: Haitians and Dominico-Haitians in Santo Domingo," *Portal* 11 (2016): 30–32.

Sabatier, Diane. "Une Haïtienne-Américaine en quête de mémoire à Haïti dans 'The Missing Peace d'Edwidge Danticat,'" *Babel* 40 (2019): 225–244.

Sairsingh, Marie. "The Archeology of Memory: Ontological Reclamation in Danticat's *Brother, I'm Dying* and *The Farming of Bones*," *International Journal on Studies in English Language and Literature* 1:1 (March, 2013): 6–10.

Samway, Patrick. "A Homeward Journey: Edwidge

Danticat's Fictional Landscapes, Mindscapes, Genescapes, and Signscapes in *Breath, Eyes, Memory*," *Mississippi Quarterly* 57:1 (1 December 2003): 75–84.

Santiago, Soledad. "Danticat at the Crossroads," *Santa Fe New Mexican* (25 November 2005): PA26.

Sartorius, David. "Paper Trails," *English Language Notes* 56:2 (2018): 25–27.

Sayers, Valerie. "Giving Grief Its Due,"' *Commonweal* 144:14 (8 September 2017): 29–30.

Schaub, Michael. "Coming to Terms with Loss and Grief in Gorgeous *Everything Inside*," *NPR* (29 August 2019).

Shank, Jenny. "Review: *Everything Inside*," (Minneapolis) *Star Tribune* (29 August 2019).

Shea, Renée. "The Dangerous Job of Edwidge Danticat," *Belles Lettres* 10:3 (Summer 1995): 12–15; *Callaloo* 19:2 (Spring, 1996): 382–389.

_____. "The Terrible Days Behind Us and the Uncertain Ones Ahead: Edwidge Danticat Talks about *The Dew Breaker*," *Caribbean Writer 2004* (2004): 241.

Simon, Daniel. "Review: *The Art of Death*," *World Literature Today* 92:2 (March/April 2018): 25.

Slone, Isabel B. "Review: *The Art of Death*," (Toronto) *Globe and Mail* (21 July 2017).

Smiley, Tavis. "Interview," *Tavis Smiley Show* (Los Angeles NPR) (6 November 2004).

Smith, Katharine Capshaw. "Interview," *Children's Literature Association Quarterly* 30:2 (Summer, 2005): 194–205.

Solomon, Lois K. "Noted Novelist Offers Writing Tips to Fourth Graders for State Exams," *South Florida Sun-Sentinel* (27 January 2017): B1.

Sontag, Deborah. "Island Magic," *New York Times* (30 August 2013).

Sorensen, Marilou. "Book Crackles with Haiti's Flavor, Tradition," *Deseret News* (20 February 1996).

Sotter, Anna O., and Sean P. Connors. "Beyond Relevance to Literary Merit: Young Adult Literature as 'Literature,'" *ALAN Review* 37 (Fall 2009): 62–67.

Spears, Crystal. "Removing the Masks of Lady Liberty: The Grotesque in the Literatures of the Defeated Americas," *CEA Critic* 75:3 (2013): 235–242.

Spratling, Cassandra. "Haitian Heritage Author Edwidge Danticat Treats Poverty and Oppression in Plain Words," *Detroit Free Press* (1 April 2002): C1.

Stevenson, Deborah, ed. "Review: *Untwine*," *Bulletin of the Center for Children's Books* 69:4 (December 2015): 192.

Strehle, Susan. "Global Fictions of Wreckage and Unsheltered Communities," *Contemporary Historical Fiction, Exceptionalism and Community*. London: Palgrave Macmillan, 2020, 189–199.

Sylvain, Patrick. "Textual Pleasures and Violent Memories in Edwidge Danticat *The Farming of Bones*," *International Journal* 2:3 (2014): 1–19.

Tillotson, Kristin. "Daughter of Haiti,"

(Minneapolis) *Star Tribune* (8 September 2013): E1.

Tobar, Hector. "Review: *Claire of the Sea Light*," *Los Angeles Times* (25 August 2013): E4.

Treisman, Deborah. "Edwidge Danticat on Her Caribbean Immigrant Experience," *New Yorker* (7 May 2018).

_____. "Edwidge Danticat on Memory and Migration," *New Yorker* (7 May 2017).

Ukani, Alisha. "Language and Activism," *Harvard Political Review* (26 March 2017).

Valbrun, Marjorie. "Haiti's Eloquent Daughter," *Black Issues Book Review* 6:4 (July/ August 2004): 42.

Verbrugge, Jennifer. "Review: *Mama's Nightingale*," *School Library Journal* 62:5 (May 2016): 61.

Villalba, Carolina. "A Newer Noir: Bringing a Classic Genre to the Caribbean," *Anthurium* 11:1 (2014): 1–4.

Vitone, Elaine. "Interview," *Publishers Weekly* 254:30 (30 July 2007): 66.

Vossoughi, Shirin, Paula K. Hooper, and Meg Escudé. "Making Through the Lens of Culture and Power," *Harvard Educational Review* 86:2 (Summer 2016): 206–232, 307–309.

Wells, Leslie. "Edwidge Danticat in Conversation at Purchase College," (Bronx) *Riverdale Press* (27 September 2019).

Wilentz, Amy. "The Other Wide of the Water," *New York Times Book Review* (10 October 2010): BR-14.

Williams, Kam. "CP2 Talks with Critically Acclaimed Author Edwidge Danticat," (Cleveland, OH) *Call & Post* (1 December 2010): CP2.

Williams, Wilda. "Interview," *Library Journal* 135:20 (1 December 2010).

Wilson, Betty. "Literature and Activism, Literature as Activism," *Caribbean Quarterly* 66:3 (2020): 405–424.

Wilson, Raffaela N. "Black Women and the Search for Spiritual Liberation," (graduate thesis) University of Georgia, 2009.

Wucker, Michele. "Edwidge Danticat: A Voice for the Voiceless," *Americas* 52:3 (May 2000): 40.

_____. "Race & Massacre in Hispaniola," *Tikkun* 13:6 (November/December 1998): 61–63.

Wynn Judith. "Cruising Through Carnival; Prejudices Hinder Look at Famous Celebration," *Boston Herald* (1 September 2002): 61.

Young, Jason R. "All God's Children Had Wings: The Flying African in History," *Journal of Africana Religions* 5:1 (2017): 50–70.

Zipp, Georg. "Selling Poverty: Junot Díaz's and Edwidge Danticat's Assessments of Picturesque Stereotypes of Poverty in the Caribbean," *Zeitschrift für Anglistik und Amerikanistik* 63:2 (2015): 229–246.

Zipp, Yvonne, "Review: *Claire of the Sea Light*," *Christian Science Monitor* (26 August 2013): 20.

Digital Sources

Brown, Jeffrey. "Edwidge Danticat on the Luxury of Creating Art" (interview) *PBS News Hours* (21 October 2020), https://www.pbs.org/newshour/show/edwidge-danticat-on-the-luxury-of-creating-art

Chambers, Kia. "Review: *My Mommy Medicine*," https://comewagalong.com/book-review-my-mommy-medicine-by-edwidge-danticat/ (12 May 20219).

Chen, Karissa. "Edwidge Danticat Wants More Haitian Storytellers" (30 September 2019): electricliterature.com/edwidge-danticat-wants-more-haitian-storytellers/

"The Dominican Republic's 'Ethnic Purging': Edwidge Danticat on Mass Deportation of Haitian Families," (interview) *Democracy Now.org* (17 June 2015).

Dowling, Brendan. "Maneuvering Myself Around a Scene: A Conversation with Edwidge Danticat," publiclibrariesonline.org/2013/10/maneuveringmyself-around-a-scene-a-conversation-with-edwidge-danticat/

"Edwidge Danticat, Author and Activist, Speaks Out Against Racialized State Violence," *UCLA Center for the Study of Women,* https://csw.ucla.edu/ 2016/05/23/edwidge-danticat-author-activist-speaks-racialized-state-violence/.

Headlee, Celeste. "Dominicans, Haitians Remember Parsley Massacre," *NPR* (1 October 2012): www.npr.org/2012/10/01/162088692/dominicans-haitians-remember-parsley-massacre.

"Interview," *BookBrowse* (2004), https://www.bookbrowse.com/author.

Jurney, Florence Ramond. "Exile and Relation to the Mother/Land in Edwidge Danticat's Breath Eyes Memory and The Farming of Bones," http:// cai.sg.inter.edu/revista-ciscla/volume31/jurney.

Laurence, Alexander. "Interview," *Alcoholreviews:* http://www.freewilliamsburg.com/still_fresh/edwidge.html.

Lee, Felicia. "Dark Tales Illuminate Haiti, Before and After Quake," *New York Times (*10 January 2011): C1.

Long, Karen R. "The Artist as Activist," *Anisfield-Wolf Book Awards* (23 March 2016): https://www.anisfield-wolf.org/2016/03/the-artist-as-activist-author-edwidge-danticat-in-cleveland/

Michel, Easmanie. "Interview," www.youtube.com/watch?v=OMpv2OzcDKQ, 3 October 2014.

Nix, Kemmie. "Review: *My Mommy Medicine*," https://www.parentschoice.org/ product/my-mommy-medicine/2019.

Racine-Toussaint. "Interview," University of California Television (31 January 2008): https://www.youtube.com/watch?v=YhMk6X3VBrE.

"Review: *My Mommy Medicine*," (London) *Daily Mail,* https://shop.dailymail.co.uk/reader link/my-mommy-medicine-by-edwidge-danti cat-hardcover-0da018a536c549fba55516b2dbee6 79c-p.html

Savaiano, Peter. "Review: "Reading Lessons," https://iiereadingcircle.wordpress.com/2013/

02/17/reading-lessons-by-edwidge-danticat/ (17 February 2013).

Shamsie, Kamila. "Memory, Ritual and Migration," *Edinburgh International Book Festival* (interview) (15 August 2020), https://www.edbookfest.co.uk/press- release/memory-ritual-and-migration-discussed-by-edwidge-danticat-and- kamila-shamsie.

"A Wall of Fire Rising," https://www.bisd303.org/cms/lib3/WA01001636/Centricity/Domain/1342/-A%20Wall%20of%20Fire%20Rising.pdf.

Index

Numbers in **boldface** indicate major entries

abortion 2, 92, 97, 150, 209
adaptation 1–2, 6, 19, 24, 32, 34,
  43–44, 54, 64, 68–69, 77, 81, 87,
  149, 156, 220, 250
Africa 1, 15, 26–27, 32, 36–37,
  45–46, 48–49, 54, 56–57, 62, 64,
  68, 70, 72, 77, 80, 88, 90–91, 108,
  114–116, 119, 126, 129, 131–133,
  136, 139–140, 147–148, 152, 160,
  172–174, 176, 178, 184, 190–191,
  194, 196–197, 200–203, 205–207,
  209, 217–219, 230–231, 236–238,
  240–241, 247, 250
The African Lookbook 80, 166,
  222–224, 256
*After the Dance: A Walk Through
  Carnival in Jacmel, Haiti* 4–6,
  21, 23, 43, **45–47**, 48, 61, 63–64,
  66, 78, 82–83, 92–94, 106, 129–
  130, 137, 140, 145, 148, 167, 172,
  178, 181–182, 195, 200, 207–208,
  215–217, 219, 227–228, 230–235,
  241, 244, 250–251, 255
The Agronomist 4, 23, 240
"AHA!" 191
"All Geography Is Within Me" 69,
  151, 210, 248
allegory 103, 119, 140
American Book Award 4, 20, 122
*Anacoana: Golden Flower,
  Haiti, 1490* 1, 4, 9, 26, 43, 45,
  47–49, 64, 68, 76, 79, 81–83, 90,
  92–95, 98, 105, 107, 109, 123, 127,
  130–131, 136, 138–139, 142, 145,
  149, 166–169, 173, 177, 181, 185,
  187, 194–195, 198, 200, 203–204,
  206, 209, 217, 220, 223, 227, 229,
  230, 232, 234
Anacaona's Genealogy 50
"Anniversary" 73, 174, 185
"Anniversary Blues" 93, 113, 248
Arawak 2, 37, 45, 92, 120, 236
Aristide, Jean-Bertrand 16, 21, 25,
  54, 58, 102, 148, 239, 242
*The Art of Death: Writing the
  Final Story* 2, 5–6, 10, 22,
  33–34, 36, 38, **50–53**, 69, 82–83,
  92–94, 97, 99, 106, 108, 113,
  123, 126–127, 144–145, 166, 185,
  193–194, 196, 198, 201, 205, 210,
  228, 230–232, 250

"The Artists of Maténwa" 224,
  227, 252

"Bajou/Dawn" 210
"Bastille Day" 6, 37, 118
Bazile, Dédée 153
"Be Unafraid" 256
"Becoming Brazilian" 63, 131,
  190, 248
Behind the Mountains 1, 4, 12,
  21–22, 44, **53–55**, 66, 80–81, 83,
  91, 97, 109, 132, 136, 139, 141, 143,
  147, 164, 167, 169, 171, 174, 177, 179,
  185, 196, 204, 211, 219–220, 227,
  229, 230, 232, 235, 248–249, 251
Behind the Mountains **Genealogy
  55–56**
"Between the Pool and the
  Gardenias" 4, 18, 65–66, 83,
  93–94, 96, 111, 137, 149, 152,
  154, 157, 167, 169, 172, 177, 179,
  184–185, 193–194, 206, 213, 220,
  229, 231
"The Book of Miracles" 66, 83, 96,
  101, 129, 138, 143, 151, 159
"The Book of the Dead" 166, 176–
  177, 208, 220, 230, 233, 235–236
Boukman Dutty 133, 153, 158, 218,
  228–229, 237, 241, 246–247
Boyer, Faidherbe "Fedo" 21–23,
  45–46, 52, 54, 83–84, 106
Boyer, Leila 18, 22, 67, 175, 191
Boyer, Mira 18, 23, 67, 175, 191

Breath, Eyes, Memory 1, 4, 7, 14,
  16–17, 19–20, 44, **56–57**, 60–62,
  65–66, 77, 80–81, 83, 85–85, 91,
  94, 97, 106, 109, 115, 131, 133, 135–
  136, 141, 145, 147, 149, 151, 160,
  163, 167, 169, 172, 174, 176, 186,
  188, 194, 198–199, 204, 206–208,
  210, 214–216, 223–225, 227–235,
  244–245, 248
"The Bridal Seamstress" 6, 97, 99,
  102, 151, 166, 176, 186, 188, 209,
  220, 228, 249, 251
Brooklyn 1, 3–4, 8, 12–14, 16,
  21–22, 27, 30, 32, 35, 53–56, 58,
  91, 99–101, 108, 119, 130, 132,
  150, 155, 179, 202, 208, 239, 243,
  245–246

Brother, I'm Dying 1, 5, 25–27, 30,
  34, 36–37, **57–60**, 80–81, 82–84,
  86, 92–94, 96, 98, 123, 128, 132–
  133, 135, 137, 140, 142, 145–146,
  158, 166–169, 171, 178–179, 181,
  186, 188, 198–199, 202, 208, 210,
  220, 224, 227–235, 244
Brown University 16–18, 26, 28,
  204

Caco Genealogy 24
Cane 2, 20, 26, 31, 48, 57, **61–63**,
  77, 109, 121–123, 125–126,
  130–131, 139, 143, 150, 162, 171,
  176–178, 182, 188, 192, 194, 200,
  202, 204, 206, 214, 238, 242, 245
Carib 48, 120, 138, 194, 206, 230,
  246–247
Carnival 1–2, 4, 11, 21, 23, 43,
  45–48, 61, **63–65**, 78, 81–82, 100,
  110, 130, 137, 148, 172, 174, 178,
  195, 204, 207, 215, 219, 242, 245,
  248, 250–252
"Carnivalia" 45
"Caroline's Wedding" 5, 34, 37,
  61, 65, 77, 80, 84, 94, 96–97, 106,
  109, 111, 132, 146, 148, 150, 152,
  156, 163, 169, 174, 177–178, 187,
  193–195, 198, 202, 204–205, 227,
  233, 235, 251
Catholicism 2, 6, 46, **65–67**, 77,
  88, 100, 112–113, 116, 129, 143–144,
  151, 157, 161, 166, 174, 185–188,
  193, 195, 197, 201, 207, 216, 218,
  221, 225, 233, 239, 243, 247
"Celia" 147, 228–229, 252
Célimène 1, 5, 43, 61, **67–68**, 76–
  78, 81, 84, 92, 97, 108, 130–131,
  137–139, 144, 147, 167–168, 162,
  178–179, 182, 186–187, 190, 194,
  198, 209, 218, 220, 223, 247
Children of the Sea (play) 19, 24
"Children of the Sea" (story) 7, 15,
  17–18, 66, 82, 84, 90, 92–94, 96,
  111, 115, 133, 138, 140, 146–147,
  149, 151, 158, 167, 169, 171, 174,
  179, 186, 193–194, 198, 201, 203,
  219–220, 227, 230, 234, 241,
  250–251
children's literature 2, 26, 36,
  68–70, 213

Index

"Clair de Lune" 74, 186
Claire of the Sea Light (novel) 2, 5–6, 31–32, 43, 63, 65, 69, **70–75**, 76, 78–80, 84–85, 90, 92–95, 97, 106, 107, 111, 115–116, 126, 128, 131, 134–135, 141, 143–144, 146, 162, 166–169, 173, 176–181, 183, 186–192, 194–195, 198, 201, 205, 208, 215, 218, 220, 223–225, 227–235, 241–244, 249, 251
"Claire of the Sea Light" (story) 5–6, 9, 28
Claire of the Sea Light Genealogy (novel) **75–76**
Claire of the Sea Light Genealogy (story) **76**, 168–169, 181, 220
Colonialism 2, 4, 10, 18, 20–21, 23, 45–46, 48–49, 55–56, 61–64, 66, 68–69, 74, **76–78**, 82, 88, 90–91, 98, 109, 110, 114–115, 130, 132–133, 136, 138–139, 150, 158, 173, 181, 187, 193, 200, 217, 236–238, 241–242, 247
Color 3, 5, 11, 56, 59, **78–80**, 98, 102, 108, 122, 131, 144, 159–160, 164, 175, 180–181, 189, 191–193, 198, 217–218, 224–225, 230
Coming of Age 2, 43, 47, 55–56, 64, **81–83**, 98, 100, 103, 127–128, 130, 136, 139, 146, 155, 174, 212
"Condolences" 63, 106, 109, 179, 230
"Connecting the Political and Personal" 256
Courage and Pain 8, 163
"Crabs" 132, 196, 235, 248
Create Dangerously: The Immigrant Artist at Work 2, 5, 9, 24, 27–31, 35, 56, 64, 79, 82–84, **85–90**, 92–93, 95–97, 106, 110, 116, 128, 137, 140, 142, 144, 147, 158, 163, 167, 169, 173, 183, 192, 196, 200, 203, 205, 208, 210, 214, 218, 221, 227–235, 242–244, 251
The Creation of Adam 17, 255
Creole 2–3, 7, 9–15, 18, 23–24, 45, 56, 58, 69, 86, **90–92**, 149–150, 158–159, 161, 164–165, 182, 201, 237, 239, 244
"A Crime to Dream" 137, 146, 222, 248

dance 1, 15, 43, 45, 47–48, 64, 66, 68, 71, 77, 90, 103, 106, 115, 118, 125, 128, 137, 139, 173, 201, 210, 222, 228, 230–231, 233, 247–248, 250
"Dangerous Unselfishness" 257
Dantica, Denise 7, 9–10, 12, 46, 140, 144, 169, 178, 188, 193, 215, 224, 241
Dantica, Joseph Nosius 3–5, 7–12, 20, 22, 24–27, 31, 43, 46–51, 57–60, 69, 80–81, 83–84, 94, 128, 133, 140, 142, 146, 158, 166, 178, 186, 192, 193, 196, 204, 209, 220, 241, 247, 250, 252

Dantica, Maxo 8, 9, 25, 28, 59, 93, 113, 128, 144, 169
Danticat, André Miracin 3, 5, 8, 12, 22, 24, 26, 51, 57–60, 69, 123, 135, 142, 166, 189, 193, 199, 220
Danticat, Eliab André "Bob" 9–12, 58, 83, 145, 163, 169, 171, 249
Danticat, Rose Souvenance 5, 8–9, 11–14, 17–18, 22, 32–34, 51, 53, 69, 84, 93–94, 111, 135, 144, 164, 168–169, 171, 179, 186, 189, 197–198, 210–211, 221, 224
Danticat Family Tree **41–42**
"Dawn After the Caribbean Tempests" 35, 77, 140
death 1, 4–6, 9, 12, 14–16, 19, 25, 27–32, 34, 44, 48, 50–54, 62, 64, 66, 70–74, 79, 82, 84, 86–88, 90, **92–97**, 98–111, 120–129, 133–136, 140, 142–150, 152, 154–156, 158, 161, 169–170, 172, 174, 179, 181–187, 192–193, 195, 199–200, 202–206, 208, 210–212, 214–215, 217–220, 222, 228, 232, 235, 238–239, 241, 243, 247
"Death by Asylum" 147
"Death Cannot Write Its Own Story" 38
"Demonstrators in Haiti Are Fighting for an Uncertain Future" 134, 194
deportation 5, 32–33, 35, 37, 44, 54, 92, 108, 128, 133, 164, 170–171
"A Despot Walks into a Killing Field" 94, 110, 137, 187, 189, 194
details 2, 4, 6, 20, 25, 48, 52, 54, 57, 63–65, 67–68, 77, 81, 87, **97–99**, 101, 104–105, 108, 137–138, 147, 151–152, 154, 156, 160, 167, 174, 181, 183–184, 190, 194, 203, 298, 216, 223, 231, 244, 249
"Detention Is No Holiday" 27, 30
The Dew Breaker (novel) 1, 4, 24–25, 28, 66, 73, 82, 86, 93, **99–105**, 115, 133, 143–144, 150, 169, 181, 187, 190, 195, 221, 227–249, 235, 241, 243, 246, 248
"The Dew Breaker" (story) 37, 44, 61, 94–95, 98, 109, 111, 127, 133, 140, 143, 169, 184, 206, 225, 227, 244
The Dew Breaker Genealogy 105
"Di Mwen, Tell Me" 73, 85, 202
diaspora 1, 3–5, 7–13, 16, 20–23, 25–30, 32–38, 44–45, 54–59, 61, 67–68, 70, 73–74, 80–82, 83–89, 91–92, 94, 97, 100, 102, 104, 110, 115, 118–120, 139, 127–129, 130–134, 138, 140, 146–149, 150, 152, 154, 156, 158–159, 161–163, 165–166, 169–171, 178–179, 181, 184, 186, 188–189, 191–192, 195–196, 201–203, 205, 207–209, 214, 219–222, 229, 236–237, 239–240, 242, 246–247, 249–252
"Dies Irae" 257
"Does It Work?" 110

Dominican Republic 8, 10, 15, 19, 26, 31–32, 49, 62–63, 121–122, 126, 143, 148–150, 158, 169, 176, 185, 191–192, 196–197, 201–203, 227, 237–238, 240–243, 245
"The Dominican Republic and Haiti: A Shared View from the Diaspora" 61, 121, 139, 191
"The Dominican Republic's War on Haitian Workers" 90, 227
"Dosas" 5–6, 61, 65, 73, 78, 84, 96–97, 106, 117, 120, 131, 142, 172–173, 176, 186, 200, 221, 223, 227–231, 233, 235, 242, 248
doubles 83–85, **105–107**, 211, 249, 251
"Dream of the Butterflies" 17, 43, 47, 79, 94, 96, 98, 108, 127, 133, 149, 166, 169, 171, 175–176, 181, 186, 214, 221, 252
dreams 2, 66, 68, 79–80, **108–110**, 124, 126, 153–155, 163, 165, 167, 201, 204–205, 221, 248
Dreams Like Me 2, 17
Duvaliers 1–2, 8–9, 16–18, 24, 26, 30, 46, 57, 64–65, 69, 82, 84, 86, 90–91, 93, 95, 98, 99–109, **110–111**, 118, 123, 133, 137, 140, 150–151, 154–158, 162, 166, 185, 187–189, 192, 194, 199, 204, 207–208, 214–216, 219, 224–225, 238–239, 241–242, 246–247, 250

earthquake 5, 9, 21, 28–30, 37, 43, 51, 65, 70, 79, 84, 89, 92–94, 98, 106, 109, **112–113**, 114, 118–119, 127, 135, 140, 142, 145, 167, 181, 184, 189, 193, 197–199, 203, 220–222, 224, 240–243, 247, 252
"Edwidge Danticat Returns to Haiti and Finds Resilience and Regeneration" 62, 197
Eight Days: A Story of Haiti 1, 5, 28–29, 43, 65, 69, 76, 78, 84, 90, 92–93, 98, 106, 109, 113, **114–115**, 126–127, 135, 145, 149, 166–167, 169, 178–179, 181, 186, 199, 201, 203, 220–221, 242, 244, 250–251
"Elsie" 6, 26, 117, 131, 142, 248
Erzulie 66, 107, **115–116**, 184, 193, 207, 216, 218–219, 224, 247
Everything Inside 2, 32, 36–38, **116–121**, 131, 142, 148, 224, 241–244

The Farming of Bones (novel) 1, 4, 18–21, 44–45, 50, 52, 62–64, 66, 74, 80, 82, 84, 92–94, 96–97, 106, 108–109, **121–125**, 126, 132–133, 136–137, 139, 142–143, 145, 150, 163, 166–167, 169–173, 175–179, 182, 185–187, 190, 192, 196, 199, 201, 203–204, 206, 209–210, 212, 214, 220–221, 227–235, 241–243, 245
The Farming of Bones Genealogy **125–126**
fear 3, 9, 11, 17–18, 28, 30, 33–34,

Index

271

43, 45, 51–52, 57, 59, 71, 73, 82, 84–86, 89, 96, 98, 100, 102–103, 107, 109, 111, 113–114, 116, **126–128**, 133, 139–141, 144, 147, 149, 157, 167, 171, 179, 192–193, 196, 201, 205–206, 208, 211–213, 220, 248, 251

"Feetfirst" 34, 53, 93, 135, 144, 179, 210, 148

"Flight" 29, 53, 89, 93, 99, 166

folklore 2, 9–10, 12, 15, 17, 54, 58, 67, 69–70, 73–74, 77, 79, 82, 101, 106, 120, 123, **128–130**, 131, 138–139, 143, 159–160, 165, 167, 172–174, 181, 202, 204–205, 208–210, 216–219, 223, 225, 228, 233

food 4, 9, 13, 15, 28, 46, 48, 54, 61, 67, 72, 76–77, 90, 113, **130–132**, 143, 152–153, 160, 163, 180, 185, 189, 196–199, 202, 206, 223, 252

The Foreigner's Home 35, 255

"Freda" 91, 218

freedom 14, 35, 103, 120, 124, **133–135**, 139–140, 152–153, 165, 181, 200–201, 207, 231, 235, 237–238

"From the Ocean Floor" 82, 151

"The Funeral Singer" 66, 77, 93–94, 104–105, 132, 143, 151, 166, 194, 209, 231, 244

genocide 19, 32, 48–49, 85, 101, 109, 123, 125, 128, 131, 150, 178, 185, 196, 203, 214, 242, 247

"Ghosts" 27, 72, 84, 94, 137, 179, 186, 195, 202, 215, 221–222

"The Gift" 6, 37, 84, 93, 118, 186, 221

Girl Rising 31, 70, 163, 248

"Giving and Receiving" 31, 70

"A Grain of Comfort" 251

grandparents 2, 7–9, 11, 13, 21, 28, 43, 48–49, 54, 56, 61, 73, 81, 83, 85, 93–94, 98, 105–107, 116, 119, 121, 126–127, **135–137**, 142–143, 145, 149–152, 154–156, 159–164, 166–170, 175–178, 182, 192, 194–196, 198, 203–204, 206–207, 210–213, 216–217, 221, 223, 225, 245

Granmè Melina 9, 11–12, 83, 136, 142, 163, 204

Granta 19, 28, 62, 106, 119

grotesque 44, **137–138**, 184, 212, 216, 222; *see also* noir

Haiti: A Slave Revolution 257, 259

"Haiti Faces Difficult Questions" 65, 112, 242

Haiti Noir 5, 28, 30–31

Haiti Noir 2 32, 118, 184, 228, 233

Haitian history 59, 81, 86, 133, 138, 159, 170

Haitian Revolution 23, 78, 88, 133, 153, 158, 200, 218, 228–229, 237, 241, 246–247

"Haiti's Quiet Beauty Captivates in Jacmel" 47

health 2, 9, 37–38, 43, 46–48, 61–62, 64, 66, 71, 74, 79–80, 90,

98, 102, 104, 107–109, 115–117, 124, 135–136, **142–144**, 145, 156, 160, 173, 174–175, 180, 199, 207, 217, 223, 227, 233; cholera 5, 29–30, 47, 140, 144, 189; coma 24, 80, 127, 136, 167, 211; herbalism 48, 54, 82, 98, 104, 109, 122, 127, 135, 142–143, 171, 210, 220, 230, 234, 251; HIV-AIDS 14, 19, 38, 46–47, 53, 79, 82, 87, 92, 118, 137, 142–144, 147, 178, 186, 191, 203, 217, 221, 240, 253; malnutrition 61–62, 131, 152, 156, 190, 200–202; scurvy 190; tuberculosis 12, 144, 152

"Home" 92

"Hot-Air Balloons" 119, 138, 143, 149, 177, 179, 186, 188–189, 192, 194, 216, 221, 223–224, 227, 230–232, 234, 252

"House of Prayer and Dreams" 71, 114, 141, 251

humor 2, 5, 46, 51, 53, 79, 104, **144–146**, 244–245, 251

Hurricane Maria 35, 240

immigration 1, 3–5, 7–13, 16, 20–23, 25–30, 32–38, 44–45, 54–59, 61, 67–68, 70, 73–74, 80–89, 91–92, 94, 97, 100, 102, 104, 110, 115, 118–120, 139, 127–129, 130–134, 138, 140, **146–149**, 150, 152, 154, 156, 158–159, 161–163, 165–166, 169–171, 178–179, 181, 184, 186, 188–189, 191–192, 195–196, 201–203, 205, 207–209, 214, 219–222, 229, 236–237, 239–240, 242, 246–247, 249–252; Krome 4, 23, 25, 59, 120, 142, 192, 242, 245–246, 252

imprisonment 3–5, 11, 18, 23, 25, 27, 30, 44, 55, 59, 82, 84–85, 94–97, 99–104, 108, 115, 120, 125, 128, 132–133, 138, 145–146, 148, 149–154, 164–165, 170, 175, 177–178, 184, 186, 188, 190, 192–194, 200–201, 206, 214–215, 222–223, 225, 236, 238–239, 241–242, 248–250, 252

In the Flicker of an Eyelid 22

"In the Old Days" 84, 92–93, 95, 110, 118, 157, 163, 174, 177, 179, 186, 199, 209, 221, 232–234, 244

"The Indigo Girl" 136, 140, 185, 197, 223, 248, 252

introductions 22, 34, 45, 67–68, 87–88, 110, 118, **149–151**, 156, 189, 204

"Je Voudrais Etre Riche" 140–141, 204, 230

"The Journals of Water Days" 65, 93, 103, 110, 137, 186–187

Kazal: The Memories of Kazal, a Photographic Approach 258

"Kettly Mars" 258

Krik? Krak! 1–2, 4, 16–18, 21, 70,

133, 149, **151–157**, 184, 193–194, 201, 223, 230, 241, 244, 248

Krik? Krak! Genealogy 157–158

language 1–3, 10, 13, 15, 38, 44, 56, 58, 64, 76–77, 79, 81–82, 90–92, 99, 104, 117–118, 127–128, 139, 144–145, 157, **158–161**, 163, 166, 173–174, 177, 188–189, 211, 227, 230–231, 236, 239; Creole 2–3, 7, 9–15, 18, 23–24, 45, 56, 58, 69, 86, **90–92**, 149–150, 158–159, 161, 164–165, 182, 201, 237, 239, 244; English 3, 13–14, 19, 26, 44, 53, 55–56, 58, 74, 90–92, 103, 117–118, 122, 144, 157–159, 163–164, 174, 177, 200, 237, 242; French 1–4, 7, 10–16, 18, 21–22, 24, 45–46, 56–58, 61, 64, 66, 70, 73, 76–78, 87, 90–91, 97, 99, 121, 130, 137–138, 146–147, 149, 152, 155, 158–159, 162, 164, 174, 177, 185, 224–225, 231, 242–243; Kwa 90; Latin 2, 180, 230; Portuguese 59, 90; Spanish 2, 7, 14, 62, 76, 90–91, 104, 123, 179, 230, 233, 242; Swahili 155, 231; Taino 1–2, 4, 9, 20, 26, 37, 45, 47–50, 63–64, 68, 76, 79, 81, 83, 90, 92–93, 95, 98, 105, 109, 120, 128, 130, 136, 138–139, 142, 145, 167–169, 174, 177, 185, 187, 192, 194–195, 198–200, 203–204, 206, 220, 223, 227, 229, 232, 15, 18, 25, 4 4,5, 62, 72, 76–77, 100, 130, 14 4,5, 178, 185, 205–207, 234, 236, 241–242, 247, 250

The Last Mapou 1, 5, 31, 43, 65, 81, 92, 97, 106–107, 127–128, 130, 135, 137, 139, 140, 142, **160–161**

The Last Mapou Genealogy **161–162**

Léogâne 8–9, 21, 26, 28, 32, 51, 54, 61, 79, 98, 108, 112–113, 136, 166, 181, 214, 221, 241–242

"Li, Li, Li" 258

literacy 2, 18, 47, 76–77, 133, 160, **162–164**, 188–189 *See also* Language

"A Little While" 89, 112

"Living and Loving Through Tragedy" 112, 167, 170, 176, 184, 199, 224

"Living with Uncertainty: Violence, Exile, and Black Life" 34

"The Long Legacy of Occupation in Haiti" 54, 242

"Look at Me" 113, 166, 210

"Lost Shadows and Stick Figures" 17

"Love, Our Only True Adventure" 117, 166

"Machandiz" 141, 180

Mama's Nightingale 5, 11, 33, 35, 84, 97, 115, 128, 133, **164–165**, 170, 175, 186, 223, 249

Marasa 106–107, 211

Index

"Marie Micheline" 4, 10, 15, 43, 79, 94, 98, 108, 151, 166, 169, 171, 176, 181, 208, 214, 221, 239, 245, 251
Maroons 114, 129, 158, 167, 201, 231, 246, 249
Massacre River 18–19, 31, 44, 63, 66, 74, 82, 96, 109, 121, 125, 127, 133, 150, 152, 154, 167, 178, 182, 192, 196, 202–203, 206, 214–215, 236, 238, 241–242, 246, 253
memory 3, 6, 10–11, 13, 16–19, 21, 31, 33, 44–45, 52, 54, 56, 58, 61, 71, 78–79, 81–83, 87–89, 91–92, 96–98, 101, 103–104, 108, 110, 114–115, 119, 124–125, 127, 129, 135–136, 139, 141, 147, 149, 151–152, 154, 157–148, **165–168**, 171, 176, 178, 181–182, 185, 194, 198–199, 201–204, 206, 208, 212–213, 221, 244, 245, 251–252
"Message to My Daughters" 197, 232, 252
Miami 1, 4, 16, 19, 21, 23–27, 29, 32–34, 36, 43, 51, 57, 59, 64–465, 69, 72, 79, 81, 92, 94, 107, 117–120, 128, 131–132, 134–135, 138, 142, 146–148, 152, 154, 157, 167, 174, 179, 182, 184, 187, 192, 197–198, 201–203, 211, 213, 214, 219, 223, 238–239, 242, 245, 247, 253
"The Missing Peace" 17, 65, 80, 92–93, 108, 136, 150, 154, 155, 164, 168, 170, 177, 179, 188, 195, 205, 221, 231, 235, 244
"Monkey Tails" 61, 65, 82, 93–94, 103, 105, 109, 127, 133, 139, 151, 164, 185–186, 200, 204, 208–209, 221, 227–229, 233, 235, 244, 248–249, 251
Morrison, Toni 15, 19, 26–27, 37–38, 51–52, 71, 87, 150, 166, 207, 248
mothers 2–5, 7–13, 15–16, 22–23, 27–28, 30, 32–34, 36, 43–44, 48–49, 51–54, 56–57, 62, 65–67, 69–74, 76–78, 80–82, 84, 90–91, 93, 96–98, 101–103, 105–107, 109, 111–112, 115–116, 119, 124, 126–130, 132, 134–138, 141, 144–147, 149–150, 152–157, 159–160, 163, 165–167, **168–172**, 173–180, 183–184, 186–188, 192–193, 195–196, 198–199, 201, 203–211, 213, 215–218, 220–221, 223–225, 231–232, 244, 253; *see also Mama's Nightingale; My Mommy Medicine*
music 2, 16, 38, 45–46, 63–64, 91, 110, 114, 117, 159, **172–175**, 182, 196, 213, 222, 227, 233–234, 238, 248
My Mommy Medicine 36, 97, 139, 160, 170, **175–176**, 211, 223, 251
"My Own Island" 47
"My Personal Journey" 259
myth 18, 26, 31, 48–49, 52, 62, 69, 77, 82–83, 86, 103, 107–108, 116, 120, 125, 127, 129, 153, 156, 158, 160, 162, 168, 176, 181, 193–194,

196, 201, 203–204, 206–209, 211, 217–219, 223, 242

names 2–4, 6–7, 9, 13, 16, 20, 26–27, 29, 52, 54, 60–61, 65–67, 70–72, 74, 76, 78–82, 85, 95–97, 99–100, 102–103, 105–106, 111, 114, 118–119, 121–122, 124, 126, 128, 134–137, 141, 146, 150, 152, 155, 161, 164, 167–170, **176–180**, 181, 184, 186, 194–196, 198–200, 202, 212, 214, 216, 233, 236–238, 241–242
National Book Award 18, 27, 36, 38, 151
nature 1, 5, 21, 23–24, 31, 37, 43, 47, 62, 65, 71, 74, 76, 81, 92, 97–98, 106–107, 116, 127–130, 134–137, 139–140, 142, 160–161, **180–183**, 209, 213, 219, 221, 244
"A New Sky" 33, 53, 94, 144, 248
New York 1, 3–4, 8–9, 11–13, 15, 18–22, 24, 26, 29–31, 34–38, 44, 54–55, 57–58, 60, 68, 80–81, 83–84, 88, 97, 100–105, 108–110, 113, 118, 125, 132, 135, 140, 146–147, 155–157, 166–167, 170, 171, 177–179, 187, 194, 198–199, 209, 215, 217, 230, 237, 239–240, 244–246, 252
"New York Day Women" 80, 150, 155, 163, 167, 170, 178, 187, 221, 235, 252
"New York Was Our City on the Hill" 8, 146, 189
"Night Talkers" 22, 44, 79, 82, 92–93, 95, 99, 101–103, 106, 133, 136–137, 140, 142, 144, 151, 159, 166, 171–172, 176, 178, 186, 199, 203, 208, 210, 214, 217, 221, 227–228, 232, 235, 244, 248–249
"Night Women" 4, 6, 84, 134, 139, 150, 153–154, 170–171, 174, 186, 187–189, 204, 221, 223, 231
"Nineteen Thirty-Seven" 132–133, 141, 152, 154, 157, 170, 177, 184, 186, 190, 194–195, 202, 206, 216, 221, 225, 231, 248
"No Greater Shame" 23, 146, 229–230, 233, 244
noirism 2, 5, 28, 144–145, 154, 158, **183–185**, 244; *see also Haiti Noir; Haiti Noir 2*
"Not Your Homeland" 59, 146, 189
Nou Bouke 29, 255

"On Borrowed Wings" 88
"On the Day of the Dead" 5, 90, 92, 99, 113, 184, 198, 218, 227, 231–232, 234
"One Thing" 94, 96, 179, 202, 223
"The Other Side of the Water" 87, 133
"Our Guernica" 9, 89
"Our Maya" 13
"Out of the Shadows" 259

"Papi" 9, 15, 206, 248, 250
patriarchy 2, 5, 56, 61, 66–67, 73,

77, 100, 116, 138, 156, 177–178, **185–188**, 194, 216, 224, 232
"A Place of Refuge" 178–179, 187, 193, 224, 252
"Plantains, Please" 21, 91, 129, 131, 163, 230
"Please Translate" 38, 177, 183–184, 244, 252
"Plunging" 120, 146, 184
"Poetry in a Time of Protest" 34
"Port-au-Prince, City of Survivors: Voices from Haiti" 141, 173
"The Port-au-Prince Marriage Special" 5, 84, 118, 144, 170, 176, 178, 186, 191, 217, 221, 227, 229, 230, 232, 241–242, 252
"The Possibility of Heaven" 32, 51, 94, 144, 186, 221, 252
"Postscript" 8, 93
Poto Mitan: Haitian Women Pillars of the Global 27, 163
poverty 4, 8, 10, 47, 61–62, 75–76, 84, 131, 139, 150, 152, 156, 159, 162, 171, 177, 187, **189–191**, 192–193, 200–202, 222, 246–247
"Prayer Before Dying" 33, 53
Providence, Rhode Island 3, 16–17, 28, 149, 227

"Quality Control" 6, 32, 46, 84, 96, 98–99, 119, 174, 183, 186, 221, 228–229

Radio Six 82, 87, 138, 140, 152, 252
"A Rain of Daffodils" 56
"Reading Lessons" 69, 73, 81, 143–144, 170, 205, 213, 228, 252
refugees 1, 4, 13, 17, 22, 25, 27, 34, 43–44, 59, 65–66, 79, 82, 96, 115, 120, 122, 127, 131, 133, 139, 147–148, 158, 169, 177–178, 185, 187, 193, 197–198, 201–203, 209, 214, 220, 245–246, 253
religion 2, 10–11, 46, 56–57, 64–66, 86, 101, 129, 159, 169, **195–197**, 207, 217, 220, 224, 227–228, 231, 233, 249; Animism 88, 173, 181, 197, 217; Baptist 8–9, 47, 57, 81, 104; Catholicism 2, 6, 46, 65–67, 77, 88, 100, 112–113, 116, 129, 143–144, 151, 157, 161, 166, 174, 185–188, 193, 195, 197, 201, 207, 216, 218, 221, 225, 233, 239, 243, 247; Evangelicalism 8, 13, 46, 81, 140, 195, 197, 228; Pentecostalism 13, 23, 232, 246; Santeria 66, 106, 116, 196, 207, 216, 233; Shamanism 48, 198; Vodou 1–2, 31, 46, 56, 65, 68, 77, 86, 88–89, 91, 106–107, 112, 115–116, 145, 151, 161, 173, 184, 193, 195–197, 201, 205, 211, 216, **217–220**, 224, 228, 230–231, 233–234, 237, 241, 247–248
"The Revenant" 62–63, 76, 94, 106, 109, 149, 179, 205, 228, 247
"A Right to Be Here: Race, Immigration, and My Third Culture Kids" 5, 35

Index

273

"Ripple Effects" 38
ritual 6, 13–14, 17, 31, 46, 48, 51, 53, 63, 66, 71–72, 81, 84, 95, 97–100, 113, 116, 124, 127–129, 139, 144, 153–154, 161, 166–167, 174, 181, 188, 196–197, **198–199**, 210, 217, 219, 229, 233, 247–248

"Sawfish Soup" 5, 93, 96, 99, 110–111, 139, 149, 180, 208, 213–214, 221, 248
"The Secret Island" 27, 90, 103, 108, 110, 170, 186
"Seeing Things Simply" 77, 91, 95, 97, 150, 155, 178–179, 186–187, 221, 223, 227, 244
"Seven" 5, 63, 85, 97, 100–101, 132, 150, 166, 179, 221, 227–228, 244, 248–251
"Seven Stories" 5–6, 32–33, 43, 45, 56, 61, 63, 65, 76, 79, 85, 90, 95, 99, 115, 119, 126, 129, 131, 133, 140, 142, 147, 162, 166, 168, 170, 172, 177, 179–180, 186, 191–193, 195, 199, 201, 209, 213, 217, 221–222, 231, 235, 248
shapeshifting 2, 68, 129, 173, 206, 219, 247
slavery 2, 32, 46, 49, 52, 56, 61, 66–67, 69, 77, 88, 90, 109, 114–116, 129–130, 132, 134, 136–139, 148, 152, 158, 165, 167, 174, 185, 187, 190, 192–193, 198, **199–202**, 205–207, 209, 213, 217–219, 224–225, 229, 231, 236–237, 241–242
"So Brutal a Death" 172
"Sole Mates" 197–198, 252
"Some of My Favorite Haitian Meals" 260
Sor Rose 65, 77, 128, 156, 193–194, 247
Standing Tall 5, 29, 192, 200, 219, 224, 227
"Starfish" 72, 186, 250
Stones in the Sun 30, 159, 208
"Storybook Ending" 10
storytelling 1, 9–10, 17, 30, 32, 35–36, 38, 47, 54–55, 64, 60, 69, 73, 81, 83, 102, 126–127, 130, 135–136, 139, 149, 151–154, 157, 161–162, 165, 169–170, 176, **202–205**, 206, 210, 221, 245, 248
"Sunrise, Sunset" 5, 78, 85, 111, 119–120, 135, 142–143, 160, 168, 170, 179, 198, 221, 223, 234, 249, 252
superstition 2, 46, 76, 106, 111, 129, 142, 156, 184, **205–207**, 211, 248; *see also* fear

Taino 1–2, 4, 9, 20, 26, 37, 45, 47–50, 63–64, 68, 76, 69, 81, 83, 90, 92–93, 95, 98, 105, 109, 120, 128, 130, 136, 138–139, 142, 145, 167–169, 174, 177, 181, 185, 187, 192, 194–195, 198–200, 203–204, 206, 220, 223, 227, 229, 232–234, 236, 241–242, 247, 250
"A Taste of Coffee" 12, 21, 78, 81, 86, 95, 102, 141, 231, 234, 244

"Tatiana, Mon Amour" 5, 15, 79, 144, 176, 195
Tent Life 30, 43, 92, 112, 139, 181, 184, 189, 194, 197, 199, 203, 218, 221, 224, 232
"Testimonial" 260
"This Is My Body" 260
Tonton Macoute 1–2, 9, 17, 27, 30, 44, 56, 61–62, 64, 81, 89, 95, 99, 103–107, 109, 137–138, 143, 149–152, 166, 171, 173, 176, 179, 184–188, 193–195, 199, 206, **207–209**, 214–216, 221, 234, 238–239, 241, 245–247, 249–251
tradition 9–10, 18, 23,46, 48, 56, 61, 64–65, 67, 81, 91, 95, 102, 106–107, 113, 116, 118, 125, 130–131, 133, 136, 139, 142, 149, 161, 165, 174, 188, 194, 199, **209–210**, 211, 215–217, 223, 225, 229–230; *see also* patriarchy
"Travelling" 130, 140
"Trimester" 97, 154
Trujillo, Rafael Leonidas 18, 20, 31, 44, 52, 63, 69, 94, 110, 121–127, 131, 133, 136, 149–150, 152, 158, 171, 173, 176, 179, 185–187, 192, 202–204, 214, 229, 238, 241–242, 247, Trump, Donald 5, 34–38, 74, 128, 147–148, 158, 171, 192, 251
"Turning the Page on Disaster" 112
twins 5, 33, 74, 80, 82, 91, 96, 98, 106–107, 109, 122, 129, 131, 133, 136, 145–146, 167, 170, 179, 182, 192, 196, 201, 206, **211–213**, 214, 218, 220–221, 231, 249

"U.S. Deportations to Haiti DURING Coronavirus Pandemic Are 'Unconscionable'" 39, 260
Untwine 1, 5, 33, 33, 37, 69, 79, 82–83, 85, 91–93, 98, 107–108, 127, 129, 131–133, 135–136, 139, 142, 145–146, 167, 170, 174, 176–179, 182, 186, 196, 198–199, 203, 206, 209, **211–213**, 214, 218, 220–221, 223, 227–235, 242, 244, 249
***Untwine* Genealogy** 213

"A Very Haitian Story" 25, 260
violence 1, 14, 25–26, 30, 34, 43, 48, 56–57, 61, 64, 66, 72–73, 81, 85, 89, 96, 99, 110, 117, 138–139, 143, 155, 166, 169, 171, 173, 187, 193–194, 207–208, **213–215**, 222, 241; arson 24, 58, 92, 98, 102, 110, 137, 140, 166, 208, 217, 247; execution 8, 16, 18, 49, 63, 76, 85–86, 93, 104, 110, 124, 128–129, 137, 140, 144, 158, 203, 205, 208, 214, 228, 241–242; gangs 22, 24–25, 49, 54, 58, 72, 78, 82, 92, 96, 111, 128, 134, 144, 166, 180, 184, 186, 194, 199, 201, 208, 215, 221, 241, 248; kidnapping 48, 52, 78, 96, 117, 177, 183, 194, 200, 208, 247; looting 24, 58, 72, 98; rape 3, 15, 18, 20, 28, 30, 44, 56–57,

62, 72–73, 77, 81, 87, 107, 109, 111, 119, 127, 134, 137–138, 146, 149, 152, 169, 179, 186–188, **193–195**, 208, 215–216, 221, 224, 250; torture 3, 11, 16, 18, 44, 76, 82, 86, 94, 98, 100–101, 103, 105, 133, 138, 150, 174, 183–186, 200–201, 209, 215, 216, 228, 238–239, 241, 250–251; *see also* Duvaliers; Tonton Macoute; Trujillo, Rafael Leonidas
virginity 1, 17, 57, 66, 81, 102, 107, 115–116, 129, 141, 146, 154, 172, 194, 196, 198, 206, **215–217**, 218, 230, 232, 234, 250
vodou 1–2, 31, 46, 56, 65, 68, 77, 86, 88–89, 91, 106–107, 112, 115–116, 145, 151, 161, 173, 184, 193, 195–197, 201, 205, 211, 216, **217–220**, 224, 228, 230–231, 233–234, 237, 241, 247–248
"Voices in a Dream" 18, 153

"Walk Straight " 11, 21, 86
A Walk Through Carnival 1, 4, 43, 63, 110, 207
"A Wall of Fire Rising" 6, 16, 62, 77, 85, 91, 96, 131, 133, 143, 149, 153–154, 157–158, 163, 170–171, 176, 186–188, 190, 206, 221, 223, 228–229, 231
"A Wasteful Approach to Detention" 260
"Water Child" 5, 21, 83, 85, 92, 97, 100, 104, 133, 150, 166, 170–171, 177, 198, 221, 227–229, 231, 233, 244, 247, 251–252
"We Are Ugly, But We Are Here" 2, 48, 187, 216
"Westbury Court" 3, 12, 14, 96, 222, 229
"When Home Hurts" 260
Winfrey, Oprah 10, 19–20, 37, 117
"Without Her" 5, 34, 53, 94, 135, 144, 179, 210, 249
"Without Inspection" 25, 43, 79, 85, 93–94, 96–97, 115, 120, 128, 133–134, 139, 146, 158, 168, 170, 172, 175, 178–180, 184, 190, 202, 205, 214, 220, 222–223, 232–235, 242, 244
women 2–4, 17–19, 22–23, 25, 27, 31, 33–34, 37, 43, 48, 56–57, 59, 62, 66, 71, 73, 76–77, 103–104, 108, 110, 115, 119, 125–126, 130, 134–138, 140–141, 143, 146, 150, 152, 154, 156–157, 163–165, 168, 171, 183, 185–191, 193–194, 196, 198–200, 204, 206, 208, 210, 215–216, **222–225**, 227, 229, 231–232, 238, 247, 250
Women: A Celebration of Strength 48
"Women Like Us" 135, 156, 224, 229, 232

"A Year and a Day" 89, 96, 189, 198, 206, 222, 229